INFORMATION RESOURCES IN
THE HUMANITIES AND THE ARTS

INFORMATION RESOURCES IN THE HUMANITIES AND THE ARTS

SIXTH EDITION

Anna H. Perrault and Elizabeth S. Aversa

with contributing authors,
Cynthia Miller and Sonia Ramírez Wohlmuth

LIBRARIES UNLIMITED

AN IMPRINT OF ABC-CLIO, LLC
Santa Barbara, California • Denver, Colorado • Oxford, England

Library of Congress Cataloging-in-Publication Data

Perrault, Anna H., 1944–
  Information resources in the humanities and the arts / Anna H. Perrault and Elizabeth Aversa ; with contributing authors Cynthia Miller and Sonia Wohlmuth. — Sixth edition.
        pages cm. — (Library and information science text series)
  Third-fifth editions, authored by Ron Blazek and Elizabeth Aversa, entitled Humanities : a selective guide to information sources; First and second editions authored by A. Robert Rogers.
  Includes bibliographical references and indexes.
  ISBN 978-1-59884-832-8 (hardback) — ISBN 978-1-59884-833-5 (paperback) — ISBN 978-1-61069-327-1 (ebook) (print)
  1. Humanities—Bibliography.   2. Humanities—Reference books—Bibliography.   3. Humanities—Information services—Directories.   4. Humanities—Electronic information resources.   5. Arts—Bibliography.
6. Arts—Reference books—Bibliography.   7. Arts—Information services—Directories.   8. Arts—Electronic information resources.   I. Aversa, Elizabeth Smith.   II. Blazek, Ron. Humanities.   III. Title.
  Z6265.B53   2013
  [AZ221]
  016.0013—dc23   2012028606

ISBN: 978-1-59884-832-8
        978-1-59884-833-5 (pbk.)
EISBN: 978-1-61069-327-1

17 16 15 14 13   1 2 3 4 5

This book is also available on the World Wide Web as an eBook.
Visit www.abc-clio.com for details.

Libraries Unlimited
An Imprint of ABC-CLIO, LLC

ABC-CLIO, LLC
130 Cremona Drive, P.O. Box 1911
Santa Barbara, California 93116-1911

This book is printed on acid-free paper ∞
Manufactured in the United States of America

CONTENTS

PART THREE—LITERATURE AND LANGUAGES

PART FOUR—PERFORMING ARTS

PREFACE

Previously published as *The Humanities: a Selective Guide to Information Resources,* this award-winning resources guide has a long history and has enjoyed a reputation for excellence in the field. Librarians in diverse environments use *The Humanities* as a trusted collection development and information services tool. Despite the availability of humanities resource lists on the Internet, the authors continue to be asked when the next edition will appear.

The first two editions of the guide, in 1974 and 1979, were produced by A. Robert Rogers. The third edition, published in 1988, began the collaboration of Professor Ron Blazek and Professor Elizabeth S. Aversa, who also produced the 4th edition in 1994 and the 5th edition in 2000. The 4th edition saw the first electronic version of the book and was the first electronic product of the publisher on CD-ROM. After the retirement of Professor Blazek in 2003, a new team was established with the addition to Professor Aversa of Professor Anna Perrault and two specialists, both of whom hold doctoral degrees in their fields: Cynthia F. Miller for Musicology and Sonia Ramírez-Wohlmuth for World Literatures and languages.

For the 6th edition, Professor Perrault has served as general editor and assumed responsibility for Parts One, Three, and Five. Professor Aversa assumed responsibility for Parts Two and Four. Sonia Wohlmuth assumed responsibility for chapter 6, World literatures and languages. Cynthia Miller assumed responsibility for Music, Chapter 9.

Although this work is in the Library and Information Science Text Series, the authors hope that it will be used by a broader audience of librarians in all types of libraries and information centers, and even more broadly by students and teachers in humanities and arts programs. The goals of this work are to provide readers with a background in the humanities and the arts and current trends in studies in those disciplines; to provide an overview of the most important current reference resources; and to provide a selection of resources that reflect the literature of the fields and disciplines included.

ORGANIZATION

Reference works and reference service have undergone much change since the 5th edition of this Guide. In addition to fewer printed works and the wide availability of online reference databases, reference has become less that of answering specific factual questions and rather more focused upon the research process. This new edition is organized more thematically than the previous editions of the Humanities text. Subjects and sub topics are not divided in the traditional reference manner of organization by categories such as dictionaries, encyclopedias, indexes, and so forth. Especially in the age of Google, users of library resources do not typically think in these terms but begin a query with "I need some information on . . ." The single search box made popular by Google has been adopted in many online catalogs and databases. It is also common for libraries to organize resources by tabs for database lists, journal title lists, access to digital collections, and also special collections to assist the user in going straight to desired types of resources. The organization of this guide is similar to these prevalent practices with regard to electronic resources. And thus, in the spirit of organization from the user's perspective this Guide departs somewhat from traditional reference practice, which is becoming less suitable in the digital age.

It can be seen in the resources included in this guide that reference materials are on the way to becoming totally digital. Nearly all of the long-running print indexing and abstracting tools are now databases. The mega databases produced by large corporate publishers have generally erased considerations of reference format. Instead databases contain bibliographic information, abstracts, and full text, and some archival materials, and multimedia. The researcher may organize searches that incorporate authors, titles, publication years, or format delimiters such as book, journal, manuscript, and many others. Searches can also limit by characteristics such as themes, genres, or by time periods. Thus, for the majority of the indexing databases, a single organizational scheme such as encyclopedia is no longer a useful designation.

It is important that information seekers understand the formats they are most likely to be accessing so that they can zero in on the best retrieval tactic. The entries in this guide give the format that the resource is being produced in, either by section headings or with the bibliographic description, e.g. print and e-book, or online subscription database, or open access resource, thus, giving the user a clear idea of the format of the resource they will be looking for.

The organization of the entries for the resources within the chapters proceeds from the general to the specific. That is, for each chapter's primary subject matter, resources that are general, covering more than one aspect of the subject are listed first. Within these general resources there is a division by format. Databases and digital collections are treated first, followed by printed resources, and then open access resources. This organization places the resources most likely to be used at the beginning of the chapter. After the general resources, specialized sub topics of the chapter primary subject matter follow. Subject terms are preferred to format terms for subtopic headings. Within the sub-topics there are usually no format breakdowns, with all formats together under the sub topical heading. While this is the usual pattern, there are variances by chapter to accommodate the organization to the subject matter and the expectation of users in the different disciplines.

CHANGES FROM THE PREVIOUS EDITIONS

In preparing previous editions, the entries from prior editions were updated and new ones added. There was significant carryover of entries from one edition to the next. In this new edition, there have been very few titles carried over from the 5th edition. For one reason, many classic and standard titles have not been revised since the last edition. For the majority of these works, the information has been newly published in online resources. Another reason is that the number of reference works being published in print has continued to diminish throughout the first decade of this century. But the total number of entries has not decreased as open access resources and a large number of databases and digital collections have been added. Thus, the 6th edition is almost an entirely new work with a much larger proportion of electronic resources. A comparison of the number of entries from the 4th, 5th and now the 6th edition shows that the number of entries has increased slightly from the previous edition, but the percentages of total have shifted among the subject areas. The following chart compares the number of entries and percentages of total by broad subject categories.

COMPARISON OF NUMBERS OF ENTRIES

	Fourth ed.		Fifth ed.		Sixth ed.	
	No.	Percent	No.	Percent	No.	Percent
General	29	2.3	35	2.5	106	7.5
Philosophy	60	4.8	63	4.4	54	4
Religion	188	15	209	15.2	120	8.5
Lit. & Lang.	354	28.3	389	28.3	476	34
Performing Arts	353	28.2	390	28.3	351	25
Visual Arts	266	21.3	288	21	299	21
Total	1,250	100.0	1,374	100.0	1,406	100.0

Taking into consideration that the majority of the entries in this edition are for works published from 2000 to present, whereas the previous editions had entries that had been published over a long span of time, the number of entries in the new edition represents an increase in coverage for recently published works. The introduction to the humanities and the chapter on general resources in the humanities and the arts has been expanded in the new edition. The subjects of World Literature and Languages and Linguistics are covered in this edition in a separate chapter (6). With the increased emphasis upon globalization currently, the greatest expansion of coverage has occurred in those subject areas. The Literature chapter (5) also has an expanded section on Genre and Reader's advisory. While some subjects still have a considerable amount of monographic publication, other subjects such as film and cinema have migrated to the Internet and there are not the large number of new publications as in previous editions.

OTHER STYLISTIC AND ORGANIZATIONAL POINTS

In an attempt to enable the reader to see relationships between resources there are references by entry numbers to other related entries. These function like "see also" references.

In this edition, organizations and societies have been given numbered entries and are in the author/title index, as opposed to the narrative approach in previous editions with indexing in the subject index. This is because most organizations are now truly "information sources," and their web presences make them far more accessible than ever before.

The majority of titles in the database sections are subscription or restricted access databases. Databases which do not require payment for access are included in the Open Access Resources sections. Digital collections can be either subscription, purchase, or open access. In the case of printed works which are also available as e-books, they are located under Printed Resources with an indication of availability in both formats. All formats are clearly indicated in order that readers can determine if a resource is likely to be available on site, free on the Internet, or a subscription product their library may not provide.

ACKNOWLEDGMENTS

The authors wish to acknowledge Professor Ron Blazek for his devotion and diligence toward the previous three editions of the Humanities Guide, ensuring the excellent reputation the work enjoys in the present day. We thank him for entrusting the future of the work to us.

Professor Perrault would like to acknowledge and thank the numerous graduate assistants from the School of Information at the University of South Florida who searched entries in the previous edition for updates, looked for new entries and reviews, and checked websites for currency. Students too numerous to list in the Humanities Sources and Services course over the years are collectively thanked for scouting out through assignments new publications for possible entries. Individually thanked are Brittany Bennett, Krystal Bullers, Barbara Cardinale, Grace Gray, Andrea La Rochelle, Sylvia Martinez, Reema Mohini, and Donna Reynolds, all of whom worked on stages in the preparation of the manuscript. After the preparation of the manuscript, a number of USF graduate students pitched in to construct the indexes to the book: Vicki Toranzo, Robert Pound, and Joy Scholing. These are especially thanked for their diligence. Professor Aversa acknowledges assistance and support from her colleagues at The University of Alabama as work on her chapters progressed. Assistance with locating resources and updating references in philosophy was provided by William Friedman, then a master's student in library and information studies. Likewise, graduate students Whitney Cornutt and Erica Durham assisted in identifying and reviewing material in the chapter on religion and mythology. In the performing arts, Professor Aversa gratefully acknowledges the work of Daniel Tackett, another graduate assistant, on the topics of dance, radio and television. Stephanie Jacobs, a student in both MLIS and Book Arts programs at Alabama, worked with the author in the area of film. The work of Richard LeComte is recognized in the byline of the section on Theater and Dance. Elizabeth Levkoff, a student in the Alabama MLIS program, also assisted Dr. Aversa in indexing. Finally, assistance with bibliographic citations and references was provided by Anthony Cox, a doctoral student in the College of Communication and Information Sciences at the University of Alabama. The authors also wish to acknowledge and thank the LU staff, especially Blanche Woolls, the editor. The production staff at BookComp, Inc. are all also thanked, especially Carol Bifulco.

PART ONE

GENERAL HUMANITIES
AND THE ARTS

CHAPTER 1

THE HUMANITIES AND THE ARTS IN THE 21st CENTURY

Anna H. Perrault

As a beginning, this chapter is devoted to fostering an understanding of the nature of the humanities; scholarship in the humanities; use and users of information resources in the humanities; the state of technology in information resources for the humanities; trends in the academy and libraries; and librarianship in the humanities and the arts. We look first at defining what constitutes the humanities.

WORKING DEFINITION OF THE HUMANITIES

Definitions of *the humanities* abound, yet there remains a certain ambiguity or rather, no one "definitive" definition. To turn first to an acknowledged authority, *The Oxford English Dictionary* (OED) provides a definition for the humanities under the noun *humanity*. Thus, *humanities* is a plural of *humanity*, that dealing with the characteristics of being human. The humanities are defined as "the study of human culture . . . literary learning or scholarship, secular letters as opposed to theology . . . the study of ancient Latin and Greek language, literature, and intellectual classical scholarship." The OED also notes that the humanities are different from the social sciences "in having a significant historical element, in the use of interpretation of texts and artifacts rather than experimental and quantitative methods." This definition is steeped in the classical tradition. Indeed, the definition of *humanist* is "A person who pursues or is expert in the study of the humanities, esp. a classical scholar" (OED 1989).

In classical and early Christian times, the scope of the humanities seemed very broad. Literature constituted the core, but virtually every discipline relating to the human mind was considered a part of the humanities. In the Renaissance period, the term *humanities* was used in opposition to the term *divinity* and seemed to embrace all areas of study outside the field of religion, the secular rather than the divine. In the nineteenth century, *humanities* included those disciplines that could not be considered part of the natural sciences. By the twentieth century, the fields of study that dealt with social, rather than natural, phenomena had emerged, along with "scientific" methods of investigation in the several social sciences. In the last decades of the twentieth century, the humanities were defined by the Commission on the Humanities as those fields of scholarship and study that are "dedicated to the disciplined development of verbal, perceptual, and imaginative skills needed to understand experience" (Commission 1980, 5).

In library and information science, the characteristics of the humanities have been described by Allen in the introduction to *The Humanities and the Library* as "concern for the individual and for the thoughts, imagination, achievement, creativity, performance, and impact of individuals. There is a concern for culture and for all kinds of human behaviors that produce cultural artifacts. And perhaps all these concerns are framed by the larger concern for values, for quality, and for expression"

(Couch 1993, xi). Allen eschews a discipline-based description and emphasizes the centrality of the individual in creativity and the impact of the creative products.

Wiberley and Jones have conducted several studies on the information seeking behavior of humanists and define the humanities as "those fields of scholarship that strive to reconstruct, describe, and interpret the activities and accomplishments of people by establishing and studying documents and other artifacts created by those people" (Wiberley 2009, 2198). They recognize that "all scholarship is a continuum from the sciences to the social sciences to the humanities. There is overlap between the social sciences and the humanities, but clear differences between the core of each area" (2198).

In "Humanities and Its Literatures," John Immroth contrasts the humanities and the sciences:

> In the mind of this writer the sciences are our study of ourselves and the world around us physically and biologically; that is to say literal, scientific, and objective studies. The social sciences appear to be the study of humankind and its relationship to other peoples, socially, economically, and politically; that is to say historical, comparative, or collective studies. Finally, the humanities are our appreciation of ourselves, our relationship to others and the world creatively, imaginatively, spiritually, and intellectually; they include ideological, esthetical, cumulative, subjective studies (Immroth 2007, 1237).

Definitions of the humanities often consist of lists of academic disciplines and those lists vary. What disciplines constitute the humanities? The question of the classification of knowledge, or of scholarly endeavors, into *fields*, *disciplines*, *research areas*, or *subjects*, is itself a humanistic problem. It is also a very practical problem for librarians and information specialists who need to categorize the literature into workable systems for storage, retrieval, preservation, and physical access to information sources, and for educators who design curricula and establish the organizational components of schools, colleges, universities, and systems of higher education. Although the Commission on the Humanities (1980) suggested that "fields alone do not define the humanities" and that "the essence of the humanities is a spirit or attitude toward humanity" (5), scholars have, at various times, classified different areas of study as "humanistic disciplines," as opposed to those in the social and behavioral sciences or those in the physical and life sciences.

"There has never been a great age of science and technology without a corresponding flourishing of the arts and humanities." Cathy N. Davidson ("Humanities 2.0: Promise, Perils, Predictions." *PMLA* 123 (May 2008): 707).

The arts fields are sometimes included in the scope of the humanities and at other times regarded as separate from the humanities, as in the National Endowment for the Arts (NEA) and the National Endowment for the Humanities (NEH). The legislation that established the NEH defines the humanities as "including but not limited to the study of the following: language, both modern and classical; linguistics; literature; history; jurisprudence; philosophy; archaeology; comparative religion; ethics; the history, criticism and theory of the arts; those aspects of social sciences which have humanistic content and employ humanistic methods; and the study and application of the humanities to the human environment with particular attention to reflecting our diverse heritage, traditions and history, and to the relevance of the humanities to the current conditions of national life" (NEH, n.d.). The NEH definition is broad and modern in describing the academic disciplines which constitute humanities studies.

The National Endowment for the Arts does not post a definition on its website. It does broadly define the arts through its funding guidelines "Grants for Arts Projects" which "support exemplary projects in artist communities, arts education, dance, design, folk and traditional arts, literature, local arts agencies, media arts, museums, music, musical theater, opera, presenting (including multidisciplinary art forms), theater, and visual arts" (NEA 2011, 5). There is some overlap in the definitions of the NEH and NEA, but the emphasis on creativity is evident in the NEA description. The NEH definition encompasses those areas that are theoretical and critical, with an emphasis upon scholarship and the historical cultural heritage.

The fields of study that we include in this guide are philosophy, religion, language, linguistics, literature, the performing arts, and the visual arts. The reader may ask, "What about history?" and that is a worthwhile question. Although many consider history to be a central humanities field, research methods in history and indications of similarities between information use in that field and in the social sciences lead us to place history closer to the social sciences than to the humanities, at least for the purpose of constructing a guide to information resources. We believe that this guide, therefore, reflects the migration during the second half of the twentieth century of history from a narrative enterprise to one using many approaches that are closely related to those of the social and behavioral sciences. This is not to suggest that the reader should overlook the

> . . . the humanities are not monolithic but, instead, are as varied as the human endeavors they study." (Knievel, J. E. and Charlene Kellsey. 2005. "Citation analysis for Collection Development . . ." *Library Quarterly 75*, (2): 166).

many studies of information-seeking behavior among historians; these works have contributed considerably to our understanding of how scholars work, and they are indeed must reading for the librarian.

In addition to those sources cited above in defining the humanities, the student wishing to explore the nature and scope of the humanities can access many useful resources in addition to such excellent general overviews as in the *Encyclopedia of Library and Information Sciences* (3rd edition, 2009). McLeish's readable *Key Ideas in Human Thought* offers brief, signed articles on the many disciplines and subfields that constitute the humanities from a 1990s perspective (Facts on File 1993). Volumes of the series *Princeton Studies: Humanistic Scholarship in America* provide a reflective look at the field over more than fifty years (Princeton, 1963–).

NATURE OF SCHOLARSHIP
IN THE HUMANITIES

At the outset, it should be remarked that humanistic research is differentiated most sharply from that in the natural sciences by the constant intrusion of questions of value. To the scientist, qua scientist, such considerations are, indeed, intrusions. They interfere with and damage the quality of research concerned with objective, empirically verifiable data, and with experimental results that can be replicated by other researchers. "Informed judgment" might play a part in determining which experiments to conduct, but "refined sensibility" would have no impact on the experimental outcome. Yet these are the "bread of life" for the humanistic scholar, whether dealing with a poem, a piece of music, a painting, a religious doctrine, or a philosophical theory. Thus, humanistic scholarship has traditionally been intimately intertwined with considerations of value.

One consequence of this connection between scholarship and value systems is the peculiarly personal and individualistic nature of humanistic research. Unlike colleagues in the natural sciences, or even, to a lesser degree, in the social and behavioral sciences, the humanist finds the research to be such an intimately personal matter that it is more difficult than in other disciplines to function effectively as a team. While the humanist has been characterized as solitary or even hermetic in the past, this is a more traditional view of the humanist than that evolving in the twenty-first century. Collaborative efforts are possible, but they require special planning and are not considered nearly as "normal" as in the natural sciences. In creativity and the arts, the writer or artist usually works alone. On the other hand, in the arts, teamwork is necessary in performances of theater, music ensembles, and dance, as well as professional practices in architecture and design. It has been suggested that while humanists and artists work alone, communities of scholars have existed throughout history and citation analysis can be utilized to study the communications among communities of scholars (Hristova 2003); and collaboration is now being urged as the concept of *digital humanities* is taking hold.

It has also been suggested that it is not necessarily the content of the scholarship in the humanities that leads to independent and solitary work, but rather that it may be that there is something different about the training and education of humanistic scholars that leads to the lack of collaborative work. For a perspective on this aspect of humanities scholarship, see the article, "Knowledge Collaboration in the Arts, the Sciences, and the Humanities" (Borden 1992).

Regardless of the reason that humanists work alone, a further result of this is the general lack of ability on the part of the humanities scholar to delegate bibliographic searching to others. The interconnections within the researcher's mind appear to be so subtle or complex that it is necessary to examine personally the index entry or abstract to identify an item of potential relevance, and to see the book or article to determine its actual relevance. Indexing tools have not provided thesauri or controlled vocabularies of the sort that are common in the pure and applied sciences. Efforts toward this goal have resulted in controlled vocabularies and thesauri for the visual arts fields produced by the Getty Research Institute (entries 11-8 through 11-11).

Part of the problem faced by the humanistic scholar also relates to the nature of knowledge in the humanities. Such knowledge is not likely to consist of hard, identifiable facts such as formulas in chemistry, population, and income statistics from census data, or the content of genetic matter. Of course, there are plenty of facts in the humanities, but their sum total is considerably less than what the humanist is searching for. To know the number of times Shakespeare used the word "mince" in *Hamlet* will tell us very little about the importance of *Hamlet*. Yet the patient accumulation and analysis of this sort of factual data, now more possible than ever with electronic text and analytical tools, can lay the foundation for knowledge of the order sought by the humanistic scholar.

Closely related to the nature of knowledge is the question of progress. In the natural sciences, knowledge tends to be progressive or "cumulative." Each successive finding confirms, modifies, or overturns some piece of existing knowledge. This is true whether the problem is the identification of a new virus that has been detected through more sophisticated laboratory equipment or a far-ranging perception of relationships, such as the replacement of Newtonian physics with Einsteinian. In the humanities, no such "progress" is observable. Neither Sophocles' *Antigone*, Wagner's *Der Ring des Nibelungen*, nor Michelangelo's *Pieta* are superseded as was the "phlogiston" theory of chemistry. This is not to say that works based upon the same or similar themes do not appear and that patterns of influence are not clearly evident. What is not cumulative is our perception of beauty, our insight into the human condition, our understanding of how people act in terms of artistic creativity.

Earlier on, C. P. Snow published a controversial work on the *Two Cultures and the Scientific Revolution* (1959). Snow saw a divide between the two cultures with the humanities in decline as the scientific culture was on the rise (18–19). This was the prevailing view after World War II as the military/industrial complex was driving scientific research. Later, Michael Moravcsik, Eugene Garfield, and others wrote of the relationships between the broad disciplines and the shared objectives of practitioners from both "cultures" (Moravcsik 1980; Garfield 1989). The latter contains a list of journals that cover the science-art connection.

The reader should not overlook the fact that, despite the differences outlined above, the sciences and the arts and humanities actually have many connections. Increasingly, scholars and educators for professions in the sciences recognize that the humanities add value to the curricula in fields such as medicine and engineering, for example, the interdisciplinary fields of bioethics or medical humanities. In questions of ethics, most any subject can be studied, such as questions of the ethics of food supply or the sustainability of the human presence in natural environments. More recently, those in the arts and design fields are collaborating with engineers in the design of electronic medical devices for prostheses. Moreover, the humanities now have interdisciplinary fields that might formerly have been considered social sciences, such as women's studies, ethnic studies, and cultural studies. These and such areas as eco-criticism are now merging with global studies in universities in the twenty-first century.

CHARACTERISTICS OF LITERATURES
IN THE HUMANITIES

Students and librarians need to understand the kinds of literature in the humanities for collection development and delivery of services. The excellent library collection will include all categories of humanities-related material and the librarian will need to be familiar with all of them.

Wiberley has defined the types of literature used in the Humanities (ELIS 2009). Whereas the social sciences and the sciences have two types of literature, that in which they write about the results of their research and that which describes and indexes the body of literature produced by the researchers, the humanities have three different kinds of literatures. The first is termed *primary literature* and consists of original works or documents that are the basis of research. The second category is *secondary literature* in which humanists publish their scholarship. We might expand the second type of literatures as defined by Wiberley and add literature designed for special groups or purposes that may be subdivided into popularizations and professional literature. These are all of special interest to the librarian or information specialist. Popularizations allow for the dissemination of special interest material to wider audiences, thus enabling libraries to play a greater educational role. The professional literature comprises publications by associations and professional societies, with journals, conference proceedings, and reports of studies about the humanities. The third type of literature in the humanities is equivalent to the second kind of literature in the social sciences and sciences and that is the tools and apparatus of bibliographic control, which provide access to the literature for purposes of research (2198). Access tools, of course, enable librarians to provide information services; here we think of bibliographies, indexes, abstracts, encyclopedias, dictionaries, handbooks, and the other finding aids needed to access information for scholarship and research. All of these make up a support literature for the humanist in addition to the primary and secondary literatures of research and other venues of publication that support the primary scholarship.

The heart of humanistic study is the original work, whether a poem, painting, symphony, or discourse on ethics. The creative contribution is what is studied by the humanist scholar. Wiberley further describes the primary literature as "that which is written by persons whose activities and accomplishments the humanist seeks to describe or interpret or by persons who observed first-hand the subject whose activities and accomplishments the humanist studies (2199). These documents or artifacts are nearly always housed in libraries, archives, or museums. When large-scale digitization was first begun, many humanists made the case that, for research, the original documents or artifacts could not be replaced by surrogates. The text of a document can be duplicated, but not the artifactual value of the material object. While digital files can be used for content, it is debatable whether or not a digital file can be considered primary literature. On the other hand, most secondary literature is studied for the text or contents and not artifactual value. In addition, as we have seen above, other kinds of literature are utilitarian rather than primary or secondary scholarship.

The centrality of the library for the humanistic researcher is still accompanied by the centrality of the monograph as distinct from the periodical article. Although there have been fewer user studies in the humanities than in other fields, the pattern of preference for books and pamphlets continues to emerge, in contrast to the ongoing preference of the natural and physical scientist for journal articles, reprints, and preprints. The most prevalent format for publication in the humanities and the arts is the printed monograph that contains both the primary, creative literature and the theoretical, critical, and textual secondary literature. For a thorough treatment of the nature of the literature of the humanities, the article by Wiberley in the *Encyclopedia of Library and Information Sciences* (3rd edition) is recommended.

INFORMATION SEEKING AND
USE IN THE HUMANITIES

The characteristics noted in the previous section on scholarship in the humanities have their impact on patterns in the use of information and library materials. They influence how humanities scholars seek information and the nature of the literature in their disciplines. For the humanist, the library remains at the heart of the research enterprise, even as electronic access allows secondary and some primary research to be done remotely. For the natural scientist, by contrast, the laboratory is at the center, with the library providing a supporting role. In this respect, the creative artist, as distinct from the researcher in the humanities, may be more nearly like the scientist—as anyone who has witnessed dialogue between a sculptor and an art historian can testify! Here the library provides support to the studio, just as the library is supportive of the lab activities of the scientist. (See chapter 11 on information seeking in the visual arts.) Regardless of the type of work the humanist engages in, the library is often an important resource. Humanities scholarship and the library's role in supporting it are discussed in Ross Atkinson's "Humanities Scholarship and the Research Library" (1995).

Another characteristic reported in user studies is the greater spread of individual titles used by researchers in the humanities. Whereas a relatively small number of journals contain a high proportion of frequently cited articles in fields such as chemistry and mathematics, the same high degree of concentration in journal or monographic titles has not been observed in the humanities. This is not to deny that critical studies tend to cluster around certain landmark works, but the spread of titles in which the criticisms appear is greater and the concentration much less intense.

A third use pattern that continues to distinguish humanistic from scientific researchers is a much wider time spread in the materials that are used. Whereas publications of the past five years seem more crucial to scientific research, with usage dropping off rapidly beyond that, the humanist is likely to be interested in works of 20, 40, 50, or 100 or more years ago. Indeed, if one considers the classics in each field, the range of interest may extend to items 200 or 300 years old, or as far back as antiquity.

This characteristic of humanities scholarship provides interesting challenges in the preservation of older materials; fortunately these challenges are being addressed by groups such as the Council on Library and Information Resources, the Association of Research Libraries (ARL), ITHAKA, and the commercial marketplace. Preservation is discussed in a section below.

A fourth distinguishing use pattern is that the humanist and artists appear to have a greater need to browse than do scientists and social and behavioral scientists. The need to browse has been found in studies of the information seeking behavior of artists and studio arts students as well as those in all the visually oriented fields. In her review of research and study of information retrieval habits of humanities scholars, Green (2000) characterizes the humanities research process as preferring informal rather than formal bibliographic approaches to information retrieval.

Finally, we must mention citation practices and studies of publication and citation data in the arts and humanities. When the Institute for Scientific Information introduced its Arts and Humanities Citation Index in 1978, Eugene Garfield pointed out that inconsistent citation practices, citations to unpublished manuscripts and catalogs, and references to original sources embedded in texts without explicit citation were but three of the problems that were considered in developing the Index. The need to "enhance" titles for the *Permuterm* subject index has also been discussed in Garfield's works (1980a, 1980b). The nature of titles in humanities publications is explored in M. Yitzhaki's (1997) "Variation in Informativity of Titles in Research Papers in Selected Humanities Journals: A Comparative Study." An argument for increased journal coverage by the Arts and Humanities Citation Index and Social Sciences Citation Index is presented in Edward Funkhouser's "The Evaluative Use of Citation Analysis for Communication Journals" (1996). Citation analysis studies in the latter 1990s and early twenty-first century are still finding that the monograph is the primary vehicle of scholarly communication in the humanities (Lindholm-Romantschuk and Warner 1996; Budd and Craven 1999; Thompson 2002). Printed works are still preferred over electronic surrogates or original electronic publication.

User studies that clarify the generalizations about humanists' scholarly practices and information seeking fall into three categories: first, the broad studies that cut across disciplinary lines; second, the more limited studies that look at a single aspect of information seeking or at one or just a few users or disciplines; and finally, the studies that focus on electronic information and how humanists respond to it. The third category has dominated work on humanities information seeking and use since the 1990s.

Among the broad and general reviews, a good starting point remains Sue Stone's "Humanities Scholars: Information Needs and Uses" (1982). Stone's findings provide what can now be considered a classic profile of the humanist. Stone established that humanists tend to work alone and in the humanities "the individual scholar's interpretation is paramount" (294). The monograph is the preferred format for publication and research; browsing is a favorite discovery method; and currency is not important in humanities scholarship. Working visual artists fit the profile of humanists in that "most artistic creation is individual and solitary" (Wenger 1998, 126).

Other general studies should enhance the librarian's basic reading on user needs and behaviors. Results of a major study by the Research Libraries Group (RLG) are presented in Constance Gould's "Information Needs in the Humanities: An Assessment" (1988). Even though the report is over 25 years old, it is still a useful reference. Stephen E. Wiberley, Jr. and William G. Jones have conducted a number of studies, following researchers in the humanities (Wiberley and Jones, 1989, 1994, 2000; Wiberley 2003, 2004). In their earlier studies in the 1980s and 1990s, the researchers found the same patterns observed by Stone and later confirmed by others (Lougee, Sandler, & Parker 1990; Tibbo 1991, 1994; Watson-Boone 1994; Bates 1996; Cory 1999; Massey-Burzio 1999). The conclusions drawn in their first report differ only slightly from Stone's, yet by 2000 they reported a widespread acceptance of electronic databases and use of communication technology.

In more specialized studies, Knievel and Kellsey conducted a citation analysis to determine which languages frequently comprise the journal citations in eight humanities fields: art, classics, history, linguistics, literature, music, philosophy, and religion (2005). The study found that citation patterns varied widely among humanities disciplines. There was a wide variance in use of foreign language sources by the different fields, higher in art, classics, history, and music. Even literature and religion had over 15 percent of citations to foreign language sources. For non-English citations, French and German comprised 15 percent. Not surprisingly, English was the major language. Overall, scholars in all eight fields cited an average of 78.2 percent English-language materials (146–147). For the relative numbers of citations to books versus those to journals, the fields of philosophy (51 percent books) and linguistics (61 percent books) showed a higher than average reliance on journals. Conversely, literature (83 percent), music (80.6 percent), and religion (88 percent) showed a higher than average reliance on books (147). The study also confirms that, in most humanities disciplines, monographs remain the dominant format of cited sources, although some fields cited monographs less frequently than expected. As of the early years of the twenty-first century, humanities scholars were not using electronic sources heavily (147). This is most likely because scholars prefer monographs, and at the time the study was done, monographic publishing was primarily in print.

East found that only 18.3 percent of humanities researchers used e-books for their research (2005). He suggested that humanities scholars may use primarily print resources because they were taught to do research that way. He recommends that librarians should at least make humanities scholars aware of what is available electronically and offer instruction (138).

While the majority of the user studies have focused on *scholars* in the humanities, Barrett (2005) conducted an exploratory study on graduate student researchers in the humanities. The study is one of a very few to look at graduate students as researchers. The study sought to find out whether there are differences between faculty and graduate students' information seeking behavior and if graduate students are, in fact, a distinct user group. The findings show that the PhD stage of a graduate student's career does entail a "unique series of stages" in which there are different needs (330). Graduate students rely a great deal on research mentors and they have time pressures such as comprehensive exams, prospectus deadlines, and expectations for completion of their research. Barrett recommends that librarians "increase their profile and relevance among graduate students" to assist them in preparing for their role as academic researchers (330).

Many specific studies of use and users in individual disciplines are covered in the remaining chapters of this guide. However, four that are not mentioned elsewhere because they are essentially addressing the area of history, may be helpful to the reader interested in humanities librarianship. The first two are by Donald O. Case: "The Collection and Use of Information by Some American Historians: A Study of Motives and Methods" (1991), and "Conceptual Organization and Retrieval of Text by Historians: The Role of Memory and Metaphor" (1991). Helen Tibbo has also studied the nature of historical scholarship and information retrieval by historians in "Information Systems, Services, and Technology for the Humanities" (1991) and *Abstracting, Information Retrieval and the Humanities* (1993).

By the last decade of the twentieth century, studies of information seeking behavior of humanists began to include the use of electronic materials and the Internet. "The Getty End-User Online Searching Project in the Humanities: Report No. 6: Overview and Conclusions," by Marcia J. Bates (1996) concludes a series of reports by describing the challenges and opportunities of providing online information for humanities researchers. Deborah Shaw and Charles H. Davis report on an investigation on the use of computer-based tools for MLA in "The Modern Language Association: Electronic and Paper Surveys of Computer-Based Tool Use" (1996) and S. S. Lazinger and others report on "Internet Use by Faculty in Various Disciplines: A Comparative Case Study" (1997).

Two studies sponsored by The Digital Library Federation (DLF) looked at scholars' use of digital libraries and electronic information resources. The DLF and the Council on Library and Information Resources in the United States sponsored the *Scholarly Work in the Humanities* Project, a qualitative study conducted at the University of Illinois-Urbana-Champaign, begun in 1999. The aim of the project was to "examine in detail how humanists work, how they are integrating technology into their work, and how future technologies might offer new opportunities in line with the goals of humanities research" (Brockman et al 2001, 1). The study was one of the first to concentrate upon the aspects of humanities research which digital libraries and electronic information resources most affect and upon gaining a thorough understanding of those aspects of humanities research. In the responses, the change to electronic texts was seen as a cultural change equivalent to the development of print.

A second study by the DLF was in collaboration with Outsell, Inc. The study results were reported in "Dimensions and Use of the Scholarly Information Environment" (Friedlander 2002). Over 3,000 educators and students from public and private research universities and liberal arts colleges in the United States were interviewed. The respondents were distributed across seven disciplines, from math to science to the arts. Thus, it was not specifically a study of humanists information seeking. The objective of the DLF survey was ". . . to collect data on the relevance of existing and possible future services as well as on student and faculty perceptions of the library's value in the context of the scholarly information environment" (Intro). One of the summarized findings from the DLF/Outsell study is that

> Respondents differ in their level of comfort with electronic information depending on discipline and status. Respondents in the arts and humanities do not feel as comfortable with electronic information as respondents in social sciences, engineering, and business . . . There continues to be a strong preference for print even if the text is electronic (Intro).

In the early years of the twenty-first century, humanists were still primarily print oriented.

In the same time frame as the two DLF studies, Palmer and Neumann conducted a qualitative study on the "Information Work of Interdisciplinary Humanities Scholars" (2002). They found that contrary to stereotype, the scholars they studied "were deliberate adopters of technology," but at that point in time for most scholars, ". . . the digital is secondary to the physical in the actual use of information sources" (110). Palmer and Neumann identify different modes of reading and accentuate that different attributes of texts satisfy different types of reading.

A meta-analysis of the literature of "Use and Users of Electronic Library Resources" was conducted under the auspices of the Council on Library and Information Resources (Tenopir 2003).

The meta-analysis included over 100 studies and found that print was still used for some reading and was a part of research in almost every discipline, especially in the humanities. Print remained the most popular medium for books; most e-journal users still printed out the articles judged to be useful; and personal subscriptions to journals continued to decrease, so users rely more on electronic subscriptions subsidized by the library and on the Internet (iv-v).

Council on Library and Information Resources. http://www.clir.org/

The Council on Library and Information Resources was formed in 1997 through the merger of the Council on Library Resources and the Commission on Preservation and Access. CLIR is an independent, non-profit organization that collaborates with libraries, cultural institutions, and communities in higher education to foster new projects in the digital age. The Council sponsors *Ruminations*, a new series of short research papers and essays that bring "a new perspective to issues relevant to planning for and managing organizational and institutional change in the evolving digital environment for scholarship and teaching."

Toward the end of the first decade of the twenty-first century, studies were beginning to find more usage of electronic texts and more sophisticated uses of technology by humanists. Sukovic (2008) looked at scholars' interaction with electronic texts and found that "Working with electronic texts combines some traditional information and research practices into new patterns of information behavior. Electronic texts were perceived as fluid entities because the electronic environment promotes seamless interactions with a variety of media and formats." These interactions are called "netchaining," or online linking to sources and people (263). The paper by Sukovic contains an excellent literature review of studies of information seeking behavior of humanists with regard to electronic resources.

TRENDS IN THE ACADEMY AND LIBRARIES

In this section a number of trends that have implications for the humanities are reviewed. The first of these is the background on the crisis in scholarly communication in the latter decades of the twentieth century and the actions that were taken by the academy. The development of digital libraries and collections is the subject of another section, followed by Digital Humanities, the use of those technologies and the changes being suggested for scholarship in the humanities in light of the impact of electronic resources.

Scholarly Communication

One of the most far-reaching changes affecting libraries and academic disciplines began in the 1980s. What started out as the "serials crisis," broadened to the "crisis in scholarly communication." Scholarly communication is the process by which research and other scholarly writings are created, peer-reviewed for quality, disseminated, and used. Some add preservation to the definition. Briefly explained, the serials crisis was caused by a precipitous rise in the pricing of print journals in the fields of science, technology, engineering, and medicine (STEM). Librarians began to push back at large publishing conglomerates, which continued raising subscription prices exorbitantly year after year. The situation with the literature of the STEM fields began to affect other disciplines and formats as academic libraries had to devote ever-larger percentages of the materials budget to STEM literatures. One of the undesirable consequences was that of the "scholarly monograph in crisis."

Scholarly communication in the humanities and some social sciences fields began to be imperiled as fewer monographs were being purchased because of the decrease in funding left over for monographs and by increasingly shorter print runs for monographs, thus reducing scholars' chances for publication. These topics occupied deliberations about funding, budgets, and the future of scholarly communication.

Association of Research Libraries (ARL). http://arl.org

The Association of Research Libraries is a not-for-profit membership organization comprising over 125 libraries of North American research institutions. Its mission is to "shape and influence forces affecting the future of research libraries in the process of scholarly communications." ARL programs and services "promote equitable access to, and effective use of recorded knowledge in support of teaching, research, scholarship, and community service." The ARL "articulates the concerns of research libraries and their institutions, forges coalitions, influences information policy development, and supports innovation and improvement in research library operations." ARL operates as a "forum for the exchange of ideas and as an agent for collective action."

Beginning in the mid-1990s, a number of conferences and studies in the United States sponsored by the ARL, the Association of American Universities (AAU), the Association of American University Presses (AAUP), the American Council of Learned Societies (ACLS) and the Modern Language Association (MLA) focused attention on the declining sales market for the scholarly monograph. The ARL, in conjunction with other scholarly societies, held a conference in 1997 on monograph publishing, *The Specialized Scholarly Monograph in Crisis or How Can I Get Tenure if You Won't Publish My Book?* The monograph crisis was described in literature-related fields by the MLA Ad hoc Committee on the Future of Scholarly Publishing as the "crisis in scholarly publishing" (MLA 2002).

American Council of Learned Societies (ACLS). http://www.acls.org

The ACLS is a private, nonprofit federation of seventy national scholarly organizations founded in 1919. The mission of the American Council of Learned Societies is "the advancement of humanistic studies in all fields of learning in the humanities and the social sciences and the maintenance and strengthening of relations among the national societies devoted to such studies." The ACLS promotes scholarship through the awarding of peer-reviewed fellowships; convening and supporting scholarly conferences; sponsoring reference works and innovations in scholarly communication; strengthening relations among learned societies; encouraging the establishment of new societies; and representing humanistic scholarship in the U.S. and internationally. The primary publication project of the ACLS is HEB (Humanities E-Book), a collection of digital editions of significant scholarship in the humanities (entry 2–32). The ACLS also sponsors the online *American National Biography* published by Oxford University Press.

The Knight Higher Education Collaborative in the United States also devoted considerable attention to the plight of scholarly publication in the humanities and social sciences. The Roundtable on Scholarly Communication in the Humanities and Social Sciences was jointly convened in March 2001 by the ARL, the National Humanities Alliance, and the Knight collaborative with funding from the NEH. A number of position papers were issued. The worry was that the speed of publication demanded by the sciences

... may overshadow a more reflective model of scholarship in which publication is the result of an individual scholar's work to develop, extend, or refine the state of thinking in a particular subject. In the constrained economics of scholarly publishing, faculty in the humanities and social sciences have found it increasingly difficult to find print venues for scholarship that make significant contributions to specialized areas of inquiry. The ultimate anxiety is that the humanities and social science will be permanently devalued within the academy (2001, 3).

The key role of the scholarly monograph was re-affirmed:

The scholarly monograph has proven to be remarkably well-suited as a vehicle for scholarly dissemination. It is not just that humanists celebrate books as objects of art important in their own right . . . but that scholarly work in the social sciences and humanities is of a different kind and hence requires a different kind of communication—one that traditional print publication has served well (2).

As a response to the crisis in scholarly publishing, proposals for electronic publication of scholarship began to emanate from the research library sector. The first of these was the Scholarly Publishing and Academic Resources Coalition (SPARC), an initiative of the ARL and allies to wrest scholarly publishing away from the publishing conglomerates and give control of scholarly communication back to the universities in which research is being generated and to encourage electronic publication of journals and texts. The American Council of Learned Societies sponsored several studies and began its own electronic books initiative (HEB entry 2-32).

SPARC (Scholarly Publishing and Academic Resources Coalition).
http://www.arl.org/sparc/

SPARC, the Scholarly Publishing and Academic Resources Coalition, is an international alliance of academic and research libraries based in Washington DC. Developed by the Association of Research Libraries (ARL), SPARC is working as "a catalyst for change to correct imbalances in the scholarly publishing system." Its charge is "to stimulate the emergence of new scholarly communication models that expand the dissemination of scholarly research and reduce financial pressures on libraries." Leading academic organizations have endorsed SPARC which is working in collaboration with publishers, authors, and libraries "to seize the unprecedented opportunities created by the networked digital environment to advance the conduct of scholarship."

The Budapest convention of the Open Society Institute (BOAI) in 2001 adopted the *Open Access Initiative* which called for the results of research produced by authors without expectation of payment to be made widely available on the Internet and to carry permissions necessary for users to use and re-use results in a way that accelerates the pace of scholarship and research. Open access literature is digital, online, free of charge, and free of most copyright and licensing restrictions. It encourages the unrestricted sharing of research results with everyone, everywhere, for the advancement and enjoyment of knowledge and society (Directory of Open Access Journals n.d.). The Initiative inaugurated the Open Access (OA) movement, recommending to researchers in the sciences self-archiving and publishing in open access journals. The Open Access movement became a worldwide effort to provide free online access to scientific and scholarly research literature, especially peer-reviewed articles and preprints. The Open Access movement gained momentum when the National Institutes of Health (NIH) promulgated a Public Access Policy in 2007 that mandated all grant project reports and resulting publications must be open access. Harvard University followed the NIH example in 2008 by requiring that faculty publish in open access journals or deposit copies of their publications in the Harvard institutional repository. Other large universities then began to join in. In 2011, there were over 160 institutions worldwide that had registered open access mandate policies with *ePrints.org*, a website that lists the institutions with copies of the policies.

Further progress was made in 2003 at the Berlin Open Access Conference where the *Berlin Declaration on Open Access to Knowledge in the Sciences and the Humanities* was drawn up. Whereas the Budapest Initiative was focused mainly on the sciences, the Berlin Declaration builds on the significant progress of the Budapest Open Access Initiative and calls for open access to knowledge in the humanities as well as in the sciences. The Declaration is a document that outlines concrete steps to promote the Internet as a medium for disseminating global knowledge. It also moves beyond the scope of primary literature, indicating ". . . open access contributions include original scientific research results, raw data and metadata, source materials, digital representations of pictorial and graphical materials and scholarly multimedia material" (Berlin Open Access Conference 2003). With the inclusion of images, graphical, and multimedia materials as well as primary research documents, open access has been extended to all disciplines and fields of knowledge.

On the way to encouraging electronic publication and open access, a number of major universities began local initiatives for the digitization and preservation of scholarly materials being produced at their institutions. Harvard, MIT, the University of Washington, and others inaugurated institutional repositories for the promulgation and archiving of scholarly resources, collections, and publications within the institution. Contents of these institutional repositories range from the faculty publications, pre-prints, theses and dissertations, teaching materials, and other unpublished research, to encompassing all of the institution's budgetary data, reports, internal correspondence, and more, all digitized (Cervone 2004, 44). In the move toward institutional repositories, librarians began to point out to scholars that they need to be concerned about the long time archiving of their own oeuvre, printed as well as born digital works.

The pros and cons of open access have been debated (see further readings section below). Cathy N. Davidson (2008), a proponent of open access, has justified it as follows:

> Once we champion openness, we enter a new world of social, intellectual, and curatorial rules. An open repository challenges the borders between disciplines as well as between professionals and amateurs, between scholars and knowledge enthusiasts. It raises questions of privilege and authority as well as ethical issues of credibility and responsibility, privacy and security, neutrality and freedom of expression (711).

As open access publishing and institutional repositories became more common, a further push was made for Green OA, a term to specifically mean immediate author archiving in an institutional repository. In Green OA the author has the capability of archiving all of published output from the author's own manuscript files. The publications are peer-reviewed, but the author can immediately archive the peer-reviewed manuscript before publication. Many publishers are beginning to agree to this arrangement. The effect is that anyone in the world can read these archived files and, in this way, an author reaches a universal audience, far beyond the numbers that only have paid subscription access. Such arrangements benefit scientific researchers who have access to everything related to their research in a timely manner. It also benefits authors in the arts and humanities who would like to reach a broader audience for their work than just the audience for academic publications. Another advantage is, if monographs are open access, they are open to web citation analysis that can demonstrate the impact of monographs just as the citation indexes have done for journal articles (Harnad 2011).

The Open Access movement began with the sciences and the research library sector and then spread to other academic disciplines, but the humanities have been slow to embrace open access. Peter Suber examined the issue in "Promoting Open Access in the Humanities"(2005). The arts fields have been even slower to adopt open access. Tomlin, in "Every man his book? An introduction to open access in the arts," addresses the reasons (2011). Open access in the arts is covered in chapter 11, the Visual Arts.

Professional and scholarly associations have endorsed open access including the Association of College and Research Libraries, the Association of Research Libraries (ARL), and the International Federation of Library Associations and Institutions (IFLA). Many have also begun to open access to their publications. By the second decade of the twenty-first century, most of the journals published by the American Library Association and its divisions had become open access journals.

Digital Libraries, Texts, and Collections

No discussion of developments in library services in the humanities could be complete without mention of digital libraries. First initiated by libraries for their collections, as digital libraries became more numerous, plans for larger digital libraries by region or countries were begun. In Europe, a number of countries have inaugurated digital library projects. The most ambitious in Europe is *Europeana* that has the goal of containing the cultural heritage from all European countries. (entry 2-52). In 2011, proposals were put forth for a Digital Public Library in North America. The Digital Public Library of America (DPLA) initiative is led by the Berkman Center for Internet and Society at Harvard University and sponsored by the Alfred P. Sloan Foundation. The DPLA is an ambitious project to provide e-books to all, especially those in areas without library services or those unable to avail themselves of library services. The proposal provoked discussion about the vision, the audience it is intended to serve, its effect on public libraries, whether or not it would be just for academics and researchers, and questions about the technological architecture to be employed.

Digital library projects abound, but they are too numerous to list in this guide. For an extensive bibliography, list of projects, journals, and conferences, consult IFLA for lists of Digital Libraries: Resources and Projects on the Web at http://www.ifla.org/II/diglib.htm.

Along with the development of digital libraries, those in the information professions became conscious of the preservation problems associated with digitized texts and born digital works. The leaders in the push to conversion of scholarly communication to electronic publishing began to turn their attention to assuring the long-term availability of digital materials. The concern for storage and preservation led to several projects.

One of the earliest was JSTOR founded in 1995 as a project at the University of Michigan, sponsored by the Andrew W. Mellon Foundation (entry 2-43). The original intent of the JSTOR project was to digitize the back files of journals in order that academic libraries that were pressed for stack space could deselect those journal runs and rely upon JSTOR for provision of the digitized text. JSTOR was such a success that it became a non-profit entity in 2003 and expanded coverage to areas in the humanities, social sciences, and sciences. JSTOR merged with ITHAKA in 2009.

ITHAKA is a non-profit agency that provides three primary services to the academic community: research on the impact of digital media through ITHAKA S+R; a digital archive of academic journals through JSTOR; and the preservation of digital scholarly literature through *Portico*. The research and consulting arm of ITHAKA produces studies and reports valuable to the scholarly and library communities. While the focus of ITHAKA's research may be more relevant for academic libraries, the organization has produced several publications that seem useful for collection development and strategic planning in general. Publications are available on the website at http://www.ithaka.org/publications.

An initiative was begun by JSTOR in 2002 funded with an Andrew W. Mellon Foundation grant to develop a model for an electronic archiving service. After several years of development, in 2005 the initiative became *Portico*, a program of JSTOR, with additional funding by the Mellon Foundation, ITHAKA, JSTOR, and the Library of Congress. While JSTOR digitizes printed materials, *Portico* preserves scholarly electronic literature originating from publishers, books and electronic journals, ensuring that those materials remain accessible to future scholars, researchers, and students. *Portico* is a dark archive, meaning the content is only available if a triggering event makes that necessary.

Charles W. Bailey, Jr., a proponent of open access, maintains several online electronic bibliographies concerning the movements and issues discussed in this section: among these are the *Scholarly Electronic Publishing Bibliography*; the *Institutional Repository Bibliography* (2011); the *Electronic Theses and Dissertations Bibliography*; *Digital Preservation and Curation* (2011); and the *Google Book Search Bibliography*. All may be found at Digital Scholarship: http://digital-scholarship.org

While these developments in preservation of digital materials were taking place in the research library community, the for-profit sector had also entered into the digitization and digital preservation arena. Companies that held large microform collections of publication output as far back as the invention of the printing press began to digitize those collections. Many of the collections are treated in chapter 2 and are important resources for librarians to know about to assist users engaged in any topic of retrospective research. But the project that has drawn the most media attention is Google Books which began as "Google print" in 2002.

In 2004, Google announced a cooperative endeavor with five major research libraries: the New York Public Library and the libraries of Harvard, Michigan, Oxford, and Stanford universities. The negotiations had been kept secret and in December 2004, when Google announced the Library Project, it stunned the library world. The libraries agreed to let Google digitize volumes from their printed book and serial collections in exchange for institutional copies of the digitized volumes. The titles to be digitized were left up to the libraries. It has been estimated that the collections of the five research libraries hold 18 million titles combined. The Google Library Project expanded to include an even larger number of research libraries, both in the United States and abroad. In this same time frame Google also entered into the Partners Project with a number of publishers to give access to recently published works that are copyrighted, as has Amazon and other companies. In 2005, "Google Print" was renamed "Google Books" which includes all of the digitized works from the various collaborative agreements. Google Books can be regarded as one of the largest digitization, preservation projects ever undertaken. (See entry 2-53)

Almost immediately upon the announcement of the Google Library Project, the question of access to copyrighted materials arose. It has been estimated that only about 15 percent of the digitized works in the Library Project are not under copyright, leaving the majority of them as copyrighted works. It is not known what percentage of the copyrighted works are orphan works, those for which the copyright owners cannot be found. In any case, under current copyright law, Google cannot give access to the complete texts of the works still under copyright. In 2005, the Association of American Publishers and the Authors' Guild filed class-action lawsuits against Google. Although a settlement was agreed to in 2008, in 2009, the U.S. Justice Department opened an anti-trust investigation into that settlement (Jones 2010, 78). The matter had not been resolved as of the publication of this work.

The primary reason for Google Books is not preservation, but content for Google's search business. Many of the same institutions in the Google Books digitization project have also entered into a private effort to ensure the long-term archiving of digitized works from their collections. The HathiTrust Digital Library was launched in October 2008 by a group of U.S. research universities as a digital preservation repository with over 50 partners including Cornell University, Yale University Library, the New York Public Library, the University of California system, the Big Ten libraries, and others. HathiTrust is administered at the University of Michigan but is supported by base funding from all of its institutional partners. The goal is to ensure long-term availability and preservation of materials to support teaching and learning for students and researchers. The HathiTrust Digital Library provides access to the digital collections of the partner universities and access services for public domain and in copyright content from a variety of sources, including Google, the Internet Archive, Microsoft, and others. In 2011, the University of Michigan Library Office of Copyright announced it would identify all of the orphan works in the HathiTrust Digital Library. An estimated 27 percent of works in the library are in public domain leaving 73 percent under copyright. Of that 73 percent, or over 6 million titles, a sample identified 45 percent as orphan works (as identified above as with copyright that an owner cannot be identified or found). HathiTrust will work to find the owners of the copyrighted texts and work with authors to authorize access rights through Creative Commons. It will take years of work, but also add access to many works not accessible because of copyright restrictions. A literature review of the background and studies that led to the formation of the HathiTrust Digital Library, along with the rationale for its formation and a thorough description of its activities, appears in the article by Christenson in *Library Resources & Technical Services* (2011).

Creative Commons. http://creativecommons.org/

The Creative Commons is "an attempt by many who create to allow others to use, manipulate, and re-use their creations legally." Current copyright law does not easily allow people to share their work in these ways as the "default" for modern copyright is to not allow a person to use or share their work with others. The Creative Commons was created to "assist creators in being able to legally declare their wishes." Creative Commons licenses, which can be as broad as to allow a person to do anything with another person's work, or to be as narrow as to only allow a person to forward or copy a work with the creator's name attached to it. The intent behind the movement is to "create a space where works of all types can be shared and used legally in the hopes of using the potential of the Internet." The founders of Creative Commons were more concerned with creating a cultural commons for art, music, literature, software programming, and more, than they were concerned with copyright of academic works.

All of these digital library programs are in the forefront in the "transformation of scholarly communication" from the print to the electronic environment. The humanities are well served by these projects as the cultural heritage of centuries is now being actively preserved. Librarians who work with students and researchers in the humanities and the arts need to be aware of the existence of these ongoing digitization projects.

Digital Humanities

While technophiles and those in the sciences may have regarded humanists as technophobes, this was a mistaken stereotype as borne out by the journal, *Computers and the Humanities*, the journal of the Association for Computers and the Humanities. The journal is an invaluable source of articles on the evolution of all aspects of computing and technology in the humanities. An informative overview of humanities computing up to the 1990s, written by the founding editor on the twenty-fifth anniversary of the journal, is Joseph Raben's "Humanities Computing 25 Years Later" (1991). In 2005, *Computers and the Humanities* was folded into another journal that traces developments in humanities computing, *Literary and Linguistic Computing* (LLC) which began in 1986 as the official journal of the Association for Literary and Linguistic Computing. LLC is now the journal of the Association of Literary and Linguistic Computing and the Association for Computers in the Humanities. The tradition is continuing with an online journal which began in 2006, *Digital Humanities Quarterly* (DHQ), published by The Alliance of Digital Humanities Organizations.

When computing in the humanities first began, only a few individuals were involved in this highly technical and expensive field, usually being involved in archiving, digitizing, and preserving texts. As the technology advanced and became more widespread, humanities computing became less concerned with the purely technical aspects and focused more on the construction of text collections and other objects of study; but research and publication were still on the individualistic model of the humanities scholar and in traditional venues. Then, as the digitization of texts and other network infrastructure were taken over and provided in libraries and institutional computer divisions, digital scholarship ". . . began to grapple with the social and collaborative aspects of computing, while continuing to explore aspects of text representation and text analysis. As it has matured, humanities computing that had been defined by a technological reliance on the computer, evolved into *digital humanities*, which is concerned more broadly with media and methods in a digital context" (Flanders and Mylonas 2009, 1559). With all of the technology available, there have been struggles and controversies among those in the humanities disciplines about how best to adjust to what has been called a paradigm shift brought about by the digital revolution.

    Digital Humanities is a term that has come into use throughout the humanities to signify the impact of information technologies upon the humanities and the use of technology to advance research in the humanities. Kamada succinctly defines digital humanities as "the application of information technologies to analyzing humanities as well as many interdisciplinary subjects" (Kamada 2008). A closely related term is *digital scholarship*. The American Council of Learned Societies' Commission on Cyberinfrastructure for the Humanities and Social Sciences' (2006) provided an all-encompassing definition of digital scholarship as "building a digital collection of information for further study and analysis; creating appropriate tools for collection-building; creating appropriate tools for the analysis and study of collections; using digital collections and analytical tools to generate new knowledge, interpretation, understanding; and creating authoring tools for presenting these new ideas, either in traditional forms or in digital form" (10). Included in this list are many activities that are in the domain of libraries and computer centers rather than the humanities researcher or scholar.

    As the early adopters of computers in the humanities realized that automation could make such scholarly compilations as concordances and corpus databases possible, librarians were working on automating their card catalogs and other technical processes. As the technical infrastructure improved, librarians had the advantage when moving into digitization of texts which required standardization of many technical aspects. "Librarians are experts at collecting and organizing information and are aware of the importance of standards and best practices. They have led the digital humanities world in advocating, developing, adopting, and documenting standards and best practices in all areas of digitization" (Flanders and Mylonas 2009, 1563). Librarians initiated the concept of the institutional digital repository and they are tackling the problems of long-term archiving, metadata management, and other attendant issues. The assumption of the areas of digitization and preservation by libraries has left the scholar the freedom to concentrate upon research.

    With digital humanities the paradigm shift has arrived. Digital humanities is now considered to be a distinct field of study at "the intersection of humanities ideas and digital methods, with the goal of understanding how the use of digital technologies and approaches alters the practice of humanities scholarship" (Flanders and Mylonas 2009, 1557). There are now programs of study or departments or institutes labeled "digital humanities," and even following the information science model, *humanities informatics*. An example is the Humanities, Arts, Science, and Technology Advanced Collaboratory (HASTAC), a national consortium founded by Cathy N. Davidson (Duke University) and David Theo Goldberg (University of California, Irvine). Both Davidson and Goldberg are heads of humanities institutes, which are interdisciplinary groupings of scholars and researchers. HASTAC ("haystack") is "a consortium of humanists, artists, social scientists, scientists, and engineers, committed to new forms of collaboration across communities and disciplines fostered by creative uses of technology"(http://hastac.org/). Belying the stereotype of humanists working alone, HASTAC is an attempt at collaboration using the possibilities afforded by new technologies to find out "what happens when we stop privileging traditional ways of organizing knowledge (by fields, disciplines, and majors or minors) and turn attention instead to alternative modes of creating, innovating, and critiquing that better address the interconnected, interactive global nature of knowledge today." Besides the academic groupings named above, HASTAC has members as varied as public intellectuals, citizen journalists, educators, software or hardware designers, scientists specializing in human-computer interfaces, gamers, programmers, librarians, museum curators, publishers, social and political organizers, and interested others "who use the potential of the Internet and mobile technologies for new forms of communication and social action . . ." The HASTAC site offers news, opportunities, competitions, blogs, and much more concerning humanities digital media (http://hastac.org/).

Digital humanities is not only concerned with the digitization of materials, e-books and so forth, but with using technology to provide fresh insights. Text mining, particularly with literature, is an increasing area of scholarly study. Another example is the new field of cultural analytics, which involves analysis and visualization of large sets of visual and spatial media: art, photography, video, cinema, computer games, space design, architecture, graphic and Web design, and product design. These fields study the pervasive cultural influence the computer and networked systems are having on society worldwide. The impact of digital humanities can be seen in the movement away from traditional humanities disciplines toward entirely new fields of study. Literature, philosophy, and cultural studies have moved closer to the arts. Interdisciplinary research in the humanities now focuses on new media studies, game studies, and digital aesthetics. Collaboration is becoming a more acceptable model for research and publication.

Discussion soon arose about the traditional promotion and tenure process which did not recognize new forms of scholarship in digital humanities. Also in the discussion of promotion and tenure was the movement within the academy toward civic engagement, an emphasis on more social and community involvement and research in which both public and traditional scholarship can dovetail and combine teaching, research, and creative activity such as writing for a general audience or civic activities that produce policy reports and "artifacts of public and intellectual value." In the humanities public scholarship became "public humanities" or "applied humanities." Woodward, in "The Future of the Humanities—in the present & in public," sees public humanities and digital humanities as intersecting (2009). The new scholarship "integrating text, image, sound, and video," are "new ways of disseminating it to ever broader publics" (121). The Open Access Movement provides another means of reaching a broader public audience.

The two trends of digital humanities and public engagement came together in discussions of re-defining requirements for promotion and tenure. The MLA report *Standing Still: the Associate Professor Survey* broadens the conception of scholarship, research, and publication to include work produced or disseminated in new media, such as digital libraries of an author's work and attendant literary criticism (MLA 2009). The Report also recommends public scholarship as an important type of work that should be welcomed in tenure considerations and supports it, stating "Scholarship is a Public good" (26).

While technology in the humanities has been around since the beginnings of the computer age, the transition to digital scholarship is being fully realized in the twenty-first century. The traditional personification of the humanist as solitary, working alone in research, creative endeavors, and publishing, is being revised through collaborative efforts in digital scholarship. The future is never predictable, but for the near future, the trajectory of digital humanities seems assured to continue.

In the academic and library worlds we are still in transition between electronic and print resources with devices to use those resources still undergoing rapid change. There is no subject or discipline for which resources have not undergone profound change in the digital era. Online databases for bibliographic access, databases of images and primary texts, tools for the analysis of texts, and the resources on the World Wide Web influence how the actual work of the humanist scholar is done. Word processing, database searching, electronic publishing, the use of analytical and statistical packages, graphical software, user friendly interfaces, and digital library collections have been discussed in the literature. The availability of all of these in digital formats on the Web has brought collaboration to scholars in the arts and humanities. And librarians, archivists, and curators are also collaborating amongst themselves and with researchers.

WORKS CITED

American Council of Learned Societies. 2006. *Our Cultural Commonwealth: Report of the Commission on Cyberinfrastructures for Humanities and Social Sciences.* http://www.acls.org/

Asheim, Lester. 1956. *The Humanities and the Library.* Chicago: American Library Association.

Atkinson, Ross. 1995. "Humanities scholarship and the research library." *Library Resources & Technical Services* 39: 79–84.

Barrett, Andy. 2005. "The Information-Seeking Habits of Graduate Student Researchers in the Humanities." *Journal of Academic Librarianship* 31 (4): 324–331.

Bates, Marcia J. 1996. "The Getty End-User Online Searching Project in the Humanities; Report No.6: Overview and Conclusions." *College & Research Libraries* 57: 514–23.

Berlin Open Access Conference. 2003. *Berlin Declaration on Open Access to Knowledge in the Sciences and the Humanities.* http://www.zim.mpg.de/openaccess-berlin/berlin_declaration.pdf

Borden, Carla M., ed. 1992. "Knowledge Collaboration in the Arts, the Sciences, and the Humanities and Social Sciences, Pt.3" in *Knowledge: Creation, Diffusion, Innovation* 14 (September): 110–32.

Brockman, William S., Laura Neumann, Carole L. Palmer, and Tonyia J. Tidline. 2001. "Scholarly Work in the Humanities and the Evolving Information Environment." Washington, DC: Digital Library Federation, Council on Library and Information Resources. http://www.clir.org/pubs/abstract/pub104abst.html

Budapest Convention of the Open Society Institute. 2002. *Budapest Open Access Initiative.* http://www.soros.org/openaccess/read.shtml

Budd, John and Catherine K. Craven. "Academic Library Monographic Acquisitions: Selection of Choice's Outstanding Books." *Library Collections, Acquisitions, & Technical Services* 23 (1): 15–26.

Case, Donald O. 1991. "The Collection and Use of Information by Some American Historians: A Study of Motives and Methods." *Library Quarterly* 61 (1): 61–82.

Case, Donald O. 1991. "Conceptual Organization and Retrieval of Text by Historians: The Role of Memory and Metaphor." *Journal of the American Society for Information Science* 42 (October): 657–668.

Cervone, H. Frank. 2004. "The Repository Adventure." *Library Journal* 129 (June 1): 44–46.

Christenson, Heather. 2011. "HathiTrust: A Research Library at Web Scale." *Library Resources & Technical Services* 55 (April): 93–102.

Commission on the Humanities. 1980. *The Humanities in American Life.* Berkeley, CA: University of California Press.

Couch, Nena and Nancy Allen, eds. 1993. *The Humanities and the Library*, 3rd ed. Chicago: American Library Association.

Davidson, Cathy N. 2008. "Humanities 2.0: Promise, Perils, Predictions." *PMLA* 123 (May): 707–717.

East, J.W. 2005. "Information Literacy for the Humanities Researcher: A Syllabus Based on Information Habits Research." *The Journal of Academic Librarianship* 31 (2):134–42.

Flanders, Julia and Elli Mylonas. 2009. "Digital Humanities." *Encyclopedia of Library and Information Sciences*, 3rd ed. 1: 1, 1557–1568. Chicago: American Library Association.

Friedlander, Amy. 2002. "Dimensions and Use of the Scholarly Information Environment: Introduction to a Data Set Assembled by the Digital Library Federation and Outsell, Inc." Washington, DC: Council on Library and Information Resources. http://www.clir.org/pubs/reports/pub110/contents.html

Funkhouser, Edward. 1996. "The Evaluative Use of Citation Analysis for Communication Journals." *Human Communication Research* 22 (June): 563–74.

Garfield, Eugene. 1980a. "Will ISI's Arts and Humanities Citation Index Revolutionize Scholarship?" in *Essays of an Information Scientist*, 3. Philadelphia, PA: ISI Press: 204–8.

Garfield, Eugene. 1980b. "Is Information Retrieval in the Arts and Humanities Inherently Different from that in Science?" *Library Quarterly* 50: 40–57.

Garfield, Eugene. 1989. "Art and Science. Part 1. The Art-Science Connection," in *Essays of an Information Scientist* 12: 54–61.

Gould, Constance. 1988. *Information Needs in the Humanities: An Assessment.* Stanford, CA: Research Libraries Group.

Green, Rebecca. 2000. "Locating Sources in Humanities Scholarship: The Efficacy of Following Bibliographical References." *Library Quarterly* 70 (April): 201–229.

Harnad, Steven. 2011. "Open Access Self-Archiving of Refereed Research: A Post-Gutenberg Compromise." *Against the Grain* 23 (April): 22–24.

Heinzkill, Richard. 2004. "References in Scholarly English and American Literary Journals Thirty Years Later: A Citation Study." *College & Research Libraries* 65 (2): 141–153.

Hristova, Mariela. 2003. "Bibliometrics & the Humanities: Analysis of Studies and Their Implications for Future Research." Independent Study. School of Information, University of Texas at Austin.

Immroth, John. 2007. "Humanities and its Literatures," in *Encyclopedia of Library and Information Science*. 2nd ed. New York: Taylor and Francis: Published online: 13 Dec 2007: 1236–1243.

Jones, Edgar. 2010. "Google Books as a General Research Collection." *Library Resources & Technical Services* 54 (April): 77–89.

Kamada, H. 2010. "Digital Humanities: Roles for Librarians." *College & Research Libraries News* 71 (October): 484–485.

Knievel, J. E. and Charlene Kellsey. 2005. "Citation Analysis for Collection Development: A Comparative Study of Eight Humanities Fields." *Library Quarterly* 75, 2 (April): 142–168.

The Knight Higher Education Collaborative. 2001. "Op Cit." *Policy Perspectives* 10 (December): 1–12.

Lazinger, S. S., et al. 1997. "Internet Use by Faculty in Various Disciplines: A Comparative Case Study," *Journal of the American Society for Information Science* 48 (June): 508–18.

Lindholm-Romantschuk, Ylva and Julian Warner. 1996. "The Role of Monographs in Scholarly Communication: An Empirical Study of Philosophy, Sociology and Economics." *The Journal of Documentation* 52 (December): 389–404.

Lougee, Wendy, Mark Sandler and Linda L. Parker. 1990. "The Humanities Scholars Project: A Study of Attitudes and Behavior Concerning Collection Storage and Technology." *College & Research Libraries* 51 (May): 231–40.

McLeish, Kenneth. 1993. *Key Ideas in Human Thought*. New York: Facts on File.

Manoff, Marlene, "Revolutionary or Regressive? The Politics of Electronic Collection Development," in *Scholarly Publishing: The Electronic Frontier*, edited by Robin P. Peek and Gregory B. Newby. Cambridge, MA: MIT Press.

Massey-Burzio, Virginia. 1999. "The Rush to Technology: A View from the Humanities." *Library Trends* 47 (Spring): 620–639.

MLA Committee on the Status of Women in the Profession. 2009. *Standing Still: The Associate Professor Survey:* Report. New York: Modern Language Association.

Moravcsik, Michael J. 1974. "Scientists and Artists: Motivations, Aspirations, Approaches, and Accomplishments." *Leonardo* 7: 255–57.

National Endowment for the Arts. 2011. *NEA Guide.* http://nea.gov/pub/pubAlpha.php?alpha=G

National Endowment for the Humanities. 2011. "What Are the Humanities? http://www.neh.gov/whoweare/overview.html

Oxford English Dictionary. Oxford, UK: Oxford University Press, 1989– . (Electronic database).

Palmer, Carole L. and Laura J. Neumann. 2002. "The Information Work of Interdisciplinary Humanities Scholars: Exploration and Translation." *Library Quarterly* 72 (1): 85–117.

Pavliscak, Pamela, Seamus Ross, and Charles Henry. 1997. *Information Technology in Humanities Scholarship: Achievements, Prospects, and Challenges. The U.S. Focus.* ACLS, Occasional Paper No. 37. Washington, DC: American Council of Learned Societies.

Princeton Studies: Humanistic Scholarship in America. Princeton University Press, 1963– .

Raben, Joseph. 1991. "Humanities Computing 25 Years Later." *Computers and the Humanities* 25: 341–50.

Shaw, Deborah and Charles H. Davis. 1996. "Electronic and Paper Surveys of Computer-Based Tool Use," *Journal of the American Society for Information Science* 47 (December): 932–40.

Snow, C. P. 1959. *The Two Cultures and the Scientific Revolution.* Stefan Collini, ed. 1993. Cambridge, UK: Cambridge University Press.

Smith, Natalia and Helen R. Tibbo. 1996. "Libraries and the Creation of Electronic Text in an Electronic Age: Scholarly Implications and Library Services." *College & Research Libraries* 57 (November): 335–53.

Stone, Sue. 1982. "Humanities Scholars: Information Needs and Uses." *Journal of Documentation*, 38 (December): 292–313.

Suber, Peter. 2005. "Promoting Open Access in the Humanities." *Syllecta Classica* 16: 231–246.

Sukovic, Suzana. 2008. "Convergent Flows: Humanities Scholars and Their Interactions with Electronic Texts." *Library Quarterly* 78 (3): 263–84.

Tenopir, Carol. 2003. *Use and Users of Electronic Library Resources: An Overview and Analysis of Recent Research Studies*. Washington, DC: Council on Library and Information Resources. http://www.clir.org/pubs/reports/pub120.pdf

Thompson, Jennifer Wolfe. 2002. "The Death of the Scholarly Monograph in the Humanities? Citation Patterns in Literary Scholarship." *Libri* 52 (3): 121–136.

Tibbo, Helen. 1993. *Abstracting, Information Retrieval, and the Humanities*. Chicago: American Library Association.

Tibbo, Helen. 1991. "Information Systems, Services, and Technology for the Humanities." *Annual Review of Information Science and Technology* 26: 287–346.

Tomlin, Patrick. 2011. "Every Man His Book? An Introduction to Open Access in the Arts." *Art Documentation* 30 (1): 4–11.

Watson-Boone, Rebecca. 1994. "The Information Needs and Habits of Humanities Scholars." *RQ* 34 (2): 203–216.

Wiberley, Stephen. 2003. "A Methodological Approach to Developing Bibliometric Models of Types of Humanities Scholarship." *Library Quarterly* 73 (2): 121–159.

Wiberley, Stephen. 2009. "Humanities Literatures and Their Users." *Encyclopedia of Library and Information Sciences*, 3rd ed. New York: Taylor and Francis: 1: 1, 2197–2004.

Wiberley, Stephen and William Jones. 1989. "Patterns of Information Seeking in the Humanities." *College & Research Libraries* 50 (6): 638–645.

Wiberley, Stephen and William Jones. 1994. "Humanists Revisited: A Longitudinal Look at the Adoption of Information Technology." *College & Research Libraries* 55 (6): 499–509.

Wiberley, Stephen and William Jones. 2000. "Time and Technology: A Decade-Long Look at Humanists' Use of Information Technology." *College & Research Libraries* 61 (5): 421–431.

Woodward, Kathleen. 2009. "The Future of the Humanities—in the Present & in Public." Daedalus 138 1(Winter): 110–123.

Yitzhaki, M. 1997. "Variation in Informativity of Titles in Research Papers in Selected Humanities Journals: A Comparative Study." *Scientometrics*, 38 (February): 219–29.

WEBSITES

American Council of Learned Societies (ACLS). http://www.acls.org

The Alliance of Digital Humanities Organizations (http://www.digitalhumanities.org) is an umbrella organization for the European Association for Literary and Linguistic Computing (ALLC) http://www.allc.org

Association for Computers and the Humanities (ACH) http://www.ach.org

Berlin Open Access Conference. 2003. *Berlin Declaration on Open Access to Knowledge in the Sciences and the Humanities*. http://www.zim.mpg.de/openaccess-berlin/berlin_declaration.pdf

Budapest Open Society Institute, *Budapest Open Access Initiative* (BOAI). http://www.soros.org/openaccess/read.shtm

Digital Public Library of America. http://cyber.law.harvard.edu/research/dpla

Directory of Open Access Journals http://www.doaj.org/

ePrints.org. Open access mandate policies. http://eprints.org/

Google Books. http://books.google.com

HASTAC. http://hastac.org/

Humanist. http://www.digitalhumanities.org/humanist/

IFLA Digital Libraries: Resources and Projects. http://www.ifla.org/II/diglib.htm

ITHAKA. http://www.ithaka.org/publications

National Endowment for the Arts. Guide, 2011. http://nea.gov/pub/2011-NEA-Guide.pdf

National Endowment for the Humanities. http://www.neh.gov/

HELPFUL RESOURCES AND FURTHER READING

Collection Development

Dillon, Dennis. 1997. "The Changing Role of Humanities Collection Development," in *Acquisitions and Collection Development in the Humanities*. Irene Owens, ed. New York: Haworth Press: 7–8.

Johns, Cecily. 1990–1994. *Selection of Library Materials in Area Studies*. Chicago: American Library Association. 2 vol.

McClung, Patricia A., ed. 1985. *Selection of Library Materials in the Humanities, Social Sciences, and Sciences*. Chicago: American Library Association.

Open Access and Scholarly Communication

McCulloch, E. 2006. "Taking Stock of Open Access: Progress and Issues." *Library Review* 55 (6): 337–343. Not a literature review, but a good review and summary of the benefits and drawbacks of the open access movement, difficulties and problems, but a positive article.

Morrison, Heather G. 2006. "The Dramatic Growth of Open Access: Implications and Opportunities for Resource Sharing." *Journal of Interlibrary Loan, Document Delivery & Information Supply* 16 (3): 95–107.

Peek, Robin P. and Gregory B. Newby, eds. 1996. *Scholarly Publishing: the Electronic Frontier*. Cambridge, MA: MIT Press. A "must-read" for those interested in scholarly publishing in the electronic age.

Schreibman, S., R. Siemens, and John Unsworth, eds. 2004. *A Companion to Digital Humanities*. Malden, MA: Blackwell Publishing.

Unsworth, John. 1996. "Electronic Scholarship or Scholarly Publishing and the Public." *Journal of Scholarly Publishing* 28 (October): 3–12.

CHAPTER 2

MULTIDISCIPLINARY RESOURCES IN THE HUMANITIES AND THE ARTS

Anna H. Perrault

As can be seen from chapter one of this guide, trends in humanities research and scholarship since the latter years of the twentieth century have become more interdisciplinary such that there are a sizable number of resources appropriate to more than one discipline in the arts and humanities. The evolutionary changes that have been brought about by online databases and digitization of texts have broadened the focus and contents of reference products so that dividing resources by reference formats is no longer useful. Included in this chapter are online reference databases, open access websites, digital collections, and printed works appropriate to more than one discipline or activity in the arts and humanities. Because they are general to all the humanities, there are tools for readers and writers as well as listings for antiquarian booksellers. Not included are very general indexes and reference works such as Academic Search Premier, Infotrac, general biographical dictionaries, and encyclopedias.

ELECTRONIC REFERENCE SOURCES

Electronic indexing databases existed before the advent of the WWW, but these were fee for service. With the rise of CD-ROMs as a distribution venue in the 1990s, electronic reference resources were at first electronic versions of the major printed indexing tools and were sold on CD-ROM. As indexing was converted almost totally to online databases, other content was added to the electronic products. Abstracts, tables of contents, and then full text were added to the indexing databases. Biographies, photographs, and book reviews were added as well. Now, for research in the humanities and the arts, it is possible to obtain much of the information one needs through the use of major online sources, even the full text of thousands of works.

With the migration to online reference sources, publishers have combined numbers of single printed publications into omnibus online databases. It is important for librarians and researchers to become familiar with electronic packages, as many librarians may subscribe selectively by publisher or distributor and not have overlapping coverage through numerous packages. In large research institutions, there will be a bewildering array of aggregated database packages with overlap in titles and content. While electronic databases have made searching easier through user-friendly interfaces, finding out about databases and knowing which product to search has become more difficult and confusing. The arrangement in this chapter is designed to assist users in identifying electronic resources databases that might be appropriate for their information need and to assist them in finding those resources in libraries.

Information seekers not affiliated with libraries and institutions that maintain access to fee-based subscription services are more dependent upon open access resources on the Internet. A section in this chapter is devoted to open-access resources.

Online Subscription Databases

The resources covered in this section are primarily online reference tools, and for the most part, commercially produced and sold. They are online only, or online with print versions. Many of the entries are electronic continuations of long-established printed indexes that have ceased being published in printed versions and are now available only online. Unlike the printed versions, many of the databases also provide full text of the items indexed as well as bibliographic information. It is common for the very large publishers and aggregators to provide links between their products and library catalogs, making it easier to use multiple databases from one site.

2-1. Arts & Humanities Citation Index. Philadelphia, PA: Thomson/Reuters, 1975– . Online subscription database. http://thomsonreuters.com

2-2. Social Sciences Citation Index. Philadelphia, PA: Thomson/Reuters, 1974– . Online subscription database. http://thomsonreuters.com

2-3. Book Citation Index. Philadelphia, PA: Thomson/Reuters, 2011– . Online subscription database. http://thomsonreuters.com

2-4. Current Contents Connect: Arts & Humanities. Thomson/Reuters 1979– . Now included with Arts & Humanities Citation Index online. Current Contents Connect: Social & Behavioral Sciences included with Social Sciences Citation Index online. http://thomsonreuters.com

While these four databases are separate, they are searched in *Web of Science*, which provides a global search interface. They are treated here as separate titles as originally published in order for the reader to understand the various indexes. Although originally designed for the sciences, Eugene Garfield's Institute for Scientific Information (ISI) citation indexes eventually included all scholarly and research fields. The underlying principles of the ISI indexes are not the same as other purely subject indexing tools. The most well-known feature of *Web of Science* **is** the ability to search for cited references by cited author, work, year, or institution. The search interface allows Boolean searching (and, or, not, same) and searching by a large number of languages and document types. The Arts & Humanities Citation Index (A&H), which began in 1975, includes art, archaeology, architecture, Asian studies, classics, dance, film, history, television, folklore, literature, music, religion, theater, and more. Besides the usual document types of books and journal articles, others include letters, scripts, poetry, creative prose, meeting abstracts and proceedings, and reviews. Types of reviews in the A&H include art exhibits, dance performances, films, TV, radio, video, theater, music performances, and scores. The A&H currently indexes some 1,200 journals fully and another 6,800 titles partially.

The Social Sciences Citation Index (SSCI), which was inaugurated in 1974 after the Science Citation Index (SCI), includes law, philosophy, history, urban studies, women's studies, as well as other social sciences fields. The SSCI has been expanded back to 1900 and fully indexes over 2,100 journals across 50 social sciences disciplines, as well as 3,500 of the world's leading scientific and technical journals. Both The A&H and the SSCI are structured the same way and include links to full text of documents indexed.

The citation indexes were designed to index the journal literature, conference proceedings, and technical reports. The indexes have always been of limited use in the humanities and the arts in which books are the primary format of scholarly communication. That is, the A&H index does not have the full record of scholarly publications in the humanities and the arts. In 2011, the Book Citation Index was introduced with indexing of over 28,000 books across all disciplines back to 2005, with 10,000 new books to be added each year. The addition of scholarly and research monographs to the citation databases has enabled researchers to search across all of the *Web of Science* resources to retrieve records from book chapters as well as journal articles. It has enabled those in the social sciences and the humanities/arts to trace the influence of their work in the same manner as the Science Citation Index (SCI) has enabled those in the sciences.

Although more useful in the sciences, Current Contents is a current awareness service providing tables of contents and bibliographic information from 1998 to the present of over 1,150 leading journals in art and architecture, performing arts, literature, language and linguistics, history, philosophy, and religion on an international basis. The module also includes relevant, evaluated websites and documents. Each issue of each journal is covered as often as it is published and each has an author index and a directory of publisher addresses. There are Arts & Humanities and Social & Behavioral editions of Current Contents.

The citation indexes are treated here as individual titles, but the search interface for all is combined under *Web of Science* which is reached through the Web of Knowledge, a website to all of the Thomson Reuters ISI products. The Web of Knowledge interface allows users to save and run searches, and manage references online with *EndNote Web* and create alerts and RSS feeds.

The ISI citation indexes are for researchers and university students. They are not designed for the needs of the general public or K-12 students. In some libraries, the citation indexes are found under Web of Knowledge in the list of databases rather than under their separate titles.

Eugene Garfield and the Institute for Scientific Information (ISI)

Eugene "Gene" Garfield is credited as one of the founders of bibliometrics and scientometrics, and was involved in the research relating to machine-generated indexing in the mid-1950s and early 1960s. Garfield founded the ISI in 1955 and began publication of the Science Citation Index (SCI) in 1963. The Social Sciences Citation Index (SSCI) followed in 1974 and the Arts & Humanities Citation Index (A&H) in 1975. Garfield used the citation index databases for his own research and contributed to a new understanding of the scholarly communication process. These databases are now searchable through *Web of Science*, which is within the Web of Knowledge portal.

The SCI was revolutionary in that the citations to other works at the end of the articles were also indexed, thus giving the indexes their name. The creation of the SCI made it possible to calculate impact factors, which measure the importance of scientific journals and allow researchers to trace the influence of their work through citation patterns. In the traditional method of indexing, humans assigned subject descriptors to articles or books. Garfield's computer-generated citation indexes use key words from the title in lieu of assigned subject descriptors. The subject indexes were *permuterm* indexing in which a term or word can be permuted throughout variations of the term, the searching equivalent of using a wild card at the end of a root term to indicate that the searcher wants all variations of the root term. The key word concept is suited to the sciences because the subject of the research is usually in the title. It worked fairly well in the social sciences, but not well at all in the humanities in which creativity in titles is highly regarded. Of particular importance to the humanities and the arts is Garfield's essay, "Is information retrieval in the arts and humanities inherently different from that in science?" In the essay, he describes the discoveries about characteristics of the humanities and the arts that were made when the A&H index was in development. Garfield saw the humanities as not being "cumulative" and not as obsessed with the new and current as the sciences are. He also points out that humanities scholars have less of a tradition of providing citations than scientists. Humanists may refer to a work of art, such as a painting or play, but not formally cite the work, i.e., allusion or implicit citation. Whereas the SCI and the SSCI were wholly computer produced, it was found necessary to employ people to scan through the materials being indexed to augment the subject descriptors and citations for the Arts & Humanities Citation Index.

The ISI products are now owned by Thomson Reuters and Dr. Garfield is Chairman Emeritus of ISI®. Under Thomson Reuters, the ISI citation indexes and products continue to be called *Web of Science.*

Garfield E. 1980. "Is information retrieval in the arts and humanities inherently different from that in science? The effect that ISI's citation index for the arts and humanities is expected to have on future Scholarship." *Library Quarterly* 50 (1): 40–57. http://www.garfield.library.upenn.edu/

2-5. British Humanities Index. London: Library Association, 1962– . Print edition quarterly. Online subscription database through ProQuest/CSA Illumina, updated monthly.

The British Humanities Index provides an index and abstracts of periodical literature from humanities journals, magazines, and newspapers published in the United Kingdom. The BHI broadly covers the humanities and arts including art and architecture, archaeology, antiques, cinema, gender studies, history, language and linguistics, literature, music, philosophy, religion, and theater. The index also includes current and foreign affairs, political science, economics, environment, and law, thus being a very good source for interdisciplinary humanities and social sciences topics. Links to full text are offered for some entries.

EBSCO Publishing. http://www.ebsco.com

EBSCO began as a serials vendor over 60 years ago and during that time, has expanded into information access and management solutions through print and electronic journal subscription services, research database development, and publishing. EBSCO now offers online access to more than 100 databases and thousands of e-journals through EBSCOhost. The company has been active in acquisitions of other publishing companies acquiring Salem Press, publisher of the popular Magill critical series, and NetLibrary, the largest e-book vendor at the time. In 2011, EBSCO Publishing and the H.W. Wilson Company merged. The H.W. Wilson indexing and full text products were added to EBSCOhost, EBSCO's suite of database products. The authoritative indexing provided by Wilson's subject thesaurus and the Wilson "names" authority file, plus EBSCO Publishing's extensive controlled vocabularies and comprehensive full-text content, were merged to form seven new "Super databases." Of the seven, three are treated here: **Humanities Source**, **Applied Science and Technology Source**, and **Biography Source**. The **Source** databases are treated first, followed by two other general Wilson databases, the Essay and General Literature Index, and the Reader's Guide. Specialized subject databases, such as Art Index and Art Source, are treated in the subject resources chapters.

2-6. Humanities Source. Ipswich, MA: EBSCO Publishing/ Wilson, 2011– . Online subscription database.

The Wilson *Humanities Index, Humanities Abstracts, Humanities Full Text,* and *Humanities Index Retrospective* were combined with the EBSCO/Whitston Publishing *Humanities International Complete* to form Humanities Source. The database has the full text of 1,450 journals. All of the databases are available as separate titles or in the combined Humanities Source product. The Wilson databases are treated separately here.

2-7. Humanities Full Text Index. New York: H. W. Wilson, 1984– . Online subscription database.

Humanities Index Retrospective. 1907–1984. New York: H. W. Wilson. Online subscription database.

Humanities & Social Sciences Index Retrospective. 1907–1984. New York: H. W. Wilson. Online subscription database

Dating from 1974 when the H.W. Wilson *Social Sciences and Humanities Index* (1965–1974) was separated into two publications. The Humanities Index is one of the leading cumulative indexes to English-language periodicals in the humanities. The contents of some 600 periodicals from all areas of the humanities and, in some cases, the social sciences, are indexed in the Humanities Index. The same can be said of the Social Sciences Index, treating interdisciplinary subjects such as anthropology. These indexes are an ideal place to begin a search. The Humanities Full Text Index includes bibliographic indexing and abstracts for full text articles from over 600 scholarly journals in the humanities. Updating is monthly.

Humanities Index Retrospective is a separate database that contains the contents of nearly 800,000 articles from the period 1907–1984. Humanities & Social Sciences Index Retrospective contains citations to more than 1,300,000 articles, including over 240,000 book reviews from 1,200 periodicals as far back as 1907.

2-8. Applied Science and Technology Source. Ipswich, MA: EBSCO Publishing/ Wilson, 2011– . Online subscription database.

The H.W. Wilson Applied Science and Technology Full Text Index, Abstracts, and Retrospective databases have been combined with the EBSCO Computer and Applied Science Complete to make up the new Source database. As with the other Wilson and EBSCO databases, they will continue to be available as separate subscriptions. While it may seem curious to have the applied science database among resources for the humanities, the database has a broad coverage of science and technology subjects, including the full text of 1,185 journals. All aspects of study in the humanities are now influenced by information technology and computer science. In the visual and performing arts are fields that have become digital such as animation, film, and television; digital media and art; architectural drawing, musical recordings, and other elements that use technology. In addition, in art, architecture, and theater, new materials are being used for construction, artworks, crafts and decorative arts, set design, lighting sources, and more. Pertinent research in all of these subjects can be found in Applied Science and Technology Source.

2-9. Biography Source. Ipswich: MA: EBSCO/Wilson, 2001– . Online subscription database.

Biography Source combines the H.W. Wilson Biography Reference Bank and Current Biography with the EBSCO Biography Reference Center. The new database contains over 600,000 biographies and obituaries. The Wilson databases are still available separately and treated in the next entry.

2-10. Biography Reference Bank. New York: H. W. Wilson. Online subscription database.

Biography Reference Bank is a single online resource that combines the content of five H.W. Wilson biographical databases: Biography Index, Current Biography, Wilson Biographies Plus Illustrated, and Junior Authors & Illustrators; as well as biographical full-text articles, page images, and abstracts from all Wilson databases. Additional content is published through agreements with other major publishers. About 1,500 new names are added each year. The graphical interface is user friendly; searching is by name, profession, place of origin, gender, ethnicity, birth/death dates, titles of works, or keywords. Both full-text articles and article citations can be retrieved. The database can be used by any level of reader in any discipline and is well suited for research in multidisciplinary fields, such as women's studies, cultural studies, media studies, and more.

Other Wilson indexes which are not included in the broader Source databases above, but containing relevant information, are treated below.

2-11. **Essay and General Literature Index.** New York: H. W. Wilson, 1984– . Online subscription database.

Essay & General Literature Index Retrospective, 1900–1984. New York: H. W. Wilson. Online subscription database.

As a long running printed tool, the *Essay & General Literature Index* (EGLI) provided indexing for articles in collections and anthologies that were not indexed in the other periodical indexes. Although other areas of the humanities are covered in this standard work, literature receives the greatest emphasis. Originally, the work succeeded the *ALA Index . . . to General Literature* (2nd ed., American Library Association, 1901–1914), that indexed books of essays, travel, sociological matters, and so forth up to 1900. A supplement covered the publications of the first decade of the twentieth century. EGLI indexes essays in books published since 1900, the initial volume covering the first 33 years. Two comprehensive printed editions have been issued covering the periods 1900–1989 (11v, 1989) and 1990–1994 (1994). The EGLI is now an online database with citations to over 86,000 essays from some 7,000 collections published in the U.S., Canada, and Great Britain. Hundreds of collections and anthologies (about 300 added annually) serve as sources of the indexed essays on authors, forms, movements, genres, and individual titles of creative works. Essay & General Literature Index Retrospective is a separate online collection that contains the publication from the years 1900–1984.

2-12. **Readers' Guide Full Text.** New York: H. W. Wilson, 1994– . Online subscription database.

Readers' Guide Retrospective. 1890–1994. New York: H. W. Wilson. Online subscription database.

The *Readers' Guide* is the most well known general indexing tool found in nearly all public, academic, and school libraries. The online version is a full-text database with articles from hundreds of magazines back as far as 1994, plus article abstracts and indexing. The Readers' Guide Retrospective is a separate file that contains the text of more than 3 million articles as far back as 1890, the beginnings of the index, "tracking modern U.S. culture and history over more than 100 years." The Readers' Guide should be included in any thorough literature search for retrospective topics in the humanities and the arts.

The H.W. Wilson Company was founded by Halsey W. Wilson in 1898 and shortly thereafter began publishing the *Reader's Guide*. Throughout the twentieth century, the Wilson indexes were ubiquitous in American libraries. With a subscription cost calculated upon the library's user base, the indexes were made affordable to the majority of public, academic, and school libraries. Up until the electronic era, the H.W. Wilson Company produced the definitive and only indexes for many subject fields. The printed indexes were simple to use with complete bibliographic information contained under one alphabetical arrangement with combined author and subject listings, called by reference librarians, a "one step" index. Wilson began producing digital versions of the print indexes in the 1980s and subsequently produced separate retrospective files for the indexes. Wilson has always been known for the quality and integrity of the indexing which was maintained as the products became online databases. Among the well-known Wilson titles were *Essay & General Literature Index*, *Humanities Index*, *Education Index*, *Library Literature & Information Science Index*, *Art Index*, *Play Index*, *Current Biography*, *Biography Reference Bank*, and *Applied Science & Technology Index*. At the time of the company's merger with

EBSCO, Wilson was offering around 80 general and specialized databases. With the EBSCO merger, a number of the long-running Wilson subject indexes were merged with the EBSCO counterparts to form new databases with added value, or at least more content to users. The new databases became Art Source (entry 8-2), Biography Source (entry 2-9), Humanities Source (entry 2-6), Applied Science and Technology Source (entry 2-8), Education Source, and Library & Information Science Source.

The H.W. Wilson Company has a legacy in American publishing. With the H.W. Wilson Foundation, the company has supported the John Cotton Dana Library Public Relations Awards, a competition to encourage improvements in library marketing and public relations. The Foundation has also granted many scholarships to those seeking to earn library and information science degrees.

2-13. FRANCIS. Institut de l'information Scientifique et Technique of the Centre National de la Recherche Scientifique (INIST-CNR), Nancy, France: 1991– . Online subscription database. http://www.inist.fr/

Previously titled (in printed form) *FRANCIS Bulletin Signaletique, Bulletin Signaletique,* and *Bulletin Analytique.* The relevant sections for arts and humanities retrospective research are: *Francis Bulletin Signaletique,* 519, *Philosophie* [1990–1994], (formerly *Philosophie Sciences Religieuses* 1969-); *Sciences Humaines* [1956-68]. *Francis Bulletin Signaletique.* 523, *Histoire et Sciences de la Litterature.* [1991–1994] and *Francis Bulletin Signaletique,* 524, *Sciences du Langage* [1991–1994]. *Francis Bulletin Signaletique,* 530, *Repertoire d'art et d'Archaeologie* (RAA). The retrospective files are each treated under the respective subjects in this guide (entries 4-2, 8–7). FRANCIS is available by subscription through EBSCOhost, ProQuest/CSA Illumina, OCLC, and OVID Technologies

FRANCIS is the computerized version of *Bulletins Signalétiques Thématiques* from CNRS, published (print version) from 1947 to 1994. Each descriptive bulletin was a set of themes with their own editorial board. In 1972, FRANCIS was created to give computerized access to the "bulletins signalétiques" and subsumes the publications of Bulletin Signaletique in the humanities and social sciences. The sciences are now subsumed by PASCHAL. Both databases are produced by INIST in partnership with several national and international organizations.

FRANCIS contains over 2.6 million bibliographic records with coverage from 1972 to present. FRANCIS is strong in religion, the history of art, psychology, and sociology. Language and linguistics are well covered with psycholinguistics, sociolinguistics, ethno-linguistics, historical linguistics, semiotics, and communications. Other subject areas include archaeology, ethnology, French literature, geography, history of science and technology, information science, and philosophy. Journal articles make up approximately 80 percent of source documents with books at 9 percent. FRANCIS also indexes books and book chapters, and offers noteworthy coverage of grey literature, including conference papers, French dissertations, exhibition catalogs, teaching materials and reports. Subject descriptors on bibliographic records in the FRANCIS database are listed in both English and French. In spite of its sponsorship, the highest percentage of references is in English at 41%, then French (31%), German (11%), Italian (5%), Spanish, (4%), and others at 8%. In FRANCIS, each file has its own specific vocabulary. All files are indexed in French and in English. The Latin America and History of Sciences files are also indexed in Spanish, and the Computer Processing and Legal Sciences file is also indexed in German. An added feature is an exhaustive list of author affiliations for all the records, making it easier to carry out bibliometric studies aimed at identifying and finding experts, and at defining research areas with a great deal of potential. With its strong emphasis of French and European literature, there is the possibility to obtain bibliographic records not contained in databases produced in the United States. Anyone endeavoring to conduct thorough research for retrospective materials in the humanities and arts needs to include FRANCIS in their research.

Gale Cengage Learning Inc. publishes a number of reference databases with similar titles, so much so as to be confusing. Also, the terms *literature* and *literary* are interpreted very broadly to include all manner of writing and publications, not just "belles lettres" and literary criticism. The offerings in the latter categories are treated in chapter five of this guide. The general and broad databases are treated in this chapter.

2-14. Gales' Literary Index. Detroit: Gale Cengage Learning Inc. http://www.galenet.com/servlet/LitIndex

2-15. LitFinder. Detroit: Gale Cengage Learning, Inc. Online subscription database.

2-16. Literature Resource Center. Detroit: Gale Cengage Learning Inc. Online subscription database.

Gale is one of the largest publishers of reference sets and series. On the website, it offers a free online index that serves as a locator for information contained within all of the Gale reference publications, print and electronic. Gale's Literary Index has a simple search engine that allows searching by author name, title, or a custom search. There are cross-references to author names, including pseudonyms, and titles, all in one source. Biographical information is given for authors as well as lists of publications. This free resource answers simple reference questions or provides information for more in-depth research. As it is an index to the various Gale literary reference series, the author information returned from a search references the Gale series in which the information is included. It is certainly the best place to begin if a library has the print volumes of the series, rather than subscriptions to the concomitant Gale online databases. It is suitable for use by the general public, students, and researchers.

Literature Resource Center (LRC) is the most comprehensive of the Gale subscription online reference databases. It is a complete literature reference database designed for both the undergraduate and graduate student as well as the general reader. LRC is a first stop Internet resource for information on literary figures from all time periods writing in such genres as fiction, nonfiction, poetry, drama, history, journalism, and more. The LRC is built on three Gale author databases: Contemporary Authors Online, Contemporary Literary Criticism series, and Dictionary of Literary Biography Online. The Merriam-Webster *Encyclopedia of Literature*, with 10,000 definitions of literary terms is also included. More than 850,000 full-text articles, critical essays and reviews from over 390 scholarly journals and literary magazines are contained in the database as well as links to over 5,000 websites focusing on major authors and their works and more than 2,800 author portraits.

LitFinder is Gale's "core repository of full-text literature." The contents span more than 660 nationalities globally containing poems, short stories, essays, speeches and plays representing the work of more than 80,000 authors. Searching is the same for both the LRC and LitFinder. As is the case with the other Gale online resources, cross-searchability is possible with resources such as Gale Virtual Reference Library, MLA International Bibliography (entry 2-20), Scribner Writers Series (entry 5-8) and Twayne's Authors Series (entry 5-9). All have the "How to Cite" feature and the ability to export to citation tools; multiple options for sorting and filtering results; enhanced Person Search and Works Search options; and ReadSpeaker audio technology. Searchers can choose from basic search, advanced search, person search, or work search. The full text of the literary work as well as the author information are returned in search results. The LRC and LitFinder will most likely be found in large public and academic libraries. The databases are also commonly provided by networks and consortia.

2-17. Biography in Context. Detroit: Gale Cengage Learning, Inc. Online subscription database.

Researchers may recall the long-running printed biographical source *Biography and Genealogy Index*, along with *Contemporary Authors*, which is now absorbed into the Literature Resource Center. These printed sources have now also been incorporated into Biography in Context, which aggregates all of the biographical products from Gale Cengage and its affiliated publishers. Biography in Context incorporates over 170 Gale reference titles with 50,000 new or updated bios added annually. While most researchers will find the authors and writers they are looking for in the literary databases treated above, Biography in Context is a broader resource and may be provided in libraries as part of Gale subscription packages while more specialized databases are not available.

2-18. International Medieval Bibliography (IMB). Turnhout, Belgium: Brepols, 1967– . Print and online subscription database. http://www.brepols.net

Brepols is an academic publisher of databases, reference works, critical works, and texts on the Middle Ages in Europe, North Africa, and the Near East. The IMB was founded in 1967 with the aim of providing a comprehensive, current bibliography of articles. The IMB draws from over 4,500 periodicals providing full bibliographical information to the entries from the publications and serves as a comprehensive cataloging and indexing system offering a wide range of search possibilities to assist the user in identifying all relevant entries. The IMB includes languages and literature, history, archaeology, theology, philosophy, Islamic studies, and the arts. A companion to the IMB is Bibliographie de civilization medieval, also published by Brepols, which indexes books and book reviews. Both of these titles are also treated in entry 6-88.

2-19. ITER: Gateway to the Middle Ages and Renaissance. Hosted by the University of Toronto Libraries. Online subscription database. http://itergateway.org

"Iter," meaning a journey or path in Latin, is a not-for-profit partnership among a number of societies and university departments for the study of the Middle Ages and Renaissance. The website provides access to medieval and Renaissance resources featuring the *Iter Bibliography*, *Iter Italicum*, bibliographies of Milton and English women writers, and a number of full text journals.

Iter's *Bibliography* includes literature pertaining to the Middle Ages and Renaissance (400–1700). Included are citations to books, journals (articles, reviews, review articles, bibliographies, catalogues, abstracts and discographies), and essays in books (including entries in conference proceedings, festschriften, encyclopedias, and exhibition catalogues).

Also available through the Iter site is an electronic file of Paul Oskar Kristeller's *Iter Italicum*, produced in cooperation with Brill publishing. Originally published in six volumes between 1963 and 1992, *Iter Italicum* is a comprehensive listing of previously uncataloged Renaissance manuscripts located in libraries and collections all over the world. It is an essential tool for any scholar working in the fields of classical, medieval, and Renaissance studies.

Also offered through Iter is the International Directory of Scholars (IDS), an online database that merges the *Directory* of the Renaissance Society of America (RSA) and *Scholars of Early Modern Studies* from the Sixteenth Century Society and Conference (SCSC). The IDS is a comprehensive resource which provides not only the usual directory contact information, but also detailed information on the research and teaching careers of scholars around the world.

2-20. MLA International Bibliography. New York: Modern Language Association of America, 1921– . Online subscription database. http://www.mla.org

In addition to the Modern Language Association (MLA) the following vendors and publisher series offer the *Bibliography* online:

CSA Illumina (ProQuest)

EBSCOhost (from EBSCO)

InfoTrac (from Gale/Cengage Learning)

Literature Online (from Chadwyck-Healey/ProQuest)

Literature Resource Center (from Gale/Cengage Learning)

2-21. **MLA Directory of Periodicals: A Guide to Journals and Series in Languages and Literatures.** New York: Modern Language Association of America, 1984– . Online database available through subscription to the MLA International Bibliography or through MLA membership.

2-22. **Literary Research Guide.** James L. Harner. 5th ed. New York: Modern Language Association of America, 2006. Print and online (2009–).

The MLA International Bibliography is the monumental bibliography known and respected by language and literature students worldwide. A standard work in the field, it has changed title and scope since its inception in 1921 as *American Bibliography*, when it was limited to writings by Americans on the literature of various countries. In 1956, it became a more expansive source of bibliographic information and was named *Annual Bibliography* from 1956 to 1962. Since 1963, it has had its present title and includes writers from a variety of languages, although still primarily American and European. Books, articles, monographs, and festschriften representing critical analyses and interpretations on folklore, language, linguistics, and literature are all included. The printed version was discontinued in 2009, with the 2008 volumes being the last printed edition. The Bibliography is now an online subscription database offered by the MLA and included in a number of publisher and vendor online reference collections.

The MLA website contains very specific information on searching the database, although the interface can change according to which vendor is supplying the database. MLA staff also offer online reference assistance to users of the database.

The database does not provide full text of the works indexed, but many of the articles in the MLA Bibliography are available in full text from Project Muse (entry 2-45), JSTOR (entry 2-43) and ProQuest digital dissertations (entry 2-27).

The *MLA Directory of Periodicals* began in 1984 as a companion to the MLA Bibliography. The Directory contains entries for over 6,000 scholarly periodicals. Entries include basic directory information plus frequency of publication, descriptions of scope, circulation figures, subscription prices and addresses, advertising information, links to online content, peer review, and submission guidelines. Other useful information on publications includes the number of articles and book reviews published each year and how many manuscripts were submitted. The Directory is available in electronic format to MLA members through the MLA website and is included in institutional subscriptions to the MLA International Bibliography through other vendors.

The 5th edition of the *MLA Literary Research Guide* (also entry 5-24) is available in print and became available online in electronic format for libraries in 2009. The online format links from the *Guide* to humanities reference sources in the subscribing library and is designed to assist users in evaluating reference sources in the humanities. Another feature allows users to save searches and citations for later use. Access is by separate subscription from MLA. Depending upon the vendor, it can be included with the MLA Bibliography. The online edition is updated regularly. While not having the advantages of the online version, the print edition is a personal handbook that can be consulted constantly as one studies or writes. Also see the *MLA Manual of Style* (entry 2-94).

2-23. **Oxford Reference Online Premium**. Oxford University Press. Online subscription database**.** http://www.oxfordreference.com/pub/views/home.html

Oxford Reference Online Premium indexes many of Oxford's reference resources in humanities and the arts as well as social sciences and natural science. Resources include encyclopedias, dictionaries, companions, and guides. The database also provides a cross-searchable language reference dictionary; subject reference for works published by Oxford University Press; and comprehensive links to other resources. Separate databases can be subscribed to by subject or topic. These books work like e-books indexed through the Oxford Reference Premium website. That is, each e-book is accessed individually. The website is very easy to use. Many, but not all of the reference titles are covered in this Guide. Examples of titles in literature included in Oxford Reference Online Premium are:

The Oxford Dictionary of Quotations

The Concise Oxford Companion to African American Literature

The Oxford Companion to American Literature

The Oxford Encyclopedia of American Literature (entry 5-32)

The Oxford Companion to Australian Literature

The Oxford Companion to Canadian Literature

The Concise Oxford Companion to Classical Literature

The Oxford Companion to English Literature

The Concise Oxford Companion to Irish Literature

The Oxford Guide to Literary Britain & Ireland (entry 5-34)

The Oxford Dictionary of Literary Terms (entry 5-31)

The Oxford Encyclopedia of British Literature (entry 5-33)

The Oxford Dictionary of Phrase and Fable

The Oxford Dictionary of Science Fiction

A Dictionary of Shakespeare

The Oxford Companion to Shakespeare

The Oxford Companion to Twentieth-Century Poetry in English

A Dictionary of Writers and their Works (entry 2-25)

2-24. Oxford Bibliographies Online. Oxford University Press. Online subscription database. http://aboutobo.com/

The Oxford Bibliographies Online series was begun in 2010 to provide subject oriented guides to online resources. The series is dubbed a "GPS for Scholars," to help navigate the vast universe of online resources of all types of electronic formats. It is a tool designed to help busy researchers find reliable sources of information quickly "by directing them to exactly the right chapter, book, website, archive, or dataset they need for their research." The entries in each subject module are authoritative and peer reviewed by experts plus a board for that particular subject. The citations contain links to full text content in the library and on the web. The online database allows users to construct their own bibliographies with personal notes. The modules are updated regularly with new entries and new discipline-based subject modules are continually being added. Subjects in the humanities in this series include Biblical Studies, Buddhism, Classics, Hinduism, Islamic Studies, Medieval Studies, Philosophy, Renaissance and Reformation, Victorian Literature, Music, Cinema and Media Studies, Linguistics, American Literature, British and Irish Literature, and Jewish Studies. The database is appropriate for both students and scholars.

2-25. A Dictionary of Writers and Their Works. 2nd ed. Christopher Riches, ed. Oxford University Press, 2010. E-book.

The first edition of the Dictionary (2001), edited by Michael Cox, was a print edition. The second edition is an electronic only work that has 63,000 new words added to the original text, including over 100 new entries dealing with authors who have risen to prominence in the 10 years since the publication of the first edition. All entries from the first edition were fully updated. In all, there are over 3,200 total entries for writers, with nationality and birth/death dates, followed by a listing of their works arranged chronologically by date of publication. The main focus of the Dictionary is "the general canon of British literature from the fifteenth-century to the present." There is also some coverage of non-fiction such as biographies, memoirs, and science, as well as inclusion of major American and Commonwealth writers. The Dictionary is a quick reference work for basic information on the authors covered.

2-26. 19th Century Masterfile: the Great Index to the Great Century. Austin TX: Paratext, 1993– . Licensed database. http://www.paratext.com

Paratext was founded in 1993 and produces a number of databases that both index a body of literature or documents and also provide links to available full text of the indexed materials. The 19th Century Masterfile collection covers literature in the sciences, technology, law, humanities, literature, and the social sciences. The Masterfile incorporates over seventy pre-1930 periodical indexes including Pooles' Index to Periodical Literature and several major newspaper indexes. The indexing covers 8,000 periodicals and newspapers, patents, U.S. and UK government documents, and millions of books, with 3 million full-text links including links to JSTOR (entry 2-43), *Accessible Archives*, and more. Other products by Paratext are Reference Universe and Public Documents Masterfile.

ProQuest Information and Learning Co. http://www.proquest.com

ProQuest is a publishing conglomerate that traces its origins to University Microfilms in Ann Arbor, Michigan. UMI was founded by Eugene Power in the 1930s. As the title implies, University Microfilms was a company that produced microfilm collections to meet the demand for copies of out-of-print titles in all fields that arose after World War II with the expansion in the number of institutions of higher education. UMI produced such series as *Early English Books I* and *II*. UMI also became the primary company collecting and filming U.S. and Canadian dissertations, an operation that expanded to become *Dissertation Abstracts International*. Bell & Howell, another microfilm company, bought UMI and created a digital operation called ProQuest. Currently ProQuest includes Chadwyck-Healey, CAS-Illumina (formerly Cambridge Abstracts), Dialog, eLibrary, and others. The general product lines produced by ProQuest of use to researchers in the arts and humanities are treated here.

2-27. PQDT. ProQuest Dissertations and Theses. Ann Arbor, MI: ProQuest. Online subscription database.

2-28. Periodicals Index Online. Ann Arbor, MI: ProQuest. Online subscription database.

2-29. Periodicals Archive Online. Ann Arbor, MI: ProQuest. Online subscription database.

ProQuest Dissertations and Theses Full text. (PQDT) continues the former *Dissertation Abstracts International*. While dissertations and theses are considered to be grey literature because they are only produced in manuscript format, the Proquest product serves as both an international bibliographic control and dissemination mechanism for theses and dissertations from over 700 academic institutions. According to the website, the database includes citations to 2.7 million dissertations and theses from 1861 to present of which over 90 percent are available for purchase as printed copies.

Throughout the twentieth century, the works were microfilmed and copies were sold in film or facsimile print from the film. In the 1990s, Proquest shifted to electronic files. Now, full text may be downloaded from the PQDT database for most of the dissertations added since 1997 and many before that date. Digitization of dissertations through UMI's Digital Archiving and Access Program is ongoing for older works.

With more than 70,000 new full-text dissertations and theses added a year, copies of dissertations can be ordered through PQDT. Online subscriptions allow unlimited searching for a set fee, and depending on an institution's subscription type, access to the full text of dissertations and theses in PDF format.

With the advent of the open access movement, authors of dissertations and theses now have the option to publish as open access and make their research available for free on the Web through PQDT Open, which provides the full text for the open access dissertations and theses free of charge.

Other ProQuest products are Periodicals Index Online and Periodicals Archive Online. Indexing is provided for almost 6,000 journals in the humanities and social sciences in Periodicals Index Online. Records are included for more than 17 million journal articles in 37 subject areas in over 50 languages and dialects. As well as indexing, access is also provided to the contents pages of the journals up to 1985. Users are able to link directly to the full text of the articles in Periodicals Archive Online, a separate but companion product from ProQuest. Direct links also take users to full text of articles in JSTOR for those institutions subscribing to JSTOR (entry 2-43). Periodicals Index Online has considerable overlap in titles with other broad humanities and social sciences indexes. The Archive Online may offer less overlap for backfiles of journal holdings in libraries.

Salem Press. http://salempress.com

Now an EBSCO subsidiary, Salem Press was founded by Frank N. Magill in 1949 to produce the *Masterplots* series. In the beginning, the *Masterplots* were intended "to provide basic reference data, plot synopses, and critical evaluations of a selection of English-language and world literature that has been translated into English." From the first critical reference series over 60 years ago, numerous other critical series followed. In addition to sets of literary criticism, Salem Press series now include history, music, government and law, philosophy, social sciences, medicine and science.

The contents for many of the printed sets were spin-offs, reprinted or revised from the *Masterplots* series. Many of them had Magill's name in the titles, e.g. *Magill's Survey of American Literature*. The *Masterplots* series are ubiquitous; they can be found in all types of libraries serving students at all levels of education. The printed sets are inevitably well worn. Each set or series has a uniform format, making them easy to use and easily recognizable as a Salem Press product. The essays are in alphabetical order by title, and each includes an annotated bibliography to aid readers in further study. Although begun as literary plot synopses, the series later expanded to include writers other than literary authors and non-narrative writings of authors and influential figures worldwide.

2-30. MagillOnLiterature Plus. Pasadena, CA: Salem Press. Online subscription database. http://www.ebscohost.com/academic/magillonliterature-plus

2-31. Salem Literature: The Database. Pasadena, CA: Salem Press. Online restricted access database. http://Literature.salempress.com

MagillOnLiterature Plus contains full text of a number of Magill titles including *Cyclopedia of World Authors*, the Masterplots series, Magill's book reviews, Magill's *Literary Annual*, and *Critical Surveys*. Over 8,500 fiction writers, poets, dramatists, essayists, and philosophers and their works are profiled in the database with approximately 35,000 critical analyses of individual works of literature, more than 15,000 biographical records, more than 5,000 images, and a glossary of 1,100 literary terms.

Another Salem Press database is Salem Literature: The Database. Salem Literature is a database indexing the content of the printed Salem Press reference sets, many of the same as in Magill-OnLiterature Plus. Along with the complete articles and sidebars from the printed sets, hundreds of photographs that may not have been available in the print versions are included in this database. Purchase of any Salem Press reference set allows free access to the Salem Literature database.

OCLC and WorldCat. Online Computer Library Center (OCLC). http://www.oclc.org/worldcat.

OCLC, a non-profit network utility, was formed in 1967 by a group of academic libraries in Ohio to develop a computerized union catalog. The project quickly gained momentum and was expanded beyond Ohio. At first strictly for use by library staff, in the mid-1980s, the database was made available for library clientele as well. In 2011, OCLC marked the 40th anniversary of the inauguration of WorldCat with a membership of more than 10,000 libraries internationally. With WorldCat, libraries can implement WorldCat Local, a single search that connects from search results directly to the library's physical, electronic and digital holdings. The single search box eliminates the need to consult separate resources and interfaces, and the search results can also be connected to interlibrary loan, social networking services, and other popular sites. This is an invaluable tool for librarians and users alike. WorldCat is available both as a subscription database and as a freely accessible online resource, although the subscription service offers more options for searching, including the Advanced Search option.

Digital Libraries and Collections

In this section are collections of resources that have been digitized, either from print or non-print collections such as microforms, manuscripts, and visual arts. The largest of these tend to be well known microform collections such as *Early English Books*. In many of these collections, the aim is to include all of the published literature from a certain time frame, e.g., The nineteenth century, or geographic area, e.g., the Caribbean. Others are by themes, such as ethnicity or genre. These collections are full-text research collections rather than reference indexing databases, although that distinction is becoming increasingly blurred. Digital collections are making research without traveling possible and are held mainly by academic research libraries. They may be subscription based, licensed, or one-time purchases. The availability of these large digital collections has brought unprecedented access to unique material, opening up new avenues for research, and the possibility of changing the landscape of research across many academic fields.

2-32. ACLS Humanities E-Book (HEB). Online subscription database. http://www.humanities ebook.org/

The American Council of Learned Societies (ACLS) sponsors the ACLS Humanities E-Book project (HEB), an online collection of over 3,000 fully searchable digitized works in the humanities with approximately 500 titles added yearly. It was launched in 2002 with a grant from the Andrew W. Mellon foundation and became a self-sustaining non-profit entity in 2005. HEB was founded to "encourage scholarly publishers to develop programs in electronic publishing; to create a not-for-profit space in e-publishing; and to encourage the acceptance of e-books for hiring, promotion, and tenure review." Collaborators in the HEB project include twenty learned societies, over 100 publishers and university presses, and the University of Michigan's Scholarly Publishing Office. The collection includes both in- and out-of-print titles ranging from the 1820s to the present. Publications include monographs, reference works, collected essays, and documentary and literary collections. Works are from the fields of history and area studies, women's studies, archaeology, art and architectural history, music and performing arts, folklore, film and media studies, language and literature, political science, religion, and more. Criteria for including works are as follows: "works selected based on the quality and longevity of the works and usefulness for teaching and research; works that remain vital to scholars and advanced students; and works that are frequently cited in the literature." Titles are linked to publishers' websites and to online reviews in JSTOR (entry 2-43), Project MUSE (entry 2-45), and other sites. There are institutional and individual subscription prices. Some titles are open access.

The ACLS and Columbia University Press also sponsor Gutenberg-e, a free site coordinated with the American Historical Association. The award winning digital editions in Gutenberg-e are multi-media and "afford emerging scholars new possibilities for online publications, weaving traditional narratives with digitized primary sources, including maps, photographs, and oral histories."

2-33. America's Historical Imprints. Newsbank/Readex. http://www.readex.com/readex/

In the print era, Newsbank was well known as a company that provided microfilm of many United States city and regional newspapers. The company subsequently switched to digital products and converted the old microfilm files. Newsbank purchased Readex, which is another of the companies formed to microfilm out-of-print titles for new library collections in the expansion era of the 1950s and 1960s. Newsbank now offers a number of Readex microform collections that have been digitized and combined into larger collections under the umbrella title of *Archive of Americana* with materials printed between 1639 and 1964. The most relevant of the collections for humanities is the America's Historical Imprints collection that contains digitized texts, primarily books, but also other types of publications. Another collection, America's Historical Newspapers contains quite a few ethnic newspapers from 25 states and in 10 languages.

America's Historical Imprints is a digital collection that in turn aggregates three Readex collections which are based on classic bibliographies: *American Broadsides and Ephemera, Early American Imprints, Evans 1639–1800, Early American Imprints, Series I; Shaw-Shoemaker, 1801–1819, Series II.* (These titles are treated in previous editions of this Guide.) The *Early American Imprints* collection was first published by Readex in cooperation with the American Antiquarian Society (AAS). For decades, the microform collections served as a foundation set for research involving early American history, literature, philosophy, religion, and more. Given the early publication dates, copies of works listed in these bibliographies will not be found in more than a few libraries or digital collections, if at all. These collections are for retrospective research and most often found in research libraries.

2-34. Cambridge Collections Online. Cambridge University Press. http://www.cambridge.org/online/cco.htm

Within Cambridge Collections Online are subject or theme-based monographic collections. Over 350 Companions titles provide introductions to major writers, artists, philosophers, topics and periods. Companions are designed not only to offer a comprehensive overview of their chosen topic, but also "to display and provoke lively and controversial debate." The online collection enhances the book series by providing cross searching of content and other standard searching features. The Complete Cambridge Companions series is available as one collection or as two sub-collections of printed monographic series: the Cambridge Companions in Literature and Classics; and the Cambridge Companions in Philosophy, Religion and Culture. Other online collections included in the database are Cambridge Dictionaries Online, Cambridge Histories Online, Cambridge Journals Online, and Cambridge Books Online. The latter was named an Excellence in Publishing award for outstanding electronic resource by Choice in 2010. Books Online is divided and can be purchased by broad subject collections. Also available through Cambridge Collections Online is Shakespeare Survey Online, the first time all of the titles published in the 62 year history of the print series are available online.

Chadwyck-Healey/ProQuest. http://collections.chadwyck.co.uk/

Founded in 1973 by Sir Charles Chadwyck in Cambridge, England as a microform publisher, Chadwyck-Healey was acquired by ProQuest in 1999. Chadwyck-Healey began with the microfilming of books from the earliest centuries of printing in England. The aim for each collection has always been to be "a comprehensive record of the literature of the period." The compilation of reproductions of texts began to accelerate when the company switched to digitizing texts and enhanced the collections with indexing and searching capabilities. Chadwyck-Healey is now the "specialist humanities imprint" of ProQuest publishing, with over 20 electronic collections offered and more being developed. In addition to the retrospective literature collections, Chadwyck-Healey has become the "leading publisher of contemporary writing in electronic form" through partnerships with living authors and print publishers. The collections do not remain static, as Chadwyck-Healey is constantly striving to add texts and improvements to them. Many Chadwyck-Healey digital resources combine numerous individual databases or sources of information to form larger and more comprehensive digital collections such as Literature Online (entry 5-1) and C19: The Nineteenth Century Index (entry 2-37). Those collections most germane to the arts and humanities are treated here, while the literature titles are in chapter five.

2-35. Early English Books Online, Chadwyck-Healey. Online subscription database. http://eebo.chadwyck.com/home

Early English Books Online (EEBO) contains "digital facsimile page images of over 125,000 titles printed in England, Ireland, Scotland, Wales and British North America; and works in English printed elsewhere from 1475–1700." This time span is from the first book printed in English by William Caxton through the age of Spenser and Shakespeare, and the English Civil War. The EEBO project began as a conversion of the microfilm series *Early English Books I & II* that aimed to include all of the titles listed in the classic comprehensive bibliographies of English literature: *The Short-Title Catalogue* (Pollard & Redgrave, 1475–1640); *The Short-Title Catalogue II* (Wing, 1641–1700); *The Thomson Tracts*, and *The Early English Books Tract Supplements*. Together the works in these bibliographies have in the neighborhood of 22 million pages, a long-term digitization project.

EEBO supports research in many subject areas, including English literature, history, philosophy, linguistics, theology, music, fine arts, education, mathematics, and science. Special materials can include prayer books, pamphlets, proclamations, almanacs, calendars, and many other primary resources. Within EEBO are special collections, such as musical exercises by Henry Purcell and Biblical Studies, which focuses on material in the database specific to church history and theology.

The search interface supports scholarly research with keyword, author, title, and Boolean searching. Subjects can also be browsed and the digitized images of original pages from all the works in the database can be viewed through features such as zooming in and out to examine particular elements more closely. The digital images accurately reflect the way the works appeared in their original printed editions. These collections are indispensable for graduate study in the humanities and are available in most research libraries in institutions with graduate degrees in the humanities.

2-36. Early European Books. Chadwyck-Healey. Online subscription database. http://www.proquest.com/en-US/catalogs/databases/detail/eeb.shtml

Following in the footsteps of Early English Books Online, Early European Books provides scholars "with extended access to more than 250 years of print culture from across Europe for the same time period 1450–1700." The project began by digitizing holdings from the Danish Royal Library's national collection of fifteenth- and sixteenth-century rare and valuable imprints. Early European Books is issued in collection units, Collection 1 has 2,600 books. The online database features "high-resolution color images of all pages, bindings and clasps, image viewing, panning and zooming, a multilingual interface, and references to bibliographic sources." Indexing extends beyond text to include features such as illuminated lettering and marginalia. The collection was a Library Journal Best Reference Pick in 2010.

Also produced by Chadwyck-Healey are a number of indexes, microfilm, and digitization projects that together comprise a compendium of indexing and documentation of nineteenth-century British and American writing and publication. These are treated in the two entries below.

2-37. C19: The Nineteenth Century Index. Chadwyck-Healey. Online subscription database. http://www.proquest.com/assets/literature/products/databases/C19.pdf

2-38. Nineteenth Century Short Title Catalogue (NSTC). Chadwyck-Healey. Online subscription database.

C19: The Nineteenth Century Index is comprised of over 22 million bibliographic records for books and newspapers, government documents, and periodical articles. For books, the records are from two major sources: The Nineteenth Century (Chadwyck-Healey's ongoing microform project at the British Library) and the Nineteenth Century Short Title Catalogue (NSTC) treated below. Over 18 million periodical articles are available in C19 from a range of sources in Chadwyck/Healey and other Proquest microform collections, including:

>*Poole's Index to Periodical Literature*
>
>*Wellesley Index to Victorian Periodicals* (1824–1900)
>
>*Periodicals Index Online* and *Periodicals Archive Online* (1790–1919): (entries 2–28, 2–29)
>
>*American Periodicals Series* (1791–1919)
>
>*American Periodicals from the Center for Research Libraries*
>
>*Palmer's Index to the Times* (1790–1905)

With the C19 Index, records to print, microform and electronic materials are linked to the full text collections that are indexed in C19 plus 70 JSTOR journals (entry 2–43). Archival records come from 62,000 collections from archives across the United States.

The Nineteenth Century Short Title Catalogue (NSTC) while incorporated into C19, is also a standalone product. ProQuest acquired the NSTC in May 2005 and "re-launched it as a Chadwyck-Healey product in November 2005." The NSTC has 1.3 million records for the nineteenth-century holdings of eight of the world's top research libraries: the Bodleian Library, British Library, Cambridge University Library, Trinity College (Dublin), National Library of Scotland, and Newcastle University Library, Library of Congress, and Harvard University Library. The NSTC covers "virtually all printed materials published in the U.S. and the British Empire from 1801 to 1919." The NSTC provides records for not only works in English but in Celtic, Gaelic, French, Welsh, and various languages from the British Empire. In addition to standard bibliographic information of author, title, and imprint, the records include library locations, subject classification, and reference number. These collections are indispensable for graduate study in the humanities.

2-39. eBooks on EBSCOhost. Ipswich, MA: EBSCO Publishing, 2011– . Online subscription database.

In the years prior to the Wilson merger, EBSCO had acquired Salem Press and NetLibrary, an e-books vendor. The e-books became available as eBooks on EBSCOhost in 2011, along with e-books from many other publishers. The e-books were given "upgraded services and integrated into the single platform user interface of EBSCOhost enabling searchers to display e-books and other types of content in the same result list." The user is able to search within the e-books and link directly to sections and chapters with zooming tools; and the user can download books for reading on portable devices. A library can choose to have one user, three users, or unlimited user subscription options. License upgrades allow for patron driven acquisition from the more than 265,000 e-books in the database. The database is likely to be available in most academic libraries.

2-40. Eighteenth Century Collections Online (ECCO). Gale/Cengage Learning, Inc. Online subscription database.

Not to be confused with EEBO (Early English Books Online (2-35) above, ECCO covers the 18th century, taking up chronologically where EEBO leaves off. Although these two digital projects are produced by different companies, content from Early English Books Online by ProQuest (entry 2-35), is cross-searchable in the Gale ECCO collection. The most striking thing about ECCO is that it offers images and illustrations, not just prose text. ECCO is based upon the bibliographic project, The Eighteen Century Short Title Catalogue (ECSTC), an online database begun with grant funding and sponsored by the British Library and subsequently the National Endowment for the Humanities, the American Antiquarian Society, and other libraries and granting agencies. The ECSTC project was conceived as a continuation of the classic bibliographies of English literature: *The Short-Title Catalogue* (Pollard & Redgrave, 1475–1640) and *The Short-Title Catalogue II* (Wing, 1641–1700). (These bibliographies were treated in previous editions of this Guide.) The scope of the ECSTC was patterned upon that of the two earlier STCs, that is, all literature published in Great Britain in all languages and internationally in English during the eighteenth century, 1701–1800.

ECCO encompasses more than 26 million pages of text from more than 136,000 titles based on the ECSTC database. The works are from such institutions as the British Library, Oxford University, Harvard University, Cambridge University, National Library of Scotland, National Library of Ireland, and the Library of Congress, including thousands of works from the Americas. Disciplines covered are literature and language, including eighteenth-century essayists, novelists, poets, playwrights, including Shakespeare's plays, poems, and collected works. Topics include drama, poetry, ballads, grammar, and so forth. The English Short Title Catalogue project is ongoing and continues to find both new titles to add and new holdings of previously unavailable titles.

Eighteenth Century Collections Online, Part II: New Editions is projected to contain 33 million pages and 180,000 titles. In 2011, the University of Michigan Library opened access to 2,229 editions of books from the ECCO collection with permission from Gale ". . . in support of the Library's commitment to the creation of open access cultural heritage archives." The databases include Citation generator and export functionality; expanded download and e-mail features; Keyword in Context feature from results list; an updated user interface, and much more.

While seemingly suited for advanced academic research, all of the collections in entries 2-35 through 2-40 can easily be used by the general reader and students in high school and college.

2-41. HathiTrust Digital Library. http://www.hathitrust.org/

The HathiTrust Digital Library is a digital preservation repository launched in October 2008 by a group of U.S. research universities, including the Committee on Institutional Cooperation (the Big Ten universities and the University of Chicago) and the University of California system with over 50 partners now including Cornell University, Yale University Library, the New York Public Library and others. HathiTrust is administered at the University of Michigan, but is supported by base funding from all of its institutional partners. HathiTrust's goal is to ensure long-term availability and preservation of materials to support teaching and learning for students and researchers. HathiTrust Digital Library consists only of digitized content, over eight million digitized books and serial volumes from multiple sources, but primarily Google's ongoing initiative to digitize millions of the books from research library collections. HathiTrust also holds significant digitized book collections from the Internet Archive and books digitized by member institutions. Full-text searching can include all of the texts or only single collections. The site has archiving tools and the ability to purchase full titles in print and electronic formats. HathiTrust also produces a monthly newsletter, which includes an update of the number of digitized collections from each contributing university or institution.

The works in the HathiTrust collection are protected by copyright. HathiTrust is not permitted to display large portions of protected works unless they have been granted permission. In cases where the copyrights have been obtained, they display the full work; that includes public domain works published before 1923 and works from the U.S. government. If the copyright cannot be determined or HathiTrust does not have permission, access to the work must be restricted. In 2011, the University of Michigan Library Office of Copyright announced it would identify all of the orphan works in the HathiTrust Digital Library. HathiTrust will work to find the owners of copyright and work with author's to authorize access rights through Creative Commons. The site has a full explanation of the different interpretations of copyright law as applied for access to digitized texts (http://www.hathitrust.org/access_use).

2-42. InteLex Past Masters. http://www.nlx.com/

Since 1989, InteLex has been publishing the Past Masters series of full-text humanities databases in both original language and in English translation. The Past Masters series encompasses "the largest collection of electronic full-text of the works of classic authors in philosophy, the history of political thought and theory, education, religious studies, economics, classics, history and philosophy of science, Germanic studies, and sociology." Letters, lectures, journals and diaries, and other manuscript materials are included in the complete collections as well as the published works. The collections are available separately by author so that only those specifically needed can be purchased.

2-43. JSTOR. Ann Arbor, MI: ITHAKA. Online subscription database. http://www.jstor.org

JSTOR is a non-profit "Journal Storage" database of back-issue serials. JSTOR began as a digital storage project to assist academic libraries with space problems in maintaining backfiles of printed journals. At first sponsored by the Andrew W. Mellon Foundation and housed at the University of Michigan, it was established as an independent not-for-profit organization in 1995 and is now a division of ITHAKA, a library consortium with over 7,000 participating libraries in 159 countries. The contents of the JSTOR corpus are only available to users affiliated with the institutions that participate in the JSTOR program on a subscription basis. The corpus has grown to include over 1,000 of the most prestigious academic journals across the humanities, social sciences, and sciences, as well as select monographs and other content types, such as letters, oral histories, pamphlets, plant type specimens, images, and 3-D models. The content is expanded continuously with a current emphasis on international publications as well as pamphlets, images, and manuscripts from libraries, societies, and museums.

In 2010, JSTOR began offering free access to searching the JSTOR content, although the full texts are still available only to users at participating institutions. And beginning in 2011, current issues for more than 150 journals became available as part of the Current Scholarship Program. Also in 2011, JSTOR opened access to content prior to 1923 without subscription fees. Libraries have several subscription options for the Archive Collections, the Current Collections and Titles, and Primary Source Collections. JSTOR has the distinction of being one of the most utilized digital collections at many institutions as the search engine provides full text searching, thus indexing all of the journals in the corpus. JSTOR content has links in the MLA Bibliography (entry 2-20), the C19 (entry 2-37) and other digital collections.

2-44. Palgrave Connect. Palgrave Macmillan, UK. Online subscription database. www.palgrave.com

Founded in 1843 in England, Macmillan is a privately owned international publishing group belonging to Verlagsgruppe Georg von Holtzbrinck GmbH, a large German publishing company with interests in publishing and media. (Palgrave Macmillan is a part of the British Macmillan publishing group and is not connected with the U.S. Collier Macmillan publishing company, which is part of

Simon and Schuster.) Palgrave Connect is a site license to access over 4,000 e-books published by Palgrave Macmillan. E-book versions of printed books are contained in the Palgrave Connect Collections by subject or by year of publication. Those collections germane to the humanities and the arts are Language and Linguistics; Literature and Performing Arts; Religion and Philosophy; History; and Social and Cultural Studies. Each collection encompasses a number of series. The database also provides links to additional resources. Palgrave permits some of the literature to be downloaded as e-books compatible with various e-book readers.

2-45. Project MUSE. Online subscription database. http://muse.jhu.edu/

Project MUSE was begun in 1993 as a cooperative project between the Johns Hopkins University Press and the Milton S. Eisenhower Library (MSEL) at Johns Hopkins, funded by grants from the Mellon Foundation and the National Endowment for the Humanities. The Project went online in 1995 with JHU Press journals. In 2000, the project expanded with journals from other publishers and more have been continually added. MUSE is still a not-for-profit collaboration between the participating publishers and MSEL, with the "goal of disseminating quality scholarship via a sustainable model that meets the needs of both libraries and publishers." For research libraries, MUSE provides full text from a selection of 500 "top-tier, heavily indexed, and widely held journals." All issues are electronically archived and accessible, now over a decade of backfiles available to subscribers as well as the current issues. In addition to the journals, there are also over 12,000 books from 70 university presses and other publishers. The book and journal collections can be searched together through the same interface. The website offers help and information for collection development on journal titles, subscriptions, and features of the project. Collections are packaged for different levels of education and type of library and academic disciplines. Many popular indexing/abstracting services and digital collections, as well as JSTOR (entry 2-43), provide links to MUSE content.

Alexander Street Press. http://alexanderstreet.com/

Alexander Street Press, L.L.C. was founded in May 2000, with the goal of "publishing large-scale digital collections of exceptional quality in the humanities and social sciences." The company now publishes more than 60 collections across the humanities that include Literature, Music, Women's History, Black History, Social and Cultural History, Drama, Theatre, Film, the Performing Arts, and Religion. In addition to many millions of pages, collections also have audio tracks, videos, images, and playlists. Alexander Street products have won numerous awards, including Best New Product and Best Content from *The Charleston Advisor*; appearances on *Library Journal*'s Best of the Year lists; Product of the Month from the History News Network; and many Choice Outstanding Academic Title awards, as well as excellent reviews in library journals.

2-46. The Romantic Era Redefined. Alexander Street Press. Online subscription collection.

In partnership with Pickering & Chatto Publishers, Alexander Street Press is publishing The Romantic Era Redefined, with over 170,000 pages of text by writers from Britain, the British Empire, and North America. Included are poetry, prose, drama, letters, and diaries, along with political, philosophical, scientific, and sociological works. In addition to Pickering & Chatto's critical editions, The Romantic Era Redefined includes the "only complete digital version of *The Wordsworth Circle*, the international academic journal devoted to the study of English literature, culture, and society during the Romantic era."

Other Alexander Street Collections reviewed in this guide are Black Short Fiction and Folklore (entry 5-206), Black Women Writers (entry 5-206), Caribbean Literature (entry 6-41), Latin American

Women Writers (entry 6-181), Black Drama (entry 8-27), North American Theater Online (entry 8-28), and Alexander Street Press music collections and streaming services, entries 9-13 through 9-16.

Open Access Resources

For people who do not have access to the subscription electronic databases and collections in the above sections, the resources in this section are all available at open access websites.

2-47. Bartleby.com. http://www.bartleby.com/

Bartleby began in 1999 and is one of the first sites to provide full text of works free of charge. It is not limited to the humanities but contains a large number of literary works. Partial and/or full text works are available. Works may be browsed or searched for via Reference, Verse, Fiction, or Non-fiction. Browsers also have the option of scrolling through an index of authors. This option is particularly helpful because it also lists the titles of the works beside them. Subject and title search options are also available. Results also include a bibliographic record citing where the text of the work originated.

2-48. Bibliomania. http://www.bibliomania.com

Bibliomania is another online resource that provides free access to literary texts. This collection includes articles, interviews, plays, short stories, and e-books with more than 2,000 Classic Texts available. The collection is continually updated with a "must read" section alerting visitors to recent additions. The site also provides study guides and reference resources (e.g., Roget's *Thesaurus*).

2-49. Electronic Literature Directory. http://directory.eliterature.org/

The Electronic Literature Organization maintains this online directory that is a unique resource for readers and writers of digital texts. It is a database of listings for electronic works, their authors, and their publishers. The entries "cover poetry, fiction, drama, and non-fiction that make significant use of electronic techniques or enhancements."

2-50. Electronic Text Center. University of Virginia Library. http://etext.lib.virginia.edu/collections/languages/

The University of Virginia Electronic Text Center is one of the first projects to convert printed works to digital. This collection holds thousands of full-text electronic materials. It can be browsed and searched by language, subject, author, genre, and period.

2-51. The European Digital Library. http://www.theeuropeanlibrary.org

2-52. Europeana. http://www.europeana.eu

Two digital library projects in Europe are both based at the National Library of the Netherlands, the Koninklijke Bibliotheek. The first of these projects was begun in 1997 at the British Library as Gabriel: the gateway to Europe's national libraries. Gabriel was subsumed by The European Library that was initiated with European funding and went live as an online service in 2005. The European Library also provided the initial organizational structure and expertise required to launch Europeana, a European Commission initiative that makes millions of digital objects from libraries, museums and archives accessible to the public via the Europeana website.

These two projects are easy to confuse from the similarity in titles and mission. The European Library offers the ability to freely search the digital resources and catalogs of 48 national libraries in Europe (A national library is the library specifically established by a country to store its information database. National libraries usually are the legal deposit and the bibliographic control center of a nation.) The libraries are all members of the Conference of European National Librarians (CENL), a foundation aimed at increasing and reinforcing the role of national libraries in Europe.

The European Library exists "to open up the universe of knowledge, information and cultures of all Europe's national libraries." Access is free to all. The European Library website has three main divisions of Libraries, Collections, and Exhibitions. Under the "Libraries" tab, libraries can be searched by country, retrieving directory and contact information, useful for planning a visit or inquiring about resources. Collections can be accessed individually or all collections browsed by subject or searched by descriptors. The site is searchable in 35 languages for full text, audio and printed music, images, manuscripts, maps, journals, children's literature, and theses and dissertations. Materials listed are both original format and digital. An "Exhibitions" tab brings up digital exhibitions. One of these is "Reading Europe," which has 1,000 books that can be searched by subject, language, or century. The European Library is a useful site to locate materials that may not easily be found through commercially published indexes or for locating titles listed in national bibliographies.

Also in 2005, the European Commission announced its intent to support the creation of a European digital library, which aims "to foster growth and jobs in the information society and media industries." The European Commission's goal for Europeana is "to make European information resources easier to use in an online environment." The digital library is envisioned as building upon Europe's rich heritage though combining multicultural and multilingual environments with technological advances and new business models. Europeana is developing a common multilingual access point which will make it possible to search Europe's distributed digital cultural heritage online. It will give users direct access to some 10 million digital objects, including film material, photos, paintings, sounds, maps, manuscripts, books, newspapers and archival papers.

The main difference between the two digital libraries is that The European Library is composed only of the collections of the European national libraries. Europeana has a much broader base, drawing from all libraries, archives, and cultural institutions in Europe.

2-53. Google Books. Google, Inc. http://www.google.com/googlebooks/

No section on free information via the Internet would be complete without an entry for Google. Google, the company; Google, the search engine; and Google Books certainly do not need any introduction to most of the world's computer literate population. Since Google announced the Google "Print Project," in 2002 to offer free access to digitized texts, the company has been embroiled in controversy over offering access to copyrighted works. Nevertheless, the Google Books project has now added millions of digitized titles from the collections of research libraries and from the output of for-profit publishers through collaborative agreements forged with these entities. In Google Books Search, the user can see the entire text of a million books that are in the public domain meaning out of copyright and download them. For those works under copyright, if the publisher has given permission, the user can see a preview of the book and, in some cases, the entire text. For those copyrighted works without permissions, the user can view bibliographic information or a description of the work. Google has added information about the digitized works, such as book reviews, web references, maps and more. Links help to find copies of the book: "Buy this book" and "Borrow this book." Copies of the new e-books can be purchased from the Google eBookstore. The e-books purchased from Google may be viewed on a variety of mobile devices.

Google Books has formed partnerships with national libraries of the Netherlands, Austria, Florence, Rome, and Catalonia, and other universities in Europe. Around 150,000 books from the sixteenth and seventeenth centuries and another 450,000 from the eighteenth century have been digitized from these collections. These books are displayed in what Google calls "full-color," that is, the images show the books as they actually appear and not a cleaned up image. This view allows for artifactual studies as well as textual studies.

2-54. **H-Net: Humanities and Social Sciences Network.** http://www.H-net.org

H-Net is an interdisciplinary, international website with over 100 edited discussion lists and blogs in the humanities and social sciences that function as electronic networks, linking professors, teachers and students for the exchange of ideas and materials. The goals of H-Net lists are "to enable scholars to easily communicate current research and teaching interests; to discuss new approaches, methods and tools of analysis; to share information on electronic databases; and to test new ideas and share comments on the literature in their fields." H-Net lists reach over 100,000 subscribers in more than 90 countries. Each network "has its own personality," is edited by a team of scholars, and has a board of editors. Most are co-sponsored by a professional society. The editors "control the flow of messages, commission reviews, and reject flames and items unsuitable for a scholarly discussion group."

H-Net has four tabs on the website: Discussion Networks, Reviews, Job Guide, and Announcements. The subjects of the discussion lists span social, cultural, and political history. Just a few of the topics gives an idea of the variety and breadth of the discussion lists germane to the arts and humanities: Art History, American Religious History, American Studies, Cinema History, Research in Folklore and Ethnology, German Literature and Philology, Philosophy of History, James Joyce Scholarship, and Museums and Museum Studies. One of the most useful features of the discussion lists is the scholarly reviews, which are written for H-Net. Review categories are for video, books, articles, multimedia, websites, and software, and also reviews for grey literature and syllabi. Each H-Net discussion network has its own review editor. Once posted to individual H-Net networks, reviews are then posted and archived to H-Review. The Reviews archive is separated into annual volumes with a search feature to assist in finding reviews. The review guidelines are excellent for teaching students to write reviews. H-Net does not have subscription charges, although donations are requested to support the site. Arrangements have been made with a number of publishers for readers of H-Net Reviews to purchase books reviewed by H-Net and earn royalties that support the Reviews program. Anyone doing research or teaching in the humanities and arts should check the site out.

2-55. **Library of Congress.** http://www.loc.gov/index.html

The U.S. Library of Congress has extensive digital collections. Clicking on the "Digital Collections and Services" tab brings up listings of the various collections of works according to their departmental location. Foremost among the collections is *American Memory* with more than 1.2 million digitized archival images of life in the United States and abroad. The items are primarily from the Prints and Photographs Division, which has more than 14 million photographs, prints, posters, and drawings from the fifteenth century to present.

Other digital collections are from the *Rare Book & Special Collections Reading Room* (http://www.loc.gov/rr/rarebook/digitalcoll.html), which includes the Manuscript Reading Room (http://www.loc.gov/rr/mss/ammem.html). Notable collections are the Lessing J. Rosenwald Collection that contains Medieval and Renaissance works, sixteenth and eighteenth century works, the works of William Blake (texts and images), nineteenth and twentieth century works, Block Books (http://www.loc.gov/rr/rarebook/rosenwald.html), and The Lewis Carroll Scrapbook Collection (http://international.loc.gov/intldl/carrollhtml/lchome.html).

Other divisions at the Library of Congress with digital collections are the Music Division and the Motion Picture, Broadcasting and Recorded Sound Division with collections of scores, sheet music, audio recordings, films, photographs, and databases for performing arts resources.

2-56. **The Modernist Journals Project (MJP).** http://dl.lib.brown.edu/mjp/

The Modernist Journals Project is a joint project of Brown University and the University of Tulsa. The MJP is intended to become a major resource for the study of the rise of modernism in the English-speaking world. The project has begun with periodical literature in a chronological range of 1890 to 1922 and a geographical range that extends to English language periodicals, wherever they were published. On the website, a list is being compiled of all the periodicals within the period. There is a database of biographies of the authors and editors of the periodicals. Another section of the site contains the text of essays about the Modernist period. The project has made a good start on a long-term endeavor.

2-57. The Online Reference Book for Medieval Studies (ORB). Hosted by the College of Staten Island-SUNY. www.the-orb.net/

The ORB is an academic site, written and maintained by medieval scholars for the benefit of their fellow instructors and serious students. Contributions to the site are peer reviewed with authors held to high standards. The online "reference book" is divided chronologically and then by topic. One of the features of the site is a section "What Every Medievalist Should Know" that contains bibliographies. A "reference shelf" provides links to textbooks and full-text translations of ancient and medieval works textbooks and links to other websites in medieval studies maintained at universities such as:

> Labyrinth. http://www8.georgetown.edu/departments/medieval/labyrinth/
>
> Internet Medieval Sourcebook. http://www.fordham.edu/halsall/sbook.html
>
> Netserf. http://www.netserf.org/
>
> World Wide Web Virtual Library/Medieval http://www.msu.edu/~georgem1/history/medieval.htm

2-58. Oxford Text Archive (OTA). http://www.ota.ox.ac.uk

The OTA is sponsored by the Oxford University Computing Services. The Archive "collects, catalogs, preserves, and makes freely accessible digital texts," holding texts in over 25 different languages. The subjects are mainly in the humanities. The collection is eclectic and miscellaneous as the texts are donated to the site.

2-59. Project Gutenberg. www.gutenberg.org

Project Gutenberg was created as a way to centralize and make freely available famous and important classic texts. It was the first and largest single collection of free electronic books that are downloaded from local FTP sites. The site has over 33,000 texts whose copyright has expired. Another 100,000 free e-books are listed as available from partners and affiliates. Project Gutenberg prominently advertises that the free e-books are compatible with the majority of e-book readers on the market and tablet, phone, and other mobile devices.

2-60. The Victorian Web. George P. Landow, ed. http://www.victorianweb.org/

Although privately maintained, this site has been in existence for many years and is continually added to. It has received recognition and awards from numerous organizations. Information can be found on all aspects of the Victorian era: economic, political, social, cultural, arts, and literature. The site mainly contains lists of resources and links to texts and critical essays that cover all aspects of the humanities during the Victorian Era. There are a few resources that reach beyond the time of Queen Victoria.

2-61. Voice of the Shuttle (VoS). http://vos.ucsb.edu

Created at the University of California at Santa Barbara, this massive open access website offers searches for various disciplines in the humanities. The "Literature in English" category has valuable links to literary bibliographies and to other associated sites such as *Bohemian Ink*, an online review site for experimental literature and poetry. The VoS site has portals to book review sites, links to other universities' humanities websites, online journals to genre literature, and links to specific genres. Some of the subjects included in the genre literature are Anglo-Radical literature, Restoration eighteenth century literature, Victorian works, and American minority literature. VoS also has literature other than English with links to Project Runeberg, foreign language resources available electronically, non-English journals, and individual links to literary resources to various foreign languages: Arabic, Chinese, Korean, Eastern European, and Japanese, among others. This popular site was listed in Forbes Magazine's Summer 2002 Best of the Web directory in the category for Academic Research.

2-62. World Digital Library. http://wdl.org

The United Nations Educational, Scientific and Cultural Organization (UNESCO) supports the World Digital Library. The site was begun in a collaborative effort between the Library of Congress, UNESCO, and major libraries from countries all over the world. The home page is a world map with nine geographic areas highlighted to click. Selecting one of the geographic areas opens a screen with images related to the region. Clicking on one of the images on the first screen brings up a menu bar on the left with lists of topics. A timeline bar across the bottom allows navigation by time periods primarily by clicking on thumbnail images. The site has books, photographs, travelogues, maps, documents, and more. While some areas do not have numerous materials, what is there does provide a picture of the culture of the region. The digital texts are accompanied by explanatory information, such as provenance and physical description, or information on an author or artist. While the World Digital Library may duplicate other cultural sites, it is an excellent collection without overwhelming numbers of documents. It is navigable by seven major languages. This is an excellent site for introductory material on cultures around the world.

Printed Resources

The titles in this section are printed monographs, sets or annuals. They may have e-book versions, but they are mainly regarded as printed works.

2-63. The Age of Milton: An Encyclopedia of Major 17th-Century British and American Authors. A. Hager, ed. Westport, CT: Greenwood Press, 2004. Print and e-book.

English literature and authors of the early modern time period of 1500–1700 are covered in this encyclopedia. The rationale for the work is that "the products of authors in all disciplines of seventeenth-century culture in Britain, in its American colony and Europe, should be taken as a whole." The encyclopedia starts with a timeline of major seventeenth-century British and American authors, followed by entries on 79 writers, scientists, and artists, arranged alphabetically. While the vast majority of the entries focus on British and American writers, European writers and artists who significantly influenced British and American literary culture are included as well. Each entry provides a biography, an overview of major works and themes, a review of the author's critical reception by his or her contemporaries and readers over the centuries, a statement of the author's significance in the age, primary and secondary bibliographies, a list of authors by birth year and an index.

2-64. Arts & Humanities Through the Eras. Detroit, MI: Thomson/Gale, 2005. 5 vols. Print and e-book.

The five volumes in this set chronologically cover Ancient Egypt; Ancient Greece and Rome; Medieval Europe; Renaissance Europe; and the Baroque and Enlightenment eras. The rationale for the set is "to provide a multidisciplinary overview of the humanities and the arts in relation to each other and set within the historical and cultural milieu of the eras." The volumes are organized with an overview of the era and a chronology of major events. Each of the disciplines: architecture and design, dance, fashion, literature, music philosophy, religion, theater, and visual arts, receives a chapter. The chapters also begin with chronologies and have articles with perspectives on movements and schools of thought, and provide biographies of significant figures in the field. Numerous photographs, maps, illustrations, and sidebars with primary source materials as well as lists of sources are included. The set is a good introduction to the European historical background of the various disciplines.

2-65. **A Dictionary of English Manuscript Terminology, 1450–2000.** Peter Beal. Oxford: Oxford University Press, 2008.

This dictionary has more than 15,000 references. The book is organized alphabetically and contains many cross references to assist users in finding what they are looking for. The entries are more essay than definition, thoroughly covering all aspects of the subject and written in clear prose. The "English" in the title can be interpreted as "British," as that is a predominant focus, along with sixteenth- and seventeenth-century manuscripts. The work is useful to scholars, librarians, archivists, and collectors.

2-66. **The Oxford Companion to the Book.** Michael F. Suarez and H.R. Woudhuyse, eds. New York: Oxford University Press, 2010.

More than a reference work, a large portion of this two-volume set is devoted to essays covering the history of the book throughout the world from ancient to modern times. Over 40 essays written by scholars from various disciplines deal with the concept of the book across time and place, and analyze how books and societies have shaped one another. Along with such subjects as bibliography, the history of printing, editorial theory and practice, and textual criticism, newer disciplines such as the history of the book and issues with the electronic book are covered. The work is organized into two parts. In the first volume are the essays. The alphabetically arranged encyclopedia of over 5,000 entries is split between the two volumes with A-C in volume 1 and D-Z in the second volume. The entries range from brief definitions and biographical entries to more extensive treatments. The essays and the alphabetically-arranged entries are interlinked to provide both depth of analysis and quick access to information. The work is suitable for both ready-reference or research. Both volumes are richly illustrated with reproductions, diagrams, maps, and examples of various typographical features. The two-volume set has been produced in a style reminiscent of fine books of the past. This fascinating work will appeal to those interested in books and book history, as well as a general international readership across a variety of disciplines.

2-67. **Oxford Dictionary of the Middle Ages.** Robert E. Bjork, ed. New York: Oxford University Press, 2010. 4 vols. Print and e-book.

The Middle Ages run from 500 CE–1500 CE in the four volume *Oxford Dictionary of the Middle Ages* with some 5,000 entries written by more than 800 scholars. The entries vary in length with thematic entries being the longest. Major areas receiving more attention are countries, art, languages, cultural issues, and historical contexts. Shorter entries are factual. Each entry has a bibliography. The 500 illustrations and 50 maps add to the information found here. The set is suitable for students and general readers.

2-68. **Oxford Dictionary of the Renaissance.** New York: Oxford University Press, 2003.

As befits its subject, this work broadly covers the Renaissance period in Europe from 1415 to 1618. The 3,000 brief articles are alphabetically arranged with a thematic index to assist in locating information. Broad subjects covered are art and architecture, history and culture, language and literature, philosophical and theological thought, war and politics, music and theater, religion, and science along with sub-topics under them. The one handy volume gives a comprehensive, authoritative look at the era and is suitable for libraries of all types and students from high school onward.

2-69. World Guide to Libraries. 25th ed. Munich: De Gruyter Saur, 2011. Print and e-book.

The 25th edition of this long running compendium contains current addresses and detailed information on the holdings of approximately 42,500 libraries in more than 200 countries. Besides contact details, entries include information regarding inter-library lending, library director, book, periodical and manuscript holdings, special holdings, areas of collection, and much more. The eBookPLUS edition facilitates finding information via search criteria.

SPECIALIZED TOPICS

These sections contain printed works and Internet sites on designated topics.

Antiquarian and Rare Books

2-70. AbeBooks. http://www.abebooks.com

AbeBooks (Advanced Book Exchange) was in the antiquarian book business long before the Internet. The site's "Rare Book Room" features choice items from the sales collection. A rare booksellers' directory is maintained in the Collector's Corner. The site also has news, information on book fairs and caring for rare items.

2-71. AcqWeb. http://www.acqweb.org/

AcqWeb is a site for acquisitions librarians. Among other services a directory is maintained of rare and antiquarian vendors and booksellers' websites at http://www.library.vanderbilt.edu/law/aqs/pubr/rare.html.

2-72. Alibris. http://www.alibris.com

Alibris is a used and out-of-print dealer that also has scarcer and rare items. It is a good place to begin searching for replacements.

2-73. American Book Prices Current. New York: Bancroft-Parkman, 1894/95– . Ann. Also Online subscription database. http://www.bookpricescurrent.com

American Book Prices Current is an annual record of books, manuscripts, autographs, maps and broadsides sold at auction that has been published since 1894/95. It is the most well-known of the pricing tools in the United States. Countries covered include North America and the UK, with sales from such other countries and Switzerland, Germany, Monaco, Holland, Australia, and many other places. It is the standard tool used by dealers, appraisers, auction houses, scholars and tax authorities and is invaluable for cataloging, collecting, pricing, seeking frequency-of-sale information, appraising, or looking for unpublished material. The online version contains over 950,000 priced reliable records available for instant easy searching.

2-74. BookFinder. Just Books Network. www.bookfinder.com

BookFinder is a book shopping search engine that scans bookseller databases to find new, used, rare, and out of print books. This website is produced by a team of high-tech librarians and programmers in Berkeley, California and Dusseldorf, Germany. They save time and money by searching every major catalog online to let people know which booksellers are offering the best prices and selection. As of 2011, the site had 150,000 entries.

2-75. Powell's Books. http://www.powells.com

Powell's is representative of the many antiquarian dealers with very good reputations who have been in business for many decades. The website has a search engine for browsing the extensive stock of rare materials with options such as searching only for first editions or particular publishers.

Conservation and Preservation

Information for conservation, preservation, and restoration for specific media are treated in the chapters covering those media: chapters 7–10, Performing Arts and chapter 11, Visual Arts.

2-76. CoOL. Conservation Online: Resources for Conservation Professionals. http://preservation-us.org/

The play on words here is for real; CoOL is a really "cool" site, a full text library of conservation information, covering a wide spectrum of topics of interest to those involved with the conservation of library, archives, and museum materials. Sponsored by the Foundation of the American Institute for the Conservation and Preservation of Historic Works (FAIC), the site has links to conservation organizations, news, job listings, directory of professionals, conferences, bibliographies, library resources, and more. Subject areas covered include cultural property such as art, books, paintings, paper, photographic materials, sculpture, wood, and textiles. Materials and formats offered are electronic media, architecture materials, archives, artifacts, manuscripts, and natural history collections. Subjects include but are not limited to biodeterioration, conservation education and training, digital imaging, disaster planning, ethics, mold, pest management, and restoration. The website will be of interest to anyone involved with or interested in conservation and preservation.

2-77. From the Hand to the Machine: Nineteenth-Century American Paper and Mediums: Technologies, Materials, and Conservation. Cathleen A. Baker. Tuscaloosa, AL: Legacy Press, 2010.

Legacy Press, founded by Cathleen Baker in 1997, publishes books about printing, paper, and bookbinding arts. This title traces the history of the U.S. paper industry from 1690 to 1900, a period of technological innovation. Printing, printmaking and drawing are reviewed in their relationship to the paper medium in which they were produced. Then the characteristics of paper, reasons for deterioration, and treatments are covered for making the best decisions for conservation.

2-78. The Getty Conservation Institute. http://getty.edu/conservation/

The Getty Conservation Institute, one of the four programs of the J. Paul Getty Trust, began operation in 1985. Since its inception, the Institute has engaged in a program of scientific research, educational activities, documentation, and the dissemination of information through publications, conferences, workshops, and public programs that include research opportunities for professionals and public lectures. In addition, the Institute has conducted international field projects in Asia, Africa, North and South America, and Europe. In its activities, "The Institute adheres to the principles that guide the work of the Getty Trust: service, philanthropy, teaching, and access." The Institute's endeavors are designed to serve the needs of the conservation profession "by undertaking work that tackles broad practical or theoretical questions of significance to the conservation field." Getty staff provides expertise in preventive conservation; monitoring and control of museum environments; methodologies for the analysis of materials and their deterioration; site management; archaeological conservation; earthen architecture and stone conservation; conservation of wall paintings and mosaics in situ; and the adaptation of technology for conservation purposes. The Institute is housed at the Getty Museum Los Angeles. Because the Getty has several locations, the LA museum is referred to as Getty Museum Los Angeles. They treat it like part of the title.

2-79. New England Document Conservation Center (NEDCC). http://www.nedcc.org/

NEDCC is a leader in providing preservation information to museums, libraries, archives, historical organizations, and other cultural institutions, as well as to private individuals. Each year, NEDCC answers more than 1,200 phone and email inquiries about general preservation issues ranging from insect infestation to basic conservation methods to sources of preservation suppliers. NEDCC's Preservation Leaflets (downloadable) cover a range of topics from planning and prioritizing for preservation to emergency management; from digital preservation, reformatting, and storage environment to care of photographs. The comprehensive suppliers list provides up-to-date contact information for providers of preservation services and supplies. Toolkits have been developed from workshops sponsored by the Institute for Museums and Library Services (IMLS) and regional library networks on these topics: Stewardship of Digital Assets; Surveying Digital Preservation Readiness; and a Preservation Education Curriculum. For anyone needing information on any aspect of preservation and conservation, the NEDCC website is a good place to begin.

Grants and Funding Agencies

2-80. National Endowment for the Humanities (NEH). http://www.neh.gov

2-81. National Endowment for the Arts (NEA). http://www.nea.gov

Two independent agencies of the U.S. government are charged with support of the Humanities and the Arts. Each has a Director and staff for grant programs in support of research, preservation, public programming, and teaching in the humanities and the arts. Both agency budgets also include funding for 56 state and territorial arts or humanities councils.

Created in 1965 as an independent federal agency, the NEH "supports research and learning in history, literature, philosophy, and other areas of the humanities by funding selected, peer-reviewed proposals from around the nation." The NEH awards competitive grants through a rigorous peer review process to the nation's museums, archives, libraries, colleges and universities, public television and radio stations, as well as to individual scholars and teachers. "To spread the wisdom of the humanities as broadly as possible," the NEH and its affiliated state councils support scholarly research, public programs, museum exhibitions, documentary films, programs for teachers, and the preservation of archives and other cultural resources.

In 1998, NEH funding began for the Digital Library Initiative, an interagency effort led by the National Science Foundation that supports research on ways to digitize collections in the sciences, the humanities, and medicine.

Also founded in 1965 along with the NEH, the NEA "encourages creativity" through support of performances, exhibitions, festivals, artist residencies, and other arts projects throughout the country. The goals of the NEA include the "creation of art meeting the highest standards of excellence, engaging the public with diverse and excellent art, and promoting public knowledge and understanding about the contributions of the arts." These elements help shape the guidelines for grant funding.

The NEA awards matching grants to not-for-profit organizations. In addition, it awards non-matching individual fellowships in literature and honorary fellowships in jazz, the folk and traditional arts, and opera. Forty percent of the Arts Endowment's funds go to the 56 state and jurisdictional arts agencies and the six regional arts organizations in support of arts projects in thousands of communities across the country.

2-82. Grants and Awards Available to American Writers. New York: American PEN Center. Online subscription database. http://www.pen.org/gandaSearch.php

The American PEN Center's Grants & Awards Available to American Writers database has more than 1,500 listings of domestic and foreign grants, literary awards, fellowships, and residencies updated every month, making it the most comprehensive online database available to writers at work in all genres. Searching is by keyword, genre, organization, or deadline. PEN members receive discounted rates.

2-83. Money for Graduate Students in the Arts & Humanities, 2010–2012. Gail Ann Schlachter, R. David Weber. El Dorado Hills, CA: Reference Service Press, 2010.

Information is provided on fellowships, grants, awards, traineeships, and other funding programs set aside to support graduate study, training, research, and creative activities in the arts and humanities. The work contains five indexes by sponsor, residency, tenability, subject, and deadline.

Museums

General information and publications for museums and museum studies are treated in this section. Art museums and related publications for more specific subject areas are included with those subject areas.

2-84. American Association of Museums (AAM). http://www.aam-us.org/

AAM is "the only organization representing the entire scope of museums and professionals and nonpaid staff who work for and with museums." Every type of museum is represented including art, history, science, military, maritime, and youth museums, as well as aquariums, zoos, botanical gardens, arboretums, historic sites, and science and technology centers. The AAM "facilitates gathering and sharing knowledge, helps to develop standards and best practices, and provides advocacy on issues of concern to the entire museum community." In 1991, the AAM Board of Directors adopted the *Code of Ethics for Museums*, a formal statement of the ethical principles museums and museum professionals are expected to observe. *The Code of Ethics* has been regularly amended, most recently in 2000. Additional standards and guidelines have been developed such as "Standards Regarding Archaeological Material and Ancient Art," and "Guidelines for Exhibiting Borrowed Objects." The AAM is a partner with National Register in publishing *The Official Museum Directory* (entry 2-87).

2-85. International Council of Museums (ICOM). http://www.ICOM

ICOM, The World Museum Community, created in 1947, is an international organization by and for museum professionals. The official languages are English, French, and Spanish. ICOM is both a network with 30,000 members and a diplomatic forum with 137 experts from countries and territories around the world to respond to challenges in museum management. ICOM is a leading force in ethical matters, including fighting illicit traffic in cultural artifacts and one of the five organizations in the Blue Shield organization (entry 11-255) for the protection of cultural heritage institutions. ICOM has an international *Code of Ethics* and publishes bibliographies and monographs on museum topics.

2-86. Museums of the World. 18th ed. De Gruyter Saur, 2011. Print and e-book.

In its 18th edition, *Museums of the World* provides information on more than 55,000 museums in 202 countries and 500 museum associations in 132 countries. Museums are listed first by country and place and within places alphabetically by name. Information in the entries includes: name of the museum in the original language with an English translation when necessary; address, phone and fax numbers; e-mail address and URL; type of museum and year of founding; staff information; and collections and facilities. The directory has an alphabetical index of museums; an index of persons covering directors, presidents, curators and academic staff of the museums; an index of artists whose works are shown predominantly in a specific museum; and a subject index.

2-87. The Official Museum Directory. National Register Publishing in partnership with the American Association of Museums. Print and online subscription database.

The Directory lists museums in the United States and has been online since 2008. The listings provide mailing address, telephone, fax, e-mail and Web site information, operating hours, admission prices, exhibit information, and more. Personnel information includes directors, curators, museum shop managers, development officers and more. A valuable feature is the Products and Services Suppliers Guide, a separate section that contains current information on unique collections and traveling exhibitions. Also listed are local cultural centers in all 50 states with the same information elements as the directory for museums. The online directory makes finding even easier through a search interface. The Official Museum Directory is suitable for any library with staff and users who need accurate directory information on museums and cultural centers.

Review Tools

Reviews can now be found in many electronic sources or websites and the online bookstores such as Amazon, Barnes & Noble, and others. Books in Print has added reviews; library vendors have databases that include reviews with listed titles. OCLC WorldCat records now include reviews cataloged as entries along with the records for the cataloged work. The reviews can be linked from the OCLC record to other databases to which libraries subscribe to access the full text of the reviews. Many of the resources treated in this chapter also can be searched for reviews such as JSTOR (entry 2-43), H-Net (entry 2-54), Project MUSE (entry 2-45), and other digital collections.

General professional review tools such as *Choice* and *Library Journal* are not included in this section, as these are known to librarians. The newspaper review magazines such as the *New York Times Review of Books*, the *New York Review of Books*, and the *London Times Literary Supplement* are also not included here as they are well known to those in the humanities.

In addition to the periodical review tools produced by library organizations and the book trade, there are two well-respected publications that list and review reference books and electronic resources. Both of these titles were long established publications in print format before becoming online databases in the twenty-first century. They both enjoy reputations for assisting librarians to select the best reference materials for their collection and informing them of the most current resources available. These two publications are treated in the next two entries below.

2-88. American Reference Books Annual (ARBA). Englewood, CO: Libraries Unlimited, 1970– . Ann. Print and online subscription database.

2-89. Guide to Reference Books. Robert Henry Kieft, ed. Chicago: American Library Association. Online subscription database.

The first of these titles is ARBA. The purpose of ARBA is to "provide high quality, critical reviews of reference publications with librarians and information professionals as its primary audience." The printed ARBA was initiated in 1970 by Bohdan S. Wynar, who continued the title for many years as the founder and publisher of Libraries Unlimited. In 2002, the first online version of the title debuted. In 2005, a new, redesigned version of ARBA online was launched with improved browsing and searching capabilities. The database contains over 20,000 reviews and is updated monthly. Both print and online reference sources are included, with an emphasis in recent years on electronic reference. Reviews are thorough and average about 200–225 words in length, although there are variations depending upon the individual reviewer or the tool being reviewed. The online database contains over 5,000 reference titles in the humanities with the option to search by author, ISBN/ISSN, subject, and title, or browse by subject. The annual printed version is the "most complete and detailed source of information on reference resources published in a single year." Each printed annual contains approximately 1,500 reviews. The work is divided into four major segments, one of which is the humanities, accounting for some 34 percent of the total coverage in ten chapters ("Decorative Arts," "Fine Arts," "Literature," "Music," and so forth). Each annual is indexed. Quinquennial indexes are available from 1970–1974, through 2005–2009 to facilitate searching the printed volumes. The online database also serves to index the contents of the printed volumes.

Another compilation concentrating on reference materials by subject is the online Guide to Reference published by the American Library Association. The Guide to Reference is also a professional tool designed to identify sources for answers to reference questions and assist with collection development. The online Guide to Reference replaces the venerable printed work known by the name of its first compiler, Constance Winchell, and later by her successors, Eugene P. Sheehy and Robert Balay. The last printed edition of this massive source, the 11th, was published in 1996. Although the coverage is international in scope, there is a known emphasis on both U.S. publications and the English language. Annotations tend to be brief and descriptive. The online tool has been shaped for electronic reference with keyword or browsing subject categories. Subscribers can give users access to interactive features such as creating and saving lists and searches. In those institutions that subscribe the Guide is available to all users.

2-90. Book Index with Reviews (BIR). EBSCO. Online subscription database.

BIR, produced by EBSCO, is primarily a tool for information professionals. The publisher's marketing materials extol the advantages of the database for collection development and Reader's Advisory. Booklists and subject guides can be searched to find new titles for acquisition, replacement copies, and reviews. BIR includes over five million book titles, with thousands of fiction series, and with more constantly being added. *NoveList*, a Reader's Advisory section, includes Reader's Advisory training, feature articles by notable librarians and subject matter experts, access to *NoveList* newsletters, genre outlines, an online product tour and more. BIR also includes the BIR Entertainment component which provides information on 450,000 music titles and over 200,000 DVD/video titles with more being added regularly. Searching is simple with a basic search by title, author, or key word. At the search results, users can further narrow their searches in a variety of ways such as by subject headings, publication date, in-print status, fiction/nonfiction and more. Reviews are linked to the works in the library catalog. Library users can have their own My BIR site with options for saving searches, lists, and alerts. The My BIR alert service lets users know about new editions, forthcoming titles from popular authors, or new releases on hot topics.

2-91. Wilson Book Review Digest Plus. New York: H.W. Wilson. 1983– . Online subscription database.

Book Review Digest Retrospective. 1905–1982. H.W. Wilson. Online subscription database.

Wilson Book Review Digest Plus is the online version of the long running *Book Review Digest*. The database contains over 100,000 full text reviews, plus review excerpts, book summaries, and bibliographic data updated daily. Entries encompass some 1,300,000 reviews from sources back to 1983, covering over 660,000 books. Book Review Digest Retrospective contains the volumes of the title from 1905–1982 with 1.5 million reviews, covering more than 300,000 books.

2-92. Charleston Advisor. Denver, CO: Charleston Comp, 1999– . Quart. Print and online journal.

The Charleston Advisor is a reviewing tool for electronic products aimed at librarians. All formal reviews are peer reviewed. The reviews are intended to be a critical evaluation, not just product descriptions. The Charleston Advisor uses a rating system based on a five-star model that scores each product based on four elements: content, searchability, price, and contract options. While other review tools may include a section of a few reviews of database products, this journal is the only one in the library field strictly devoted to electronic products.

Tools for Writers

2-93. Writer's Reference Center. New York: Facts on File. Online subscription database.

The Writer's Reference Center database is designed to assist users to become better writers. The database covers the fundamentals of quality writing with an in-depth grammar section that defines grammatical terms and gives examples of use, while another section explains the meaning and usage of frequently confused words. Useful to any user are almost 100,000 definitions from more than a dozen thematic dictionaries, encyclopedias, and other reference books published by Facts on File. The interface is easy to use with a "Did You Mean . . . ?" search feature. The database can be used by students or those who need to write for job requirements.

2-94. MLA Style Manual and Guide to Scholarly Publishing. 3rd ed. New York: Modern Language Association of America, 2008.

The *MLA Style Manual* is generally accepted as the standard style manual for the Humanities. The 3rd edition of the *Manual* has been updated to accommodate electronic publishing, citation of web resources, submission of electronic files, and the like. One change from older style manuals is that the format of the cited work is now specified, as Print, PDF file, Map, and so forth as part of the bibliographic citation. The *MLA Style Manual* is also available in large print.

The *Chicago Manual of Style* is also accepted for journals and publications in some fields in the Humanities. The 16th edition (2010) of the *Chicago Manual* actually includes two different referencing and citation styles: one for the humanities and social sciences and another for the sciences and technology.

2-95. The Oxford Guide to Library Research. 3rd ed. Thomas Mann. New York: Oxford University Press, 2005.

In this general guide to library research, the author provides explanations of both print and online searching that are suitable for any student, scholar, or researcher. A large number of important resources and databases are explicated in the work. In addition, the Guide is especially strong on reference strategies as well as information retrieval strategies, with examples drawn from the author's experience in reference work at the Library of Congress. Even experienced researchers can learn a great deal from this work. It is recommended for personal ownership to go along with a style manual.

2-96. The Oxford American Writer's Thesaurus. Christine Lindberg, comp. New York: Oxford University Press, 2009.

Reviewers practically wax poetic about this work. Often mentioned is that the work is so entertaining and fascinating that one can set out to look up a word and end up reading for quite some time. Rick Moody has written a humorous foreword and sometimes amusing mini-essays on their favorite words are offered by nine distinguished contemporary writers. One popular feature is lists of words that link opposites, e.g., fat and thin, comic and tragic, interesting and boring. The 2004 edition was a Reference and User Services Association "Outstanding Reference Sources" selection in 2005.

2-97. WritersMarket.com. Cincinnati: Writer's Digest Books**.** Online subscription database.

2-98. Writer's Market. Cincinnati: Writer's Digest Books**.** 1922– . Ann.

2-99. Guide to Literary Agents. Cincinnati: Writer's Digest Books. 1991– . Ann.

2-100. Literary Market Place: The Directory of the Book Publishing Industry with Industry Yellow Pages (LMP). Medford, NJ: Information Today. 1940– . 2 vols. Ann. Print and online editions.

A number of annual directories inform writers as to possible venues to submit their work. In these, the terms *writer* and *literary* are used in the broadest sense for any kind of writing or *literature* to be submitted for publication. The most well-known of these are LMP and several guides by Writer's Digest Books.

LMP, the most well-known and frequently used directory of this type on the market, was published by Bowker beginning in 1940. LMP is now published by Information Today, Inc. in two print volumes, LMP and the *International Market Place* (IMLP). LiteraryMarketPlace.com is the online version of the two print LMP titles. Some access to company directory information is free on the website, including small press information, but only subscribers have access to full information on publishers and agents. LiteraryMarketPlace.com provides up-to-date listings of organizations, periodicals, and some 3,000 publishing houses with officers and key personnel, all of whom are involved in the placing, promotion, and marketing of literary property. Also included is information on book clubs, associations, book trade events, conferences and contests.

LMP directory information includes 54 sections on publishers, agents, and ad agencies to associations, distributors, and events, services, and suppliers. In all there are more than 12,500 listings with names, addresses, and numbers; key personnel, activities, specialties; e-mail addresses and websites. Similarly, the IMLP "covers the publishing scene in more than 180 countries worldwide." There are up-to-date profiles for publishers and literary agents, booksellers and book clubs, major libraries and library associations, trade organizations, distributors, dealers, literary associations and prizes, trade publications, book trade events, and other resources conveniently organized by country.

Both LMP and ILMP include two publisher indexes, "Types of Publications Index and Subject Index," and a "Personnel Yellow Pages" section.

Writer's Digest Books publishes several annual printed guides aimed at writers of different literary formats and genres. Whereas the LMP is aimed at businesses and libraries, the Writer's Digest products are tailored to the individual writer with costs set appropriately. The separate print guides do not have electronic counterparts, but the publisher offers Writer'sMarket.com, an online subscription database, which contains the information in the printed guides and more. The online database is a one-stop shopping place for writers needing information published in more than one Writer's Digest title. WritersMarket.com has over 8,000 market listings for book publishers, magazines, contests, literary agents, greeting card publishers, screenwriting markets, playwriting markets, conferences, newspapers, online publications, syndicates, and organizations. Besides providing information on markets to submit manuscripts, the site has a search feature to allow custom searches. The best aspect is that subscribers can set up a personal database for listings and search results can be saved. The Submission Tracker lets the subscriber input information on all of their manuscript submissions and to track the status of each one. Payments can also be tracked. There are other resources to assist writers in their work and advice on how much to charge. Market Watch Updates provides news and online help is available. Subscriptions to the site are nominal and set at the individual level in order that writers can use the site as a working tool.

The annual, printed general Writer's Market, as the publisher describes it, ". . . is the writer's bible to freelance success." Writer's Market treats issues of authors' rights, negotiation with publishers and editors, and dealing with agents. The coverage of the markets is detailed. In addition to directory information, there are interviews with successful writers in each issue. The most recent editions have added new articles on topics such as how to use social media and online freelance writing. A deluxe edition of the print publication includes an online subscription access code to WritersMarket.com.

The Guide to Literary Agents is part of WritersMarket.com; there is a print version as well. The work provides names and specialties for more than 750 individual agents around the United States and the world to assist writers in finding an agent to represent them. Agents listed represent authors to publishers and purchasers. The format is similar to other Writer's Digest publications and opens with several introductory essays about literary agents relative to their activity, selection, and responsibilities to their clients. The work is divided into sections treating fee and non-fee literary agents, script agents, over 100 conferences of interest to writers and both a glossary and several indexes. As with other Writer's Digest publications, purchase of the print edition includes online access to WritersMarket.com.

Organizations and Societies

Listed here are organizations generally concerned with the humanities. Organizations for specific disciplines and specialized topics are in the chapters devoted to those subjects.

2-101. **The American Academy of Arts and Sciences (AAAS).** http://www.amacad.org/

The AAAS, founded in 1780, is an "international learned society composed of the world's leading scientists, scholars, artists, business people, and public leaders." Academy projects focus on critical issues in science and technology policy, national security, social policy, education, and humanities and culture. *Dædalus*, the journal of the AAAS, was founded in 1955 and is published by the MIT Press. Articles on libraries at the close of the twentieth century and the implications of the changes for scholars are collected in *Daedalus* 125 (Fall 1996). http://www.mitpressjournals.org/loi/daed

2-102. **The American Society for Information Science and Technology (ASIST).** http://asist.org/SIG/ah.html

ASIST has a special interest group (SIG) on Arts and Humanities that explores the applications of information science to scholarship and creative endeavors in the humanities and fine arts.

2-103. **Association for Computers and the Humanities (ACH).** http://www.ach.org

ACH claims to be *the* professional society for digital humanities, supporting computer-assisted research, teaching, and software and content development in humanistic disciplines such as literature, philosophy, and history.

2-104. **The Museums, Arts, and Humanities Division of the Special Libraries Association (SLA).** http://mah.sla.org/

The Museums, Arts, and Humanities Division encompasses librarians and information specialists from all types of museums; from historical societies, institutions, and other organizations having special departments or special collections devoted to the arts, decorative and performing arts, architecture and humanities; and from both public and private organizations having libraries or subject collections devoted to the creative arts and/or other branches of the humanities.

2-105. **The National Humanities Alliance (NHA).** http://www.nhalliance.org

The NHA is a coalition of 88 organizations concerned with federal programs that affect the humanities. The membership includes scholarly and professional societies; associations of museums, libraries, universities, state humanities councils; university-based and independent centers and institutes; and other groups with interests in the humanities. The mission of the NHA is to advance the cause of the humanities with regard to national policy, programs and legislation that affect the humanities.

2-106. **Society for the History of Authorship, Reading and Publishing: A Global Society (SHARP).** http://www.sharpweb.org/

SHARP was founded "to create a global network for book historians working in a broad range of scholarly disciplines. Research addresses the composition, mediation, reception, survival, and transformation of written communication in material forms including marks on stone, script on parchment, printed books and periodicals, and new media." With more than 1,000 members in over twenty countries, SHARP works in concert with affiliated academic organizations around the world to support the study of book history and print culture.

PART TWO

PHILOSOPHY AND RELIGION

CHAPTER 3

PHILOSOPHY

Elizabeth S. Aversa

INTRODUCTION

The study of philosophy remains a cornerstone of a liberal arts education. Said to include all knowledge or "learning" exclusive of practical arts and technologies, philosophy is a discipline that is unique in both breadth *and* precision. Philosophers ask questions that are introspective (about *us*) and truly universal (about all things external to us). The scope of philosophy is broad, but when the philosopher's work begins, attention to the finest detail is required in making observations and developing arguments.

Working Definition of Philosophy

Although the term *philosophy* is derived from the Greek words usually translated to mean "love of wisdom" (PhilosophicalSociety.com), there is reason to believe that the original usage was somewhat broader, connoting free play of the intellect over a wide range of human problems and even including such qualities as shrewdness, curiosity, and practicality. McLeish, in fact, suggested that the definition "love of knowledge acquired by the exercise of the intellect" is more appropriate to the original meaning (1993, 556).

The meaning of the term *philosophy* has had a gradual narrowing beginning in antiquity and proceeding in stages up through the present time. Socrates differentiated his activity from that of the sophists by stressing the raising of questions for clarification in the course of discussion, as distinct from giving answers or teaching techniques for winning arguments. This distinction sets philosophy up more as an activity than a process. An emphasis on critical examination of issues remained central to philosophic method in the succeeding centuries. Stanley Chodorow, in "Transformations in the Humanities," stated it more simply: "The one thing nearly all philosophers agree on is . . . that philosophical investigation rests on the making and analysis of arguments" (1994, 27).

The encyclopedic concepts of philosophy as encompassing all knowledge were shattered by the rise of modern science in the seventeenth century. First the natural sciences emerged as separate disciplines, then the social and behavioral sciences effected their separation from philosophy, and eventually the social sciences migrated into distinct scholarly and applied fields. It has been noted that the meaning of the term *philosophy* has changed significantly over the years, "with many inquiries that were originally part of it having detached themselves from it" (Honderich 2005, 702).

Stripped of the natural and social sciences, what remains now of philosophy? It has been suggested that the shortest and most direct definition may be that philosophy is "thinking about thinking" (Honderich 2005, 702). First there are questions about the nature of ultimate reality. Then there is the matter of knowledge as a whole as well as the interrelationships of the specialized branches of it. There are questions of methodology and presuppositions of the individual disciplines. (The phrase "philosophy of . . ." is often assigned to this type of endeavor: philosophy of science, philosophy of education, and the like.) Finally, there are those normative issues for which there are not scientifically verifiable answers.

It may be said, then, that philosophy is the discipline that is concerned with basic principles of reality; methods for investigation and study; and the logical structures, systems and interrelationships among all fields of knowledge. For additional definitions of philosophy and discussions of some of the problems of defining the discipline, the reader should see Ted Honderich's *Oxford Companion to Philosophy* (2005), and the introductory chapter of Susan Haack's *Putting Philosophy to Work* (2008).

Major Divisions of the Field

Philosophy may be divided in several different ways. No longer are information resources or academic programs in philosophy organized around just the traditional subfields of epistemology, metaphysics, ethics, aesthetics, and logic—although students of philosophy will need to understand these categories and the differences among them. While these are outlined here, it is useful to recognize that the field may also be divided by philosophical traditions, historical categories, and other groupings, all of which are introduced below.

Epistemology is concerned with the theory of knowledge, and the scope and limits of human knowledge. It poses the question "what can we know?" and "how certain is our knowledge?" Rationalists focus on the role of human reason as the source of all knowledge, while empiricists hold that knowledge is derived from experience. Philosophers are interested in propositional knowledge and it is generally agreed that there are two fundamental types of propositional knowledge: *a priori*, which is knowable without reference to experience and which alone possesses theoretical certainty, as in the principles of logic; and *a posteriori*, which is derived from experience, as in the findings of scientific research, but possesses only approximate, rather than absolute, certainty. Questions of belief, truth, evidence, and objectivity are among the interests of those who focus on epistemology. Over the past three decades, there has been a convergence of humanistic and social scientific disciplines, and this is very evident where cognitive science, psychology, and epistemology meet. Indicative of this convergence is the biographical note on the editor of the online *Dictionary of Philosophy of Mind*: "I'm jointly appointed in Philosophy and Systems Design Engineering, and cross-appointed to Computer Science (I have supervised students in each of these departments and Psychology)" (Smith n.d.). Increasing numbers of papers, and even books, address the idea that epistemology is multidisciplinary and that understanding how we know requires some understanding of the mind's architecture. It is an exciting time to be in the vortex of this branch of philosophy.

The beginner who wants to learn about the basic concerns of epistemology might enjoy reading, "How do philosophers think critically about knowledge?" in *Philosophy: The Big Questions* by Frank Cunningham and co-authors (2003, 278–295). The reader who wishes to explore the convergence of epistemology and cognitive science should see the now classic *Epistemology and Cognition* by Alvin I. Goldman (1986).

Metaphysics is the branch of philosophy that is concerned with identity, matter, time and human nature. It is also concerned with questions of being and simply put, existence. Metaphysics may be further subdivided into *ontology* and *cosmology*. *Ontology* is concerned with the nature of ultimate reality, sometimes referred to as "being." It includes consideration of whether reality has one, two, or many basic components (monism, dualism, or pluralism, respectively). Monistic philosophies consider whether reality is ultimately mental or spiritual (idealism), or physical (materialism). Dualistic philosophies commonly regard both matter and mind as irreducible ultimate components, while pluralistic philosophies allow for many possibilities. Pluralistic ideas are most often argued in the political realm.

Cosmology is concerned with questions of origins and processes. The nature of causality has been a frequent topic of debate. Although a few have argued for pure chance, more philosophers have emphasized antecedent causes; (that is, preceding events that cause the event under consideration to happen) or final causes (ends or purposes that exert influence on the outcome of events).

Many of the former persuasion are convinced that there is no room for either chance or freedom in the chain of causality. The determinists are called *mechanists* if they also believe that reality is ultimately physical. Those who emphasize final causes are known as *teleologists*. *The Blackwell Guide to Metaphysics,* edited by Richard M. Gale, provides articles on metaphysical issues for consideration and future debate (2002).

The division of philosophy that is most familiar to the general public is ethics. *Ethics* is concerned with questions of right and wrong; and the standards of individual, group, or society's behavior in the moral context. Also known as "moral philosophy," ethics is sometimes studied in the broad domain of values in which we consider, for example, aesthetics.

In ethics, the questions relate to human nature and to matters of conduct. Can certain actions be considered morally right or wrong? If so, on what basis? Should the interest of self have priority (egotism) or should the interest of others be the driving principle (altruism)? Or is there some greater good to which both self- and other-interest should be subordinate? Ethical theories may be classified by the manner in which criteria for right actions are established or by the nature of the highest good.

Andrew Jack suggested that ethics can be conveniently divided into three parts: "normative ethics, practical ethics, and meta-ethics." The first deals with normative principles or moral rules, such as "The Golden Rule." Meta-ethics considers the nature of metaphysical issues that can arise for any moral principle. Practical ethics considers specific applications of ethical thinking to particular problems (Jack 1993, 248–249).

Discussions in the popular literature have brought the consideration of practical ethics to newspaper readers and viewers of the television evening news. Such issues as euthanasia, assisted suicide, the death penalty, abortion, equality of the sexes or races, and the use of animals for biomedical research are but a few topics. Peter Singer's *Practical Ethics*, first published in 1979 and thoroughly revised for a 2nd edition in 1999 (Cambridge University Press), is a highly acclaimed work on the subject and includes chapters on equality and discrimination, treatment of animals, and environmental concerns, as well as an excellent discussion of the nature of ethics. Singer was the focus of controversy in the popular press. An accounting of that is an article by Paul Zielbauer, "Princeton Bioethics Professor Debates Views on Disability and Euthanasia," in the *New York Times* (October 13, 1999, p. 8). For practical, applied ethics, see the *New York Times* column "The Ethicist" in the Sunday *New York Times Magazine*. Readers of the weekly feature inquire about their ethical dilemmas at work, in the home, in relationships and in commerce, and "the ethicist" answers, providing perspective, food for thought, and occasional solutions.

Readings by major philosophers in ethics can be found in *Introducing Philosophy Through Film* edited by Richard Fulmerton and Diane Jeske (2010). Films that confront ethical questions are listed along with the mostly classical essays. Films such as *Sophie's Choice, Saving Private Ryan, Dirty Harry,* and *Titanic* are recommended under the heading "Act Consequentialism and its Critics" along with readings of John Stuart Mill, Immanuel Kant, and Thomas Nagel, while a section on "Obligations to Intimates" lists films *The English Patient, Casablanca,* and *High Noon* with readings by Aristotle and Railton, among others. Although *Introducing Philosophy through Film* was designed to introduce philosophy to students as young as high school-age, it can easily serve a general audience, especially one interested in ethics.

The nature of beauty is the subject matter of *aesthetics*. Concerns of the philosopher may be differentiated from those of the psychologist and those of the critic. The psychologist concentrates on human reactions to aesthetic objects. The critic focuses on individual works of art or on the general principles of criticism, usually within the confines of a particular discipline. The philosopher is broadly concerned with beauty per se, whether in art or in nature. Does beauty adhere in the beautiful object? Are there objective criteria by which it may be determined? Or is beauty a subjective experience with no universally valid norms? Classical theories stress objectivity, while romantic theories emphasize individualism and subjectivity. Further, aesthetics explores the nature of the arts and considers similarities and differences between the visual and performing arts, and questions concerning what art represents and expresses.

It should be noted that some contemporary editors have classified aesthetics with other subfields of philosophy in what are called "theories of value." *The Oxford Companion* article on philosophy suggests that ethics, political philosophy and aesthetics are in the domain of "theory of values" (2005, 706). This trend deserves watching over the next few years.

To gain a greater understanding of aesthetics and the arts–and the questions about different kinds of values—moral, utilitarian or truth—the student beginning the exploration of philosophy will enjoy chapters 7 and 8 of *Philosophy: The Big Questions*, referenced above.

Logic deals with the principles of correct reasoning or valid inference. It differs from psychology in that it does not describe how people actually think but rather prescribes certain canons to be followed if they wish to think correctly. *Deductive logic,* sometimes known as Aristotelian or traditional logic, is concerned with the process by which correct conclusions can be drawn from a set of axioms known or believed to be true. Its most familiar form is the syllogism, which consists of three parts: the major premise, the minor premise, and the conclusion.

Major premise: All men are mortal.

Minor premise: Socrates is a man.

Conclusion: Therefore, Socrates is mortal.

Inductive logic is a result of the development of modern scientific methods. It deals with the canons of valid inference, but is concerned with probabilities rather than certainties and often involves the use of statistics. In a sense, the opposite of deductive logic, inductive logic attempts to reach valid generalizations from an enumeration of particulars.

Although logic arose in antiquity and was summarized in Aristotelian works, few advances were made until the last half of the nineteenth century, when symbolic and Boolean logic provided forms of notation useful in mathematical reasoning and later in computer science and information retrieval. Today, logic is sometimes regarded as more closely aligned with mathematics than with philosophy. However, the systematic rules of inference are essential to the arguments in all other branches of philosophy and actually predate the divisions of the field proposed here. Condron and co-authors note that tools to support the teaching of philosophy have largely concentrated on logic "which is ideally suited to the new medium for delivery and assessment of courses" (2001).

Having introduced the five classical divisions of philosophy, epistemology, metaphysics, ethics, aesthetics, and logic, we cannot ignore other organizing principles. For example, the *Internet Encyclopedia of Philosophy* uses broad categories, such as "Metaphysics and Epistemology," that incorporate philosophy of language, philosophy of religion, and philosophy of mind. The category "Value Theory" is set up to include aesthetics, bioethics, ethics, philosophy of law, and political philosophy. The heading "Science, Logic and Mathematics" predictably takes in the fields of logic and the philosophy of science. Finally, a catch-all grouping of "Philosophic Traditions" is organized around geography (by countries) or grouping (e.g., Feminist Philosophy).

Other organizational schemes for dividing philosophy may be completely by "tradition" (American, Continental, Indian, Chinese, and so forth) or by historical periods (Ancient, 15th–17th Centuries, Modern, and Contemporary, for instance). Steven Cahn, in his chapter in the book *Teaching Philosophy: Theoretical Reflections and Practical Suggestions,* edited by Tziporah Kasachkoff (2004), describes ways of organizing a beginning philosophy course and he notes both advantages and disadvantages of the topical approach, the "great texts" approach, the historical approach, and the secondary source approach.

The editors of *The Oxford Handbook of Contemporary Philosophy* (2005), when organizing the topics to be covered, selected topics that they believed would give readers "a sense of the range and excitement of contemporary analytic philosophy" and "inform them of . . . interesting recent development" (Jackson and Smith 2005, *v*). The articles in this handbook are categorized under seven headings: moral philosophy; social and political philosophy; philosophy of mind and action; philosophy of language; metaphysics; epistemology; and philosophy of the sciences. While logic is excluded, so noted by the editors, the essays cover recent developments across almost all of the traditional divisions of the field.

Use and Users of Philosophy Information

A search of the literature of use and user studies indicates that very little research has been done on literature use by philosophers. There is evidence, however, that the literature of the field is widely used and that particular authors are well-cited both within the humanities and by writers in the sciences and social sciences.

Citation represents one of several measures of literature use. Eugene Garfield, over the years since the advent of *The Arts and Humanities Citation Index* (entry 2-1), has published a number of papers affirming that a few philosophers are among the most cited authors covered in the databases. Plato and Aristotle will always be highly cited, but philosophers such as Karl Popper and John Rawls make the "highly cited" category (Garfield 1980). Not only articles, but also books were found to be well-cited in the last quarter of the twentieth century (Garfield 1989, 101). Journals including *Journal of Philosophy* are cited across many fields, suggesting the influence that philosophy makes on all fields of knowledge (Garfield 1983, 763).

The numbers of books published annually provides another indicator of use. Among humanities fields, philosophy produces fewer titles than visual arts, performing arts, and language and literature, but the number of both titles and hardcover books published in philosophy has remained stable over the past five years. The 2011 *Library and Book Trade Almanac* reported that the number of book titles across all fields published in the U.S. has declined steadily since 2006. In the field of philosophy, the number of titles has remained relatively consistent with an increase from 2044 titles in 2006, to 2631 in 2007, followed by a steep decrease in 2008. The number of book titles published again increased in 2009 to level off at 2267 in 2010. The number of titles in philosophy remains above the 2006 level despite the economic downturn that has affected publishers, libraries, and vendors in the book trade in recent years (Bogard 2011, 492).

John W. East reported in 2003 that recent, English language books were frequently cited in the journals *Noûs* and *Philosophical Quarterly*. The article, "Australian Library Resources in Philosophy: A Survey of Recent Monograph Holdings," suggests that English has become the *de facto* language of philosophy in the twenty-first century. The author was also surprised to note that the newer book titles were the most highly cited in his study, suggesting that philosophical writers value both the old and the new (East 2003, 92–99).

An older study by Jean-Pierre V.M. Herubel at Purdue University, "Philosophy Dissertation Bibliographies and Citations in Serials Evaluation," provides insight into the literature used by philosophy scholars in preparing dissertations in one university environment. Reflecting Garfield's earlier findings, *Journal of Philosophy* and *Philosophical Review* were among the most highly cited journals (first and fourth) with 63 and 44 citations respectively. The dissertations, which are dated between 1970 and 1988, reflect the humanist's heavy reliance on monographs (71.3 percent of all references) and lesser use of the journal literature, 28.7 percent (Herubel 1991, 67).

The importance of monographs is reaffirmed in a later study by Ylva Lindholm-Romantschuk and Julian Warner, "The Role of Monographs in Scholarly Communication: An Empirical Study of Philosophy, Sociology and Economics" (1996).

Studies of scholars' information seeking for the Research Libraries Group by Constance Gould, *Philosophy: Information Needs in the Humanities: An Assessment*, suggested that relatively few philosophers use traditional reference sources to stay current in their field, particularly when compared to researchers in other disciplines (Gould 1988). This notion is confirmed when one considers the approaches to philosophy that teachers use; most of the emphasis is on the works *of* philosophers, not *about* them. Furthermore, types of reference tools in philosophy have changed so that digital collections and the bibliographic apparatus supporting the literature have begun to merge into online portals and encyclopedias and dictionaries that link directly to the literature of the masters.

The practice of acknowledgement by authors was investigated by Cronin and co-authors in 2003. Comparing acknowledgement in articles in the psychology journal *Psychological Review* and the philosophy journal *Mind*, the authors found that while 49 percent of the articles in *Psychological Review* contained one or more acknowledgements, only 25 percent of the *Mind* articles did so. The study also showed that collaborative authorship is increasingly common in the psychology articles and that co-authorship is less prevalent (although it does occur) in philosophy (Cronin et al. 2003).

Wayne Blivens-Tatum offers insight into the kinds of reference tools philosophers need in order to do their work. Blivens-Tatum, who is the philosophy and religion librarian at Princeton University, observed:

> Philosophers, like most scholars in the humanities, rarely seek research help from librarians. There are several reasons for this. First, rather than gather immense amounts of data or read large numbers of books and articles for their research, philosophers tend to analyze a few sources and arguments in great depth. Except for historians of philosophy, philosophers rarely need to do exhaustive searches . . . Blivens-Tatum goes on to say that another possible reason is "philosophy has a remarkably robust bibliographic and reference apparatus and sources are easy to find" (Blivens-Tatum 2011, 318).

It is also well-documented that "philosophy continues as an academic discipline because philosophers earn their living, for the most part, by being teachers of philosophy" (Kasachkoff, 5). The teachers who develop next-generation philosophers are among the important users of a broader array of philosophy resources to support pedagogy. Several resources that may whet the appetite of students for the discipline have been mentioned in this chapter: *Introducing Philosophy Through Film* (Palmer 2001); *Looking at Philosophy: The Unbearable Heaviness of Philosophy Made Lighter* (Fulmerton and Jeske 2010); and *Philosophy: The Big Questions* (Cunningham et al. 2003) are especially provocative for students, teachers, and other readers with a beginning interest in philosophy.

Libraries, Information Centers, and Special Collections in Philosophy

Because philosophy is the subject that is most concerned with knowledge and its fields, subfields, and organization, it is appropriate to include in this chapter a brief mention of the relationship between classification of knowledge and classification of library materials. The basics of library classification schemes, the purpose of subject headings and the material on cross-references is appropriate to the literature and information resources of all fields, but should not be confused with the categorizations of knowledge that developed earlier in the field of philosophy. Taylor and Joudrey distinguish between general categorizations of knowledge and bibliographic classification systems; the reader wishing additional detail should consult pages 379 through 384 of *The Organization of Information* by Arlene G. Taylor and Daniel N. Joudrey (3rd ed. Libraries Unlimited, 2009).

Methods of describing, indexing, and searching are rapidly changing to accommodate the enormous mass of information that is being made available electronically and the many links among the sources. Humanities librarians continue to be involved in developing the systems by which philosophical materials, both books for shelves and electronic resources for databases, can be organized for convenient access by users. Their work in these areas is enhanced by a basic knowledge of categorization and classification from both philosophical and bibliographical domains.

It has become a truism to say that the competent librarian will employ information sources far beyond the collection of a single library. Indeed, since the last editions of this guide, emphasis has increasingly been on "access to" rather than "ownership of" information resources. The role of bibliographies, indexes, portals and online library catalogs is familiar. Special collections in philosophy may attempt to cover the discipline as a whole, a period of history, a special topic, or the works of a single philosopher. A few library special collections of note in North America are listed here.

> The Hoose Library of Philosophy at the University of Southern California contains over 40,000 volumes and covers all time periods from medieval manuscripts to contemporary publications.

The Renaissance period is the topic of the Professor Don C. Allen Collection at the University of California, San Diego.

The University of Pittsburgh Special Collections Department collects in the history of scientific philosophy.

The General Library of the University of Michigan has a large collection dealing with Arabic philosophy.

The Weston College Library attempts to be comprehensive in collecting works of Catholic philosophy, and Dominican College Library specializes in Thomist works and attempts to collect all works by Dominican authors.

The Van Pelt Library at the University of Pennsylvania holds nearly 3,000 manuscripts of fifteenth- through nineteenth-century Hindu philosophy, religion, and grammar.

McMaster University Library in Hamilton, Ontario, holds the papers of Bertrand Russell, more than 250,000 items. Information is disseminated in *Russell: The Journal of the Bertrand Russell Archives*.

The University of Missouri Thomas Moore Johnson Collection of Philosophy holds more than 1700 titles dating from 1494 through the nineteenth century.

These are just a few special collections in philosophy. With the advent of digital collections, many more works are being made available to scholars around the globe. Texts and collections available through sources like the Oxford and Cambridge bibliographies with links to texts and the offerings of resources like the Philosophy Documentation Center's *E-Collection* (entry 3-1) and *Philosophy on the EServer* (entry 3-12) will make it increasingly possible for researchers to access the literature they need without visiting a physical library.

The next section introduces some of the most important resources for meeting the needs of the philosophers, students, teachers, as well as general readers.

Works Cited

Blivens-Tatum, Wayne. 2001. "The Compleat Philosophy Librarian." *Reference and User Services Quarterly* 50, 4 (Summer): 318.

Bogard, David. 2011. *Library and Book Trade Almanac*. 56th ed. Medford, New Jersey: Information Today.

Chodorow, Stanley. 1994. "Transformations in the Humanities." In *Perspectives on the Humanities and School-Based Curriculum Development*. American Council of Learned Societies, Occasional Paper No. 24: 27–48.

Condron, Francis, Michael Fraser, and Stuart Sutherland. 2001. *Oxford University Computing Services Guide To Digital Resources for the Humanities*. Morgantown, WV: West Virginia University Press.

Cronin, Blaise, Debra Shaw, and Kathryn La. 2003. "A Case of Thousands: Co-authorship and Sub-authorship Collaboration in the 20th Century as Manifested in the Scholarly Journal Literature of Psychology and Philosophy." *Journal of the American Society for Information Science & Technology* 54, 9 (July): 855–871.

Cunningham, Frank et al. 2003. *Philosophy: The Big Questions*. Toronto: Canadian Scholars' Press.

East, John W. 2003. "Australian Library Resources in Philosophy: A Survey of Recent Monograph Holdings." *Australian Academic and Research Libraries* 3, 2 (June): 92–99.

Fulmerton, Richard and Diane Jeske. 2010, *Introducing Philosophy Through Film*. Malden, MA: Wiley-Blackwell.

Gale, Richard M., ed. 2002. *The Blackwell Guide to Metaphysics*. Oxford: Blackwell Publishing.

Garfield, Eugene. 1980. "Is Information Retrieval in the Arts and Humanities Inherently Different from That in Science . . . ?" *Library Quarterly* 50 (1980): 40–57.

Garfield, Eugene. 1983. *Journal Citation Studies* 38. "Arts and Humanities Differ from Natural and Social Sciences Journals—But Their Similarities Are Surprising." In *Essays of an Information Scientist*. Vol. 5. ISI Press.

Garfield, Eugene. 1989. "A Different Sort of Great-Books: The 50 Twentieth-Century Works Most Cited in the *Arts and Humanities Index*, 1976–1983." in *Essays of an Information Scientist*. Vol. 10. ISI Press.

Gould, Constance. 1988. *Information Needs in the Humanities: An Assessment*. Stanford, CA: RLG, 1988.

Herubel, Jean-Pierre V.M. 1991. "Philosophy Dissertation Bibliographies and Citations in Serials Evaluation." *The Serials Librarian* 20: 65–73.

Honderich, Ted. 2005. *Oxford Companion to Philosophy*, 2nd ed. Oxford: Oxford University Press.

Jack, Andrew. 1993. "Ethics." In *Key Ideas in Human Thought*, Kenneth McLeish, ed. New York: Facts on File: 248–49.

Jackson, Frank and Michael Smith, eds. 2005. *The Oxford Handbook of Contemporary Philosophy*. Oxford: Oxford University Press.

Kasachkoff, Tziporah. 2004. *Teaching Philosophy: Theoretical Reflections and Practical Suggestions*. Lanham, MD: Rowman and Littlefield Publishing Group.

McLeish, Kenneth, ed. 1993. *Key Ideas in Human Thought*. New York: Facts on File.

Palmer, Donald. 2001. *Looking at Philosophy: The Unbearable Heaviness of Philosophy Made Lighter*. Mountain View, CA: Mayfield Publishing Company.

Romantschuk, Ylva and Julian Warner. 1996. "The Role of Monographs in Scholarly Communication: An Empirical Study of Philosophy, Sociology, and Economics." *Journal of Documentation* 52 (December): 389–404.

Singer, Peter. 1999. *Practical Ethics*. 2nd ed. Cambridge, UK: Cambridge University Press.

Taylor, Arlene G. and Daniel N. Joudrey. *The Organization of Information*. 3rd ed. Westport, CT: Libraries Unlimited, 2009.

Zielbauer, Paul. "Princeton Bioethics Professor Debates Views on Disability and Euthanasia." *New York Times* (October 13, 1999): 8.

Websites

The Internet Encyclopedia of Philosophy (IEP). http://www.iep.utm.edu/

PhilosophicalSociety.com. http:philosophicalsociety.com/What%20Philosophy%Is.htm

SELECTED INFORMATION SOURCES IN PHILOSOPHY

This section introduces some of the most important resources for meeting the needs of philosophers, students, and teachers, as well as general readers.

Information resources for the field of philosophy, one of the "literary humanities" fields, are generally centered on the writings of philosophers (the texts) or around topical divisions of the field. Increasingly, the "great texts" are available electronically, so a number of online tools link from entries in bibliographies, histories, dictionaries, and encyclopedias to the texts by philosophers, ancient and modern. Both open access resources and those that require a subscription or purchase are listed below.

Databases and Digital Collections

3-1. E-Collection. Philosophy Documentation Center. Online subscription database.

The E-Collection contains complete electronic coverage of 90 journals and other series publications, with each article accompanied by permission and copyright information. Libraries are also offered a Collection Development Bundle consisting of access to some 20 journals in the field. Most of those that are offered are recent (1990 forward), but a few date back to the 1920s.

3-2. InfoTrac Religion & Philosophy. Gale Cengage. Online subscription database. http://www.gale.cengage.com

Over 250 magazines and academic journals have been selected for this collection that covers philosophy and related areas such as religion. Indexing began for most selections in 1980 and full texts of many articles are available from 1983 to the present.

3-3. InteLex Past Masters. Online subscription database. http://www.nlx.com/home

This is an online database that provides full-text access to a comprehensive collection of works in Classical Philosophy, Medieval Philosophy, Continental Philosophy, and British and American Philosophy. The database description states that "InteLex Corporation's PAST MASTERS series encompasses the world's largest collection of full text electronic editions in philosophy." Further, InteLex acquires and develops "definitive editions of the full corpora of the seminal figures in the history of the humanities, including published and unpublished works, articles and essays, reviews and correspondence." The files are available online directly and also in a format suitable for installation on a library's server. Authors' works are procured individually and purchasers are billed separately. Some libraries may purchase an entire package while others may select specific authors to include in their digital offerings.

3-4. International Directory of Philosophy. Charlottesville, VA: Philosophy Documentation Center. Online subscription database. http://secure.pdcnet.org/idphil

This source is a searchable online database comprised of two traditional print-on-paper directories: *Directory of American Philosophers* and the *International Directory of Philosophy and Philosophers*. The new consolidated resource with over 30,000 entries contains information on university philosophy departments; academic programs; philosophical societies, associations, and congresses; journals and philosophy publishers around the world; and individual philosophers. The overall goal of this online resource is to facilitate communication about philosophy and among philosophers on a worldwide scale.

3-5. Oxford Bibliographies Online (OBO). Online subscription database. http://oxfordbibliographiesonline.com/

This resource indexes bibliographic resources of all types and makes them accessible to the researcher. OBO is primarily designed to provide bibliographic information, but the organization and introductory descriptions serve an encyclopedic function as well. The publisher's description of the resource states that OBO is "A scholar-curated library of discipline-based subject modules." Each article has subject headings related to the topic, a commentary essay, citations to relevant resources with annotations, and links where available. The user is guided through the resource to the chapter, book, website, archive, or data set needed. The philosophy section added just fewer than 50 new articles in July 2011 alone. It was the intention of the editors to combine the best aspects of online bibliographic databases and print bibliographies and their goal has been realized in this helpful and unique resource.

3-6. Philosopher's Index. Philosophers Information Center, 1970– . Online subscription database. http://philindex.org

This is the standard bibliographic index to the philosophical literature in the Anglo-American tradition, going back as far as 1940. The Index covers close to 700 journals representing 15 fields of philosophy. Over one-dozen languages are covered, including a good number of non-western ones. Abstracts are written by the authors. The print Index is published quarterly. There are both subject and author listings for all entries, with the abstracts appearing in the author section. There is a separate index for book reviews. Originally, the index covered only the periodical literature, but books in English were added in 1980. The Philosopher's Index is provided online by subscription through several vendors and on CD-ROM through Ovid.

The Philosopher's Information Center. http://philinfo.org

The Philosopher's Information Center, founded by Dr. Richard H. Linebeck, is a non-profit organization whose purpose is stated as "providing the finest scholarly resources to philosophers and individuals interested in philosophy and related disciplines." The scholarly resource for which the Center is responsible is The Philosopher's Index (entry 3-6), the standard index to the philosophical literature.

3-7. Philosophy Research Index. Charlottesville, VA: Philosophy Documentation Center (PDC). Online subscription database. http://secure.pdcnet.org/pri

The Philosophy Research Index is another subscription-based database of bibliographic information on articles, books, reviews, dissertations, and other resources in philosophy. The mission of its developer, the Philosophy Documentation Center and former publisher of *Philosopher's Index*, is to "use the best available technology to provide searchable bibliographic coverage of a definable portion of the known philosophical literature in several western languages." Covering 1460 to the present, the database includes references in English, Spanish, German, French, Italian, Latin, and other languages. A translation tool assists with searches across languages. This has been noted as an up-and-coming competitor of the *Philosopher's Index*, described above.

The Philosophy Documentation Center (PDC). http://www.pdcnet.org/

Located in Charlottesville, VA, the PDC provides access to information resources in philosophy, applied ethics, religious studies, classics, and fields related to the discipline of philosophy. The non-profit Center, which began its work in 1966, has grown over the years to offer membership management for professional organizations, secure hosting of full-text, service as a fulfillment house for print and electronic journals, rights and permissions management, conference registration management and other wide ranging services to the philosophy researcher, associations, and libraries.

New products of the PDC include the Philosophy Research Index (entry 3-7). This is advertized on the Center's website as "the new standard for bibliographic research in philosophy," and it will compete with the older Philosopher's Index (entry 3-6). Another new product offered by the PDC is the "E-Collection," which contains complete electronic coverage of 90 journals and other series publications, with each article accompanied by permission and copyright information. Libraries are also offered a "Collection Development Bundle" consisting of access to some 20 journals in the field. Most of those that are offered are recent (1990 forward) but a few date back to the 1920s. Finally, the newly available (since 2010) online International Directory of Philosophy (entry 3-4) consolidates the long-running print tools *Directory of American Philosophers,* and the *International Directory of Philosophy and Philosophers.* The print directories continue to be published by PDC as well. The PDC is still growing in its offerings, and so the librarian will do well to make contact about the host of products and services available to the discipline and those interested in it.

3-8. Poiesis: Philosophy Online Serials. Charlottesville, VA: Philosophy Documentation Center. Online subscription database. http://secure.pdcnet.org/pdc/bvdb.nsf/journal?openform&journal =poiesis

This online database contains the full text of current, recent, and back issues of a growing number of print philosophy journals. Every word in every journal issue in the database is fully searchable, including all articles, book reviews, footnotes, announcements, and notices. Users can view up to a paragraph of text of each item retrieved; many journal titles also allow full text display.

3-9. Routledge Encyclopedia of Philosophy (REP). Edward Craig, ed. 2000. http://www.rep.rout-ledge.com

Although this encyclopedia was first a print product in 10 volumes, it has adapted to online easily, and the user will find it more convenient to use online. The entries carry a substantial number of cross-references and excellent bibliographic information so the user can consult the referenced material without needing to work with the multi-volume print set. Articles are updated quarterly by subject specialists. Another resource is the *Shorter Routledge Encyclopedia of Philosophy* (Edward Craig, ed. 2005). This handy resource brings together 900 of the most important entries in the 10-volume encyclopedia, many updated with new reading suggestions, and adds new articles on timely topics. This work is designed for the student or general reader; the multi-volume *Encyclopedia* will continue to serve the needs of scholars and specialists.

Open Access Resources

Archives and Texts

3-10. Internet Sacred Text Archive: Western Philosophy. http://www.sacred-texts.com/phi/index.htm

This section of the acclaimed archive contains texts by the most important writers who have defined the philosophy of modern Western society. Texts here discuss ethics, metaphysics, epistemology, and political philosophy. The user should be warned that most of these are large text files, which may take a while to download, particularly on a slow connection.

3-11. Greek Philosophy Archive. http://people.clemson.edu/~knox2/archive/Greek.html

This is the resource at which the user will find texts for the ancient Greek philosophers' works. Dialogues of Plato, the works of Aristotle, Meditations of Marcus Aurelius, and other texts are a click away. Along with these pages, there is a "sculpture garden" page with photos related to ancient Greek culture: sculpture, architecture, and ceramics.

3-12. Philosophy on the EServer. http://philosophy.eserver.org

The EServer is a digital humanities project based at Iowa State University. Its goal is to provide published works across the disciplines "free of charge." The Philosophy pages are especially rich, offering links to out-of-copyright canonical texts and articles as well as newer contributed papers that authors provide to the site. In addition to the widely available works of Aristotle and Plato; Kant, Descartes, and even Derrida are represented in Philosophy on the EServer.

3-13. PhilPapers: Online Papers in Philosophy. http://philpapers.org/

PhilPapers is a comprehensive directory with links to online articles and books by academic philosophers designed to facilitate the exchange and development of philosophical research through the Internet. It gathers and organizes philosophical research from journals, archives and personal papers, and provides tools for philosophers to access, organize, and discuss this research. Manuscripts can be submitted for discussion, too. PhilPapers started in 2006 as part of *MindPapers*, and now includes much of the material from Online Papers in Philosophy. The developers of this resource understand that philosophy is about "the argument" and so they make available opportunities for discussion, categorization, and editing of papers. The coverage is good, too: a search on "animal ethics" yielded 402 items and they were categorized into a handy group of five sub-topics ranging from "animal cruelty" to "vegetarianism." Some features require that users sign in, but creating an account is easy and free.

Included with PhilPapers is *Contemporary Philosophy of the Mind: An Annotated Bibliography* (http://consc.net/mindpapers). This is a collection of the texts of over 28,000 papers in *Philosophy of Mind* and the *Science of Consciousness*. The library is organized by eight major themes, and then further subdivided by topic. Both online and print items are included with links to those that are freely available online.

Other Open Access Resources

3-14. A Dictionary of Philosophical Terms and Names. http://www.philosophypages.com/dy/

This dictionary is a concise guide to technical terms and personal names often encountered in the study of philosophy, with links to entries and information found in standard reference works. The site has not been updated since 2006, so some links are broken. Despite this disadvantage, the resource serves a needed dictionary function along with offering biographical sketches of philosophers, more detailed biographies for well-known figures, a timeline, study guides, and a survey of the history of philosophy. Its organization is easy to follow, making this a good source for ready reference queries.

3-15. Dictionary of Philosophy. Dagobert D. Runes. New York: Kessinger Publisher's Rare Reprints, 2006. Print and e-book online at http://www.ditext.com/runes/index.html

This is a reprint edition of an old standard first published in 1942 to furnish clear and concise definitions and descriptions and to do so in a comprehensive fashion, functions that the work still serves. Entries are signed by the contributors, and the work is of value now for its historical character as well as its comprehensive and accurate nature in treating various thinkers, issues, and ideological systems of the past. The online version, prepared by Andrew Chrucky, is an easily searchable tool.

3-16. EpistemeLinks. http://www.epistemelinks.com/

EpistemeLinks is a free site of links to philosophy resources on the Internet. The number of links is close to 20,000 and the fact that this site began in 1997 makes it a popular source with its regular users. It should be noted that EpistemeLinks.com is not currently being maintained or updated with new links. The site provides this notice on the home page: "The site can still provide some value to visitors, but expect to find broken links on various pages." As time goes on, the value of this "old favorite" will decline, but for the time being, it remains a helpful resource.

3-17. ETHX on the Web: A Bibliographic Database on Bioethics and Professional Ethics. http://bioethics.georgetown.edu/databases/index.html

Georgetown University Libraries provides extensive free access to databases on ethics. The ETHX web continues to serve the purposes previously served by the print *Bibliography of Bioethics* that was published for over 30 years by the same institution. The 35th volume of the *Bibliography of Bioethics* is the last volume to be published because the Bibliography ceased publication as of 2009. The final volume includes abstracts from periodicals and bibliographic information for journal and newspaper articles, government reports, reports of international organizations, and book chapters. A fact sheet provided by the Bioethics Library at Georgetown points the user to the ETHX on the Web database, which "will cover the entire time span of the Bibliography of Bioethics." The fact sheet also provides an interesting brief history of this important resource. See http://bioethics.georgetown.edu/publications/Bibliography%20of%20Bioethics%20Fact%20Sheet%202010.pdf.

3-18. The Internet Encyclopedia of Philosophy (IEP). http://www.iep.utm.edu/

The IEP was founded in 1995 as a non-profit organization to provide open access to detailed, scholarly information on key topics and philosophers in all areas of the field. It operates through the volunteer work of the staff (http://www.iep.utm.edu/eds/), which consists of editors, authors, and technical advisers, and is housed at the University of Tennessee, Martin. Most of the articles in the IEP are original contributions by specialized philosophers and identified by the author's name at the foot of the article. Others are temporary, or "proto articles," that have largely been adapted from older sources, and identified by the initials "IEP." Original ones will eventually replace the placeholder articles. Use of the IEP is free of charge and it is available to all users of the Internet. The present editors and authors hold doctorate degrees and are professors at colleges and universities around the world, most notably from the United States, Great Britain, and Australia.

3-19. The Ism Book. http://www.ismboook.com

Easy to search compendium of "-ism"s, retrieving short definitions of theories, doctrines, movements, and approaches in philosophy, religion, politics, science and the arts. The user needs only to click on the "ism" on an alphabetical list. New "-isms" are added continuously. This resource claims to be the longest-running dictionary of philosophy on the Internet (since 1996) and was placed in the public domain by its author, Peter Saint-Andre.

3-20. Meta-Encyclopedia of Philosophy. http://www.ditext.com/ http://www.ditext.com/encyc/frame.html

This is a dynamic resource that enables the user to compare topics in key online philosophy reference tools. The user can compare entries in Runes, IEP, SEP, *Dictionary of the Philosophy of the Mind*, *The Ism Book*, the 1913 *Catholic Encyclopedia*, and *Dictionary of Philosophical Terms and Names*. Arranged alphabetically, the *Meta-Encyclopedia* retrieves entries and associated sources in a simple data format that can be clicked for full information. While this resource lacks visual appeal and extensive documentation, the feature allowing for comparisons across seven electronic tools is worthwhile.

3-21. Notre Dame Philosophical Reviews. http://ndpr.nd.edu

Managed by an editorial board and produced by philosophers at Notre Dame, this resource publishes book reviews in the field of philosophy. Between 10 and two-dozen reviews appear monthly in the online only resource. The reviews are generally between 1,500 and 2,500 words, a substantial length for academic reviews. The aim of the publishers is to keep the reviews current within a year of a book's publication. This is a free resource, available either on the website or by an e-mail list if the user prefers to receive reviews to the e-mailbox.

3-22. Philosophy Around the Web. http://users.ox.ac.uk/~worc0337/philindex.html#philos

This site is an all-around resource that provides links to many philosophy-related materials. Organized around 14 main categories, the site provides links to journals, texts, pages about philosophers, pages about philosophy, jobs, reference works, and more. While many of the links work, still, there is no evidence that the site has been updated since 2005–2006. Links to use-net groups are not useful, but the list of journals and links out to other contemporary resources allow this site to retain some usefulness. The developer, Peter J. King, stated that he never meant this to be a comprehensive site; he also editorializes about some of the resources to which his site points; but it is still useful and it is still free.

3-23. Philosophy News Service. http://www.philosophynews.com

This is just what the title implies: a news service alerting the readership to new developments (papers, conferences, publications, current issues) in the field of philosophy. The information from the source can be had from the website or one can subscribe to receive it through other alerting systems (RSS feeds, etc.). There is an alphabetical list with links to the archives, and a feature called "table talks" for online discussion of issues that are of current interest. Essays and interviews are posted as well, making this a thoughtful source for philosophy faculty members, students, and generalists or journalists with philosophical interests.

3-24. Stanford Encyclopedia of Philosophy (SEP). Edward N. Zalta, ed. 1995. http://plato.stanford.edu

The SEP is a full text academic online reference work published by the Metaphysics Research Lab at the Center for the Study of Language and Information (CSLI) at Stanford University. An editorial board of over 100 subject experts maintains and updates the free resource. Since its earliest beginnings in 1995, the structure and organization of this tool have consistently met the highest standards. An expert or group of subject specialists in the field keeps each entry current. They include documentation on previous versions, bibliographic references and extensive cross-references to other entries. Since 1997, the encyclopedia has maintained a "fixed archive" every three months that can be consulted for historical purposes and cited as one would cite a journal or other continuing publication. The encyclopedia has been supported by a number of impressive grants and a history of the encyclopedia project has been maintained over the years and continues to be open-access. Updates are noted, and the notifications of updates are available through several means, including RSS feeds. When an entry is updated, the notification states specifically which aspect of the entry has been updated, the bibliography, web links, main text, and so forth. The encyclopedia's editorial group is responsive to new research. This is one of the most professionally written and best-organized philosophy resources available on the web.

Print Resources

3-25. A to Z of Philosophy. Alexander Moseley. London: Continuum Publishing Group, 2008.

This small paperback provides a concise and easy-to-use dictionary for the general reader. Important concepts (e.g., absolute, fallacies), subfields (e.g., ethics, metaphysics), and people (e.g., Aristotle, Popper) are defined simply and efficiently. A list of references for further reading, a list of entries, and a list of names (with dates and a brief identifier) follow the main text. Another compact reference source for the generalist or student is *Great Thinkers A-Z.* (Julian Baggini and Jeremy Stangroom, Continuum, 2004). This title covers 100 "great thinkers" from the last 2,500 years with brief signed entries. A chronology and thematic guide based on subdivisions of philosophy are found at the back of the book, along with a list of the contributors and their affiliations. Neither of these sources from Continuum Publishing professes to be exhaustive or scholarly; they provide quick "snapshots" of important concepts and thinkers in the Western tradition.

3-26. Biographical Dictionary of Twentieth-Century Philosophers. Stuart Brown et al., eds. New York: Routledge, 2002.

This is an important, informative, and lucid source, in a new edition, providing background information for college students and specialists on more than 1,000 philosophers from all over the world. Over 100 scholars have contributed the entries, with an emphasis on Anglo-American and European personalities; representation is also given to philosophers from China, Japan, Russia, and the Mid-East. Entries vary in length from 250 to 1,250 words and identify demographics, field of study, and accomplishments; and provide a bibliography along with an essay describing the individual's life and thought. Handy indexes allow the resource to be accessed by the country of origin, major influencers, and division of the field represented by the philosophers covered.

3-27. Cambridge Dictionary of Philosophy. 2nd ed. Robert Audi, ed. New York: Cambridge University Press, 1999.

This is an important and highly regarded dictionary. The 2nd edition expands on the first by some 400 new articles, including a limited number of entries for living philosophers. The Cambridge dictionary is authoritative and, in some respects, encyclopedia-like.

3-28. Concise Encyclopedia of Western Philosophy. J.O. Urmson. New York: Routledge, 2003.

This is a revision of another highly reliable and popular resource. This particular work is especially noted for its good coverage of individual philosophers.

3-29. Dictionary of Philosophy. Andrew Flew and Stephen Priest. London: Pan, 2002.

This is a classic dictionary that has undergone revision. It is an A-to-Z guide that is suitable for students and laypersons as well. Terms are defined, persons are identified, and concepts are given brief, clear explanations.

3-30. Encyclopedia of Bioethics. 3rd ed. Stephen Garrard Post, ed. New York: Simon & Schuster/Macmillan, 2003. 5 vols.

This is a revision of the 1995 revised work in the field of bioethics, updating the treatment of the ethical and social issues of life sciences, medicine, health care, and the health professions. Philosophical perspectives are provided, among others, since the work is interdisciplinary in nature. Elements are included that embrace the study of history, theology, science, law, and the social sciences. For the philosopher, there is value not only in the specialized area of bioethics, but also in the excellent coverage given general ethical theory, which can still be used to supplement other works. Entries are arranged alphabetically and include major issues of modern times (AIDS, sexuality and gender, animal welfare and rights, bioterrorism, managed care, and other timely topics). In many cases, the perspectives of different authors are presented. There is an attempt to avoid technical language and to achieve a universal perspective, with contributions from experts from across the globe. The work has a comprehensive index and cross-references are supplied. This new edition has over 100 totally new articles and substantially revised older entries.

3-31. Encyclopedia of Ethics. 2nd ed. Lawrence C. Becker and Charlotte B. Becker, eds. New York: Routledge, 2001. 3 vols.

This edition updates a classic encyclopedia. Over 300 experts worked with the husband and wife team of editors to revise and update both the entries and bibliographies. New entries have been added.

3-32. Encyclopedia of Indian Philosophies. Karl H. Potter. Delhi: Motilal Banarsidass, 1995– . 9 vols.

This revised and continually expanding version of the Encyclopedia remains a standard for the encyclopedia. According to the general editor, Karl Potter, "For purposes of control, 'Indian philosophical works' as understood for the project is confined to treatises which are (1) of philosophical interest throughout; (2) theoretical rather than purely practical in their intended function, and (3) polemical or at least expository in a context where defen[s]e of one view among alternatives is appropriate." This multi-volume set, organized topically and then chronologically, contains for each volume, an introduction by its editor and summaries of all texts known to exist in Western language translation. The current work is listed not as a publication but as an "ongoing project" of The Infinity Foundation in Princeton, NJ. Volume 1, the bibliography, a fixed document pointing to print sources, is online at http://faculty.washington.edu/kpotter/.

3-33. Encyclopedia of Philosophy. 2nd ed. Donald Borchert, ed. Macmillan Reference USA, 2005. 10 vols.

This is a 10-volume second edition of the encyclopedia that was first published in 1967 with Paul Edwards as editor. The new edition includes more than 450 entries on new topics and 300 new entries on topics included in the earlier addition. This edition's articles are by leading authorities in the field. Arranged alphabetically, the entries vary in length with some described by reviewers as "the equivalent of a small book." Borchert, the editor of the project, is an Ohio State scholar and edited the supplement to the first edition. Each volume in this set ranges in length from about 700 to more than 850 pages; the last volume (v.10) is comprised of an index to the set and a bibliography of philosophical journals. The virtues of this encyclopedia are its breadth of coverage and the balance between old and new and analytic and continental traditions.

3-34. Philosophy: A Guide to the Reference Literature. 3rd ed. Hans E. Bynagle. Westport, CT: Libraries Unlimited, 2006. Print and e-book.

Like its predecessors, the first and second editions, this is a highly valuable tool for researchers in philosophy. Bibliographic resources receive careful attention through coverage, although in this edition, the resources are arranged primarily by subject rather than by type of reference tool. Bynagle discusses the pros and cons of the new arrangement in the preface to this edition, concluding that the subject arrangement, with entries organized under top-level headings like general sources, histories of philosophy, branches of philosophy, and miscellany, works best for today's users. The guide continues as a leading source of information regarding reference material in the field.

Histories

3-35. Grundriss der Geschichte der Philosophie. Friedrich Ueberweg. Berlin: Mittler, 1916–1928; Repr. Basel, Switzerland: Schwabe, 1951–1956, 1960–1961. 5 vols. Pap. ed. issued by Nabu Press, 2010.

An important history of philosophy first appearing in the 1860s, this work has received even more attention through the years for its rich bibliographic coverage. For this reason, it is considered a necessary tool for philosophical study and has often appeared in the bibliographic sections of literature guides. The coverage represents ancient to modern philosophy. It should be noted that the English translation of this work was completed in the nineteenth century from the fourth edition and it lacks the bibliographies. This work's 1863 edition, in the original German, is also available online at http://www.archive.org/details/grundrissderges00erdmgoog.

3-36. A History of Philosophy. Frederick Charles Copleston. New York: Continuum, 2003–2006. 11 vols.

Written from the standpoint of a scholastic philosopher (Copleston was a Jesuit priest and Professor of the History of Philosophy at Heythrop College, Oxford), this work first appeared in 1945. It has become a standard history of philosophy in the English language through frequent addition and reprinting. Beginning with ancient times (Greece and Rome), the coverage progresses through the various schools of Western philosophy, Neoplatonism, Scholasticism, Rationalism, Empiricism, Romanticism, and Utilitarianism, using representative philosophers as labels for each of the volumes. Each volume was published with a good bibliography and index. The current reprint treats the single volumes individually. This is still a useful work and reviews have been written of individual volumes.

3-37. The Oxford Illustrated History of Western Philosophy. Anthony Kenny, ed. New York: Oxford University Press, 2001. Pap.

Initially published in 1994 without *Illustrated* in the title, this remains an excellent one-volume product from Oxford. It furnishes a brief and readable yet informative survey describing idea systems, writings, and important developments from ancient times through the twentieth century. The work is organized chronologically into six major divisions, each by a different scholar, beginning with ancient philosophy and ending with political influences. Color and black-and-white illustrations are provided, along with maps and a chronological table. If philosophy can be illustrated at all, this resource does it.

3-38. Routledge History of Philosophy. New York: Routledge, 1993–1999. 10 vols. Pap. ed., 2003.

Now available in paperback, this leading multi-volume English-language work is among the best of its kind. Each volume of the *History* is edited by an individual scholar who has worked with 10 to 20 experts who have contributed chapters of approximately 40 pages each to the topical coverage. Volume 1 (1997) treats the early beginnings of Western philosophy to Plato; volume 2 will cover Aristotle to Augustine; volume 3 (1998) examines medieval philosophy; volume 4 (1993), the Renaissance and rationalism; volume 5 (1996), British philosophy/Enlightenment; volume 6 (1993), German Idealism; and volume 7 (1994), the nineteenth century. The final three volumes deal with the twentieth century; volume 8 (1994), continental philosophy; volume 9 (1997), science, logic, and mathematics; and volume 10 (1999), meaning, knowledge, and value.

Initiated by the same publisher and utilizing similar style and format is the series, *Routledge History of World Philosophies*, which examines the nature and development of the philosophies of the world in individually edited volumes with numerous contributors. The series now includes Islamic, Jewish, Latin American, and Chinese philosophy.

Series

Several extensive series are available in the area of philosophy and they are all excellent sources in which to find overviews of topics, references to pursue, and expert essays in important concepts, schools, and people. These will help the researcher to establish a structure for further searching. Only a few individual titles, published after 2000, are mentioned in the list below, but the reader should consult title lists for the Cambridge Companions to Philosophy, Religion, and Culture series (156 titles to date with about half specific to philosophy), the Blackwell Philosophy Guides Series (37 titles), the Great Minds series (24 titles), and the Oxford Handbooks and Companions.

3-39. A Companion to Ethics. Peter Singer, ed. Oxford: Blackwell Reference, 2000.

This is but one example of the companion volumes offered by Blackwell in the subfields of philosophy. Lengthy articles on a wide range of ethics topics and issues are brought together from expert authors by a well-known editor. Theoretical and applied issues are taken up, giving the reader a broad sweep of this subfield. In the same series are companion volumes for epistemology, philosophy of language, and aesthetics, among many others.

3-40. The Blackwell Companion to Philosophy, 2nd ed. Nicholas Bunnin and E.P. Tsui-James, ed. Malden, MA: Blackwell Publishers, Ltd., 2003. (Blackwell Companions to Philosophy)

This one-volume companion is organized into two areas: Part I, "Areas of Philosophy" and Part II "History of Philosophy." Within the former section, there are articles on the disciplinary branches and "Philosophy of . . ." entries; the latter section is organized chronologically beginning with the ancient Greeks and concluding with a chapter on Sartre, Foucault, and Derrida, with most chapters focusing on a particularly influential philosopher. Further reading is recommended and each entry has a list of references and discussion questions. This title is part of the Blackwell Companions to Philosophy series, which now offers more than two-dozen companion volumes.

3-41. Companion to Philosophy in the Middle Ages. Jorge J.E. Garcia and Timothy B. Noone, ed. Malden, MA: Wiley-Blackwell Publishers, 2003. (Blackwell Companions to Philosophy)

Another in the Blackwell Companion to Philosophers Series, this one, with articles by renowned scholars, contains essays on important concepts in philosophy between the fourth and fifteenth centuries and also offers 140 entries on individual philosophers of that period of history. Cross-references and bibliographies enhance the value of this resource.

3-42. The Oxford Companion to Philosophy. 2nd ed. Ted Honderich, ed. Oxford: Oxford University Press, 2005. Print. E-book available through Oxford Reference Online by subscription.

This work continues to stand out as one of the most useful and informative single-volume companions to philosophy. The real improvement, however, is the inclusion of the *Oxford Companion*, and the *Oxford Dictionary of Philosophy*, in the group of resources now online through Oxford Reference Online. Cross-references link among the Oxford resources. As is true of similar works in philosophy, Oxford treats personalities, topics, branches, schools, concepts, and terms, but it does so in a readable, informative, accurate, and interesting fashion. Maps, a chronological table, and an index are included. Entries include brief bibliographies.

3-43. Philosophical Perspectives. Malden, MA: Blackwell Publishing, 1996– . Print and e-book.

This is an annual publication that provides new essays by leading thinkers in the various subfields of philosophy. Each annual volume is devoted to a particular topical area. The series has run since 1987. Volumes one through nine are available through Ridgeview Publishing Company and volumes 10 forward from Blackwell. The publication is billed as "a supplement to *Noûs*." Both the journal *Noûs* and *Philosophical Perspectives* are now available online through the Wiley Online Library, a digital library of thousands of scholarly, scientific, and medical journals.

Organizations

3-44. American Philosophical Association. http://www.apaonline.org/

The Association was founded in 1900 to promote the exchange of ideas among philosophers and to encourage scholarly and creative activity in the field. It is the most comprehensive philosophical society in the United States. National and regional groups elect officers and sponsor annual conferences and meetings. The Association publishes several newsletters. The reader may learn more by consulting the Association's website at http://www.apaonline.org/, or by readings James Campbell's *A Thoughtful Profession: the Early Years of the American Philosophical Association* (Peru, IL: Open Court Publishing Company, 2006).

3-45. Phi Sigma Tau, philosophy's honor society, was founded in 1931 to promote ties between philosophy students and departments of philosophy. It is the publisher of *Dialogue* and an association newsletter. The website for the organization is at http://phi-sigma-tau.org/.

3-46. American Catholic Philosophical Association, an example of a more specialized association in the field, was founded in 1926. It publishes *American Catholic Philosophical Quarterly* and its *Proceedings, New Scholasticism Philosophy*, and *Studies of the American Catholic Philosophical Association*. The organization holds annual conferences and has a Web site at http://www.acpaweb.org/Links.htm.

3-47. International Council for Science. The Hague. http://www.icsu.org/

Over the years, UNESCO has provided support for many international philosophical activities. In 1946, it recognized the International Council of Scientific Unions (The Hague) as coordinating body. This organization was renamed in 1998 and is now recognized as the International Council for Science. One of its branches is the International Union of the History and Philosophy of Science, which maintains affiliations with both national and international organizations. The purpose of the organization is to facilitate international exchanges and understanding in the scientific and research fields through conferences and congresses and the like. The IUHPS is made up of two different suborganizations: the Division of the History of Science and Technology; and the Division of Logic, Methodology, and Philosophy of Science.

3-48. The American Association of Philosophy Teachers.
http://philosophyteachers.org/index.shtml

The American Association of Philosophy Teachers promotes teaching of philosophy and sponsors professional development opportunities for philosophy teachers. There is a syllabus sharing initiative to assist those new at teaching or who are teaching new courses. The course sharing is for members only. The association was founded in 1976. Another is the Association of Philosophy Journal Editors, which was founded in 1971 and later disappeared only to have been "revived" in 2009 by Thom Brooks and others. There appears to be no current web presence as the association organizes itself again, but it is mentioned in recent blog posts by Brooks and others.

A few examples of societies devoted to individual philosophers are given in the next three entries.

3-49. C.S. Pierce Society. http://www.piercesociety.org/

The Pierce Society is but one example of the many societies organized around the work and influence of a single philosopher. The Pierce Society was founded in 1946 and publishes its *Transactions* quarterly.

3-50. The Kant Society (http://www.keele.ac.uk/kant/) furthers the study of Immanuel Kant by conducting research and publishing studies of Kant and his work.

3-51. The Hegel Society of America (http://www.hegel.org/) promotes the study of Hegel and his philosophical works.

A number of organizations are for women in philosophy such as the two below.

3-52. Society for Women in Philosophy (SWIP). http://www.uh.edu/~cfreelan/SWIP/

The Society for Women in Philosophy was begun in 1972 to promote women in philosophy and their activities. The Society has a website that includes statistics on women philosophers, publications, courses, and special areas of philosophy related to women. Links to feminist sites and to other associations are provided.

3-53. The International Association of Women Philosophers (IAWP).
http://www.iaph-philo.org/e_iaph.php?lang=1

The International Association of Women Philosophers is a professional association and network that provides a forum for discussion, interaction, and cooperation among women engaged in teaching and research in all aspects of philosophy, with a particular emphasis on feminist philosophy. The IAWP holds conferences and publishes its proceedings.

Some associations are organized around a particular subdivision of philosophy. Examples are included in the last entry here.

3-54. The Ancient Philosophy Society (http://www.ancientphilosophysociety.org/); **North American Society for Social Philosophy** (http://www.pitt.edu/~nassp/nassp.html); **Radical Philosophy Association** (http://home.grandecom.net/~jackgm/RPA.html); and the **Society for Business Ethics** (http://www.societyforbusinessethics.org/). These associations generally sponsor meetings, conferences, or congresses and publish newsletters or full-fledged journals. A more comprehensive listing of specialized associations may be found at the Philosophy Documentation Center website or on the pages of philosophy web portals.

CHAPTER **4**

RELIGION

Elizabeth S. Aversa

INTRODUCTION

The study of religion, supported by diverse information resources, is important to achieving an understanding of nearly every human interest. In the disciplines of the humanities, social sciences, and even the sciences, religion is integral. Every thoughtful reader can give examples of the impact of religion on several representative disciplines: art, music, literature, sociology, economics, and environmental sciences. All discussions of society's contemporary topics, such as diversity and tolerance, terrorism, war and the search for peace, law and jurisprudence have roots somewhere in religion. Colleges from Swarthmore to Washington University in St. Louis to the University of California Davis have web pages that inform students on the question of "Why Study Religion?" This chapter addresses the breadth of the field and the resources that support its study.

Working Definition of Religion

The word religion is thought to have come from the Latin term *religare,* which means "to bind." The more recognizable Middle English *religioun* is directly related to concepts of piety and conscientiousness, and influences modern definitions of the term (Online Etymology Dictionary). The notion of recognition and worship of an "unseen power" dates to the 1500s. Contemporary definitions include "belief in, worship of, or obedience to a supernatural power or powers believed to be divine or to have control of human destiny," and "any formal or institutionalized expression of such belief" (Collins English Dictionary).

Humanities bibliographer and scholar Lester Asheim suggested an even more familiar definition: "the study of man's beliefs and practices in relation to God, gods, or the supernatural" (1956, 2). John F. Wilson and Thomas P. Slavens later suggested that religion is a set of beliefs and behaviors that "express as a system the basic shape or texture of the culture . . ." (Wilson and Slavens 1982, 4).

More recently, scholars have avoided a specific definition of the term *religion,* instead suggesting that all definitions of the term carry cultural biases. Winston King, in fact, suggests that even the notion of defining religion as a discreet aspect of human life is a product of Western religious thought (King 2005, 7701).

Regardless of whether one accepts a traditional or a more contemporary definition, the study of religion includes, at minimum, examination of a belief system, some type of spirituality, and the relationship of the belief system and accompanying behaviors to a culture or cultures.

Religion influences other disciplines in a way no other discipline, with the possible exception of language, does. Every student will be able to identify religious influences and themes in art, music, literature, drama, history, anthropology, law, sociology, and psychology. Religious influences are increasingly considered in the sciences and multidisciplinary studies as well, as in medicine and environmental studies, to name just two examples. Walter Kaufmann's chapter on religion in *The Future of the Humanities* is still timely as he suggests that the only way to teach religion in colleges and

83

universities is to use an interdisciplinary approach. In recommending that mode, he states, "Religion is far too important to be left to theologians" (1977, 152). John R. Hinnells, in his article entitled "Why Study Religions? " expresses doubt that "one can understand any culture and history, political or social, without understanding the relevant religions" (2005, 6).

One can study religion from many positions; the most prevalent include the historical approach, the social science approach, and the study of the spiritual/phenomenological aspects. Two sources provide especially good coverage of diverse aspects of the study of religion for the general reader. *The Routledge Companion to the Study of Religion* covers 11 "key approaches" to the study of religion along with more than a dozen contemporary issues associated with such study (Hinnells 2005). Donald Wiebe's article "Religious studies" reviews the development of the field of religious studies and provides over 50 references to works that define religious studies and demarcate it from religious education (2005).

Major Divisions of the Field

Religions are commonly classified as being predominately sacramental, prophetic, or mystical. Sacramental religion places emphasis on the observation of ritual and on the sacredness of particular objects. Eastern Orthodoxy and Roman Catholicism are familiar examples. Prophetic religions emphasize the communication of divine will in verbal form, often with strong moralistic emphasis. Islam and Protestantism reflect this approach. Mystical religions stress direct encounter with a god and view words, rituals and sacred objects as auxiliary at best, or even hindrances, to the full communion that is seen as the ultimate goal of all religious striving. Certain branches of Hinduism and Buddhism are examples of the predominately mystical.

Librarians and information specialists are concerned with the literature generated by the religions of the world. These may be conveniently analyzed under six major headings: traditional headings include (1) personal religion, (2) theology, (3) philosophy of religion, and (4) science of religion. More recently, (5) sociology of religion, and (6) anthropology of religion have emerged as categories with expanding literatures.

Personal religion is the primary and most direct source of religious writing. It is intimately related to the experiences of individuals and reflections about their significance. A major class of documents in this category would be the sacred scriptures of the world's great religions. Related to the sacred writings are those documents of explication and interpretations commonly known as commentaries. Then there is another larger body of literature that does not have the same authoritative standing as the scriptures and their respective commentaries. Works in this category may be devotional, autobiographical, or biographical. In this group would be a large body of popularizations.

Theology is an attempt to express in intellectually coherent form the principal doctrines of specific religions. David Ford defines it at its broadest as "thinking about questions raised by, about and between religions" (2005, 61). It is the product of reflection upon the primary sources of religion. It differs from philosophy in that the basic truth of the religious position is accepted first, and then attention is given to its thoughtful and systematic exposition. The field of theology has many subdivisions. Within the Christian tradition, systematic theology and biblical theology have been especially important, but there is a substantial body of literature on moral, ascetic, mystical, symbolic, pastoral, liturgical, and natural theology as well. It should be noted that the concept of theology is not a part of all religious traditions. Ford provides further delineation of the field of theology (Ford 2005, 61–79).

The *philosophy of religion* is an attempt to relate religious experience to other spheres of experience. It differs from theology in that it makes fewer assumptions about the truth of a religious position, at least in the beginning. Philosophy of religion has been described as a bridge between philosophy and religion, with religion as the area for speculative investigation. William J. Wainwright, editor of *The Oxford Handbook of Philosophy of Religion*, traces the term to the nineteenth century, and suggests that earlier interest died down after the emergence of analytical philosophy and the decline of interest in idealism as the main focus of inquiry. However, he goes on to describe a revival of interest by "young analytic philosophers of religion" who address a wide array of objectives from the epistemological to ontological arguments and beyond (2005, 1–11). For a broad list of arguments taken up by the philosophers of religion, see *Philosophy of Religion: a Guide to the Subject* (Davies 1998).

The *science of religion* has also generated a substantial body of literature, one that has grown since the last edition of this guide. Here, emphasis is placed on comparative and historical methods with no presumptions about, and perhaps no interest in, the truth or falsity of the religions being examined. Whereas the locus of interest in the categories of literature listed above is usually one of the world's living religions, this is not always the case in the scientific study of religion where a purely objective approach to the description and comparison of religious phenomena represents the ideal. *The Oxford Handbook of Religion and Science* provides helpful essays on methodological approaches, major fields, and contemporary debates in the science-religion relationship (Clayton and Simpson 2006). Brief essays illustrating the diversity of topics within science and religion are found in Harper's *Spiritual Information–100 Perspectives on Science and Religion,* a collection of essays in honor of Sir John Templeton (Harper 2005), while *The History of Science and Religion in the Western Tradition: An Encyclopedia* offers well-documented scholarly articles on the topics covered in the field as well as the intellectual foundations and philosophical backgrounds that provide the framework for this division of the field (Ferngren 2000).

Sociology and *anthropology* of religion both emerged in the twentieth century, and there remains some tension over the territories occupied by each. However, these social scientific approaches to the study of religion are supported by growing literatures and thus must be considered by the librarian. Religion's relationships to culture, environment, globalization, gender, secularization, and behaviors are considered by both divisions of the field. For further reading, see *The Anthropology of Religion: an Introduction* (Bowie 2000) and *The New Blackwell Companion to the Sociology of Religion* (Turner 2010).

Use and Users of Information in Religion

As compared to other literary fields of the humanities, there continues to be a lack of attention to use and user studies in the area of religion. This may be, in part, the result of the very diverse nature of the literature of religion and the multiple viewpoints represented by its literature. Furthermore, the audience for the literature of the field is as vast and varied as the literature itself. Users of scholarly historical materials, for instance, are unlikely to be readers of devotional literature; and users of online prayer lines or inspirational materials are probably not accessing peer reviewed journals or the indexes that cover them. More studies look at information seeking and use among scholars than other audiences due to our limited ability to study, in depth, other users of religious materials.

The study of users of religious material is further complicated by the fact that citation analysis, a method used in other disciplines, is rarely appropriate to the field of religion. Many uses of religious materials do not result in publication where sources are routinely cited or they support implicit references in sermons, presentations, and publications that are not under any kind of bibliographic control. However, several new studies provide a few insights into what is used by religious scholars.

Knievel and Kellsey's "Citation Analysis for Collection Development: A Study of Eight Humanities Fields" confirms that among the fields studied, religion had fewer citations than the other disciplines in the humanities, but the citations per article topped the field of philosophy (2005). The authors suggest, rightly, that "The wide variety of subfields in religion (from theology and biblical studies to Islam, Buddhism, etc.) makes this a field in which further study would be fruitful" (164). Rong's "Citation Characteristics and Intellectual Acceptance of Scholarly Monographs" reports that monographs remain important in religion, and that the citations observed were to more recent materials than had been expected (2008). Rong and Knievel and Kellsey had similar findings with regard to the high level of dependence by religion scholars on the monograph.

Research has found that books, journals, and dissertations were the most preferred sources of information for theology students at the International Baptist Seminary in Prague, and that the students there displayed basic skills in the use of information technologies to identify sources. The same study found that theology students use resources across disciplines and employ a variety of search strategies, including browsing (Penner 2009).

According to research over the past several decades, information seekers and users in religious studies continued to exhibit traditional information seeking behaviors. They also continue to use traditional forms of resources.

Information seeking has been addressed by several recent studies. In a study of the Catholic religious in Nigeria, researchers found that the primary information needs were for information about the Catholic Church, information and communications technology, and information about school curricula (Adetimiriin 2010). The author observed that the use of information technology was important to the 124 religious who were surveyed as to their information seeking. In another study of information-seeking behavior, this one of Jewish studies scholars, it was found that the scholars used different information seeking strategies depending on the phase of the research process they were in (Bronstein 2007). "From Intention to Composition: How Seminarians Conceptualize Research," addresses questions of resource seeking as part of the research process of seminarians, and concurs with the finding that different strategies are employed at different phases in the research process (Lincoln and Lincoln 2011). More recently, studies of specific literatures were undertaken on the Baha'I religion (Faxel 2003) and the new interdisciplinary field of MSR (management, spirituality, and religion) by Fornaciari and Dean (2009).

As scholars increasingly utilize digital libraries and open source materials on the web, as well as traditional print materials, studies of use and users will reveal much-needed information to guide collection development and library services in the field of religion.

Works Cited

Adetimiriin, A.E. 2010. "Information Seeking Behaviour of the Catholic Religious in Ibadan, Nigeria." [Summary of a research note delivered at the ISIC 2004 conference, Dublin, 1–3 September, 2004] *Information Research* 10, no. 1, summary 5 (Available at http://InformationR .net/ir/10-1/abs5).

Asheim, Lester. 1956. *The Humanities and the Library*. Chicago: American Library Association.

Bowie, Fiona. 2000. *The Anthropology of Religion*. Oxford: Blackwell Publishers.

Brian S. Turner, ed. 2010. *The New Blackwell Companion to the Sociology of Religion*. Malden, MA: Wiley-Blackwell.

Bronstein, J. 2007. "The Role of the Research Phase in Information Seeking Behaviour of Jewish Studies Sholars: A Modification of Ellis's Behavioural Characteristics." *Information Research* 12, 3 (April): paper 318.

Clayton, Philip and Zachery Simpson. 2006. *The Oxford Handbook of Religion and Science*. Oxford: Oxford University Press.

Davies, Brian. 1998. *Philosophy of Religion–A Guide to the Subject*. Washington: Georgetown University Press.

Faxel, Seena. 2003. "Contemporary Developments in Baha'I Studies" in *Occasional Papers in Shaykhi, Babi and Baha'I Studies* 7, 1 (January) at www.h-net.org/~bahai/bhpapers/vol7/trends.htm.

Ferngren, Gary B., ed. 2000. *The History of Science and Religion in the Western Tradition: An Encyclopedia*. New York: Garland Publishing, Inc.

Ford, David F. 2005. "Theology," in the *Routledge Companion to the Study of Religion*. London: Routledge: 61.

Fornaciari, Charles J. and Kathy Lund Dean. 2009. "Foundations, Lessons, and Insider Tips for MSR Research." *Journal of Management, Spirituality & Religion* 6, 4 (October): 301–321.

Harper, Charles L., Jr., ed. 2005. *Spiritual Information–100 Perspectives on Science and Religion*. Philadelphia: Templeton Foundation Press. http://InformationR.net/ir/12-3/paper319.html.

Harper, Douglas. "Religion," in *Online Etymology Dictionary*. Dictionary.com at http://dictionary .reference.com/browse/religion.

Hinnells, John R. 2005. *The Routledge Companion to the Study of Religion.* London: Routledge.

Kaufmann, Walter. 1977. *The Future of the Humanities.* New York: Thomas Y. Crowell.

King, Winston. 2005. "Religion," in *Encyclopedia of Religion.* 2nd ed. Lindsay Jones, ed. Detroit: Macmillan Reference USA, 11: 7701.

Knievel, Jennifer E. and Charlene Kellsey. 2005. "Citation Analysis for Collection Development: A Comparative Study of Eight Humanities Fields." *Library Quarterly* 75, 2 (April): 142–168.

Lincoln, L. and T. Lincoln. 2011. "From Intention to Composition: How Seminarians Conceptualize Research." *Theological Librarianship: An Online Journal of the American Theological Library Association* 4 (March). https://journal.atla.com/ojs/index.php/theolib/article/view/178/468.

Penner, Katherina. 2009. "Information Needs and Behaviours of Theology Students at the International Baptist Theological Seminary." *Theological Librarianship* 2, 2 (December): 51–80.

"Religion." *Collins English Dictionary–Complete & Unabridged 10th Edition.* HarperCollins Publishers. Dictionary.com at http://dictionary.reference.com/browse/religion.

Rong, Tang. 2008. "Citation Characteristics and Intellectual Acceptance of Scholarly Monographs." *College & Research Libraries* 69, 4 (July): 356–369.

Wainwright, William J. 2005. *The Oxford Handbook of Philosophy of Religion.* Oxford: Oxford University Press.

Wicks, Albert Donald. 1997. "The Information Seeking Behavior of Clergy: A Study of Their Work Worlds and Work Roles." PhD dissertation, University of Western Ontario.

Wiebe, Donald. 2005. "Religious Studies," in *The Routledge Companion to the Study of Religion.* London: Routledge: 98–124.

Wilson, John F. and Thomas P. Slavens. 1982. *Research Guide to Religious Studies.* Chicago: American Library Association.

INFORMATION SOURCES IN RELIGION, MYTHOLOGY AND FOLKLORE

GENERAL SOURCES ON RELIGION

Databases and Digital Collections

4-1. **ATLA Religion Database with ATLASerials.** American Theological Library Association. Online subscription database.

The American Theological Library Association (ATLA) database provides the most extensive access to information on religion of any source. ATLA is the full text version of the ATLA Religion Database, which is the combination of two separate products of the Association. Covering 1949 to the present, the ATLA database is *the* bibliographic source for those interested in religious studies, Biblical studies, archaeology, and antiquities; religion in human culture and society; church history, missions, and ecumenism; pastoral ministry; world theology, and philosophy and ethics.

Coverage, as reported by ATLA, is more than 1.82 million records, including the following: 598,000 journal article records, 250,600 essay records from 18,000 multi-author works, about 52,000 book reviews, and over 1,700 journal titles, 552 of which are indexed. Some journal indexing goes back further than the 1949 start date. Journals that are indexed in ATLAs are carefully considered and chosen for their scope and standing among scholarly journals. Journals are representative of a wide array of faiths, denominations and language groups. ATLA indexes individual essays in books, rather than whole volumes, so that discreet works are accessible. The database has some unique features, including scripture citation indexing that enables users to identify articles that cite particular scriptural passages.

Print predecessors of the ATLA Religion Database with ATLASerials are *Religion Index One: Periodicals; Religion Index Two: Multi-Author Works*; and *Index to Book Reviews in Religion*. ATLA databases are available through EBSCO and other vendors.

4-2. **FRANCIS.** Institut de l'information Scientifique et Technique of the Centre National de la Recherche Scientifique (INIST-CNR), Nancy, France: 1991– . Online subscription database. Previously titled (in printed form) *FRANCIS Bulletin Signaletique, Bulletin Signaletique, and Bulletin Analytique*. The relevant sections for arts and humanities retrospective research are: *Francis Bulletin Signaletique, 519, Philosophie* [1990–1994], (formerly *Philosophie Sciences Religieuses* 1969–).

FRANCIS is a multi-disciplinary database that indexes materials on religion, art history, literature, and psychology, among other topics. The database offers bilingual descriptors, and provides researchers with articles, serials, books, conference papers, book chapters, dissertations (in French), catalogs, legislation, and reports. For a more detailed description of FRANCIS, see entry 2-13.

4-3. **Oxford Reference Online.** Oxford, UK: Oxford University Press. Online subscription database. http://www.oxfordreference.com

To the benefit of scholars everywhere, Oxford University Press has made hundreds of its reference publications in all subjects available online. Oxford Reference Online provides two comprehensive collections by subscription. The publisher's website describes the online options as follows: "The Core Collection contains about 100 dictionary, language reference, and subject reference works published by Oxford University Press. It is a fully-indexed, cross-searchable database of these books . . . The Premium Collection enhances the 100+ books in the Core Collection with an expanding range of key titles from the acclaimed *Oxford Companions Series*, plus the *Oxford Dictionary of Quotations*. These publications, in print or online, are of great value to the humanities scholar, librarian, or non-specialist reader. While several print items are included in this guide, the titles available online in religion and religious studies are listed here. The user will rarely go wrong in consulting these sources.

The following titles address the area of religion. After consulting the appropriate dictionaries or companions in this series, the researcher should see the sources on the specific subject for the search in the list under the appropriate subject heading in this guide.

> *A Dictionary of the Bible*
>
> *The Oxford Companion to the Bible* (entry 4-63)
>
> *The Oxford Guide to People and Places of the Bible*
>
> *The Dictionary of Buddhism*
>
> *The Oxford Dictionary of Byzantium*
>
> *The Oxford Dictionary of the Christian Church*
>
> *A Dictionary of Hinduism*
>
> *The Oxford Dictionary of Islam*
>
> *A Dictionary of Popes* (entry 4-80)
>
> *The Oxford Encyclopedia of the Reformation*
>
> *The Oxford Dictionary of Saints*

4-4. Proquest Religion. Proquest. Online subscription database. www.proquest.com

Proquest Religion has more than 220 journals, with many titles from religious publishing bodies and nondenominational organizations, most of them available with full-text. The content goes back to 1986 and is scholarly, designed to meet the needs of both religious studies programs and general library collections. The database covers formal theological studies and commentary on topics of general interest from the perspectives of many, worldwide religions. In addition, journals on related religious studies, such as philosophy, ethics, and international perspectives are included.

4-5. Religion & Philosophy INFOTRAC. Gale Cengage. Online subscription database. http://www.gale.cengage.com

Over 250 magazines and academic journals have been selected for this collection that covers religion and related areas such as anthropology. Indexing began for most selections in 1980, and full texts of many articles are available from 1983 to the present.

4-6. Religion & Philosophy Collection. EBSCO. Online subscription database. http://www.ebsco host.com

This is a comprehensive database of full-text articles and reviews on topics such as world religions, major religious denominations, biblical studies, religious history, epistemology, political philosophy, moral philosophy and the history of philosophy. The collection provides access to more than 300 full-text journals and its coverage of the subject areas listed is extensive. Religion & Philosophy Collection is an essential tool for scholars searching for journal articles, librarians seeking book reviews, or the general user wanting magazine articles or photographs and other graphical materials. Searching through the EBSCO system is familiar to librarians and scholars and allows for differentiation between scholarly journals that are peer reviewed or not, magazines, and book reviews; limiting by document type, date of publication, and type of image; and the choice of EBSCO's "visual search" or other search options, e.g. Boolean or Smart Text Searching.

4-7. World Religion Database (WRD). Todd M. Johnson and Brian J. Grim, eds. Leiden, Netherlands: Brill Publishers. Online subscription database.

According to reviews and the database description, the WRD offers detailed statistics on religious affiliation for every country in the world and is the major source of a definitive picture of religious demography worldwide. Current and historical data are available along with estimates or forecasts of future membership in denominational organizations. (Forecasts to the year 2050 are included, as are historical estimates back to 900.) The database draws upon a broad array of surveys, including census data, for the statistical data it offers. The WRD provides direct access to the sources on which figures in the database are based. The main page provides a search box and links to five directories: the main query home page; the religion home page; the religious freedom home page; census and survey homepage; and a "top 20" lists page. Data may be extracted by multiple attributes and sorted and resorted to produce the reports sought. The output of a search can be exported to a spreadsheet of the users' choice for further manipulation. Another useful source of data on religions is the *Association of Religion Data Archives* (entry 4-32).

Print Resources

4-8. A Bibliographic Guide to the Comparative Study of Ethics. Mark Juergensmeyer and John Braisted Carman. Cambridge: Cambridge University Press, 2009.

This guide provides bibliographic access to primary and secondary works on ethics within a religious tradition. It is a reissue from the 1991 hardback of the same title, but holds up under the test of time as an excellent source.

4-9. ARBA in-depth. Philosophy and Religion. Martin Dillon and Shannon Graff Hysell, eds. Westport, CT: Libraries Unlimited, 2004.

The publisher's description states that "this work is designed to assist academic, public, and religious special libraries in the systematic selection of suitable reference materials for their collections. Its purpose is to aid in the evaluation process by presenting over 300 critical and evaluative reviews in all areas of philosophy and religion." This is the third in this special series published in conjunction with the standard *American Reference Books Annual* (ARBA) (entry 2-88).

4-10. Angels A to Z. James R. Lewis, Evelyn Dorothy Oliver, and Kelle S. Sisung. Canton, MI: Visible Ink Press, 2002.

This is a revision of the 1996 compilation of information treating angels in various religious traditions and systems of belief, including the occult. Arranged alphabetically, the work furnishes entries on angels by name and by relevant topics to enhance the study and understanding of them. Angels are treated in relation to art, folklore, literature, music, film, and television. Bibliographical references are included as is an index. A bibliography and filmography provide additional resources.

For a readable resource, see *Angels: a History* by David Albert Jones (Oxford University Press, 2010). This slim volume consists of eight brief chapters on the history, appearance, definition, and descriptions of angels, both good and fallen. The best features of this work are the references and an index of references to angels in the Bible and the Quran.

4-11. Annual Review of the Sociology of Religion (ARSR). Leiden, Netherlands: Brill Publishing, 2010– .

Brill Publishing states that the purpose of the ARSR is "to investigate the 'new' role of religion in the contemporary world, which is characterized by cultural pluralism and religious individualism." The editors focus on a specific subject in each volume. Volume 1, appearing in 2010, was devoted to the topic of Youth and Religion.

4-12. Atlas of the World's Religions. Ninian Smart and Frederick Denny, eds. Oxford: Oxford University Press, 2007.

This is a heavily updated edition of an atlas published in 1998. This edition contains more maps and textual material than the previous work and has updated statistical information as well. It covers indigenous religions, place names and religious sites, and other topics of contemporary interest. The atlas has a handy glossary as well.

4-13. The Book of Miracles. Kenneth L. Woodward. New York: Simon & Schuster, 2000.

This volume is a guide to miracles in monotheistic and Indian religions. The author retells classic miracle stories as they are described in sacred texts in an array of western and eastern religions, and provides commentary on the place of miracles in the various traditions. The miracles covered are limited to those attributed to human beings and those that, in the word of the author, "in principle were witnessed by others." Extensive notes and a useful bibliography of books and articles are included.

4-14. The Encyclopedia of Apocalypticism. Bernard McGinn, John J. Collins, and Stephen J. Stein, eds. New York: Continuum, 1999. 3 vols.

This encyclopedia is devoted to the topic of the *apocalypticism*, or the "belief that God revealed the imminent end of the ongoing struggle between good and evil in history." The three volumes, separately edited, address the topic from the perspective of the origins of the concept in Judaism and Christianity (Collins), the concept in western history (McGinn), and apocalypticism in contemporary times (Stein). Entries by individual scholars from a wide array of universities across the globe are well documented and include bibliographies. Indexes, with reference to ancient texts, accompany the work. The growing interest in the apocalypse and "end times" is reflected in popular media, but this encyclopedia documents the serious scholarship behind the topic. This is an indispensible resource for the individual beginning study of the topic or the serious scholar seeking references and resources to further the study of the subject.

4-15. Encyclopedia of Religion. 2nd ed. Lindsay Jones, ed. Detroit: Macmillan Reference USA, 2005.

This work is a monumental revision of Mircea Eliade's 16-volume Encyclopedia that was published in 1987. It was aimed at the student or nonspecialist, but the quality of the scholarship behind that work made it appealing to the serious scholar as well. The same can be said for this new 2nd edition edited by Jones.

      The remarkable aspect of this revision, aside from the size of the project, is the way revised material is organized and distinguished from original material. According to the publisher, all entries from the first edition were examined for revision and two-thirds of them were deemed relevant without revision. If an article is reprinted with few or no changes, the name of the scholar is followed by the date 1987 in the new edition. Where entries were updated for the second edition by the original author or by another scholar, a single name will be followed by two dates (1987 and 2005) or two names will be listed, each followed by one of the two years. "The editors considered some articles from the first edition worthy of inclusion in the second but no longer state-of-the-art (e.g., Mysticism, Rites of Passage, Sexuality). In such instances, the entry is reprinted with the title qualified by 'First Edition' and is then followed by a completely new article with the same title but the qualifier 'Further Considerations.'" Even the bibliographies note new references if material within the entry was revised in the least. Totally new articles reflecting contemporary interests include Bioethics, Cybernetics, Ecology and Religion, Genetics and Religion, Healing and Medicine, Medical Ethics and Secular Medicine.

4-16. Encyclopedia of Religion in America. Charles H. Lippy and Peter W. Williams, eds. CQ Press, 2010. 4 vols.

Described by the publisher as "a multidisciplinary examination of religion in American life," the *Encyclopedia of Religion in America* examines how religious history and practices are woven into the political, social, cultural, and historical landscape of North America. Edited by well-known experts in the field, the work explains the origins, development, adaptation, influence, and interrelations of the many faiths practiced, including major world religions, new religious sects, cults, and religious movements that originated or had an influence in the United States.

4-17. The Literature of Theology: A Guide for Students and Pastors. Rev. ed. John A. Bollier and David R. Stewart. Westminster: John Knox Press, 2003.

This guide provides access to more than 500 bibliographies of religious resources, such as encyclopedias, theology, biblical and historical studies, electronic sources, and dictionaries. It is an updated and revised work and one recommended for the lay person, pastors and students. This source provides a Christian viewpoint but the tools identified are useful for studies of other faith traditions.

4-18. Melton's Encyclopedia of American Religions. 8th ed. Farmington Hills, MI: Gale/Cengage Learning, 2009.

The first edition of this work was issued in 1975, attesting to its importance as a standard reference work over the years. Hundreds of religious bodies on the North American continent are treated. A categorical arrangement places the various religious families under various chapter headings. Entries provide information on the various bodies (history, development, and organizational aspects) as well as a bibliography and bibliographic notes.

Encyclopedia of American Religions is an essential resource for students and scholars researching issues in a wide variety of social science disciplines, from American history to cultural studies, political science, gender studies, psychology of religion, and more. It reflects new scholarly research and interpretation that have emerged over the last two decades, as well as significant new areas of study, such as post-9/11 America, the role of gays and lesbians in church, gender, and the role of the evangelicals in American political life.

4-19. Routledge Companion to the Study of Religion. John R. Hinnells, ed. New York: Routledge, 2005.

In 30 chapters by almost as many subject specialists, the diverse areas of the study of religion are discussed in thoughtful essays with excellent bibliographies. Hinnells begins with an essay on the why of religious studies, and important scholars, mostly affiliated with British and U.S. institutions, address a variety of approaches to the study of religion and what Hinnells calls "key issues" in the study of religion. The handbook provides a good background for both the lay person and student of religion. Routledge publishes additional encyclopedias in the religious area; two that are recommended are Routledge's *Encyclopedia of Christian Theology*, a translation of the French *Dictionnaire Critique de Théologie* 2nd Edition and the *Encyclopedia of Modern Jewish Culture* edited by Glenda Abramson. Both were published in 2005.

4-20. Religions of the World: A Comprehensive Encyclopedia of Beliefs and Practices. 2nd ed. J. Gordon Melton and Martin Baumann, eds. Santa Barbara, CA: ABC-CLIO, 2010. 6 vols.

This encyclopedia addresses religions in over 200 countries with entries placed in the country and geographic context. The work includes current information on membership in religious communities in the various countries, and the total number of alphabetically arranged entries is over 1,200. Produced by scholars and edited by J. Gordon Melton, an expert, this work has been recommended for high school through college level collections, as well as for those serving the lay public. Another reference tool edited by Melton and others and scheduled for publication by ABC-CLIO is *Religious*

Celebrations: an Encyclopedia of Holidays, Festivals, Solemn Observances and Spiritual Commemorations in two volumes.

4-21. **Science and Religion in the English-Speaking World: 1600–1727: A Bibliographic Guide to the Secondary Literature.** Richard S. Brooks and David K. Himrod. Lanham, MD: Scarecrow Press, 2001.

This bibliographic guide provides information about the secondary literature of the period 1600–1727. Topics covered by the guide include theology, science and Christianity, technology, philosophy, religion and the relations among them. Very positive reviews confirm the utility of this guide.

4-22. **World Religions in America.** 4th ed. Jacob Neusner, ed. Louisville, KY: John Knox Press, 2009.

The chapters in this comprehensive handbook reflect the place of various world religions in the U.S. and the increasing number of non-Christian religions is reflected in the entries. Improvements in this edition include the addition of timelines and study questions for the chapters, and new essays on timely topics including "the Unification Church" and women in religion.

4-23. **Worldmark Encyclopedia of Religious Practice.** Thomas Riggs. Detroit: Thomson Gale, 2006. 3 vols. Print and e-book available through Gale Virtual Library Online.

This encyclopedia uses a relatively uniform format to address historical, demographic, geographic, spiritual, and social aspects of 13 major religions and 28 subgroups. The three-volume format has Volume 1 covering the religious groups, and Volumes 2 and 3 addressing the religious situation in countries across the globe. The encyclopedia is illustrated with maps, drawings, and photographs; there are tables comparing aspects of the religions, a glossary, a subject and name index, and a general index to all entries.

4-24. **Yearbook of American and Canadian Churches.** Eileen Lindner, ed. Nashville: Abingdon Press, 1916– .

Since this publication began in 1916, the Yearbook has provided information about churches, denominations, finances, contacts, histories, church membership and participation, and the like. The 2011 directory covers 237 denominations. It is a publication of the National Council of Churches (entry 4-34).

Open Access Resources

4-25. **A History of the Crusades.** 2nd ed. Kenneth M. Setton, ed. http://digicoll.library.wisc.edu/History/

This digital library is part of the University of Wisconsin's digital history collection. The resource provides, in six volumes, the entire history of the crusades. Categories under which the collection can be browsed are the first hundred years; the later crusades, 1189–1311; the fourteenth and fifteenth centuries; art and architecture of crusader states; impact of the crusades on the Near East; impact of the crusades on Europe. Boolean searching provides precise location of texts and illustrations.

4-26. **Interfaith Online .** http://www.interfaith.org/

Interfaith is an online, free and independent resource with information on matters related to religion, spirituality, and faith. The site provides very brief entries on the world's major religions, with specific sections on the beliefs, the canon, and themes of the religion. The more valuable aspects of this website are the very active and free-to-join interfaith forum, the news that is updated continuously, and the links to important texts.

4-27. International Religious Freedom. Washington, DC: U.S. Department of State. http://www.state.gov/g/drl/rls/irf/

This resource is part of the extensive and informative Department of State website. Annual reports, dating from 2001 to the present, on *International Religious Freedom* provide a running history of religious freedom and tolerance around the globe. The user will find the reports organized chronologically, with each followed by a list of countries for which details are available by one click. In addition, there is an executive summary for each report that gives a broad observation on activities related to religious freedom for the year reported. Documents like the Universal Declaration of Human Rights and the International Religious Freedom Act are also provided as appendixes to the annual report.

4-28. Religious Worlds: An Internet Portal for Information about Religions and Religious Studies. Gene R. Thursby. http://www.religiousworlds.com/index.html

Religious Worlds is an efficiently organized gateway to internet resources on religion. The links are organized under clear headings related specifically to religion, for example, Religion in Cyberspace; Religious Experience; Religious Traditions or by the type of materials linked, e.g., Bibliographies, Reference Sources, Portals. The home page does not indicate the frequency with which the resource is updated, but the "featured sites" link suggests that updates occur regularly and often.

4-29. Virtual Religion Network (VRN). Mahlon H. Smith. 1999–2008. http://virtualreligion.net/

The VRN provides, in the developer's words, "resources for research and reflection." The four resources are (1) Virtual Religion Index–Premier Gateway to Research Quality Websites, (2) Synoptic Gospels Primer–Source Analysis of Matthew, Mark & Luke, (3) Into His Own–Sourcebook for Interpreting the World of Jesus and (4) Jesus Seminar Forum–Gateway to Research of the Jesus Seminar. The first of these will be of greatest interest to the librarian, in that the Virtual Religion Index provides hyperlinks to the homepages of a large number of religion-related resources. Categories of resources, many of which provide full text of articles and other documents, include denominational groups (Confessional Agencies), Christian tradition, Biblical Studies, Islamic Studies, Jewish Studies, Buddhist Studies, and American Studies. There are also categories of links to Academic Sites, Comparative Study of Religion, area studies (e.g., East Asian), and related areas (e.g., Archaeology and Religious Art, Anthropology and Sociology, Philosophy and Theology, and Psychology of Religion, to mention just a few). The developer's objective, stated on the opening page of the site, is to analyze and highlight important content of religion-related websites to speed research. While not comprehensive, the website provides valuable links and opens the door to additional searching on the web.

4-30. Voice of the Shuttle: Religion (VoS). Alan Liu and colleagues at The University of California Santa Barbara. http://vos.ucsb.edu/browse.asp?id=2730

VoS has provided links to websites in a wide range of subject areas since 1994. The Religion page contains hundreds of links to reference sources, texts, specific religious groups, and academic departments and courses in religious studies. This is a valuable free website that is continuously improved.

4-31. Wabash Center Internet Resources in Theology and Religion. Charles K. Bellinger. http://www.wabashcenter.wabash.edu/resources/guide-headings.aspx

The Wabash Center provides broad support for teachers of religion and theology in institutions of higher education. Along with grants, workshops, consulting, and publication of a peer-reviewed scholarly journal, the Center has a selective, annotated guide to internet resources. Subject headings for the guide include best of the web; aspects of religion; religious thought, archaeology, Bible and classics; religions (organized by faith tradition); geographical or demographic groups; Christianity; and pedagogy. An especially useful feature from the latter is the "Syllabi Collection," a collaborative project between the American Academy of Religion and the Wabash Center that provides access to and sharing of syllabi on a variety of topics from teachers at numerous universities and seminaries.

4-32. Religion Data Archive. The Association of Religion Data Archives (ARDA). http://www.thearda.com/

The ARDA, which was founded as the American Religion Data Archive in 1997, provides statistical information on all manner of religious topics, both U.S. and international in scope. Housed at the Pennsylvania State University, the ARDA Data Archive is a collection of surveys, polls, and other data submitted by researchers and made available online by the ARDA. Among the materials are statistical data on denominational memberships, data from surveys of the public and denominational members, and geographical information. Especially useful are the denominational family trees and profiles. This collection of data archives is available on the organization's free website. It is funded by the Lilly Endowment, the John Templeton Foundation and the Pennsylvania State University. The best approach to locating needed data is to browse files by category, alphabetically, view the newest additions, most popular files, or search for a file. After a file has been selected, the user can preview the results, learn about how the data were identified and collected, save survey questions, and download the data file. The ARDA website also includes materials and ideas for teachers (the learning center), information for the press (the press room), and resources for congregations.

Organizations

Religious organizations, both popular and scholarly, are valuable sources of information. They may be denominational, ecumenical, or academic. The number of denominational organizations is immense and diverse in terms of mission, size, and functionality. However, certain useful generalizations can be made about larger religious groups and related scholarly organizations and societies.

Generally, religious organizations maintain national offices and have extensive publishing programs. Much of the publishing effort of denominational groups is designed to serve the needs of local congregations for devotional and educational materials. A number of the denomination-specific groups maintain research staffs at the national level and nearly all gather basic statistical data such as size of membership, number of congregations, and attendance at religious education programs. They issue directories, though these are increasingly published online, along with proceedings of national, regional, state, or diocesan conferences. Almost all organizations now have Web sites, although some remain more basic than others. The proportion of web material that is open to subscribers or members varies as well.

Many national organizations maintain historical materials or archives pertaining to the denomination and some actively promote church or congregational libraries. Digital libraries are increasing in number, and many of these are open to all.

While the number of organizations is too large to cover here, a sampling of religious organizations and library associations related to religion here suggest the possibilities for the information seeker.

4-33. The International Society for the Study of Religion, Nature and Culture (ISSRNC). http://www.religionandnature.com/

ISSRNC is an organization devoted to facilitating collaboration and dissemination of research findings on the relationships among people and their cultures, nature and the environment and religion and the practice thereof. The association's journal is the *Journal for the Study of Religion, Nature and Culture.*

4-34. National Council of Churches of Christ in the USA (NCC). http://ncccusa.org/

Ecumenical cooperation is exemplified by the work of the NCC, which was founded in 1950. The NCC has been "the leading force for ecumenical cooperation among Christians in the United States." The NCC collects and analyzes statistical data and publishes the *Yearbook of American and Canadian Churches* in print and online. The publication is now in the 78th edition. The NCC is also a provider of church bulletin inserts on a wide range of topics.

4-35. The Religion Communicators Council. http://www.religioncommunicators.org/

The Religion Communicators Council, founded in 1929, was previously known as the Religious Public Relations Council. This organization holds conferences and competitions in the area of public relations for religious groups. Recent topics covered in the organization's web material included "branding" and awards for the promotion of faith values.

4-36. Religious Education Association (REA). http://www.religiouseducation.net/

Specialized organizations serving the religious community can provide information on very focused topics. For example, the REA states that its mission is "to create opportunities for exploring and advancing the interconnected practices of scholarship, research, teaching, and leadership in faith communities, academic institutions, and the wider world community." Members are professors and researchers in the field of religion. The association publishes a journal entitled *Religious Education* that is a membership benefit.

4-37. The World Council of Churches (WCC). http://www.oikoumene.org/

The WCC is the broadest and most inclusive among the many organized expressions of the modern ecumenical movement. The WCC publishes two online journals, *The Ecumenical Review* and *The International Review of Mission.* The WCC maintains two important research resources: the Ecumenical Centre in Geneva and the Ecumenical Institute in Bossey. These facilities are responsible for maintaining the records of the ecumenical movement worldwide. Books, documents, journals, and archival materials are maintained; over 130,000 monographs and millions of archival documents are held. The catalog of the library and archive can be accessed at http://library.oikoumene.org/indix. php?id=395.

Library Associations

4-38. The American Theological Library Association (ATLA). http://www.atla.com/

ATLA is the professional association that supports all aspects of theological and religious studies librarianship. ATLA's membership represents many religious groups and faith traditions; the purpose of the association is to support the libraries and librarians. The association publishes an online journal, *Theological Librarianship,* and maintains a job openings page for religious studies and theological library positions. Conferences and professional development opportunities are offered as well. Perhaps ATLA's greatest contribution to religious studies librarianship is its publication of the *ATLA Religion Database* and its companion *ATLA Serials* (ATLAS). *Library Journal* called ATLA with ATLAS "the essential resource, bar none." The database and its evolution are described more fully elsewhere in this Guide (entry 4-1)

4-39. Association of Christian Librarians. http://www.acl.org

The mission of the Association of Christian Librarians, whose primary members are academic librarians, is "to empower evangelical librarians through professional development, scholarship, and spiritual encouragement for service in higher education."

4-40. The Association for Jewish Libraries. http://www.jewishlibraries.org/main/

The Association for Jewish Libraries promotes Jewish literacy and literature through support of libraries.

4-41. Catholic Library Association. http://cathla.org/

Additional support for librarians working with religious collections is offered by the Catholic Library Association, one of the oldest such organizations. It publishes *Catholic Library World.*

4-42. The Church and Synagogue Library Association. http://cslainfo.org/

The Church and Synagogue Library Association provides a valuable service to congregational libraries across denominations by publishing affordable guides and bibliographies on topics such as financing the church library, cataloging and classification, and archiving. A quarterly journal, *Congregational Libraries Today,* is the organization's major publication.

Lastly, Ellen Bosman's web page identifies additional religious library associations as well as providing a guide of selection sources for congregational collections: http://web.nmsu.edu/~ebosman/church/index.shtml.

SACRED WORKS

A special type of materials in religion is what are called sacred works or sacred scriptures. These works have words that are considered *sacred* by believers or followers of the faith. The words "differ from ordinary words in that they are believed either both to possess and convey spiritual and magical powers or to be the means through which a divine being or other sacred reality is revealed." The origins of the sacred works are sometimes oral. The truly sacred works may become, through time or by a decision of the followers, part of a religion's canon. Other works that support those that are part of the canon may be termed semi-sacred literature. For more detail see: *Encyclopædia Britannica Online,* s. v. "scripture," at http://www.britannica.com/EBchecked/topic/530020/script.

4-43. The Internet Sacred Text Archive (ISTA). Evinity Publishing, 1999– . http://www.sacred-texts.com/index.htm

Although this website lacks highly sophisticated search capabilities, it nonetheless claims to be "the largest freely available archive of online books about religion, mythology, folklore and the esoteric on the Internet." Begun over a decade ago by John Bruno Hare, who died April 27, 2010, the site is maintained by Evinity Publishing Inc. The ISTA, as the resource is known, is dedicated to religious tolerance and scholarship. It is inclusive, providing access to well-known texts as well as the more obscure. From African religions to Zoroastrianism, sacred texts, or accounts of them, are listed and links provided to the scanned or linked documents. Material is believed to be in the public domain, available through fair use, or already on the Internet. A special goal of this resource is to remedy "the under-representation of traditional cultures on the Internet." Thus the site has an impressive collection of transcriptions of complete books on Native American, African, Asian and other non-Western religions, spiritual practices, mythology and folklore." The sources of the text versions are identified;

for example, the Greek New Testament is accompanied by the note: "The text given here . . . is that of the Nestle-Aland 26th/27th edition." The user can click on broad categories on the left of the page to search by country names, e.g., England; religion or belief system, e.g., Jainism, Mormonism, Judaism, Astrology, New Thought; concepts related to religion, e.g., evil, time; or major text titles, e.g., I Ching, Bible. A review of the site called it among the closest to being all inclusive and comprehensive in its coverage.

The Bible and Bible Study Tools

Since the 5th edition of *The Humanities* was published, great advances have been made in making online Bibles accessible to everyone. Most versions and translations are now available on the Internet, and Bibles and their supportive materials have been among the first electronic resources to be widely available for smart phones and other handheld and mobile information technology devices. One of the most comprehensive sources for electronic versions of the Bible is BibleGateway, the next entry.

4-44. **Biblegateway.com.** http://www.biblegateway.com

This website is a one-stop place to go for full-text versions of the Bible. It offers about 100 different versions of the Bible, in languages from Arabic to Vietnamese, in English, Spanish, Slovak, and Farsi, with audio versions for those who would prefer to listen than to read. One special feature of the site is the passage lookup. There are additional resources, devotionals, reading plans, and more.

Librarians will want to refer users to sites like BibleGateway, but they will also continue to hold print versions in their book collections. The list here gives the principal English-language versions and the dates of initial translation/publication. They are listed in chronological order.

King James or Authorized Version (1611)

Douay Bible (1582–1610, revised 1749–1750)

American Standard Version or American Revised Version (1901)

Revised Standard Version (1952)

The Jerusalem Bible (1966)

The New English Bible (1971)

The New American Bible (1971)

New International Version (NIV) (1978)

Contemporary English Version (CEV) (1995)

English Standard Version (2001)

A vast number of aids to Bible study are available including commentaries, concordances, and reading plans and notes developed by biblical scholars, preachers, and lay persons. The following are printed resources.

Concordances and Commentaries

It should be noted that a number of Bible commentaries and concordances are available both in print and online formats. The increasing number of electronic publications of these particular resources is testimony to the fact that their utility is greatly enhanced by the availability of convenient means of manipulating, sorting, and comparing resources one against another. The fact that such comparisons, or use of parallel sources, can now be made "on the fly" is a benefit to the user. Also, the availability of Bible study tools online and in audio and video formats adds to the appeal for today's readers.

4-45. Cruden's Complete Concordance to the Old and New Testament. Alexander Cruden. Peabody, MA: Hendrickson Publishers, 2007.

This edition of the ever-popular concordance is compact, convenient and concise. It is comprised of three sections: Common Words, Proper Names, and Apocryphal Words.

4-46. The ESV (English Standard Version) MacArthur Study Bible. John MacArthur. Wheaton, IL: Crossway Bibles, 2010.

The ESV provides MacArthur Bible study notes alongside verses in this newly available version in the MacArthur Bible Study collection. Along with the complete Bible text, the study Bible includes MacArthur's notes numbering over 25,000; maps, charts and timelines in color; introductions to each book of the Bible; extensive cross references; a concordance and a Bible reading plan.

4-47. Harper's Bible Commentary. James Luther Mays, ed. San Francisco: Harper, 2000.

The commentary covers Old and New Testaments as well as the books of the Apocrypha. By its coverage, it addresses the biblical canons of Judaism, Catholicism, Eastern Orthodoxy, and Protestantism. Books of the Bible are covered in three ways: general essays provide a context for the entire Bible; articles introduce major sections of the Bible; and commentaries on the individual books themselves follow. An additional commentary revised during the same period is *Peake's Commentary on the Bible* (Arthur Peake et al., ed. Routledge, 2001). Peake's is a scholarly commentary that involved contributions from 60 subject experts in this 2001 revision. This publication is strong on its reliance of recent research, documentation, and new texts. The complete library collection will also add *The Oxford Bible Commentary,* edited by John Barton and John Muddiman (Oxford University Press, 2001).

4-48. Nelson's Biblical Cyclopedic Index. Nashville: Thomas Nelson, 2010.

This index consists of a concordance, a Bible dictionary, and a Bible. Its indexes list more than 8,000 names, subjects, doctrines, events, and other details found in the Bible. User reviews suggest that this is an excellent source for the everyday Bible reader—50 of 54 reviewers posting on Amazon gave the Cyclopedic Index four or, most often, five stars.

4-49. The New Interpreter's Bible: general articles & introduction, commentary, & reflections for each book of the Bible, including the Apocryphal/Deuterocanonical books. Nashville: Abingdon Press, 1994–2004. 12 vols.

Intended for Bible study, *The New Interpreter's Bible* is a completely new work from the older version of the *Interpreter's Bible* (1951–57). This work contains full texts and critical notes of the *New International Version* and the *New Revised Standard Version* of the Bible in parallel columns.

4-50. Old Testament Commentary Survey. 4th ed. Tremper Longman, Grand Rapids, MI: Baker, 2007.

This work is not a commentary itself but rather a guide to them. The fourth edition of the *Old Testament Commentary Survey* provides information about established commentaries. Listed are a number of works on each book of the Old Testament and brief indications of their emphases and viewpoints are given. Longman provides a serious evaluation of each and suggests the most likely users for them. A summary list amounts to Longman's recommendations for those who need advice on building a collection of good commentaries on the Old Testament.

4-51. The New American Bible Concise Concordance. John R. Kohlenberger III, ed. New York: Oxford University Press, 2003.

This concordance is to the *New American Bible*. It is arranged alphabetically by word and provides not only book, chapter and verse for each, but a few contextual terms associated with the words are also provided.

4-52. Multi-Purpose Tools for Bible Study. Federick Dankar. Minneapolis, MN: Fortress Press, 2003. Print and CD-ROM.

This is regarded as a reliable guide for students and scholars to the foundational texts of biblical study. It provides concordances, Hebrew and Greek texts, grammars, lexicons, Bible dictionaries and commentaries. This resource has been published for over 40 years and remains popular today.

4-53. Ryrie NASB–New American Study Bible. Charles Ryrie. Chicago: Moody Publishers, 2010.

This is hailed as a comprehensive source containing "10,000 explanatory notes, in-text graphics, and thorough book outlines, extensive cross-references, expanded topical index and a concordance."

4-54. Strong's Exhaustive Concordance of the Bible. James Strong. Peabody, MA: Hendrickson Publishers, 2007.

This is an updated version of a widely available and highly respected concordance. The publisher highlights that "This edition includes new typeface making it more readable, updated and improved Hebrew and Greek dictionaries, maps and additional Bible study aids, the words of Christ in red, and clear edge-tab indexing . . ." An interactive CD-ROM is included with purchase of the print resource.

Guides, Handbooks, and Reference Works

4-55. All the People in the Bible: An A-Z Guide to the Saints, Scoundrels, and other Characters in Scripture. Richard R. Losch. Grand Rapids, MI: William B. Eerdmans, 2008.

This source can be aptly described as a biographical source as it covers both individuals who are identified in the Bible, but also individuals who influenced events in the Bible in the first place. The organization of the guide is clear, an alphabetical listing of what the author calls saints, scoundrels and other characters. Gods and other spiritual beings are identified and described in this work, too. Reviewers found this source to be a helpful work for both students and lay persons.

4-56. The Anchor Yale Bible Dictionary. Davis Noel Freedman, ed. New Haven, CT: Yale University Press, 2008. 6 vols.

This Bible dictionary has now been brought out under the new Anchor Yale imprint. It is the first major Bible dictionary to come out in the last three decades and it has been hailed as the most extensive such work ever created. The dictionary consists of 6 volumes of approximately 1,200 pages each; more than 6,000 entries; and more than 7,000,000 words. Based on the work of 1,000 contributors, this publication is multicultural and interdisciplinary in scope and coverage and includes illustrations, endpaper maps, and bibliographic references.

4-57. Biblical Studies on the Internet: A Resource Guide. 2nd ed. Roland H. Worth, Jr. Jefferson, NC: McFarland Publishing, 2008.

This source covers 4,800 resources at over 10,000 Web sites for an audience the developer describes as "the average internet user." The broad reach of the guide's content is, according to one reviewer, "made possible by a unique method of indexing and cataloguing the web sites with the use of a code." When a particular threshold number of sources appear on one web page, that page is designated for coverage in the guide, thus managing the number of URLs efficiently. Bible translations, dictionaries, commentaries, and information in other languages are included.

4-58. Eerdmans Dictionary of the Bible. David Noel Freedman, ed. Grand Rapids, MI: W.B. Eerdmans, 2000.

This one-volume dictionary contains 5,000 alphabetically arranged entries on books, persons, places, and significant terms in the Bible. It explores the background of each biblical book and related writings in cultural, natural, geographical, and literary contexts. Nearly 600 scholars and experts contributed to the Eerdmans Dictionary. Charts, maps, and photographs are included, as are what the publisher calls "supplementary aids:" lists of abbreviations, a pronunciation guide, a transliteration key, and concise bibliographies. This work is based on the *New Revised Standard Version* of the Bible.

4-59. Encyclopedia of Biblical Ethics. R.K. Harrison. New York: Testament Books, 2003.

Previously published (in 1992) as *The Encyclopedia of Biblical and Christian Ethics*, this reference source has entries on a wide array of moral issues and concerns of the modern world. These are arranged from A to Z and each is discussed in light of what would be a Biblical interpretation. Over 50 scholars contributed to the encyclopedia that covers complex topics that are of increasing interest in the twenty-first century.

4-60. Index to Periodical Literature for the Study of the New Testament: New Testament Tools and Studies. Watson E. Mills. Leiden, Netherlands: Brill Publications, 2004.

This index covers 175 different periodicals and contains over 15,000 citations to twentieth century articles in the journals. References are arranged by canonical order. The periodicals are primarily English-language but they represent a broad array of theological viewpoints.

4-61. The International Standard Bible Encyclopedia. Geoffrey William Bromiley, ed. Grand Rapids, MI: W.B. Eerdmans, 2009.

Designed for teachers, students, pastors and laypersons, this revised encyclopedia contains articles that vary in length from several lines to many pages. Entries include pronunciation, etymology, and definitions as they have evolved through history. Many cross references connect entries in a thoughtful and logical way. The work is illustrated.

4-62. The New Unger's Bible Handbook. Merrill Frederick Unger and Gary N. Larson, ed. Chicago: Moody Press, 2005.

This is a single-volume Bible handbook that covers all books of the Bible, providing commentary on each along with color illustrations, photographs, maps, diagrams, and charts. It is a popular resource for students of the Bible since the contents are inclusive of the latest scholarship in biblical history, archaeology, and geography.

4-63. The Oxford Companion to the Bible. Bruce M. Metzger, and Michael D. Coogan, eds. Oxford: Oxford University Press, 1993. Print and e-book available through *Oxford Reference Online.*

This popular one-volume reference to the people, places, events, books, institutions, religious beliefs, and secular influences of the Bible was written by more than 250 scholars from diverse places and religious backgrounds. Along with the expected entries, there are also longer articles on religious concepts (e.g., sin) and on timely issues such as homosexuality or politics. This is a standard, well-respected source that was most recently thoroughly revised in 1993.

Maps and Atlases

4-64. C.E.B. Bible Map Guide: Explore the Lands of the Old and New Testaments. National Geographic Society, ed. Nashville: Common English Bible, 2011.

This full-color publication provides maps to the areas of the Bible during biblical times. The maps are based on the *Common English Bible.*

4-65. Oxford Bible Atlas. 4th ed. Adrian Curtis, ed. Oxford: Oxford University Press, 2009.

The *Oxford Bible Atlas* has undergone revision to bring it up to date with regard to biblical scholarship and to archaeology, topography, and geography. With color maps, it guides the user through the geography of the Holy Land from Exodus to New Testament times. The *Atlas* includes an illustrated survey of the relevance of archaeology for the study of the Bible and a chronology. A place name index, list of further reading, and a general index follow the maps and texts accompanying them. This is regarded as a useful atlas for students and laypersons with an interest in the Bible and the history of the Holy Land.

4-66. The Sacred Bridge: Carta's Atlas of the Biblical World. Anson F. Rainey and R. Steven Notley. Jerusalem: Carta, 2006.

This atlas is a highly regarded work consisting of about 300 maps depicting all aspects of the Biblical world in light of contemporary scholarship. Migration and trade routes, settlements, battles, and other events appropriate to cartographic representation are found in this atlas, and the maps are accompanied by commentaries that illuminate the maps themselves. A comprehensive chronological table, bibliographic references to every item used in preparation of the entries, and an index that, according to the description from the publisher, "contains every place name that has been mapped and, in addition, names that still defy exact location but can be shown in relation to specific biblical episodes." Another less costly but still very well-received, recently published atlas is *The IVP Atlas of Bible History* by Burton MacDonald (Oxford: Lion Hudson PLC, 2007).

RELIGIOUS BELIEF SYSTEMS

Like Bibles, the sacred texts of non-Christian religions are now available in a wide variety of electronic formats for delivery through diverse technologies. Several recent editions are listed here but the reader will also want to search the web for other versions, old and new. As with Biblegateway (entry 4-44), the Internet Sacred Text Archive provides the text for many different religions and belief systems throughout the world (entry 4-43).

Buddhism

4-67. Encyclopedia of Buddhism. Robert E. Buswell, ed. New York: Macmillan Reference USA, 2004. 2 vols.

This 2-volume encyclopedia has 500 entries that vary in length from a paragraph or two, to four to six pages on broad topics related to Buddhism, its practices and its influences. The articles are signed, and brief bibliographies accompany each entry. Over 250 contributors were responsible for the encyclopedia. From Abhidharma to Zongmi, concepts, influences, people, places, events; and text, documents, and methods of study of Buddhism are defined and discussed in understandable, clear language. The encyclopedia includes a synoptic outline that places the entries in 24 broad categories and a useful timeline. This reference source is useful to secondary and college students as well as the general reader.

4-68. BuddhaNet: Buddhist Studies. Buddha Dharma Education Association, Inc. 1996–2011. http://www.buddhanet.net/.

This free web resource is packed with timely information for the user interested in all things Buddhist. This comprehensive guide to Buddhism answers many basic questions, while the Buddhism e-Library provides a multilingual online resource suitable for the librarian or researcher. News from the Buddhist world is updated daily. A directory of Buddhism worldwide; annotated video, audio, and e-book lists; and resources for meditation are included. Buddhist weblinks to blogs, meditations, and other internet resources, and a daily readings link to the word of the Buddha complete this comprehensive web resource.

Christianity

Databases

4-69. ATLA Catholic Periodical and Literature Index (CPLI). Online subscription database. Quart. Available through the American Theological Library Association (ATLA) and EBSCOhost.

The Catholic Periodical and Literature Index is now a publication of the American Theological Library Association (ATLA). It provides indexing of periodicals, collections of essays, church and papal documents and electronic resources related to the practice and intellectual and historical traditions the Catholic Church. ATLA's CPLI provides indexing from 1981 to the present and is updated quarterly. Like other similar indexes, this one began as a guide, *Guide to Catholic Literature 1888–1940*, that identified books and booklets of Catholic interest with periodical updates to this work. Meanwhile, the Catholic Library Association began *Catholic Periodical Index*, a quarterly that covered journal literature back through 1930. The current product was derived from the first electronic offering that the Catholic Library Association issued on CD-ROM in the 1990s.

Printed Resources

4-70. The Book of Saints: A Comprehensive Biographical Dictionary. 7th ed. Basil Watkins, ed. New York: Continuum, 2004.

This is the 7th edition of this classic resource, entirely revised and reset. This is one of the standard sources for biographies of the saints. The book's content includes an introduction, alphabetically arranged entries on the saints, illustrations, a bibliography, a list of websites on saints, a glossary, and a list of martyrs. *The Oxford Dictionary of Saints* (5th ed. David Hugh Farmer, ed., Oxford University Press, 2004) is another highly respected source on the saints, due for revision in June 2011. The revised 5th edition is set to include appendices containing maps of pilgrimages, a list of saints' patronages and iconographical emblems, and a calendar of feasts.

4-71. Butler's Lives of the Saints: New Full Edition Supplement of New Saints and Blesseds. Volume 1. Paul Burns, ed. Collegeville, MN: Liturgical Press, 2003. (Butler's Lives of the Saints series, 13).

This volume updates the 12 volumes that cover the saints associated with the 12 months of the year in the Butler's Lives of the Saints series. This volume brings together those who were canonized or beatified between 1999 and 2003, and presents them in chronological order. Saints who have been canonized since their mention in previous volumes have new expanded entries. It should be noted that *Butler's Lives of the Saints* is one of the oldest and most trusted reference sources and most libraries will keep one or another of the editions, either multi-volume or concise. As beatifications and canonizations occur, librarians and readers alike will need new supplements.

4-72. Cambridge Dictionary of Christianity. Daniel Patte, ed. Cambridge, UK: Cambridge University Press, 2010.

The editorial concepts for this monumental dictionary were stated when development of the work began: "The goal of the *Cambridge Dictionary of Christianity* is to make understandable the complexity of present-day Christianity by clarifying the contextual character of Christian theological views, practices and movements through history and cultures," and the intended result was to document "the range of understandings of theological concepts and practices" so that users could recognize the range of these choices and the effects on their contextual and religious character. Over 800 scholars contributed to the dictionary, and entries include bibliographies. The emphasis throughout is to highlight the diversity of understanding of the Christian traditions in different environments while remaining respectful of all. This source is both authoritative and comprehensive.

4-73. Concise Encyclopedia of Amish, Brethren, Hutterites, and Mennonites. Donald B. Kraybill. Baltimore: Johns Hopkins University Press, 2010.

Both the religious views and the lifestyles of these very private religious groups are uncovered in this unprecedented encyclopedia. The author is a scholar of renown who has published extensively on the Amish community. The encyclopedia provides not only information on the beliefs of the religious communities studied, but it also includes entries on groups that have been assimilated into the mainstream culture. Statistical information, bibliographic sources, and directory information about groups with three or more members are included.

4-74. Encyclopedia of Christian Literature. George Kurian and James Smith. Lanham, MD: Scarecrow Press. 2010.

This source is comprised of two parts: 40 essays on different genres of Christian literature (e.g., apologetics, systematics, mission literature, etc.) with bibliographies. Each essay is several pages in length and provides a good introduction to the literature type. The second part of the encyclopedia consists of 400 biographical essays, averaging a full page in length, on Christian authors and their works. Authors are defined broadly: writers, preachers, poets, theologians, and hymn writers are among those for whom brief biographical entries appear. The time period covered by this two-volume set with over 175 contributors is 2,000 years of Christianity.

4-75. Faith Reads: A Selective Guide to Christian Non-Fiction. David Rainey. Westport, CT.: Libraries Unlimited, 2008.

This resource is designed to serve both librarians and readers. It lists over 600 books that address topics such as life stories, Christian self-help, prayer and spiritual growth, the arts, nature, and even business. Besides informative annotations of the titles described in the chapters, the guide indexes authors, titles, and subjects at the back of the book. Appendices include listings of Christian publishers, awards, and review sources.

4-76. Historical Dictionary of Jesus. Daniel J. Harrington. Lanham, MD. Scarecrow Press, 2010.

Consisting of three parts, this dictionary contains a section on Jesus as an historical figure; a dictionary containing over 400 entries that are cross referenced and that detail actions and words associated with Jesus according to a number of scholars and sources; and a bibliography of the important books about the historical Jesus. The user of this resource will learn about the methods, disciplines and approaches to the study of Jesus. The people, places, and events associated with Jesus are identified and defined in this highly regarded source. Another more exhaustive work on this topic, in four volumes, is *Handbook for the Study of the Historical Jesus*, edited by Tom Holman and Stanley E. Porter (Brill, 2010).

4-77. Mormonism: A Historical Encyclopedia. W. Paul Reeves and Ardis E. Parshalls, eds. Santa Barbara: ABC-CLIO, 2011.

This encyclopedia is organized around eras, events, people, and issues of the Church of Jesus Christ of Latter-Day Saints. The Eras section consists of long essays on six eras between the 1820s and the present. Events, people and issues sections have from two dozen to several dozen entries. There are sidebars that illuminate the topics of the primary entries. A chronology and bibliography complete the work. It should be noted that this encyclopedia is designed to cover the most prominent aspects of the religion for general readers, not to be a comprehensive source.

4-78. New Catholic Encyclopedia. 2nd ed. Catholic University of America and Gale Research, 2002. 15 vols.

This 2002 revision of the 1967 set is thorough and now covers recent developments in the Church leadership; individuals such as popes, canonized and beatified persons; and changes in basic Catholic law, liturgy, and influence. This is a standard work that will be called upon for its authority and coverage.

4-79. The Official Catholic Directory Anno Domini. P.J. Kennedy and Sons, National Registry Publishing, NJ: New Providence, 1817– . Ann.

The *Official Catholic Directory Anno Domini* is the standard annual reference tool that provides information on all aspects of the U.S. Roman Catholic Church. This publication contains the following: updated diocesan entries that were confirmed and approved by the dioceses; listings for religious orders of men and women, missionary activities, and foreign missions; a user's guide and glossary with definitions; statistics for the 209 US dioceses; E-mail and Web site information for Catholic institutions; a map detailing diocesan and province boundaries in the US; a products & services guide advertising goods specific to the Catholic Church and its patrons; an index that lists priests alphabetically; a necrology index. A Part II Supplement volume will include listings of Archdioceses and Dioceses of the World and updates to the main volume.

4-80. The Oxford Dictionary of Popes. J.N.D. Kelly. Oxford: Oxford University Press, 2003.

This is a chronologically arranged dictionary covering the popes from Peter to the present. Antipopes, pretenders, and even Joan, the alleged female papal aspirant, are included. Entries include information about pre-papacy lives of the popes, their backgrounds, careers, and families as well as coverage of their activities as pope. Bibliographic information is provided for each pope. J.N.D. Kelly is Canon of Chichester Cathedral and author of several other works on religious topics.

4-81. Prophecy and Apocalyptic: An Annotated Bibliography. D. Brent Sandy and Daniel M. O'Hare. Ada, MI: Baker Academic, 2007.

This bibliography guides researchers to 550 titles in the Apocalyptic and Old Testament prophetic literature. The publication is sponsored by the Institute for Biblical Research, an organization that promotes excellence in biblical scholarship from within an evangelical faith environment. About three-quarters of the titles relate to prophecy and the remainder to the apocalyptic literature.

4-82. A Research Bibliography in Christian Ethics and Catholic Moral Theology. James T. Bretzke. Lewiston, NY: Edwin Mellen Press, 2006.

This bibliography has several thousand entries covering over two centuries of books and journal articles. Entries are organized under broad subject headings and most topics are also subdivided into books and journal articles. While useful due to its size and scope, the user should note that annotations vary considerably in length and that the index is difficult to use because there are no subdivisions under the terms indexed. There is no list of journals covered.

Open Access Resources

4-83. Catholic Reference Sources. http://cathrefbooks.wikidot.com/b162

The purpose of this online bibliographic resource is to update James McCabe's *A Critical Guide to Catholic Reference Books* that has been a standard tool since 1989. The updating is made possible by a joint project of the Roman Catholic Denominational Group of the American Theological Library Association and the Academic Section of the Catholic Library Association. This may serve as a model for revising and updating, and, indeed continuing to make useful valuable resources previously only available in print.

4-84. The Cooperative Digital Resources Initiative of the American Theological Library Association and **Association of Theological Schools** (http://www.atla.com/cdri/) provides access to "digital images of woodcuts, photographs, slides, papyri, coins, maps, postcards, manuscripts, lithographs, sermons, shape-note tune books, and various forms of Christian art, architecture, and iconography." The collections in this digital resource have been contributed by major divinity schools, including those at Harvard, Yale, Vanderbilt, Emory, Duke, and Princeton Universities.

4-85. Symbols in Christian Art and Architecture. Walter E. Gast. http://www.planetgast.net/symbols/symbolsc/symbolsc.html

This free website contains "a gallery of images you are likely to find in many Christian churches along with explanations to help you understand their meaning and significance." Church features and architectural symbols are also explained. An alphabetical search leads to images with explanations, while it is even easier to find items by browsing. It is also possible to search on basics like color, numbers, and patterns. Referrals to Amazon's offerings on symbols and symbolism help support the costs of maintaining the website.

Hinduism

4-86. Brill's Encyclopedia of Hinduism. Knut A. Jacobsen, Helene Basu Malinar, Angelika Malinar, and Vasudha Narayanan. Leiden, Netherlands: Brill Publishing, 2009–2013. 5 vols. projected.

The *Encyclopedia of Hinduism* will be a five-volume set, one volume published annually, over the period 2009–2013. Volume 1 is on Regions, Pilgrimage and Deities; Volume 2 covers Sacred Texts, Ritual Traditions, Arts, and Concepts of Hinduism; Volume 3 covers Society, Theology and Philosophy. Volume 4 will take up historical periods, philosophers, poets and saints, relations between Hinduism and other religions, politics and contemporary issues; and the final volume will cover religious symbolism, missions and global Hinduism, religious movements as well as the Diaspora communities outside South Asia.

4-87. The Illustrated Encyclopedia of Hinduism. James G. Lochtefeld. New York: Rosen Publishing Group, 2002. 2 vols.

This is a two-volume dictionary with brief entries, arranged alphabetically, on both broad and narrow topics related to Hinduism. However, there are a number of encyclopedia-like characteristics that make this resource more valuable than an ordinary dictionary. A classified index of the contents is provided at the beginning of the work, enabling the user to search for terms as they relate to such categories as art, architecture and iconography; geography; language; and yoga and tantra. Numerous cross references within the entries appear in boldface. Volume 2 includes a pronunciation guide for Hindi and Sanskrit terms, a bibliography, a "back-of-the-book" index, and credits for the many black and white photographs included in the encyclopedia. Another source that offers insight into the Hindu religion is *Dictionary of Hindu Lore and Legend* by Anna L. Dallapiccola (W. W. Norton, 2002). This small dictionary carries a punch; over 1,000 topics on all aspects of Hinduism's stories, lore, and legend are covered. Sanskrit equivalents are given, and even the introductory material on the region and its people proves to be helpful. Reviewers agree that this is a highly recommended dictionary. Finally, the more recent *A Dictionary of Hinduism* by W.J. Johnson (Oxford University Press, 2009) provides authoritative varying length articles on all aspects of Hinduism. Much of the material is contemporary, and even treatment is given to the sects within Hinduism. Following the entries, there are a pronunciation guide, maps, and a chronology of the religion.

Islam

4-88. Index Islamicus. Leiden, Netherlands: Brill, 1958– . Print. Available online through EBSCOhost.

This is an increasingly important database that grew out of *Index Islamicus, 1906–1955*, an index of journal articles that was authored by J.D. Pearson and published in 1958. After its publication, there were several supplements issued; and, by 1975, Pearson began editing a quarterly index that treated both articles and monographs. The supplements were later cumulated and that cumulation was published in separate monograph and article volumes. By the 1990s, the publisher changed and the print database included access to thousands of articles in books, periodicals, anthologies, and other publications. Now available online, the index is an indispensable resource for materials in European languages on all aspects of the Islamic world: history, religion, society, and culture are covered here, and the more than 3,500 sources indexed contain material by authors from an expanding range of social science and humanities disciplines.

4-89. Al-Quran: A Contemporary Translation. Rev. ed. Ahmed Ali. Princeton, NJ: Princeton University Press, 2001.

As with all sacred texts, there have been many editions of the *Quran* in the modern era, now many of them translations. In this edition of the Quran, originally published in 1985, the text is in Arabic with a parallel English translation. Reviewers praise the translation as being more rhythmic than others they had read.

4-90. Encyclopaedia Islamica. Farhad Daftary and Wilferd Madelung, eds. Leiden, Netherlands: Brill Publishing, 2008. 16 vols. projected.

Material in this projected 16 volume set will includes information about all aspects of Islam focusing on the heritage of Shia Islam. Three volumes of the alphabetically organized set have been published as of this date, with 13 additional volumes projected. The publisher's description for the entire set states that it is "due to become one of the major comprehensive reference works on Islam and the Muslim world."

4-91. Encyclopedia of Islam and the Muslim World. Richard C. Martin, ed. New York: Macmillan Reference USA, 2004. 2 vols.

A review of this 2-volume set in *Booklist* places it rightly between large scholarly encyclopedias and one-volume popular treatments of Islam and Muslim cultures. The encyclopedia is essentially a sourcebook for historical and contemporary information. Just over 500 articles are arranged alphabetically, and the illustrated entries are meant to serve readers with limited knowledge of Islam, secondary and college-level teachers, and librarians needing basic information to proceed with additional readings or reference tools. The articles are authoritative and signed by scholars and subject experts. Brief bibliographies accompany the articles.

4-92. Islamic Civilization: History, Contributions, and Influence: A Compendium of Literature. Shaikh Ghazanfar. Lanham, MD: Scarecrow Press, 2006.

The history and influence of Islam are the topics of the 600 books and numerous articles in this compendium. The humanities and social sciences are the primary areas of influence covered although science is also a heading represented by fewer entries. The bibliography is organized around the disciplinary headings except for two additional major subjects: Islam-West Linkages and General. Annotations are thoughtful and thorough, so much so that reviewers comment on their quality. The compendium is indexed by authors and titles.

Judaism

4-93. Cambridge Dictionary of Jewish History, Religion and Culture. Judith Reesa Baskin, ed. New York: Cambridge University Press, 2011.

According to the publisher's description, this set is for a twenty-first-century audience. The entries that are written by leading scholars define both spiritual and intellectual aspects of Judaism. The entries provide material on central people, events and places, and the literary and cultural contributions of the Jewish people. Examinations confirms review reports that entries in the *Dictionary* "explore Jewish history from ancient times to the present and consider all aspects of Judaism, including religious practices and rituals, legal teachings, and legendary traditions and rationalism, mysticism and messianism." Secular and political movements; Jewish contributions to literature, art, music, theater, dance, film, broadcasting, sports, science, medicine and ecology; and a differentiation between the religious and secular life are among many other topics covered here. Articles are several pages in length, on average, and have good reference lists.

4-94. The Cambridge History of Judaism. William David Davies, ed. Cambridge University Press, 2008. 4 vols.

This work's primary focus is the history of the Jews from 586 B.C. onward. Volumes published prior to 2000 included The Persian Period and the Early Roman Period, published in 1984 and 1999 respectively. The latest volume was Volume 4, published in 2006. The period covered is the Late Roman Rabbinic Period. The history is one of the hundreds of titles in the Cambridge History series, many of which are now available electronically.

4-95. Dictionary of Jewish Terms. Ronald L. Eisenberg. Rockville, MD: Schreiber Publishing, 2008.

Unlike the Cambridge Dictionary edited by Baskin, this is a true dictionary of *terms* with brief definitions suitable for everyone. Arranged alphabetically, the terms range from near slang (e.g., Borscht Belt) to Hebrew (Ru'ach) to conceptual (e.g., false accusations). Place names are defined, and Yiddish pronunciations are given for some familiar terms (e.g., Shabbos). References and notes follow the main dictionary.

4-96. Encyclopedia of Jews in the Islamic World. Norman A. Stillman, ed. Leiden, Netherlands: Brill Publishing, 2010. 5 vols.

More than 350 scholars provide coverage of topics such as Jewish history, culture and religion. This set focuses specifically on Jews in Muslim lands dating from medieval to modern times: late medieval, early modern, and modern periods are covered. Maps, graphs, and illustrations are included in this alphabetically organized encyclopedia. Volume 5 is a resource list and extensive index.

4-97. Historical Atlas of Judaism. J. Bacon and I. Barnes, eds. Secaucus, NJ: Chartwell Books, 2011.

This historical atlas contains over 100 maps outlining the history, struggles, and culture of the Jewish people. The publisher's description states that the maps were "specially commissioned" for this publication that covers Jewish history from ancient Palestine to the modern state of Israel.

4-98. Jewish Encyclopedia. Kopelman Foundation.
http://www.jewishencyclopedia.com/index.jsp

This is a free encyclopedia online taken from the 12-volume *Jewish Encyclopedia* that was published between 1901 and 1906. The work is now in the public domain and will support scholarship needing an historical source. The 15,000 plus entries are alphabetically organized. Entries include source references. Basic keyword searching is supported.

4-99. Judaica Reference Sources: A Selective Annotated, Bibliographic Guide. 3rd ed. Charles Cutter. Santa Barbara, CA: ABC-CLIO, 2004.

This source has been expanded and updated to include over 1,000 annotated entries on reference sources dealing with all aspects of Jewish life and religion. The work includes lists of websites in five different languages, including Hebrew and Yiddish. The second edition of this title was awarded the Outstanding Reference Award from the Association of Jewish Librarians.

4-100. The New Encyclopedia of Judaism. 2nd ed. Geoffrey Wigoder, ed. New York: New York University Press, 2002.

This resource is a comprehensive, one-volume encyclopedia. Reform, Conservative, and Orthodox points of view are reflected in the articles on hundreds of aspects of Judaism, including women's roles, religious movements, and customs and folklore, to name just a few examples. Biographical entries are included as are commentaries on specific prayers and rituals. This revised and expanded edition of the encyclopedia updates the original entries and adds some 250 new ones. The edition is enhanced by a new introduction and a fully revised annotated bibliography.

4-101. The Oxford Handbook of Jewish Studies. Martin Goodman et al., eds. Oxford: Oxford University Press, 2002. Pap. 2005.

The publisher accurately describes this award-winning handbook: the work "begins with an examination of Jewish Studies as an academic discipline in its own right. The first half of the volume is organized chronologically, followed by sections on languages and literature, general aspects of religion, and other branches of Jewish Studies, which have each accumulated a considerable corpus of scholarship over the past half-century." The latter group of essays includes entries on a wide array of topics including mysticism, Jewish women's studies, demography, theater and film studies, and anti-Semitic research. The contributors are scholars from across the globe. Extensive bibliographies/reading lists accompany the entries and a thorough back-of-the-book index is included.

4-102. Torah: the Pentateuch: Interlinear Hebrew/English. Philadelphia: Jewish Publication Society, 2007.

The Torah is composed of the five books of Moses. Authorized editions are in Hebrew and there are many editions published in a variety of languages. The Jewish Publication Society has been responsible for quite a few editions, translations, and commentaries. This edition may be especially useful to those wanting to know more about the Torah, for those learning Hebrew, as well as those of the Jewish faith.

Sikh

4-103. International Bibliography of Sikh Studies. Rajwant Singh Chilana. Dordrecht, Netherlands: Springer, 2005. Print and online.

This bibliography of over 10,000 sources, organized into 30 categories, provides extensive access to all types of material on the Sikh religion and culture. The categories under which the materials are organized include the gurus, scripture, saints, philosophy, and history of the faith and culture. Additional categories on Sikh leaders and the arts are included, too. Bibliographic entries within the categories are listed by author, and there is an author index. Coverage is to 2004 and the bibliography is also available online.

NEW RELIGIONS AND SECTS

4-104. Dictionary of Gnosis & Western Esotericism. Wouter Hanegraaff et al., eds. Leiden, Netherlands: Brill Publishing, 2006.

Esotericism has been defined as a set of more-or-less related movements, personalities, and volumes of writings that have appeared through the centuries and that offer a quite distinct religious vision from that professed by "orthodox Christianity." More than 180 experts contributed the 400 articles in this dictionary. Topics covered include people, movements, and ideas. For example, there are entries for Christian Theosophy, the Hermetic tradition, Freemasonry, illusionism, and a history of Gnosis and Western Esotericism.

4-105. Encyclopedia of New Religions: New Religious Movements, Sects and Alternative Spiritualities. Christopher Partridge. Oxford: Oxford University Press, 2004.

This guide provides brief informative articles on what are termed "new religions" or sects and alternative spiritualities, arranged by broad religious traditions in which the new religions are rooted (e.g., Christianity, Islam, Indian, East Asian, New Age). Within the broad categories, the religious groups are arranged chronologically. The articles are mostly less than a page in length, but they provide critical information that can be used in subsequent searches. Most articles give information on the founding, structure, and basic belief system of the religions or sects. The authors of the articles are "scholars, each of whom possesses special knowledge of individual new religions," according to J. Gordon Melton who wrote the foreword to the guide. Color photographs accompany the text.

MYTHOLOGY AND FOLKLORE

A large number of resources are available for mythology and folklore as they overlap with a number of other disciplines, such as classical studies, art history, and literature. These two fields are indexed in the *MLA International Bibliography,* which has been treated in chapters 2, 5, and 6. The reader is reminded to check these chapters for other resources that may contain relevant materials.

Open Access Resources

4-106. Bulfinch's Online. 1855 ed. Thomas Bullfinch.
http://www.greekmythology.com/Books/Bulfinch/bulfinch.html

Bulfinch's standard on myth and legend is available at both greekmythology.com and through the University of Pennsylvania's site that provides a collection of links to Bullfinch's books online (http://onlinebooks.library.upenn.edu/webbin/book/lookupname?key=Bulfinch%2c%20Thomas%2c%201796-1867).

4-107. The Library of Congress American Folklife Center.
http://www.loc.gov/folklife/index.html

The American Folklife Center is a research center of the Library of Congress. The Center's website provides a guide to the archival collections of the Library, both print and online, with links to the electronically available ones. A wealth of information on the study of folklife (research methods and practices, for example), a *Folklife Sourcebook* with listings of over 150 other resources on the subject of folklore and folklife, and an informative newsletter are also available at this free website.

4-108. Folklore and Mythology Electronic Texts. D.L. Ashliman, ed.
http://www.pitt.edu/~dash/folktexts.html

This is a straightforward alphabetical link list to full-text resources on Folklore, Folk and Fairy Tales; and Germanic myths, legends and sagas. It was developed at the University of Pittsburgh by D.L. Ashliman and was last revised in 2004. Links checked appear to be stable.

4-109. Greek Mythology.com. http://www.greekmythology.com/index.html

GreekMythology.com provides links to many aspects of Greek mythology including sites on gods, goddesses, heroes, places, creatures, and full-text of important myths. A handy family tree of the gods is on the home page for reference. This online resource is logically organized but lacks visual appeal. However, it does provide some links to the basics of mythology in the Greek tradition and the site is free. Links to *Bulfinch's Mythology* and other classic sources are valuable for students and those with curiosity about Greek mythology. The website sponsors a discussion forum whose threads are categorized under the topical areas that organize the resources on the website: Olympian Gods, Titans, The Myths, Creatures, etc.

4-110. Theoi Greek Mythology. Aaron J. Atsma. Auckland, New Zealand. http://www.theoi.com/

This free website explores Greek mythology and the gods in classical literature and art. The developer states the aim of the project: "to provide a comprehensive, free reference guide to the gods (*theoi*), spirits (*daimones*), fabulous creatures (*theres*) and heroes of ancient Greek mythology and religion." This site is visually attractive and well organized, and serves as a guide to web resources and an encyclopedia, with well-documented entries. The organizational scheme is simple: Greek Mythology Introduction has definitions and links on A-Z Gods, Cults, Bestiary, and similar topics;

Greek Mythology and Biographies links to more information on gods, goddesses, heroes, and other "persons" important to mythology (e.g., giants); and a Gallery provides access to photographs of art, such as vases, that depict mythological events, persons, and stories. An impressive Library provides links to important works by major authors, such as Aeschylus, Homer, and other less popular ones as well. A gods and heroes family tree and a list of most popular links are included. While there are many mythology websites, a large proportion of them have not been recently updated. The website appears to be well maintained.

Print Resources

General sources in language and literature should also be consulted in order to broaden a search for material on folklore, folklife, mythology, and the classic literatures related to these fields. See chapters five and six.

4-111. Creation Myths of the World: An Encyclopedia. 2nd ed. David A. Leeming. Santa Barbara, CA: ABC-CLIO, 2009. 2 vols.

This two-volume work introduces five kinds of creation myths and then has entries on over 200 culturally and religiously based creation myths from all over the world. Theme and motifs are identified and discussed, and the myths are placed in a cultural context.

4-112. A Dictionary of World Mythology. Arthur Cotterell, ed. Oxford: Oxford University Press, 2003. Print and e-book.

This is one of the nine mythology and folklore titles in the Oxford Reference Collection. Available in print and online through *Oxford Reference Online,* there are entries on the gods of Greece, Rome, and Scandinavia; deities of Buddhist and Hindu India; and the entities of other cultures and countries.
Other dictionaries in the Oxford series on Mythology and Folklore, revised or updated since 2000 and available through the Online Reference programs, include *A Dictionary of African Mythology: the Mythmaker as Storyteller* (Harold Scheub, 2000); *A Dictionary of Asian Mythology* (David Leeming, 2001); *A Dictionary of Celtic Mythology* (James MacKillop, 2000); *A Dictionary of Creation Myth* (David Leeming and Margaret Leeming, 2009); *A Dictionary of English Folklore* (Jacqueline Simpson and Steve Roud, 2000); *The Oxford Dictionary of Phrase and Fable* (Elizabeth Knowles, 2006); and *The Oxford Companion to World Mythology* (David Leeming, 2005).

4-113. Brewer's Dictionary of Phrase and Fable. 17th ed. John Ayto and Ebenezer Cobham Brewer, eds. Edinburgh: Chambers, 2008.

This has been a standard source in the field since 1870. This edition is a complete revision, with new entries numbering over 1,500. Words, sayings, expressions and phrases that are used in mythology and in ordinary literature and popular culture are examined and explained in this work that serves as both a reference source and a readable addition to a personal library.

4-114. Facts on File Encyclopedia of World Mythology and Legend. 3rd ed. Anthony Mercatante and James Dow, eds. New York: Facts On File, 2009. 2 vols.

This Facts on File resource provides an extensive survey of myths, legends, and folklore from around the world. This revision adds new entries on non-western topics such as Tibet, and an updated bibliography provides access to more materials. A list of websites is a helpful aspect of this reference tool.

4-115. Folklore: An Encyclopedia of Beliefs, Customs, Tales, Music and Art. 2nd ed. Charlie T. McCormick and Kim Kennedy White, eds. Santa Barbara, CA: ABC-CLIO, 2010. 3 vols.

Both ancient and contemporary folklore are covered in this 2nd edition. An extensive bibliography and photographs are included in this encyclopedic work with entries by scholars. This encyclopedia is suitable for academic and general readers, and the first edition was hailed as a "one-stop" source of information on folklore.

4-116. Handbook of Classical Mythology. William Hansen. Santa Barbara, CA: ABC-CLIO, 2003. (World Mythology Series).

This handbook is appropriate for high school and college audiences or for the interested non-specialist. It covers Greek and Roman mythology, and provides documented entries on the figures, the myths, and related topics across the disciplines. The influence of these myths on culture is explored. Longer general essays precede the main body of the work and cross references and suggested readings follow the entries.

The ABC-CLIO World Mythology Series includes 10 titles that address the same audience as that for the *Handbook of Classical Mythology*. All the handbooks are organized with background essays followed by alphabetically arranged entries. The titles are: *Handbook of Chinese Mythology* (Lihui Yang and Deming An, 2005); *Handbook of Egyptian Mythology* (Geraldine Pinch, 2002); *Handbook of Japanese Mythology* (Michael Ashkenaji, 2003); *Handbook of Mesoamerican Mythology* (Kay A. Read and Jason J. Gonzolez, 2000); *Handbook of Native American Mythology* (Dawn E. Bastian and Judy K. Mitchell, 2004); *Handbook of Norse Mythology* (John Lindow, 2001); and *Handbook of Polynesian Mythology* (Robert D. Craig, 2004).

4-117. Lexikon Iconographicum Mythologiae Classicae. (LIMC). Zürich: Artemis, 1981–2009. 8 vols. 2 vols. supp.

The Lexikon is a pictorial dictionary of classical mythology compiled by international scholars in nearly forty countries over three decades. LIMC provides access to the entire iconographical tradition of classical art, cataloging representations of mythology in the plastic arts of antiquity. A fuller entry is provided in the Visual Arts chapter (entry 8-120).

4-118. Mythology of Asia and the Far East: Myths and Legends of China, Japan, Thailand, Malaysia and Indonesia. Rachel Storm. Leicester: Anness, 2003.

Although this is a very short book, it is helpful in that it explores East Asian, as opposed to Greek and Roman, mythological traditions.

4-119. The Times World Mythology. William G. Doty. New York: Times Books, 2002.

With authoritative articles on Greek, Roman, Norse, Egyptian, and Far Eastern mythologies, this one-volume work includes maps and illustrations.

4-120. Who's Who in Classical Mythology. Michael Grant and John Hazel, eds. London: Routledge, 2001.

This resource identifies and defines, in thorough entries with sources, Greek gods, goddesses, and other entities, along with the myths and legends associated with them. Another excellent resource from Routledge is the *Routledge Handbook of Greek Mythology: Based on H.J. Rose's Handbook of Greek Mythology* (Robin Hard, 7th ed., 2003). This source provides classic coverage of mythological topics. Reviews note its comprehensiveness and readability.

PART THREE

LITERATURE AND LANGUAGES

CHAPTER 5

LITERATURE AND LITERARY STUDIES

Anna H. Perrault

INTRODUCTION

In this chapter, we look at the reference resources for the study of literature. The entries are more specific than those in chapter 2 on multidisciplinary resources. Because of the broad nature of many interdisciplinary studies, we advise that both chapters 1 and 2 should be used in tandem with this chapter. Those two chapters relate more closely to literature than to any of the other subject chapters in this guide. There is very little overlap between the entries in chapter 2 and this chapter. Librarians working with literature collection development and reference will need to know the scope of the resources from both chapters.

In the introduction to this chapter, the definitions of literature are covered followed by the divisions and forms of literatures. Different sections highlight use and users in literary studies, electronic texts and digital collections, and resources for librarians. We begin with describing what literature is and the various forms of literature.

Working Definition of Literature

The earliest literature developed out of myths, legends, and folk tales that were passed down orally long before they were written down. The beginnings of literature have been traced back to the *Epic of Gilgamesh,* a Babylonian epic poem, that was probably composed around 1900 BC from stories in the Sumerian language that date much farther back in time. The ancient civilizations of China, India, Persia, Greece, and Rome all had well-developed literatures with epics, lyric poetry, songs, dramas, satires, histories, and didactic writings. Throughout the centuries, other forms were added such as novels and critical works. With computer technology and the Internet, digital poetry as well as digital media and art have added new dimensions to the traditional forms. With such a variety of forms, we turn first to defining the meaning of the term *literature.*

For purposes of this chapter, we can look to the definition of literature that Helen Haines offers in the now-classic *Living with Books*: "Literature, in familiar library classification and definition, embraces the whole domain of imaginative and creative writing as well as the history, philosophy, and art of literary expression and various distinctive forms in which literary art finds manifestation" (Haines 1950, 418). In this definition, literature includes all manner of artistic or imaginative writing. Some are inclined to define literature by the genre or forms that are usually included: fiction, poetry, and drama, what might be considered "literary art." Now, in a broad sense, *literature* also includes non-fiction such as essays, journals, memoirs, and historical and critical literature. The issue of value in literature is an important one. Sometimes definitions of literature suggest a value judgment; that is, the literature has "lasting value" or is of "permanent interest." Literary criticism of one work may ultimately become a part of the body of literature itself as is most evident in the area of literary scholarship. The critical literature is then subject to criticism itself.

In *Information Needs in the Humanities*, Constance Gould found that distinctions between *literature* and *non-literature* were being ignored in research, as "New Historicism" had encouraged interest in such works as "medical texts, ecclesiastical court records, house-wifery manuals, homilies, and other contemporary texts" (Gould 1988, 22). A body of literature can also be described as *canonical* or *non-canonical*, traditional classical literature and then broader writings as in the previous sentence.

Another use of the term *literature* is to describe the body of written work in a discipline or field. These "literatures of . . ." refer to writings in a special discipline or field of study. The role of the literatures, as vehicles for scholarly communication in various academic disciplines is made apparent in the curricular offerings of graduate schools of library science, information science, and information studies in such courses as "Social Sciences Literature," "Resources in the Humanities," and "Sources and Services: Science and Technology," as a few examples. Such courses include coverage of structures of the literature, the roles of various types of publications, and the unique forms of communications that one finds in the field under study.

Lastly, the terms *literature* and *author* are now used in many reference works to connote those who write and any type of writing. In the present age, the term *literature* can mean any written work, whether printed, published, or not. Reference works with these broad parameters as their scope are included in chapter 2 of this guide. This chapter uses the definitions of *literature* and *literary* as defined by Haines above.

Divisons and Forms of Literatures

The basic forms of literature are usually considered to be poetry and prose. Prose is normally divided into novels, short stories, and essays. Poetry is normally treated as a single unit, but it can be subdivided by type, e.g., lyric poems, epic poems, and so forth. The drama, as a literary record of what is to be performed on the stage, has an independent life of its own and may also be considered as a major literary form. Modern drama is ordinarily prose, but it may also be verse, or it may consist of both prose and verse. In this guide, drama is included in chapter 8, Dance and Theater, and in chapters 5 and 6.

Another approach to the organization of literature is by historical periods or literary movements, often combined with the forms outlined above. One approach to the division of languages and literature is offered by the Modern Humanities Research Association in *ABELL: The Annual Bibliography of English Language and Literature* (entry 5-2). Many of the divisions and subdivisions in ABELL can be applied to literature other than English materials. UNESCO organizes literature by regions of the world and the Library of Congress classification is also first geographical and then by forms and time periods.

For collection development forms of literature are described as primary texts, critical editions, and electronic texts and websites. Each of these can be further divided: Primary source materials can be published texts or manuscripts and archival materials. Electronic texts can be either primary or secondary. Images can also be primary or secondary resources.

Haines's *Living with Books* should be consulted for the classic librarian's view of the fields of literature, drama, poetry, and fiction (1950). Also directed to the librarian is James K. Bracken's "Literature," in *The Humanities and the Library* (1993). The chapter provides a fine introduction to the traditional printed literature, including sections on bibliography.

In addition to the forms long established for printed literature, new forms are springing up in digital literature. In chapter 1, *digital humanities* is considered as the transformation of scholarship and research into new areas of research using computer technology. Digital humanities has fostered collaboration in scholarship and research, setting a new paradigm for the humanities. The treatment of digital humanities in chapter 1 does not explore the use of digital technology for generating creative works. On its official website, the Electronic Literature Organization explains *electronic literature* as more than just literature or poetry created with a computer, but it can be multimedia activities, such as animated poetry presented in graphical forms or computer art installations that are interactive and have literary aspects, or interactive novels and collaborative writing projects through emails, SMS messages, wikis, or blogs. The description goes on to say that, "These activities, unbound by pages and the printed book, now move freely through galleries, performance spaces, and museums. Electronic literature often intersects with media and sound arts, but reading and writing remain central to the literary arts" (http://eliterature.org/). While the reference literature is now predominantly electronic and creative works embrace the capabilities afforded by technology, the printed work still rules in scholarly literary criticism and in art history. The findings of studies of the use of the literature by literary scholars are detailed next.

Use and Users in Literary Studies

Of all the disciplines covered in this guide, literature is the one in which scholars have been subjected to the greatest scrutiny in terms of their information needs and information-seeking behaviors. Surveys, observational studies, and unobtrusive citation analyses provide an interesting and varied picture of the literary scholar's work habits and literature use. A number of these studies are treated in chapter 1 because many of the studies that include literature are broader studies of information seeking behavior of humanities scholars. The reader is referred to those studies that established the traditional profile of the humanities scholar that obtain for scholars in literature, with Stone being the study most often cited (1982). The library is central to literary research with browsing as a discovery method and the monograph being the most cited publication format. Studies that looked more specifically at literary scholarship are reviewed here beginning with the most cited studies from the 1980s.

Richard Heinzkill looked at English literary works in "Characteristics of References in Selected Scholarly English Literary Journals" (1980). He updated the study 20 years later and it is reviewed below. Madeline Stern's "Characteristics of the Literature of Literary Scholarship," is another frequently cited article. Stern focused on three literary authors and three movements of literary theory, reporting on format, primary versus secondary sources, and age distribution, finding citations to books for the literary authors in the 80 percent range and slightly lower from the mid-70 percent range for literary theory (Stern 1983). In 1985–1986, three significant studies were published: John Cullars' "Characteristics of the Monographic Literature of British and American Literary Studies" (1985); John Budd's "Characteristics of Written Scholarship in American Literature: A Citation Study" (1986); and also by Budd "A Citation Study of American Literature: Implications for Collection Management" (1986). In this last study Budd looked at citations from books, book articles, journal articles, and dissertations, principally to try to identify core books and journals, finding that the majority of the citations were to books. Cullars compared references from 30 monographs to the findings from previous studies of the journal literature. He found the main difference to be a much greater use of manuscripts, but books were still the major research resource. Cullars also found a greater citation rate to sources more than 10 years old in monographs, than in the journal literature (521). By the mid-1980s, Constance Gould found that emphasis on individual authors had diminished, literary scholarship was becoming increasingly interdisciplinary, and that "some theoretical work is informed by deconstructionism, feminism, and Marxism" (1988, 22).

In addition to looking at British and American literature, John Cullars also investigated the characteristics of other special literatures in "Characteristics of the Monographic Scholarship of Foreign Literary Studies by Native Speakers of English" (1988); "Citation Characteristics of French and German Literary Monographs" (1989); and "Citation Characteristics of Italian and Spanish Literary Monographs" (1990).

These earlier studies found the monograph to be the dominant format by far with a significant use of primary sources and use of older secondary materials. In terms of bibliometric studies, findings are that the literature of literary scholarship is not as subject to "obsolescence" as that of the sciences.

Later studies continued to add to the profile of information seeking by literary scholars. Chu conducted a qualitative study of the research behavior of literary critics using a phased model approach (1999). She found that those interviewed relied upon academic libraries and their own personal collections for the majority of their research. They used both formal and informal channels for obtaining information. The ideas for future work most often arose from previous work or teaching, suggesting they did little searching for information to generate new ideas. Familiarity with library systems and collections was indicated by the majority having had some form of bibliographic instruction and experiencing little difficulty in finding information (265–266). Chu found that the model of research conducted by the literary critics followed the model presented by Stone of humanists' information seeking and not the "scientific" approach of scientists and social scientists that could have as many as eleven stages. Rather, Chu found that the model for literary critics had six stages: idea, preparation, elaboration, analysis and writing, dissemination, and further writing and dissemination (266–268). The research process was not a clearly defined step-by-step process as was that of scientists and social scientists.

Thompson examined citations in studies of nineteenth century British and American literature from both books and journals (2002). She divided out primary and secondary sources cited; among the secondary sources she found that 67 percent were to books, 14 percent were to book articles and 18 percent were to journals, with remaining miscellaneous categories having less than 1 percent each (128). Thompson found that the citation patterns in literary scholarship in earlier studies still persisted at the beginning of the twenty-first century. The monograph was still the dominant form of publication in literary studies with primary sources the most significant and that use of materials was from "a broad age spectrum" (130). Another finding was that at the time of the study, literary scholars were hardly citing websites at all (132).

As a follow-up to his earlier research, Richard Heinzkill conducted a citation analysis of journals in English and American literature published in 2003 (2007). His findings were not very different from those of Thompson and earlier studies. Books were cited far more often (75.8%) than journal articles (19.8%). Over half of the monographs cited (55.4%) were less than 20 years old. In general, journal articles published within the past 20 years were the most frequently cited (141). As in previous studies, he found that there were almost no citations to websites or electronic texts, explaining that use is suspected, but not cited (150). Findings for citations in other languages were congruent with those of Thompson with respect to French and German (144–147). Heinzkill found that literary scholars use a diversity of monographs which fall outside of the core classifications for literature, over 40 percent being outside (141). Thompson also found that the scholars used a broad range of literature.

Knievel and Kellsey conducted two citation studies that together included eight disciplines: art, classics, history, linguistics, literature, music, philosophy, and religion (2004, 2005). The studies looked at which languages frequently make up the citations in the journal literature of those fields. Literature, more than all the other fields in the study except religion, was strongly dominated by monographs, with 83 percent of all citations referring to monographs. Literature was also more dominated than average by English language citations, with nearly 84 percent of all citations referring to materials in English. Citations in literature included almost no German language sources, but literature scholars cited 12 percent French materials, the highest concentration of French material in any of the disciplines in the studies. While articles about literatures in languages other than English tended to have more non-English sources cited, most topics in American or British literature had few or none (158–160).

Wiberley and Jones conducted several studies on the information seeking habits of humanists. In "Time and Technology: A Decade-Long Look at Humanists' Use of Information Technology" they found that critical editions with hypertext links were turning out to be very useful to humanities scholars (2000). But scholars were concerned about having to live without journals. They were willing to use technology if it did not consume too much of their time and they could clearly see the benefits. They all felt that technology had revolutionized the way they do research in a positive and powerful way (429).

Ellis and Oldham conducted a study of the use of the Internet by English literature researchers (2005). They contacted researchers in British universities and in United States, Canada, New Zealand, and Australian universities. At the time of the study, respondents indicated reluctance to publish in electronic journals, but preferred long established and reputable peer-reviewed print journals. For monographs, most respondents preferred to have a printed book, rather than a digital copy. They did, however, acknowledge the convenience of digital works. Indications were that electronic works were making an impact on their research.

The use of the literature, both primary and secondary, by literary scholars has not varied much since the 1980s. Older sources are still cited; foreign language sources are used infrequently; and the ratio of monographs to journal articles and other types of materials has remained fairly constant. Citations to both monographs and primary sources are usually more than 50 percent. For literary research, primary materials are almost always published works as opposed to history in which unpublished sources make up a considerable percentage of resources. Citations studies found almost no citations for websites or electronic texts. Heinzkill speculated that the scholars were searching for and reading electronic sources, but that they then found printed copies to cite. Thus, citation analysis may not reveal all of the literature and formats that scholars employed in their research. When questions of the use of technology were added to studies in the 1990s, the general findings were that the scholars used technology and saw advantages, but they still preferred print monographs.

Electronic Texts and Digital Collections

Technology in the humanities was at first centered in developing collections of digitized texts. Electronic text projects, such as Michael Hart's Project Gutenberg (entry 2-59), the Electronic Text Center at the University of Virginia (entry 2-50), and the Oxford Text Archive (entry 2-58), have made the full text of many great literary works available. Author projects such as Dartmouth's Dante Project or the Blake project provide the full text of works such as *The Divine Comedy*, along with commentaries on the work and other related texts and criticism, in searchable form. Helen R. Tibbo's "Information Systems, Services, and Technology for the Humanities," provides a good starting point for the history of the development of text collections and the technical considerations and hurdles that were undergone and an extensive list of sources with an excellent review of literary texts (1991). Another article that will provide background on the topic is Anita Lowry's "Electronic Texts in English and American Literature" (1992). Here the reader can find information about Shakespeare and other English-language text files and also about basic considerations such as descriptive markup language and encoding. Avra Michelson and Jeff Rothenberg discuss all aspects of electronic texts in "Scholarly Communication and Information Technology" (1992). The article describes projects such as the *Thesaurus Linguae Graecae* (TLG) (entry 6-82) and American and French research on the *Treasury of the French Language* (ARTFL entry 6-141). The impact of electronic text is covered in *Literary Texts in an Electronic Age: Scholarly Implications and Library Services*, edited by B. Sutton (1994) and by Susan Hockey in "Evaluating Electronic Texts in the Humanities" (1994).

In tandem with the founding of academic text centers for the collection of digital texts, companies that held large stores of texts in microform began to reformat those materials into digital texts. Such well-known microform sets as *Early English Books* I and II, *Early American Imprints*, and other collections organized by centuries were converted and became subscription databases. Now it is possible for retrospective research to view much of the publication output of the United States and Western European countries from the beginning of printing well up into the twentieth century through these omnibus databases. Retrospective collections are essential for literary study, the reason collections of electronic texts exist. Many of these databases and collections are treated in chapter 2 of this guide as they serve a number of disciplines in the humanities and social sciences.

The movement to the digitization of texts by libraries, cooperative projects, and companies has freed the scholar from the task of creating a critical mass of digital texts and the worries of preservation and access. The preservation of primary "born digital" materials is essential for the future of literary scholarship. Major repositories, such as HathiTrust (entry 2-41) and Portico have been developed for this purpose. The trends in digital preservation and open access during the twenty-first century are covered in more detail in chapter one.

By the twenty-first century, the use of computers and networked technology was affecting the production of creative works in literature. Electronic literature such as hypertext fiction, digital poetry, interactive novels and poetry, performance poetry, and other new hybrids of technology and traditional forms of literature have developed. These are both creative outlets and subjects for literary criticism and scholarship. The Internet resources related to literature are vast and include blogs, discussion lists, and electronic journals on many literary genres, writers, and special topics. Search the Web for any contemporary writer and most likely they will have a website. Finally, as can be seen in the resources treated in chapter 2 and in this chapter, scholars are now able to access a wide variety of databases and digital collections without leaving their workplace.

Resources for Librarians

A number of guides to literature and literary studies include essays helpful to an understanding of research in literature and reference resources: *Critical Terms for Literary Study* (Frank Lentricchia and Thomas McLaughlin, eds., 1990); *Introduction to Scholarship in the Modern Languages and Literatures* (Joseph Gibaldi, ed., 1992); and *An Introduction to Bibliographical and Textual Studies,* (3rd. ed. William Proctor and Craig S. Abbot, 1999). *Literature in English: A Guide for Librarians in the Digital Age* (Betty H. Day and William A. Wortman, eds., 2000) is divided into two parts: Resources and Collections and Readers and Services. The guide contains chapters on Primary Source Material; Critical Editions; Literary Reference in the New Century; and Management of Electronic Text Collections, among others. The broader and more current MLA *Literary Research Guide,* by James L. Harner is kept up-to-date in an online version (2006 print, 2009– online, entries 2-22, 5-24). The divisions in the Harner guide are first according to literatures and then by reference formats. Overview essays in the *Encyclopedia of Library and Information Sciences* (3rd edition, 2009), are good basic introductions to topics in literature and literary studies.

Works Cited

Budd, John. 1986. "Characteristics of Written Scholarship in American Literature: A Citation Study." *Library and Information Science Research* 8 (April): 189–211.

Budd, John. 1986. "A Citation Study of American Literature: Implications for Collection Management." *Collection Management* 8 (Summer): 49–62.

Chu, Clara M. 1999. "Literary Critics at Work and Their Information Needs: A Research-phases Model." *Library & Information Science Research* 21 (2): 247–273.

Cullars, John. 1985. "Characteristics of the Monographic Literature of British and American Library Studies." *College and Research Libraries* 46 (November): 511–522.

Cullars, John. 1988. "Characteristics of the Monographic Scholarship of Foreign Literary Studies by Native Speakers of English." *College and Research Libraries* 49 (March): 157–170.

Cullars, John. 1989. "Citation Characteristics of French and German Literary Monographs." *Library Quarterly* 59 (October): 305–325.

Cullars, John. 1990. "Citation Characteristics of Italian and Spanish Literary Monographs." *Library Quarterly* 60 (October): 337–356.

Day, Betty H. and William A. Wortman, eds. 2000. *Literature in English: A Guide for Librarians in the Digital Age*. Chicago: Association of College and Research Libraries. (ACRL Publications in Librarianship, 54).

Ellis, David and Hanna Oldman. 2005. "The English Literature Researcher in the Age of the Internet." *Journal of Information Science* 31 (1): 29–36.

Gibaldi, Joseph, ed. 1992. *Introduction to Scholarship in the Modern Languages and Literatures*. New York: Modern Language Association.

Gould, Constance. 1988. *Information Needs in the Humanities: An Assessment*. Stanford, CA: Research Libraries Group.

Haines, Helen E. 1950. *Living with Books*. 2nd ed. New York: Columbia University Press.

Harner, James L. 2006. *Literary Research Guide*. 5th ed. New York: Modern Language Association of America. (Also online 2009–).

Heinzkill, Richard. 1980. "Characteristics of References in Selected Scholarly English Literary Journals." *Library Quarterly* 50 (July): 352–365.

Heinzkill, Richard. 2007. "References in Scholarly English and American Literary Journals Thirty Years Later: A Citation Study." *College & Research Libraries 68* (March): 141–153.

Knievel, Jennifer E. and Charlene Kellsey. 2004. "Global English in the Humanities? A Longitudinal Citation Study of Foreign Language Use by Humanities Scholars." *College & Research Libraries* 65 (3): 194–204.

Knievel, Jennifer E. and Charlene Kellsey. 2005. "Citation Analysis for Collection Development: A Comparative Study of Eight Humanities Fields." *Library Quarterly* 75, 2 (April): 142–168.

Lentricchia, Frank and Thomas McLaughlin, eds. 1995. *Critical Terms for Literary Study*. Chicago: University of Chicago Press.

Lowry, Anita. 1992. "Electronic Texts in English and American Literature." *Library Trends* (Spring): 704–723.

Michelson, Avra and Jeff Rothenberg. 1992. "Scholarly Communication and Information Technology: Exploring the Impact of Changes in the Research Process on Archives." *American Archivist* 55 (Spring): 236–315.

Proctor, William and Craig S. Abbot. 1999. *An Introduction to Bibliographical and Textual Studies*. 3rd. ed. New York: Modern Language Association.

Stern, Madeline. 1983. "Characteristics of the Literature of Literary Scholarship." *College and Research Libraries* 44 (July): 199–209.

Sutton, B. 1994. "Literary Texts in an Electronic Age: Scholarly Implications and Library Services." Urbana-Champaign: ASLIS, University of Illinois.

Thompson, Jennifer W. 2002. "The Death of the Scholarly Monograph in the Humanities? Citation Patterns in Literary Scholarship." *LIBRI* 52, 3 (September): 121–191.

Tibbo, Helen R. 1991. "Information Systems, Services, and Technology for the Humanities." *Annual Review of Information Science and Technology* (ARIST) 26: 287–346.

Wiberley, Stephen and William Jones. 2000. "Time and Technology: A Decade-Long Look at Humanists' Use of Information Technology." *College & Research Libraries* 61 (5): 421–431.

Website

Electronic Literature Organization. http://eliterature.org/).

SELECTED RESOURCES IN LITERATURE AND LITERARY STUDIES

Many resources that were included in the Literature chapter in previous editions of this guide have been placed in the second chapter, "Multidisciplinary Resources in the Humanities and the Arts," in this edition. The term *literature* is defined or interpreted in different ways. The most general definition is of literature as any form of poetry, prose, or narrative text. So too, the terms *author* and *writer* are used for any type of writing. Many of the online reference databases use the term *literature* in this sense. We speak of the "literature" of particular fields or disciplines such as the "literature of information science." Thus reference sources that include authors or works that are more general are included in chapter 2 in this Guide. Also included in chapter 2 are reference sources that cover more subjects than any one chapter in the book, such as the *MLA Bibliography* (entry 2-20). Then there is the use of *literature* to refer to creative endeavors, literature as *belles lettres*. This chapter more narrowly covers creative literature, literary criticism, and the study of literary writings in English. Chapter 6 treats literature written in languages other than English.

The first portion of this chapter covers general resources in literature by format. The sections that follow are by literary form: Fiction, Genre and Reader's Advisory, and Poetry. Lastly, there are two special topics sections for Ethnic Studies and Gender Studies.

GENERAL RESOURCES FOR LITERATURE

Databases and Digital Collections

The resources covered in this section are, for the most part, commercially produced and sold. They are online only, or online with print versions. The organization is mainly by publisher with all appropriate titles by the publisher for literature listed together in order for the reader to be able to see the titles as a grouping. In many cases single print titles or digital collections have been combined into larger electronic entities by the publisher and the user is aided in locating titles by knowing they are available separately or under a larger database grouping.

Entries 5-1 through 5-3 are databases produced by **Chadwyck-Healey/Proquest.**

5-1. Literature Online Reference. Chadwyck-Healey/Proquest. Online subscription database. http://collections.chadwyck.co.uk/

Literature Online is a reference database, rich in content, containing a large number of separate databases, digital collections, and reference works. The database combines and indexes the texts of over 357,250 works of poetry, drama, and prose fiction in the English language written from the 7th century to the present. In addition to classic and standard works, Literature Online includes all of an author's works that can be found to make as complete a corpus as possible. Literature Online also contains the complete text of a number of reference works including *The Concise Oxford Dictionary of Literary Terms* and the *New Princeton Encyclopedia of Poetry and Poetics* (entry 5-170). Also within the database are the full texts of 312 current literature journals that are indexed in *The Annual Bibliography of English Language and Literature* (ABELL) (treated below). The Literature Online database also includes multi-media with a collection of nearly 1,000 videos of poetry readings.

The Literature Online database is an all-encompassing resource for the historical study of English literature, but as it continues to grow, increasing numbers of works by the major authors of the twentieth century are being added as well as new reference works and digital collections. The scope of the database can more easily be seen through the publisher's listing below of the databases and reference works included in Literature Online:

Webster's Third New International Dictionary, Unabridged, 1993 edition

Early American Fiction, 1789–1875 (entry 5-56)

Early English Prose Fiction 1500–1700 (entry 5-57)

18th Century Fiction (entry 5-57)

African-American Poetry, 1760–1900 (entry 5-211)

American Poetry (entry 5-165)

English Poetry (entry 5-167)

20th Century African-American Poetry (entry 5-211)

20th Century American Poetry (entry 5-166)

20th Century English Poetry (entry 5-169)

The Chadwyck-Healey digital collections contained within Literature Online are also available individually and should be searched by title in libraries that do not subscribe to the Literature Online database.

The next two entries are the two major bibliographies contained within Literature Online: ABELL: *the Annual Bibliography of English Language & Literature* (entry 5-2) and *Bibliography of American Literature* (entry 5-3).

5-2. The Annual Bibliography of English Language & Literature (ABELL). London: Modern Humanities Research Association. Available in print from the MHRA. Included in Literature Online Reference and also available separately as an online subscription database through Proquest/Chadwyck-Healey. http://www.mhra.org.uk/Publications/Journals/abell.html

ABELL has been the standard bibliography for literature written in English in Great Britain and the Commonwealth countries since 1920. All aspects and periods of English literature are covered, from Anglo-Saxon times to present. The bibliography contains more than 880,000 records for monographs, periodical articles, critical editions of literary works, book reviews, collections of essays, and doctoral dissertations published anywhere in the world, including scholarly material in languages other than English, and also records for unpublished doctoral dissertations for the period 1920–1999.

5-3. Bibliography of American Literature (BAL). New Haven, CT: Yale University Press for the Bibliographic Society of America, 1955–1991. New Castle, DE: Oak Knoll Press, 2003. 9 vols. This reference is included in Literature Online Reference or available separately as an online subscription database through Chadwyck-Healey/Proquest.

Between 1955 and 1991, Yale University Press published the nine volumes of BAL for the Bibliographical Society of America. A selective index to the set was published in 1995. A new printing was issued by the Oak Knoll Press in 2003. BAL's accuracy is widely recognized. Jacob Blanck led a team of bibliographers over the years of the project and the bibliography became known by his name. Originally projected for eight volumes, this monumental but highly selective series was finally concluded with publication of the ninth volume some 36 years following volume 1. The *Bibliography* complements the work of the early American bibliographers Charles Evans and Joseph Sabin. Some 300 American writers, dating from the Federal period to moderns who died before 1930, are covered. BAL contains close to 40,000 records of nearly 300 American writers' literary works. The works of about 30 writers are covered in each volume in systematic fashion, including first editions, reprints containing textual or other changes, and a selected listing of biographical, bibliographical, and critical works. Only authors of literary interest (popular in their time but not necessarily recognized today as major writers) are included. The online BAL allows researchers to search all volumes together. Each author is searchable with lists of works divided into sections, including principal works, reprints, and references. Each primary book listed has a title-page transcription along with information about the collation, pagination, binding, and publication history. The location of at least one copy is given, as well as a selected list of bibliographical and biographical works. The database also provides a list of general references, principal periodicals consulted, and initials and pseudonyms. The printed BAL is usually found in academic libraries and is now available in electronic form through the Literature Online database.

EBSCO produces quite a few databases available through **EBSCOhost.** The main database for literature is Literary Reference Center in the next entry.

5-4. Literary Reference Center. EBSCO. Online subscription database. http://www.ebsco.com

Literary Reference Center is a full text database that combines information from major respected reference works, books, and literary journals as well as original content from EBSCO Publishing. The publisher's description of Literary Reference Center is that the database includes more than 10,000 plot summaries, synopses and work overviews; 75,000 articles of literary criticism; 130,000 author biographies; full text of more than 300 literary journals; 500,000 book reviews; 25,000 classic and contemporary poems; over 11,000 classic and contemporary short stories; full text of more than 7,500 classic novels; over 3,000 author interviews; and over 1,000 images of key literary figures. Of particular note, the database contains the Bloom Series of more than 500 books from Chelsea House Publishers edited by renowned literary critic Harold Bloom (entry below). Literary Reference Center was selected as a 2006 Library Journal Best Reference Resource.

   Also contained within Literary Reference Center is MagillOnLiterature Plus from Salem Press, a subsidiary of EBSCO (entry 2-30). Unlike the free Salem Literature: the Database (entry 2-31), MagillOnLiterature Plus is a subscription database that contains the full text of Magill literary criticism sets.

Facts on File produces print reference works in a variety of subject areas. Digital versions of the literary criticism works are collected into the Bloom's database.

5-5. Bloom's Literary Reference Online. New York: Facts on File. Online subscription database. http://factsonfile.com

Bloom's Literary Reference Online contains the published works from Facts on File's print literature monographs and series. A major portion of the contents are from the Bloom's monograph series of critical articles by noted scholars and also hundreds of Harold Bloom's essays on the lives and works of great writers throughout the world. In the database there is information on more than 46,000 characters; extensive entries on literary topics, themes, movements, genres, and authors; almost 170 video segments; and more. It has a "Did You Mean . . . ?" search feature. MARC records can be downloaded to a library's catalog. The database is suitable for schools and public libraries, for which it would be a major resource. Listed below in brief titles are print sets and series contained within the database.

> *A to Z of African-American Writers*; *A to Z of Latino American Writers and Journalists*; *A to Z of Women Writers*

> Banned Books

> Harold Bloom's Canon of Literature; Professor Bloom's selections of the major works of Western literature; Bloom's Bio Critiques; Bloom's Classic Critical Views; Bloom's Major Dramatists; Bloom's *Guides* (to individual works); Bloom's Literary Themes; Bloom's Major Novelists; Bloom's Major Poets; Bloom's Major Short

Story; Bloom's Modern Critical Interpretations; Bloom's Modern Critical Views; Bloom's Shakespeare Through the Ages

Facts on File Companions to Literature; Encyclopedias of . . . American Literature, Ancient Literature, British Writers, Medieval Literature, Political Thought, Renaissance Literature, the Enlightenment, the Harlem Renaissance, World Writers, and Literary Movements

Gale Cengage Learning publishes a number of reference databases with similar titles that include the terms *literature*, *literary*, and *authors*. The databases, which are broad in scope and coverage and not restricted to the critical study of literature, are listed in chapter 2 of this guide: Gales' Literary Index entry (2-14), LitFinder (entry 2-15), and Literature Resource Center (entry 2-16). The reader is advised to refer to these resources as well as those listed in this section, which treats databases that are for information on literary authors or literary criticism. Also in this section are several critical series from publishers which Gale has purchased, but the series have retained those publishers' names. The literary resources are placed together here in order that the coverage, contents, and differences among them can be seen.

5-6. **Dictionary of Literary Biography Complete Online.** Farmington Hills, MI: Gale Cengage Inc. Online subscription database.

5-7. **Literature Criticism Online.** Farmington Hills, MI: Gale Cengage Inc. Online subscription database.

5-8. **Scribner's Writer's Series.** Farmington Hills, MI: Gale Cengage, Inc. Online subscription database.

5-9. **Twayne's Author Series.** Farmington Hills, MI: Gale Cengage, Inc. Online subscription database.

Dictionary of Literary Biography Complete Online includes the *Dictionary of Literary Biography* (more than 345 vols.); *Dictionary of Literary Biography Documentary Series* (more than 50 vols.); and the *Dictionary of Literary Biography Yearbook* (23 vols.) The print series has volumes for specific types of literature or time periods covering writers from all eras and genres. Entries are written and signed by academic experts and include bibliographies and illustrations. Intended for students in secondary schools and university-level coursework, the database allows the student "to follow the development of an author's canon and the evolution of his/her reputation." The entire text of articles can be searched by Named Authors or keyword and other search terms. Results can be narrowed by limiting to year(s) of publication, series, and number of results per page. The database is widely available in academic and public libraries.

Also included in the Dictionary of Literary Biography Complete Online is the four-volume *Nobel Prize Laureates in Literature* set from the *Dictionary of Literary Biography series* (volumes 329–332). In addition to the biographical essays, many entries include materials from the Swedish Academy award presentation such as banquet speeches by the recipients. The Nobel Laureates set is also available as an e-book through the Gale Virtual Reference Library.

Literature Criticism Online, unlike the LitFinder (entry 2-15) and Literature Resource Center (entry 2-16), is more limited in scope to just the Gale Literary Criticism series. This database aggregates and indexes these Gale printed literary criticism series: *Contemporary Literary Criticism; Twentieth-Century Literary Criticism; Nineteenth-Century Literature Criticism; Shakespearean Criticism; Literature Criticism from 1400–1800; Classical and Medieval Literature Criticism; Poetry Criticism; Short Story Criticism*; and *Drama Criticism*. While there are many published sets of literary criticism that consist of entries written especially for those works, these series by Gale give a historical perspective by reproducing the criticism of an author's works ranging from contemporary reviews up to the present, both scholarly and popular, gathered together. The criticisms come from a range of publications including broadsheets, pamphlets, encyclopedias, books and periodicals, replicated to produce "the exact look and feel of the print originals." The database is a time-saver for students, allowing them to retrieve many references from one source and see the development or changes in an author's reputation over time.

Two similar online series from publishers acquired by Gale contain critical essays on authors and their works: Scribner's Writers Series and Twayne's Author Series. Both series are intended for secondary school and university readers and general or specialized research. The Scribner's Writers Series contains over 2,000 critical biographies of 15 to 20 pages each that place an author's work in historical context. Scribner print titles included in the online series are: *European Writers; Ancient Writers: Greece and Rome; British Writers; American Writers; African-American Writers; Modern American Women Writers; Supernatural Fiction Writers;* and *Writers for Young Adults*. (All but the latter of these titles are treated in the 5th edition of this Guide.) The Scribner's database covers many topics, including the Bible as sacred literature, Renaissance and short fiction, African-American literature, gay and lesbian mystery fiction, Anglo-Saxon poetry, writing and nature, and the Gothic novel. As with other Gale databases, documents can be translated through the site into a number of languages. The database gives the capability to generate citations in MLA or APA format and export to bibliographic support software.

The Twayne's Author Series database has similar features to those of the Scribner's Writers Series. The Twayne database includes *Twayne's English Authors, Twayne's U.S. Authors*, and *Twayne's World Authors*. Each of these resources gives literary criticism for about 200 authors. In the database, an author search results in a wide-ranging list of bibliographies, chronologies, critical discussions, and more, containing information on the author's works and literary career. The database also allows searches to be narrowed by genre, nationality, gender, time period, and more. Lists of related research topics and of authors writing on a particular topic are also provided. Both the Scribner's and Twayne's Authors Series are available independently or as an integrated, add-on module of the Literature Resource Center (entry 2-16), providing simultaneous searching of several Gale databases all at once. For those using libraries not subscribing to the Gale online series treated above indexing for all of the print and database series is in the free online database from Gale Cengage Learning, Gales' Literary Index (entry 2-14) at http://www.galenet.com/servlet/LitIndex.

5-10. Johns Hopkins Guide to Literary Theory and Criticism. Baltimore, MD: Johns Hopkins University Press. Online subscription database. http://litguide.press.jhu.edu

Compiled by 275 specialists from around the world and including more than 240 entries, this online subscription database provides a "comprehensive historical survey of the field's most important figures, schools, and movements." Some specific subjects include African-American feminist literary criticism, British New Left criticism, Classical literary criticism, literary criticism on fantasy fiction, historical novel criticism, modernist literature criticism, and gay literary criticism, among many others. This resource is updated annually to "reflect rapidly changing scholarship."

5-11. Oxford Reference Online Premium. Oxford University Press. Online subscription database. http://www.oxfordreference.com/pub/views/home.html

Oxford Reference Online Premium indexes many of Oxford's reference resources, including encyclopedias, dictionaries, companions, and guides (also entries 2-23, 4-23). Resources are for the humanities as well as social sciences and natural sciences. Oxford Reference Premium offers over 20 of the Oxford literature resources. The database also provides a cross-searchable language reference dictionary; subject reference for works published by Oxford University Press; and comprehensive links to other resources. The site provides a large amount of information on American, Canadian, English, and Irish literature as well as art and design topics. The database covers prominent writers, prose, literary magazines, publishers, poetry, and other topics. These books work like e-books indexed through the Oxford Reference Premium website. That is, each e-book is accessed individually. The organization of each resource is the same, arranged in alphabetical order. The website is very easy to use. Separate databases can be subscribed to by subject or topic. Many, but not all of the reference titles contained in the Reference Premium database are covered in this Guide. Examples of titles in the database are:

The Oxford Dictionary of Quotations

The Oxford Encyclopedia of American Literature (entry 5-32)

The Oxford Companion to Australian Literature

The Concise Oxford Companion to Irish Literature

The Oxford Dictionary of Literary Terms (entry 5-31)

The Oxford Encyclopedia of British Literature (entry 5-32)

The Oxford Dictionary of Phrase and Fable

The Oxford Dictionary of Science Fiction

The Oxford Companion to Shakespeare

The Oxford Companion to Twentieth-Century Poetry in English

5-12. Palgrave Connect: Literature and Performing Arts. Palgrave Macmillan, UK. Online subscription database. http://www.palgraveconnect.com/pc/collections/literatureperformingarts.html

Palgrave Connect is a site license to e-books published by Palgrave Macmillan (see also entry 2-44). The subscription database aggregates a number of Palgrave collections by subject. As a part of the Literature and Performing Arts collections, series include the New Middle Ages; Palgrave Studies: Nineteenth Century Writing and Culture; Palgrave Studies: Enlightenment, Romanticism and Cultures; Nineteenth Century Major Lives and Letters; and American Literary Readings in the Twenty-first Century, among others. The series and the e-books are also available separately.

Printed Resources

The majority of the entries in this section are printed works, but many are also available as e-books. A number of publishers' series are also included in this section.

5-13. An Author Index to Little Magazines of the Mimeograph Revolution. Christopher Harter. Metuchen, NJ: Scarecrow Press, 2008.

Approximately 100 little magazines published between 1959 and 1980 are indexed in this work. Over 500 authors are represented and 20,000 works indexed. As many poets and writers publish in small press and even more cheaply produced media, finding all of their works has always been a challenging task. This one volume index greatly facilitates the location of many well-hidden pieces of literature.

5-14. The Bedford Glossary of Critical and Literary Terms. 3rd ed. Ross Murfin and Supryia M. Ray. Boston: Bedford/St. Martin's Press, 2009.

This book does the basic job of defining terms used in literature and literary criticism. But unlike most works of its kind, there are unusual features that help explain the terms, such as contemporary examples drawn from movies, TV shows, and best sellers, some with illustrations. It even has a few examples in the way of cartoons by Matt Groening and Garry Trudeau to make a point. The work is authoritative and yet appeals to students.

5-15. Cambridge Guide to Literature in English. 3rd ed. Dominic Head. Cambridge, UK: Cambridge University Press, 2006.

This guide includes literary and non-literary authors who were important within the literary culture of their era, such as theologians, philosophers, scientists, and critics. The scope extends beyond the narrow confines of "English Literature" and includes many women writers, and non-British and non-American authors working in English around the world. Geographically, the work spans areas of the world in which English is a major language from Africa, Australia, Canada, Caribbean, India, New Zealand, South Pacific, the U.S., Ireland, and the United Kingdom. Entries are organized alphabetically into categories of literary works by format, literary groups or school, critical schools or movements, literary genres, poetic forms and sub-genres of drama and fiction, rhetorical terms, theatres, and literary magazines.

5-16. The Cambridge History of Twentieth-century English Literature. Laura Marcus and Peter Nicholls. Cambridge: Cambridge University Press, 2004.

This title is not intended as a reference work, but as a history for those interested in 20th century literature, its cultural context, and relation to the contemporary. The publisher describes it as "the first major history of 20th Century English literature to cover the complete range of writing in England, Scotland, Wales and Ireland." In addition, the work "explores the impact of writing from the former colonies on English literature of the period and analyzes the ways in which conventional literary genres were influenced by the technologies of radio, cinema and television." The information is organized into five chronological time periods: Pt. 1: Writing Modernity "traces Modernism in the pre-history of fin-de-siècle Decadence." Pt. 2: The emerging Avant-Garde is the "second phase of Modernism's pre-history." Pt. 3: Modernism and its aftermath, 1918–1945. Pt. 4: Post war cultures, 1945–1970, "investigates the role of writers and intellectuals in the projects of cultural reconstruction." Pt. 5: Towards the Millennium "explores literature and culture during the last 30 years of the 20th Century."

5-17. The Companion to Southern Literature: Themes, Genres, Places, People, Movements, and Motifs. J. M. Flora, L. H. MacKethan, and T. Taylor, trans. Baton Rouge, LA: Louisiana State University Press, 2001.

An encyclopedic approach to Southern literature, the Companion contains over 500 entries arranged alphabetically. The entries cover subjects as varied as people, movements, places, and genres, examining how each contributes to a better understanding of the literature of the American South. Unlike similar sources which focus primarily on Southern authors, this companion covers a considerably broader topic range.

5-18. Encyclopedia of Literature and Politics: Censorship, Revolution and Writing. M. Keith Booker, ed. Westport CT: Greenwood Press, 2005. 3 vols.

This encyclopedia has over 500 entries on authors and works ranging from ancient Greece to the present in its attempts to address the world history of literature related to politics. Entries include biographical information on authors and discussion of major works. Political theater, poetry, and newspapers/journals are also discussed. The work includes entries on genres as they relate to politics and information on important historical events and political movements with strong ties to literature. The focus is mostly on American and British writers, but writers and works from many other areas of the world are included.

5-19. Gale Contextual Encyclopedia of American Literature. Gale Cengage, 2009. 4 vols. Print and e-book.

This four-volume set is designed to give readers the context for greater understanding of the authors and literary works profiled. Biographical, historical, literary and critical information are presented to show the author's personal life and beliefs as well as events and the culture of the times in which they lived. Attention is paid to themes and literary devices that define a writer's style and place the author in a larger literary critical tradition. Suggested topics and questions make the set suitable for classroom use. As e-books they are fully searchable and can be cross-searched with other literature resources published by Gale.

5-20. A Glossary of Contemporary Literary Theory. 4th ed. Jeremy Hawthorn. New York: E. Arnold, 2001.

The appearance of the first edition of this scholarly work in 1992, along with the online *John Hopkins Guide to Literary Theory & Criticism* (entry 5-10), bears witness to the increased interest in the field regarding literary theory. Its revision and update only two years after publication was impressive. The focus of this work is theory not criticism because there has been much discussion of literary theory in recent years. Many of the terms in this work are not found in other literary dictionaries and therefore add to the value of the work. Entries vary in size from a few sentences to several pages on topics such as "modernism." It has no index but there are numerous cross-references. The work is most suitable for academic libraries with graduate programs in literature.

5-21. A Glossary of Literary Terms. 9th ed. M. H. Abrams and Geoffrey Galt Harpham. Boston: Wadsworth Cengage Learning, 2009.

The Glossary is an established reference work, begun by the distinguished critic and scholar M.H. Abrams. It has been recognized as an outstanding tool since its initial publication in 1957. The 9th edition represents a good revision, updating, and slight expansion of material. It continues the useful added feature of a separate section containing several articles examining important critical movements since the 1920s. This reference has good illustrations and a number of references to literary and critical material have been furnished. Rather than a list of entries with definitions, the work is more of a handbook, providing a series of essays bringing together related terms in the body of a textual narrative. An alphabetical index at the end facilitates access to the desired term and related passages. The work is clearly written, comprehensive in coverage, and well-developed stylistically and substantively, and is a valuable addition to the reference collection.

5-22. Greenwood Press Literary Masterpieces. Westport, CT: Greenwood Press. Monographic series. Print and e-books.

The individual volumes in this monographic series each focuses on a particular time, place, or genre as can be seen in the title list below. Each volume has an introductory essay "defining and giving an overview of the highlights and important contributions of the era or genre." Each of the volumes is organized chronologically. For authors, there is brief biographical background, plot synopses, thematic analyses and character development, literary style, and a summary of critical reception and interpretations of a single major work. Further reading lists include criticism, reviews, and other related works of fiction. The volumes both provide an overview of the period or movement and place the individual authors into the cultural milieu of the time. The volumes are available in print and as e-books.

Masterpieces of 20th-Century American Drama, 2005

Masterpieces of American Romantic Literature, 2006

Masterpieces of Beat Literature, 2006

Masterpieces of British Modernism, 2006

Masterpieces of Classic Greek Drama, 2005

Masterpieces of French Literature, 2004

Masterpieces of Jewish American Literature, 2007

Masterpieces of Modern British and Irish Drama, 2005

Masterpieces of Non-Western World Literature, 2007

Masterpieces of Philosophical Literature, 2006

5-23. A Handbook to Literature. 11th ed. Hugh Holman. Upper Saddle River, NJ: Pearson Prentice Hall, 2009. Print with companion website. http://www.prenhall.com/harmon

The Prentice-Hall Handbook has been a standard personal reference for students of literature at all levels for many years with such well known persons as Addison Hibbard, William Harmon, and William Flint Thrall formerly serving as editors. The work alphabetically lists over 2,000 literary terms. A companion website is maintained by the author that includes additional information including an interactive timeline of important literary and historical events, web links to Pulitzer and Nobel Prize-winning authors, and for teachers, flashcards to assist in studying important terms.

5-24. Literary Research Guide. James L. Harner. 5th ed. New York: Modern Language Association of America, 2006. Print. Online 2009– .

Literary Research Guide, published by the MLA, is a selective, annotated guide to reference sources, essential to the study of British literature, literature of the United States, other literature in English, and related topics. This guide evaluates important bibliographies, surveys of research, indexes, databases, catalogues, dictionaries, encyclopedias, handbooks and more. Also included are lists of major journals and background studies that are listed but not evaluated. The author has provided only what he characterizes as "reasonably thorough, accurate, effective, organized, and adequately indexed work." The information is organized into divisions for general literary reference works, national literatures, and topics or sources related to literature. Each division is further subdivided and each subdivision is classified by type of reference work. The Guide is aimed at college literature majors and graduate students. Although the Guide is online, literature majors may want printed copies.

5-25. Literary Research: Strategies and Sources. Landham, MD: Scarecrow Press. Monograph series. Print and e-book.

The works in this monograph series each focus on a particular period or national literature. The volumes are suitable for graduate and professional research, outlining the best strategies for research in a specialized area. Reference resources and databases are compared in a narrative style. A sampling of titles includes:

The American Modernist Era (2008)

British Modernism (2010)

The British Romantic Era (2005)

The Era of American Nationalism and Romanticism (2007)

Irish Literature (2009)

The Literatures of Australia and New Zealand (2010)

5-26. Magill's Survey of American Literature. Rev. ed. Steven G. Kellman, ed. Pasadena, CA: Salem Press, 2007. 6 vols.

An effort was made to cover even more minority and women writers in the revised edition of this title. The set contains profiles of major authors of fiction, drama, and poetry, each with sections on biography, general analysis, and analysis of the author's most important works: novels, short stories, poems, plays, and nonfiction. Given for each writer are birth and death data; a brief summary; biography; then an analysis of the writer's style, themes, and literary characteristics. The works are analyzed with a summary description and analysis and bibliography. Many entries include photographs and thumbnails of the book. Each volume in the series includes a glossary of literary terms and a list of all authors included in the set. A sidebar to each essay is called "Discussion Topics" with questions to encourage discussion. A handy aid is a pronunciation key that appears at the beginning of all six volumes.

5-27. The New York Public Library Literature Companion. Anne Skillion, ed. New York: The Free Press, 2001.

Intended as a desktop resource for literature, this work is divided into three sections: Creators, Works of Literature, and Literary Facts. The Creators section has brief biographies of authors, biographers, critics, editors, publishers, thinkers and translators, plus author awards. The Literature section has brief descriptions of novels, plays, poems, stories and essays, along with book awards, reading lists, and landmarks in literary censorship. Literary Facts includes brief descriptions of characters in literature, literary terms, and a chronology of world literature. Additional sources of information are provided such as websites for literature, bibliographies, and libraries that have significant literary holdings. While this work is valuable for quick reference, it is over 10 years since publication and websites and award lists may not be current.

Oxford University Press reference works—Oxford University Press publishes numerous companions, dictionaries, encyclopedias, and guides. The majority of these works are printed, but also indexed and available as e-books through Oxford Reference Online Premium (entries 2-23, 4-3), an online subscription database (http://www.oxfordreference.com/pub/views/home.html). A number of Oxford reference titles in literature are separately treated here in entries 5-28 through 5-34.

5-28. Oxford Chronology of English Literature. Michael Cox, ed. Oxford: Oxford University Press, 2002. 2 vols.

The two volumes of this work cover 1474 through 2000, from the first book printed in England by William Caxton, to J.K. Rowling's work. One of the chief accomplishments of the Chronology is to place works into a context of time and place with other notable writings. Within each year, the entries are alphabetical by author's name and dates, followed by the type of the work, e.g., fiction, non-fiction, poetry, and so forth. For each work, the main title, other title page elements, the imprint, and a note on the publishing history of the work, comprise the entry. The author index gives the author's dates, his/her genre, and a list of works with publication dates. The title index provides the author's names and date of publication. There is also an index for translated authors. While any such compilation cannot be comprehensive, the aim is to include works from every period "whose influence has been decisive and permanent." The Chronology is a good purchase for all libraries serving students of literature.

5-29. The Oxford Companion to English Literature. 7th ed. Dinah Birch, ed. Oxford: Oxford University Press, 2009. Print and e-book.

This revision of the 6th edition (2000) has more than 1,000 new entries. Four introductory essays precede the entries which range from short to more extensive treatment of major figures. The entries contain plot summaries and information on literary works, authors, themes, archetypes, journals, and forms. Concepts are clearly explained for those not immersed in literary jargon. Appendices include a chronology, lists of literary awards, and a list of the revised entries with authors. Also, the *Concise Oxford Companion to English Literature* (2nd ed., 2003), edited by Margaret Drabble and Jenny Stringer, based upon the 6th edition of the *Companion to English Literature*, is available. The concise works are more suitable for personal libraries than the larger editions.

5-30. **The Oxford Concise Companion to Canadian Literature.** 2nd ed. William Toye. Oxford: Oxford University Press, 2011.

The Concise Companion is the most up-to-date Oxford reference work on Canadian literature. The first edition was based upon the critically acclaimed *Oxford Companion to Canadian Literature*, published in 1998, of which William Toye was general editor. This second concise edition has been fully updated and contains over 900 entries covering major writers, significant works, awards, genre surveys, and other aspects of the Canadian literary scene, past and present.

5-31. **Oxford Dictionary of Literary Terms.** 3rd ed. Chris Baldick. New York: Oxford University Press, 2009. Print in paperback, with companion website.

With over 1,200 entries the 3rd edition has been updated and expanded to include "increased coverage of new terms from modern critical and theoretical movements, such as feminism, and schools of American poetry, Spanish verse forms, life writing, and crime fiction." The dictionary also includes coverage of traditional drama, versification, rhetoric, and literary history, as well as recommended further readings and a pronunciation guide to more than 200 troublesome terms. The companion website keeps web links up-to-date and active. In addition to being a standard reference tool, the paperback edition is easily affordable for the personal library.

5-32. **The Oxford Encyclopedia of American Literature.** Jay Parini, ed. Oxford: Oxford University Press, 2004.

The Oxford Encyclopedia of American Literature contains 350 essays from the leading scholars in the field, spanning the range of American literary history from the seventeenth century to the present. Essays on poets, playwrights, novelists, and significant American works are among the entries. Additionally, essays on literary movements, periods, and themes provide historical perspective and social context.

5-33. **The Oxford Encyclopedia of British Literature.** David Scott Kastan, ed. Oxford: Oxford University Press, 2006. 5 vols.

This five-volume set is a collection of over 500 substantial articles, arranged alphabetically, that cover the entire history of British Literature in English. The set focuses on the writers, conventions, and institutions of the United Kingdom and the Republic of Ireland. It does not include writing in English for American, Canadian, or South African writers. The majority of entries focus on authors, but some consider particular themes, movements, genres, or institutions "whose impact on the writing or reading of literature has been significant." Articles are listed in chronological order and include selective bibliographies of relevant primary and secondary sources. An index, at the end of volume 5, lists all the topics covered in the Encyclopedia. The work was a RUSA Outstanding Reference Sources selection in 2007.

5-34. **Oxford Guide to Literary Britain and Ireland.** 3rd ed. Daniel Hahn and Nicholas Robins, ed. Oxford: Oxford University Press, 2008.

First published in 1977, this Guide is a gazetteer of almost 2,000 places including villages, towns, cities, and landscapes in Britain and Ireland detailing their connections with the lives of famous writers. The organization is by regions of England and then by country for Wales, Scotland, and Ireland. For the first time, entries are included for living writers. The entries interweave information with anecdotes and quotations to create a vivid picture of the day-to-day lives of the writers. New to this edition are special feature entries on writers associated with particular places, including the Brontes, Walter Scott, and James Joyce, contributed by such well-known authors as Margaret Drabble and John Sutherland. The Guide also provides an index of author names, with mini biographies, enabling the reader to track down all the places associated with their favorite writers. The Guide is an ideal resource and companion for any literary pilgrimage in Britain or Ireland or for the armchair literary traveler.

5-35. The Routledge Dictionary of Literary Terms. 2nd ed. Peter Childs and Roger Fowler, ed. New York: Routledge, 2006.

The Routledge Dictionary is a new title based on the revised edition of the 1987 publication of *A Dictionary of Modern Critical Terms*, edited by Roger Fowler. This is an important and unique work due to the depth of coverage it gives to terms associated with modern literary criticism. Definitions are provided through thorough accounts of critical terminology and analyses of contemporary academic debates in essay-length articles. The history and significance of such terms as *cybercriticism* and *globalization* are traced as well as their relationship to modern criticism; and topics such as post structuralism, feminist criticism, and Marxist criticism are examined in-depth.

5-36. Social Issues in Literature. Detroit, MI: Greenhaven Press, Gale Cengage, Inc. Monographic series.

Political or social issues are prominent in many of the masterpieces of literature. Each book in this Greenhaven Press series examines the role that a given social issue plays in one author's major work or body of work. The series has an interdisciplinary perspective focused on "the intersection between literature and sociology." The format for each book has the initial three chapters beginning with biographical and critical information about the author, emphasizing the influences upon that author. Next is a chapter in which the relationship between the work and the social issue it explores is examined. The final chapter looks at the social issue from a contemporary perspective, assessing its significance in society today. Each book also includes: a timeline of the author's life; a Further Reading section that suggests other works on the same social issue; a bibliography of books, periodicals, and websites on that issue; and a subject index. A selective list of the titles gives an idea of the breadth of coverage of the series:

Bioethics in Mary Shelley's *Frankenstein*, 2010

Censorship in Ray Bradbury's *Fahrenheit 45*, 2011

Gender in Lorraine Hansberry's *A Raisin in the Sun*, 2010

Mental Illness in Ken Kesey's *One Flew Over the Cuckoo's Nest*, 2010

Politics in George Orwell's *Animal Farm*, 2010

Social and Psychological Disorder in the Works of Edgar Allan Poe, 2010

Tyranny in William Shakespeare's *Julius Caesar*, 2010

Women's Issues in Alice Walker's *The Color Purple*, 2011

Bioethics in Aldous Huxley's *Brave New World*, 2010

Civil Rights in Richard Wright's *Native Son*, 2009

Colonialism in Chinua Achebe's *Things Fall Apart* , 2010

The Environment in Henry David Thoreau's *Walden*, 2010

> Genocide in Elie Wiesel's *Night,* 2009
>
> Male/Female Roles in Ernest Hemingway's *The Sun Also Rises,* 2008
>
> Patriarchy in Sandra Cisneros's *The House on Mango Street,* 2010
>
> Political Issues in J. K. Rowling's Harry Potter Series, 2009
>
> Racism in Harper Lee's *To Kill a Mockingbird,* 2008
>
> Women's Issues in Amy Tan's *The Joy Luck Club,* 2008
>
> Worker's Rights in Upton Sinclair's *The Jungle,* 2008

5-37. Traveling Literary America: A Complete Guide to Literary Landmarks. B. J. Wellborn. Jefferson Press, dist. Independent Publishers Group, 2005. http://www.ipgbook.com

Information and directions to historic sites connected with American authors are contained in this work. Additional information includes other places of interest such as bookstores and libraries near the sites covered.

5-38. Twayne Companion to Contemporary Literature in English from the Editors of the Hollins Critic. R.H.W. Dillard and Amanda Cockrell, eds. New York: Twayne Publishers, 2002. 2 vols.

The Hollins Critic is published at Hollins University in Roanoke, Virginia, where an internationally famous writers-in-residence program is based. The journal runs critical essays of contemporary writers with complete checklists of their works. The contents of this two-volume set are revised and contain updated essays on approximately 100 writers of poetry and fiction from the latter half of the 20th century.

Open Access Resources

Prior to commercial publishers entering the field of online reference, a number of websites were developed to give free access to full texts and information on literary authors. A few of the best sites that have stood the test of time are briefly reviewed in this section.

5-39. A Bibliography of Literary Theory, Criticism and Philology.
http://www.unizar.es/departamentos/filologia inglesa/garciala/bibliography.html

This is a bibliography of literary studies, criticism and philology, listing well over 150,000 items–books, book chapters, articles, films, websites, and so forth, with a main focus on English-speaking authors and criticism or literary theory written in English, although there are many listings on linguistics, cultural studies, discourse analysis, and other philological subjects.

5-41. Luminarum: Anthology of English Literature. http://www.luminarium.org/

Luminarum combines several sites first created in 1996 to provide a starting point for students and enthusiasts of English literature. The site is not affiliated with any institution nor is it sponsored by anyone other than its maintainer. The information in this site, including authors, essays and articles, and additional resources, are organized by time periods:

> Middle English Literature (1350–1485) http://www.luminarium.org/medlit/
>
> 16th Century Renaissance (1485–1603) http://www.luminarium.org/renlit/
>
> Early 17th Century (1603–1660) http://www.luminarium.org/sevenlit/
>
> Restoration and 18th Century (1660–1785) http://www.luminarium.org/eightlit/

In addition, there are sections dedicated to religious writers, Renaissance drama, and 17th century poets.

5-42. Literary Resources on the Net. Jack Lynch, ed. Newark, NJ: Rutgers. 2005– . http://andromeda.rutgers.edu/~jlynch/Lit/

Resources for all major time periods in literary history: e.g. Classical, Medieval, Romantic, Victorian, and so forth, are covered on this site. It also covers women's literature and the history of the book. Each section includes bibliographies, dictionaries, periodicals, sub-genres, and journals. This reference holds a plethora of information within these pages.

5-43. The Literary Encyclopedia. http://www.litencyc.com/

This is an expanding global literary reference work written by over 1,800 specialists from universities around the world. It currently provides more than 4,800 authoritative profiles of authors, works, and literary and historical topics. The site grows by over 60 articles per month. It also lists more than 21,000 works by date, country, and genre.

5-44. The Modern Word. http://www.themodernword.com/default.aspx

The Modern Word website includes information about experimental twentieth century authors, such as Pynchon, Kafka, Joyce and others. Searchable through an index of authors, the website also contains biographies, reviews, interviews, literary criticism and essays. The website is valuable for information about innovative authors as well as more mainstream writers.

5-45. The Online Books Page. http://onlinebooks.library.upenn.edu/

This resource facilitates access to full texts of books that are available over the Internet by providing links for each work. Titles are listed in sections by Library of Congress call numbers. The titles listed are mounted on a vast variety of websites. The site both organizes the titles by subject so that the user gets listings by subject and provides a direct link to an electronic copy.

5-46. PAL: Perspectives in American Literature–A Research and Reference Guide.
http://www.csustan.edu/English/reuben/home.htm

The Perspectives in American Literature (PAL) guide is maintained by California State University professor Paul P. Reuben. The project began as a book, but is now available online. The guide is divided into chapters and appendices. It is free, quite easy to use, and is updated regularly. The resource covers American literature from 1700 to the late twentieth century. The appendices include selected bibliographies on poetry, fiction, folklore, and drama, as well as literary history. The resource also provides an alphabetical listing of 452 American authors. Each of these pages includes a brief biography, a list of primary works, and a selected bibliography

5-47. Virtual salt. www.virtualsalt.com/litterms.htm

Common literary terms used in fiction are listed along with their definitions. For each term there is an example of a fictional work in which the term is used or applied.

5-48. Yahoo! Directory: Arts & Humanities: Humanities: Literature
http://dir.yahoo.com/Arts/Humanities/Literature/

This site is an online guide to Web-based sources. It is a catalog of sites created by a staff of editors who visit and evaluate web sites, and then organize them into subject-based categories and sub-categories including Literature.

Major Organizations

5-49. Modern Language Association of America. http://www.mla.org

Founded in 1883, the MLA is the oldest, largest, and best known of the organizations in the U.S. that promote the study and teaching of languages and literatures. It has more than 30,000 members, in 100 countries, primarily university or college teachers. The MLA conducts an immense range of programs and activities. The MLA International Bibliography, covered in detail in chapter 2, is among the world's most important bibliographic resources covering drama, English, folklore, foreign languages, humanities, language, linguistics, and literature (entries 2-20, 6-3). Other publications include the journal PMLA (quarterly) and Job Information Lists in both English and Foreign Language versions available on the Web. An important contribution of the Association is its style manual, available in high school and scholar's versions, and also on the Web (entry 2-94).

5-50. The American Comparative Literature Association. http://www.acla.org

The American Comparative Literature Association is the principal learned society in the United States for scholars whose work involves several literatures and cultures. It promotes the study and teaching of comparative literature in American universities, cosponsors the Yearbook of Comparative and General Literature, and maintains a list of links to Web sites concerned with comparative literature.

5-51. British Comparative Literature Association (BCLA). http://www.bcla.org/

Founded in 1975, BCLA aims to "promote the scholarly study of literature without confinement to national and linguistic boundaries, and in relation to other disciplines."

5-52. American Literature Association.
http://www.calstatela.edu/academic/english/ala2/intro.html

The American Literature Association was founded in 1989 as a coalition of societies devoted to the study of American authors. The major activity of the American Literature Association is its annual conference, providing opportunities for scholarly interaction.

5-53. African Literature Association. http://www.africanlit.org/

The African Literature Association, founded in 1975, publishes the *Journal of the African Literature Association* (JALA) and its ALA Newsletter.

5-54. Council of Literary Magazines and Presses. http://www.clmp.org/about/index.html

The Council of Literary Magazines and Presses "serves one of the most active segments of American arts and culture: the independent publishers of exceptional fiction, poetry and prose. Literary magazines and presses accomplish the backstage work of American literature: discovering new writers; supporting mid-career writers; publishing the creative voices of communities underrepresented in the mainstream commercial culture; and preserving literature for future readers by keeping books in print." The Council assists "little magazines" in a variety of ways, including the website that has links to many small presses.

5-55. The Electronic Literature Organization (ELO). http://eliterature.org/

The ELO was founded in 1999 "to foster and promote the reading, writing, teaching, and understanding of literature as it develops and persists in a changing digital environment." Membership of the ELO includes writers, artists, teachers, scholars, and developers. The organization maintains the *Electronic Literature Directory* (entry 2-49) for open source, semantic web-based development, and an Electronic Literature Awards program that recognizes exemplary works of poetry and fiction.

FICTION
Databases and Digital Collections

5-56. Early American Fiction, 1789–1875. Ann Arbor, MI: Proquest. Licensed or purchased database. http://www.proquest.com

The contents of Early American Fiction, 1789–1875 are based upon two standard bibliographies: *The Bibliography of American Literature (BAL)* (entry 5-3) and *Lyle H. Wright's American Fiction 1774–1850.* The collection began with a microform collection published by Research Publications and later digitized by Chadwyck-Healey. This collection incorporates the contents of the Chadwyck-Healey collection based upon the Wright bibliography and extends the coverage up to 1875, adding more than 300 additional titles and over 50 new authors. The collection was sponsored by the Andrew W. Mellon Foundation and the University of Virginia Library and published in collaboration with the University of Virginia. Early American Fiction 1789–1875 contains the full text of more than 730 first editions of American novels and short stories by such authors as Louisa May Alcott, Herman Melville, Harriet Beecher Stowe and Mark Twain, as well as minor writers of the period. Not typical of many digital collections, the pages of the texts are available in full color, enabling the viewer to see details of the originals such as their illustrations, typography, bindings, design, and construction. The collection will most likely be found in research libraries serving graduate programs in American literature.

5-57. Early English Prose Fiction. Ann Arbor, MI: Proquest. Licensed or purchased database. http://www.proquest.com

The "Early English" period in this case is defined as "those writings before the inauguration of the fiction novel in the 18th century." This digital collection has more than 200 works from the period 1500–1700, a larger number than one might expect for a time period in which religion and politics occupied much of the printed output. Included in the collection are the full text of works by key writers such as John Bunyan, Sir Philip Sidney, Thomas Nashe, and Aphra Behn. The collection has been produced in association with the Salzburg Centre for Research on the Early English Novel (SCREEN).

The Eighteenth Century Fiction collection, also a subscription database from Proquest, continues with 96 works by writers from the British Isles from 1700 to 1780. Both of these collections will most likely be found in research libraries serving graduate programs in literature.

Printed Resources

Many major publishers and university presses have companion or guides series for literary criticism. A few of these are represented in this section. These works are not reference works, but collections of critical essays that explicate the authors and their works in the political, literary, and social milieu of the period. The reader can use the information in these entries to search for similar titles in the respective series.

5-58. The Cambridge Companion to the Twentieth Century English Novel. Robert Caserio, ed. Cambridge UK: Cambridge University Press, 2009. Print and e-book (Cambridge Companions to Literature).

The history and development of the novel in Britain in the twentieth century are traced in this work. Since the twentieth century is usually divided into two halves separated by World War II, 17 of the topical essays "aim to unite pre-1945 fiction with that which followed." As well as various chronological periods (Edwardian and Georgian, the Great War, the 1920s and 1930s, World War II and the post-war years), the essays discuss the role of the Empire, regionalism, the role and importance of Ireland, feminism, working-class fiction, the importance of history in fiction, postmodernism, detective and spy books, the 'post-consensus novel,' minority cultures in English fiction, the different types of satire, and finally the role of fantasy, romance, horror and science fiction. The work is an example of others in the Cambridge Companions to Literature series.

5-59. The Columbia Companion to the Twentieth-century American Short Story. Blanche H. Gelfant, ed. New York: Columbia University Press, 2001. Print and e-book.

The essays in this critical work are divided into two parts. Part 1 concentrates upon stories that share a particular theme, such as Working Class Stories or Gay and Lesbian Stories. The larger portion of the book is Part 2, which contains more than 100 entries on individual writers and their work. In addition to well-known authors, promising new writers at the end of the century are covered. There are not many reference works devoted to the short story. This one is recommended for undergraduates and public libraries.

5-60. A Companion to the Victorian Novel. Patrick Brantlinger and William B. Thesing, eds. Boston: Blackwell Publishers, 2005. Print and e-book. (Blackwell's Companions to Literature and Culture).

The novel became the prime literary reading for the Victorians, from the intellectual classes to the working classes. The era produced the Brontes, Dickens, Eliot, Hardy, Scott, and Thackeray, among others. This work has 26 essays written by "renowned and emerging scholars in the field of Victorian studies." The first section on Historical Contexts and Cultural Issues provides overviews of key historical contexts, such as religion, class, gender, and the publishing world. The second section, Forms of the Victorian Novel, surveys the various genres and subgenres of the Victorian novel: the Newgate Novel, Sensation Novel, industrial novel, children's fiction, and science fiction, among others. The third section deals with Victorian, modern, and postmodern theories of the novel and looks at how Victorian novels and novelists were critically received, both then and now. Each chapter has bibliographies with recommendations for further reading, and there is a detailed index.

Two other similar collections of essays were published around the same time. *The Cambridge Companion to the Victorian Novel* (2001) and *A Companion to the Victorian Novel,* issued by Greenwood Press (2002). Another in the Blackwell series is *Companion to the Eighteenth-century Novel and Culture* edited by Paula R. Backscheider and Catherine Ingrassia (2005).

5-61. Facts on File Companion to the American Short Story. Abby H.P. Werlock. 2nd ed. New York: Infobase Publishing/Facts on File, 2009. 2 vols. Print and e-book.

According to the publisher, this work is one of the few devoted to the short story and to analyze the genre as a whole with coverage from the beginnings of the short story in the early 19th century to the present. This updated edition has hundreds of new entries for major Canadian, classic American writers, and individual stories, with modern and current writers emphasized. The entries include brief author biographies, synopses of individual stories, and topics. An informative introduction "surveys the history of the short story in the United States, interprets the current literary landscape, and points to new and future trends." A bibliography, list of prize-winners, thematic index, and cross-references complete the set. The work is suitable for students from high school through undergraduate work.

5-62. Novel & Short Story Writer's Market. Cincinnati: Writer's Digest Books. Ann. Print and online.

Novel & Short Story Writer's Market is an annual print publication with the contents also online in Writersmarket.com (entry 2-97). In addition to the annual, Writer's Digest publishes many monographs on various aspects of writing, selling, and publishing, including separate titles for genre fiction. As with others of the Writer's Market titles, in this one there are listings for over 1,100 book publishers, magazines, literary agents, writing contests and conferences, each containing current contact information, editorial needs, schedules and guidelines that save writers time and "take the guesswork out of the submission process." Also in this work are more than 100 pages of listings for literary journals and another 100 pages of fiction book publishers. The Writer's guide also features original interviews with working editors and writers, how-to's on the craft of fiction, and articles on the business of getting published. Purchase of the print edition includes online access to Novel & Short Story Writer's Market, part of WritersMarket.com.

Salem Press publishes the Magill's critical series as well as the Masterplots series. All of the Magill critical works for fiction are gathered below in entries 5-63 through 5-67, except those for world authors in chapter six. These works are also contained in the MagillOnLiterature Plus database (entry 2-30).

5-63. Magill's Critical Survey of Long Fiction, 4th ed. Carl Rollyson, ed. Salem Press, 2010. 10 vols.

5-64. Critical Survey of Short Fiction. 2nd rev. ed. Charles E. May, ed. Pasadena, CA: Salem Press: 2001. 7 vols.

5-65. Short Story Writers, rev. ed. Charles May, ed. Salem Press, 2007. 3 vols.

The Magill's sets began with literary criticism and that is what they are best known for. These three sets are all revisions and are typically described as the entries having been reviewed and revised with new entries added. They are all organized alphabetically by author with basic information such as dates and places of birth and death. For each author, there is a list of works. The main portion of the profile is an Analysis section that "describes the author's work and examines it in terms of themes, typical concerns, characters, and motifs using the author's works to illustrate these themes." The Further Readings section has "authoritative, up-to-date resources." Many of the literary criticism sets are made up of entries pulled from larger sets upon the same subject with newer entries added and different titles as is noted in the entries here below.

 According to the publisher's description, the 4th edition of Magill's *Critical Survey of Long Fiction* expands the set to 10 volumes covering literary fiction from over 60 countries and from the tenth century to the twenty-first. "Women writers comprise half of the new authors and many authors with works in English translation are included for the first time." Volume 10 contains a general bibliography; a timeline; a list of Major Awards; a chronological list of authors; and Category, Geographical, and General Subject Indexes. This is one of the largest of the critical sets and can suffice for smaller library collections instead of numerous publications for the same coverage.

 The second edition of the *Critical Survey of Short Fiction* received an ALA/RUSA Outstanding Reference Source designation. Volume 7 contains "29 topical essays devoted to theory, history, subgenres, and world cultures (including ethnic groups both within and outside of the U.S.)." The final volume also includes an Awards section for The Best American Short Stories, the O. Henry Awards, and other honors.

 Short Story Writers is drawn from Salem Press's *Critical Survey of Short Fiction* and includes the "most frequently studied and researched short fiction writers." The new edition adds 44 more articles and covers 146 authors and 800 works reflecting the "range and diversity of nineteenth and twentieth century short-story writing." Twenty-one new women authors were added to this edition. Libraries that own the *Critical Survey of Short Fiction* may choose not to own both titles, but smaller libraries may choose this three-volume set.

5-66. **Notable American Novelists,** rev. ed. Carl Rollyson, ed. Salem Press, 2007. 3 vols.

5-67. **Notable British Novelists.** Carl Rollyson, ed. Salem Press, 2001. 3 vols.

The essays in the 2007 revised edition of *Notable American Novelists* first appeared in the first edition of *Notable American Novelists* and in the 2nd edition (2000) of *Critical Survey of Long Fiction*. Both American and Canadian writers of long fiction from the 19th and 20th centuries are included. A range of genres and styles are represented. Beat writers and a number of writers from such disparate genres as detective fiction and science fiction are included. In addition, the "diversity of the American experience is also represented in African American writers, Hispanic authors, American Indian novelists, Jewish writers, and Chinese American novelists."

Notable British Novelists consists of entries for the best-known and most studied English, Scottish, and Irish writers of long fiction from the fifteenth century through the twentieth, with a wide range of genres and styles represented. This three-volume set is made up of a combination of new and updated essays from the *Critical Survey of Long Fiction*, *Second Revised Edition* (2000). The set examines the works most often studied in high school and undergraduate literature classes.

GENRE AND READER'S ADVISORY

In the library literature and in practice, genre and reader's advisory are inextricably linked. While encompassing mostly various genres of fiction, the definition of *genre* has become very broad and also sometimes includes ethnic and gender literature. It is important for librarians to understand genre fiction in order to be able to meet readers' preferences. In recent years, attention to reader's advisory has intensified and there have been numerous guides published for librarians dealing with reader's advisory and genre fiction. Publishers have inaugurated new series and there has been growing attention paid to genre fiction in high schools and university courses. Also several databases are now available for both librarians and readers that are constantly updated with reviews, lists of recommendations, blogs, and other value added services.

The traditional genres are eight types of popular fiction: Adventure, Crime Fiction, Fantasy, Historical Fiction, Horror, Romance, Science Fiction, and Westerns. More recently new genres have emerged such as Christian Fiction, Chick Lit, and Street Lit/Urban Fiction. Another kind of genre is narrative non-fiction, which tells a story while blending fiction with fact. Also included are those books that blend more than one genre, termed *cross-genre fiction*. These pose problems for librarians in classification and shelving as to where to assign a title. This information is culled from a useful article in the *Encyclopedia of Library and Information Sciences* (3rd ed.), "Popular Literature Genres," by Barry Trott (2009, 4242–4250).

Genre fiction books have generally been shelved separately from literary fiction within library organizational schema and also generally not classified in public libraries. As genre has become broader and inclusive of other categories than popular fiction, problems have arisen in organization and management. The growing popularity of genre books has also led to databases to assist with the workload of providing reader's advisory services.

The entries in this section concentrate on the traditional genres of fiction. The organization places reader's advisory databases first, followed by general print sources, and then open access resources. After the general resources, there are sections by specialized genres that include both print and electronic resources.

Databases

Several publishers offer online reader's advisory databases, which are aimed at librarians, but are also suitable for readers to utilize. It is likely that readers will find at least one of the following databases offered by their local library.

5-68. Books & Authors. Gale Cengage Learning, Inc. Online subscription database.

Formerly "What Do I Read Next?" the Books & Authors database is a one-stop destination for readers, RA librarians, and book clubs. The genres included in the Books & Authors database are fantasy fiction, historical fiction, horror stories, inspirational fiction, mystery fiction, popular romance, science fiction, and western fiction. Users can browse to select books by genre, titles, authors, best sellers, award winners, and recommended lists. Searching by author results include, birth date, awards, personal information, career, writings, and more. Title results give plot summaries, main characters, setting, subjects, reviews, author information, Read-a-likes, and recommendations for further reading. There are features for users, such as their own personal reading room and user communities. Searching is menu driven and the user can be guided through a "Who? What? Where? When?" feature that helps discover books by graphing results from answering the questions. Search limiters can also help narrow results. American or Canadian best seller lists and lists of award-winning books are included as well as lists of recommended titles compiled by reader's advisory experts.

5-69. NoveList. EBSCO. Online subscription database. http://www.ebsco.com

NoveList is a database designed to be an aid to librarians for reader's advisory services to adults, teens, and younger readers. According to the publisher's description, the database provides access to information on 155,000 fiction titles, over 60,000 being juvenile fiction records. The database goes beyond just records for fiction titles and has several built-in features which make it suitable for teachers and readers including curriculum-driven material designed to help integrate NoveList into the classroom. The Reader's Advisory section includes RA training, NoveList newsletters, Genre Outlines, hundreds of reading lists, book talks, and feature articles by notable librarians and subject matter experts. Lists of award titles and recommended reading lists by genres and topics are included. The database has an easy to use interface with a single search bar. Results can be sorted by popularity and/or Lexile scores. Records can be linked to a library catalog, making it easy to find a desired title in the local library. Several different customized versions of NoveList can be subscribed to including NoveList Plus and NoveList K-8 and K-8 Plus.

5-70. The Reader's Advisor Online. Santa Barbara, CA: Libraries Unlimited/ABC-CLIO. Online subscription database.

The Reader's Advisor Online was begun with Libraries Unlimited's *Genreflecting* monograph series (entry 5-71). The purpose and scope of the database were broadened and it not only contains all of the volumes in the Genereflecting series, but also essays from other Libraries Unlimited publications, *The Readers' Advisor's Companion,* and more. The database covers over 400 genres, subgenres, and reading interests, fiction and nonfiction. Titles included are based upon recommendations of experts in reader's advisory. A number of features are included such as "Read-Alike Quick list" and searches for suitable titles for book groups. Titles recommended can be linked to the library catalog to take the user right to local bibliographic records to make finding the book easy. The publisher maintains "The Reader's Advisor Online Blog" which is updated bi-weekly on important reader's advisory issues. The blog includes This Week's Hottest Fiction, Hitting the Shelves, In the News, RA Tips and Online Product News, list of authors, and more.

Printed Resources

5-71. Genreflecting Advisory Series. Diana Tixier Herald, ed. Santa Barbara, CA: Libraries Unlimited/ABC-CLIO. Print and online. Monographic series.

Libraries Unlimited's Genreflecting Advisory Series features a number of titles covering various areas of world literature. These titles are included in the Reader's Advisor Online database profiled above (5-70). The books in this series are written from the "reading interest" point of view. Although some of the volumes treat traditional popular reading genres, other volumes treat a theme so that within that theme, more than one of the traditional genres can be represented (see list below). Each volume covers about 700 titles and has sections on collection development, reader's advisory, and publishers specializing in that area of literature. Each volume also includes lists of award winners and relevant journals and databases for that subject. Entries are arranged by genre and each section begins with an overview of the genre and how it has been addressed in that particular field of literature. Entries provide the title of the work, the author(s), the publisher, year and place of publication, plot summaries, subject keywords, and any awards won. Some volumes flag entries of potential interest to YAs. Volumes are indexed by author, by title, and by subject. They are also excellent tools for acquisitions and collection development. A selection of titles published in the series, but not separately treated in this guide, is listed here:

> *Blood, Bedlam, Bullets, and Badguys: A Reader's Guide to Adventure/Suspense Fiction*, 2004
>
> *Canadian Fiction: A Guide to Reading Interests*, 2005
>
> *Caught Up In Crime: A Reader's Guide to Crime Fiction and Nonfiction*, 2009
>
> *Christian Fiction: A Guide to the Genre*, 2002
>
> *Fluent in Fantasy: The Next Generation*, 2006
>
> *Genrefied Classics: A Guide to Reading Interests in Classic Literature*, 2006
>
> *Graphic Novels: A Genre Guide to Comic Books, Manga, and More*, 2006
>
> *Jewish American Literature: A Guide to Reading Interests*, 2004
>
> *Latino Literature: A Guide to Reading Interests*, 2009
>
> *Nonfiction Reader's Advisory*, 2004
>
> *The Real Story: A Guide to Nonfiction Reading Interests*, 2006
>
> *Romance Fiction: A Guide to the Genre*, 2nd ed., 2011

The Read On . . . series from Libraries Unlimited also has titles that relate to genre. The next two entries are titles from the Genreflecting Advisory Series.

5-72. Genreflecting: A Guide to Popular Reading Interests. 6th ed. Diana Tixier Herald and Wayne A. Wiegand. Westport, CT: Libraries Unlimited, 2006. Print and online. (Genreflecting Advisory Series)

The popularity and wide acceptance of this guide is evident in that this is the sixth edition of the text. More than 5,000 titles are listed by genre. This edition has new chapters on Christian fiction and emerging genres.

5-73. Now Read This: A Guide to Mainstream Fiction, 1978–1998. Nancy Pearl. Englewood, CO: Libraries Unlimited, 1999. Print and online. (Genreflecting Advisory Series)

Now Read This II: A Guide to Mainstream Fiction, 1990–2001. Nancy Pearl. Englewood, CO: Libraries Unlimited, 2002. Print and online. (Genreflecting Advisory Series)

Now Read This III: A Guide to Mainstream Fiction. Nancy Pearl and Sarah Statz Cords. Santa Barbara, CA: Libraries Unlimited/ABC-CLIO, 2010. Print and online. (Genreflecting Advisory Series)

These guides to mainstream fiction have become a series within the Genereflecting Advisory series and the standard in reader's advisory. The stated purpose in the first volume is that the book "provides a method of understanding by what criteria a reader judges a novel and therefore makes it easier to recommend titles that fit those criteria." The third in the series describes 500 of the most popular works published since 2000, all new to the series. The distinguishing characteristic of these guides is the "Now Try" recommendations that are purposely aimed "at mid-list and lesser known award-winning titles that may not have come to readers' attention." For each entry there are suggestions for further reading based upon the elements of settings, plot, character, and other features that readers liked about that title. Each volume in the series contains lists of award winning books, indications of titles appropriate for young adult readers, and author/title indexes.

5-74. The Best American Novels of the Twentieth Century Still Readable Today. Eleanor Gehres. Golden, CO: Fulcrum Publishing, 2001.

The 150 novels from the twentieth century reviewed in this book are the personal choices of Gehres, former Director of the Denver Public Library's Western History Department. Many of them are award winners, but one of Gehres' criteria was that "the book should still be a good read today." The worth of the book lies in the reviews of the books, as the majority of the entries are modern classics. The titles are grouped by decade, with a list of important historical events leading off each chapter, followed by a short synopsis and the review. The book is suitable for readers in public libraries, book clubs, and school libraries.

5-75. The Novel 100: A Ranking of the Greatest Novels of All Time. Daniel S. Burt. New York: Facts on File, 2003.

Burt's choices are based upon his definition of a great novel as one that "has defined or modified the genre and remained influential over time." Thus, not unexpectedly, the majority are nineteenth and twentieth century works from Western countries. The selections are diverse, however, with regard to gender, race, and ethnicity. This reference also offers a list of 100 "honorable mentions," which doubles the number of titles covered. The work is interesting to read and could be used for class or book club discussion.

5-76. 100 Most Popular Genre Fiction Authors. Bernard A. Drew. Littleton, CO: Libraries Unlimited, 2005.

In addition to having favorite genres, readers also have favorite authors and look for information about them. Authors from all major genres (mystery/detective, crime, adventure/suspense, thriller, horror, fantasy, science fiction, western, historical, women's, and romance) are profiled in this work. In addition to information about the personal and writing lives there is a complete list of the author's published works, fiction and nonfiction. Many of the profiles also have black and white photos. The work is suitable for adults and YAs.

5-77. The Reader's Advisory Guide to Genre Fiction. Joyce Saricks. Chicago: American Library Association, 2009. Print and e-book.

Readers tend to have a favorite type of character, setting, or storyline. These "appeal characteristics" are reflected in the four divisions of this guide: Adrenaline, which includes adventure, suspense and thrillers; Emotions, which has gentle reads, romance, and women's lives; Intellect, which is comprised of literary fiction, mysteries, and science fiction; and Landscape genres, which include fantasy, westerns, and historical fiction. The guide also suggests lists of genre characteristics and provides additional author referrals.

Another ALA work is the *Readers' Advisory Handbook* by Jessica E. Moyer and Katie Mediatore Stover (2010). Unlike most of the reader's advisory books for the librarian, this one includes information on more than just finding appropriate titles for readers' needs. From reading in 10 minutes to assess a book, to writing reviews, to marketing, collection development, programming, and managing selectors, the book offers practical advice for the busy librarian. It is suitable for all librarians who are involved in reader's advisory and related aspects.

5-78. Sequels: an Annotated Guide to Novels in Series. 4th ed. Janet G. Husband and Jonathan F. Husband. Chicago: American Library Association, 2009.

The authors have three criteria to define the series included in this work. 1) Primarily, a series shows development of plot or character from book to book; 2) Books in which a chronology is minimal or debatable, but share a cast of characters and/or location; 3) Books that were conceived as a series by the author. The series are those likely to be found in a medium-sized public library. In addition to being helpful for reader's advisory, the book may also be useful in acquisitions and reference.

5-79. The Short Story Reader's Advisory. Brad Hooper. Chicago: American Library Association, 2000.

Unique among genre reader's advisory, this book is an introduction to short story writing helping to increase understanding of short story elements and writers. More than 200 critical essays cover short story writers past and present. In addition, there is also a guide for RA's on how to interview readers in order to make specific recommendations that match their reading interests.

Open Access Resources

5-80. Book Muse. Book Muse Network. http://www.thebookmuse.com

Book Muse offers in-depth notes for avid readers of all ages. These notes include questions that spark discussion, thoughtful commentaries, author biographies, leader's tips, and suggestions for further reading. The goal at the Book Muse is to enhance the joy and satisfaction that comes from reading, musing on, and discussing good books. To accomplish this, the site offers guidance for the reading and discussion of books.

5-81. Booklist Online. Chicago: American Library Association. Online subscription database also available to members of the ALA. http://www.booklistonline.com

Booklist is a review tool for librarians mainly in public libraries and school media. Coverage of genre and reader's advisory is extensive. Booklist Online is both a free website and a subscription database. The free site offers a selection of Booklist content, plus some Web-only features, and is updated daily or weekly, depending on the portion of the site. Reviews and articles on the home page are free, but to read full text of all reviews and features, it is necessary to subscribe. The subscription database contains archived reviews and features that are interlinked.

5-82. BookRags: Biographies. http://www.bookrags.com/browse/biography/

Book Rags is a research resource for students with over 5.8 million pages of literature summaries, literary essays, encyclopedias, e-books, and bibliographies drawn from over 100 respected education databases.

5-83. **The Compulsive Reader.** http://www.compulsivereader.com/html

This open access website contains reviews about the most current and popular authors in fictional literature. It also provides interviews with the authors, literary news, and criticisms.

5-84. Fiction_L. Readers' Advisory List. http://www.webrary.org/rs/flmenu.html

Morton Grove (IL) Public Library maintains this website of reader's advisory for fictional works. The site was created by and for fiction librarians but it is open to all readers. It functions as a standard discussion list in that users subscribe via email. Discussions center primarily upon compiling lists, such as Mysteries Without a Murder or Social Media in Fiction and once a list is completed, it is posted to the Booklist section of the site. Users may also search the archives, dating from 1995 to present.
Booklist: http://www.webrary.org/rs/FLbklistmenu.html
Archive: http://www.webrary.org/rs/FLarchive.html

5-85. **Knowledge Rush.** http://www.knowledgerush.com

This open access website includes a directory of authors from a variety of genres. The site includes reading lists, keyword searches and books by category. Topics included are banned books, romance, horror, mystery, and science fiction, among other popular genres of literature. Additionally, the website links specific works to public domain websites. It also contains an encyclopedia of many topics including literature.

5-86. **The Literature Network.** http://www.online-literature.com/

This database offers online literature for students, educators, and anyone who loves to read. It provides 1,900 full books and over 3,000 short stories and poems by over 250 authors.

5-87. **Overbooked: A Resource for Readers.** http://www.overbooked.org/

Begun in 1994 by Chesterfield County (VA) public librarian Ann Chambers Theis, Overbooked aims to provide book alerts for "ravenous readers" based on starred reviews from Booklist, Kirkus, Library Journal, or Publishers' Weekly. Books are sorted into the All-Stars category (those receiving three or more starred reviews) or by genre and year, and include bibliographic information as well as an annotation and the publication that gave the book a starred review. Downloadable Hotlists of new and notable books and a new section called Bookings contain trailers and other book-related special features. While the site primarily focuses on fiction, "readable non-fiction" is also included at Theis' discretion.
Hotlists: http://www.overbooked.org/hotlists/index.html
Bookings: http://overbooked.com/bookings/

5-88. **Reading Group Choices.** www.readinggroupchoices.com/

Informative, intellectual, creative, and interactive material of interest to book clubs is offered on this website. It selects discussible books and suggests discussion topics for reading groups. An annual guide is distributed to libraries, reading groups, book stores, community book festivals, and individuals.

GENRE SPECIALIZED BY TOPIC

Gothic and Horror

5-89. **Encyclopedia of the Vampire: The Living Dead in Myth, Legend, and Popular Culture.** S. T. Joshi, ed. Santa Barbara, CA: Greenwood/ABC-CLIO, 2010. Print and e-book.

Nearly 240 A-Z entries on all aspects of vampirism are contained in this book on the very popular topic. Entries include examples from literature, film and television, and folklore, plus photographs and illustrations.

5-90. Fang-tastic Fiction: Twenty-first Century Paranormal Reads. Patricia O'Brien Mathews. Chicago: American Library Association, 2011.

The ghoulish title of this work says it all. The book is a guide to the literature but is also a good read for RA librarians and horror enthusiasts.

5-91. Gothic Literature: A Gale Critical Companion. Jessica Bomarito, ed. Detroit: Gale, 2006. 3 vol. Print and e-book.

As a part of the Gale Critical Companions Collection, *Gothic Literature* is a three-volume set that spans all aspects of Gothic literature. Topics include visual and performing arts, Gothic society and culture, and Gothic themes and settings. The book covers 37 Gothic genre authors with complete critical analysis of their works. The electronic version of the book includes primary source documents, full text commentaries of Gothic literature, and recommended reading lists. Links to associated sites such as authors, themes and titles are also provided.

5-92. Hooked on Horror: A Guide to Reading Interests in Horror Fiction. A. J. Fonseca and J. M. Pulliam. Englewood, Colorado: Libraries Unlimited, 2003.

Hundreds of new and classic horror titles are described and organized according to reading preferences in this book. The work focuses on titles published in the last decade of the twentieth century and older classics that are commonly available in libraries. It covers 13 subgenres of horror fiction: vampires and werewolves, techno horror, ghosts and haunted houses, small town horror, and more.

5-93. The Readers' Advisory Guide to Horror. 2nd ed. Becky Siegel Spratford. Chicago: American Library Association, 2012.

The usual lists of recommended titles, authors, and sub-genres are included in this updated guide as well as new advice for RA librarians. This edition has an expanded resources section with an overview of the current state of horror lit.

5-94. Twenty-First Century Gothic: Great Gothic Novels Since 2000. Danel Olson, ed. Lanham, MD: Scarecrow Press, 2011.

Fifty-three original works from around the world written since 2000 are discussed in this informative work. The essays explain how each of the novels are Gothic and also how "they advance or change Gothicism."

5-95. The Vampire Book: The Encyclopedia of the Undead. 3rd ed. J. Gordon Melton. San Diego, CA: Visible Ink, 2010.

Updating the second edition of 1999, this edition expands coverage in 500 entries and 200 photographs of vampires in books, movies, television and more. Coverage is worldwide, and both popular and scholarly, historical and current. Entries for the Twilight books and movies, as well as the Buffy series are included. The edition does not however, contain the appendix of listings for organizations and websites from the previous edition.

5-96. The Horror's Writers Association. http://www.horror.org

The Horror Writer's Association, founded by Robert R. McCammon, is a professional organization specifically geared to the needs of writers of fear. The Association is dedicated to promoting reading interests in horror and dark fantasy. The association sponsors the Bram Stoker Awards, publishes anthologies, and has a recommended reading list.

5-97. Necropsy: The Review of Horror Fiction. Baton Rouge: Louisiana State University. http://www.lsu.edu/necrofile

Necropsy is an online journal that reviews novels, films, anthologies, and plays in the horror genre. It is edited by Pulliam and Fonseca (authors of *Hooked on Horror: a Guide to Reading Interests in Horror Fiction,* entry 5-92 above). Author, title index, reviewer, and publisher indexes are provided.

Graphic Novels

Once considered underground or cult subjects, comic books and graphic novels have become mainstream best sellers and popular culture icons that have influenced American life and culture. Graphic novels have emerged as the fastest growing segment of book publishing and have been accepted by librarians and educators because they encourage reading among all ages, reading levels, and females and males. Some contend that graphic novels are not a genre, but rather a medium within which various genres are represented. The genres and formats of anime, manga, and comics are included in this section. While these genres are not all the same, they are related literary and art forms. They are all treated in this section because they are often included together in works concerning them. Comics are an especially popular genre and there have been a large number of publications about these works. Only a few titles can be treated here. Animation as an art form is included in Chapter 10, along with film and cinema.

5-98. Underground and Independent Comics, Comix, and Graphic Novels. Alexandria, VA: Alexander Street Press. Online subscription database.

This digital comics collection is claimed by the publisher to be the first ever scholarly, primary source database focusing on adult comic books and graphic novels. According to the publisher's description, the collection "documents the entire spectrum of underground and independent North American and European comics and graphic novels, with 75,000 pages of original material from the 1950s to today along with more than 25,000 pages of interviews, commentary, theory, and criticism from journals, books, and magazines, including *The Comics Journal.*" Among the notable contents is *The Seduction of the Innocent* by Dr. Frederick Wertham, the book that led to one of the largest censorship programs in U.S. history, and the complete transcripts of the senate subcommittee hearings that resulted in the Comics Code Authority and, inadvertently, the underground comix movement. These publications were not generally collected by academic or even public libraries. The database provides a complete collection in the genre all at once. Because of the adult content it is most suitable for academic libraries and research.

5-99. Graphic Novels Core Collection. New York: H.W. Wilson. Online subscription database.

Although the title implies that this is a full-text database, it is actually a review database that contains recommendations for over 2,000 comic book titles. Full bibliographic information is provided as well as annotations, reviews, awards the title has won, and illustrations of cover art. All titles are searchable by author, title, subject, genre, and grade level with standards for "rating material by age appropriateness strictly applied." Entries link to additional review excerpts from Wilson's *Book Review Digest Plus* database and to the library's online catalog. Other Wilson Core collections can be searched simultaneously as well as other Wilson subject databases. The database is very helpful for collection development and as a means of keeping up with new publications. It also can be useful for reader's advisory.

5-100. **Comic Book Encyclopedia; The Ultimate Guide to Characters, Graphic Novels, Writers, and Artists in the Comic Book Universe.** Ron Goulart. New York: HarperCollins, 2004.

The *Ultimate Guide* has been described as entertaining and "chock-full of trivia." The mostly short entries include characters, heroes, villains, writers, artists, series, and companies. The most interesting aspect of this volume may be the reproductions of the original artwork from the comics. Several reviewers commented upon the quality of the reproductions that form a history of illustration in comics throughout the twentieth century. The entries are mainly short, making the book suitable for library collections as a reference work.

5-101. Comics Buyer's Guide. Kraus Publications. 2004– . Mo. http://cbgxtra.com/

This title began as a monthly compilation of comic ads published in tabloid format that became a monthly bound magazine in June 2004. From 2004–2009, a price guide list was included in the publication in order to appeal to comic book investors. Since 2009, Krause Publications has reduced the number of pages and removed the pricing guide from the monthly publication, publishing a separate *Comic Book Checklist & Price Guide* annually instead. The monthly version includes "Commentary from industry insiders and experts, market analysis with new issue sales, back-issue sales, and auction results, comic book reviews and "retroviews," as well as author profiles and a calendar of upcoming events. The website also contains comic book reviews and access to sales charts, as well as columns, blogs, classifieds, and other resources geared to appeal to comics fans.

5-102. Comics, Manga, and Graphic Novels: A History of Graphic Narratives. Robert S. Petersen. Santa Barbara, CA: ABC-CLIO, 2010.

While the three formats of comics, manga, and graphic novels are included in the title to this work, the author's emphasis is on his interpretation of them as "graphic narratives," or the "ability to narrate through graphic images," an alternative term to the use of *comics*. Using this term the history of the genres is traced from their beginning with cave paintings up through the latest developments in digital comics. The work includes numerous illustrations ranging from British satirical prints to Japanese woodblock prints; examples of the work of well-known contemporary illustrators are also included. Some reviewers point out a lack of illustrations in some chapters, which could be due to copyright restrictions. The book is not a reference work, but could be of interest for the author's point of view on the history of the genres or to look for more information than reader's advisory guides provide.

5-103. Encyclopedia of Comic Books and Graphic Novels. M. Keith Booker, ed. Santa Barbara, CA: Greenwood, 2010. 2 vols. Print and e-book.

The emphasis in this encyclopedia is comics, which were first published in the United States, with special emphasis on the new graphic novel format that emerged in the 1970s, although there are entries for European comics and manga. Coverage ranges from the debut of Superman in 1938 to the present day. The set contains articles written by eighty contributors dealing with the genre's history and its profound influence on American life and culture. With 340 signed entries by 78 comics scholars, the encyclopedia covers significant writers, artists, comic book imprints, major genres and themes, landmark titles, and specific characters in the field. The well-known superhero comics such as Superman, Batman, and Spiderman, are included, but lesser-known creators and artists are also included. In addition to factual information, there are critical analyses and attention to the cultural impact of comic books and individual works. Entries are arranged alphabetically with a general index, an alphabetical list of entries, and a topical entry guide. Some entries have references and a selected bibliography (listing more than 100 Web sites, magazine articles, and books) is in the second volume.

5-104. **500 Essential Graphic Novels.** Gene Kannenberg. New York: Collins, 2008.

Anyone interested in graphic novels will enjoy reading this work. Gene Kannenberg directs Comicsresearch.org (entry 5-113). The listings in this work are those determined by the author as being "essential." The 10 alphabetically organized theme chapters go from adventure through fiction and humor to war. This approach by reader themes makes the work suitable for reader's advisory. Each chapter contains a thoughtful introduction and features ten essential reads with additional genre-defining works, all from 1987 onward. The one- to two-page entries contain a plot synopsis and a qualitative review with the novel cover shown and for some, a page excerpt. This book pairs well with Serchay's Guide (entry 5-106).

5-105. **Graphic Novels and Comics in Libraries and Archives: Essays on Readers, Research, History and Cataloging.** Robert G. Weiner. Jefferson, NC: McFarland, 2010. Print and e-book.

The 29 essays in this work are written by librarians maintaining graphic novel collections in various types of libraries. The essays address multiple aspects of collections from basic background information, history of manga in Japanese libraries, surveys of teen readers, to an introduction, to webcomics. Other essays for the professional treat audiences, recommended titles, promotion of selections and programming, cataloging, and evaluating library comics collections. The book is a good introductory work and also useful to professionals for collection development and management.

5-106. **The Librarian's Guide to Graphic Novels for Adults.** David S. Serchay. New York: Neal-Schuman Publishers, Inc. 2009.

Not a reference book, this work by Serchay is a complete guide written for librarians to assist with establishing a brand-new collection, fully understanding what graphic novels are, where to purchase them, how to catalog them, and how to review, promote, and maintain the new collection. One chapter defends why graphic novels should be collected in academic libraries. The work includes an annotated bibliography, recommended readings, and indexes. This book is well written and appealing. In other words, the Guide is perfect for those who know little about graphic novels.

Another work written for librarians is *The Reader's Advisory Guide to Graphic Novels* by Francisca Goldsmith (American Library Association, 2010). Although written for reference librarians, this book provides a solid background as well as a helpful list of professional tools that would be useful for collection development.

5-107. **Mostly Manga: A Genre Guide to Popular Manga, Manhwa, Manhua, and Anime.** Elizabeth F.S. Kalen. Santa Barbara, CA: ABC-CLIO/Libraries Unlimited, 2012.

As can be seen from the title, this work includes Japanese, Korean, and Chinese "manga." Also included are author, title, subject, and genre indexes and an appendix about the films of Studio Ghibli.

Another work on graphic novels from Libraries Unlimited, this one for adults, is in the Read On series, *Graphic Novels: Reading Lists for Every Taste* by Abby Alpert (2012). With 70 thematic lists and over 500 original annotations, the work provides perspective on graphic novels as an art form. Award winners and titles suitable for young adults are indicated.

And *Mangatopia: Essays on Manga and Anime in the Modern World*, also issued by Libraries Unlimited is a critical work edited by Timothy Perper and Martha Cornog (2011). Essays cover various topics from fantasy to sex to politics and what manga and anime means to artists, readers, and fans.

5-108. **The Superhero Book: The Ultimate Encyclopedia of Comic-Book Icons and Hollywood Heroes.** Gina Misiroglu and David Roach, eds. Detroit: Visible Ink, 2004.

As its title indicates this book concentrates just on superhero characters. Almost 300 entries cover the most well-known and best-loved superheroes from comic books, movies, television, and novels. Not just the iconic names are treated, but also "counterculture, not so well known, and the worst of the genre." The work is organized into eras: the Golden Age (1938–1954), the Silver Age (1956–1969), the Bronze Age (1970–1979), and the Modern Age (1980-present), detailing the growth of the genre and development of the superhero concept. The 150 full-color illustrations include many classic comic covers. In addition to entries on the individual characters there are several articles about superheroes as a genre character, such as their vulnerabilities, creators, and appearance in prose. Since it focuses on the most popular types of comics characters, the work is worth owning in addition to the broader comics encyclopedias.

5-109. UXL Graphic Novelists. Tom Pendergast, Sara Pendergast, and Sarah Hermsen. Chicago: ALA, 2007. 3 vols. Print and e-book.

The defining feature of this three-volume work is that it is written for a young adult audience and does not contain adult material, although it is suitable for anyone interested in the topic. The set profiles contemporary novelists and fifteen of the graphic novelists profiled are women; seventeen are Japanese, of whom most were interviewed. The work is attractively formatted with sidebars, reproductions of artworks, and photographs of the novelists. Entries are lengthy and include references to newspaper and magazine articles and a few scholarly articles. Each volume has a bibliography, glossary and index for the set. All the introductory materials are reproduced in each volume, including a history of the graphic novel and discussion of manga.

5-110. Akemi's Anime World. http://www.Animeworld.com

Akemi is a fun website devoted to all things anime. It contains reviews of older and new anime and quite a bit of information on the Japanese language. Reviews cover suitability or not for YAs and children.

5-111. Anime and Manga Research Circle. http://tech.groups.yahoo.com/group/amrc-l

This is an open Yahoo! Group, primarily focused on Japanese comics and culture.

5-112. Comic Book Resources. http://www.comicbookresources.com

Comic Book Resources is an online comics magazine containing daily comics news, reviews, columns and blogs, and links to help comics fans find comics shops, upcoming events, and other resources. Perhaps the biggest draw for comic book lovers is the very active user forums, categorized by publisher, media type, and column.

5-113. Comicsresearch. http://www.Comicsresearch.org

Maintained by Gene Kannenberg, author of *500 Essential Graphic Novels* (entry 5-104), this site is a comprehensive bibliography with listings and reviews of works about comics, organizations, library resource guides, and more. Included on the site is *Comic Art in Scholarly Writing: A Citation Guide* by Allen Ellis, a guide to citing comic art as suggested by the Popular Culture Association.

5-114. Comix-Scholars Discussion List. http://www.english.ufl.edu/comics/scholars

This discussion list is hosted by the University of Florida's Comics and Visual Rhetoric program and is open to all scholars of comics.

5-115. Diamond Comic Distributors. Comic book/comics. Bookshelf Glossary. http://www.diamondbookshelf.com/

Many comics publishers have exclusive distribution contracts with Diamond Comic Distributors. Diamond offers both comic books and comic related merchandise and is the primary source of comics for libraries and retailers. Diamond publishes "Previews," a catalog of forthcoming publications as well as book lists and reviews. Another distributor is Haven Distributors that works with independent publishers (http://havendistro.com).

5-116. Don Markstein's Toonopedia: a Vast Repository of Toonological Knowledge.
www.toonopedia.com.

Another comprehensive site, this encyclopedia provides character histories, publication information, and creator related details. Entries are thorough and detailed.

5-117. Finding Scholarly Literature on Graphic Novels.
http://library.columbia.edu/eguides/graphic_novels.html

From Columbia University, this open access site provides bibliographic information for scholarly materials on graphic novels. The electronic links include *Modern Language Association's International Bibliography* (entry 2-20), *Annual Bibliography of English Language Literature* (ABELL) (entry 5-2), and *The Comics Research Bibliography* (entry 5-113), among others. The site also provides information about print format bibliographies of relevant works.

5-118. Grand Comics Database (GCD) http://docs.comics.org/

The slogan for the GCD is "Indexing every comic book ever made from all over the world." The GCD is a non-profit, non-commercial, fan-based volunteer effort with the goal of documenting and indexing all comics for the free use of scholars, historians, researchers, and fans. The GCD is an ongoing project to build a detailed comic-book database that is international, accurate, and complete from the beginning of the art form to the present. It is truly international with comics series in almost 50 languages, quite a few of them minor. The database includes information on creator credits, story details, and other information useful to comic-book readers, fans, collectors, and scholars. Over 7,000 publishers, 3,000 brands, 300,000 covers and 900,000 stories are represented in the database. Searches for covers show the cover images that are copyrighted by their respective current copyright holders. The GCD is a fully searchable wiki that is easy to use and understand, and also easy for contributors to add information to it. A disclaimer warns about content that may be objectionable. The GDC is only one of many comics databases. The various comics publishers each have their own database: DC Comics Database, Marvel Comics Database, also characters, Spiderman, Batman, and so forth.

5-119. Graphic Novel Reporter. http://www.graphicnovelreporter.com

Part of the Book Report Network, this site contains summaries, reviews, resources, and opinions on graphic novels.

5-120. Indy Aisle. http://havendistro.com

Independent publishers submit upcoming publications to this web catalog, an alternate distribution channel to Diamond (entry 5-115).

5-121. Lambiek Comiclopedia. http://www.lambiek.net/artists/index.htm

Originating in the Netherlands, the strength of the Comiclopedia is information on British and European creators of comics. The site also offers a history of Dutch comics. The focus is on artists rather than writers and the site has information on over 10,000 artists from around the world. It is a good site to remember if searching other sites has not turned up the information sought.

5-122. The Librarian's Guide to Anime and Manga. Gilles Poitrass. Berkeley, CA: 2005– . Online subscription magazine.

The Guide describes Japanese animation (anime) and comics (manga) and reviews and links to websites, books, magazines, and other resources.

Historical Fiction

5-123. Historical Dictionary of Westerns in Literature. Paul Varner. Lanham, MD: Scarecrow Press, 2010. (Historical Dictionaries of Literature and the Arts)

The fascinating history of the Western emerges in this work through a chronology, a bibliography, an introductory essay, and through hundreds of cross-referenced dictionary entries on authors, titles, and series to new trends, stock characters, themes, criticism, and historical events. Entries include "Pre-Westerns," beginning with a captivity narrative from 1692, but the focus of this dictionary is on classic Westerns and other types such as "antimyth Westerns" and "alternative Westerns." An extensive bibliography provides title lists for major authors and resources for further study. Varner is also the author of *The Historical Dictionary of Westerns in Cinema* (2008) in the same Scarecrow series.

5-124. Historical Fiction: A Guide to the Genre. Sarah. L. Johnson. Westport, CT: Libraries Unlimited, 2005.

5-125. Historical Fiction II: A Guide to the Genre. Sarah. L. Johnson. Westport, CT: Libraries Unlimited, 2009.

For Johnson, historical fiction must be set prior to 1950 and be written from research, not personal experience. Since historical fiction is such a large genre, the first volume focuses on books published between 1995 and mid-2004, with the second extended to 2008. In both volumes, an introductory chapter discusses appeal factors such as time period, setting, historical content, level of realism, pacing, characterization, subject, and dialogue. The titles are organized into 13 subgenres: traditional historical novels, multi-period epics, romance, sagas, westerns, mysteries, adventure, thrillers, literary fiction, Christian fiction, time-slip stories, alternate history, and fantasy. Each subgenre is then divided by time, place, or subject. The listings for books give author, title, publisher, publication date, number of pages, keyword subject headings, and an annotation summarizing the story and the appeal factors, thus showing librarians how each title relates to readers' interests. Symbols identify award winners, biographical stories, and classics and indicate whether a title is appropriate for reading groups and young adults. Series each have an entry as well as individual titles. In volume II, chapter introductions have been updated to reflect changes. This volume continues rather than replaces the earlier work, adding more than 2,700 new titles. A section on historical-fiction blogs has been added to the chapter on resources.

5-126. Read On . . . Historical Fiction; Reading Lists for Every Taste. Brad Hooper. Westport, CT: Libraries Unlimited, 2006. Print and e-book. (Read On Series)

Historical fiction is divided into chapters according to "underlying" appeal characteristics in this guide. The chapter themes are Settings, Character, Story, Language, and Mood and Atmosphere, but the subdivisions are not the usual. Each chapter has many subdivisions determined by the titles being listed, such as under character, "Women with True Grit" and under mood and atmosphere,

"Flights of Fancy." The book is fun to browse through and there is a chance that titles may be listed but are not known to the advisor or reader.

5-127. Read the High Country: Guide to Western Books and Films. John Mort. Westport, CT: Libraries Unlimited, 2006. (Genreflecting Advisory Series)

Mort's guide is not only a reader's and selection guide for librarians, but it is a history of the West. There is a Western TimeLine up to 1929. The entries include books written about the West as well as *Westerns*, and there is a great deal of information on Native Americans and the development of the West. A Settings index provides for those seeking works about particular locales. Helpful information also includes icons to indicate titles that are "woman-friendly," suitable for young adults, Christian-themed, or considered a classic. Divisions include Traditional Westerns, Nontraditional Westerns, The Contemporary West, and Western Mysteries and Romances.

5-128. Read West. http://www.readwest.com

The ReadWest Foundation is a nonprofit organization with the mission of identifying the best in Western literature and creating an increased awareness of the genre. The organization holds an annual conference, as well as book signings, and hosts an online bookstore powered by Amazon. The bookstore highlights categories within the genre, ranging from "new" and "classics" to "mountain man," as well as well-known Western authors, such as Louis L'Amour and Elmer Kelton.

5-129. Historical Fiction Network. www.histfiction.net

Summaries of books, links to historical fiction sites, and resources for historical fiction writers are offered in this database of historical fiction authors. Also included is a list and reviews of the top 100 historical fiction novels. This website has a useful timeline that helps place books within the flow of history from B.C. to the 20th century.

5-130. Historical Fiction Review. Historical Novel Society. Quart. http://www.Historicalnovelsociety.org/the-review.htm

The Historical Novel Society, founded in 1997, promotes all aspects of historical fiction, through providing opportunities for new writers, a community for authors, readers, agents, and publishers, and information for students, booksellers and librarians. The *Historical Fiction Review* is furnished to all members of the society. About 800 reviews are published per year. It is purported to be "the only magazine of its kind, the best and most complete guide to the latest historical fiction in the world."

Mystery and Detective Fiction

5-131. British Crime Writing: An Encyclopedia. Barry Forshaw, ed. Santa Barbara, CA: ABC-CLIO/Greenwood, 2009. 2 vols.

According to the publisher's description, the contributors to this set are academics, critics, and practitioners who have written 475 signed and authoritative entries on British crime writers, magazines, films, and topics such as pieces depicting how crime writing has changed. All of the well-known crime writers are represented as well as newer and lesser-known authors with portraits and illustrations and a "preliminary guide to related topics." There are a bibliography and an index. Forshaw is also the author of *Rough Guide to Crime Fiction* (2007) and *Stieg Larsson: The Man Who Left too Soon* (John Blake, 2010). The work is suitable for all levels of reader.

Another work on crime fiction is *Crime Writers: a Research Guide,* by Elizabeth Haynes (Libraries Unlimited, 2011). This resource provides information for researching fifty top crime writers including websites and other online resources. Ten writers are covered more thoroughly with suggestions for other writers with similar styles or themes. This reference has a time line for authors and events in the development of the crime fiction genre.

5-132. Critical Survey of Mystery and Detective Fiction. Rev. ed. Carl Rollyson, ed. Pasadena, CA: Salem Press, 2008. 5 vols.

The set contains 37 overview essays and 393 author essays. The organization is the same as all Salem Press critical works. The set has seven appendices: Bibliography; Genre Terms and Techniques; Crime Fiction Jargon; Major Awards; Web Resources; a Timeline of Mystery & Detective Fiction; a Chronological List of Writers, plus four indexes. As with other Salem Press products, this set is appropriate for both public and academic libraries. The work was a Choice Outstanding Academic title in 2008.

5-133. The Dark Page: Books that Inspired American Film Noir (1940–1949). Kevin Johnson, ed. New Castle: DE: Oak Knoll Press, 2007.

5-134. The Dark Page II: Books that Inspired American Film Noir (1950–1965). Kevin Johnson, ed. New Castle, DE: Oak Knoll Press, 2009.

Kevin Johnson, cinephile and rare bookseller, has assembled two extraordinary volumes which trace the literary sources of the American film noir cycle. Both volumes identify every film noir during the time periods that had a literary source and give detailed bibliographic information on the first editions of these novels. Whether the novels are considered hard-boiled, mystery, crime, or suspense, they are organized chronologically and each one is paired with a full-color image of the first edition book, the majority of them in their original lurid, and often surreal, dust jackets. The volumes are each well-researched, organized, and stunningly illustrated with images that most readers would otherwise never see elsewhere.

5-135. Icons of Mystery and Crime Detection: From Sleuths to Superheroes. Mitzi M. Brunsdale. Santa Barbara, CA: ABC-CLIO /Greenwood, 2010. 2 vols. Print and e-book.

Twenty-four characters and their creators from comic strips, detective fiction, movies and television series are profiled in this work. Each chapter contains a chronology for the character, author, or show with images. The essays discuss historical and cultural contexts, defining characteristics and legacy of the subject. Accompanying bibliographies contain primary works of authors and criticism. The set will appeal to students and general readers.

Greenwood produces several series with the "Icons" title. Each title focuses on twenty-four figures that "embody the values and reflect the essences of a particular culture." The series provide "fresh insights for the student and popular reader into the power and influence of icons . . ." The works are designed for students and to provide more information than "conventional reference articles but . . . less intimidating and more accessible than a book-length biography." The Icons titles profile persons in the humanities and the arts as well as other professions, pop culture, race and ethnicity, science and technology, and more.

5-136. Mystery Ink. http://www.mysteryinkonline.com

In spite of the dot com address, Mystery Ink is an open access website with crime fiction book reviews, author interviews, and list of awards. Perhaps the best aspect of the site is the links to author websites, crime fiction websites, blogs, and bookstores. Anyone wanting to keep up with the crime fiction scene will enjoy this site.

5-137. The Mystery Reader. Dede Anderson. http://www.themysteryreader.com

The Mystery Reader offers hundreds of book reviews for mystery novels. One who indulges in this website can also meet new authors and learn about forthcoming mystery novels. It reviews books in six categories: Latest Police/Detective, Latest Romantic Suspense, Latest Thrillers, Latest Cozy, Latest Suspense, and Latest Historical. Each book is priced, reviewed, and given from 5 stars (outstanding) to 1 star (don't bother). Its other features include New Faces (introducing new authors), Eagerly Awaited (upcoming releases), Author Directory, Small Press, Mailbag, News, Crime Scene (news from authors), and Author Freebies.

5-138. **100 Most Popular Contemporary Mystery Authors.** Bernard A. Drew. Santa Barbara, CA: ABC-CLIO/Libraries Unlimited, 2011.

This reference work contains both biographical information and bibliographies of the authors' works with over sixty photographs. Drew is also the author of *100 Most Popular Genre Authors* (entry 5-76).
    Libraries Unlimited has also published a number of other titles to aid in reader's advisory. *Make Mine a Mystery II* (2011) is a sequel to the award-winning original by Gary Warren Niebuhr covering the best authors in mystery writing and providing a bibliography of mystery series.

5-139. **The Readers' Advisory Guide to Mystery.** 2nd ed. John Charles, Candace Clark, Joanne Hamilton-Selway, and Joanna Morrison. Chicago: American Library Association, 2012. Print and e-book.

This updated edition covers the latest, along with the most popular classic titles in mystery fiction.

5-140. **Reference and Research Guide to Mystery and Detective Fiction.** 2nd ed. Richard Bleiler. Westport, CT: Libraries Unlimited, 2004.

This updated work significantly expands the first edition. It contains annotated primary and secondary reference sources specific to the mystery and detective genre. The work also contains media references to magazines, radio programs, television and movies. Specific author websites are also provided.

5-141. **Stop** *You're Killing Me!* (Electronic Version). L. Surber and S. Ulrich. http://www.stopyourekillingme.com

This website and newsletter is a resource for lovers of mystery, crime, thriller, spy, and suspense books. The site lists over 2,400 authors, with chronological lists of their books (over 28,000 titles), both series and non-series. Other links include: What's New, Award Winners, Location Index, Diversity Index, Job Index, Historical Index, Genre Index, Read-A-Likes, Magazines, and What We Read.

5-142. **Whodunit? A Who's Who of Crime and Mystery Writing.** Rosemary Herbert and Dennis Lehane. Oxford: Oxford University Press, 2003.

With 380 signed entries the book covers classic and contemporary mystery writers and characters. In addition to the entries on authors and characters there are entries on character types, such as the clerical sleuth, culinary sleuths, elderly sleuths, gentlemen thieves, the Femme Fatale, the coroner, and the con artist. In addition to these sleuth types, there is an article on "the corpse." Although the OUP is in the business of producing scholarly works, it can be seen that this work is a fun read and suitable for general library collections.

Pulp Fiction

5-143. **The Classic Era of American Pulp Magazines.** Peter Haining. Chicago, IL: Chicago Review Press, 2000.

The period between the World Wars: the era of Prohibition, the Great Depression, sexual liberation, and the spread of organized crime, are covered in this critical history of American pulp literature. The literature, which was mass-produced in cheap pulp magazines, had an incredible popular appeal. The stories span a number of genres, including the hard-boiled detective story, science fiction, fantasy, and the Western. The work is fully illustrated, with biographical entries of most of the important pulp authors, and bibliographic information on hundreds of pulp magazines published between the early 1920s and the 1950s. The work is recommended for both academic and public libraries.

Romance

5-144. A Companion to Romance: From Classical to Contemporary. Corinne Saunders, ed. Malden, MA: Blackwell, 2004. Print and e-book. (Blackwell Companions to Literature and Culture, 27).

This work begins with a theoretical background about what constitutes romance fiction. The author addresses classical romance themes and characters through the Victorian romance novels and on to modern romance traditions. Essays on each era of romantic literature written by various scholars in the field include the history of the genre and literary criticisms.

The development of the romance as a genre is the subject of *Women and Romance Fiction in the English Renaissance* by Helen Hackett (Cambridge University Press, 2000). The author traces the progress of Renaissance romance from "a genre addressed to women as readers, to a genre written by women." This is a critical work most suited to academic libraries.

5-145. Romance Fiction: A Guide to the Genre. 2nd ed. Kristin Ramsdell. Santa Barbara, CA: ABC-CLIO/Libraries Unlimited, 2012.

The genre of Romance fiction is defined in this guide that has an extensive bibliography of the genre with a suggested core collection listed in chronological order. In addition to the two editions of *Romance Fiction*, the author also published *Happily Ever After: A Guide to Reading Interests in Romance Fiction*.

5-146. The Romance Reader. http://theromancereader.com

It has only been in recent years that romance novels have been taken seriously by those who don't read them, even though they are the most popular form of genre fiction with over half of mass market paperback fiction being romance novels. This site is one of the oldest review sites and it is organized into contemporary, historical, paranormal, series, and eclectic. The reviews rank the works according to one to five hearts. Other features are author interviews and a section where readers can ask questions and get answers. The site can help readers and librarians alike to be "in the know."

5-147. Romance Writers of America. http://www.rwa.org

The Romance Writers of America (RWA) website is dedicated to advancing the professional interests of career-focused romance writers through networking and advocacy. The association represents more than 10,000 members in 145 chapters offering local or special-interest networking and education. The RWA sponsors conferences and the RITA and Golden Heart awards. The searchable website provides information on author appearances, new book releases, and lists of titles based on geography, genre, or time period.

5-148. The Romantic Reader. Dede Anderson. http://www.theromancereader.com

Thousands of book reviews for romance reading pleasure can be found on this site. Categories of reviewed books include: Latest Historical, Latest Time Travel (Futuristic and Fantasy), Latest

Contemporary, Mystery/Suspense, Latest Regency, and Latest Eclectic Themes. Other links include: Author Freebies, Eagerly Awaited, Author Address Book, Mailbag Archives, and Romance Features (top reads). The website is for fans of the romance genre.

Science Fiction and Fantasy

5-149. Anatomy of Wonder: A Critical Guide to Science Fiction. 5th ed. Westport, CT: Libraries Unlimited, 2004.

Now in its fifth edition, this award-winning work is the most well known and highly regarded as the best guide to science fiction literature. Offering an overview of the English-language science-fiction field for a wide audience, the work is divided into three parts: a history of science fiction; a critical examination of novels, single-author collections, and anthologies; and a survey of the secondary literature. Annotations outline each work's plot, historical significance, and theme, and include cross-references to similar works. Numerous lists will aid librarians, readers, and teachers: listings of the best books chosen by the contributors, major awards, important series, young adult books, translations, library research collections, publishers and organizations, and a list of online resources. Indexes are provided for titles, authors, and themes. The work is recommended for all sizes and types of libraries.

5-150. Brave New Words: The Oxford Dictionary of Science Fiction. Jeff Prucher. Oxford: Oxford University Press, 2007.

Jeff Prucher is an editor for the Oxford English Dictionary's science fiction project. This work is the first historical dictionary devoted to science fiction. It manages to be a history of the genre, in addition to being a fun read as the play on words of the title indicates. The history of each word, term or expression is documented. Citations are included for each definition, starting with the earliest usage that can be found. Citations are drawn not only from science fiction books and magazines, but also from all forms of media, from mainstream publications, fanzines, screenplays, newspapers, comics, film, songs, and the Internet. In addition to illustrating the different ways each word has been used, citations also show when and where words have moved out of the science fiction lexicon and into that of other subcultures or mainstream English. This work received rave reviews and won the Hugo Award for Best Related Book in 2008. It was also a RUSA Outstanding Reference Sources selection in 2008. This is one work that will be purchased by libraries and many fans for their personal library.

5-151. Classics of Science Fiction and Fantasy Literature. Fiona Kelleghan. Pasadena, CA: Salem Press, 2002. 2 vols.

The entries in *Classics of Science Fiction and Fantasy Literature* discuss 180 individual books and series, arranged alphabetically by title. The work begins with an introductory essay by the noted scholar T.A. Shippey on developments in the science-fiction and fantasy fields. The critical essays are divided into two sections, the first being "The Story" with plot details and the major characters. The second section concerns themes and literary interpretation of the work. The set also includes an annotated bibliography and up-to-date lists of major science-fiction and fantasy award winners, an annotated list of websites, a time line of titles and a general index. Author, title, and genre indexes are also provided.

5-152. Dictionary of Fantasy Literature. Brian Stableford. Lanham, MD: Scarecrow Press, 2005. (Historical Dictionaries in Literature and the Arts)

As described by the publisher, the dictionary includes cross-referenced entries on more than 700 authors, ranging across the entire historical spectrum with more than 200 other entries that describe "fantasy subgenres, key images in fantasy literature, and technical terms used in fantasy criticism." The chronology tracks the evolution of fantasy from the origins of literature to the twenty-first century. The introduction explains "the nature of the impulses creating and shaping fantasy literature, the problems of its definition, and the reasons for its changing historical fortunes." The work concludes with an extensive bibliography that ranges from general textbooks and specialized accounts of the history and scholarship of fantasy literature, through bibliographies and accounts of the fantasy literature of different nations, to individual author studies and useful websites.

5-153. **Dictionary of Science Fiction Literature.** Brian Stableford. Lanham, MD: Scarecrow Press, 2004. (Historical Dictionaries in Literature and the Arts)

One of the unusual features of this reference work is the attention paid to speculative fiction, i.e., "works that may not ordinarily be classified as 'sci-fi' because they are scientific writing and are thought-provoking regarding the possibilities that the future may hold." The dictionary tracks the development of speculative fiction influenced by the advancement of science and the idea of progress from the eighteenth century to the present day. It also includes the mainstream authors of works marketed as science fiction, various subgenres, significant magazines and their editors, and words or terms coined by sci-fi writers. Also included are an introductory essay, a chronology covering the literature from the 1700s through the present, a list of acronyms and abbreviations and also an extensive bibliography that includes books, journals, fanzines, and websites. The dictionary provides general readers and enthusiasts as well as serious writers and critics with an understanding of the genre of science fiction literature. Another reference work by Stableford is *The A-Z in Science Fiction Literature* (Scarecrow Press, [2005]), a historical dictionary of science fiction literature, terms, and authors with shorter entries. Both titles are recommended for academic and public library collections. The covers of these dictionaries by Stableford are both striking and good examples of the genre.

5-154. **Science Fact and Science Fiction: An Encyclopedia.** Brian Stableford. New York: Routledge, 2006.

Both science writers and science fiction are included in this work. The concentration is on the real science behind the themes and plots of science fiction: acoustics, chemistry, engineering, paleontology, physics, zoology, and more. The entries are by topic or person and there is a subject index for finding subjects among the entries. The thorough bibliography includes non-science fiction science writers. The work is recommended for all science fiction collections and general collections as well.

5-155. **The Science in Science Fiction: 83 SF Predictions that Became Scientific Reality.** Robert Bly. Dallas, TX: BenBella, 2005.

Robert Bly is a science fiction writer. His similar title to that of Brian Stableford above is a less scholarly work aimed at a more popular audience. As the title suggests, the focus is narrower and much less hard science. The 83 predictions discussed include anti-gravity, cloning, genetic engineering, X-rays, holograms, nanotechnology, neutron stars, and parallel universes. It is Bly's contention that these scientific discoveries were foretold in science fiction before they became scientific discoveries or accomplishments. The work is a good read for all ages. It is especially useful to spark an interest in science among young people.

5-156. **Strictly Science Fiction: A Guide to Reading Interests.** Diana Tixier Herald and Bonnie Kunzel. Englewood, Co: Libraries Unlimited, 2002. (Genereflecting Advisory Series)

From the publisher's description, over 900 titles are included in Strictly Science Fiction, mostly from the 1990s, but ranging from 1818 to 2002. Each title has a brief annotation. The chapters are divided into sub-categories that have catchy and sometimes humorous titles. The chapters are not organized according to established sub-genres, but into groupings with similar qualities and appeal to readers so that similar titles can be found. The last chapter, "Resources for Librarians and Readers," is a guide by formats to online resources, bibliographies, biographies, dictionaries, and more. In addition to the titles covered, there is a chapter for YA titles and a chapter of short story anthologies. Appendices include lists by awards, one of "best" authors and their "best" writings, and author, title, and character indexes. This work is valuable, both for the titles it covers and for the information about advisory for science fiction.

5-157. Fantastic Fiction. http://www.fantasticfiction.co.uk/

Users can search by author or title, or browse by genre or category, such as new or most popular for over 350,000 books on this website. Clicking on a title brings up a page showing the various formats offered by Amazon (hardcover, Kindle, etc.), a summary of the book, similar books by other authors, and other purchase options, including Abebooks and eBay listings for the title. In addition to the books, there are over 30,000 author pages with short bios, bibliographies, and awards listed for each.

5-158. Locus Magazine Online. Science Fiction and Fantasy. http://www.locusmag.com

Locus Magazine publishes reviews and listings of new and upcoming science fiction and fantasy books and magazines, as well as interviews, convention reports, an annual year-in-review, recommended reading lists, and survey. The website includes cumulative indexes to the book reviews and interviews included in the monthly magazine, but most of the content is available only via the print issues.

5-159. Science Fiction and Fantasy Research Database. http://sffrd.library.tamu.edu/

Sponsored by Texas A&M University, this open access science fiction collection website is searchable by author, subjects or titles. It provides full text articles on science fiction or fantasy movies, television, comics and other forms of literature.

5-160. SyFy Channel. http://www.blastr.com

This website provides up-to-date information on science fiction books, television programs, and movies from Blastr, an affiliate of the SyFy channel.

5-161. Science Fiction Studies. http://www.depauw.edu/sfs

From DePauw University, this open source website is an electronic version of the *Science Fiction Studies Journal* which is published three times yearly. The electronic version publishes abstracts and full text articles, reviews on science fiction works, historical documents and essays. It has a normal one-year delay between the reviews in the print format and the electronic version. Full text articles appear when the journal has sold out. It is searchable by keyword, publishers, authors and topics within the genre of science fiction. The website also provides links to other science fiction links, known as *wormholes*.

5-162. SF Site. The Home Page for Science Fiction and Fantasy. http://www.sfsite.com

The site is colorful with new reviews posted on the home page accompanied by copies of the book covers. Reviews can be searched by authors and Topical Lists compiled by others. In addition to reviews there are interviews with authors and artists. The site has links to podcasts and a discussion board. Enthusiasts and librarians can keep up with the latest on the site.

Street Lit

5-163. The Readers' Advisory Guide to Street Literature. Vanessa Irvin Morris. Chicago: American Library Association, 2012.

One of the newest genres, street lit, or urban fiction, portrays the gritty details of urban living. The genre has been controversial, but also wildly popular. The work is by street lit advisory expert Vanessa Morris, with a foreword by Teri Woods. It covers the history of the genre, subgenres, major authors and works, and suggestions for reader's advisory.

Oriented to young adults is *Urban Grit: A Guide to Street Lit* by Megan Honig (Libraries Unlimited, 2010). The history of one of the newest genres and the development of the genres are explained. More than 400 titles are classified according to subgenre with reader's advisory.

POETRY

Interest in poetry crosses all echelons of society, from the intellectuals who make up the literary elite, to students and teachers, to the general public. Poetry has enjoyed a boom since the advent of the Internet with sites too numerous to list. Quite a few sites post a "poem of the day" and give more sites for information on poets and original poetry texts. A significant portion of current publications of poetry are available either only online or via some combination of online and offline publication.

The introduction to this chapter has described electronic literature as a growing phenomenon. *Digital poetry* is a new form of electronic literature, displaying a wide range of approaches to poetry. As the term implies, digital poetry is written with the use of computers and the Internet. Computers allow the creation of art that utilizes different media: text, images, sounds, and interactivity. Works so created synthesize both arts and media to create communities of collaborative writing and publication (as in poetical wikis). Many types of digital poetry are available such as "hypertext, kinetic poetry, computer generated animation, digital visual poetry, interactive poetry, code poetry, holographic poetry (holopoetry), and experimental video poetry." Digital poetry can be available online, as installations in art galleries, in certain cases also recorded as digital video or films, or as "digital holograms" (Digital Poetry, *Wikipedia*).

The resources in this section are somewhat more mundane than the exciting sphere of digital poetry, but are the best, whether for students and researchers or for those who just love poetry. Sources in this section treat poetry in English or from more than one language.

Databases

5-164. Columbia Granger's World of Poetry Online. New York: Columbia University Press. Online subscription database.

In 1995, the Columbia University Press began producing a CD-ROM product that incorporated the content of two standard reference works in print, both *Columbia Granger's Index to Poetry* and *Columbia Granger's Dictionary of Poetry Quotations*. That earlier electronic database is now the Columbia Granger's World of Poetry Online. The difference from the earlier indexing tool and dictionary is that the World of Poetry Online contains the full text of poems as well. The publisher's description of the database enumerates the contents beginning with over 250,000 poems in full text, including major works that are considered too long by other websites, e.g. Chaucer's *Canterbury Tales*, Milton's *Paradise Lost*, Wordsworth's *The Prelude*, and many others. In addition to poems in English, the database also contains poems in Spanish, French, German, Italian, Portuguese, Latin, and other modern and ancient languages. There are also the full text of 10,000 of the most anthologized non-copyrighted poems, as well as indexing to more than 135,000 poems by more than 20,000 poets in more than 700 anthologies and 70 collected and selected works. In addition current poetry is drawn from some of the best poetry periodicals, such as *Poetry* Magazine, *The Southern Review*, and *Poetry Northwest*.

Granger has over 1,000 commentaries on best-known poems and biographies of well-known poets. Commentaries are written by the editor, William Harmon, and a team of scholars. Each commentary puts the poem in its historical context and describes, when necessary, "what happens" in the poem. Notes on proper names and difficult terms are provided and explication of the form of the poem and the author's technique. Throughout the commentaries are links "to other poems by the same poet, to other poems on the same subject, and to other poets." Also included are over 100 audios of selected poems with more being added and a glossary of 600 terms defined with examples from poems. Full text of 14 award-winning Columbia University Press books of and about poetry are included, such as *The Columbia History of American Poetry*, *The Columbia History of British Poetry*, and *Modern East Asian Literature*, to name a few. *The Columbia Granger's* print indexes are also included: *The Columbia Granger's Index to Poetry in Anthologies* editions 8–13; *The Columbia Granger's Index to Poetry in Collected and Selected Works*, editions 1-2; and *The Columbia Granger's Index to African-American Poetry*.

The user is able to browse the database by poems, poets, anthologies, biographies, commentaries, and subjects and search by author, title, subject, first line, last line, key word, or category. Subject searches can be run by era or school, nationality, language, cultural identity, gender, and form. The subject thesaurus also makes it easy to find poems for special occasions. Commentaries, biographies, and glossary terms are linked. The database is appropriate for students at all levels and the general public. It is essential for libraries serving students of poetry in literature programs.

Digital Collections

A number of collections produced by Chadwyck-Healey that were first made available in CD-ROM (some previously microforms) are now available as separate databases and are also included in the mega database Literature Online (entry 5-1). For American poetry there are two databases: American Poetry (entry 5-165) and 20th Century American Poetry, Second Edition (entry 5-166). For English poetry other than American, English Poetry, Second Edition (entry 5-168) includes poetry up to the early twentieth century, followed by 20th Century English Poetry (entry 5-169).

In addition, Literature Online also includes multimedia to support poetry study, offering Poets on Screen, a growing collection of video clips including over 900 filmed poetry readings of contemporary poets reading their own poems or classic poems. Also contained within the Literature Online database is the *New Princeton Encyclopedia of Poetry and Poetics* (entry 5-170). Complete descriptions and editorial policies of all of the collections can be found on the Chadwyck-Healey website: http://collections.chadwyck.co.uk/marketing/.

5-165. American Poetry. Chadwyck-Healey/Proquest. Online subscription database. http://collections.chadwyck.co.uk/

According to the publisher's description, The American Poetry collection contains more than 40,000 works from over 200 poets from the Colonial era to the twentieth century. In addition to the most studied and well-known poets, there are also the works of less familiar poets. The principal bibliographic source used for selection was the *Bibliography of American Literature* (entry 5-3), supplemented with selections of additional poets by an editorial board "to provide a more thorough and rounded collection." The complete text of each poem is included. Any accompanying text written by the original author and forming an integral part of the work, such as notes, dedications, and prefaces to individual poems, is also generally included. The database is suitable for all type of libraries for students, teachers, and the general public.

5-166. **20th Century American Poetry, Second Edition.** Chadwyck-Healey/Proquest. Online subscription database. http://collections.chadwyck.co.uk/

Two existing Chadwyck-Healey literature collections have been combined to comprise the Second Edition database: Twentieth-Century American Poetry and Twentieth-Century African American Poetry (entry 2-11). The collection "brings together the most important and influential poems representing the full range of movements and traditions in American poetry from 1900 to the present day." The database covers African-American writers from both the North and South. The database is also available as an add-on to the Literature Online database.

5-167. English Poetry. Chadwyck-Healey/Proquest. Online subscription database. http://collections.chadwyck.co.uk/

English Poetry, according to the publisher's description contains the full text of poetry for over 160,000 works from the eighth century up to the twentieth century by 1,350 poets listed in the *New Cambridge Bibliography of English Literature.* The database aims "to encompass the complete published corpus by all poets listed in NCBEL who were active between 1100 and 1900." The full text of multi-volume sets and anthologies are included in the collection as well as single books of poetry. Included in addition to the poetry are epigraphs, dedications, notes, and bibliographical details pertinent to the edition used in the database. Also included in the English Poetry full-text database is *The Faber Poetry Library,* a collection of 140 volumes containing the works of 50 of the most influential poets of the twentieth century, including Sylvia Plath, James Joyce, and Seamus Heaney.

5-168. English Poetry, Second Edition. Chadwyck-Healey/Proquest. Online subscription database. http://collections.chadwyck.co.uk/

English Poetry, Second Edition contains over 183,000 poems, "essentially comprising the complete canon of English poetry of the British Isles and the British Empire from the 8th century to the early 20th." The scope of the collection has been broadened to include works representing "both of the literary heritages of Commonwealth and ex-colonial countries, and of writers that have only been brought back to scholarly attention during the end of the twentieth century, including previously neglected women poets." The poems are drawn from close to 5,000 printed sources, with more than 2,700 poets represented.

5-169. Twentieth Century English Poetry. Chadwyck-Healey/Proquest. Online subscription database. http://collections.chadwyck.co.uk/

The Twentieth Century collection primarily includes British poets or poets based in Britain, although selected major Commonwealth authors who are based outside the British Isles are also included. The collection contains the poetry of over 280 poets from 1900 to the present. Many of the poets, publishers, and their living relatives have cooperated in contributing to the collection to further the aim of providing as full a collection of the published works of each poet as possible. When available, a poet's collected edition has been included.

5-170. The New Princeton Encyclopedia of Poetry and Poetics. Princeton University Press, dist. by Gale, 2007. Print and e-book. Also included in Literature Online by Chadwyck-Healey.

This new e-book edition of the indispensable Princeton Encyclopedia assesses 106 national poetries, with coverage of "every significant poetry tradition in the world." Many entries such as "sonnet" are virtually unchanged from the earlier edition; others, such as Feminist poetics, are brand-new. This is an essential purchase for any library supporting the study of poetry.

5-171. Irish Women Poets of the Romantic Period. Alexander Street Press. Online subscription database. http://alexanderstreet.com/

The description of this collection stresses that this group of women poets has been neglected in studies of the Romantic period in England and Ireland. This thought is borne out in that the names of the 50 poets, such as Henrietta Battier, I. S. Anna Liddiard, Adelaide O'Keeffe, and Elizabeth Ryves, are not generally recognized by even those with an advanced graduate degree in literature. The collection contains 80 rare works owned by only a small number of libraries in the world. In addition to the original texts, there are critical essays written by prominent scholars on the subject, especially commissioned by Alexander Street Press. Other elements of the collection include a critical introduction providing context for the poetry; a bibliographical introduction and a general bibliography; criticism, reviews, and links to related Web resources. The collection was carefully compiled and edited by Stephen Behrendt, the George Holmes Distinguished Professor of English at the University of Nebraska, along with a board of distinguished scholars. Irish Women Poets of the Romantic Period is available on the Web, either through subscription or one-time purchase of perpetual rights.

Printed Resources

5-172. Critical Survey of Poetry. 4th ed. Pasadena, CA: Salem Press. 10 vols. Print and e-book.

The Critical Survey of Poetry is comprised of a number of printed sets organized into five subsets by geography and essay type: a 4-volume subset on *American Poets*; a 3-volume subset on *British, Irish, and Commonwealth Poets*; a 3-volume subset on *European Poets*; a 1-volume subset on *World Poets*; and a 2-volume subset of the *Topical Essays*. The *Cumulative Indexes* volume covers all five subsets and is free with purchase of more than one subset. The complete set is also available online through the Salem Literature database.

5-173. The Facts on File Companion to British Poetry before 1600. New York: Facts on File, 2008.

5-174. The Facts on File Companion to British Poetry, 17th and 18th Centuries. New York: Facts on File, 2008.

5-175. The Facts on File Companion to British Poetry, 1900 to the Present. James Persoon and Robert R. Watson, eds. New York: Facts on File, 2009.

Each of these titles is issued separately, although they form a set. "British" in the title of these works includes poetry of the Commonwealth countries, both former and current, but not American poets. In addition to entries on individual poets and poems, there are entries for movements such as cubism, feminism, new criticism, surrealism, and performance poetry. The entries vary in length from 500 to 2,500 words and contain "see also" references and bibliographies. A glossary of poetic terms and a bibliography include works on more than one writer and anthologies. It lacks a subject or thematic index and has only a general index. The titles are designed for high school students and undergraduates.

5-176. Encyclopedia of American Poetry: 19th Century. Eric L. Haralson, ed. Chicago: Fitzroy Dearborn Publishers, 2007.

5-177. Encyclopedia of American Poetry: 20th Century. Eric L. Haralson, ed. Chicago: Fitzroy Dearborn Publishers, 2011.

These encyclopedias focus on individual poets. The signed articles provide biographical information and critical discussion of the literary and historical significance of each poet, excellent bibliographies of both works and criticism, and suggestions for further reading in the topical entries. Both a general index and a title index are included. While major poets are profiled there are others included who may have faded from popularity or are otherwise not well known. The works are suitable for academic and large public libraries.

5-178. Encyclopedia of the New York School Poets. New York: Facts on File, 2008. Print and e-book. (Literary Movements Series)

The New York School started in the 1950s and was one of the most influential movements of American poetry from the last half of the twentieth century to today. *Encyclopedia of the New York School Poets* is an A-to-Z reference with more than 400 entries. The work broadly includes the central figures, plus poets and artists who influenced the movement or were influenced by it, such as Andy Warhol, the Beat poets, W.H. Auden, and Robert Lowell. In addition to poetry, related literary works, New York locales, small presses and magazines, and the visual arts are covered. Each entry has a bibliography, with a general bibliography at the end of the volume. The work has cross-references, an index, a timeline, and a list of entries by subject. The work is specialized but is suited to all poetry and research literature collections.

5-179. Greenwood Encyclopedia of American Poets and Poetry. Jeffrey Grey, ed. Westport, CT: Greenwood, 2006. 5 vols.

Although there are other sources for biographical and critical essays on American poets, this encyclopedia is comprehensive in the attention devoted to schools and movements in the twentieth and twenty-first centuries. The encyclopedia contains over 900 articles by approximately 350 scholars. American poets are covered from Colonial times through the twentieth century, tracing the development of American poets and poetry. The set is well indexed with lists of the pre-twentieth century poets, as well as the twentieth and twenty-first century poets. Even with the current emphasis on digital resources, this printed set is still a worthwhile addition for libraries serving high school and college students.

5-180. Index to American Periodical Verse. Metuchen, NJ: Scarecrow Press, 1971– . Ann.

Although this title has been a long running publication, the last volume published was for 2006. The usual pattern is that the volumes are two years behind the publication year. Nearly 7,000 poets are indexed from a broad cross section of publications: literary, popular, scholarly, and general magazines and journals published in the U.S., Canada, and the Caribbean. A section for the periodicals indexed gives publication information and indications of what volume(s) are indexed in the work. The title is a good acquisition for smaller libraries that lack the expensive databases in literature.

5-181. Poetry Criticism. Detroit: Gale/Cengage Learning. 1991– . Print and e-book.

This series focuses on English-language poets, although foreign-language poets who have been widely studied and translated into English are also included. Each volume treats a varying number of major poets, but the volumes are not organized by eras or themes, nor are the poets related in any way. Entries supply an introductory biographical sketch and description of important works. Also included are listings of critical analyses, with excerpts of commentary concerning major poems. Entries conclude with a brief bibliography of secondary sources for further reading. It is necessary to use the cumulative indexes by author and nationality to find particular poets one is searching for. The cumulative title index to the entire series is published separately. The series is also indexed in the free Gale's Literary Index database.

5-182. Poetry for Students. Detroit: Gale/Cengage Learning. Print and e-book.

As the title implies, this series is designed specifically to meet the needs of high school and undergraduate college students studying poetry. Each volume provides an analysis of approximately

20 poems that teachers and librarians have identified as the most frequently studied in literature courses. For each poem, there is an overview essay on the poem with an analysis of the work's construction and form; an examination of key themes addressed in the poem; a discussion of the historical and cultural context in which the poem was composed; selected criticism on the poem or poet; and a brief author biography with a list of sources for further study and suggested research topics.

5-183. **Poet's Market.** Cincinnati: Writer's Digest Books, 1985– . Ann.

One of the few guides focusing on the needs of the poet, the intention of this work is to help serious poets find the right outlets and "derive appropriate rewards for their labor." With over 1,000 listings, the book gives guidelines for submissions, the type of publication, type of poetry considered, and other salient bits of information (such as pay rates or no pay). Included here are small-circulation literary journals, mass circulation magazines, and book publishers, both small press and trade. The editors supply a code to identify what might be the most receptive publishers, and identify specialties. Additionally, there are listings of greeting card companies, writing colonies, and poets' organizations. Suggestions are given for promoting one's work, giving readings, social networking, and self-publishing. The contents are accessed through indexes of various types, including geographic region and subject.

5-184. **Thematic Guide to American Poetry.** Westport, CT: Greenwood, 2002. Print and e-book.

5-185. **Thematic Guide to British Poetry.** Westport, CT: Greenwood, 2002. Print and e-book.

These guides are organized by familiar themes such as love, death, patriotism, music, nature, and more. The topics are explored in detail in lengthy essays with references to specific poems. Historical context and biographical sketches offer insight into the poets' lives as well as the time periods in which they lived. Included in each volume is a list of anthologies in which the referenced poems can be found and works offering interpretations of numerous poems. Author, title, and subject indexes aid in locating poems referenced in the essays. These guides are useful for students, both high school and undergraduate, or the general public.

Open Access Resources

5-186. **The Academy of American Poets.** http://www.poets.org/page.php/prmID/41

Marie Bullock founded The Academy of American Poets in 1934 after discovering that most poets were unable to make a living as poets in the United States. She vowed to nurture American poets and promote contemporary poetry through the Academy. In keeping with this mission, the organization created National Poetry Month, hosts forums and poetry readings, and publishes *American Poetry* magazine and maintains poetry archives in both audio and written formats. It sponsors awards to over 200 prizes to novice and veteran poets.

5-187. **British Electronic Poetry Centre (BEPC).** http://www.soton.ac.uk/%7Ebepc

The BEPC "serves British poetry's diverse traditions of innovation." It was launched in May 2002. The guide section includes an index of poets with links to their biographies, critical readings and examples of their work as text and audio files. Readings contain an audio archive of poetry reading. There is a gateway which contains links to other sites, a forum, and further information on BEPC.

5-188. **British Poetry 1780–1910: A Hypertext Archive of Scholarly Editions.** http://etext.lib.virginia.edu/britpo.html

This archive of Romantic and Victorian British poetry is a subset of the holdings of the Electronic Text Center at the University of Virginia Library. The archive currently holds works by Coleridge, Tennyson, and Lewis Carroll among others and also by lesser-known women writers of the late eighteenth century, such as Ann Batten Cristall and Mary Robinson. The archive contains the texts themselves, made accessible as linear HTML documents, plus facsimile and other illustrative material in a hypertext structure. The texts are marked up in SGML according to the TEI guidelines, and the project intends to make the source files downloadable from the site for use with the user's own text analysis software.

5-189. Electronic Poetry Center. http://epc.buffalo.edu/

With links to other electronic poetry sites as well as to authors' poetry, this website exists to promote contemporary, experimental, and innovative poetry.

5-190. Contemporary American Poetry Archive. http://capa.conncoll.edu/

Although the title may imply that the Contemporary American Poetry Archive (CAPA) would be devoted to recently written poetry, the archive's purpose is "to make freely available on the Internet out of print volumes of twentieth century American poetry." The site provides limited biographical information about the poets. Books from commercial, university, and small presses are eligible for archiving; copyright information on reprinting the works is provided. Self-published and vanity press books are not considered for inclusion. The archive is supported by Connecticut College, Department of English, and Connecticut College Libraries.

5-191. Modern American Poetry. http://www.english.uiuc.edu/maps/

This online resource is provided as a companion to the *Anthology of Modern American Poetry* published by Oxford University Press, and maintained by the University of Illinois. It contains sites for over 150 individual American poets. For each poet, the site provides a photo, brief biography, selected criticism of major works, and links to further information. For most poets, a bibliography is also provided. If available, excerpts of interviews and autobiographical writings are published. The biographical notes are concise but useful, and the critical selections are well chosen and edited, providing a brief but comprehensive view of the range of critical views on each writer. The site is easily navigable and well-presented, despite some ugly fonts. Links are current. The site is most useful for undergraduates and general readers and as a first point of reference for all. It is especially useful for its coverage of more obscure figures that might not have another site of such accuracy devoted to them.

5-192. National Book Awards. http://www.nationalbook.org/nbapoetrywinners.html

This site is a collection of each of the books that has won the National Book Award for poetry since the award's inception in 1950 (excluding the years 1984–1990). The NBA created the site as a retrospective for the 2009 National Book Awards with the intention of creating a permanent "digitized literary archive" of the award winning books, funded by the National Endowment for the Arts. Each year is represented by an image of the cover of the winning book. Clicking on a cover leads to a page showing bibliographic information, the author's photograph, suggested links, and purchase information for the book, as well as the finalists and judges for that year. The best part, however, is the essay on the book written by other poets describing their reactions to the work.

5-193. PENNsound. http://www.writing.upenn.edu/pennsound/

PENNsound was launched in January 2005. It is a non-commercial project to make available what is described as the largest collection of poetry sound files on the Internet. It is part of the University of Pennsylvania's Center for Programs in Contemporary Writing and includes sound recordings to download, videos of performances, and texts about authors.

5-194. Poetry 180. Library of Congress. http://www.loc.gov/poetry/180/

The purpose of this site is to expose students to one poem a day throughout the school year.

5-195. Poetry Archive. http://www.poetryarchive.org/poetryarchive/home.do

The Poetry Archive holds audio recordings of well-known, mostly British, poets reading their own work. The earliest are of Alfred Tennyson and Robert Browning, recorded towards the end of the nineteenth century. Notable twentieth-century poets featured in the archive include: John Betjeman, Edmund Blunden, Simon Armitage, Fleur Adcock, U. A. Fanthorpe, Allen Ginsberg, Seamus Heaney, Elizabeth Jennings, Rudyard Kipling, Louis MacNeice, Christopher Logue, Hugh MacDiarmid, Peter Porter, Kathleen Raine, Michael Rosen, Siegfried Sassoon, George Szirtes, Anthony Thwaite, Hugo Williams, and W. B. Yeats. The archive was initiated by Richard Carrington and the Poet Laureate Andrew Motion, who were concerned that people should have the opportunity to listen to poets recite their own poems. The Poetry Archive is extensive and growing. It may be searched and browsed by poet or poem and also browsed by the region of Britain that each poet is associated with. Included are sections for teachers and students, and a Children's Archive for younger users. Video recordings of interviews with contemporary poets are also hosted on the site. This is a well-designed site and a key resource for those studying modern British poetry.

5-196. Poetryclass. http://www.poetryclass.net/index.htm

Poetryclass is an online resource for teachers wanting to spark the interest of younger children in poetry. Hosted by The Poetry Society, it is likely to be of interest to undergraduate education researchers or teachers. The site offers a broad selection of material from poetry lessons, interviews with poets, and poetry by children. It also includes an analysis of a project run by The Poetry Society with poet Ann Sansom for teacher training with students at Exeter University, offered as a model for use by others. There is plenty of feedback from schools that have been involved in Poetryclass projects, as well as resource material, articles, and recommendations for classroom books. This site is very easy to use and offers useful resources for planning and analysis, as well as links to sites of further interest.

5-197. Poetry Daily. http://www.poems.com/

Poetry Daily is an online and non-profit poetry anthology, newsletter, and bookstore. Every day a new contemporary poem is featured, complete with information about the (usually American) author. An archive makes all past poetry available to readers and includes work by well-known poets such as A. R. Ammons, Yves Bonnefoy, and Seamus Heaney. However, of most interest to poetry scholars will be the archive of interviews with writers and the newsletter. Robert Bly, David Lehman, and Ruth Stone have all submitted to interviews, which although pitched at the general reader are illuminating and probing. The newsletter is primarily a review section and probably Poetry Daily's most impressive aspect. Some 30 or so reviews are carried at any one time, making the site an invaluable resource for those interested in contemporary poetry.

5-198. The Poetry Foundation. http://www.poetryfoundation.org

The Poetry Foundation's mission is to "discover and celebrate the best poetry" and "put it before the largest possible audience." The website is a collection of articles from the foundation's *Poetry* magazine, as well as announcements, articles, podcasts, and videos about poetry. Resources range from a searchable database of poems and poets to the Learning Lab for students and teachers. It even has a mobile poetry application for smart phones allowing users to search through the sizable archives on the go.

5-199. Poetry Society of America. http://www.poetrysociety.org/

The Poetry Society of America (PSA) was founded in 1910. It organizes readings, seminars and competitions, details of which are available on the website. Its current members include a number of major contemporary American poets, although membership is open to all. The main research resource on this site is PSA Resources and consists of links to external sites under the following headings: Poetry Conferences and Festivals, Poetry Journals, Poetry Book Publishers, MFA Programs in Poetry, Literary Organizations and Miscellaneous Resources, and Independent Literary Bookstores. The listing under Poetry Journals currently includes links to the web pages of a number of literary and arts periodicals which publish poetry. Some of these titles have online content; others are simply the home pages of publications with subscription information and current contents. The category Literary Organizations and Miscellaneous Resources also contains much useful information. The Society publishes a journal, *Crossroads,* and this site includes some of its content online. The PSA is a partner with Boston University and the Library of Congress in "The Favorite Poem Project" which is linked from this site. While the PSA site is aimed at the general public, there is sufficient content to make it of use to those undertaking research into modern and contemporary American poetry.

5-200. Poets.org. http://www.poets.org/

The website of The Academy of American Poets contains biographies and electronic texts of poems by over 200 poets writing in English (not just Americans). It also provides a news service for American poets, prizes and awards, poetry discussion forums, and poetry "exhibits" (essays with hypertext links to information, images, and related materials). The site contains a large audio section where users can download sound files of authors reading their poetry. This is a large, well-presented site that offers a great deal to those interested in poetry in the USA. The site is targeted more toward the enthusiast than the scholar, but the information and electronic texts it provides should ensure it is not without usefulness to the academic.

5-201. Representative Poetry On-line. http://rpo.library.utoronto.ca/display/index.cfm

Representative Poetry On-line is an anthology of British poetry from Caedmon in the seventh century to the present. Over 2,000 poems are included by over 350 different poets. The database of poetry may be searched by: poet, title, first line, keyword, or date. Bibliographic details are given for the source of each inclusion, along with some annotations. In addition to the poems, the site includes many key texts on poetics in both prose and verse, and an extensive glossary of poetic terms, which should prove a useful reference guide for the student. This site is based on the printed editions of *Representative Poetry,* published by the University of Toronto Press between 1912 and 1967. The electronic version includes some works that were not included in print and are difficult to obtain from other sources. Representative Poetry On-line is clearly presented and easy to use and has received several awards.

5-202. Sackner Archive of Visual and Concrete Poetry.
http://www.rediscov.com/sacknerarchives/

Founded by Ruth and Marvin Sackner in 1979, the Sackner Archive in Miami is one of the best and most complete collections of concrete and visual poetry in existence. Visual Poetry, an international movement, has its origins in work by Mallarme and Apollinaire and came to prominence in the 1950s and 1960s. Featuring work by artists and writers from around the world, the archive represents a unique resource. The collection includes books, prints, objects, texts, manuscripts, paintings and more. There are works from major art movements such as Futurism, Surrealism, the Bauhaus and significant artists, including Ian Hamilton Finlay and Eugen Gomringer. It is possible to browse the online collection by keyword, author, or title. Many works are represented by images and there is extensive additional cataloguing.

5-203. Ways to Celebrate National Poetry Month with the *New York Times*. http://learning.blogs. nytimes.com/2010/04/01/11-ways-to-celebrate-national-poetry-month-with-the-new-york-times/

Shannon Doyne, Katherine Schulten, and Holly Epstein Ojalvo first published this *New York Times* blog article as "Eleven Ways to Celebrate National Poetry Month" in March, 2010. In 2011, they decided to add ideas to it each year, amending the title to create a permanent collection of ideas for exploring poetry in creative ways. Suggestions vary from creating "found poetry" by using the words from another work to comparing the lyrics from rap songs to traditional poetry. The ideas are geared toward teachers and written with lesson plans in mind, although many easily could be adapted for personal poetry adventures.

SPECIALIZED TOPICS IN LITERATURE
Ethnic Studies

5-204. African American Literature: A Guide to Reading Interests. Alma Dawson and Connie Van Fleet. Westport CT: Libraries Unlimited, 2004. (Genreflecting Advisory Series)

Part of the Genreflecting Advisory Series, this is a general reference guide to African-American literature published between 1990 and 2003. The guide does include some older books that the authors considered classics in the field. This book is aimed at adults (but possibly useful to YAs). Only African-American writers are featured; the authors chose to focus on writers "who have spent their formative years in the United States" (xv). The book includes a section on trends in African-American publishing. Genres covered include detective/crime fiction, frontier literature, historical fiction, inspirational literature, mainstream fiction, romance fiction, and speculative fiction. The inspirational and frontier literature sections contain some nonfiction entries. There is also a "life stories" section with biographies and autobiographies.

5-205. American Ethnic Writers. Pasadena, CA: Salem Press, 2008. 3 vols.

This revised edition of American Ethnic Writers has been expanded to three volumes to include more new writers. Contents described in the publisher's description give the numbers as 225 ethnic writers, among them 94 women. Writers included are African American (102), Asian American (32), Jewish American (31), Hispanic/Latino (46), and Native American (21). Arranged alphabetically by author, each essay begins with information pertinent to the ethnicity of the writer (e.g., Asian American novelist), a summary description of the writer's significance, and biographical information. A section of analyses focuses on the writer's works and includes a Suggested Readings section for more information. Each essay is signed by the scholar or other expert contributor who wrote the piece. At the end of volume three is a General Bibliography and a list of Web Sites, as well as five indexes: Author Index, Title Index, Authors by Ethnic Identity, Titles by Ethnic Identity, and Titles by Genre. The set is a good resource of basic information for students and the general public.

    Another critical work by Salem Press is *Notable African American Writers* (2006), a three-volume set that contains approximately 80 essays on African-American novelists, poets, playwrights, short-story writers, and writers of nonfiction from colonial America to today. This volume offers a comprehensive overview of each author's biography and literary career as well as listings of their major works in all genres. Through discussions of their lives and literature, this work "helps readers to better understand the experience and influence of African Americans in the history of their country." Indexes include genre, personages, title, and subject.

5-206. Black Short Fiction and Folklore. Alexander Street Press. Online subscription database. http://alexanderstreet.com/BLFI

This database is a far-ranging compilation of literature from Africa and the African Diaspora that includes all manner of writings from fables, parables, ballads, and folktales, to short fiction and novellas. Over 30 percent of the items in the collection have never been published before from archives and personal collections. New materials are continuously being found and added to the database. It is a rich resource, not only for the literature contained in it, but for cultural, social, and political research. The collection received the Best Reference Database designation by Library Journal in 2004.

The Black Women Writers database is another collection from Alexander Street Press. It contains materials drawn from the Black Short Fiction and Folklore collection and others, augmented with writings from contemporary women writers.

5-207. The Columbia Guide to Contemporary African-American Fiction. D. Dickson-Carr. New York: Columbia University Press, 2005.

This is a general reference guide to African-American fiction published from 1970–2000. The book includes American-born authors and black Caribbean authors who immigrated to the United States. The guide opens with an overview of developments in African-American fiction and publishing over the 30-year period covered in the entries. Entries include 114 authors with biographical information and plot summaries and reviews of their works. Major works have separate entries. There are also entries on relevant journals and magazines, literary movements as they are addressed in African-American fiction of the period, and discussion of many different genres and African-American writers' work in them. An index allows searching by author, title, and subject.

5-208. Encyclopedia of African-American Women Writers. Yolanda Williams Page, ed. Greenwood Press, 2007. 2 vols. Print and e-book.

Novelists, playwrights, poets, essayists, literary critics, and authors of children's works from the eighteenth to the twentieth-first centuries are profiled in this two-volume set. Included are 168 African American (and some Caribbean) women writers. Each entry has a section on the life of the writer, her major works, critical responses to them, and a bibliography, which lists the author's works and critical articles about the works. Volume 1 contains two lists of authors, the first organized by genre and the second by date. A four-page bibliography on African American women writers is in volume 2, as well as an index, list of awards won by the women, and biographical data on each of the contributors. A similar work also published by Greenwood is *Writing African America Women: An Encyclopedia of Literature by and about Women of Color* (2006). The work covers many of the same authors, but is more focused on a feminist perspective. Yolanda Williams Page has also edited *Icons of African-American Literature: the Black Literary World* (Greenwood, 2011) containing just 24 entries on the most notable figures in African-American literature and cultural topics related to the literature. Both works by Page are suitable for students at all levels and the general public.

5-209. The Greenwood Encyclopedia of Multiethnic American Literature. Emmanuel S. Nelson. Westport, CT: Greenwood Press, 2005. 5 vols.

While there are many publications devoted to one or another ethnic literature, this is a good resource, especially for smaller libraries, as it provides at least basic information about many different literatures. "Multiethnic" is a broad category that includes African Americans, Finnish Americans, Jewish Americans, Native Americans, Amish Americans, and 34 other ethnic groups. Major authors and works, events, concepts, and publishers are covered in entries by more than 300 contributors. The value of this set lies in the focus on the impact of ethnic identity on American literature and the inclusion of lesser known writers as well as those to be found in less comprehensive works. Black and white images and further readings are provided. The Encyclopedia was a RUSA Outstanding Reference Sources selection in 2006.

From the same publisher is the *Greenwood Encyclopedia of African American Literature* edited by Hans Ostrom and J. David Macy, Jr. (2005, 5 vols). In this set, there are over 1,000 articles contributed by 200 scholars, with additional sources following each article. In addition to writers, literary forms, genres, and movements, there are articles on historical and social issues that impacted African American literature, important newspapers and literary journals, regions and locations.

5-210. **Harlem Renaissance: A Gale Critical Companion.** J. Witalec. Detroit: Gale, 2002. 3 vols.

Volume 1 in this set contains an introduction to the Harlem Renaissance, written by a noted scholar in the field, a descriptive chronology of events, and essays on five major topics related to the movement. Volumes 2 and 3 include approximately 35 entries on the major literary figures and their works from the period. These entries include a biographical/critical introduction, a complete bibliography of the author's works, and full text reprinted of criticism about the author or individual works. Authors covered in Harlem Renaissance include Langston Hughes, Zora Neale Hurston, and many more. Another work on the same topic is the Routledge *Encyclopedia of the Harlem Renaissance* (2005).

5-211. **20th Century African-American Poetry.** Chadwyck-Healey. Online subscription database. http://collections.chadwyck.co.uk/

African-American Poetry, 1760–1900. Chadwyck-Healey. Online subscription database. http://collections.chadwyck.co.uk/

Together these two digital collections contain over two centuries of the poetical writings of African-American poets. The 20th century collection has over 10,000 poems by 75 poets including acclaimed poets throughout the century and young poets near the end of the century. The complete collections are included as well as related prose writings. Indexes include titles and first lines. Selections for African-American Poetry, 1760–1900 are based upon the bibliography of William French et al., *Afro-American Poetry and Drama, 1760–1975: A Guide to Information Sources* (Gale Research, 1979). The collection includes nearly 3,000 poems written by poets from all walks of life. The collections are available separately and also included in Literature Online (entry 5-1).

Gender Studies

5-212. **Orlando.** Cambridge University Press. In Cambridge Collections Online. Online subscription database.

Orlando is a comprehensive electronic database relating to women's writing in the British Isles. It offers a wealth of biographical and critical information on more than 1,200 writers, together with entries on literary and historical events. The database offers entries on authors' lives and writing careers, contextual material, timelines, internal links and bibliographies. Entries are tagged, enabling searchers to focus not only on author, date, and place but also on such issues as genre, intertextuality, and relations with publishers.

5-213. **Emory Women Writers Resource Project.** http://womenwriters.library.emory.edu/

Texts by and about women, from the 17th through the early 20th century, are available on this website. The site is divided into collections and each collection can be searched or browsed. Searching can be by ethnicity, genre, region, period, publisher, or subject. Collections include Genre Fiction;

Early Modern through the 18th Century; World War I Poetry; Native American; Abolition, Freedom, and Rights; and Women's Advocacy. Some collections also contain essays to aid in the comprehension of particular authors, works, or eras.

5-214. Encyclopedia of Feminist Literature. Kathy J. Whitson. Westport, CT: Greenwood Press, 2004.

The treatment of feminism in this work emphasizes the creative rather than the theoretical. There is a short history of feminism as a concept endorsing the social, political and economic equality of women. Biographical and contextual information is included for 70 women writers who challenged traditional gender roles with their writings. Both well-known and relatively obscure American and English creative writers are profiled. Besides biographical information, each entry contains a summary with commentary on one major work. Entries include related references and suggested readings. In addition to the author entries, there are 20 articles covering topics related to feminism, such as Abolition and Amazon, to Spirituality, Silence and Voice, and Woman Question. The book is a good introduction to the topic for students.

Two other similar works are available on the topic. One is another work with the same title by Mary Ellen Snodgrass (Facts on File, 2006). The second one is *Encyclopedia of Feminist Literary Theory* by Elizabeth Kowaleski Wallace (Taylor & Francis, 2009. E-book).

5-215. Encyclopedia of Contemporary LGBTQ Literature of the United States. Emmanuel S. Nelson. Greenwood Press/ABC-CLIO, 2009. 2 vols. Print and e-book.

Hundreds of alphabetical entries discuss authors, literary works, movements, genres, and social contexts and issues in this two-volume work. An alphabetical list of the entries makes it easy to find a topic quickly. The work is a Choice 2010 Outstanding Academic Title selection.

5-216. Feminism in Literature: A Gale Critical Companion. Jessica Bomarito and Jeffery Hunter, eds. Detroit: Gale, 2005. 6 vols. Print and online.

The history of women's and feminist thought is traced through women writers from antiquity through the modern era. Various topics include misogyny and women's roles in ancient civilizations, sixteenth century women's devotional and religious literature, seventeenth and eighteenth century women's captivity material, the women's suffrage campaign of the nineteenth century in the United States, women authors of the 'Lost Generation,' and lesbian literature, among other topics specific to female authors. In addition to the important female literary figures, this work also provides information about the culture, society and historical situation of the authors. The set is a basic information resource on the topic for public and academic libraries.

5-217. Gay, Lesbian, Bisexual, and Transgendered Literature: A Genre Guide. E. Bosman and J. Bradford. Westport CT: Libraries Unlimited, 2008. (Genreflecting Advisory Series)

This is a general guide to gay, lesbian, bisexual, and transgender (GLBT) literature. Most of the books discussed were published after 1969, but a few older works are included. All featured works have either GLBT main character(s) or main themes. This book is aimed at adults, but entries on books of potential interest to YAs have been flagged. The work includes a section on the history of GLBT literature and a discussion of how librarians can handle special issues (e.g. censorship). Genres covered include classics, general fiction, historical fiction, romance, fantasy, science fiction, horror, mystery/crime, comics and graphic novels, and drama. Also included are sections on books addressing coming out and HIV/AIDS and a "life stories" section with biographies and autobiographies.

5-218. Historical Dictionary of Lesbian Literature. Meredith Miller. Lanham, MD: Scarecrow Press, 2006. (Historical Dictionaries of Literature and the Arts)

The Historical Dictionary of Lesbian Literature has been compiled both to provide further information to those who are already familiar with the field and to explain it to those who are just getting acquainted. Through an introduction on the development of the genre and the entries, the work provides an idea of the factors which have influenced the lesbian identity in all kinds of literature. Several hundred cross-referenced dictionary entries cover important writers such as Sappho, Colette, Mary Wollstonecraft, and many others who are less well known. Other entries deal with the styles, themes, literary movements, publishers, and outstanding works of the genre. Also included are a chronology and a bibliography for further research.

5-219. Women in Literature: Reading Through the Lens of Gender. Jerilyn Fisher and Ellen S. Silber, eds. Westport, CT: Greenwood Press, 2003.

The focus of this work is not women writers, but women as characters in literature. Ninety-six of the most frequently taught works of literature by both male (Dickens, Faulkner) and female (Shelley, Chopin, Harper Lee) authors are analyzed by scholarly contributors to construct a feminine perspective on the works.

CHAPTER 6

WORLD LITERATURE AND LANGUAGES

Sonia Ramírez Wohlmuth

The chapter on world literature and languages is new for this 6th edition of the Humanities Guide. In the latter years of the 20th century, there was an increased emphasis upon globalization in business and in education. The Internet and subsequent mobile technologies have been catalysts for drawing people across the world closer together and fostering the study of different countries and cultures.

As with the other chapters in this Guide, the works listed in this chapter exclude retrospective items in favor of more current works (that is, year 2000 or later). The reader is referred to earlier editions of the Guide for works published prior to 2000. The process of selection draws on works reviewed in academic and professional publications, publishers' brochures and catalogs, as well as searches in the online catalogs of major academic and research libraries.

The organization and entries in this chapter should be helpful to librarians, teachers, and students. The chapter has two major divisions, the first, World Literature and the second, World Languages and Linguistics. Within these divisions general resources are placed first then followed by more specific resources organized by geographic regions according to the United Nations Statistics Division geographic scheme.

WORLD LITERATURE

For the purpose of this guide, world literature is an umbrella term that encompasses all literary works initially produced in a language other than English. Damrosch succinctly describes the process of dissemination of works that become part of the canon of world literature, "A work enters into world literature by a double process: first, by being read as literature; second, by circulating out into a broader world beyond its linguistic and cultural point of origin" (David Damrosch, *What Is World Literature?* Princeton University Press, 2003: 6).

One mechanism for circulation beyond the point of origin has been translation. In the West, there is a long-standing tradition of literary translation best exemplified by the dissemination of the Greek and Roman classics in all languages of Europe and beyond, as well as translations of the Bible to modern European languages. Because of the importance of translation as a vehicle of dissemination, the Special Topics section at the end of this chapter includes Literary Translation as one of its subheadings.

This chapter contains a number of anthologies in addition to reference works. In developing a global literature collection, anthologies can play a larger role than for collections of literature written in English. Anthologies can offer a wide coverage of the best writings by authors who may not be well known beyond their native countries. Anthologies usually contain both biographical information and criticism in addition to the writings of the authors included. They tend to be focused upon authors of a certain country or region, time period, literary movement, or genre. Anthologies can constitute a basic literature collection without the necessity to offer individual titles for a large number of authors. Bilingual anthologies can be offered for library clientele who are trying to learn another language whether it be English or non-English languages. As such, anthologies can be the core of a worldwide literature collection.

In terms of organization, World Literature begins with general resources, works that address world literature in general or more than one region. The general resources are followed by more specific resources by geographic divisions. The first geographic divisions are by continent subdivided by regions or countries with further subdivision by literary genre. Works dealing with the narrative are grouped together followed by drama and poetry. The last section on Special Topics is organized thematically and addresses those subjects which are salient in modern literature. The first subdivision includes works that can be viewed as testimonial literature and focuses on historical events such as the Holocaust, other historical genocides, war and conflict. Works that address the literary production of women or themes related to the role of women in society, as well as issues of gender and sexuality, form the second set of entries. Literary Translation treats the transmission of works beyond the immediate scope of their linguistic community. Works that deal with literary translation in general or translation of a particular language or genre are treated in that section. The final section of Special Topics deals with the presentation of the unreal or imagined and includes both works that reflect a specific genre, science fiction, as well as works with elements of fantasy, the fantastic, or magic realism.

RESOURCES IN WORLD LITERATURE

The first grouping for Resources in World Literature includes general works that deal with literature written in languages other than English. These works include databases and digital collections containing either primary sources, that is, literary texts themselves, or critical works about specific authors and their literary production. Monographs and monographic sets include bibliographies, frequently updated on an annual basis; encyclopedias and dictionaries; histories; and criticism. To avoid repetition of a large number of resources covered in other chapters, described below are subscription databases and digital collections reviewed in both chapter 2 and chapter 5 that may include texts and critical works germane to studies in world literature.

Literature is addressed broadly in the resources in chapter 2, "Multidisciplinary Resources in the Humanities and the Arts." Many databases and collections reviewed in that chapter contain titles pertaining to subjects in world literature. In particular, the reader is referred to the general database products listed here:

Cambridge Collections Online (entry 2-34)

Chadwyck/Healey: Early European Books digital collection (entry 2-36) as well as other collections devoted primarily to literature and publications in English, such as Early English Books Online (entry 2-36), and C-19: the Nineteenth Century Index (2-37), along with the Nineteenth Century Short Title Catalog (2-38)

EBSCO/Wilson Humanities indexes (entries 2-7, 2-9, 2-12); and Salem Press Literature: The Database (entry 2-31)

FRANCIS—one of the most comprehensive indexes to literature in Europe; coverage is primarily Western Europe (39%), France (28%), and the United States (17%); (entry 2-13)

Gale/Cengage databases: Litfinder has a broad chronological scope extending from the Middle Ages to the present day (entry 2-15) and Literature Resource Center (entry 2-16)

Oxford Reference Online Premium entry (2-23)

Resources in chapter 5 cover literature in English which also can be useful in searching for criticism of works published worldwide and some of which do include global literature translated into English.

Chadwyck-Healey offers Literature Online Reference, a database that aggregates many other separate Chadwyck-Healey collections (entry 5-1).

Gale Cengage databases include Dictionary of Literary Biography Complete Online (entry 5-6); Literature Criticism Online (entry 5-7); Scribner's Writer's Series (entry 5-8); and Twayne's Author Series (entry 5-9), which includes Twayne's World Authors.

MagillOnLiterature Plus (entry 2-30) is a database of Salem Press critical works. It includes the five-volume *Cyclopedia of World Authors*. In addition, the three-volume *World Philosophers and Their Works* provides valuable background information for literary movements and theories. Magill's *Critical Survey of Long Fiction*, 4th ed. includes many authors with works in translation (entry 5-63).

Palgrave Macmillan, UK offers Palgrave Connect: Literature and Performing Arts, a site license to e-books (entry 5-12).

The reader is encouraged to consult these sources and others in chapters 2 and 5 in addition to those in this chapter. The general resources in world literature begin next with databases and digital collections.

Databases and Digital Collections

E-books on Demand Service (EOD). http://search.books2ebooks.eu/

The EOD is an e-books on demand service provided by over thirty European national libraries, city libraries, and university libraries. A person can request through one of the library catalogs a work that is not under copyright. The library will digitize the work and send the digital file to the requestor. The libraries are being encouraged to then add these works to their digital libraries and send metadata to Europeana (entry 2-52). The EOD service also has a Facebook page.

6-1. The Cambridge Companions to Literature and Classics. Cambridge: Cambridge University Press. Monographic series. Online subscription database.

This online collection corresponds to the more than 250 titles published as individual monographs under the series title. The database allows searching of the contents of all volumes simultaneously thus providing access to over 2,000 individual essays that treat literary movements, genres, national literatures, as well as specific authors and their works.

6-2. IBZ Online (Internationale Bibliographie der geistes-und sozialwissenschaftlichen Zeitschiftenliteratur). Berlin: Walter De Gruyter. Online subscription database.

International and interdisciplinary (social sciences and humanities) in scope, the IBZ now indexes some 11,500 journals and more than 3 million articles. The search interface is available in both English and German. Users can undertake key word searches of both article titles and abstracts (feature inaugurated in 2011).

Also published by De Gruyter is the **IBR Online** (*Internationale Bibliographie der Rezensionen geistes-und sozialwissenschaftlicher Literatur/International Bibliography of Book Reviews of Scholarly Literature in the Humanities and Social Sciences*). Since 1971 the bibliography has published reviews of books in the humanities and social sciences gleaned from nearly 7,000 journals, mostly published in Europe. The database contains more than 570,000 reviews, and some 60,000 new entries are added every year.

6-3. MLA International Bibliography. New York: Modern Language Association of America, 1926– . Online subscription database. http://www.mla.org

The MLA International Bibliography is a classified listing and subject index of scholarly books and articles on modern languages, literatures, folklore, and linguistics, which has been compiled by the Modern Language Association of America since 1926. The electronic version includes the entire print run of over 2,000,000 records in the Bibliography. It also provides access to the MLA Directory of Periodicals, a guide to some 7,100 journals and monographic series. For fuller information see entries 2-20 and 2-21.

Open Access Resources

As with databases and digital collections, there are also a number of open access resources covered in chapter 2 that are germane to world literature. Foremost among them is the European Digital Library and Europeana (entries 2-51 and 2-52); Project Gutenberg (entry 2-59); the Oxford Text Archive (entry 2-58); Voice of the Shuttle (2-61); and the World Digital Library (entry 2-62). More specialized websites include the Online Reference Book for Medieval Studies (ORB) (entry 2-57). In chapter 5, open access resources germane to world literature include Literary Resources on the Net (entry 5-42), the Online Books Page (entry 5-45), Poetry Foundation (entry 5-198), and the Sackner Archive of Visual and Concrete Poetry (entry 5-202). Below are open access resources that more directly focus on world literature.

6-4. Bibliotheca Augustana. http://www.hs-augsburg.de/~Harsch/augustana.html

The Bibliotheca Augustana is a digital library of world literature e-texts in many of the world's languages. The electronic texts are in Latin, Ancient Greek, English, French, German, and Italian and range in date from classical times to the modern age. Also, this site provides links to many other foreign language literature sites.

6-5. World Book Club. http://www.bbc.co.uk/podcasts/series/wbc

Approximately 50 interviews with well-known authors discussing their work are archived on this BBC website. Although the English language format limits the scope of authors, there are interviews with authors who do not regularly publish in English.

6-6. World Oral Literature Project. http://oralliterature.org/

This project is primarily the work of researchers at Cambridge University although Yale University has been a co-site since 2011. Oral literature in the scope of this project includes epic poems, folk tales, creation tales, myths, legends, proverbs, word games, autobiographical and historical narratives, as well as ritual texts and curative chants. The texts themselves are in the form of sound files. Access is facilitated by an interactive world map that shows the location of the field and archival recordings.

Organizations

As in the foregoing sections, attention is called to organizations and associations germane to world literature that have been treated in other chapters in this Guide. In chapter 5, there is an entry for the Modern Language Association as an organization in addition to entries for MLA publications (entry 5-49). Two comparative literature associations are The American Comparative Literature Association (entry 5-50) and the British Comparative Literature Association (entry 5-51). The Electronic Literature Organization (entry 5-55) also concerns literature worldwide. Many organizations are included which are international but primarily operate in the language of the country in which they are based. A few of the organizations that operate in English are included here.

6-7. International Association for Philosophy and Literature. IAPL. http://www.iapl.info/

The IAPL was founded to provide a forum for discussion and research about the interplay of humanistic disciplines concerning philosophy, literary theory, and cultural, aesthetic, and textual studies. The headquarters is at Stony Brook University.

6-8. International Society for Folk-Narrative Research. http://www.folklore.org.il/ISFNR/

The International Society for Folk Narrative Research, based at the Nordic Institute of Folklore in Turka, Finland, is a scholarly and professional organization of international specialists in the areas of folk narrative, popular literature, folklore, and related fields. In recent years, the focus of the society has broadened to cover all aspects of narrative "as representing the pivotal category of human communication."

6-9. **The European Society for Textual Scholarship. ESTS.**
http://www.textualscholarship.eu/index.html

The ESTS is an international and interdisciplinary society for the study and promotion of textual scholarship in Europe. It holds an annual conference and publishes a journal, *Variants*. ESTS has a close collaboration with the Society for Textual Studies in the United States (http://www.textual.org/).

Printed Monographs, Sets, and Series

Literature Worldwide—History and Criticism

6-10. **Approaches to Teaching World Literature.** New York: Modern Language Association. Monographic series.

This series now contains more than 100 titles of which approximately 70 were published in 2000 or later. While the series also includes both American and English literature, there are many works that focus on specific authors or literary works, mostly European, known through translation to English.

6-11. **Contemporary World Fiction: A Guide to Literature in Translation.** Juris Dilevko, Keren Dali, and Glenda Garbutt. Santa Barbara, CA: Libraries Unlimited, 2011. Print and e-book.

This guide to literature in translation lists over 1,000 annotated titles in contemporary world fiction with nine introductory essays about classic titles in world fiction.

6-12. **Encyclopedia of World Authors: 19th and 20th Centuries.** Marie Josephine Diamond, ed. New York: Facts on File, Inc., 2003.

The introduction in this encyclopedia summarizes major literary and aesthetic currents by time and place. A timeline of authors included in the encyclopedia begins with year of birth 1749 and extends to 1962. Entries are arranged alphabetically by author name and include brief biographical information and lists of noted works.

Although the focus of the *Encyclopedia of Literary Modernism* (Paul Poplawski, ed. Greenwood Press, 2003) is on English literary production from 1890 to 1939, it also includes many authors who do not write in English. The alphabetical organization includes author entries as well as literary themes, movements, and articles on particular geographic regions.

6-13. **Gale Contextual Encyclopedia of World Literature.** Gale Cengage, 2009. 4 vols. Print and e-book.

This set provides readers with the necessary background to understand authors and their works within a historical and aesthetic context. Selected authors are presented with biographical, historical, literary and critical information to connect them to the events and culture of their time. Recurrent themes and stylistic devices in authors' works are highlighted as these show connections to a broader literary tradition. The e-book version is fully searchable and cross-searchable with other Gale products.

Although the title is *Concise Dictionary of World Literary Biography*, this work issued by Gale (1999–2000) is a 4-volume set that covers Greek and Roman classics, German literature, Eastern European literature, and selected authors from Africa, the Caribbean, and Latin America. Each volume covers 30 to 40 major authors in the form of a biographical essay and critical evaluation of major works with an author index for each volume of the series.

6-14. **International Who's Who of Authors and Writers 2010.** 25th ed. London: Routledge, 2010. Ann.

The 25th edition of the *International Who's Who of Authors and Writers* provides biographical information on major literary figures as well as literary organizations throughout the world. This reference tool contains nearly 8,000 entries for authors of literary works, journalists, major literary organizations, international literary awards, and national libraries. Updated annually, the current volume covers established authors as well as those who have first received critical acclaim.

6-15. **Magill's Survey of World Literature.** Steven G. Kellman and Frank N. Magill. Pasadena, CA: Salem Press, 2009. 6 vols. Print and e-book.

Magill's Survey of World Literature contains more than 300 writers from 45 different countries whose period of literary productivity extends from the 6th century BCE to the 21st century. The author profiles include biographical information as well as a critical overview of their major literary works. The authors presented here have written in all literary genres: narrative, drama, poetry, and essay.

Another Salem Press product is *Cyclopedia of World Authors* (4th rev. ed. Frank N. Magill and Tracy Irons-Georges, 2004. 5 vols.). This revision of the 1997 edition provides summary information on over 2,400 authors and their major works. Coverage is broad in scope and includes authors from the ancient world up to the present. A brief bibliography is included at the end of each article that provides guidelines for further study. The fifth volume includes an author index, a geographical index, as well as a timeline organized by author's year of birth.

6-16. **The Reader's Companion to World Literature.** Lillian Herlands Hornstein and G. D. Percy, Leon Edel, Horst Frenz, and Sterling Allen Brown. New York: New American Library, 2002.

This concise guide to world literature provides lists of authors, titles, literary and aesthetic currents, historical events, and technical terms and phrases.

6-17. **Reference Guide to World Literature.** 3rd ed. Sara Pendergast and Tom Pendergast, eds. Detroit: St. James Press, 2003. 2 vols. Print and e-book.

This reference work, recognized by both RUSA as an Outstanding Reference Source and by Choice (September 2003) as an Outstanding Academic Book for the scope of its coverage, provides bio/bibliographical entries on some 500 authors and their major works. The chronology of this guide extends from ancient Greece to the 21st century. Author entries provide an overview of the writer's life and the trajectory of his or her literary production. The title entries discuss a particular literary work in depth.

6-18. **A Very Short Introduction.** Oxford: Oxford University Press, 2001– . Monographic series.

As indicated by the title, this series provides the reader with summary information about national literatures, regional literatures, or the literature of a particular language. Recently published titles are listed below. All have *"A Very Short Introduction"* as a subtitle.

Colonial Latin American Literature. Rolena Adorno. 2011.

German Literature. Nicholas Boyle. 2011.

Modern Latin American Literature. Roberto González Echevarría. 2011.

Russian Literature. Catriona Kelly. 2001.

Chinese Literature. Sabina Knight. 2012.

Spanish Literature. Jo Labanyi. 2010.

French Literature. John D. Lyons. 2010.

6-19. What Is World Literature? David Damrosch. Princeton: Princeton University Press, 2003.

This collection of essays on world literature focuses on three areas: circulation, translation, and production. The author uses diverse examples in discussion of these issues including Gilgamesh, Kafka, and Rigoberta Menchú.

       Damrosch has also edited *Teaching World Literature* (Modern Language Association, 2009). Part of the Options for Teaching series, this collection of 32 essays offers insights from different perspectives to the complex subject of world literature. The first group of essays deals with questions of definition and the particular problems posed by literature in translation. The need to provide a context and cultural explanation for works of world literature is the focus of the second set of essays. The last two sets of essays address teaching strategies and the development of a curriculum for world literature.

6-20. World Authors, 1995–2000. Mari Rich, Olivia J. Smith, and Clifford Thompson. New York: H.W. Wilson, 2003.
World Authors, 2000–2005. Jennifer Curry. New York: H.W. Wilson, 2007.

The World Authors series contains biographical articles on major literary figures as well as major writers of non-fiction, essays in the humanities and social sciences. The series is updated frequently. The 1995–2000 volume includes biographical and bibliographical information for some 300 authors in all genres. Many authors contributed autobiographical statements specifically for this publication.

6-21. World Literature and Its Times. Detroit: Gale, 1999–2006. Monographic series.

This monographic series is intended to establish a relationship between the sociopolitical context of a literary work and the literary work itself. The 8-volume series focuses on the literary output in all forms, including fiction, poetry, and nonfiction essay, of a selected country or region. Each volume covers approximately 50 major works in depth. The inclusion of a substantive bibliography at the end of the discussion of each work provides a valuable guide for further reading and investigation.

     Latin American Literature and Its Times. Vol. 1, 1999.

     African Literature and Its Times. Vol. 2, 2000.

     British & Irish Literature and Its Times: Celtic Migrations to the Reform Bill (Beginnings–1830s). Vol. 3, 2000.

     British & Irish Literature and Their Times: The Victorian Era to the Present. Vol. 4, 2001.

     Spanish & Portuguese Literatures and Their Times. Vol. 5, 2001.

     Middle Eastern Literatures and Their Times. Vol. 6, 2004.

     Italian Literature and Its Times. Vol. 7, 2005.

     Classical Literature and Its Times. Vol. 8, 2006.

6-22. World Literature Today (WLT). 1927– . Print and online.
http://www.ou.edu/worldlit/faqs.html

WLT, a major source of reviews of world literature translated into English, was founded as *Books Abroad* in 1927. The journal is still published at the University of Oklahoma, now in both print and digital editions by subscription. In the last 10 years, the content has been expanded to include essays, original writings, interviews, and news. The scope has been broadened to embrace other arts and culture. WLT has won numerous awards, among them a Pushcart Prize. It is an excellent venue to keep current with the latest trends in literature worldwide.

Twayne's Companion to Contemporary World Literature (Gale/Twayne, 2003) is a two-volume set that contains book reviews from *World Literature Today*. The reviews cover the period from 1977 to 2001. In addition, there are critical essays for the period 1927 to 1976. This work provides good coverage of world literature in the second half of the twentieth century, especially for those libraries that do not have access to the journal.

Literature Worldwide—Narrative

6-23. Contemporary World Fiction: A Guide to Literature in Translation. Juris Dilevko, Keren Dali, and Glenda Garbutt. Santa Barbara, CA: Libraries Unlimited, 2011. Print and e-book.

This work is an overview of recent fiction translated to English. The nine chapters are organized geographically: Africa; the Arab world; East Asia; South Asia; the Mediterranean; Russia, Central and Eastern Europe; the Iberian Peninsula and Latin America; Northern Europe; and Western Europe (including the French-speaking Caribbean). Each chapter contains an appendix of representative works with annotations.

6-24. The Facts on File Companion to the World Novel 1900 to the Present. Michael Sollars and Arbolina Llamas Jennings. New York: Facts on File, 2008. 2 vols. Print and e-book.

This resource, from the Companion to Literature series, is a two-volume set arranged alphabetically by author (volume I, A–L; volume II, M–Z). Some 600 individual articles cover major novelists and outstanding works. The author entries include biographical information and a summary of the author's major works. At the end of the second volume is a list of authors by region.

Literature Worldwide—Drama and Poetry

6-25. Columbia Encyclopedia of Modern Drama. Gabrielle H. Cody and Evert Sprinchorn, eds. New York: Columbia University Press, 2007. 2 vols.

This resource surveys the development of modern theatre in Europe, Latin America, Africa, Asia, and the English-speaking world from 1860 to the present. The individual essays cover over 600 authors and place them within the historical and social contexts that shape their work. A fuller treatment of the work is in entry 8-55.

Also in theater and drama, Routledge has published *Who's Who in Contemporary World Theatre* (2000, entry 8-83) and *World Encyclopedia of Contemporary Theatre* (1998, entry 8-39).

6-26. The Poetry of Our World: An International Anthology of Contemporary Poetry. Jeffrey Paine, ed. New York: Harper Collins Publishers, 2000.

This anthology begins with an introduction to recent trends in poetry followed by representative texts organized geographically. Part 1 is the English-speaking world, part 2 Latin America, part 3 Europe, part 4 Africa, and part 5 Asia. A title index and a general index follow at the end.

LITERATURE BY REGION OR COUNTRY

The organization in this section is geographical. Within the geographical regions, the literature is usually divided into History and Criticism, Narratives, and Drama and Poetry. The resources are not divided by formats as in the general resources above, but all formats are included together under the various subheadings with databases or digital collections listed first followed by print resources.

Africa

6-27. African Writers Series. Ann Arbor, MI: Chadwyck/Healey Proquest. Online subscription database. http://collections.chadwyck.com/marketing/home_aws.jsp

This collection is based on the Heinemann African Writers Series and covers works published from 1973. Although some were written decades earlier to the end of the twentieth century, the series includes works from authors of all regions of Africa. Many authors' works appear in English translation for the first time in this series. Each volume contains introductory materials and glossaries to aid in the understanding of the work. The collection is indexed by author name, gender, nationality, and dates of birth/death.

6-28. Literary Map of Africa. Ohio State University Libraries. Open Access resource. http://library.osu.edu/sites/aflitmap/aflitmap.php.

This website has a map interface as well as an author index to the literature of Africa. Clicking on a country name on the map leads to a list of authors from that country. The author links provide access to the major works of the author and the languages in which that work is available.

Africa—History and Criticism

6-29. African Literature: Overview and Bibliography. Jonathan B. Smithe, ed. New York: Nova Science Publishers, 2002.

This introduction to African literature is based on a jury selection of the 100 best examples of literature of the continent. In addition to coverage of these 100 literary works, indexes are arranged by author and country. This reference provides a comprehensive bibliography of studies of African authors and literatures.

6-30. The Cambridge History of African and Caribbean Literature. F. Abiola Irele and Simon Gikandi, eds. Cambridge, UK: Cambridge University Press, 2004. 2 vols. Print and e-book.

The major focus of this two-volume history is African literature and the African diaspora in the Caribbean. The first volume discusses the importance of the oral tradition in African literature and Afro-Caribbean literature. Also included are chapters on the literary traditions of Ethiopia and South Africa as well as African literature written in Arabic. The second volume focuses on literature written in European languages, English, French, Portuguese, and Spanish, as well as Caribbean literature written in French and Spanish. Essays on post-colonialism and post-modernism conclude the volume.

Diaspora

Diaspora literature or diasporic literature is sometimes viewed as a type of testimonial literature with focus on separation, either forced or voluntary, from the homeland. The diaspora can be large scale and systematic such as the Jewish diaspora from Spain and Portugal after the institution of the inquisition in 1493; the centuries long African diaspora as a result of slavery; and the establishment of European administrative structures in colonial possessions far from the homeland. Diaspora literature often includes an idealized vision of the homeland and attempts to recreate that homeland in another time and place resulting in conflicts for the protagonist in terms of identity and linguistic loyalty.

6-31. **The Companion to African Literatures.** Douglas Killam and Ruth Rowe, eds. Bloomington: Indiana University Press, 2000.

This A-Z handbook provides author entries, title entries, and subject entries for all aspects of African literature. Although the focus is on those authors who write in English, the Companion also includes authors who have been translated to English.

6-32. **Encyclopedia of African Literature.** Simon Gikandi. London: Routledge, 2003. Print and e-book.

This comprehensive reference work on African literature has over 600 entries arranged alphabetically that include both well-known and emerging authors, their texts and criticism as well as concepts of literary theory.

Covering these topics in more depth is *African Literature: An Anthology of Criticism and Theory* (Tejumola Olaniyan and Ato Quayson, eds. Oxford: Blackwell, 2007). This anthology contains over 90 individual essays on various aspects of African literature including literary histories of particular regions, oral traditions, the role of the writer, issues of identity, post-colonialism, and sexuality.

6-33. **Literature of Africa.** G. D. Killam. Santa Barbara, CA: Greenwood, 2004.

This introductory guide to the literature of modern Africa focuses on 10 authors and their works. Entries include both those authors who write in English as well as those who write in other languages. The 10 chapters include biographical information about the author and the important historical, political, and social events that emerge as literary themes and motifs. An introductory chapter describes the history and development of literature in Sub-Saharan Africa and offers a geographic organization of the continent as part of the discussion of the colonial experiences and challenges of the postcolonial period.

Another reference on Sub-Saharan Africa is *Southern African Literatures* by Michael Chapman (University of Natal, 2003). The essays in this volume cover all aspects of the literatures of Southern Africa from the ancient oral traditions of the Bushmen to the 21st century. The volume is organized in six parts. The first deals with the oral tradition; part 2 concerns the writings of the age of European settlement; part 3 covers African or Colonial literature (late 19th century); part 4 treats post-independence literature; and part 5 covers the interregnum in South Africa (1970–1995). The final section discusses future studies. An extensive bibliography at the end of the reference also includes a guide to authors cited.

6-34. **The Rienner Anthology of Africa Literatures.** Anthonia G. Kalu, ed. Boulder, CO: Lynne Rienner Publishers, 2007.

This comprehensive anthology of African literatures covers both oral and written traditions from ancient times to the present. The nearly 1,000-page anthology is divided into four sections. The first deals with the oral tradition. The second focuses on autobiographies from the early slave trade. The final two sections cover historical perspectives of colonialism and post colonialism as reflected in literary production.

A complementary work is *Gods and Soldiers: The Penguin Anthology of Contemporary African Writing* (Rob Spillman, ed. Penguin Books, 2009). This anthology of 30 African writers brings together fiction and non-fiction from the entire continent. The works included were originally published in other languages: Arabic, Zulu, and French, among others. Recurrent themes are politics, repression, and exile.

6-35. **West African Literatures: Ways of Reading.** Stephanie Newell. Oxford: Oxford University Press, 2006.

This collection of essays focuses on the literature of West Africa written both in English and French, as well as the native language oral traditions. The 14 chapters are organized thematically and deal with the oral tradition, issues of translation, post-colonialism, and nationalism and identity.

Africa—Narrative

6-36. The Cambridge Companion to the African Novel. Abiola Irele, ed. Cambridge, UK; New York: Cambridge University Press, 2009. Print and e-book.

This overview of the African novel begins with a chronological orientation followed by discussion of the oral and written traditions. Subsequent chapters treat particular authors, the novel in Afrikaans, the novel in Francophone Africa, the autobiographical novel, and emerging themes such as the post-colonial condition.

     A complementary critical work is *Contemporary Francophone African Writers and the Burden of Commitment* (Odile Cazenave and Patricia Célérier. University of Virginia Press, 2011). This specialized volume treats the historical and political issues that permeate literary production in Francophone Africa.

6-37. New Novels in African Literature Today: A Review. Ernest N. Emenyonu, ed. Ibadan, Nigeria: HEBN; Woodbridge, UK; Rochester, NY: James Currey, 2010. (African Literature Today).

The essays in this concise guide offer an overview of the most recent narratives of African writers including African writers who now reside elsewhere.

     A more specific work on a contemporary subject is *Islam in the Eastern African Novel* by Emad Mirmotahari (Palgrave Macmillan, 2011) that explores the works of three novelists from Eastern Africa: Nuruddin Farah, Abdulzarak Gurnah, and M. G. Vassanji, in terms of the rising identity with Islam. The various essays explore themes of colonialism, nationality, diaspora, and exile.

Africa—Drama and Poetry

6-38. African Theatre. Oxford, UK: James Currey, 1999– . Monographic series.

This publisher's series treats the history of theatre in Africa, individual authors, and themes such as the role of women, politics, and diaspora.

6-39. Modern African Drama: Backgrounds and Criticism. Biodun Jeyifo. New York: W. W. Norton, 2002.

This anthology offers representative works from all regions of Africa. Each selection is accompanied by background information and criticism and ends with a chronological guide and a selected bibliography for further reading.

6-40. Yoruba Poetry. Enl. and rev. Ulli Beier, with Timi Laoye, eds. Bayreuth, Germany: E. Breitinger, Bayreuth University, 2002.

This revised edition of a classic anthology of Yoruba poetry in English translation offers a perspective of the broad range of genres including sacred texts, folk poetry, and modern social commentaries. The introductory essay is a reader's guide to the history and development of Yoruba poetry.

     Also issued by the same publisher is *Yorùbá Royal Poetry: A Socio-historical Exposition and Annotated Translation* by Akíntúndé Akínyẹmí (2004). This specialized volume is an introduction to the tradition of laudatory poetry written in Yoruba. Many examples are available here for the first time in English translation.

Americas

6-41. Caribbean Literature. Alexandria, VA: Alexander Street Press. Online subscription database or perpetual license. http://alexanderstreet.com/products/cali.htm

The focus of this collection is the literary production of the entire Caribbean region from 1900 to the present. All genres are represented in the works selected for inclusion. In addition, there are manuscript and archival materials, photographs, and interviews. Multiple versions of a work are often included—original language, as well as translations to English or other European languages.

6-42. Harry Hoijer's Chiricahua and Mescalero Apache Texts. Open access resource. http://etext.virginia.edu/apache/

This online project is based on the book of the same name published by the University of Chicago Press in 1938. The texts, in bilingual format with informative notes, reflect the broad folkloric tradition.

Americas—History and Criticism

6-43. A Companion to Latin American Literature. Stephen M. Hart. Woodbridge, UK: Tamesis Books, 2009.

This companion volume offers a chronological approach to Latin American Literature beginning with a chapter on the Amerindian legacy followed by chapters on colonial literature, the early nineteenth century, the late nineteenth century, the early twentieth century and the late twentieth century. The final chapter deals with postmodern literary developments. Included also are a comprehensive bibliography as well as a list of items for further reading.

Historical literature and historiography in Latin America are treated in *Colonialism Past and Present: Reading and Writing about Colonial Latin America Today* (Alvaro Félix Bolaños and Gustavo Verdesio, eds. State University of New York Press, 2002). Topics include indigenous histories of the conquest, colonial histories, early newspapers, and selected historical novels.

6-44. A Companion to Spanish American Modernismo. Aníbal González. Woodbridge, UK: Tamesis Books, 2010.

This volume is a concise history of Modernismo, often cited as the first major literary movement to originate in the Americas. The seven-essay chapters treat the origins of Modernismo and its manifestation in all literary genres as well as journalistic texts. The final chapter is dedicated to the legacy of Modernismo.

Modernismo

Modernismo is widely recognized as the first major literary movement to originate in Latin America. The beginning of modernismo is signaled by the publication of *Azul* in 1888 by the Nicaraguan poet, Rubén Darío. Influenced by the French literary currents symbolism and Parnassianism, modernismo is concerned with the development of a new aesthetic that emphasizes the ideal in contrast with the quotidian. Elements of modernismo are present in the works of the precursors, José Martí, Julián del Casal, Salvador Díaz Mirón, José Asunción Silva, and Manuel Gutiérrez Nájera. Although modernismo finds paramount expression through poetry it also finds expression in the prose works of José Enrique Rodó. The poets of modernismo at its apogee include Leopoldo Lugones, Julio Herrera y Reissig, Ricardo Jaimes Freyre, Guillermo Valencia, José Santos Chocano, and Amado Nervo. The rise of vanguardism in the 1920s signals the end of modernismo.

6-45. Cubanísimo! The Vintage Book of Contemporary Cuban Literature. Cristina García, ed. New York: Vintage, 2003.

The editor, the well-known novelist Cristina García, brings together disparate elements of Cuban literature, both in Cuba and in the Cuban diaspora, through a common theme, music. The different sections are organized according to Cuban musical forms: the danzón, the rumba, the son, the mambo, and the salsa. Within each section are short stories, poems, extracts from novels, and essays of 25 Cuban authors including the well known and those little known in English translation.

6-46. Encyclopedia of Caribbean Literature. D. H. Figueredo, ed. Westport, CT: Greenwood Press, 2006. 2 vols.

This two-volume encyclopedia covers the entire Caribbean region and includes authors who write in Spanish, French and Creole as well as English. The 700 entries provide biographical information and include a bibliography of the author's works or critical studies about the author. The individual articles provide a historical context for the author's life and works.

By the same publisher, *Literature of the Caribbean* (Lizabeth Paravisini-Gebert, ed. 2008) is an anthology of 15 texts that exemplify current trends in Caribbean literature. The authors whose works appear here in translation represent the English speaking Caribbean as well as Francophone and Hispanophone traditions.

6-47. Encyclopedia of Latin American and Caribbean Literature, 1900–2003. David Balderston and Mike Gonzalez. London: Routledge, 2004.

This guide to the last century of Latin American and Caribbean literary production provides over 200 brief entries on authors, their works, recurring themes, and literary currents. A schematic chronology of events and corresponding literary achievements helps to orient the reader. An index provides ready access to the entries, and a bibliography at the end guides future reading and research.

The *Concise Encyclopedia of Latin American Literature* (Verity Smith. Fitzroy Dearborn, 2000) is available as a printed work as well as an e-book and includes entries by topic, country, authors, and literary works. An alphabetical list of entries at the beginning of the encyclopedia and a title index and general index at the end help users find entries. The volume represents a condensation of the original *Encyclopedia of Latin American Literature* published in 1997.

6-48. Historical Dictionary of Latin American Literature and Theatre. Richard Young and Odile Cisneros. Lanham, MD: Scarecrow Press, 2011.

An extensive introduction to the history of Latin American literature and a detailed timeline orient the reader to the authors covered in this biographical dictionary. Author entries are arranged alphabetically. The introduction explains the complexities of Spanish and Portuguese double surnames.

6-49. Literature of Latin America. Rafael Ocasio. Westport, CT: Greenwood Press, 2004.

This volume is part of the Literature as Windows to World Culture series. It deals primarily with major themes in Latin American literature from the nineteenth century to the present: the indigenous legacy, the emergence of modern Latin America and its literature, the "Boom," and women writers.

The tensions between traditionalism and modernity seen in contemporary Latin American literature are treated in *Latin America Writes Back: Postmodernity in the Periphery (An Interdisciplinary Perspective)*. In terms of genre, focus is on theatre and the narrative (Emil Volke, ed. Routledge, 2002).

6-50. Literatures of Latin America: From Antiquity to the Present. Willis Barnstone, ed. Upper Saddle River, NJ: Prentice Hall, 2003.

This anthology of Latin American literature (translated to English) was previously published as part of *Literatures of Africa, Asia, and Latin America* (1999). The present volume is organized chronologically and thematically. It begins with a section on Native American literature extending from pre-Colombian times to the present. The next section includes texts from the periods of discovery, conquest, and colonization. This is followed by the final section that covers 19th and 20th centuries.

 Literary Cultures of Latin America (Mario J. Valdés and Djelal Kadir, eds. Oxford University Press, 2004) is a three-volume set of individual essays which provide an overview and comparison of the literatures of Latin America from the period of discovery and conquest to the present. The essays offer important historical perspectives within the framework of different literary currents and theories. Each article offers an extensive bibliography.

6-51. Words of the True Peoples: Anthology of Contemporary Mexican Indigenous-Language Writers. Carlos Montemayor and Donald Frischmann, eds. Austin: University of Texas Press, 2004–2007. 3 vols.

This bilingual anthology of indigenous writers in Mexico reflects the movement to recover and preserve indigenous culture and identity. The three volumes offer texts from 13 different indigenous languages with side–by–side translations to Spanish. Volume 1 contains prose texts, volume 2 poetry, and volume 3 theater.

Americas—Narrative

6-52. The Cambridge Companion to the Latin American Novel. Efraín Kristal, ed. Cambridge, UK: Cambridge University Press, 2005. Print and e-book.

The individual essays in this volume constitute an overview of the Latin American narrative from the 19th century to the present. The first part contains essays dedicated to the 19th century novel. The second part addresses the heterogeneity of the regional novel. Part III contains essays on issues of gender and sexuality followed by an in-depth discussion of six novelists and their signature work. The epilogue by well-known translator Jill Levine deals with issues of translation. A general bibliography is found at the end of the volume.

 A study by Naomi Lindstrom, *Early Spanish American Narrative* (University of Texas Press, 2004), follows the native American narrative tradition through a chronological treatment of narratives in the Spanish language through the end of the nineteenth century including *modernismo*.

6-53. The Columbia Guide to the Latin American Novel Since 1945. Raymond L. Williams. New York: Columbia University Press, 2007.

This comprehensive guide to the contemporary Latin American novel includes works written in English, Spanish, Portuguese, French, Dutch, and Haitian Creole. The first part presents a chronological and regional survey. The second part addresses national literatures and includes an A-Z guide to particular works.

 Whistler in the Nightworld: Short Fiction from the Latin Americas (Thomas Colchie, ed. New York: Plume, 2002) includes 21 different authors whose works have been published since the 1980s. The editor notes that this new generation of authors is more global in that many have traveled widely and nearly half now live outside of Latin America.

6-54. Latin American Mystery Writers: An A-to-Z Guide. Darrell B. Lockhart, ed. Westport, CT: Greenwood Press, 2004.

This alphabetical guide includes 54 authors representing, principally, Argentina, Mexico, and Cuba. The editor has also taken care to include female mystery writers. The entries include biographical information, discussion of the author's principal works and a bibliography of primary and secondary sources.

A study of crime fiction that complements the A to Z is *Contemporary Hispanic Crime Fiction: A Transatlantic Discourse on Urban Violence* (Glen S. Close. New York: Palgrave Macmillan, 2008). The division into four metropolitan centers favors Spanish America: Mexico City, Buenos Aires, Bogota, and Barcelona.

Americas—Drama

6-55. Encyclopedia of Latin American Theater. Eladio Cortés and Mirta Barrea-Marlys, eds. Westport, CT: Greenwood Press, 2003.

Two works on Latin American theater were published in 2003, one from Greenwood Press and one from Praeger. Both of the works are treated in the theater chapter 8 in this Guide. The first is *Encyclopedia of Latin American Theater*, an overview that includes the Nuyorican and Chicano traditions in the United States but excluding the non-Spanish-speaking Caribbean, with chronological coverage from the pre-Columbian period to the present. See also entry 8-94.

The second title is *Latin American Dramatists since 1945: A Bio-bibliographical Guide* by Tony A. Harvell, a comprehensive guide organized alphabetically by country that includes Spanish America and Brazil, with an author index as well as a title index that provide ready access to the materials covered (also entry 8-95).

Adding to the information in these two reference works are anthologies and critical works on the theater in three different countries:

> *Columbian Theatre in the Vortex: Seven Plays.* (Judith A. Weiss, ed.; intro. essay by María Mercedes Jaramillo. Lewisburg, PA: Bucknell University Press, 2004). This concise anthology presents an overview of Columbian theatre since its inception and particularly in the last 30 years. Extensive background notes are included for each of the representative works presented.

> *Five Plays in Translation from Mexican Contemporary Theater: A New Golden Age.* (Salvador Rodríguez del Pino. Lewiston, NY: Edwin Mellen Press, 2001). This brief anthology introduces the work of five contemporary Mexican dramatists: Marcela del Río, Carlos Olmos, Eduardo Rodríguez Solís, Pablo Salinas, and Tomás Urtuasástegui. In addition to the translated texts, this volume includes biographical information as well as interviews with each author.

> Concentrating on three aspects of Brazilian theatre: the postmodern period, women playwrights, and the training of playwrights and scholars, is *Flash & Crash Days: Brazilian Theater in the Postdictatorship Period* (David S. George. Garland, 2000).

Americas—Poetry

6-56. The FSG Book of Twentieth-century Latin American Poetry: An Anthology. Ilan Stavans, ed. New York: Farrar, Straus, Giroux, 2011.

This extensive anthology presents the work of 84 authors who write in Spanish, Portuguese, Latino, Spanish, and indigenous languages. Representative poems are in the original language with side-by-side English translations. Two other anthologies of modern poetry are treated here:

> *An Anthology of Spanish American Modernismo.* (Kelly Washbourne, ed. and trans.; Sergio Gabriel, trans. MLA, 2007). This anthology provides access to poetry (Spanish and English texts) representative of the literary esthetic of *modernismo*, the first

literary movement to originate in Spanish America. A general introduction as well as notes on the process of translation are followed by the anthology of 18 different poets.

Reversible Monuments: Contemporary Mexican Poetry (Mónica de la Torre and Michael Wiegers, eds. Copper Canyon Press, 2002). The generations of Mexican poets born since 1950 constitute the focus of this comprehensive bilingual anthology. Many authors are accessible to English readers for the first time in this anthology. The selected works of each author are preceded by a brief biographical sketch.

6-57. The Oxford Book of Latin American Poetry: A Bilingual Anthology. Cecilia Vicuña and Ernesto Livon-Grosman. New York: Oxford University Press, 2009.

The chronological scope of this anthology begins with indigenous poetry about the conquest and extends to the end of the twentieth century. More than 120 poets are included here with English translations of representative poems originally written in Spanish, Portuguese, or indigenous languages. The original text appears below the translation. Below are three other anthologies of Caribbean poets:

Open Gate: An Anthology of Haitian Creole Poetry (Paul Laraque and Jack Hirschman, eds.; Jack Hirschman and Boadiba, trans. Curbstone Press, 2001). This is the first bilingual anthology of Haitian Creole poetry that makes representative works available to English-speaking readers. The anthology is divided into three sections; the first deals with the founders of the modern Haitian Creole tradition; the second, the literary outpouring of the Duvalier dictatorship embodied by the "Society of Butterflies;" and finally, the new generation and the poetry of the Haitian diaspora.

Burnt Sugar = Caña quemada: Contemporary Cuban Poetry in English and Spanish (Lori Marie Carlson and Oscar Hijuelos, eds. Free Press, 2006). This specialized bilingual anthology includes recent Cuban poets, those writing in Cuba or writing in exile.

Puerto Rican Poetry: An Anthology from Aboriginal to Contemporary Times (Roberto Márquez, ed. and trans. University of Massachusetts Press, 2007). This anthology, in English, offers an extensive introduction to the poetry of Puerto Rico beginning with accounts of native verse in early Spanish chronicles. The first three chapters are divided chronologically: the conquest to 1820, 1820 to the 1950s, and the 1950s to the present. The last chapter treats the production of Puerto Rican poets outside of Puerto Rico.

Asia

6-58. Bibliography of Asian Studies. Ann Arbor, MI: Association for Asian Studies. 1992– . Online subscription database.

This online bibliography, initiated in 1992, includes and continues the print-based *Bibliography of Asian Studies* (1971–1991). The now approximately 800,000 citations cover all disciplines but with emphasis on the humanities and social sciences. The items cited represent works about Asia published in Western-language monographs and journals. The entries are searchable by author, title, year of publication, subject, country, journal title, ISSN, as well as key word. Many of the journals included here are not indexed elsewhere. The yearly updates add over 30,000 new items to the bibliography.

Asia—Eastern and South-Eastern Asia

6-59. Japanese Text Initiative. Open access resource. http://etext.lib.virginia.edu/japanese/index.html

The goal of this University of Virginia-based project is to put online the major works of classical Japanese literature in the original published form. However, whenever possible, English translations of the texts are included. The original scope of the collection is being expanded to include twentieth century Japanese literature when it is possible to obtain permission from authors or publishers.

6-60. The Cambridge History of Chinese Literature. Kang-i Sun Chang and Stephen Owen, eds. Cambridge, UK: Cambridge University Press, 2010. 2 vols. Print and e-book.

This comprehensive history covers Chinese literature from the first century of the Christian era to the end of the 20th century. The chapters are organized chronologically and treat all literary genres as well as non-fiction prose. The inclusion of these materials aids in situating literature in its historical context. Each volume includes a glossary, bibliography, and index.

Another similar two-volume work is *A Concise History of Chinese Literature* (Yuming Luo; Ye Yang, trans. Brill, 2011). This comprehensive history of Chinese literature from antiquity to the present provides access to the tradition of literary criticism as well as information about the literature itself. Organization is chronological by dynasties with subdivisions for genre.

An earlier and more concise work is *Chinese Literature: Overview and Bibliography* (James L. Claren, ed. Hauppauge, NY: Nova Science Publishers, 2002). This introduction to the history of Chinese literature begins with the classical period in the 6th century BCE and extends to the present. An extensive bibliography of primarily English language sources for further reading is included as well as subject/author/title indexes.

6-61. The Canon in Southeast Asian Literatures: Literatures of Burma, Cambodia, Indonesia, Laos, Malaysia, the Philippines, Thailand, and Vietnam. David Smyth, ed. Surrey, UK: Curzon, 2000.

Sixteen individually authored essays cover a diversity of topics related to the less-studied literatures of Southeast Asia. The identification of national literary classics, the role of religious texts, women's writings, literary histories, and the emergency of preferred genres are among the topics treated.

6-62. The Columbia Companion to Modern East Asian Literature. Joshua S. Mostow, ed. New York: Columbia University Press, 2003.

The three major literary traditions of East Asia are the focal points of this comprehensive volume: Japan, China, and Korea. The work begins with a brief overview of East Asian literature followed by three detailed sections on each of the literatures. The individual sections provide a history of the literary tradition of that language followed by a discussion of modern themes, literary movements, and particular authors and their works.

6-63. Historical Dictionary of Modern Chinese Literature. Li-Hua Ying. Langham: The Rowman & Littlefield Publishing Group, 2010. Print and e-book.

The introductory chapters to this dictionary of twentieth-century Chinese literature include reader's notes and a chronology. The dictionary itself is an alphabetical arrangement of major authors, works, and literary movements.

Concentrating upon literature produced after 1949 is *A History of Contemporary Chinese Literature* (Hong Zicheng; Michael M. Day, trans. Brill, 2007). The first half of the book examines fiction, poetry, drama, and non-fiction prose until 1976. The second half looks at the development of literary arts and literary criticism from 1976 to the present.

6-64. Historical Dictionary of Modern Japanese Literature and Theater. J. Scott Miller. Lanham, MD: Scarecrow Press, 2009.

The chronological point of departure for this dictionary is the Meiji Restoration of 1868 in which there was a flourishing of literary forms under the influence of Western novels, poems, plays, and journalistic texts. The subsequent developments in Japanese literature and theatre are chronicled here. This volume offers a general introduction and chronology followed by over 4,000 entries on authors, literary movements, genres, and concepts important to the development of a modern literary tradition in Japan. Also published by Scarecrow Press is the *Historical Dictionary of Japanese Traditional Theatre* by Samuel L. Leiter (2006, entry 8-85).

Earlier literature is collected in *Traditional Japanese Literature: An Anthology, Beginnings to 1600* (Haruo Shirane, ed. Columbia University Press, 2007). This extensive anthology is arranged chronologically and offers an introduction to each literary period. It includes all genres and essays on special topics such as women's writings and the development of secular prose and also a bibliography of studies written in English on Japanese literature.

Asia—Western

6-65. Literatures of the Middle East: From Antiquity to the Present. Willis Barnstone and Tony Barnstone, eds. Upper Saddle River, NJ: Prentice Hall, 2003.

This anthology, as indicated by its title, covers literature in the Middle East from the earliest times to the present. The work is enhanced by extensive introductions, reading notes, and bibliographies related to the texts presented. All literary genres are presented here in addition to major religious, philosophical, historic, and political essays.

An anthology concentrating upon the twentieth century is *Tablet & Pen: Literary Landscapes from the Modern Middle East.* (R. Aslan, ed. W. W. Norton, 2011). Part of the Words without Borders Series, this anthology presents authors from the beginning of the twentieth century to the present. The anthology is organized by chronology and language and includes translations from Arabic, Persian, Turkish, and Urdu.

Literature in Arabic

6-66. Database of Arabic Literature in Western Research. OxLit Literary Publication and Documentation. Open access resource. http://www.oxlit.co.uk/oxlit/index.pl

This database records recent publications related to Arabic literature that have been published in the West. Primary sources and secondary sources are included in the database which is searchable by genre. The user is also able to search for critical materials and author biographies.

6-67. The Cambridge History of Arabic Literature. Cambridge, UK: Cambridge University Press, 2006–2010. 6 vols. Selected volumes available as e-book.

The first four volumes of this series reflect a chronological organization of Arabic literature; the first volume ends with the Umayyad period at the end of the 7th century and the fourth treats modern Arabic literature. The fifth volume of this series is dedicated to the literature of Al-Andalus, and the final volume is an overview of the history of Arabic literature.

Another work from Cambridge University Press is *An Introduction to Arabic Literature* (Roger Allen, 2000). This overview of Arabic literature begins with a chapter on the difficulties of transliteration and translation. The following six chapters address sacred texts, poetry, narrative, drama, and the tradition of literary criticism.

A similar work is *Arabic Literature: An Overview* (Pierre Cachia. RoutledgeCurzon, 2008). The author's preface indicates that this volume is meant to introduce readers to Arabic literature, both classical and popular, across time and space. The introductory chapter discusses the difficulties in transliterating Arabic and the variation encountered in personal names. Subsequent chapters include an essay on Arabic literature in the Iberian Peninsula.

6-68. **Iraq's Modern Arabic Literature: A Guide to English Translations Since 1950.** Salih J. Altoma. Lanham, MD: Scarecrow Press. 2010.

This bibliographical guide to the last 60 years of Iraqi literature begins with introductory chapters on issues of transliteration and translation. The bibliographic entries are organized by genre: autobiographical essays, drama, fiction, and poetry. An appendix provides information on Iraqi writers now living in the West and a second appendix covers women writers. In addition to an author index, there is also an index on translators.

An anthology from another country in the Middle East is *Beyond the Dunes: An Anthology of Modern Saudi Literature* (Salma K. Jayyusi, Mansour al-Hazimi and Izzat Khattab, eds. London: I. B. Tauris, 2006). This is one of the few anthologies restricted to a particular region or nation in the Arabic-speaking world. Following the introductory essay, sections are dedicated to particular genres: poetry, short stories, and excerpts from novels, plays, and autobiographical literature

6-69. **The Routledge Encyclopedia of Arabic Literature.** Julie Scott Meisami and Paul Starkey. London: Routledge, 2010.

This comprehensive encyclopedia contains more than 1,300 entries that cover authors, works, genres, literary terms, and issues related to Arabic literature. The chronological scope is broad and includes the traditions of both classical and modern Arabic literature. The geographic coverage includes Africa, the Middle East, Spain, and Turkey. The reader is guided by a chronological table at the beginning as well as notes on transliteration. Each entry contains suggested works for further reading.

A more concise work is *Modern Arabic Literature in Translation: A Companion* (Salih J. Altoma. London: Saqi, 2004). This brief guide to modern Arabic literature in English offers summary chapters on fiction, drama, poetry, and autobiographical writing. The author also discusses to what degree modern Arabic literature has become known in the western world.

Another concise introduction to Arabic literature is *Modern Arabic Literature* (Paul Starkey. Edinburgh University Press, 2006). This introduction to Arabic literature of the nineteenth and twentieth century is an appropriate handbook for both undergraduate students as well as general readers. Although this volume focuses on modern Arabic literature it discusses the influence of traditional medieval literary forms as well as innovations from the West. Separate chapters address poetry, prose fiction, and drama.

Literature in Hebrew

6-70. **The Anthology in Jewish Literature.** David Stern, ed. Oxford, UK: Oxford University Press, 2004.

The importance of the anthology in the propagation of Jewish literature is the focus of this collection of essays. The essays address literature in Hebrew as well as literature in Yiddish.

6-71. **Translating Israel: Contemporary Hebrew Literature and Its Reception in America.** Alan L. Mintz. Syracuse: University of Syracuse Press, 2001.

This collection of essays is organized thematically and treats historical, social, and literary topics that emerge in modern Israeli literature such as Zionism, the Holocaust, and the development of a postmodern aesthetic.

Producing the Modern Hebrew Canon: Nation Building and Minority Discourse by Hannan Hever (New York University Presses, 2002) addresses the question of literature in Hebrew as a literature of exile. Literature as a vehicle of political satire is also treated as is the relationship of Hebrew literature to contemporary Arabic literature.

Asia—Southern

6-72. The Oxford India Anthology of Bengali Literature: 1861–1941; The Oxford India Anthology of Bengali Literature: 1941–1991. Kalpana Bardhan, ed. Oxford, UK: Oxford University Press, 2011.

This two-volume anthology of Bengali literature covers a period of 130 years and includes multiple genres: poetry, short story, novel, memoir, and essay. Also included are chronological lists of authors and representative works.

Another Oxford work is *Representing India: Literature, Politics and Identities* by Mukesh Williams and Rohit Wanchoo (2008). The essays in this volume focus on literatures that depend on the Sanskrit heritage, that is, literature in Hindi and Bengali. The role of films in Hindi as a vehicle of cultural dispersion is also treated.

6-73. The Oxford India Anthology of Modern Urdu Literature: Poetry and Prose Miscellany; The Oxford India Anthology of Modern Urdu Literature: Fiction. Mehr Afshan Faroqi, ed. Oxford, UK: Oxford University Press, 2011.

These two companion volumes represent an overview of literature published in Urdu (of both Indian and Pakistani authors). Many of these works appear in English translation for the first time. The first volume begins with a general introduction followed by a selection of poetry, a prose miscellany including essays and sketches, autobiographical sketches, drama, humor and satire, letters, and literary anecdotes. A glossary at the end is followed by a bibliography.

The second volume offers an anthology of short stories and excerpts from novels and novellas. The introduction provides an outline of modern Urdu literature and provides a historical context. The chronological list of authors has biographical information about each. As with the first volume there is an end glossary and bibliography.

In addition to the two works above, *Modern Indian Theatre: A Reader* is treated in chapter 8, entry 8-85.

Europe

6-74. European Writers Collection (Scribner Writers Online). Gale/Cengage. Online subscription database. http://www.gale.cengage.com/ScribnerWriters/index.htm

The 2010 web version of European Writers Collection contains 14 volumes arranged chronologically (Vols. 1–2 Middle Ages and Renaissance, Vols. 3–4 Age of Reason/Enlightenment, Vols. 5–7 The Romantic Century, Vols. 8–13 The Twentieth Century, Vol. 14 Index). It is based on the 1991 publication edited by George Stade. Entries treat individual authors and their works as well as literary genres and literary motifs. The index volume provides access by name, date of birth, and language. It also contains a bibliography arranged by chronology and nationality of authors.

6-75. WESSWeb: Online Text Collections in Western European Literature. Open Access resource. http://wessweb.info/index.php/Online_Text_Collections_in_Western_European_Literature

Western European literature is defined broadly by the Western European Studies Section of the ALA Association of College and Research Libraries to include the majority of the countries in Europe. The WESSWeb site provides links to online collections of literary texts from Europe. The organization is by language. Within the language areas, headings describe electronic texts (primary materials), literary criticism (secondary materials), as well as resources on language and linguistics and online library or museum exhibits. The links to the literary texts themselves includes both original language versions and English translations.

Europe—History and Criticism

6-76. Comparative History of Literatures in European Languages. Margaret R. Higonnet. Amsterdam: John Benjamin Publishing Co., 2008.

Sponsored by the International Comparative Literature Association, this resource is a series of volumes of literary history from an international point of view. It covers literature of European languages from all over the world; and, in time, it spans the period from the Renaissance to the present day.

Another approach to European literature is *Writing Europe: What is European about the Literatures of Europe?* (Ursula Keller and Ilma Rakuša, eds. Central European University Press, 2004). The 33 essays in this volume, originally published in German, cover literature from all geographic areas of Europe. They treat the issue of local/national versus regional versus universal focus in modern European literary expression.

6-77. History of European Literature. Annick Benoit-Dusausoy and Guy Fontaine, eds.; Michael Wooff, trans. London: Routledge, 2000.

Originally published in French, this extensive collection of essays surveys major issues in European literature from Greco-Roman literature to the present. The essays are organized chronologically and include all major European literatures. The final essay looks at contemporary authors and trends in the twentieth century.

Europe—Greco-Roman Classics

6-78. L'Année philologique on the Internet (AnPhilNet). Société Internationale de Bibliographie Classique. Online subscription database. http://www.annee-philologique.com/

L'Année philologique (APh), the long running and foremost bibliography of the classics begun in 1924, is still published in a print edition; but it also has a companion database published in collaboration with the French Centre National de la Recherche Scientifique (CNRS) and the American Philological Association (APA). AnPhilNet contains the printed bibliography from volume 1 to within a year of the current volume. Anyone conducting research in classical studies will find the bibliography to be indispensable.

6-79. Blackwell Reference Online: Classics. Hoboken, NJ: Wiley-Blackwell. Online subscription database.

The collection of titles offered in this online source list recent publications also available in print and published primarily after 2005. This reference deals with various aspects of classical studies. The titles cover history, archaeology, and literature including specific authors and works.

6-80. Lectrix. Cambridge, UK: University of Cambridge Press. Online subscription database.

This collection of Greek and Latin texts offers selected texts in the original language together with tools to enable reading and understanding the texts while including an English translation. Each text is accompanied by a dictionary, a grammatical parser, commentaries from the Cambridge Greek and Latin Classic series and web pages containing explanatory material on the language of the text and its historical context.

6-81. Perseus Digital Library. http://www.perseus.tufts.edu/hopper/. Open access resource.

Dedicated to the Greco-Roman classics in its inception, the multi-media Perseus Digital Library now offers access to early texts in Arabic and Germanic languages as well as Renaissance texts in English and Latin. In addition to the texts, there are tools for those who wish to read works in the original languages including Greek and Latin dictionaries, language handbooks, and critical guides to texts.

6-82. Thesaurus Linguae Graecae. University of California, Irvine. Online subscription database. http://www.tlg.uci.edu/

The Thesaurus Linguae Graecae began in 1972 with the goal of producing a digital corpus of literary texts written in Greek from the time of Homer to the end of the Byzantine Empire. At present, this corpus represents 4,000 authors and 10,000 works. While the TLG is a subscription database, an abridged version is available without subscription.

6-83. A Bibliographical Guide to Classical Studies. Graham Whitaker. Hildesheim: Olms-Weidmann, 2007. 5 vols.

This resource provides a comprehensive subject guide to books published from 1873 forward. The text includes descriptions of general subject encyclopedias and handbooks as well as periodical literature and bibliographies that deal with classical literature. Interdisciplinary in scope, this guide also includes bibliographical information on studies of classical languages, history, art, archaeology, religion, philosophy, and science.

6-84. Classical and Medieval Literature Criticism. Detroit: Gale. 1987– . Monographic series.

This extensive series covering the Greco-Roman classics and early European literature has more than 140 volumes, each containing essays dedicated to particular authors or literary works. The scope of the volumes is not limited chronologically or geographically.

6-85. Classical Studies: A Guide to the Reference Literature. Fred W. Jenkins. Westport, CT: Libraries Unlimited, 2006.

This user guide provides information about both print and electronic handbooks, encyclopedias, and bibliographies. The over 1,000 entries contained in this handbook are covered in a title and author index.

Another guide is the *Undergraduate's Companion to Ancient Greek and Roman Writers and Their Web Sites* (James Galbraith. [S.I.]: Libraries Unlimited, 2004). This introductory resource is intended for use by undergraduates who are studying the classics and would like to locate relevant texts, study guides, and critical materials online.

6-86. A Guide to Greek Theatre and Drama. Kenneth McLeish; completed by Trevor R. Griffiths. London: Methuen Drama, 2003.

The works of Aeschylus, Sophocles, Euripides, Aristophanes, and Menander are examined in depth in this comprehensive guide to Greek theatre. The introductory chapters provide background information on the performance of drama including discussion on the use of verse, music, and chorus.

A more concise work is *Greek Drama and Dramatists* by Alan H. Sommerstein (Routledge, 2002). The first chapters of this guide to classical Greek drama provide an overview of the origins of the genre and its major exponents. The introductory chapter provides a chronological overview and covers minor authors. An anthology of excerpts from key works follows. The work is available both in print and as an e-book.

6-87. The Oxford Companion to Classical Literature. 3rd ed. M. C. Howatson, ed. New York: Oxford University Press, 2011.

The third edition of this work represents the continuation of a handbook first published in 1937 and highly regarded as a tool for students and scholars. It is interdisciplinary in nature with a focus in literature as well as classical antiquity. The latest edition represents considerable revision and expansion of previous editions. The index provides access to classical authors, literary forms, subjects, and individual works as well as historical events and figures, institutions, and cultural manifestations. The volume is further enhanced by inclusion of a chronological table and maps of the ancient world.

Complementing the *Companion* is the *Oxford Classical Dictionary* (4th ed. rev., 2012), available as an e-book. The latest edition in print is the 3rd revised edition. The *Dictionary* is a standard reference for classical study and needs no further explanation.

Europe—Medieval and Renaissance

6-88. International Medieval Bibliography Online. Turnhout, Belgium: Brepols Publishers. Online subscription database. http://www.brepolis.net/

This online bibliography includes more than 300,000 articles published from 1967 to the present. The selection of articles reflects the interdisciplinary nature of medieval studies; likewise, the coverage is extensive both chronologically (400 to 1500) and geographically (all of Europe as well as the Middle East and North Africa). In addition to issues related to European languages and literatures, the bibliography includes history, archaeology, theology, philosophy, Islamic studies, and the arts. The bibliography is updated on a quarterly basis.

The Bibliographie de civilization médiévale, also published by Brepols, is a companion to the International Medieval Bibliography Online. It indexes books and book reviews that treat any aspect of medieval studies. The online database provides an interface in English as well as French to access the more than 100,000 titles indexed.

Another online subscription database is Iter: Gateway to the Middle Ages and Renaissance (http://www.itergateway.org/). Iter offers access to bibliographies, journals, critical editions, and literary criticism related to the European Middle Ages and Renaissance with a focus on women writers. For a fuller treatment of Iter see entry 2-19. A related open access website is The Online Reference Book for Medieval Studies (ORB), hosted by the College of Staten Island-SUNY (http://www.the-orb.net/), (entry 2-57).

6-89. The Cambridge Companion to the Epic. Catherine Bates, ed. Cambridge, UK: Cambridge University Press, 2010.

The coverage of this companion volume is worldwide in scope and extends from the epic of Gilgamesh to the present. The individual chapters treat Greek and Roman epics, epic poems of the Middle Ages, the Renaissance, and the modern era. The final chapter discusses the tradition of translation of epic literature.

6-90. Of Reynaert the Fox: Text and Facing Translation of the Middle Dutch Beast Epic Van den vos Reynaerde. Andre Bouwman. Amsterdam: Amsterdam University Press, 2009. Available as e-book.

This is the first bilingual edition of the medieval epic that recounts the exploits of the crafty fox. It offers readers the original text with side-by-side English translation.

Another translation is *Dutch Romances III: Five Interpolated Romances from the Lancelot Compilation* edited by David F. Johnson and Geert H. M. Claassens (Rochester, NY: D. S. Brewer, 2002). Planned as a three-volume set, the third volume is the only one published thus far with volumes I and II predicted for 2012 publication. The set offers parallel translations of the Arthurian tradition in Middle Dutch. Volume III offers a collection of five romances not attested in other versions of the exploits of Lancelot. They appear in this critical edition in English translation for the first time. This reference has extensive notes and an informative introduction.

6-91. Encyclopedia of Medieval Literature. Robert Thomas Lamdin and Laura Cooner Lambdin, eds. Westport, CT: Greenwood Press, 2000.

This guide to literature between 500 and 1500 focuses primarily on the early literature of England but also includes other European literatures (Hispanic, Celtic, Germanic, Italian, and Russian) as well as Islamic and Mongolian literary works. The organization by author and title entries provides easy access to authors and their works. A guide to further reading is found at the end.

Another work with the same title, *Encyclopedia of Medieval Literature* is a quick reference encyclopedia spanning the time period from 500 to 1500 (Jay Ruud, Facts on File, 2006). The approximately 700 entries are arranged alphabetically. A timeline and list of authors covered in the reference are arranged by geographical area.

6-92. Encyclopedia of Renaissance Literature. James Wyatt Cook. New York, NY: Facts on File, 2007.

This quick reference source to literature from 1500 to 1660 provides ready access to an alphabetical list of authors and titles represented in the literature of Europe (English, French, German, Italian, Spanish) as well as works from China, India, Japan, the Islamic world, and the New World. Entries also include literary and historical terms.

From the same time period, *Ghost Stories in Late Renaissance France: Walking by Night* by Timothy Chesters (Oxford University Press, 2011) has a corpus of ghost stories produced in the period 1550 to 1610. The author uses the framework of history to explain the rise in this genre, which explores religious doctrine, awareness of New World belief in the supernatural, and love and courtship.

Europe—Eastern

6-93. American Bibliography of Slavic and East European Studies: ABSEES 1990-present. Online subscription database. http://www.ebscohost.com/academic/american-bibliography-of-slavic-eastern-european-studies

This bibliography, covering East-Central Europe and the former Soviet Union, is produced at the University of Illinois at Urbana-Champaign and made available through EBSCOhost. It includes articles, books, dissertations, and journals in all disciplines as well as online resources and government publications from the United States and Canada that focus on Eastern Europe.

Also useful is *Bibliography of Slavic Literature* (Dasha Culic Nisula, Scarecrow Press, 2001). The bibliographical entries in this volume represent literature from the middle ages to the present. The selection is based on a survey of bibliographies as well as library holdings.

6-94. Central and Eastern European Online Library. Frankfurt am Main: CEEOL. Open access resource. http://www.ceeol.com/index.aspx

This collection provides full text access in PDF format to 687 journals published in Central and Eastern Europe as well as other selected documents that have been digitized for this collection. The journals cover all disciplines and there is an index by subject matter to the periodicals that are included.

The index all includes the languages of articles published in these journals. As many publish articles in English this is a valuable resource to work that may not be indexed elsewhere.

6-95. Yiddish Digital Library. Open access resource.
http://www.yiddishbookcenter.org/yiddish-books

The Steven Spielberg Digital Yiddish Library has as its mission to provide open online access to out-of-print Yiddish books. At present, there are nearly 11,000 full-text works available online and by author, title, or Library of Congress subject heading. Users are able to download or print the texts in PDF format.

6-96. An Anthology of Jewish-Russian Literature: Two Centuries of Dual Identity in Prose and Poetry. Maxim Shrayer. Armonk, NY: Sharpe, 2007.

This anthology, winner of the 2007 National Jewish Book Award, Eastern European Studies, provides readers a variety of readings that include short stories, excerpts from novels, memoirs, poems, and essays from 130 Jewish writers who write in the Russian language. The authors include those who lived in Russia as well as those who had emigrated. For each author included in the anthology, pertinent biographical information is given as well as a commentary on the range and scope of his or her work. In addition, there are introductory essays on Jewish history in Russia for each chronological period.

6-97. The Cambridge Introduction to Russian Literature. Caryl Emerson. Cambridge: Cambridge University Press, 2008.

This introductory history of Russian literature treats recurring themes from the earliest traditional narratives to the present. The organization of the volume is both chronological and thematic with discussions of representative literary texts for each period.
For more in-depth analysis, *The Cambridge Companion to Twentieth Century Russian Literature* (Evgeny Dobrenko and Marina Balina, 2011) can be consulted. Through a series of chapter-length essays, this companion reviews the major literary currents of the twentieth century in all genres. The final chapter covers Russian critical literary theory.

6-98. The Columbia Guide to the Literatures of Eastern Europe Since 1945. Harold B. Segel. New York: Columbia University Press, 2003.

This is a reference guide to literature in post-World War II eastern Europe and includes the literary production of Albania (and Kosovo), Bosnia-Herzegovina, Bulgaria, Croatia, Czech Republic, German Democratic Republic, Hungary, Macedonia, Poland, Romania, Serbia (and Montenegro), Slovakia, and Slovenia. The handbook includes authors who work in all genres. Bibliographical information for each author includes works translated to English as well as critical studies. Access to the volume is facilitated by an author index.

6-99. Polish Literature from 1864–1918: Realism and Young Poland: An Anthology. Michael J. Mikos, ed. Bloomington, IN: Slavica, 2006.
Polish Literature from 1918–2000: An Anthology. Michael J. Mikos, ed. Bloomington, IN: Slavica, 2008.
Polish Romantic Literature: An Anthology. Michael J. Mikos, ed. Bloomington, IN: Slavica, 2002.

These three anthologies provide an overview of Polish literature in the 19th and 20th centuries. Each volume contains informative introductory essays that describe major historical events and place Polish literature within the literary currents of the time. The presentation of authors and representative texts offers biographical notes and annotations to ensure comprehension of the texts. Each volume contains a bibliography of materials available in English for further study.

6-100. The Routledge Companion to Russian Literature. Neil Cornwell. London: Routledge, 2001. Print and e-book.

This handbook surveys Russian literature from its beginnings to the post-Soviet period. The period of the great Russian novel is given special attention. Comprehensive in nature, this history also treats Russian literary theory, socialist realism, works of émigré authors, and women's writings. For each section there are lists of recommended readings and critical studies.

Another introductory work, *Russian Literature: Overview and Bibliography* includes both well-known and lesser-known authors (Gene V. Palmer, Nova Science Publishers, 2002). The bibliographical references include both Russian and language sources. Access to the work is provided by indexes of authors, titles, and subjects.

6-101. Russian Literature. Andrew Wachtel and I. Vinitskii. Cambridge, UK: Polity, 2009.

This concise history of Russian literature offers 10 chapters that proceed chronologically from the Middle Ages to the present. Each chapter contains an introductory essay followed by a closer examination of particular authors or literary works that embody the cultural and historical significance of that time period. Parallel events in Russian art and music are used to provide a full historical context.

A mosaic of literary forms from medieval sagas to the present is offered in *An Anthology of Russian Literature from Earliest Writings to Modern Fiction: Introduction to a Culture* (N. Rzhevsky, ed. Armonk, NY: Sharpe, 2004). In addition to omnipresent authors such as Tolstoy, Gogol, Dostoevsky, and Chekov, there are less-known authors who have not received wide attention outside of the Russian-speaking world. An introductory essay begins each section of the anthology; there are also bibliographies that provide a guide to further study.

6-102. Writers under Siege: Czech Literature since 1945. Jiří Holý. Brighton, UK; Portland, OR: Sussex Academic Press, 2008.

This English translation of a work previously published in Czech and German offers to English readers biographical and bibliographical information about the most important post-war Czech writers. Included in the volume are references to secondary sources about the authors treated.

Covering much of the same geographic area is *Literature of Post-Communist Slovenia, Slovakia, Hungary and Romania: A Study* (Robert Murray Davis, McFarland & Co., 2008). This critical work is based on interviews with authors from four central European countries. Bibliographical citations for primary and secondary works are treated in each chapter.

Narrative

6-103. Contemporary Russian Fiction: A Short List. Kristina Rotkirch and Charles Rougle, eds. Moscow: Glas, 2008.

This volume consists of interviews with 11 leading Russian authors. They represent diversity in themes and style, though the works of all show the effects of political and societal changes in Russia in the last two decades.

Another anthology of contemporary authors is *Russian Love Stories: An Anthology of Contemporary Prose* (Nadya L. Peterson, ed. New York: Peter Lang, 2009). This thematically organized anthology represents the work of 12 Russian narrators who began publishing their works in the late 1960s. The stories represent all aspects of love and sexual expression including sexual fantasy and incest.

6-104. Russian Pulp: The Detektiv and the Russian Way of Crime. Anthony Olcott. Lanham, MD: Rowman & Littlefield, 2001.

This history of modern Russian detective fiction introduces the reader to the rise of pulp fiction in the post-Soviet era. Detective fiction is not, however, a new genre. Rather, in the absence of cultural controls that promoted the utilitarian and didactic, crime fiction flourished. The Russian detective novel is surprisingly introspective at times. Both the "detektiv" and the criminal are seen as imperfect beings, the product of their circumstances.

In *The Greatest Russian Stories of Crime and Suspense* (Otto Penzler, ed. Pegasus Books, 2010), the 19 short stories include works of Chekhov, Dostoevsky, Gogol, Gorky, Nabokov, Pushkin, and Tolstoy.

6-105. A Handbook of Czech Prose Writing, 1940–2005. Bohuslava Bradbrook, ed. Brighton, UK; Portland, OR: Sussex Academic Press, 2007.

This handbook provides an introduction to 35 Czech authors from the period of World War II to the beginning of the twenty-first century. Each chapter treats an individual author and provides biographical information as well as an overview of the author's major works.

A more in-depth treatment is *An Introduction to Twentieth-century Czech Fiction: Comedies of Defiance* (Sussex Academic Press, 2001). The works of nine Czech authors form the focus of this concise history of Czech fiction in the last 100 years. The first six chapters are dedicated to the work of a single author: Jaroslav Hašek, Karel Čapek, Bohumil Hrabal, Josef Škvorecký, Ota Pavel, and Ivan Klíma. The final chapter introduces three new authors.

6-106. In a Maelstrom: The History of Russian-Jewish Prose (1860–1940). Zsuzsa Hetényi. Budapest; New York: Central European University Press, 2008.

This history of Russian-Jewish prose begins with essays that define the scope of this literature and its linguistic complexity. The following chapters review major authors and their works. The final chapter deals with authors as émigrés in other European countries or in the Americas.

Drama and Poetry

6-107. The Cambridge Introduction to Russian Poetry. Michael Wachtel. New York: Cambridge University Press, 2004.

This concise handbook is well suited to students and researchers who desire a brief overview of Russian poetry. The introductory text deals with issues of translation and transliteration. The first section, labeled Concepts, describes Russian metrics, the poetic lexicon, use of tropes and topoi. The third chapter ends with a section on genre. The second half of the book, titled Interpretation, treats different poetic forms and themes such as the ode and elegy, the ballad, love poetry, nature poetry, and patriotic verse.

6-108. Contemporary Russian Poetry: An Anthology. Evgeny Bunimovich and J. Kates, eds. Champaign, IL: Dalkey Archive Press, 2008.

This volume is one of the first comprehensive anthologies of poetry from the post-Soviet era. The 44 authors presented here include many whose works are available in English for the first time; women authors are well represented. The side-by-side Russian/English texts make this anthology equally useful for students of Russian literature. The authors selected exhibit a wide range of poetical styles and themes.

A critical work on the same period is *Lyric Poetry and Modern Politics: Russia, Poland, and the West* (Yale University Press, 2009). This volume takes a comparative approach to major poets in Russian and Poland and the influences on their works from West Europe and the United States. It is a valuable introduction to modern Polish poetry, which is less available through English translation or critical studies.

6-109. The Modern Russian Theater: A Literary and Cultural History. Nicholas Rzhevsky. Armonk, NY: M.E. Sharpe, 2009.

In the introductory essay to this history of Russian theater in the twentieth century, Rzhevsky establishes the necessity of treating theater performance and theater as literature as a whole rather than separate cultural manifestations. A particular focus of this history is the adaptation of literary works, both Russian and foreign, for the stage. See also *Historical Dictionary of Russian Theater* by Laurence Senelick (Scarecrow Press, 2007), entry 8-96.

Europe—Northern

6-110. Project Runeburg. Open access. http://runeberg.org/

The goal of Project Runeburg is to provide open access to the classic literature of the Nordic countries. The project began in 1992 with a student group from Linköping University in Sweden who digitize and edit literary texts that are now in the public domain. The scope of the collection includes both primary and secondary sources as well as encyclopedias works, dictionaries, glossaries, and grammars. Although most of the collection is in the original Scandinavian language, there are some English titles as well.

6-111. A Companion to Old Norse-Icelandic Literature and Culture. Rory McTurk, ed. Oxford, UK: Blackwell, 2005.

This companion provides an overview of the literary traditions of Icelandic literature beginning with Christian texts. Several chapters treat epic poetry and metrics and this reference offers a discussion of the development of modern genres both narrative and poetic.

6-112. Historical Dictionary of Scandinavian Literature and Theater. Jan Sjavik. Lanham, MD: Scarecrow Press, 2006.

This reference tool provides information on literature and theater from the Scandinavian countries. In addition to the chronologically organized articles, there are bibliographies for further reading.
    Northern Arts: The Breakthrough of Scandinavian Literature and Art: From Ibsen to Bergman (Arnold L. Weinstein, Princeton University Press, 2008) is a complementary critical work.

6-113. Histories of Scandinavian Literature. Lincoln: University of Nebraska Press, 1993–2007. Monographic series.

This monographic series contains histories of the literature of the various Scandinavian countries.

> *A History of Danish Literature.* Sven H. Rossell, ed. 1993.
> Danish literature has long held a position of dominance among the Scandinavian literatures. This work traces its origins from the earliest Runic inscriptions to the present, including genres as diverse as the children's tales of Hans Christen Andersen, the autobiographical narrative of Karen Blixen (Isak Dinesen), and the philosophical essays of Søren Kierkegaard.

> *A History of Icelandic Literature.* Daisy Nejmann, ed. 2007.
> This volume surveys Icelandic literature from the ninth century to the present. Medieval Icelandic literature is represented by the sagas and Eddic poetry. Other chapters highlight less-known Icelandic genres including drama, children's literature, and women's literature.

A History of Norwegian Literature. Harald S. Naess, ed. 1993.
This overview of Norwegian literature begins with the epic poets of the ninth century who narrated the exploits of the Vikings, in verse, and continues to the twentieth century. Special sections are devoted to the works of Nobel Prize winners Sigrid Undset, Knut Hamsun, and Bjornstjerne Bjornson, as well as chapters on children's literature and women writers.

A History of Swedish Literature. Lars G. Warme, ed. 1996.
This history provides coverage of Swedish literature from the Middle Ages to the twentieth century. The importance of Swedish literature, despite the geographic isolation of the nation and the limited dissemination of the language, is made apparent in the discussions of historical and social issues reflected in literary works. An in-depth treatment of feminist themes is included as well as a chapter on children's literature.

Europe—Southern

Greece

6-114. The Cambridge Companion to Greek Lyric. Felix Budelmann, ed. Cambridge, UK; New York: Cambridge University Press, 2009.

This comprehensive work treats the Greek lyric from its beginnings until the twentieth century. The individually authored chapters treat lyric and gender, the relationship of meter and music, as well as particular authors and genres.

6-115. Encyclopedia of Modern Greek Literature. Bruce Merry. Westport, CT: Greenwood Press, 2004.

This encyclopedia offers readily accessible information to more than 800 authors and their works as well as entries about genres and themes. The chronological coverage is from the Byzantine period to the present. A chronological table serves to orient readers to the time periods covered.
A complementary study is *Modern Greek Literature: Critical Essays* (Gregory Nagy and Anna Stavrakopoulou, eds. Routledge, 2003). The 10 chapter-length essays address the influences from classical and Byzantine literature, women writers, the development of the modern Greek novel, and the interface between historiography and literature.

6-116. From Byzantium to Modern Greece: Medieval Texts and Their Modern Reception. Roderick Beaton. Aldershot, England; Burlington, VT: Ashgate/Variorum, 2008.

This specialized study treats Greek literature from the Byzantine period until the modern era. The development of a national literature is a major focus in the work.

6-117. Step-mothertongue: From Nationalism to Multiculturalism: Literatures of Cyprus, Greece and Turkey. Mehmet Yaşın. London: Middlesex University Press, 2000.

The essays presented in this collection consider questions of national and culture identity as well as language choice in Cypriot literary works. Contemporary writers and poets are represented among the authors of the essays.

6-118. Surrealism in Greece: An Anthology. Nikos Stabalis. Austin: University of Texas Press, 2008.

The introductory essay defines the scope of this anthology as limited to authors who wrote and lived in Greece from the 1930s to the 1960s. The works presented here in English translation place Greece definitively within the Surrealist movement. The editor establishes three time periods for this anthology of 18 different authors: the founders, the second generation (post World War II) and the Pali group which is based on the name of the literary review, *Pali*, which came to an end with the rise of the military junta in 1967. Each section contains a brief background essay. In terms of genre, poetry is best represented here although there are also limited examples of the visual arts as well.

Italy

6-119. **Encyclopedia of Italian Literary Studies.** Gaetana Marrone, ed. New York: Routledge, 2007. 2 vols.

This two-volume reference work contains over 600 entries that address all aspects of Italian literature including authors, genres, literary movements, major themes as well as critical responses to specific works. The encyclopedia also includes references to journalism, film, and popular culture. In the case of specific authors, the entries contain a brief biography, an overview of the author's major works, and a bibliography for further reading.

6-120. **Italian Literature before 1900 in Translation: An Annotated Bibliography, 1929–2008.** Robin Healey. Toronto: University of Toronto Press, 2011.

The introductory essay to this volume indicates its scope; it is a compilation of all known translations to English, published between 1929 and 2008, of Italian literature originally written before 1900. Therefore, there is a broad spectrum of Italian literature extending from the Middle Ages to the end of the nineteenth century. All genres are represented here including the essay and religious/philosophical texts. A statistical table of authors is included at the end of the introduction.

6-121. **Modern Italian Literature.** Ann Hallamore Caesar and Michael Caesar, eds. Cambridge: Polity, 2007.

This history covers the period from 1690 to the present with a focus on cultural aspects of literary production including discussions of the intended reading audience, a history of publishing, and the competing currents of public/private art. The content is arranged in three periods of time: the first is the eighteenth century, a period of national identity formation; the second period covers the nineteenth century and the emergence of industrial Italy; the third period extends from the beginning of the twentieth century to the present and is characterized by constant renegotiation of national cultural identity.

6-122. **The Oxford Companion to Italian Literature.** Peter Hainsworth and David Robey, eds. New York: Oxford University Press, 2002.

In this guide, most titles are listed in Italian with some in English. Nearly 2,400 entries are alphabetically arranged and were written by a team of international Italianists. Only the lengthier entries include supplemental bibliographies and usually provide no more than one or two references. Literary genres and movements are also outlined as well as textual criticism, publishers, and literary magazines. Entries also treat Italian literature written in Latin and various dialects as well as the influence of classical and patristic writings on Italian literature. Some reference is given to political background, historical events and philosophies. It is recommended for academic and large public library collections.

ITALY—NARRATIVE

6-123. **The Cambridge Companion to the Italian Novel.** Peter Bondanella and Andrea Ciccarelli. Cambridge, UK: Cambridge University Press, 2003.

The collection of essays in this guide to the Italian novel is from the Middle Ages to the present. Introductory materials provide a chronology and an overview of the development of prose fiction as an independent genre. The essays treat the late medieval and renaissance narrative, the historical novel, literary realism, and the development of popular fiction. Contemporary themes addressed in the individual studies include testimonial literature, feminist writing, exile and migration, and the intertwining of film and novel.

6-124. Crimini: The Bitter Lemon Book of Italian Crime Fiction. Giancarlo De Cataldo, ed.; Andrew Brown, trans. London: Bitter Lemon Press, 2008.

This anthology of Italian crime fiction makes available to English readers the work of nine emerging authors. Crime fiction is a genre that has made its presence known in popular fiction.

Another study of detective fiction is *The Novel as Investigation: Leonardo Sciascia, Dacia Maraina, and Antonio Tabucchi* by JoAnn Cannon (University of Toronto Press, 2006).

6-125. Italian Tales: An Anthology of Contemporary Italian Fiction. Massimo Riva, ed. New Haven, CT: Yale University Press, 2004.

The generation of authors who have come of age since World War II is the focus of this anthology of short stories. The introductory essay considers the role of Italy in a new, unified Europe and the globalization of culture. The stories of 18 different authors are organized thematically and deal with Italy's historical past, memory, and emigration and exile.

ITALY—DRAMA AND POETRY

6-126. An Anthology of Modern Italian Poetry in English Translation, with Italian Text. Ned Condini, ed. and trans. New York: Modern Language Association of America, 2009.

This dual-language anthology offers a sampling of 38 Italian poets including authors who are well known in English translation as well as those whose works appear here in English for the first time.

A similar anthology is *A Selection of Modern Italian Poetry in Translation,* edited by Roberta L. Payne (McGill-Queen's University Press, 2004). Also available as an e-book, this dual-language anthology offers a sampling of 38 Italian poets including authors who are well known in English translation as well as those whose works appear here in English for the first time.

6-127. A History of Italian Theatre. Joseph Farrell and Paolo Puppa, eds. Cambridge, UK: Cambridge University Press, 2011.

This history begins with the Middle Ages and extends to the present. The organization is largely chronological. Some chapters are dedicated to particular authors and one chapter treats women authors. The final chapters present the tradition of dialect theatre in Northern Italy, Naples, and Sicily.

Iberian Peninsula

6-128. A Comparative History of Literatures in the Iberian Peninsula. Fernando Cabo Aseguinolaza, Anxo Abuín González, and César Domínguez, eds. Amsterdam; Philadelphia: John Benjamins, 2010.

This first volume of an intended two-volume history of the literatures of the Iberian Peninsula begins with an overview of Iberian literary history followed by thematically organized essays. The first section provides a geo-cultural account of literary manifestations in the Iberian Peninsula. The second section focuses on identity and isolation. The third section on the multilingual nature of the Iberian Peninsula is an appropriate continuation of the theme of identity. The oral tradition (section 4) includes epic poetry and the ballad tradition. The final section discusses the development of literary traditions beginning with the court of Alfonso X in the thirteenth century and ending with the transition to democracy after the fall of the dictatorships in Spain and Portugal.

6-129. **Hispanic and Luso-Brazilian Detective Fiction: Essays on the** *género negro* **Tradition.** Renée W. Craig-Odders, Jacky Collins, and Glen S. Close, eds. Jefferson, NC: McFarland, 2006.

This volume treats detective fiction in Spain and Portugal as well as Latin America. The individual essays treat a particular author and his or her work. Major divisions within the book correspond to geography—the Iberian Peninsula and Latin America.

6-130. **A Companion to Portuguese Literature.** Stephen Parkinson, Cláudia Pazos Alonso, and F. T. Earle. Woodbridge: Tamesis, 2009. Print and e-book.

This handbook is an introduction to European Portuguese literature from the Middle Ages to the present. It contains brief essays on major authors and genres and more extensive essays on key authors and their work. It has a greater emphasis on the modern period. Despite its traditional approach and coverage of the well known, there has been a conscious effort to include female writers. The exclusion of Brazilian and African literature corresponds to the editors' view that these literatures are extensive enough to require separate study. Bibliographical information includes sources of Portuguese literature in translation.

A quick reference work to go along with the *Companion* is *A Chronology of Portuguese Literature: 1128–2000* (Rogério Miguel Puga, Newcastle upon Tyne, UK: Cambridge Scholars, 2011). This volume is the first comprehensive chronology of Portuguese literature; it extends from the Middle Ages to the end of the twentieth century. Representative works are listed for each time period together with brief biographical information about the author.

Spain

6-131. **Biblioteca Virtual Miguel de Cervantes.** Fundación Biblioteca Virtual Miguel de Cervantes. Open access resource. http://www.cervantesvirtual.com/

The Biblioteca Virtual Miguel de Cervantes began as a pedagogical Project of the University of Alicante with the goal of providing ready access to students of the foundational works in Spanish in the areas of literature and the humanities. The Biblioteca now includes a broader scope of literature and humanities with titles in many languages, including English translations of well-known Spanish language authors (Spain and Spanish America).

6-132. **The Cambridge History of Spanish Literature.** Vol. 1. David T. Gies (ed.). Cambridge, UK: Cambridge University Press, 2004. Print and e-book.

This overview of the literary history of Spain begins with an introductory essay on the formation of a literary canon. Subsequent chapters address literary genres within each major literary period ending with post Franco literature and film. The section on modern literature includes two chapters dedicated to literature in Catalonia.

A Companion to Catalan Literature by Arthur Terry (Woodbridge, UK; Rochester, NY: Tamesis, 2003) is more specific to Catalonia. This specialized volume is one of the few that addresses literature in Catalan. It is broad in chronological scope beginning with the Middle Ages and ending with the 20th century. Also included are authors from Valencia and Mallorca who write in Catalan. This study offers lists of works available in English for further reading.

6-133. Literary Adaptations in Spanish Cinema. Sally Faulkner. London; Rochester, NY: Tamesis, 2004.

The organization of this volume is thematic rather than chronological. Following the introduction is a chapter on post-Franco cinema. The remaining chapters deal with representations of the city, the nineteenth century novel represented in film, a separate chapter on Buñuel and Galdós, and a final chapter on the representation of history in film.

6-134. A New History of Spanish Writing, 1939 to the 1990s. Christopher Perriam. Oxford; New York: Oxford University Press, 2000.

This volume is an introduction to authors and themes from the Civil War to the end of the twentieth century. Chapters are organized thematically and address the depiction of history in literature, issues of power, and the emergence of a new literary paradigm.

    A similar work is *New Spain, New Literatures* (Luis Martín Estudillo and Nicholas Spadaccini, Vanderbilt University Press, 2010). This collection of essays presents the plurality of modern Spanish literature. The chapters deal with specific themes and representative authors. Chapters introduce authors who now write in minority languages such as Basque, Galician, and Catalan. Other essays treat the representation of history and memory, the new immigrants, and issues of gender and class.

6-135. Spanish Literature: Current Debates on Hispanism; Spanish Literature from Origins to 1700; Spanish Literature: 1700 to the Present. David William Foster, Daniel Altamiranda, Carmen Carmen Urioste-Azcorra, eds. New York: Garland, 2001. 3 vols.

This three-volume set provides an overview of Spanish literature from its origins to the present. The first volume focuses on the twentieth century and the tradition of literary criticism. The second volume begins with one of the earliest known poetic forms, the *jarcha*, and ends with the Baroque dramatist Pedro Calderón de la Barca. The final volume begins with chapters on three 18th-century authors (Torres Villarroel, Caldalso, and Fernández de Moratín) and ends with two women representative of the post-Franco generation.

    A more specialized work within the history of Spanish literature is *The Scroll and the Cross: 1,000 Years of Jewish-Hispanic Literature* (Ilan Stavans, ed. Routledge, 2003). The centuries-long mutual influence of Jewish culture and thought on Hispanic literature is the focus of this collection of essays. Included are historical authors such as Maimonides and Miguel de Cervantes as well as modern authors from both sides of the Atlantic including Unamuno, García Lorca, Borges, as well as more recent writers such as Jacobo Timerman, Mario Vargas Llosa, and Ariel Dorfman.

Spain—Narrative

6-136. The Cambridge Companion to the Spanish Novel from 1600 to the Present. Harriet S. Turner and Adelaida López de Martínez. Cambridge: Cambridge University Press, 2003.

This work traces the development of the modern Spanish novel from 1600 to the present and shows the coalescence of influences from Cervantes' Don Quijote and the traditions of the picaresque novel. The essays note the importance of invention and experimentation. Additionally, these studies look outside the process of writing to examine the role played by historical events and cultural contexts in the evolution of the Spanish novel. A chronology of the novel and a guide to further reading are also included.

    Contemporary Spanish Fiction: Generation X (Dorothy Odartey-Wellington, University of Delaware Press, 2008) focuses on the work of six novelists whose works were published between 1994 and 2001. The role of societal changes—globalization, consumerism, and media saturation—are seen as important factors in the rise of a new narrative that is highly connected with popular culture.

6-137. Madrid Tales. Helen Constantine and Margaret Jull Costa, eds. and trans. Oxford, UK; New York: Oxford University Press, 2012.

This collection of short stories translated to English is one of a series of anthologies that focus on European capitals. The authors include well-known figures from the 19th century such as Pérez Galdós and Pardo Bazán as well as new authors whose work has been previously unavailable in English translation. As with the previous volumes in this series the reader is placed in context through the inclusion of maps and photographs. Also see entry 6-149 for French tales.

Spain—Drama and Poetry

6-138. Out of the Wings: Spanish and Spanish American Theatres in Translation.
http://www.outofthewings.org/

This project represents a collaboration of King's College London, Queen's College Belfast, University of Oxford, and the Arts & Humanities Research Council (UK). The database provides an author index, a title index, and a translator index to the online texts. The works selected reflect primarily the Golden Age or Baroque and modern drama in Spain and Spanish America.

6-139. The Cambridge Introduction to Spanish Poetry: Spain and Spanish America. D. Gareth Walters, ed. Cambridge, UK: Cambridge University Press, 2002.

This history of poetry in the Spanish language is organized thematically. The various chapters deal with poetic subgenres such as the epic, ballads, songs and sonnets, love poetry, religious and moral poetry, and poetic satire. The appendix contains a chronological list of authors cited.

The texts of many classic works are contained in *The Golden Age: Poems of the Spanish Renaissance* (Edith Grossman, W. W. Norton, 2006). This edition of 40 poetic works of the Spanish Renaissance presents side-by-side translations of the work of well-known authors such as Garcilaso de la Vega, Fray Luis de León, Lope de Vega, San Juan de la Cruz, and the Mexican author Sor Juana Inés de la Cruz. Accompanying materials include brief biographical information about each author included in the anthology.

6-140. Modern Spanish Dramatists: A Bio-bibliographical Sourcebook. Mary Parker, ed. Westport, CT: Greenwood Press, 2002. Print and e-book.

This reference work covers the period from the 18th century to the present. The 33 Spanish dramatists treated in this work include well-known authors as well as those who are little known outside of Spain. An introductory essay explores the development of Spanish drama since the Golden Age. The author entries include a brief biography, discussion of major works, and critical reception of the plays.

Europe—Western

France

6-141. ARTFL. American and French Research on the Treasury of the French Language. Department of Romance Languages and Literatures, University of Chicago. Online subscription database.

The Project for American and French Research on the Treasury of the French Language (ARTFL) is a cooperative enterprise of the Laboratoire ATILF (Analyse et Traitement Informatique de la Langue Française) of the Centre National de la Recherche Scientifique (CNRS) and the Division of the Humanities and Electronic Text Services (ETS) of the University of Chicago. ARTFL offers a full-text database of nearly 2,000 works in French dating from the 15th to the 20th centuries. Included are works of literature, literary criticism, history, philosophy, and economics. Also found in the database are a number of open access resources such as the *Dictionnaires d'autrefois*, the *Encyclopédie* of Diderot and d'Alembert, and the *Bibliothèque Bleue de Troyes*.

6-142. The Cambridge Companion to French Medieval Literature. Simon Gaunt and Sara Kay, eds. Cambridge, UK: Cambridge University Press, 2008.

This survey of French medieval literature begins with the Song of Roland and ends with texts written in Middle French. All genres are represented including a chapter on various editions of the Vulgate in Old French as well as discussions of recurring themes such as the treatment of religion, marriage and sexuality.

A *New History of Medieval French Literature* (Jacqueline Cerquiglini-Toulet, Johns Hopkins University Press, 2011) is on the same subject. Previously published in French in 2007, this history of medieval French literature offers new perspectives. The first chapters deal with questions of authorship and readership. The actual mode of writing and dissemination of works are subjects of subsequent chapters. The chronology of authors and works helps to orient the reader.

6-143. The Cambridge History of French Literature. William E. Burgwinkle, Nicholas Hammond, and Emma Wilson, eds. Cambridge; New York: Cambridge University Press, 2011.

This single volume yet comprehensive history of French literature begins with the Occitan troubadours and ends with a discussion of current film and new media. The intervening chapters are organized by chronology and genre. Essays are included on more specialized topics, such as women writers, travel literature, the concept of Francophonie, and the Holocaust.

6-144. French XX Bibliography Critical and Bibliographical References for the Study of French Literature Since 1885. French Institute-Alliance Francaise de New York: French Institute in New York. 1969– . Published by Susquehanna University Press for the French Institute 1986– . Ann.

This annual publication provides listings of books, articles, and reviews that deal with French literature from the late 19th century to the present.

Francophone literature

The term *francophone* literature encompasses the literary production of all countries in which French is used as the language of cultural expression. This includes France and other European countries where French is widely spoken, such as Belgium, Switzerland, and Luxemburg. Outside of Europe, francophone literature is identified with French speaking Canadian authors, primarily from Quebec. In the Caribbean, French is the literary language of Haiti, Guadeloupe, and Martinique. The production of francophone literature in Africa is a complex question. The sphere of influence of the French language has both North African and Sub-Saharan exponents. However, the loss of power and prestige of the French language has diminished its use in post-colonial Africa. Similarly, political changes account for the now limited use of French as a literary language in southeast Asia.

6-145. French Global: A New Approach to Literary History. Christie McDonald and Susan Rubin Suleiman, eds. New York: Columbia University Press, 2010.

This volume attempts to review the literary history of France both within the European context and beyond. The various essays explore the concepts of "Francophonie," cultural spaces, mobility, and migration. The editors offer new interpretations of well-known texts within this global paradigm and emphasize the diverse views of language, text, and nation that inform the study of literature in the present century.

A similar work is *French Literature: A Cultural History* (Alison Finch, Polity Press, 2010). The 10 chapters in this volume survey French literature from its beginnings to the present with a focus on historical and social context. The final chapter expands the concept of French literature to include Francophone writers throughout the world.

Francophone literature worldwide is also treated in *The Cambridge Introduction to Francophone Literature* (Patrick Corcoran, ed. University of Cambridge Press, 2007). The five chapters cover the Maghreb, Sub-Saharan Africa, the Middle East, Canada, and the Caribbean. A bibliography and suggestions for further reading are included.

6-146. The Literature of Provence: An Introduction. Daniel Vitaglione. Jefferson, NC: McFarland. 2000.

Since the literature of Provence is less known to the English reader, this concise volume is a welcome introduction. Organization is chronological and begins with the troubadour tradition of the Middle Ages. The last of the seven chapters treats the most recent writers who continue to prefer Provençal or Occitan as the language of literary expression.

6-147. Masterpieces of French Literature. Marilyn S. Severson. Westport, CT: Greenwood Press, 2004.

This resource is a summary guide to the major works of French literature. It includes in-depth essays on eight French masterpieces. The analyses of literary works focus on plot, character development, recurrent themes, style, and historical context. In addition, there is biographical information on the authors treated.

FRANCE—NARRATIVE

6-148. The Facts on File Companion to the French Novel. Karen L. Taylor. New York: Facts on File, 2007.

This A-Z guide to the French novel begins with an extensive introduction to the history of the novel. More than 500 entries (authors and their works, key concepts and themes) follow. Each of the entries contains a short list of references.

6-149. The Oxford Book of French Short Stories. Elizabeth Fallaize, ed. Oxford, UK: Oxford University Press, 2002.

This anthology of 28 short stories begins with the late eighteenth century and ends with new and emerging writers of today. Although the selected stories are primarily from France, there are also representative texts from Quebec, Africa, and the French Caribbean. Women writers are well represented in this anthology.

Also published by Oxford University Press are a number of anthologies of French short stories or tales compiled by Helene Constantine. In each, the reader's experience is enhanced by the presence of photographs and maps to put the literary tour in context.

> *French Tales* (2008) contains 22 short stories of both well-known and lesser-known authors. The organization is geographical.

> *Paris Metro Tales* (2011) contains 22 short stories that have the metro as focal point. The introductory essay offers a brief history of the metro and its historical role, for example, as place of refuge and resistance in the Second World War.

Paris Tales (2004) is a collection of 22 short stories that provide a portrait of the arrondissements and quartiers of Paris as seen through diverse protagonists from well-known authors from the nineteenth century to the present.

FRANCE—DRAMA AND POETRY

6-150. Act French: Contemporary Plays from France. Philippa Wehle, ed. New York: PAJ Publications, 2007.

Although this anthology contains only seven plays it is significant because it presents current, cutting edge dramatists to the English speaking public: Valère Novarina, Olivier Cadiot, Michel Vinaver, Michèle Sigal, José Pliya, Emmanuelle Marie, and Philippe Minyana.

6-151. The Cambridge Introduction to French Poetry. Mary Lewis Shaw. Cambridge, UK: Cambridge University Press, 2003.

This comprehensive survey of French poetry covers the period from the eleventh century to the present. The geographical scope includes authors from Francophone countries throughout the world. The introduction contains a glossary of poetic terms to guide the reader through the detailed discussion of authors and their works. Citations from the works themselves are given in the original French with an English translation.

6-152. Six Nineteenth Century French Poets. A. M. Blackmore and E. H. Blackmore, eds. and trans. Oxford, UK: Oxford University Press, 2009.

This bilingual anthology of the poetry of Lamartine, Hugo, Baudelaire, Verlaine, Rimbaud, and Mallarmé is part of the Oxford World Classics series. The translations have been praised by reviewers and also the explanatory notes that guide the reader through difficulties in understanding the original verses.

6-153. Twentieth Century French Poetry: A Critical Anthology. Hugues Azérad and Peter Collier, eds. Cambridge, UK: Cambridge University Press, 2010.

This anthology is well suited for students of French literature because the chapter-long essays offer a detailed analysis of the French language poem that is the point of departure. However, an English translation of the original text is not available although the explication is in English. Each chapter closes with an extensive list of references.

A more specialized work is *Surrealist Painters and Poets: An Anthology* (Mary Ann Caws, ed. MIT Press, 2001). The artists and writers selected for this anthology represent those who reflect on their own artistic production and identify it with a particular esthetic. The texts include formal essays as well as memoirs written by or about André Breton, René Char, René Magritte, Guillaume Apollinaire, and Antonin Artaud, and others.

Holland/Belgium

6-154. A Literary History of the Low Countries. Theo Hermans. Rochester, NY: Camden House, 2009.

This text offers a comprehensive overview of the literatures of the Netherlands and former Flanders. The seven chapters are organized chronologically; the first covers the period from the Middle Ages to 1400 followed by a chapter on the late Middle Ages; the third chapter treats the Baroque; the fourth chapter the Enlightenment. The final chapters cover the nineteenth century, the period of esthetic renewal at the end of the nineteenth century, and the first two decades of the twentieth century. The final chapter treats the period before and after World War II.

Germany/Austria/Switzerland

6-155. Germanistik Online Datenbank. Berlin: Walter de Gruyter. Online subscription database. http://www.degruyter.com/view/db/germanistik

This bibliography is both retrospective and ongoing. Beginning with 1961, Germanistik provides access to works published about German literature, theatre, media studies, cultural history, and linguistics. The online interface, available in both German and English, allows full-text search as well as guided searches by author, title, public year, and keyword. At present, approximately 350,000 items are indexed. While the majority of these entries are in German, contributions in other languages are not excluded.

6-156. The Cambridge Companion to German Romanticism. Nicholas Saul. Cambridge, UK: Cambridge University Press, 2009.

This multidisciplinary approach to German Romanticism includes chapters on all genres of literature, recurring themes, as well as the fine arts, philosophy, religion, and social sciences.

6-157. Camden House History of German Literature. Rochester, NY: Camden House, 2001–2007. 10 vols.

This 10-volume set covers German literature from its origins to the twentieth century. Most of the volumes, with the exception of volume, 10, *German Literature of the 20th Century*, consist of a series of individually authored essays that treat major authors and genres within the chronological scope of that volume. The final volume in the series, the twentieth century, is individually authored by Ingo Stoehr. Particularly notable is the interdisciplinary nature of the essays in this comprehensive history of German literature; there is a conscious attempt to link literature to historiography, the social sciences, philosophy, and the fine arts.

6-158. Encyclopedia of German Literature. Matthias Konzett. Chicago: Fitzroy Dearborn Publishers, 2000. 2 vols.

This work is arranged alphabetically by author. The individual entries contain a list of major works of the author, translations to English, and secondary scholarship. Selected works are highlighted and have a separate article following the main author article. An effort is made to trace recurrent themes and relate them to major historical events and cultural currents. Articles are also provided on nonliterary topics and concepts, philosophy and social theory, that are intimately bound with the literary output of an era.

6-159. Historical Dictionary of German Literature to 1945. William Grange. Lanham, MD: Scarecrow Press, 2010. Print and e-book.

Historical Dictionary of Postwar German Literature. William Grange. Lanham, MD: Scarecrow Press, 2009. Print and e-book.

These titles are compilations of authors, literary works, genres, movements, and historical events in the period from prior to 1945 and from 1945 to 2008, arranged chronologically. All authors who write in German are included, regardless of nationality or country of residence. Each volume offers an introductory essay for each major period. Also included are some nonliterary works that are considered to be integral to the history of German literature. The Postwar book was also issued in paperback with the title *A to Z of Postwar German Literature*.

6-160. Literature and Film in the Third Reich. Karl Heinz Schoeps. Columbia, SC: Camden House, 2010.

This work, based on the second German edition of *Literaturur im Dritten Reich (1933–1945),* constitutes the first work available in English that surveys literary and cinematic production during the Third Reich. It reflects works that supported National Socialism as well as those that resisted the totalitarian regime. The historical context is well covered through presentation of key historical and philosophical works.

6-161. Modern German Literature. Michael Minden. Cambridge, UK: Polity Press, 2011.

This concise history covers works written from 1750 to the present in the framework of international cultural impact such as the propagation of Romanticism throughout European literary circles. Other major currents are seen in Modernism, the literature corresponding to the Third Reich, and creative responses to the open multi-media cultures of the Weimar and Federal Republics.

6-162. A New History of German Literature. David E. Wellbery, Judith Ryan, Hans Ulrich Gumbrecht, et al., eds. Cambridge, MA: Belknap Press of Harvard University Press, 2004.

The 200 essays in this comprehensive literary history focus on particular authors, historical events, artistic currents, and even the effect of technology. The chronological scope of the essays begins with the Middle Ages and extends to the twentieth century.

GERMANY/AUSTRIA/SWITZERLAND—NARRATIVE

6-163. Cambridge Companion to the Modern German Novel. Graham Bartam, ed. Cambridge, UK: Cambridge University Press, 2004. Print and e-book.

This collection of essays deals with all aspects of the contemporary German narrative. The individually authored studies explore reflections of society and politics, gender issues, the Bildingsroman, World War II and its aftermath, and questions of identity in the Swiss and Austrian novel.
     Also published by Cambridge University Press is *Contemporary German Fiction: Writing in the Berlin Republic* (Stuart Taberner, ed., 2007). This volume of essays deals with various aspects of contemporary German fiction including coming to terms with the Nazi past, the unification of Germany, and the position of the Jewish minority in today's Germany.

6-164. Crime Stories: Criminalistic Fantasy and the Culture of Crisis in Weimar Germany. Todd Herzog. New York: Berghahn Books, 2009.

The emergence of crime fiction as a popular genre during the period preceding the rise of National Socialism is the focus of this study. The thematically organized chapters treat themes such as the criminal as outsiders of society, the psychology of criminality, mass culture, and crime detection and investigation. The final chapter deals with criminalistic fantasy after the Weimar Republic.

GERMANY/AUSTRIA/SWITZERLAND—DRAMA AND POETRY

6-165. Contemporary German Plays. Margaret Herzfeld-Sander, ed. New York: Continuum, 2001. 2 vols.

This anthology of contemporary German drama presents the work of seven different authors in English translation. The second volume in particular offers works that address contemporary views of German history and the Second World War.

6-166. Dictionary of German Theater. William Grange. Lanham, MD: Scarecrow Press, 2006.

This reference guide to German theater opens with a chronology and introduction to German theater, followed by an alphabetical guide to playwrights and their works, dramatic genres and literary movements, as well as directors, producers, and actors.

A more in-depth treatment of a significant period is *Theatre under the Nazis* (John London, ed. Manchester University Press, 2000). This volume presents an overview of German Theatre from the end of the Weimar Republic to the end of World War II. The introductory essay is followed by chapters on Nazi drama, Jewish theatre, and German theatre in exile.

6-167. Twentieth-Century German Poetry: An Anthology. Michael Hofmann, ed. New York: Farrar, Straus and Giroux, 2006.

This comprehensive anthology of contemporary German poetry, originally published as *The Faber Book of 20th-Century German Poems* (2005) presents a wide range of themes: personal tragedy and triumph, the struggle of dissent and protest, responses to Germany's troubled history and reunification. Because German poetry is little known to English readers, this work is a welcome addition to the repertory of modern European poetry.

Few studies of German literature are dedicated exclusively to the literary production of Austria as is *Poetry in a Provisional State: The Austrian Lyric 1945–1955* (Anthony Bushell, University of Wales Press, 2007). This study of Austrian poetry covers the period between the fall of the Third Reich and Austria's reassertion of independence in 1955. Of particular interest is the absence of references to the Nazi era in the poetry of the first decade following the end of the Third Reich.

SPECIALIZED TOPICS IN WORLD LITERATURE

Holocaust, Genocide, and Testimonial Literature

6-168. Literature of the Holocaust. Open access. http://www.writing.upenn.edu/~afilreis/Holocaust/holhome.html

This website is maintained by Al Filreis, Director of the Center for Programs in Contemporary Writing at the University of Pennsylvania. Organization of materials is alphabetic and contains links to other websites as well as some full text documents. The scope of the website is broad and includes texts on the Holocaust in general as well as excerpts from testimonies and diaries.

6-169. Yad Vashem. http://www.yadvashem.org

The Yad Vashem is an international organization with the world center for Holocaust remembrance and education located in Jerusalem. The website provides information on a variety of topics related to the Holocaust. The online catalog to the institute's library offers the researcher an overview of the scope of studies that exist on the Holocaust. Some digital collections are provided as well including photographs and some short literary works.

6-170. Bearing Witness: A Resource Guide to Literature, Poetry, Art, Music, and Videos by Holocaust Victims and Survivors. Philip Rosen and Nina Appelbaum. Westport, CT: Greenwood Press, 2002.

An introductory essay provides a historical context for the Holocaust and the persecution of Jews and "undesirable" segments of the population. The five chapters contain over 800 references to individual writers/artists and their work. The first chapter treats memoirs, diaries, and fiction. Poetry is the focus of the second chapter; chapters on art and music follow. The final chapter reviews videos of the holocaust experience, in particular, those that feature testimony by survivors. Included at the end is an index organized by age-appropriate level which makes this guide particularly useful for K-12 instruction.

6-171. Contemporary Jewish Writing in the World. Lincoln, NE: University of Nebraska Press, 1998– . Monographic series.

This series focuses on the Jewish diaspora outside of the United States. The series consists of anthologies, organized by country, that present the works of Jewish authors who struggle with issues of identity in the context of nations where Jews form a clearly delineated minority population.

> *Contemporary Jewish Writing in Austria.* Dagmar C. G. Lorenz, ed. 1999.
>
> *Contemporary Jewish Writing in Brazil.* Nelson H. Vieira, ed. 2010.
>
> *Contemporary Jewish Writing in Britain and Ireland.* Bryan Cheyette, ed. 1998.
>
> *Contemporary Jewish Writing in Canada.* Michael Greenstein, ed. 2004.
>
> *Contemporary Jewish Writing in Germany.* Leslie Morris, ed. 2002.
>
> *Contemporary Jewish Writing in Hungary.* Susan Rubin Suleiman, ed. 2003.
>
> *Contemporary Jewish Writing in Poland.* Antony Polonsky, ed. 2001.
>
> *Contemporary Jewish Writing in South Africa.* Claudia Bathsheba Braude, ed. 2001.
>
> *Contemporary Jewish Writing in Sweden.* Peter Stenberg, ed. 2005.
>
> *Contemporary Jewish Writing in Switzerland.* Rafael Newman, ed. 2003.

6-172. Encyclopedia of Holocaust Literature. David Patterson, Alan L. Berger, and Sarita Cargas. Westport, CT: Greenwood Press, 2002.

The introductory essay provides notes on the scope of the encyclopedia and the process of selection. The alphabetical entries follow a uniform organizational structure. The first question addressed is why the author or work holds a significant place in Holocaust literature. Biographical information about the author is also included followed by a critical review of major works. At the end of the encyclopedia are three appendixes. The first lists authors by date of birth and is followed by the second author appendix organized by country of birth. The third appendix provides the original name of authors who are better known under a pseudonym.

6-173. German Writers in French Exile, 1933–1940. Martin Mauthner. London: Vallentine Mitchell in Association with the European Jewish Publication Society, 2007.

This specialized volume is the story of a group of German writers who emigrated to France at the onset of the Nazi regime, including well-known authors such as Thomas Mann, Lion Feuchtwanger, and Stefan Zweig. Their efforts to undermine German authority and alert the West of impending catastrophe are documented here as well as their internal struggles and disagreements.

6-174. Historical Dictionary of "The Dirty Wars." 2nd ed. David Kohut and Olga Vilella. Lanham, MD: Scarecrow Press, 2010.

This is a much-expanded version of the first edition of the work. The new edition presents background information necessary for anyone who is studying South American literature of the second half of the twentieth century (1954–1990). The dictionary begins with a chronological index of events in each of the six countries studied: Argentina, Bolivia, Brazil, Chile, Paraguay, and Uruguay.

Following the chronology are the dictionary entries of individuals who have a place of prominence during this period: government officials, artists, musicians, and writers.

6-175. Holocaust Literature: An Encyclopedia of Writers and Their Work. S. Lillian Kremer. New York, London: Routledge, 2003. 2 vols.

This comprehensive two-volume encyclopedia contains over 300 entries on Holocaust authors. The authors selected for inclusion represent a broad spectrum and include a variety of languages and nationalities as well as second and third generation writers. Also included are a glossary of terms and maps. The appendices include authors by birthplace and language of works, literary themes, list of ghettoes referenced in authors' texts, literary themes, and historical events.

6-176. The Oryx Holocaust Sourcebook. William R. Fernekes. Westport: Greenwood Publishing Group, 2002.

This volume provides an overview of available materials for study of the Holocaust. The 17 chapters cover reference books; scholarly works in history and the social sciences; audiovisual materials in multiple formats, including art works and music; museums and memorials; and online resources. In addition, there are chapters dedicated to non-fiction narratives and literary texts in all genres, as well as works for children and young adults.

6-177. Spirit of Resistance: Dutch Clandestine Literature during the Nazi Occupation. Jeroen Dewulf. Woodbridge: Boydell & Brewer, 2010. Print and e-book.

This specialized study deals with the clandestine literature that flourished in the Netherlands during the Nazi occupation. The introductory chapter deals with the literature of resistance throughout Dutch history. Subsequent chapters treat the rise of antifascist literature in the decade preceding the Second World War, clandestine printing during the German occupation, and the postwar period.
A Family Occupation: Children of the War and the Memory of World War II in Dutch Literature of the 1980s is an introduction to the recurrent theme of Nazi occupation in Dutch literature (Jolanda Vanderwal Taylor, Amsterdam University Press, 2009). The horrors of war are seen from the point of view of the child. The final chapters deal with the aftermath of war in the search for justice for victims and collaborators alike.

6-178. Testimonio: On the Politics of Truth. John Beverly. Minneapolis, MN: University of Minnesota Press, 2004.

This specialized volume offers an overview of the genre known as *testimonio* in Spanish American literature. The work focuses on the post-Cold War period and the emergence of testimonial narratives that deal with civil war and internal struggles throughout Latin America. One of the chapters treats the controversy surrounding the story of Rigoberta Menchú.

6-179. The Theatre of Genocide: Four Plays about Mass Murder in Rwanda, Bosnia, Cambodia, and Armenia. Robert Skloot, ed. Madison, WI: University of Wisconsin Press, 2008.

The introduction to this concise anthology discusses the origins of the term genocide and provides historical background for the four twentieth-century genocides that form the common subject matter of the four dramatic works offered in English translation.

Women Writers

6-180. A Celebration of Women Writers. Mary Mark Ockerbloom, ed. Open access resource. http://digital.library.upenn.edu/women/

This website is a portal for online access to women authors throughout the world. Some of the links lead to online full texts translated to English of earlier authors whose works are now in public domain. The lists of authors are organized by chronology and by geography.

6-181. Latin American Women Writers. Alexandra, VA: Alexander Street Press. Online subscription database. http://alexanderstreet.com/products/laww.htm

This collection offers a broad overview of literary works by women from 20 different countries, extending from colonial times to the present. Although most of the works in the collection are in the original language, this database is included here because it interfaces with other Alexander Street collections. The works selected for inclusion represent all literary genres as well as memoirs and essays. The sophisticated indexing of the collection offers not only the traditional points of access: nation, dates of birth/death, and literary movements, but also key words that deal with issues of gender, politics, slavery, and the struggle for independence.

6-182. African Women Writing Resistance: Contemporary Voices. Jennifer Browdy de Hernandez, Pauline Dongala, Omotayo Jolaosho, and Anne Serafin, eds. Madison, WI: University of Wisconsin Press, 2010.

This anthology of contemporary African women writers begins with an essay on the topics explored in the selections and how they constitute a break with tradition or resistance to societal norms. The texts that follow are organized thematically. Major themes include acceptance or rejection of tradition; issues of sexuality; challenges to the institution of marriage; women's health issues; women as activists against war and the degradation of the environment; exile and diaspora; and perspectives of the past, present, and future.

6-183. An Anthology of Nineteenth-century Women's Poetry from Spain: In English Translation, with Original Text. Anna-Marie Aldaz, ed.; Anna-Marie Aldaz and W. Robert Walker, trans. New York: Modern Language Association of America, 2009.

This anthology presents 21 women poets in English translation, many for the first time, although a few of the authors such as Gertrudis Gómez de Avellaneda and Rosalía de Castro are well represented in anthologies of Spanish literature.

6-184. Twentieth-Century Chinese Women's Poetry: An Anthology. Julia C. Lin, ed. and trans. New York: M. E. Sharpe, 2009.

This anthology covers a century of women's poetry in Chinese. The selected poems are organized geographically, China and Taiwan, and chronologically. Many authors are made accessible for the first time in this English language anthology. The introductory essay offers an overview of Chinese poetry and of the authors selected for this anthology.

6-185. Woman Critiqued: Translated Essays on Japanese Women's Writing. Rebecca L. Copeland, ed. Honolulu, Hawaii: University of Hawaii Press, 2006.

This specialized volume provides an excellent overview of Japanese women writers and the critical response to their work. The sections of the book are organized thematically and treat issues related to the negative stereotype of the woman writer, such as her womanliness, her narcissism, as well as other subjects such as writing as resistance.

6-186. Women's Writing from the Low Countries 1200–1875: A Bilingual Anthology. Lia van Gemert. Amsterdam University Press, 2010. Print and e-book.

This bilingual Dutch-English anthology provides an overview of works by women writers in the period 1200 to 1875. The anthology begins with two introductory essays; the first covers the period 1200 to 1575 and the second the period 1575 to 1875. The anthology is organized both chronologically and thematically. The first sections deal with religious themes ranging from the contemplative to the harsh realities of Catholic/Protestant religious conflict. In the modern period themes include the education of women, social inequalities, and the role of the woman writer.

6-187. Writing to Delight: Italian Short Stories by Nineteenth-Century Women Writers. Antonia Arslan and Gabriella Romani, eds. Toronto: University of Toronto Press, 2006.

This anthology begins with a background essay on nineteenth century Italy followed by short stories of both well-known and less-known women authors.

After the War: A Collection of Short Fiction by Postwar Italian Women treats more openly topics previously considered taboo such as domestic abuse, mental illness, and sexual relationships (Martha King, ed. New York: Italica Press, 2004).

Also from Italica Press is *Contemporary Italian Women Poets: A Bilingual Anthology* (Cinzia Sartini Blum and Lara Trubowitz, ed. and trans. 2001). This anthology offers a collection of poetry written in the 20th century by Italian women authors. The introductory chapters treat the issue of translation. Representative texts are given in the original Italian with English translation. An extensive bibliography is found at the end of the volume.

Literary Translation

6-188. Index Translationum–World Bibliography of Translation. UNESCO. Open access resource. http://portal.unesco.org/culture/en/ev.php-URL_ID=7810&URL_DO=DO_TOPIC&URL_SECTION=201.html

This database contains cumulative bibliographical information on books that have been translated and published in approximately 100 UNESCO Member States since 1979 and includes more than 2,000,000 entries for translated works in literature, social and human sciences, history, art, as well as natural and physical sciences. The database is updated every four months. Information is compiled based on submissions to bibliographic centers and national libraries in participating countries. The Index Translationum does not include periodical literature, brochures or patents.

6-189. Encyclopedia of Literary Translations into English. O. Classe, ed. London; Chicago: Fitzroy Dearborn Publishers, 2000. 2 vols.

This comprehensive encyclopedia contains articles related to the art and practice of literary translation in general as well as entries for specific authors and their works.

A similar work is *Literary Translation: A Practical Guide* by Clifford E. Landers (Clevedon, UK: Multilingual Matters, 2001). This handbook provides a concise overview of the issues involved in the translation of literary works such as issues of adaptation, tone and register, the replication of metric forms in poetry, and translating for a particular audience as in the case of children's literature. The text contains examples of translations to English from several different languages although the preponderance is from Portuguese.

6-190. The Oxford History of Literary Translation in English. Peter France and Stuart Gillespie, eds. Oxford and New York: Oxford University Press, 2005–2011. 5 vols.

This multivolume history covers the time period from the Middle Ages to the beginning of the 21st century. The work treats the role of translators and their translations in defining the literary culture of the English-speaking world. It examines the factors that coalesced in creating a demand for translation and the process of dissemination. Each volume provides extensive bibliographies for further reading and research.

> *To 1500.* Vol. 1. Roger Ellis, ed. 2008.
>
> *1550–1660.* Vol. 2. Gordon Braden, Robert Cummings, and Stuart Gillespie, eds. 2011.
>
> *1660–1790.* Vol. 3. Stuart Gillespie and David Hopkins, eds. 2005.
>
> *1790–1900.* Vol. 4. Peter France and Kenneth Haynes, eds. 2006.

An earlier work also edited by Peter France is *The Oxford Guide to Literature in English Translation* (2001). This volume is a compilation by experts in many areas of classical and modern literary history. The first part of the book offers an overview of the history of translation into English. The second part is arranged by language of origin and offers critical essays with bibliographies on the translations of specific texts, authors, and genres as well as national literatures.

6-191. Decolonizing Translation: Francophone African Novels in English Translation. Kathryn Batchelor. Manchester, UK: St. Jerome Publishing, 2009.

This corpus-based study reviews translation practices of rendering into English narratives from Francophone Africa. Among the issues studied are the representation of dialect and register in the framework of post colonialism and translation theory.

6-192. Translation and the Rise of Inter-American Literature. Elizabeth Lowe and Earl E. Fitz. Gainesville: University of Florida Press, 2007.

This volume deals with literary translation, reception theory, and comparative literature. In particular, the role of translation in placing Latin American literary works among the masterpieces of world literature is viewed as a key development.

On the same subject is, *Voice-Overs: Translation and Latin American Literature* (Daniel Balderston and Marcy Schwartz, eds. Albany: State University of New York Press, 2002). This collection of 31 essays addresses all aspects of literary translation with a focus on the literature of Latin America. The first section, the most extensive, contains essays of well-known authors who have written on the difficulty of translating creative works. The second section deals with the problem of representing cultures in another linguistic context. The final section utilizes a case history approach to elucidate particular translation dilemmas by illustrating the problems in translating particular authors and particular works.

Gregory Rabassa's Latin American Literature: A Translator's Visible Legacy is a specialized volume dedicated to one of the most highly regarded translators of the Latin American in Portuguese and Spanish (María Constanza Guzmán, Bucknell University Press, 2010). Rabassa has translated the works of Julio Cortázar, Gabriel García Márquez, Jorge Amado, and Clarice Lispector, among others. Included in this discussion of literary translation are chapters that provide insight into the translator's transactions with the authors as he developed English versions of their texts.

Science Fiction and Fantastic Literature

6-193. Brazilian Science Fiction: Cultural Myths and Nationhood in the Land of the Future. M. Elizabeth Ginway. Lewisburg, PA: Bucknell University Press, 2004.

This specialized study provides an excellent introduction to the science fiction of Brazil produced in the period 1960 to 2000. The author views science fiction as a vehicle of social criticism. The first wave of authors can be viewed as anti-technological; they prefer to perpetuate the myth of Brazil as an agrarian society. The second group of authors corresponds to the decade (1970s) of the military regime; science fiction is used to describe a dystopian world, a thinly veiled satire of life in a dictatorship. The generation of authors who emerge in post-dictatorship Brazil in the mid-1980s reflects the increasing complexity of Brazilian society in a new global context.

6-194. A Companion to Latin American Magic Realism. Stephen M. Hart and Wen-chin Ouyang, eds. Woodbridge, UK: Tamesis Books, 2005.

The four-part division of the individual essays contained in this volume reflects the major themes that the editors have identified in Latin American magic realism. The first section deals with works that use magic realism to construct genealogies, family histories, and family myths. The second section explores how magic realism can be used to retell history and deform realities through nightmare and fantasy. The concept of magic itself is the topic of the third set of essays and the final set of essays views nation and empire within the context of magic realism. While the major focus is on Latin American authors, the essays show how this literary aesthetic has influenced others in Europe, Africa, and the Middle East.

Magic Realism

The term *magic realism* as applied to Latin American literature appears for the first time in an essay, "El cuento venezolano" published in 1948 by the Venezuelan author Arturo Úslar Pietri. In this essay, Úslar Pietri notes the fusion of the mythical and the real in the Latin American narrative, beginning perhaps with the earliest chronicles that recounted travels and explorations in the New World. In addition to the short stories of Úslar Pietri himself, this literary current is identified with authors such as Miguel Ángel Asturias and Gabriel García Márquez (both recipients of the Nobel Prize in Literature), Juan Rulfo, Laura Esquivel, Alejo Carpentier, and Isabel Allende. The birthplace of magic realism is appropriate for Latin America whose history, especially as construed by the first chroniclers, contains fabulous and fantastic elements. Other characteristics include the dislocation of time, syncretism and hybridity, as well as different perspectives of narration.

6-195. The Emergence of Latin American Science Fiction. Rachel Haywood Ferreira. Middletown, CT: Wesleyan University Press, 2011.

This concise history of the development of science fiction literature in Latin America offers an historical overview in the introductory chapter. The following chapters are thematically organized and treat in depth the works of selected authors. The first thematic chapter treats the concepts of utopia and dystopia; the second examines the impact of Darwinism in scientific thought and its reflection in science fiction; the third chapter explores the limits of science; and the last the emergency of technology as an alternative to science. A chronology of science fiction works follows at the end of the volume together with a bibliography of primary sources and a bibliography of secondary sources.

Also issued by Wesleyan University Press is *Cosmos Latinos: An Anthology of Science Fiction from Latin America and Spain* (Andrea L. Bell and Yolanda Molina Gavilán, eds., 2003). The stated purpose of this anthology is to make known through English translation the body of science fiction literature written in Spanish and Portuguese. Although the anthology includes authors already known through English translation, some of the newest authors are made accessible to English readers for the first time. The scope of the anthology begins with the late nineteenth century precursors and ends with works published as late as 2000.

6-196. **French Science Fiction, Fantasy, Horror and Pulp Fiction: A Guide to Cinema, Television, Radio, Animation, Comic Books and Literature from the Middle Ages to the Present.** Jean-Marc Lofficier and Randy Lofficier. Jefferson, NC: McFarland, 2000.

This encyclopedic work is divided into two parts. The first provides background information, lists, and summaries of works produced as film, television, radio, animation, comic books, and graphic novels. The second part covers major authors and works of French science fiction, fantasy, and horror. The chronological scope of this section is extensive and covers the Middle Ages to the present. In all, there are over 3,000 entries in this reference work.

6-197. **The Italian Gothic and Fantastic: Encounters and Rewritings of Narrative Traditions.** Francesca Billiani and Gigliola Sulis, eds. Cranbury, NJ: Associated University Presses, 2007.

This collection of essays provides an introduction to gothic and fantastic narratives written in Italian from the late nineteenth century through the twentieth century. Essays are divided into three parts; the first attempts to define and categorize the genre; the next two sections are organized chronologically into nineteenth and twentieth century.

6-198. **Latin American Science Fiction Writers: An A-to-Z Guide.** Darrell B. Lockhart, ed. Westport, CT: Greenwood Press, 2004.

This guide to Latin American science fiction writers portrays 70 authors and their works. There is an introductory essay followed by the individual author entries. For each author there is biographical information and a description of major works followed by separate bibliographies of works and criticism. In addition to a general index there is also a bibliography of anthologies of science fiction and criticism.

Also published by Greenwood Press is *The Supernatural in Short Fiction of the Americas: The Other World in the New World* by Dana Del George (2001).

6-199. **The Lights of Home: A Century of Latin American Writers in Paris.** Jason Weiss. London/New York: Routledge, 2003.

The century encompassed by Weiss's essays begins in 1893 and ends in the 1990s. Weiss contemplates the effect that Paris had on the formation of identity and aesthetic sensibility in the case of numerous Latin American writers including, among others, Rubén Darío, Ricardo Güiraldes, Alfonso Reyes, Teresa de la Parra, Lydia Cabrera, César Vallejo, and Miguel Angel Asturias. Weiss suggests that the development of magic realism was enhanced by the contact with European surrealists in the decade of the 1920s.

6-200. **Robot Ghosts and Wired Dreams: Japanese Science Fiction from Origins to Anime.** Christopher Bolton, Istvan Csicsery-Ronay (Jr.), and Takayuki Tatsumi, eds. Minneapolis, MN: University of Minnesota Press, 2007.

This collection of essays offers an overview of the development of Japanese science fiction and the most recent manifestation, anime. The time period covered by these studies begins before the Second World War and continues to the beginning of the 21st century. The first group of essays treats the use of horror and machines in prewar science fiction. The following section deals with science fiction animation.

6-201. **Science Fiction Literature in East Germany.** Sonja Fritzsche. New York: Peter Lang, 2006.

This specialized study treats East German science fiction from 1949 to the present. The chapters are organized chronologically and present detailed descriptions of major authors and their works.

Because of the years of isolation that followed the Second World War, many of the authors presented in this study are little known in the West.

6-202. **The SFWA European Hall of Fame: Sixteen Contemporary Masterpieces of Science Fiction from the Continent.** James Morrow and Kathryn Morrow, eds. New York: Tor, 2007.

This anthology of contemporary European science fiction presents English translations of works from a variety of European authors. An introductory essay surveys trends in European science fiction. At the end of the volume there is a bibliography of European science fiction authors in translation.

6-203. **Worlds Apart: An Anthology of Russian Fantasy and Science Fiction.** Alexander Levitsky, ed. New York; London: Duckworth, 2007.

This comprehensive and scholarly anthology of Russian science fiction covers a period of over 200 years beginning with the first fantastic stories that suggest other worlds and ending in the 1950s. The editor has preferred to focus on little known authors rather than those well known through translation such as Pushkin and Dostoevsky. The introductory essays provide a historical context for the reader.

Contemporary writers are featured in *Rasskazy: New Fiction from a New Russia* (Mikhail Iossel and Jeff Parker, eds. Portland, OR; Berkeley, CA: Tin House Books, 2009). This anthology presents the new generation of 22 Russian writers who came of age in the post-Soviet era. The themes treated here represent new realities such as economic concerns, criminal organizations, and the war with Chechnya. In stylistic terms, the editors point to the influence of magic realism in several of the authors.

WORLD LANGUAGES AND LINGUISTICS

Because language is an integral part of literary studies, this section is devoted to works that treat language in general or that study specific languages. Included are reference works on language and linguistics, reference grammars, histories of specific languages or language families, and specialized dictionaries. Outside of the scope of this section are textbooks, materials for language learners, student dictionaries, and ordinary bilingual dictionaries. The limitation to works published in English is at times a disadvantage because studies about a particular language are often written in that language when it is one that has wide readership in the academic community.

The study of language is one of the oldest intellectual endeavors of man and dates from the time of the Sanskrit scholar Pānini (500 BC). The first extant grammar of a European language, a Greek grammar by Dionysius Thrax, does not emerge until several centuries later. The grammars of the late Roman Empire such as those of Varro, Donatus, and Priscan were highly influential in the late Middle Ages and became models for the prescriptive grammars that began to emerge for the modern European languages. Many have attributed the rise of modern linguistics to the work of William Jones whose fortuitous discovery in the 18th century of the relationship between Sanskrit and the classical languages, Greek and Latin, became the basis of the modern scientific study of the Indo-European language family.

Today, linguistics is an all-encompassing field that interrelates with many disciplines such as philosophy, psychology, computer science, and acoustics among others. It is not possible within this chapter to include all of the subfields of modern linguistic studies. Therefore, selection has been guided by consideration of the need for succinct factual information about a specific language, its history and relationship to other languages, as well as a summary of grammatical features.

GENERAL RESOURCES

Online Dictionaries and Databases

6-204. Cambridge Dictionaries Online. Cambridge, UK: Cambridge University Press. Online subscription database. http://dictionary.cambridge.org

The online dictionaries from Cambridge University Press include monolingual dictionaries for British English, American English, business English, as well as three student-oriented dictionaries: *Learner's Dictionary*, *Essential British English*, and *Essential American English*. Three bilingual dictionaries are provided for English-Spanish; español-inglés; and English-Turkish.

6-205. CORPUS.BYU.EDU. Provo, UT: Brigham Young University. Open access resource. http://corpus.byu.edu

Seven open access online corpora now are hosted by Brigham Young University and developed under the direction of faculty member Mark Davies. The corpora are primarily based on English texts both American and British English; there is also a corpus for Spanish and one for Portuguese. The corpora cover a broad range of chronological periods. They are valuable resources for linguists, lexicographers, and historians.

> **Corpus of Contemporary American English (COCA).** http://corpus.byu.edu/coca/
>
> **Corpus of Historical American English (COHA).** http://corpus.byu.edu/coha/
>
> **TIME Magazine Corpus of American English**. http://corpus.byu.edu/time/
>
> **BYU-BNC: British National Corpus**. http://corpus.byu.edu/bnc/
>
> **Google Books (American English) Corpus**. http://googlebooks.byu.edu/

Corpus del español. http://www.corpusdelespanol.org/

O corpo do português. http://www.corpusdoportugues.org/

6-206. CSA Linguistics & Language Behavior Abstracts (LLBA). Available by subscription from ProQuest. http://www.proquest.com/en-US/catalogs/databases/detail/llba-set-c.shtml

Published by Cambridge Scientific Abstracts, LLBA provides access to abstracts of journal articles and books, book chapters, and dissertations as well as citations to book reviews selected from over 1,500 periodical publications. The chronological scope of coverage extends from 1973 to the present with monthly updates. As of April 2012, LLBA contained over 480,000 records. LLBA covers all subfields of linguistics as well as related disciplines such as psychology, speech and hearing sciences, cognitive psychology, and educational psychology.

6-207. Ethnologue: Languages of the World. M. Paul Lewis, ed. Dallas, TX: SIL International, 2009. Online subscription database. http://www.ethnologue.com/

Based on the 16th edition of the printed work, Ethnologue provides information on the languages of the world. Various access points to information are provided: by language or language family and by country or geographical area. For example, for each country, it is possible to obtain a list of all languages spoken, the linguistic families represented, and the number of speakers of any given language.

6-208. Oxford English Dictionary. Oxford; New York: Oxford University Press. Online subscription database. http://www.oed.com

The Oxford English Dictionary (OED), initiated in 1857 by the Philological Society of London, is the most comprehensive dictionary of its kind containing more than 600,000 words that reflect the past and present of the English language. Each entry contains information on pronunciation, etymology, and meaning. The documentation of word uses constitutes one of the unique features of this dictionary. The first uses of a word in any of its meanings are documented from various sources including literature, academic and scholarly publications, and popular media. In many ways, the OED constitutes a selective diachronic corpus of the English language since the first occurrences of a word in any of its acceptations are documented. The online OED is regularly updated and includes the latest technical vocabulary as well as neologisms and emerging innovative uses of existing words in popular language.

6-209. Oxford Language Dictionaries Online. Oxford; New York: Oxford University Press. Online subscription database. http://oxfordlanguagedictionaries.com

This collection of bilingual dictionaries is designed to support language students, but is useful to the general reader as well. At present dictionaries and other materials are available for Chinese, French, German, Italian, Russian, and Spanish.

6-210. Thesaurus Linguae Latinae. Berlin: Walter De Gruyter. Online subscription database. http://www.thesaurus.badw.de/english/index.htm

A project of the Bayerische Akademie der Wissenschaften, the Thesaurus is a comprehensive dictionary of ancient Latin from earliest documentation to approximately 600 AD. The entries in the dictionary are based on documentation of collected occurrences of words in all acceptations that are part of the lexicographical archive that has been painstakingly converted into the print (and digital) versions of the dictionary. The last published printed volume was for 2009.

Scholarly and Professional Associations and Institutes

6-211. American Council on the Teaching of Foreign Languages (ACTFL). http://www.actfl.org/

The ACTFL has been instrumental in setting standards for the evaluation of foreign language competency. The ACTFL has also published many position papers and reports on foreign language instruction in the United States.

In addition to the ACTFL, numerous other associations focus on the teaching of foreign languages. The following list provides access information for associations based in the United States that are dedicated to the study of foreign languages. These websites typically offer information about the language that is the object of study as well as publications of the association and pedagogical materials. Most contain hyperlinks to outreach programs from foreign embassies or international organizations that promote the study of the target language.

> **American Association of Teachers of Arabic**. http://www.aataweb.org/
>
> **American Association of Teachers of French**. http://www.frenchteachers.org/
>
> **American Association of Teachers of German**. http://www.aatg.org/
>
> **American Association of Teachers of Italian**. http://www.aati-online.org/
>
> **American Association of Teachers of Japanese**. http://www.aatj.org/
>
> **American Association of Teachers of Korean**. http://www.aatk.org/
>
> **American Association of Teachers of Slavic and East European Languages**.
> http://www.aatseel.org
>
> **American Classical League**. http://www.aclclassics.org/
>
> **Chinese Language Teachers Association**. http://clta-us.org/

6-212. American Dialect Society (ADS). http://www.americandialect.org/

Founded in 1889, this society is primarily concerned with the study of English in North America. However, the sphere of interest also includes languages in contact with English. The ADS sponsors several publications including *American Speech* and *Newsletter of the American Dialect Society*. The ADS is also a collaborator on the *Dictionary of American Regional English* (entry 6-241).

6-213. American Philological Association (APA). http://www.apaclassics.org/

The APA, founded in 1869, is a learned society for the study of Latin and classical Greek as well as ancient literatures and civilizations. Several publications are sponsored by the APA including *Transactions of the American Philological Association (TAPA)*, *Amphora*, and various newsletters.

6-214. European Language Resources Association (ELRA). http://www.elra.info/

ELRA is a resource for the study of language engineering technologies. However, the association offers language resources that are also of use to linguists and language researchers. The website provides information on the development of new language tools such as software, evaluation systems, and processes for standardization. This association also has a newsletter and announcements of forthcoming conferences.

6-215. The Linguist List. http://linguistlist.org

The Linguist List has been managed under the auspices of the Institute for Language Information and Technology (ILIT) at Eastern Michigan University since 2006. The purpose of the List is to provide a forum for discussion of linguistic issues and exchange of information related to research in the discipline. Linguist List regularly publishes book notices and book reviews as well as calls for papers and conference announcements, and a directory of linguists accessible by area of specialization.

6-216. Linguistic Society of America (LSA). http://www.lsadc.org

Founded in 1924, the Linguistic Society of America is dedicated to the study of language within a scientific framework. The LSA serves an advocacy role as well and has issued position statements on language rights, the English-only movement, bilingual education, and Ebonics. LSA also supports ongoing research on the documentation and preservation of endangered languages. The website provides information about LSA publications such as *Language* and the digital version *eLanguage* which offers open access to some materials such as publication notices.

6-217. Linguistics Research Center. http://www.utexas.edu/cola/centers/lrc/

The Linguistics Research Center has been a funded research center in the College of Liberal Arts at the University of Texas since 1961. The website focuses on Indo-European languages and cultures, and offers resources for study such as books online, lesson modules on Indo-European languages, an Indo-European lexicon, maps and atlases, as well as ongoing bibliographies of publications about Indo-European language and culture.

6-218. SIL International (Summer Institute of Linguistics, Inc.). http://sil.org

Founded in 1934, SIL is a faith-based nonprofit organization that works with communities throughout the world to maintain their language through the development of research projects and training materials. SIL has collaborated in studies of 2,590 distinct languages spoken in nearly 100 countries. The SIL website offers linguistic materials in several languages and tools for the linguist such as specialized, downloadable fonts.

Printed Monographs, Sets, and Series

6-219. The Cambridge Encylopedia of Language. 3rd ed. David Crystal, ed. Cambridge, UK: Cambridge University Press, 2010.

This revised and expanded edition of the *Cambridge Encyclopedia of Language* contains 11 thematically organized sections that treat topics such as myths and popular ideas about language, issues of language and identity, the structure of language, the medium of language (oral communication, reading, writing, and sign) child language acquisition, language and the brain, language typology, and communication. To facilitate access, the end of the volume offers a glossary, a table of languages of the world, and indexes by language, author, and subject as well as a bibliography for further reading.

6-220. The Cambridge Encyclopedia of the World's Ancient Languages. Roger D. Woodward, ed. Cambridge, UK: Cambridge University Press, 2004.

This volume is an authoritative reference work on the world's ancient languages. It is unique in the scope of coverage; all well-documented ancient languages are represented here. The chapter-length articles on individual languages or a group of closely related languages provides information on writing systems, phonology, morphology, syntax, and the lexicon. Discussions of language classification, geographic dispersion, and chronology place the language in historical context.

6-221. **Cambridge University Press Monographic series.**

Cambridge University Press publishes a number of monographic series in languages and linguistics, several of which are listed in this entry.

> **Cambridge Handbooks in Language and Linguistics** (2007–). Each volume in this series is dedicated to a particular aspect of linguistics such as phonology, pragmatics, sociolinguistics, syntax, child language, second language acquisition, and language policy.

> **Cambridge Language Surveys** (P. Austin, I. Roberts, S. Romaine et al., eds. 1981–). With over 20 published volumes, this ongoing series provides an overview of the major languages of the world. The individual volumes treat language families or cohesive geographic areas. Extant titles cover Indo-European languages, Chinese, Korean, the languages of Japan, Dravidian languages, as well as indigenous languages of the Americas and a two-volume set on pidgins and creoles.

> **Cambridge Reference Grammars** (1999–). The coverage of languages in this ongoing series is broad in scope with volumes treating Dutch, Hebrew, Arabic, Tamil, Thai, Spanish, French, and Russian.

> **Cambridge Syntax Guides** (P. Austin, B. Comrie, J. Bresnan, D. Lightfoot, I. Roberts, N. V. Smith, eds. 2001–). This series responds to the growing interest in comparative syntax and the development of formal structures for the analysis of syntax. While most of the texts in this series treat European languages there are also studies dedicated to Arabic, Chinese, and Chichewa (a Bantu language).

6-222. **Concise Encyclopedia of Languages of the World.** Keith Brown and Sarah Ogilvie, eds. Oxford, UK: Elsevier, 2009.

This is a comprehensive guide to languages of the world. Individually authored articles offer information about the typology of the language, where it is spoken, the number of speakers, structural features (phonology, morphology, and syntax) as well as a brief bibliography for further reading.

6-223. **Dictionary of Languages: The Definitive Reference to More Than 400 Languages.** Rev. ed. Andrew Dalby. New York: Columbia University Press, 2004.

This reference source to languages of the world is highly accessible to readers. A glossary of linguistic terms defines the limited specialist terms used in the discussions of the world's languages. The 200 maps included provide geographic orientation for discussion of the dissemination of a language and its proximity to other languages. The individual articles include examples of the script, alphabet, and system of numerals used by each language.

6-224. **The Dictionary of Historical and Comparative Linguistics.** R. L. Trask, ed. Chicago: Fitzroy Dearborn, 2000.

This dictionary is particularly helpful for students of historical linguistics. The A to Z arrangement of terms includes many that are peculiar to early studies of Indo-European linguistics that came from a tradition of German scholarship. Many of these terms of German origin are rarely used in modern linguistic terminology.

6-225. **A Dictionary of Linguistics and Phonetics.** 6th ed. David Crystal, ed. Malden, MA; Oxford, UK: Blackwell, 2008.

The new edition of this standard dictionary on linguistics with a focus on phonetics includes recent changes and innovations in linguistic terminology. The editor has taken care to make the dictionary accessible. The introductory materials include a comprehensive list of abbreviations that are used in the dictionary entries as well as a chart of the International Phonetic Alphabet, diacritics, and suprasegmentals.

Additional publications are in the monographic series *Blackwell Handbooks in Linguistics* available in print and as e-books. The handbooks deal with a broad range of topics in all subfields of linguistics with volumes dedicated to specific languages with over 40 titles published. Several comprehensive, multi-volume sets are included such as *The Blackwell Companion to Syntax* (5 vols. 2006) and *The Blackwell Companion to Phonology* (5 vols. 2011).

6-226. Encyclopedia of Linguistics. Philipp Strazny, ed. New York: Fitzroy Dearborn, 2005. 2 vols.

The introduction to this encyclopedia discusses the development of linguistics as a field of study and particularly the creation of new subfields such as computational linguistics. The 500 essay-length entries cover the diverse areas of study within linguistics, contributors to the discipline, specific languages, and linguistic regions throughout the world.

A more specialized work by the same publisher is *The Dictionary of Historical and Comparative Linguistics* (R. L. Trask, ed. 2000). This dictionary is particularly helpful for students of historical linguistics. The A-to-Z arrangement of terms includes many that are peculiar to early studies of Indo-European linguistics that came from a tradition of German scholarship. Many of these terms of German origin are rarely used in modern linguistic terminology.

6-227. Facts about the World's Languages: An Encyclopedia of the World's Major Languages, Past and Present. Jane Garry and Carl Rubin, eds. New York: H. W. Wilson, 2001.

This reference work of the languages of the world contains nearly 200 articles arranged alphabetically by language name. Each article provides information about the phonological, morphologic, and syntactic systems of the language. Accompanying materials include a discussion of the ethnolinguistic groups that use the language, sociopolitical factors that affect the dissemination and use of the language, and issues of language and identity. There is a brief bibliography for further reading. This volume also includes a glossary of linguistic terminologies and indexes by country, language families, and alternative names of languages.

6-228. International Encyclopedia of Linguistics. 2nd ed. William J. Frawley, ed. Oxford, UK: Oxford University Press, 2003. 4 vols. Print and e-book.

The revised edition of this encyclopedia, originally published in 1992, contains 850 entries that offer a comprehensive overview of all subfields of linguistics, including those that interface with other disciplines, such as computer science, philosophy, literary studies, and social and behavioral sciences.

By the same publisher is *The Concise Oxford Dictionary of Linguistics* (2nd ed. P. H. Matthews, ed. 2007). This expanded edition offers definitions of over 3,000 terms related to language and linguistics. The introductory essay explains criteria for inclusion of terms and discusses the relationship between linguistics and other fields of study, such as communication, literature, philosophy, and psychology.

6-229. The Linguistics Encyclopedia. 3rd ed. Kirsten Malmkjær, ed. London: Routledge, 2009.

The latest edition of the Routledge *Linguistics Encyclopedia* provides coverage of all major areas of linguistics. There are 79 entries alphabetically arranged. Each article provides references for further writing. Entries that are new or substantively revised include, among others, artificial languages and computational linguistics, corpus linguistics, language and gender, and writing systems.

Two monographic series are also published by Routledge: the *Routledge Handbooks in Applied Linguistics* and *Essential Grammars*. The handbooks offer a comprehensive overview of the various subfields of applied linguistics including second language pedagogy, pragmatics, intercultural communication, corpus linguistics, and forensic linguistics.

More than 30 volumes have been published in the *Essential Grammars* series. They include less-studied languages, such as Georgian and Latvian as well as major European languages and widely disseminated languages such as Arabic. Some of the volumes are revised editions of earlier publications. The grammars represent a reference tool for language learners as well as those who desire a brief overview of the major aspects of a particular language.

6-230. A Little Book of Language. David Crystal. New Haven, CT: Yale University Press, 2010.

This concise introduction to the study of language addresses language acquisition; endangered languages; and the effect of technology on reading, writing, and speech. This volume offers an excellent introduction to language for the non-specialist.

6-231. London Oriental and African Language Library. Theodora Bynon, David C. Bennett, Masayoshi Shibatani, eds. Amsterdam: John Benjamins, 1994– . Monographic series.

This ongoing series of reference grammars on the languages of Asia and Africa is broad in range and includes a variety of language families over a wide geographical area. Both major languages and less studied languages are included in the series.

LANGUAGE RESOURCES BY GEOGRAPHIC REGION

The resources cited in this section are grouped by the recognized place of origin of a language. Thus, resources related to English are listed under Europe unless the scope of the work is specifically limited to another geographic area, as for example, a reference work on Indian English. Specialized dictionaries that are specific to one language are also placed in this section.

Africa

6-232. African Languages: An Introduction. Bernd Heine and Derek Nurse, eds. Cambridge, U.K.; New York: Cambridge University Press, 2000.

This text provides an overview of languages spoken in Africa. The four chapters that follow the introduction treat the major language families: Niger-Congo, Nilo-Saharan, Afroasiatic, and Khoisan. Subsequent chapters deal with phonology, morphology, syntax, typology, and comparative linguistics. The final chapters discuss the historical and societal role of language in Africa. Access to information is facilitated by an index of languages.

6-233. African Voices: An Introduction to the Languages and Linguistics of Africa. Vic Webb and Kembo-Sure, eds. Cape Town: Oxford University Press, 2000.

Envisioned as a textbook for courses that deal with the languages of Africa, this volume provides overviews of major linguistic issues such as languages in context and languages in competition. There are also chapters on phonology, lexicography, cross-cultural communication, and language pedagogy in Africa.

A more recent and specialized treatment is *Language and National Identity in Africa* (Andrew Simpson, ed. Oxford University Press, 2008). This volume offers a geographic approach to the subject of language in Africa. Each chapter treats the linguistic situation of a distinct nation or geographic region.

6-234. Guinea Languages of the Atlantic Group: Description and Internal Classification. William A.A. Wilson, Anne Storch, eds. Frankfurt am Main; New York: Lang, 2007.

This specialized volume is a study of one of the subgroups of Niger-Congo languages. In addition to languages that are better known and documented, such as Fula and Wolof, there are some 60 lesser-known languages in danger of extinction. This study provides an overview of the Atlantic language group through descriptions of the phonology, morphology, and syntax of these languages, as well as comparative wordlists.

6-235. An Introduction to African Languages. G. Tucker Childs. Amsterdam; Philadelphia: John Benjamins, 2003.

This handbook provides an overview of African languages including a history of the study of African languages. Several chapters are dedicated to classification and comparison of the four major language phyla. Subsequent chapters treat issues of phonetics and phonology, morphology, syntax, semantics, typology, and sociolinguistics.

6-236. Language in South Africa. Rajend Mesthrie, ed. Cambridge, UK; New York: Cambridge University Press, 2002.

This collection of studies offers a comprehensive overview of the complex linguistic situation in South Africa. The first part deals with the major language groups in South Africa: Khosean and Bantu as well as Afrikaans and South African English. The second section explores the situation of languages in contact and the final section addresses issues of language planning, policy, and education.

Americas

Indigenous Languages

6-237. Society for the Study of the Indigenous Languages of the Americas (SSILA).
http://www.ssila.org/

SSILA is an international scholarly organization founded in 1981 and dedicated to the study of the indigenous languages of the Americas. The Society publishes the *SSILA Newsletter* on a quarterly basis and provides an annual award for an unpublished monograph that significantly contributes to existing knowledge about indigenous languages. The website offers many links to institutes and academic programs that study indigenous languages.

6-238. California Indian Languages. Victor Golla. Berkeley: University of California Press, 2011.

This concise volume provides a comprehensive overview of the indigenous languages of California. The first section defines California as a sociolinguistic area and introduces the language families present in its confines. Subsequent sections treat the history of the study of indigenous languages in California, the major language families, typological and area features, and linguistic prehistory. Appendixes provide comparative word lists for the major languages.

6-239. Mexican Indigenous Languages at the Dawn of the Twenty-First Century. Margarita Hidalgo, ed. Berlin: Mouton de Gruyter, 2006.

This collection of essays provides an overview of the status of indigenous languages in Mexico today as well as historical perspectives of languages in contact. The chapters are organized thematically into four sections: history and theory, language policy, bilingualism and bilingual education, and conclusions: past, present and future of indigenous languages.

6-240. Native Languages of the Southeastern United States. Heather K. Hardy and Janine Scancarelli, eds. Lincoln: University of Nebraska Press in cooperation with the American Indian Studies Research Institute, Indiana University, Bloomington, 2005.

This volume is a comprehensive history of the native languages of the southeastern United States. Chapters are individually authored and begin with an overview of the history of research on native languages in the southeast. Subsequent chapters treat the individual languages of the Muskogean family. Several chapters are dedicated to languages that are not part of the Muskogean language group.

American English

6-241. Dictionary of American Regional English. Cambridge, MA: Harvard University Press, 1985–2012.

The fifth and final volume (SI-Z) of the *Dictionary of American Regional English* (DARE) completes DARE with 60,000 definitions of current and obsolete words and expressions and provides information on word origins and variant pronunciations. Additionally, the DARE indicates locations where a word is used as well as variants in different regions. A companion website for DARE is housed at the University of Wisconsin: http://dare.news.wisc.edu/.

American Spanish

6-242. A Dictionary of New Mexico and Southern Colorado Spanish. Rev. and expanded 2nd ed. Rubén Cobos. Santa Fe: Museum of New Mexico Press, 2003.

The new edition of the dictionary first published in 1983 constitutes the most complete reference work for Spanish spoken in the southwestern United States. The dictionary includes lexical items that reflect the archaic nature of the Spanish spoken in the region as well as the words of indigenous origin chiefly from Nahuatl and the later adaptation of English words that resulted from the languages in contact situation. The dictionary also includes some texts to exemplify usage such as popular poetry, anecdotes, or lyrics to songs.

6-243. A History of Afro-Hispanic Language: Five Centuries, Five Continents. John M. Lipski. Cambridge, UK: Cambridge University Press, 2005. Print and e-book.

This comprehensive study of Afro-Hispanic language begins with a chapter on the presence of Africans in the Iberian Peninsula prior to the new world expansion. Subsequent chapters deal with early Portuguese language texts and early Spanish texts, as well as Afro-Hispanic texts from Latin America from the 16th to the 20th centuries. The final chapters provide an overview of major African language families and the phonological and grammatical characteristics of Afro-Hispanic language.

6-244. Spanish in the Americas. Eleanor Greet Cotton and John M. Sharp, eds. Washington, DC: Georgetown University Press, 2001. Print and e-book.

This volume provides a comprehensive overview to varieties of Spanish in the Americas. Introductory materials include tables and maps to orient the reader. The first few chapters deal with definition of language varieties or dialects followed by a linguistic introduction to the Spanish language and the linguistic situation of Spain today. Subsequent chapters cover the transmission of Spanish to the Americas and the grouping of contemporary language varieties.

6-245. Varieties of Spanish in the United States. John M. Lipski. Washington, DC: Georgetown University Press, 2008. Print and e-book.

In recognition of the more than 30 million people in the United States that use Spanish as their preferred language, this volume studies the persistence of Spanish since the 16th century in the area north of the Rio Grande. Following the introductory chapters, each chapter describes the major characteristics of a particular immigrant group: Mexican, Cuban, Puerto Rican, Dominican, Salvadoran, Nicaraguan, Guatemalan, and Honduran as well as varieties of Spanish with a long-standing tradition such as New Mexican Spanish and the now endangered variety, *isleño*, in Louisiana.

Canadian French and Haitian Creole

6-246. The French Language in Canada. John Hewson. Munich: LINCOM EUROPA, 2000.

This concise volume is one of the few works available in English on Canadian French. The work treats the history of French in the New World and develops topics such as the persistence of archaisms, borrowings from Amerindian languages, and contact with English. In addition, there are chapters that cover specific grammatical aspects of Canadian French such as phonology and sociolinguistic variation.

6-247. The Haitian Creole Language: History, Structure, Use, and Education. Arthur K. Spears and Carole M. Berotte Joseph, eds. Lanham, MD: Lexington Books/Roman & Littlefield, 2010.

This essential introduction to Haitian Creole offers background information on the history of Haiti from its beginnings to the contemporary diaspora. Subsequent chapters discuss essential features of the language, such as its orthography as well as sociolinguistic issues including regional and social varieties and code switching.

Asia

6-248. A Dictionary of Chinese Characters: Accessed by Phonetics. Stewart Paton. Abingdon, UK: Routledge, 2008.

This dictionary is intended to be used in conjunction with a traditional Chinese-English dictionary. It presents 934 characters arranged alphabetically by standard transliteration to Roman characters.

6-249. Encyclopedia of Arabic Language and Linguistics. Kees Versteegh, Mushira Eid, Alaa Elgibali, Manfred Woidich, Andrzej Zaborski, eds. Leiden; Boston: Brill, 2005–2009. 5 vols.

This comprehensive encyclopedia deals with all aspects of the Arabic language in its various chronological stages as well as differentiation of current language use by register and geography. The five volumes are organized alphabetically with individually authored articles on Arabic scholars, topics in linguistics, and geographic variants.

6-250. Japanese/Korean Linguistics. Stanford, CA: CSLI Publications, 1989– . Monographic series.

Seventeen volumes have now been published in this series on Japanese and Korean linguistics. The publisher's website maintains a cumulative index of articles published in the series.

Europe

6-251. **Accademia della Crusca**. http://www.accademiadellacrusca.it/index_eng.php

The website for the Accademia della Crusca provides an interface in English, although the majority of the hyperlinked documents and web pages are in Italian. Founded in 1583, the Accademia has worked to establish and document a national language. Summaries are provided of the five editions of the *Vocabolario degli Accademici* as well as other resources related to the Italian language.

6-252. **The Cambridge History of the Romance Languages**. Martin Maiden and John Charles Smith, eds. Cambridge, UK: Cambridge University Press, 2011– . Vol. 1: Structures.

The first volume of the projected multivolume History of the Romance Languages contains 14 individually authored chapters that cover a broad range of topics in the historical development of the Romance languages from Latin. Following the introductory chapter on historical linguistics and Romance linguistics in particular, there are four chapters dedicated to phonological and morphonological processes and three chapters on morphosyntax. The remaining chapters treat lexicography and pragmatics.

6-253. **A Dictionary of European Anglicisms: A Usage Dictionary of Anglicisms in Sixteen European Languages**. Manfred Görlach, ed. Oxford, UK: Oxford University Press, 2001.

This specialized dictionary demonstrates the widespread usage of words of English origin in European languages today. The dictionary presents the forms, meaning, and usages of words borrowed from English. It is a useful resource for lexicographers and students of languages in contact.

6-254. **An Encyclopedia of the Languages of Europe**. Glanville Price, ed. Oxford, UK; Malden, MA: Blackwell, 2000.

This encyclopedia surveys the languages of Europe. The individual entries vary in length but the longer entries provide an overview of the language under discussion and include information on the history of the language, its dissemination, major grammatical features, and literary tradition. This work is inclusive in nature and extends coverage to languages not indigenous to Europe but now present as a result of immigration. The entries also include geographical areas as well as individual languages. The many enhancements to the encyclopedia make it more accessible such as maps, a guide to the International Phonetic Alphabet, and images of different writing systems.

6-255. **Francophone Studies: The Essential Glossary**. Margaret A. Majumdar, ed. London: Arnold, 2002.

This reference work is particularly useful to students of Francophone culture and literature. It includes approximately 400 entries that refer to major historical events and figures, literary movements, cultural institutions, as well as popular culture and politics.

6-256. **Language in the British Isles**. David Britain, ed. Cambridge, UK: Cambridge University Press, 2007.

This volume treats the languages and varieties of English currently spoken in the British Isles in a coherent collection of 25 individually authored essays. The first section concerns varieties of English; the second section the Celtic languages; and the third section other languages including Caribbean creoles, Indic languages, Chinese, and other European languages. The final section addresses socio-linguistic issues.

6-257. The Languages and Linguistics of Europe: A Comprehensive Guide. Bernd Kortmann and Johan van der Auwera, eds. Berlin: Mouton/de Gruyter, 2011. (The World of Linguistics, vol. 1).

This first volume of a projected multi-volume work provides an overview of the language families of Europe. It is comprehensive in scope and includes non-traditional varieties of language such as sign language. The 49 individually authored chapters are organized in five sections. The first addresses the typology of the languages of Europe followed by a section on area typology and languages in contact. Section 3 treats issues of language policy and language politics. The final two chapters deal with the history of European languages and the linguistic research tradition in Europe.

PART FOUR

PERFORMING ARTS

CHAPTER 7

PERFORMING ARTS

Elizabeth S. Aversa

INTRODUCTION

As much as any broad discipline in the humanities, the field of Performing Arts has seen unprecedented change since the 2000 edition of this guide. The changes relate to both the technologies used within the performing arts, e.g., digital recordings, as well as the web technologies that allow for the "publication" and distribution of material, such as sound recordings, movies, television shows, and animated pieces. The performing arts broadly defined include dance, theatre, music, general performing arts, radio, television, animation, and film. This introductory chapter contains the definitions and references to the literature about librarianship and treats general resources in the performing arts. Each division of the performing arts is treated in turn in chapters eight, nine, and ten, each beginning with brief introductions.

Working Definition of the Performing Arts

The term *performing arts* has not become standardized in its usage. It is used to differentiate the arts or skills which, by their nature, require public performance, as opposed to those whose beauty is appreciated through the sense of sight or some surrogate, as in the visual arts. McLeish states: "In the performing arts . . . the performer, the intermediary, is a crucial part of the process." Generally, there are three elements necessary for consideration as a performing art: the piece or work being performed; the performer or performers; and an audience hearing, viewing, or experiencing the performance. Sometimes the three elements originate in the same individual, as in the case where songwriters compose the work and perform it for themselves in the privacy of the practice room or studio. Most often, however, the entities are different individuals or groups, and we treat the performing arts in that sense in this guide. New forms of performance that have developed in recent years involve the piece or work being presented and an audience, but the performers or performer may be invisible to the audience. For example, animation involves performers, e.g., the voice of characters, but what the audience sees may be devoid of human "performers."

Major Divisions of the Field

In this guide, music, opera, dance, theater, radio, television, film, and animation are covered as performing arts. The division into chapters may appear arbitrary to the reader, but the rationale for the full chapter on music is two-fold: the volume of resources suggests the need for a separate chapter and the formats of music resources, in many cases, are unique to the field. The fields associated with recorded or technologically delivered performance (radio, television, film, animation) are grouped together as are dance and theatre. Recorded music, dance, and theater productions are covered in the separate chapters.

Music is commonly defined as the art of organizing sound. Its principal elements are melody (single sounds in succession), harmony (sounds in combination), and rhythm (sounds in a temporal relationship). The two major divisions are vocal music and instrumental music. Vocal music includes songs, opera, oratorios, and so forth, while instrumental music includes solos, chamber music, and orchestral music. Musical instruments may be classified as stringed (violin, harp, guitar), woodwind (flute, bassoon, oboe, English horn), brass (trumpet, cornet, bugle, trombone), percussion (drums, bells, gongs, chimes), keyboard (piano, organ). A system of musical notation came to be used in about 1700.

The librarian responsible for a music collection will need to keep in mind three major elements: 1) the music itself, which follows to some degree the divisions outlined above; 2) the literature about music, which is divided more along the conventional lines for all disciplines, but with some special characteristics; and 3) the vast array of recordings on records, discs, tapes, cassettes, and video, which are a part of any modern music library and which pose problems in terms of organization, preservation, retrieval, and use. Downloadable music from Internet sources adds to the complexity for the librarian.

The *dance* may be defined as movement of the body to a certain rhythm. The three major divisions of the field include folk dancing, ballroom dancing, and theater dancing. Folk dancing, which originated in open-air activities, is characterized by great vigor and exuberance of movement. Ballroom dancing had its origin in the European courts of the Renaissance and is an indoor participant activity that is gaining popularity today. Theater dancing is a spectator activity that may be traced to religious dances in the ancient world and to performances known as masques in the courts of Renaissance Europe. Its most characteristic form is the ballet. The dance is usually, though not always, accompanied by music. The subject of dance notation is of ongoing interest and new material on dance notation can be accessed on the Internet. Increasingly, the dance librarian will rely on media such as DVDs and downloadable material, particularly as they relate to teaching dance.

Theater is the art of presenting a performance to a live audience. In modern usage, the term is restricted to live performances of plays. A distinction is sometimes drawn between theater and drama; theater is restricted in meaning to those matters having to do with public performance, while drama includes the literary basis for the performance, that is, the text of plays. The texts are often classed with literature in libraries, leading to the seemingly illogical separation of the texts of plays from works about performance of those plays. Topics that are closely related to theatrical performance, and that help to differentiate it from drama, are acting, costume, makeup, directing, and theater architecture. These topics are covered here.

Film may be divided into two types: feature length, an hour or longer, and shorts. Many feature length films are fictional, often based on books of some popularity. Others, known as documentaries, are prepared for informational purposes. The fictional and documentary form may be combined to make colorful travelogues or the so-called docu-dramas, in which real situations are presented in fictional, or partly fictional, form. Two other forms of film are animated cartoons and puppet features. Recent technology has allowed for the melding of live action and animated cartoons, so that cartoon characters mix with live casts. Shorts are often filmed by independent producers and sold to distributors of feature length films or video to complete an "entertainment package" for viewing in theaters or homes.

Films are widely used in schools, universities, churches, and other institutions for informational, educational, and training purposes. Films of this type are likely to constitute the bulk of many library collections, although popular videos are increasingly available for library circulation. Video and DVDs are later entries to the performing arts field, particularly as forms available to most of the public. Feature length films, educational films, "how-to" instructions in a variety of fields, and music performance are all widely distributed on DVD for home consumption. Their inclusion in public library collections, while attracting some new users to libraries, may pose problems from the standpoint of preservation, censorship, and fees for services.

Radio, which depends entirely on sound for its effects; and television, relying on sound and visuals, can be presented either "live" or in a prerecorded form. For libraries, it is the residual audio and videos or DVDs that may be included in collections. These materials share with the other performing arts some of the problems of organization and preservation.

Increasingly, libraries are depending on the Internet for recording of all kinds of performances. This provides unprecedented access for users but it also presents issues for the organization, storage, preservation, and retrieval of library materials in all areas of the performing arts. Some of these issues are discussed in the sections below.

Many helpful resources are available for students, librarians, and general readers who wish to understand more about materials on the performing arts, how they are selected for libraries, and how they are organized for both preservation and retrieval. Although some of the readings on these topics date to the 1990s, the basic information is still useful if the reader overlooks references to specific bibliographic sources that have not been updated or revised. Of course, if a historic perspective is needed, the older sources will serve the reader well.

Many resources that were previously available only in print form are now accessed in electronic formats. A review of hundreds of World Wide Web sites related to the performing arts reveals the widest array of offerings encountered by this author in any subject area; resources range from well-organized and maintained sites to poorly designed and outdated resources that do little but muddy the research waters. An outstanding example of a helping resource is the comprehensive Indiana University *Worldwide Internet Music* at http://www.music.indiana.edu/music_resources/.

Use and Users of Performing Arts Information

Of the performing arts, music has been the most studied in terms of use and users of information. Malcolm Jones' *Music Librarianship* introduced, very generally, types of music libraries and their users in "Music Libraries and Those They Serve" (1979, 13–23). The chapter on music by Elizabeth Rebman in *The Humanities and the Library* offered a brief user perspective in the section entitled "The Work of Composers, Performers, and Music Scholars" (1993, 136–137). R. Griscom, "Periodical Use in a University Music Library: A Citation Study of Theses and Dissertations Submitted to the Indiana University School of Music from 1975–1980" (1983); R. Green, "Use of Music and Its Literature Over Time" (1978); and David Baker, "Characteristics of the Literature Used by English Musicologists" (1978) are now classics. Lois Kuyper-Rushing's "Identifying Uniform Core Journal Titles for Music Libraries: A Citation Study" (1999) is a study to benefit collection development in music as well as a contribution to the use/user literature.

Recent looks at use and users include Audrey Laplante and J. Stephen Downie, "The utilitarian and hedonic outcomes of music information-seeking in everyday life" (2011). In this study, it was found that users respond favorably to a search when they find pleasure in retrieving the material and when they actually find the music sought. Charlie Inskip, Andy MacFarlane, and Pauline Rafferty's "Creative professional users' musical relevance criteria" considers user relevance judgments for music as compared with text (2010). The paper has an extensive and helpful bibliography on retrieval in music and in general. The same collaborators, Inskip, MacFarlane and Rafferty, also published "Meaning, Communication, Music: Toward a Revised Communication Model" (2008) and "Towards the Disintermediation of Creative Music Search: Analyzing Queries to Determine Important Facets" (2009). Catalog searching is addressed in David M. King's "Catalog User Search Strategies in Finding Music Materials" (2005).

The interest in both retrieval and organizing for retrieval, especially of non-text material in the performing arts, has grown over the years and now is a major research area. Patricia Sasser investigates the use of digital sheet music collections in "Sounds of Silence: Investigating Institutional Knowledge of Use and Users of Online Music Collections" (2009). A survey of users established what some of the issues are connected with accessing such collections. Other relevant papers include: J. Kim and N. Belkin, "Categories of Music Description and Search Terms and Phrases Used by Non-music Experts" (2002); Gwen Evans and Susannah Cleveland, "Moody Blues: The Social

Web, Tagging, and Nontextual Discovery Tools for Music" (2008); Jenn Riley and Michelle Dalmau, "The IN Harmony Project: Developing a Flexible Metadata Model for the Description and Discovery of Sheet Music" (2007).

Organizing music and performing arts material is addressed in Tracey Snyder, "Music Materials in a Faceted Catalog: Interviews with Faculty and Graduate Students" (2010). Finally, Elizabeth Kelly sums up the present state of music indexing and cataloging in her paper "Music Indexing and Retrieval: Current Problems" (2010). She says, "Academics and librarians have not yet reached a consensus on the indexing of print resources about music, nor have they developed satisfactory means of indexing sheet music. With the increasing presence of audio music on the Internet, the need to properly index MP3s and other audio files has reached a new level of urgency and with it the need to label these items satisfactorily to enable retrieval. While the importance of these fields has been constant since the beginning of indexing and cataloguing, increased availability of sources means that there is more music available to users than ever before, but little in the way of sorting through it. Luckily, studies are being undertaken with the aim of solving these problems" (Kelly 2010, 163). The sheer number of studies addressing these issues suggests that the organization of information in the arts will continue to be a major research focus well into the future.

In the area of film studies, "Citation of Cinematic Examples in Film Studies: The Interface of Scholarship, Technology, Law and the Market," examines how the practice of scholarship, copyright, and technology converge (Kiss 2011).

Works Cited

Baker, David. "Characteristics of the Literature Used by English Musicologists," *Journal of Librarianship* 10 (July): 182–200.

Couch, Nena and Nancy Allen. 1993. *The Humanities and the Library*. 2nd ed. Chicago: American Library Association.

Evans, Gwen and Susannah Cleveland. 2008. "Moody Blues: The Social Web, Tagging, and Nontextual Discovery Tools for Music." *Music Reference Services Quarterly* 11, 3/4 (2008): 177–201.

Green, R. 1978. "Use of Music and Its Literature over Time," *Notes* 35 (September): 42–59.

Griscom, R. 1983. "Periodical Use in a University Music Library: A Citation Study of Theses and Dissertations Submitted to the Indiana University School of Music from 1975–1980." *Serials Librarian* 7 (Spring): 35–52.

Inskip, Charlie, Andy MacFarlane, and Pauline Rafferty. "Creative Professional Users' Musical Relevance Criteria." *Journal of Information Science* 36, 4 (August): 517–29.

Inskip, Charlie, Andy MacFarlane, and Pauline Rafferty. 2008. "Meaning, Communication, Music: Toward a Revised Communication Model." *Journal of Documentation* 64, 5: 687–706.

Inskip, Charlie, Andy MacFarlane, and Pauline Rafferty. 2009. "Towards the Disintermediation of Creative Music Search: Analyzing Queries to Determine Important Facets." *Proceedings of ECDL Workshop on Exploring Musical Information Spaces* (Corfu, Greece, October 1–2, 2009).

Jones, Malcolm. 1979. "Music Libraries and Those They Serve," in *Music Librarianship*. Munich: K. G. Saur: 13–23.

Kelly, Elizabeth. 2010. "Music Indexing and Retrieval: Current Problems." *The Indexer* 28, 4 (December): 163–166.

Kim, J. and N. Belkin. 2002. "Categories of Music Description and Search Perms and Phrases Used by Non-music Experts." *Proceedings of the 3rd International Conference on Music Information Retrieval IRCAM*. Paris, France, 13–17 October.

King, David M. 2005. "Catalog User Search Strategies in Finding Music Materials." *Music Reference Services Quarterly* 9 (4): 1–24.

Kiss, E. 2011. "Citation of Cinematic Examples in Film Studies: The Interface of Scholarship, Technology, Law and the Market." *EDULEARN11 Proceedings*: 7169–7171.

Kuyper-Rushing, Lois. 1999. "Identifying Uniform Core Journal Titles for Music Libraries: A Citation Study." *College and Research Libraries* 60 (March): 153–163.

Laplante, Audrey and J. Stephen Downie. 2011. "The Utilitarian and Hedonic Outcomes of Music Information-seeking in Everyday Life." *Library & Information Science Research* 33, 3 (July): 202–10.

MacLeish, Kenneth. 1993. "Performing Arts," in *Key Ideas in Human Thought.* New York: Facts on File.

Rebman, Elizabeth. 1993. "The Work of Composers, Performers, and Music Scholars" in *The Humanities and the Library.* 2nd ed. Nena Couch and Nancy Allen. Chicago: American Library Association: 136–137.

Riley, Jenn and Michelle Dalmau. 2007. "The IN Harmony Project: Developing a Flexible Metadata Model for the Description and Discovery of Sheet Music." *The Electronic Library* 25, 2 (2007): 132–147.

Sasser, Patricia. 2009. "Sounds of Silence: Investigating Institutional Knowledge of Use and Users of Online Music Collection." *Music Reference Services Quarterly* 12, 3/4 (July/December 2009): 93–108.

Snyder, Tracey. 2010. "Music Materials in a Faceted Catalog: Interviews with Faculty and Graduate Students." *Music Reference Services Quarterly* 13, 3/4 (July/December 2010): 66–95.

Website

Worldwide Internet Music. http://www.music.indiana.edu/music_resources/

Major Organizations, Information Centers, and Special Collections

The number of national and international organizations in the performing arts is so great that attention can only be given here to those that are most significant to the librarian. Guides to the specific fields in the performing arts will offer additional information in much greater detail, as will the many directories now available on the web or, in increasingly rare cases, in print. The reader should consult the websites of the relevant organizations for additional information about their activities, publications and electronic resources.

Regardless of the performing art of interest, a good place to begin a search for both state and national organizations is with the website of the National Endowment for the Arts (NEA) (entry 2-81). The site offers a list of Film/Video/ Radio Resources at http://www.nea.gov/resources/disciplines/media/resources.html. Music societies, organizations, and service groups are listed at http://www.nea.gov/resources/disciplines/music/resources.html, while dance organizations are listed at http://www.nea.gov/resources/disciplines/dance/resources.html. The main site for the NEA is at http://www.nea.gov.

Other specialized organizations are treated in the sections within this chapter in tandem with the appropriate subjects.

Collections

The most outstanding music collection in the United States is at the Library of Congress, which benefits from copyright deposit. The Music Division issued numerous catalogs, several of which are listed elsewhere in this book. Another notable collection is found in the Music Division of the Research Library of the Performing Arts in Lincoln Center (part of the New York Public Library). In Europe, the Austrian National Library (Vienna), the Royal Library of Belgium (Brussels), the Biblioteque Nationale (Paris), the Deutsche Staatsbibliothek (Berlin), the British Museum (London), the Biblioteca Nazionale Centrale (Florence), and the Vatican Library (Rome) all have outstanding collections.

The Dance Collection in the Research Library of the Performing Arts (New York Public Library) includes photographs, scores, programs, prints, posters, and playbills, as well as instruction manuals and other literature on the dance. The Archives of Dance, Music and Theatre contain about 20,000 similar memorabilia related to the performing arts in the twentieth century.

The Theater Arts Library (University of California at Los Angeles) has screenplays and pictures in addition to the general collection of English and foreign language books on film. The Harvard Theatre Collection (Houghton Library) has rare letters, account books, diaries, drawings, promptbooks, and playbills from the United States, Great Britain, and continental Europe. Similar materials relating to British and American theater from 1875 to 1935 (especially the Chicago Little Theatre Movement, 1912–1917) are found in the Department of Rare Books and Special Collections, University of Michigan. The Theatre Collection in the Research Library of the Performing Arts (New York Public Library) is one of the most notable anywhere. Bibliographic access is provided through its published catalog. The Free Library of Philadelphia has over a million items relating to the theater, early circuses, and minstrel and vaudeville shows.

The Library of Congress has several notable film collections. Some of the materials have been received on copyright deposit through the National Film Registry.

This is only a small sampling of the performing arts collection in the United States and Europe that contain specialized information in a rich diversity of formats. The World Wide Web offers a wealth of information on the performing arts. This must now be the first resource consulted by the researcher beginning a search on associations, special collections, or performing arts societies.

SELECTED INFORMATION SOURCES
IN THE PERFORMING ARTS

PERFORMING ARTS, GENERAL

Databases

7-1. **International Index to the Performing Arts (IIPA).** Alexandria, VA: Chadwyck-Healey. 1999– . Online subscription database.

IIPA full text covers a broad spectrum of the arts and entertainment industry including dance, film, television, drama, theater, stagecraft, musical theater, broadcast arts, circus performance, comedy, storytelling, opera, pantomime, puppetry, magic, and more. Prior to the IIPA full-text edition with abstracts, the product was issued in CD-ROM. The database, begun in 1999, indexes 200 scholarly and popular periodicals in the performing arts and other content, such as biographical profiles, conference papers, obituaries, interviews, discographies, reviews, and events.

7-2. **Performing Arts Yearbook (PAYE).** Manchester, UK: Impromptu Publishing. Ann. Subscription includes access to the online database at http://www.artsDB.net.

As of 2010, this international directory, published annually, combines the *Performing Arts Yearbook Europe* and the *Performing Arts Yearbook for Asia, North America & Pacific*. Subscription to PAYE gives online access to this directory. Subscribing organizations can add their own information to this database and create a profile for their business. The directory presents descriptive and contact information for cultural organizations of all kinds, including ministries of culture and funding agencies, opera companies, dance companies, theatres and theatrical companies, orchestras and instrumental ensembles, festivals, producers and promoters, and venues. The publication is very similar to *Musical America* (entry 9-174).

Open Access Resources

The number of open source materials in the performing arts expands daily with entries from fans, schools, university departments, and organizations. Websites on the Emmys, Oscars, and Tony awards are examples, as are websites on individuals, organizations, and fan-generated lists, far too many to mention here. For sites in addition to the larger and currently stable ones listed in this chapter, the reader should simply search for the topic of interest and he or she will likely find a web source to support their research.

7-3. **Creating Digital Performance Resources: A Guide to Good Practice**. Barry Smith, ed. Oxford: Oxbow Books, 2001. Print and online at http://www.ahds.ac.uk/creating/guides/.

This work is part of the Arts and Humanities Data Service series of guides to good practice. The guides are meant to educate those in the humanities and arts who create, preserve, and use digital resources. Guides in the series address a number of humanities disciplines and the arts; this one relates to performing arts resources. According to the publisher's website, this resource "covers various issues related to digital resources in the performance arts. It examines the construction of web-based databases, digital archives, e-journals and teaching applications, all in the context of performing arts datasets." Three sections with individual chapters by expert editors give practical advice. Finally, a section on the use of electronic resources in the practice of the performing arts is included. A glossary and bibliography, including web resources, complete this small volume.

7-4. Entertainment Weekly. http://www.ew.com. New York: Entertainment Weekly.

The print version, which began in 1990, was designed to cover the trends and developments in the entertainment industry in this country, and furnished feature stories, reviews of books, motion pictures, musical recordings and television programs of all kinds. It was partner to the television show of the same name. Now online, Entertainment Weekly provides television, film, and theater information, as well as professional reviews and viewer comments, sometimes hundreds of them. The website user can select "TV Recaps" to find out what happened on the week's television shows and see what viewers thought. Or the "Stage" tab leads to theater reviews and listings of plays on and off Broadway. If the user selects "Movie and DVD Guide," he or she can watch movie trailers, see synopses and reviews, read numerous viewer comments, and even consult a matrix comparing the ratings of a half dozen professional critics for a given film. This is a good source for lots of popular culture information and for reading what the audiences think of performances live and recorded.

7-5. Global Performing Arts Database. http://www.glopac.org

This database is sponsored by the Global Performing Arts Consortium (GloPAC). The organization is international in scope and is committed to using digital technology to make performing arts artifacts accessible so that they can be studied, preserved, and known to future generations. The database offers images, texts, video clips, and recorded sound on various people, pieces performed, locations, objects, and records such as scripts. There is a video on how to search the database, and browsing is both informative and fun.

7-6. Great Performances. http://www.pbs.org/wnet/gperf/index.html

This website is all about the Great Performances series on the U.S. Public Broadcasting System. Schedules of programming, upcoming presentations, program companions, videos of selected programs, and special features are available at the site. Links are provided to affiliates in the system. A wealth of information, as well as selected whole programs, is brought to the user at this site.

7-7. Performing Arts Encyclopedia (PAE). http://www.loc.gov/performingarts/

This PAE website of the Library of Congress is a rich resource for information across the performing arts. The following divisions at the Library are represented in this rich web resource: the Music Division; the Motion Picture, Broadcasting and Recorded Sound Division; the American Folklife Center; the Manuscript Division; the Rare Books and Special Collections Division; and the Prints and Photographs Division. The Library's description of the site states that the encyclopedia provides information about the Library's "collections of scores, sheet music, audio recordings, films, photographs, and other materials." Users can find digitized items from the collections; special Web presentations on topics and collections; articles and biographical essays; finding aids to collections; databases for performing arts resources; information on concerts at the Library; and a special Performing Arts Resource Guide which contains entries for hundreds of Library collections, Web sites, databases and exhibits. This free resource will open the door to the wealth of performing arts information, including programs and web presentations, of the Library of Congress.

Print Resources

7-8. African Americans in the Performing Arts. Steven Otfinoski. New York: Facts on File, 2003.

One of the A to Z of African Americans series, this consists of 190 biographies (usually one to one-and-a-half pages in length) of African Americans in the arts and entertainment arena. Every performance discipline is covered: music, dance, theater, and all types of entertainers and creators are included. The biographies are not all cut and dried; they are infused with the personal stories of the individuals as well as career facts about them. This has an index and also a list of individuals, along with their fields and birth and death dates as an additional point of reference, and also a bibliography and some photographs.

7-9. The Art of Clowning. Eli Simon. New York: Palgrave Macmillan, 2009.

This resource is more of a text than a reference tool, but it is a helpful resource nonetheless. Chapters offer explanations of tasks, techniques, and exercises that the clown-to-be should understand, but it is also rich with history of clowning and clown-like characters. Clowning as a state of mind is introduced early on in a chapter on Finding Your Own Clown. This is followed by the specifics: mask techniques, white-face, appearance, music, and voice and text are all taken up in the chapters, and exemplars are noted. Familiar clowns from Emmett Kelly to Ronald McDonald find mention in this book. Beyond the chapters there is a detailed back-of-the-book index.

7-10. Bibliographie des Arts du Spectacle–Performing arts bibliography. Nicole Leclercq and Alain Chevalier. New York: Peter Lang, 2000.

This is a scholarly bibliography of books in the French language in all areas of the performing arts. Its scope is books published between 1985 and 1995. It covers the expected fields of theater, musical theater, dance, cinema, and radio and television, but it also has sections on mime, circus, puppetry, and light entertainment. The sections are further subdivided, making this an easy resource to consult. Collections with depth in performing arts will need to have this comprehensive resource.

7-11. Obituaries in the Performing Arts, 2010. Harris M. Lentz III. Jefferson, NC: McFarland, 2010. Ann.

This annual publication, edited by Lentz since 1994, consists of obituaries of individuals in the performing arts who died in the previous year. The birth and death dates, location of death, and cause are listed, along with recaps of the deceased's career. Filmographies are supplied for film and television personalities and there are copious photographs. This reference resource is sold as a subscription journal.

7-12. The Oxford Encyclopedia of Theatre and Performance. Dennis Kennedy. New York: Oxford University Press, 2003, 2005. Print and e-book available in Oxford Reference Online.

This work covers a wide sweep of performing arts with authoritative entries on dance, opera, broadcasting (radio and television), film, as well as popular performance formats, such as circus and carnivals. The entries range from brief dictionary-like definitions to long, scholarly entries by more than 300 contributors. This volume is an award-winner, having taken the Choice Outstanding Academic Title award in 2004.

7-13. The Performing Arts: A Guide to the Reference Literature. Linda Keir Simons. Englewood, CO: Libraries Unlimited, 1994.

This guide, which was very helpful when it first appeared, is listed here only for its coverage of some historically important bibliographies and catalogs. Under bibliographies and catalogs, the reader will find items that are probably now available only in remote storage at research libraries, but they can be useful to the researcher nonetheless. If a library has this guide it should be kept for the purposes noted, or if it's missing, a used copy might be procured.

7-14. The Performing Arts Business Encyclopedia. Leonard DuBoff. New York: Allworth Press, 1996.

This slim volume serves a very specific purpose, and that is to define and explain words and phrases that one meets in the business of the performing arts. The book is subtitled "For Individuals and Organizations as well as the Attorneys and Advisors who Assist Them." The author, an attorney himself, covers terminology specific to the performing arts (grip, green room), to performing arts law (performing rights, block-booking), and to business (accrual basis, audit). The entries are arranged alphabetically and the terms are explained so anyone can understand them. Some entries date this book: computer hardware and software, for example, would probably not need definitions in an updated edition. Despite the age of the work, it is useful.

7-15. Performing Arts: Fergusons' Careers in Focus. New York: Infobase Publishing, 2006. Print and e-book.

This is one of a series of career guides for young adults. It provides information plus sound advice for the individual seeking to make a living in the performing arts. A related source is *Performing Arts Ferguson Career Launcher* by Celia Watson Seupel (Checkmark Books, 2010).

7-16. Queer Encyclopedia of Music, Dance, and Musical Theater. Claude J. Summers, ed. Berkeley, CA: Cleis Press, 2004.

Many aspects of the performing arts are covered in this authoritative encyclopedia: music, dance, opera, and musical theater are represented as expected, but so are drag shows and performers. Topical and name indexes enable the user to find people within topical entries, and topics as they appear in individual entries. Biographical entries make up a good proportion of the 200-plus entries that are signed and contain helpful references.

CHAPTER 8

DANCE AND THEATER

Elizabeth S. Aversa and Richard LeComte

DANCE

Dance information resources have changed considerably over the recent years. Old indexes are still useful, but several of the major tools have ceased publication. Notably, the GK Hall publications formerly produced for the New York Public Library's Dance Collection are no longer being published. These are noted below, but we have retained the titles because of their value as finding tools for literature pre-dating 2001. The New York Public Library's Dance Division reported to this author that "All our records are currently available through New York Public Library's online catalog (http://catalog.nypl.org/)." The reader is further referred to the titles in "Performing Arts General" above for additional coverage of the dance.

Indexes and Serials

8-1. Dance Magazine. 1927– . Macfadden Performing Arts Media, LLC. Online subscription.

This long-running magazine, which began as *The American Dancer,* is a valuable source for all kinds of information about the dance. The magazine is now available electronically, and the publisher also offers the ballet specific magazine *Pointe* as well as an annual college guide. This is a must for nearly every library; it is a good buy (under $40 US for new subscriptions) with excellent value for the investment. Articles appeal to dancers, people in the dance community, and audiences as well. Back issues, in print, can be purchased, and their availability is noted on the magazine's website. Links to the publisher's dancemedia.com will lead the reader to video collections both freely available and for purchase.

Dictionary Catalog of the Dance Collection; Index to Dance Periodicals; Dance on Disc. New York Public Library for the Performing Arts. Boston: G.K. Hall.

These resources were special catalogs and indexes produced by the Dance Division of the New York Public Library's Performing Arts Research Center. They were published and distributed by G.K. Hall. The Dictionary Catalog, which covered items cataloged prior to 1973 and then was supplemented from 1976 until 2000, was one of the most comprehensive tools of its kind. *The Index to Dance Periodicals*, which began in 1990, also ceased publication in 2001. A CD-Rom title, *Dance on Disc*, was produced until 2004 when GK Hall stopped publishing and distributing it.

Print Resources

8-2. Appreciating Dance: A Guide to the World's Liveliest Art. Harriet Lihs. Hightstown, NJ: Princeton Book Company, 2009.

This tome provides eight chapters on the dance, beginning with definitions of dance, dance in its many contexts (religion and dance, social dance, court and theatrical dance, modern dance, and dance in musicals and film). All are placed in historical perspectives. The final chapters take up careers in dance and dance in the twenty-first century and all have ample footnotes for each chapter and an extensive index. The back-of-the-book index will enable users to find people, productions, companies, and types of dance in the chapters. From the earliest dance, through hip-hop and break-dancing, this volume proves to be a helpful and contemporary resource.

8-3. The International Encyclopedia of Dance. Selma Jeanne Cohen, ed. Dance Perspectives Foundation Inc. New York: Oxford University Press, 2004. 6 vols.

This important encyclopedia was published in 1998 and released in paperback in 2004. It is broad in scope, covering all forms of dance from the world over throughout recorded history. Alphabetically arranged, the entries are by experts and scholars in the various forms of the dance. With over 2,000 entries, and as many illustrations of different types, the user will find every aspect of dance covered here: forms and movements, music, staging, costumes, performances, dance techniques, dance notation, and historical topics are among the hundreds of topics addressed here. Unexpected topics appear as well, e.g., ice dancing. There are biographical and career histories of dancers, choreographers, and producers, among other people associated with dance in its many forms. The work has an extensive index that assists the user in accessing multiple places to look for information, from different perspectives, on a topic.

8-4. The Oxford Dictionary of Dance. 2nd ed. Debra Craine and Judith Mackrell, eds. New York: Oxford University Press, 2010. Print and e-book in Oxford Reference Online.

This second edition of the Dictionary, containing more than 25,000 entries, with more than 150 of them new, covers all aspects of dance with particular emphasis on performance. The focus is on theatrical dance, not native dance. Here we find brief entries on dance history, types of dance from ballet to hip-hop, dance companies, dance traditions of different countries, technical aspects of the dance, as well as coverage of dancers, choreographers, and even musicians and composers. The coverage is broad and timely. Entries are brief and to the point and they are arranged alphabetically. Individual entries do not have bibliographic references but a selected bibliography is included for the volume. The only negative to this handy work is its lack of illustrations.

Open Access Resources

8-5. Critical Dance. http://www.ballet-dance.com/

Critical Dance is (according to its "about" page) "an international non-profit entity founded for the purpose of promoting and supporting the dance arts, including dance arts professionals, organizations, companies, presenters, writers and audiences." Its website is a valuable resource that has both the critical dance forum and *Ballet-Dance Magazine*.

8-6. Cyber Dance: Ballet on the Net. http://www.cyberdance.org/index.html

According to the brief and accurate description on the site's Home Page, "CyberDance is an extensive internet dance database containing thousands of links to classical ballet and modern dance resources on the Internet." Here the user will find hundreds of portals and web sites about the dance. The site is not limited to the ballet, and has links for schools of the dance, colleges, dance companies, people, professional associations, and vendors and suppliers. This site provides more links than any encountered on the dance.

8-7. Voice of Dance. http://www.voiceofdance.com

Voice of Dance is a resource for dance fans, dance professionals, and dance students. The history of the site states that it began as a forum at a time when message boards and discussions were the way to communicate within a community. The site now covers multiple areas of interest, from finding tickets to criticism to finding classes and more. The developers state that "the database technology at the core of the site cross-references this information in a fully integrated way that is not possible in the off-line world." This site is a true mix of directory, newsletter, resource guide, and encyclopedia.

8-8. Global Dance Directory. http://globaldancedirectory.com/

Copyrighted by danceScape, this web resource has tabs for businesses, classified ads, and even articles about the dance business. The site lists more than 2,500 schools and studios, 100 dance companies, and over 300 retail establishments that serve the dance community. There are events and job opportunities listed here as well. Although the directory is headquartered in Ontario, Canada, the listings cover the U.S. and other areas as well. This online directory provides a good place to find contacts in many aspects of the dance.

8-9. Dance USA. http://www.danceusa.com

A set of commercial directories are brought together here for the dance, drill team, and team spirit community. The user will find choreography, fundraising services, team travel companies, music and sound editors, video- and photographers, camps and competitions, and other listings of services and organizations (such as college dance teams).

Specialized Topics in Dance

8-10. The Language of Spanish Dance: A Dictionary and Reference Manual. Matteo Marcellus Vitucci, Louis Gioia, and Nancy Ruyter. Hightstown, NJ: Princeton Books, 2003.

This encyclopedic volume explains and defines, with illustrations, dance steps, positions, and techniques of Spanish dancing. It also provides a wealth of information on dance genres, people, music of the dance, and movements associated with the various dances. The more than 800 entries are alphabetically arranged, and there is a supplemental chapter on guitar music for flamenco, a bibliography of over 200 sources, and an index. The authors state in the preface that this reference is not designed to teach Spanish dance; rather it is meant to document and authenticate aspects of the dance for scholars, practitioners, and students of the future.

8-11. Stage Combat Resources and Materials. Michael Kirkland. Westport, CT: Praeger Press, 2006.

Stage combat could be covered in the theater resources section of this guide but it is placed here because stage fighting is sometimes considered a form of choreography. An historical essay on combat and the use of various weapons (swords, daggers, etc.) is followed by a numbered, copiously annotated bibliography covering books, articles, and videos. All types of combat are covered from barroom brawling to dueling to military combat. There is a glossary and list of films as well. The website of the Society of American Fight Directors at http://www.safd.org/about/history may be of interest as will be *Fight Choreography: A Practical Guide for Stage, Film and Television*, by F.B. McAsh

(Ramsbury: Crowood, 2010). This comprehensive book explains the artistic process of creating the fight scene from scripted page to finished performance.

Ballet

8-12. ABT Online Ballet Dictionary. http://www.abt.org/education/dictionary/index.html

Terms from the print *Technical Manual and Dictionary of Classical Ballet* (Dover, 1967) have been carried over and enhanced by demonstrations of many positions and movements by members of the American Ballet Theatre. The site is easily used, with an alphabetical list of terms to select from; one click and the definition and associated media (photograph or video) appear. The media can be opened or downloaded at the user's preference.

8-13. Ballet and Modern Dance: A Concise History. Jack Anderson. Hightstown, NJ: Princeton Book Company, 1993.

Even though this is an older source it remains useful, particularly for public and school libraries, where concise, easy-to-access histories are needed. The profiles at the back are generally brief, but the volume has a good index and a large bibliography. This history is divided into 11 chapters and covers dance from the primeval and Ancient Greek time through to contemporary dance from an international perspective. It is still useful after nearly 20 years.

8-14. Classical Ballet Terms: An Illustrated Dictionary. Richard Glasstone. Hightstown, NJ: Princeton Books, 2005.

This slim volume provides definitions, historical perspectives, and correct spellings for terms used in the ballet. As the publisher's description points out, the dancer may not care about the appropriate spelling of a French term, but for those who write and publish on the dance, the information in this volume is essential.

8-15. The Video Dictionary of Classical Ballet: Kultur Distributor. Released 1991. DVD (270 minutes on two DVDs).

This DVD is the filmed/recorded version of a standard ballet dictionary. Over 800 movements are demonstrated by well-known dancers, giving the student or the audience member information about positions, movements, and their directions in a variety of styles: French, Russian, and so forth. Although the release date is 1991, this is a favorite that continues to be sold.

Biomechanics and Conditioning

8-16. Conditioning for Dance. Eric Franklin. Champaign, IL: Human Kinetics, 2003.

This volume will serve the needs of dancers, martial artists, and athletes who need balance, flexibility, and alignment along with what the author calls "whole body conditioning." Starting with the mind and continuing to all kinds of movements, Franklin calls upon the literature of conditioning, biomechanics, anatomy, and a host of other fields as background. Ten chapters make for precise, focused reading. Along with the impressive bibliography, there is an extensive index. Reader reviews have been almost uniformly positive. *Conditioning with Imagery for Dancers* by Jordana Deveau and Donna Krasnow may also be of interest (Toronto: Thompson Educational Pub. 2011).

Ballroom Dancing

8-17. Ballroom Dance Resource http://www.ballroomdancers.com

This resource is one in which there is much information to be had at the basic site, but additional videos and information beyond the basic requires a "premium" membership for which there is a fee, presently $99 U.S. The basic membership (free) provides access to a forum for discussion (example: how to best end a waltz?) and to videos of dance steps with instruction and text coverage as well. In an age of TV's "Dancing with the Stars," this is a good resource for audiences, amateurs, as well as professional dancers and teachers.

Dance Notation

Over the years, there has been much conversation and controversy in the dance education and choreography communities over whether there is need for dance notation. Several systems exist today and their basics are available on the websites listed below. As technology is increasingly used to record the dance and as costs of the technology plummets, the need to notate the dance may again come into question. Databases provide archives of notated dance. Supporters of dance notation argue that it enables teachers and performers to access specific dance performances, to study them, and to recreate them long after the parties involved are no longer active. Three systems are listed below.

8-18. Benesh Institute Notation. http://benesh.org

This website is sponsored by the Royal Academy of Dance and it offers an overview of the Benesh Dance Notation System. The notation system was developed and first published in the mid-1950s and, according to the website, the Royal Academy of Dance publishes its set exercises and dances in its examination syllabi in Benesh notation.

8-19. Dance Notation Bureau (DNB). www.dancenotation.org

The Dance Notation Bureau's website states that their mission is to "advance the art of dance through the use of a system of notation by creating dance scores using the symbol system called "Labanotation." The site contains dance notation basics and a catalog of notated dances along with a discussion forum. The DNB has a long (70+ year) history and its website gives background on both the issue of dance notation and its practical applications. The website is well organized and attractive, making it a pleasure to use.

8-20. The Dance Writing Site. http://www.dancewriting.org

This site covers the Sutton Dancewriting system that is one of five types of "movement writing" notation. The Sutton system includes DanceWriting, SignWriting, MimeWriting, SportsWriting, and ScienceWriting. The DanceWriting system records on paper the movements involved in the dance. The website has several examples and downloadable texts for the user who wishes to learn more.

History of the Dance

8-21. Dance History. Adshead Layson Staff. New York: Routledge, 2010. E-book.

This book is now available, fully revised and updated, as an e-book. It is listed here because of its long history as a print text that, as the publisher stated, ". . . remains the only book to address the rationale, process, techniques and methodologies specific to the study of dance history." The main chapters are produced by dance experts. Helpful chapters discuss the literature of the dance and dance history resources. The original text was first published in 1983, but updating and availability as an e-book continue to make it a standard.

8-22. Society of Dance History Scholars Website. http://www.sdhs.org/

This is a web site devoted to the promotion of all aspects of the study of dance through research, publication, performance, and outreach. The society has seven "working groups" that contribute to the mission: Dance History Teachers, Early Dance, Ethnicity and Dance, Interdisciplinary Approaches to Nineteenth Century Dance, Popular, Social and Vernacular Dance, Practice-as-Research and Students in SDHS. The primary publication of the Society is *Studies in Dance History* that started as a journal and now appears as a monograph series.

Tap Dancing

8-23. Tapworks: A Tap Dictionary and Reference Manual. Beverly Fletcher. Hightstown, NJ: Princeton Book Publishers, 2003.

This book is an official reference of the Dance Masters of America, an organization of "artists and educators committed to the elevation of the art of dance and to provide innovative artistic experiences for the advancement of dance worldwide." Although it is a slim volume (less than 200 pages) it has more than 1,500 entries on all aspect of tap dance. The entries include the history of the genre, biographical material on dancers, and information on tap dancing itself. This dictionary offers technical terms and instructions on how to perform steps and movements in tap dancing. Readers' reviews are very positive, suggesting that tap aficionados have found a helpful reference.

Organizations

The number of organizations devoted to dance is small; those that do exist seem to be largely concentrated in the areas of ballet and the teaching of dance.

8-24. The Imperial Society of Teachers of Dancing. http://www.istd.org/about-us/

The Imperial Society of Teachers of Dancing, which has a branch in the United States, publishes *Dance Magazine*, a long-established standard in the field and also publishes *Imperial Dance Letter*.

8-25. The Dance Educators of America (http://www.deadance.com/us/index.htm) and **Dance Masters of America** (http://www.dma-ational.org/pages/about/201) both consist of dance teachers and have regional groups that supplement the activities of the national groups. The Dance Educators of America was established in 1932. Dance Masters is an older organization that was established in the 1890s and continues to be concerned with teaching of the dance.

THEATER

Databases

8-26. American Drama, Third Release. Ann Arbor, MI: ProQuest Information and Learning Co. Online subscription database. http://www.proquest.com/en-US/catalogs/databases/detail/american_drama.shtml

This ProQuest database offers online access by play, title, keyword, character, place, date of first performance, and genre to more than 1,500 plays by 500 playwrights from 1714 to 1915, although plans seem to be afoot to expand the scope. ProQuest also lists several other theater databases: *Source Materials in the Field of Theater*, *Twentieth-Century Drama* (2,500 plays in English from around the world), and *English Drama*, which contains more than 3,900 plays from 1280 to 1915.

8-27. Black Drama. James V. Hatch Will Whalen and Jeremy Caleb Johnson, eds. Alexandria, VA.: Alexander Street Press. Online subscription database or purchase. http://solomon.bldr.alexanderstreet.com/

This database contains the full text of more than 1,200 plays by more than 100 playwrights, along with biographical information on the writers. According to the website, more than a quarter of the documents represent plays previously unpublished and released to the publisher at the discretion of the playwrights themselves. The scope of the database reaches back to 1846, with *The Black Doctor* by Ira Frederick Aldridge. The editors are theater scholars who based their selections on black theater bibliographies, including *Black American Playwrights 1800 to the Present: a Bibliography* (Scarecrow, 1976). The database contains many key and lesser-known playwrights. It advertises itself as deeply indexed, and the scripts and biographies are accessible by production company, subject headings, characters (by sex, sexual orientation, nationality, and other criteria), and genre, among other elements. Alexander Street offers a drama package that includes *Asian American Drama* (more than 250 plays), *Latino Literature* (including plays), *North American Indian Drama*, *North American Women's Drama* (1,500 plays back to the Colonial era), and *Twentieth Century American Drama* (2,000 plays from the United States and Canada).

8-28. North American Theatre Online. Alexandria, VA.: Alexander Street Press. Online subscription database. http://asp6new.alexanderstreet.com/atho/index.shtml

This is an essential tool for ferreting out plays, performers, theater artists, and other information on theater in the United States and Canada. The site provides online access to dozens of theater reference works going back into the nineteenth century (categorized either as primary or secondary material), including a 1919 history of the American theater, *The Oxford Companion to the American Theatre* by Gerald Bordman (entry 8-46), *A Record of the Boston Stage* (published in 1853), *Notable Women in the American Theatre: A Biographical Dictionary* (Greenwood 1989), and *American Theatre: A Chronicle of Comedy and Drama 1969–2000* by Thomas Hischak (entry 8-40). Information can be found on most theatrical professionals from the twentieth century and many from the nineteenth century, through either a simple search or in an alphabetical listing. Calling up names gives the user access to their mentions in the indexed reference material; for playwrights, users also may find complete play texts, because the database accesses the other drama full-text databases published by Alexander Street. The interface is basic and easily usable; a table of contents gives access to a list of works indexed as well as indexes of people, plays, productions, companies, years, characters, and subjects. The site also features photos and playbills from image databases, including the Theatre Scrapbook Collection at Virginia Tech. This resource is a great place to start when researching an American theater, performer or artist, and it is a fair substitute for a basic collection of theater reference. The database is as good as the material fed into it, and the works used are among the foundations of theater research.

8-29. Play Index. H.W. Wilson/EBSCO. Print and also online subscription database. http://www.hwwilson.com/Databases/playindex_e.htm

H.W. Wilson began offering its renowned published-play index database on the Web, where it is available by subscription, in 2006. The index boasts that it has about 31,000 play citations in its database; its scope encompasses plays written or translated into English published from 1949 to the present (many plays written before 1949 are in the index because they were published in post-1949 editions). The user can search by title, author, subject, keyword, and genre, including mysteries, monologues (the database has more than 600 indexed), plays in verse, radio plays, and pantomimes. Searchers can also limit the scope of their searches by number and sex of characters and audience age group (pre-kindergarten to sixth grade, seventh to 12th grade, and adult). Books of plays are indexed along with individual titles within anthologies or stand-alone scripts, including the acting versions published by Dramatists Play Service. The bibliographic citations contain a brief description of the play's plot as well as several publication citations. This resource will aid researchers looking for lists of plays by specific playwrights as well as producers looking for scripts within certain parameters of cast size, audience, or subject.

8-30. Theatre Communications Group Tools & Research. New York: Theatre Communications Group. Online subscription database. http://www.tcg.org/tools/index.cfm

Founded in 1961 with a grant from the Ford Foundation, the Theatre Communications Group serves as a national organization and advocacy group for regional theaters in the United States. The group has more than 700 member theaters and 12,000 individual memberships. In addition to its extensive publications division, the group features a website with numerous resources for researching trends in employment and theatrical production. The advantage to the researcher lies in the picture the site gives of American theater outside of New York City. The Theatre Profiles section features a search-able database of profiles of member theaters; some of the profiles go back to 1995. Information pro-vided includes an annual budget figure, seating capacity and an artistic statement. The Theatre Facts series provides a yearly overview of the financial state of American nonprofit theaters. In addition, the site has an index to American Theatre. Some materials are open only to members. A recent addi-tion, New Plays in Production, features production information and press on world premiere plays presented at member theaters.

Open Access Resources

8-31. Folger Shakespeare Library. Washington, D.C.: Folger Shakespeare Library. http://www.folger.edu/

This extensive website provides a comprehensive "Discover Shakespeare" page, which offers visi-tors links and guides to the Folger's resources. Users are introduced to Shakespeare through a brief biography and other materials on his plays and poetry. The Collection Highlights gallery is an enter-taining look at some of the print and visual materials housed at the library, including David Garrick and Mrs. Bellamy in *Romeo and Juliet*. The links section offers direction to several key Shakespeare websites, including the MIT Shakespeare Project and Shakespeare's grave at Stratford-on-Avon. This site is a strong starting point for Shakespeare studies.

Also available from Folger is *World Shakespeare Bibliography Online* edited by James L. Harner (http://www.worldshakesbib.org/index.html). This online bibliography gives access to sur-rogate records for more than 125,000 annotated entries. The scope of the database reaches from 1960 to 2010 and includes works in more than 120 languages. The database, updated quarterly, covers both literature and criticism on Shakespeare and his times and production records. Advanced search allows users to limit searches to articles or productions. The database also includes materials on recorded Shakespeare productions so students can find them in WorldCat or other catalogs.

8-32. Canadian Theatre Encyclopedia. Gaetan Charlebois, founder. Athabasca, Alberta, Can.: Atha-basca University Press. http://www.canadiantheatre.com/dict.pl?action=index

Charlebois, editor of *Hour Magazine* in Montreal, founded the site in 1996 with an eye toward devel-oping an ongoing database about Canadian theater. The site presents a simple, alphabetical listing of entries; playwrights, actors, directors, plays, and theaters are mixed together. The site also has a basic search that allows users to find words either in entry titles or in full text. The site includes articles on some actors familiar to American audiences, including Eric McCormack, Roy Dupuis, Martin Short, and William Shatner, as well as well-known writers, including Robertson Davies, and theater com-panies, including the Shaw Festival. Noted Canadian plays, including *Fortune and Men's Eyes* and *La Duchesse de Langeais*, are mentioned in articles about their playwrights. All the articles are short and they emphasize their relevance to the Canadian theater scene. For example, a brief article on Toronto's Tarragon Theatre describes how it has fostered Canadian playwriting since 1971. Entries include information on when they were last updated.

8-33. Intute Theatre and Drama Web site. Bristol, U.K.: Joint Information Systems Committee. http://www.intute.ac.uk/theatre/

This British website, part of a much larger framework of recommendations for online academic information, is a production of faculty at several universities, including Oxford, Birmingham, and Bristol. The site offers links to hundreds of sites the board members have reviewed and certified fit for viewing. For example, under playwrights, the site gives a link to the Early Modern Drama Database, the Royal Court Theatre (a noted new-plays venue in London), and a Sam Shepard website. Under theatre history, the site takes users to the American Variety Stage database at the Library of Congress, the Appia Project (re-creating on computers the designs of Adolphe Appia), and Puppet India, which describes itself. The site even has an RSS feed that sends out bulletins on new resources. This umbrella site will be a solid addition to a reference list of theater sources and a place where students may turn when searching for up-to-date Internet resources.

8-34. Irish Theatre Online. Dublin, Irish Theatre Institute. http://www.irishtheatreonline.com/

This site offers up-do-date, searchable lists of theater companies throughout Ireland, Irish theater artists, and festivals. Of perhaps more interest to students is the Irish Playography companion site at http://www.irishplayography.com/. This resource uses data gleaned from two main databases: the Irish Playography catalog, whose scope includes plays produced in English dating back to 1904, and the growing *Playography na Gaeilge*, listing plays produced in Irish. It offers a database of Irish playwrights and plays accessible by playwright and title (it even provides a list of plays and playwrights that can be scrolled alphabetically); more advanced searches allow users to search by actor or actress, director, theater company, cast breakdown, year of production, genres, and other elements. The database also lists first productions outside of Ireland where appropriate; for example, Leonard's play *Da* opened first at a theater in Maryland. This provides a good addition to world theatre collections.

8-35. Yale University Library Theater and Dance Research Guide. New Haven, CT: Yale University. http://guides.library.yale.edu/content.php?pid=8564&sid=55015

Dr. Tobin Nellhaus, Yale librarian for performing arts, media, and philosophy, has compiled a thorough guide both to theater bibliography and research as well as links to contemporary theater companies and productions. The beginning researcher will find this site useful because Nellhaus offers a librarian's perspective to finding materials; he provides a primer page on how to find books, articles, and videos on theater and dance (for example, in keyword searching, use "theater" instead of "theatre"). Convenient drop-down menus guide users to "Areas and Topics of Study" (acting, playwriting, producing, dance, history and criticism, and design and technology) and "Reference Sources." The section under theater history and criticism provides an invaluable list of online sources broken down by eras and types of resources, including photo and playbill archives. The site depends heavily on Yale's collection, so some of the sources may not be readily available locally. Another, more specialized theater site is the *New York University Research Guide Subjects: Theater* (http://nyu.libguides.com/cat.php?cid=8604). It covers a broad range of topics and appears to be updated regularly.

Print Resources

8-36. The Continuum Companion to Twentieth Century Theatre. Colin Chambers, ed. London: Continuum, 2002.

The unusual aspect of this single, un-illustrated volume is that some of the 280 contributors are theater professionals rather than academics. The editor is a former journalist and literary manager. The contributor list for the *Continuum Companion,* which has more than 2,500 entries, includes actors Ben Kingsley, Ian McKellen, and Jessica Lange; directors Harold Prince and Arthur Penn; lighting designer Jennifer Tipton, and a wide range of theater academics. The work's scope encompasses the twentieth century, but includes how previous eras, including the Greek and Elizabethan, influenced the modern era. Theater in Great Britain and the United States make up the bulk of the entries. The strict alphabetical scheme makes finding entries on people, countries, theater companies, and more general topics easy, and most entries conveniently provide a few book titles for further reading.

8-37. History of the Theatre. 10th ed. Oscar G. Brockett and Franklin J. Hildy. Boston: Pearson Education, Inc., 2008.

This edition marks the 40th anniversary for *History of the Theatre*, the perennial go-to textbook for theater history. This is an ideal narrative sourcebook for students of theater. In the preface, the authors note that they lean more toward detail than theory and invite professors to discuss theories mentioned in the text further with their classes. In this edition, the authors updated each chapter. The book is ordered chronologically, making it easy to find a particular period with the help of a detailed, period-oriented table of contents. The volume includes illustrations, an extensive, chapter-by-chapter bibliography, and an index that allows access by performer, play title, theater company, and even genre.

8-38. Oxford Encyclopedia of Theatre & Performance. Dennis Kennedy, ed. Oxford, UK: Oxford University Press, 2003. 2 vols. Print and e-book in Oxford Reference Online.

This two-volume 1,500-page encyclopedia (with a few illustrations) attempts to cover the full breadth of theater and performance throughout the world. The preface notes that the editors attempted to include contemporary theatrical and performance theory as well as a range of types of performance, including para-theatrical activities, agitprop, mass media, and pornography. The table of contents breaks down entries on theatrical concepts and styles by era or country of origin; theatrical companies and individuals given separate articles are organized by country as well (although without referent page numbers). There follows alphabetical listings of entries, including many two- or three-paragraph entries on world theatrical figures, cities, countries, and theater companies with a slight bias toward British figures. Americans and figures from around the world are also covered; Arthur Miller, the Marx Brothers, and Fanny Brice are mentioned, along with the 16th century Chinese playwright Tang Xianzu and the Polish playwright Stanislaw Witkiewicz. Longer breakout sections are included for such broader topics as Carnival, London, Lighting and Film, and Theatre. Volume II features a timeline of world theater history, which is helpful for the beginning theater student, as well as an index of the plays, musicals, operas, and other works mentioned in the volumes and a list of works for further reading.

8-39. World Encyclopedia of Contemporary Theatre. Don Rubin, gen. ed.; Anton Wagner, director of research, managing ed. New York: Routledge, 1998. 6 vols. Print and e-book.

This massive, six-volume, illustrated encyclopedia is the product of the World Encyclopedia of Contemporary Theatre Corp. and received backing from a variety of state agencies and patrons, including UNESCO, the International Theatre Institute, and the International Society of Libraries and Museums for the Performing Arts. The volumes represent a multinational endeavor with roots going back to the late 1970s. In 1983, with the help of York University in Toronto, the World Encyclopedia was incorporated as a nonprofit corporation and drew grants from the Ford Foundation, among other organizations. The scope covers the theaters of the world since 1945, and the volumes explore individual areas: Europe, the Americas, Africa, the Arab World, and Asia-Oceania. The sixth volume is a bibliography and cumulative index. Each volume begins with a table of contents by country and introductory material that gives an overview of theater during the 50-year span of coverage as well as musical theater, theater for young audiences, and dance and puppet theater. Each volume has its own index providing access by name, play title, and company name, among others. Numerous illustrations give users a feel for the theaters they're reading about. The volumes also are available online in the Ebrary Academic Library Complete collection.

SPECIALIZED TOPICS IN THEATER

American Theater

8-40. **American Theatre: A Chronicle of Comedy and Drama, 1969–2000**. Thomas S. Hischak. New York: Oxford University Press, 2001. Continues Gerald Bordman's *American Theatre: A Chronicle of Comedy and Drama, Volumes 1–3* (entry 8-46).

Following up the first three volumes by Gerald Bordman, this work continues a play-by-play chronicle of each New York theater season from 1969 to 2000. The editor notes that, during this period, the New York theater scheme atomized; many key productions were staged off-Broadway or off-off Broadway, making the seasons difficult to chronicle in a blow-by-blow manner. The scope of the reference work excludes musicals, which Bordman covered elsewhere. The title of the volume also is something of a misnomer: It covers only the New York theater scene. Hischak attempts to break the volume up first by titled thematic periods—1969–1975 ("Getting Through by the Skin of Our Teeth"), 1975–1984 ("Everything Old is New Again"), and so forth. He then writes, in narrative fashion, a history of the seasons (fall 1974-spring 1975, for example). For each play covered the editor summarizes the plot, gives a taste of the play's background, says how long the play ran, and summarizes critical reaction. He also offers asides about individual playwrights, directors, actors, and designers to show how the productions fit into their careers. A table of contents and indexes complete this resource that gives valuable information about the shape of a theatrical season and how individual plays fit into the theatrical milieu of their time.

8-41. **Best Plays Theatre Yearbook, 2008–2009.** Jeffrey Eric Jenkins, ed. New York: Limelight; London: dist., Eurospan, 2010.

This reference source serves both as an honor to the plays or musicals deemed among the ten best for a theatrical season and a yearbook similar to *Theatre World* but without lots of photographs. Often the series is known as "Best Plays" or by its noted previous editors, Burns Mantle and Otis Guernsey Jr. Earlier editions, including those published in the 1970s, usually included extensive dialog taken from the plays; nowadays, however, we get critical assessments along with illustrative snippets of dialog and a handful of photographs. The volume also covers the theatrical season, recounting productions on Broadway, off Broadway, and off-off Broadway and around the United States. As in *Theatre World* (entry 8-50), listings include cast and crew members, number of performances, cast replacements for long runs, theater information, and a brief synopsis. At the back, the editor provides almanac-like lists of award winners going back many years and an index to the best plays going back to the first edition back in 1894. Finally, an index provides access by play title, theater company, person, or key words. Although not as visually stimulating as *Theatre World*, *Best Plays* provides an introduction to the best new scripts, which can be accessed through play indexes or online catalogs.

8-42. **The Cambridge Guide to American Theatre.** 2nd ed. Don B. Wilmeth, ed. Cambridge, UK: Cambridge University Press, 2007.

This second edition, lightly illustrated, displays extensive revision and updating to accommodate new material, more than 340 new entries. After a historical introduction to the American theater, the guide lists more than 2,700 entries under a strict alphabetical scheme that mixes general articles

(Asian-American theater, theater in Atlanta) with notable American stage artists (actors, playwrights, directors, designers and producers, among others), productions, and stage companies. The articles can become chatty and opinionated. Most articles are two or three paragraphs; broader themes get a longer treatment, as with vaudeville or feminist theater. The play listings contain brief production histories and descriptions rather than a full plot synopsis.

8-43. The Cambridge History of American Theatre. Don B. Wilmeth and Christopher Bigsby, eds. New York: Cambridge University Press, 1998–2000. 3 vols. Print and e-book in Cambridge Histories Online.

The editors have compiled a series of narrative essays on aspects of American theater during the scope of the resource: Volume 1 covers American theater history from beginnings to 1870; Volume 2 from 1870 to 1945; and volume 3, Post World War II to the 1990s. The entries include playwriting, musicals, directing, acting, theater design, the development of regional theater, and so forth. Although of varying quality, the essays detail the main trends of theater during the time periods: decentralization, the growing costs and safe choices of Broadway, the eclectic experimental movements, off- and off-off Broadway, and the emergence of fascinating artists. The differences in tone and emphasis arise from using multiple contributors. Included is a handy timeline matching theatrical events to events in American and world cultural history. The online edition does not have an index, but each chapter is searchable by keyword in a PDF reader format. The print version, which features a few illustrations, does have an extensive index for the third volume as well as an extensive general bibliography.

8-44. Historical Dictionary of African American Theater. Anthony D. Hill with Douglas Q. Barnett. Lanham, Md.: Scarecrow Press, 2009 (Historical Dictionaries of Literature and the Arts Series).

Here is a compilation of more than 600 entries on African-American theaters, plays, artists, and movements that covers 1816 to the present, even as the timeline provided with the other titles in the Historical Dictionaries series goes back to the 18th century. The volume offers a robust cast of performers, authors, plays, and projects, from Rosetta LeNoire, founder of the Amas Musical Theatre, to Denzel Washington, to the musical *Jelly's Last Jam*. Topics include African American Folklore, "miscegenation," and Mythic Theme, a style that arose from the Black Power movement of the 1960s. The volume includes a timeline at the beginning, an introduction that summarizes the history of African American theater, and a bibliography organized by subject.

8-45. Lortel Archives: The Internet Off-Broadway Database. New York: The Lucille Lortel Foundation. http://www.lortel.org/LLA_archive/index.cfm

Echoing the Internet Broadway Database (entry 8-51), the Lortel Archives attempts to provide users the same kind of searchable resource for off-Broadway productions. The scope of the database includes play titles, casts, and crews from productions that appeared in houses with between 100 and 499 seats, the range of seating that defines off-Broadway in labor contracts. The site states that its staff members have entered complete off-Broadway seasons going back to 1958 (more than 5,000 shows as of January 2009). Through an advanced search, the database is accessible by actor name, company name, play title, playwright, crew members, or awards. Like the IBDB, search results produce first a clickable name; once clicked, a list of productions from the individual appears (in reverse chronological order). A further click on the show title brings up the listings from the programs. A click on individual names or company names will yield a list of credits. Clicking on a venue will produce a list of plays produced there; for example, clicking on the New York Theatre Workshop brings up a list of productions as well as a link to the company's official Web site. If used in conjunction with the IBDB, the Lortel site will give researchers a fuller picture of the careers of actors, playwrights, production companies, and other theatrical practitioners on the New York City scene.

8-46. The Oxford Companion to American Theatre. 3rd ed. Gerald M. Bordman and Thomas S. Hischak. New York: Oxford University Press, 2004. Print and e-book in Oxford Reference Online.

This volume includes new entries on each Broadway theater, some off-Broadway theaters, and many regional houses in addition to performers, playwrights, designers, and plays; included are some assessments of careers. The entries tend to be brief. On the other hand, entries now exist for movements and subjects, including Asian-American theater, AIDS, and the American theater and Hispanic-American theater. The online edition has extensive hyperlinks to other entries in the volume. The printed version does not have an index, but because all the entries are in alphabetical order, most actors, theater, shows, or playwrights will be easy to find, provided the user knows the spelling. Also, the print volume has "see" references where no full entry on a person appears.

8-47. The Shuberts Present: 100 Years of American Theater. Maryann Cach, Reagan Fletcher, Mark E. Swartz, and Sylvia Wang. New York: Harry N. Abrams, Inc., 2001.

This coffee-table-ready volume presents material from the Shubert Archives; its authors are staff members. Starting in 1900, the Shubert brothers built an empire of theater ownership based on Broadway, and in the 1970s, the papers and memorabilia of the corporation were consolidated into archives by the Shubert Foundation. This book begins with the story of the organization, including family photos, posters, and publicity material. It then moves uptown, starting with 45th Street, to present histories and photos of each Shubert Theater, including former out-of-town theaters. The production photos from shows at each theater and architectural details of the theaters are unique aspects of this work. The volume has a table of contents for access by theater as well as an index for access by name, show title, or other topic. Lists include one of all Shubert theaters, past and present, with an asterisk marking theaters still owned by the organization. A similar resource, the book *At This Theatre: 100 Years of Broadway Shows, Stories and Stars* (Applause Theatre and Cinema Books, 2002), describes informally the history of forty active Broadway theaters, among them those owned by the Shuberts and other organizations, and includes many illustrations.

8-48. Theater Photography From the Theresa Helburn Collection. Bryn Mawr, PA: Tryptich Tri-College Digital Library. http://triptych.brynmawr.edu

Helburn, a Bryn Mawr graduate, co-founded the Theatre Guild in New York, worked there for many years, and gave her memorabilia collection to her alma mater. Many of the photos now are online. The collection features more than 1,100 photos from productions produced by the guild, including *Oklahoma*. Unfortunately, many of the photos are restricted to library patrons. The photos are searchable by keywords. In addition, "19th Century Actors and Theater Photographs" at the University of Washington (http://content.lib.washington.edu/19thcenturyactorsweb/) presents a series of more than six hundred photos of U.S. theatrical figures searchable by name and profession; for example, "comedians" or "dramatists."

8-49. Theatre Research Resources in New York City. Amy Hughes. New York: Martin E. Segal Theatre Center Publications, 2004.

Researchers headed to New York City or needing primary sources on American theater can use this booklet to ascertain which theater collection may hold what they're looking for. The publication is the product of the doctoral program in theater at the City University Graduate Center and lists alphabetically libraries, collections, or museums. For those collections, it lists contact information, addresses, operating hours, and what their collections hold, including notes on what's accessible and catalogued. The slim volume contains a table of contents listing the collections covered in the text for a quick perusal.

8-50. Theatre World. Ben Hodges and Scott Denny, eds. (v. 66, 2009–2010). 1944/45– . Montclair, NJ: Applause Theatre & Cinema Books; Milwaukee, WI: an imprint of Hal Leonard Corp., 2010.

A favorite of browsers and scholars alike, this source offers photos from theater productions in New York City and, to a lesser extent, the rest of the United States for each theatrical season. After starting in the 1940s as *Theatre World*, it changed its name often, usually to honor its longtime editor, as in *John Willis' Theatre World*. Ben Hodges took over as editor in chief in 1998, and Willis now is listed as editor emeritus. For many years published by Crown, *Theatre World* now comes out under the imprimatur of Applause. The annual undertaking provides the most vivid pictorial depiction of the theatrical season in the United States, drawing from thousands of photographs sent in by press agents and resident theaters. The work now includes extensive off-off Broadway company listings as well as synopses of shows. As before, the book lists cast and crew credits including designers, stage managers, publicity agents, among others for each show, the theater in which it played, and the number of performances. The Broadway entries are chronological by opening date; the off-off Broadway and regional entries are by company. Lists of awards and obituaries complete the work.

Broadway

This section contains general works about Broadway. Musical theater is placed within the Music chapter (9) entries 9-103 through 9-113.

8-51. Internet Broadway Database. www.ibdb.com. Karen Hauser, conception and direction; Jennifer Stewart, manager. New York: The Broadway League in association with Theatre Development Fund and New York State.

This free Web resource is probably the single greatest advance in theater reference in the 21st century. The easily searchable site provides access to hundreds of Broadway production cast and crew lists. The Broadway League's research department began processing and expanding the data for the site in 1996; the data are gleaned primarily from opening-night programs. As the League continues to input productions, the scope of the resource now goes back to the 19th century while moving forward, adding new productions as they open on Broadway. The productions covered are limited to those that appeared on Broadway. Students need to realize this fact when they research any of the figures found on this site; the credits probably include only a fraction of their output. Also, because the resource is produced by one entity and not in a vast, Wiki-like collaboration such as the Internet Movie Database, biographical materials on individuals generally is limited to their credits, and many names have no attached biographies. For a given show, statistics show how many performances the original ran as well as the much later revival. A pop-up provides information on cast changes during the run as well as the list of musical numbers from the program. In addition to "title page" credits for shows, practically all professional practitioners on each production are findable for each production, including fight captain, marketing, puppet designer, and dialect coach. The site is constructed with an eye toward usability. A FAQ and contact list are easily found on the site's tabs as well as a feedback form and a handy orientation guide under "help."

Tony Awards. The American Theatre Wing. http://www.tonyawards.com

The American Theatre Wing for more than 70 years has been dedicated to celebrating excellence and supporting education in the theatre through programs and activities which help students, audiences and members of the theatrical community "to learn more about what makes theatre tick from the people who make it so vital." The Tony Awards got their start in 1947, when the Wing established an awards program to celebrate excellence in the theatre. The award is named for Antoinette Perry (Toni), an actress, director, producer, and the "dynamic wartime leader of the American Theatre Wing." The official medallion of the Tony awards depicts the masks of comedy and tragedy on one side and the profile of Antoinette Perry on the other. The awards are presented annually by Tony Award Productions, a joint venture of The Broadway League and the American Theatre Wing. The two organizations have jointly administered the Tonys since 1967, the year of the first Tony telecast. Under *Tony Legacy*, the website lists all the nominees and winners from its inception in 1947. (http://www.tonyawards.com/en_US/index.html)

8-52. Broadway: An Encyclopedia. Ken Bloom. New York: Routledge, 2004.

This work presents long articles on just about every Broadway theater and many selected theater professionals. Most Broadway practitioners are covered in entries on the theaters in which their efforts went on display. The book opens with a description of the work as a reference source (more for browsing than scholarship) along with a brief history of how the theater district gradually moved uptown to its current position in the West 40s. Entries are in alphabetical order by subject (thus Rodgers and Hammerstein are in the Rs), and an index provides access by shows or names that appear in the entries. The book is a fun, interesting read, as well as a serious information source.

8-53. Broadway Musicals and Plays: Descriptions and Essential Facts of More Than 14,000 Shows Through 2007. Thomas S. Hischak. Jefferson, NC: McFarland & Company, 2009.

This reference work, drawn from a number of sources, including *Theatre World* and previous works by Stanley Green and Gerald Bordman, describes each Broadway production, be it play or musical, from 1919 to the present. The first part of the book offers descriptive paragraphs on each show; they are arranged in alphabetical order, so a user seeking a specific play or musical should be able to find it easily. Revivals are listed beneath the main entry. The second part arranges the titles chronologically, so users can see when the shows opened. The long index provides access to the entries by actor, director, or writer depending if that information appears in the descriptions.

8-54. The Routledge Guide to Broadway. Ken Bloom. New York, NY: Routledge, 2007.

The history of Broadway is condensed here in an introduction and a series of dictionary-like entries in alphabetical order, mixing theaters, composers, playwrights, performers, lyricists, and producers. The entries are informative and brief descriptions of the major events in individual theaters or in the careers of Broadway figures. The volume is most useful for the descriptions of Broadway theaters of the past and the present. Large academic libraries probably will have reference works that go far beyond this offering, but the book may be useful for public libraries and smaller collections.

Drama, Theory, and Criticism

8-55. The Columbia Encyclopedia of Modern Drama. Gabrielle H. Cody and Evert Sprinchorn, eds. New York: Columbia University Press, 2007. 2 vols.

This encyclopedia presents articles on playwrights, plays, and companies that have influenced major trends in dramatic literature and performance, starting with Henrik Ibsen and continuing to the present day. Probably the most important aspect of this encyclopedia is how the authors of the articles place the play, the movement, or the playwright into a historical context, allowing users to gain an understanding of works beyond names and dates. The preface notes the departure of the encyclopedia from other theater references with its emphasis on dramaturgy. The editors include many more obscure authors from around the world, including African and South American playwrights. This two-volume set is strictly alphabetical, scattering individuals and plays among longer articles on national drama histories and movements. The index features a list of the entries in alphabetical order, repeating the arrangement of the volumes, and a more helpful index that gives page numbers for people, plays, and other figures.

8-56. Critical Survey of Drama. 2nd rev. ed. Carl Rollyson, ed. Pasadena, CA: Salem Press, 2003. 8 vols.

This edition combines the *Critical Survey of Drama English Language Series* and *Foreign Language Series*. This extensive work amounts to an encyclopedia of drama: The revised edition contains 602 essays, of which 538 examine individual dramatists, from Aeschylus to Christopher Durang, and 64 cover broad topics. This revised edition completes a series of revamping for Salem's series of critical surveys of literature, including *Critical Survey of Long Fiction* (entry 5-63) and *Critical Survey of Poetry* (entry 5-172). After a list of contributors (more than 350 academics) and a table of contents listing featured dramatists and topics, the book launches into its essays, arranged alphabetically by dramatist. The resource is international in scope. The entries list dates, and places of birth and death; a list of principal dramas with production and publication dates; and descriptions of their achievements and biography. Later, playwrights get photos with their entries. After the biographies, the contributors offer analyses of the writers' careers as well as descriptions of individual plays and how they fit into the authors' overriding themes. The entries end with a list of other major works and a bibliography of criticism. Volumes 7 and 8 contain overviews on American and British drama, European Drama, World Drama, Dramatic Genres, and Dramatic Techniques. Each is broken down into subcategories, such as Restoration Drama, Spanish Drama Since the 1600s, and Adapting Novels to the Stage. A large contingent of access aids brings up the rear: an overall bibliography; a timeline of dramatic milestones; chronological, geographical, and categorized lists of playwrights; and a subject index, which includes playwright names. These volumes provide a comprehensive look at major and some nearly forgotten dramatists as well as solid overviews of dramatic ideas. The essays that place the playwrights in context and the extensive indexing offer quick access to the great figures, movements, and ideas of playwriting.

8-57. Drama Criticism. Janet Witalic, ed. Farmington Hills, MI: Gale Group, 1983– .

Each volume in this continuing series features in-depth coverage of three to 10 playwrights combined with an extensive index of cumulative authors, topics, nationality, and title indices that cover the full range of Gale publications on literature, including *Contemporary Authors, World Literature Criticism,* and *Literature and its Times.* Beginning students may find the author index a bit troublesome to use, particularly with its extensive use of confusing acronyms, which sends searchers back frequently to the keys. The cumulative title index, however, is especially helpful, because it guides students to articles on authors by way of title, in case the playwright of a particular work is not known. If libraries are collecting the full print set, they need to start at the beginning; one or two volumes aren't all that useful, because they deal with so few writers and refer to the rest of the collection frequently. Volumes 21 and 22, for example, feature only four dramatic figures. The introductions to the volumes state clearly the intent of the volumes and contain a helpful paragraph on how to cite the essays contained in the volumes.

   The entries themselves divide into a biographical introduction, including an overview of critical reception, principal works, general commentary, and commentary on individual titles. Libraries may have discontinued subscriptions to the series because the material in *Drama Criticism,* along with many of Gale's other series, is available online as part of Gale's Literature Resource Center (entry 2-16). The Literature Resource Center features a guided tour to show students how to use the resources, but the Gale interface is straightforward and productive; results are broken down by type, literature criticism, biographies, overviews, news and reviews, primary sources and multimedia.

8-58. Drama for Students: Presenting Analysis, Context and Criticism on Commonly Studied Dramas. Anne Marie Hacht, project editor. Detroit: Gale. Monographic series.

Each volume in the series features coverage of 14 or 15 plays with an eye toward interpreting the dramatic works for students in literature classes. Entries feature an introduction about the play's place in the dramatic canon; a biography of the playwright; a synopsis of the play; a breakdown of the characters; and critical analysis, focusing on themes, style, criticism, a bibliography, historical context, suggestions for reading, and topics for further study. Short, signed critical essays are included; the authors are academics and theater professionals. The style of the articles is fairly simple, so the resource is useful for high school students. The volumes have a cumulative author and title index, so users can find which volume contains the play or playwright they seek. Online, the volume also contains a glossary of literary terms, a subject and theme index, and a cumulative ethnicity and nationality index. Online access serves this reference well, because users can access articles from all the volumes at once. As of 2010, the series was up to Volume 28.

8-59. Masterplots II: Drama Series, Revised Second Edition. Christian H. Moe, ed. Pasadena, CA: Salem Press, 2004. 4 vols.

This *Masterplots* is one of 17 in a series of Salem Press literary reference works. The scope of *Masterplots II* has no overlap with the 1996 *Masterplots: 1,801 Plot Stories and Critical Evaluations of the World's Finest Literature*, which carries about 400 play titles. The current drama volume features plays most-often studied in colleges and high schools, according to the Publisher's Introduction. The revised edition adds 92 titles, including 20 produced after 1990. The plays in *Masterplots II* are arranged alphabetically across the four volumes. After a list of play titles used as a table of contents in the first volume, the books break the plays down by title (alternative titles included), type of plot (political, melodrama, absurdist or expressionist, for example), time of plot (when the play occurs), locale, date and location of first production, and first printing. The editors then provide a cast of characters, a detailed plot synopsis, and an analysis of the play's meaning, theatrical devices, context, and further resources. The entries on each play are about four or five pages long and are provided by more than 200 academics. Most of the plays were written in the 20th century. The fourth volume provides key tools for multiple access points for *Masterplots II*: A chronology of the plays summarized in the volumes; a list of screen adaptations of the plays; a list of play titles in *Masterplots, Revised Second Edition* in case a user doesn't find the title she or his is looking for; an author index; and a Type of Plot (or genre) index. Although no substitute for reading the plays, *Masterplots II* will give users an idea of what the play's about, a rudimentary overview of its place in the dramatic canon, and an idea if the script is worth checking out, reading in full, or even producing.

8-60. Theatre in Theory: 1900–2000: An Anthology. David Krasner, ed. Malden, MA.: Blackwell Publishing, 2008.

This volume takes a more conventional approach to anthologizing theatrical theory than *Twentieth-Century Theatre: A Sourcebook* (entry 8-62). The scope of this volume reaches from 1900 to some essays written after 2000. The Table of Contents lists the theorists and the essays from which excerpts are drawn; Krasner places the essays in chronological order for more intuitive access. Each entry begins with a biographical examination of the author, then presents the author's words. An index will aid users in finding names and titles included in the essays. Krasner also includes a breakdown of author by movement (Avant-Garde and Happenings, Comedy, Feminism and Queer Theory, and so forth) and a bibliography.

8-61. Theatre/Theory/Theater: The Major Critical Texts From Aristotle and Zeami to Soyinka and H el. Daniel Gerould, ed. New York: Applause Books, 2000.

This volume tries to fill a gap in theater reference as an introductory anthology to theories of drama and theater. It begins with Aristotle's *Poetics* and the *Natyasastra* by Bhararta, then moves on to No drama, theories about theater brought about by the Renaissance revivals of the art in Europe, and "The Whole Art of the Stage," an essay by Francois Hedelin describing neoclassical drama. The volume then has significant essays on Romanticism ("The Stage as a Moral Institution" by Schiller), naturalism and modernism ("Naturalism in the Theatre" by Emile Zola), and twentieth-century musings by Gordon Craig and Bernard Shaw. Gerould's introduction places the works in context. Unfortunately, much larger anthologies, including *Dramatic Theory and Criticism: Greeks to Grotowski* by Bernard F. Dukore, are out of print, so Gerould's volume will suffice for librarians building a new collection.

8-62. Twentieth-Century Theatre: A Sourcebook. Richard Drain, ed. New York: Routledge, 1995.

Because the volume's scope encompasses the twentieth century, the book can provide many more voices than a work attempting to span all of theater history. The volume is not arranged chronologically; instead, Drain has arranged the readings by themes. An easily scanned table of contents and an index provide access by author, play title, terms, and genres (comedy, for example), and company names. The snippets of theatrical commentary, ranging from theories of the stage to directions on how to present a theatrical protest-event for optimum media coverage, are very brief, rarely longer than two pages. These pieces may not be enough to give the user a robust knowledge of the chosen practitioner or theorist's ideas; but the snippets are ideal for use by the Internet generation, and the volume presents biographical paragraphs for each author and an extensive bibliography.

Plays and Playwrights

8-63. Doollee.com. Weymouth, Dorset, UK: Julian Oddy. http://www.doollee.com/index.htm

The "about" section of this website admits that this database is the avocation of Oddy, who aims to catalog all plays by playwrights from 1956 to the present. He lists more than 100,000 modern plays and hundreds of playwrights. The site, however, does not appear to have a search engine. Instead, Doollee has a clickable alphabet that acts as an index. Because the playwrights are alphabetized left-to-right in tables rather than down rows, searchers may find the playwrights index difficult to use. Also, many entries give merely a title and some idea of where the first production took place. Other titles, more fully presented, offer character breakdowns, first publications, and plot summaries. The site also lends access to the plays list by character name and offers a list of theaters, play publishers, and literary agents as well. Where possible, Doollee also includes contact or agent information for the playwrights and invites authors to apply for inclusion. Unfortunately, the table format for organizing information on each playwright makes the website difficult and confusing to read. As a supplement to the Plays Index, this site will work for searchers looking for more obscure playwrights or plays.

8-64. Dramatists Play Service. New York: Dramatists Play Service. http://www.dramatists.com/

Dramatists Play Service, one of the main licensers of stock and amateur rights for plays, was formed in 1938 by members of the Dramatists Guild. The service also publishes plays in acting editions, thus making it, along with Samuel French, one of the key play publishers in the United States. The service's website offers an extensive search engine called the Play Finder, in which users may seek out plays by title, author, keyword, and cast breakdown. The advantage of this site is that it gives searchers access to many plays not produced on Broadway and some hot-off-the-stage plays; a few haven't even been published in book form yet. Given the scope of the search is limited to those plays Dramatists Play Service handles, this resource is extremely helpful for patrons producing plays on the amateur stage, readers looking for playscripts, or for students keeping up on contemporary drama. This volume has worth, both for a theater and in a literature reference collection.

8-65. Dramatists Sourcebook. 25th ed. New York: Theatre Communications Group, 2008.

This perennial guide published by Theatre Communications Group provides pertinent information for beginning playwrights: who produces new works, how to get an agent, and where to apply for prizes, grants (both from private foundations and state arts agencies), writers' colonies and membership organizations. Just about all the theaters listed in the 25th edition, members of the service organization for regional theaters, do not take unsolicited scripts, but many do take synopses and several pages of dialog. The book is useful as a directory of theaters in the United States that handle new work. The list of agents is handier, especially with the prolog describing how to approach an agent. The special-interest index breaks down theaters and organizations down by what kinds of plays they support, e.g., Hispanic, translations, and their nature, e.g., nonprofit, university-based theater which is a useful companion to the general index. The 25th edition includes a how-to introduction by Tony Kushner, author of the *Angels in America* plays.

8-66. Inter-Play. Portland, Ore.: Portland State University. http://www.lib.pdx.edu/systems/interplay/

This free Internet resource at Portland State University offers a quick way of looking up a play by author or title; a search brings up a simple list of manifestations complete with Portland State's Library of Congress classification number and title, publisher, and year of the volume or journal in which the title appears. The humanities librarians at Portland State created the database, which contains more than 44,000 play citations. The library's Web site notes that the database is updated regularly, although some recent titles, including the Pulitzer-winner *Rabbit Hole* by David Lindsay-Abaire, were not listed. Basically, the database provides a quick assurance that a play exists and enough information with which to search Amazon.com or WorldCat.

8-67. The Ivan R. Dee Guide to Plays and Playwrights. Trevor R. Griffiths. Chicago: Ivan R. Dee, 2003.

Griffiths has compiled an annotated guide for more than 550 playwrights. The orientation of the volume is toward the London theater. Contemporary American playwrights, including Wendy Wasserstein, Christopher Durang, Richard Greenberg, and Eric Overmyer, are presented within the context of which plays have been performed in London. Each entry (most are no more than a quarter-page) includes a brief critical evaluation of the playwright, a list of plays, and a list of "Try these" plays related to the themes of the playwrights in the entries. The book includes a how-to-use paragraph and an extensive index for access by terms or names other than the playwrights.

8-68. Notable Playwrights. Carl Rollyson, ed. Pasadena, CA: Salem Press, 2005. 3 vols.

This highly focused reference work provides extensive biographies of 106 playwrights. The editors culled the biographies from Salem's more extensive *Critical Survey of Drama, Revised Edition* (entry 8-56). The introduction notes that most of the playwrights are from the United States or Great Britain, but a number of playwrights from elsewhere are featured, including Aeschylus, Yukio Mishima, and Moliere. Contributors are drawn from a range of universities in the academic community, including some independent scholars. Each section begins with the principal works by the playwright, followed by entries on works in other literary forms, achievements, biography, and analysis, including paragraphs on major works. This extensive treatment will aid students in beginning to study major playwrights; the bibliographies at the conclusion of each playwright's entry will be helpful. The list of playwrights chosen seems somewhat eclectic; Stephen Sondheim is included, for example, but not Oscar Hammerstein. The third volume has a wealth of ancillary material including a Dramatic Terms and Movements glossary and playwright indexes by geography and category, i.e., absurdist and restoration comedy.

8-69. The Oxford Dictionary of Plays. Michael Patterson. New York: Oxford University Press, 2005.

Patterson presents what amounts to an annotated list of the 1,000 key plays in world theater, covering every era from the Greeks to *Angels in America*. The plays are presented alphabetically by title, but the author presents a number of alternative access tools. The first breaks the plays down by era in a section called "Plays Selected for Entry." He then provides an index of characters, so users can find the plays in which Willy Loman and Falstaff appear, and an index of playwrights. Entries for each play list the playwright, the date, and location of the first production, if known; the date of publication; the date of translation into English if applicable; a description of the genre; the setting; the cast breakdown by sex; a brief summary of the plot; and, finally, a brief overview of the play's significance. The paperback edition is titled *The Oxford Guide to Plays*; its description appears identical to this volume.

Performances and Performers

8-70. Enter the Actors: New York Stage Actors in the Twentieth Century. Thomas S. Hischak. Landham, MD: Scarecrow Press, 2003.

This book goes the Internet Broadway Database one step further. It provides short biographies for 986 New York stage actors and a list of shows they appeared in during the twentieth century. The author adds a number of asides about each performer that lend depth and charm to an otherwise dry listing of birth dates and list of appearances. This reference will supplement online databases, giving students additional information on performers they may encounter in cast lists.

8-71. Profiles of African American Stage Performers and Theatre People, 1816–1960. Bernard L. Peterson Jr. Westport, CT: Greenwood Press, 2001. (5th and final volume in Greenwood Press's series of reference works on African-American theater).

Theater fans may get lost in this volume, because of the wealth of information not found elsewhere. The book provides biographical information on 340 African-American theater artists who flourished during the time period in the title, with additional names in two appendices: a list of 100 names of people mentioned in the main entries, and a list of 320 additional figures. An introduction notes that the scope of the volume ends in 1960 because African-American entertainers after 1960 are documented heavily in other volumes. Main entries include a summary that hits the highlights of the stage professional's career, then goes into details on birth, education, and major achievements. The main entries are in strict alphabetical order, as are the appendices. Appendix C offers a classified list of artists by discipline, including composers, critics, singers, television/radio performers and professionals, and so forth, although without page references. An extensive list of abbreviations used in the biographies is followed by authors and a long catalogue of symbols showing how to interpret the many dots, squares, and bold-type listings used in the text. A useful index, including play titles, is provided, offering fast access to specific terms within the biographies, as is a bibliography. This volume may be the only source for information on many of these key figures in American theater history.

8-72. The Gay and Lesbian Theatrical Legacy: A Biographical Dictionary of Major Figures in American Stage History in the Pre-Stonewall Era. Billy J. Harbin, Kim Marra and Robert A. Schanke, eds. Ann Arbor, MI: University of Michigan Press, 2005.

The introduction notes that this book is the third in a series on gays and lesbians in the American theater brought out by the University of Michigan Press, called *Triangulations: Lesbian/Gay/Queer Theater/Drama/Performance*. More than 50 academics contributed to the volume. The dictionary describes the lives of a series of gay theatrical personalities, openly or not, with some figures from music and dance. The problem the volume takes on involves whom to include. The scope of the volume takes into account figures who flourished before 1969, but the editors do include some individuals who came later. The biographies stress how the subjects' sexuality affected their work and their lives. The entries are alphabetical by artist, but the editors also include a breakdown of subjects by profession and an index. Most of the entries include photos.

Stagecraft, Production, and Education

8-73. **Back Stage Actors' Handbook.** Sherry Eaker, ed. New York: Back Stage Books, 2004.

Eaker, longtime editor of *Back Stage*, the weekly newspaper that theater people in New York and Los Angeles consult for happenings and auditions, has compiled a reference source for actors making contacts with casting agents, directors, producers, acting teachers, and a host of other people who may help them with their careers. Like the newspaper, the book contains a lot of advertising, and contacts may go out of date. A Table of Contents gives users access to the book's clearly outlined subjects: Training, Basic Tools (head shots, resumes, promotion, money), Finding the Work (agents, auditions), The Work (descriptions of how to break into soaps, commercials, student films, cruises, and other venues open to fresh faces), and The Life (advice on how to get by in New York, Los Angeles, and less expensive places). The *Handbook* has no index, but the back of the book has directories of theater companies and casting directors and talent agents.

8-74. **The Back Stage Guide to Stage Management: Traditional and New Methods for Running a Show From First Rehearsal to Last Performance.** 3rd ed. Thomas A. Kelly. New York: Back Stage Books, 2009.

This updated volume by Kelly, a professional stage manager for more than 40 years, presents a how-to manual for anyone who wants to take on the responsibilities for this critical and difficult assignment. Primarily a textbook, the volume contains a glossary of theater-management terms, including "Sitzprobe," a sit-down reading of a score with the singers, and "brush-up rehearsals," a run-through of a long-running show to rid the production of actors' bad habits. In addition to an index, this volume contains several graphics, many in the appendices, showing examples of production schedules, cue sheets, prompt books, and automation diagrams. In effect, the volume represents a comprehensive description of just about all backstage activities.

8-75. **The Directory of Theatre Training Programs: Profiles of College and Conservatory Programs Throughout the United States.** P.J. Tumielewicz and Peg Lyons. Dorset, VT: Theatre Directories, 2007.

The reference book contains listings for more than 475 conservatory and college training programs as well as more than 440 summer theaters and 85 summer training programs, according to a Theatre Directories release. An index provides access to the degrees offered by the institutions, and the articles offer information on admissions, programs and philosophy.

8-76. **Encyclopedia of Stage Lighting**. Jody Briggs. Jefferson, NC: McFarland & Co., 2003.

Briggs, a lighting designer, has compiled a dictionary-like reference that defines many key terms in stage lighting. The author organizes the book alphabetically by entry title; the entries range from short definitions of devices to long descriptions of how to plot lights or, more useful to the general reader, the kinds of lighting used for different styles of theater and difficult lighting problems. In addition, readers can learn how to use trigonometry in calculating lighting coverage and the basics of computer-based light boards. The highly technical nature of theatrical lighting, which must be learned from the ground up with heavy emphasis on practice, means that a textbook will be more helpful for the beginning lighting student. This volume goes way beyond what a stage crew member needs to know about stage lighting. The book lacks an index but has a bibliography.

8-77. Illustrated Theatre Production Guide. John Holloway. Woburn, MA: Focal Press, 2002.

This is an illustrated how-to reference for people building stage sets. The volume begins with a description of theater types (proscenium, thrust, theater in the round, and so forth) and an extensive breakdown and description of theatrical equipment, including rigging, draperies and drops, hardware, ropes and knot tying, and hand tools. Holloway describes how to build flats, doors and windows, steps, platforms, coffin locks, and a host of other designs and devices, all under the philosophy of simple construction done in a shop, then hoisted or carried onto the stage for final assembly.

8-78. Making Stage Props: A Practical Guide. Andy Wilson. Ramsbury, Marlborough, Wiltshire: Crowood, 2003.

This book by a British property master outlines the fundamentals of building stage props. It includes an introduction that describes when props should be built and not rented or bought (unavailable, too costly, or thrown about the stage), then gives detailed descriptions of construction in such chapter titles as Working with Mild Steel, Modeling, and Upholstery. Illustrations help prop makers visualize what they need to do. The volume is more how-to book than reference source, but a glossary and index will allow readers to look up techniques, tools, or items they may need to accomplish backstage tasks. The supplier section lists U.K. firms.

8-79. Producing Theatre: A Comprehensive Legal and Business Guide. 3rd rev. ed. Donald C. Farber. Pompton Plains, NJ: Limelight Editions, 2006.

This book describes the producing process from obtaining a property to opening night, royalties, and beyond. The volume's extensive appendices contain sample contracts and agreements for musicals and plays that will be of help to anyone interested in the creative artist-producer relationship; they include the Literary Purchase Agreement, the Collaboration Agreement, Limited Liability, Articles of Organization, and the Approved Production Contract for Plays from the Dramatists Guild. The Table of Contents lists the broad categories of the chapters, after which Farber goes into detail on all manner of possible producing activities—adapting a work in the public domain for the stage, for example, or signing contracts with theaters and professional unions, or coveted movie deals and how producers participate in them. The volume lacks an index, but the Table of Contents should be a sufficient navigation tool.

8-80. Stage Makeup. 10th ed. Richard Corson, Beverly Gore Norcross and James Glavan. Boston: Allyn & Bacon, 2009.

The latest edition of the classic makeup reference adds more than 100 new images and expands references to new products and websites. The volume is arranged by process. Part One describes Basic Principles (Bones of the Face, Construction of a Head) and moves through Light and Shade, Color in Pigment, and Lighting and Makeup. Part Two goes into planning, including relating the makeup to character. Part Three, the longest part, deals with applications and covers equipment, stippling—meaning pressing makeup on rather than painting, modeling, prosthetics, facial hair, hair and wigs, makeup for film and television, and nonrealistic makeup, e.g., zombies, the Wicked Witch of the West, and Fagin. An extensive list of appendices includes a Health and Safety section and makeup fashions through the ages, up to the twentieth century. A table of contents and an index of illustrations help users access information in the volume by subject and photo, and an index at the back aids in more specific searches. Some sections are arranged alphabetically, including Appendix A (Makeup Materials, arranged by name of substance or function); others are in order of process. This volume is an essential reference for any library attached to a theater department with an active production program.

8-81. **Theatrecrafts.** com. http://www.theatrecrafts.com/index.shtml

Although the site does not seem to have an "about" page, it does provide links to dozens of sites with information on theater crafts, including production management, makeup, scenery, lighting, and stage humor.

8-82. **The What, Where, When of Theatre Props**. Thurston James. Cincinnati, OH: Betterway Books, 1992.

This fascinating, five-part reference work attempts to label material objects by when they were introduced into civilization. This seemingly vast undertaking is useful to property masters who want to avoid anachronism, having someone in a play set in medieval times, like *Beckett*, use a fork, for example. The author, a former property master, draws from a clips file he maintained to help him get period accoutrements right. James divides the material into five categories: daily living (by far the longest), civil authority (standards, flags and, most intriguingly, punishments), warfare, science and technology, and religion. Under food, James outlines when forks, spoons, and knives came into use in the West and when such potables as beer from grains and bourbon were invented. Particularly interesting are the charts James includes to show when furniture and games came into fashion or were invented. Use of this book can extend into all areas of creative endeavor, including the writing of historical fiction and the study of nutrition, military history, or religious practice. The book comes with line illustrations, particularly helpful in areas that have little to do with everyday life, as in the alchemy section.

INTERNATIONAL THEATER RESOURCES

8-83. **Who's Who in Contemporary World Theatre**. Daniel Meyer-Dinkgrafe, ed. New York: Routledge, 2000.

The volume covers more than 1,400 living theatrical artists from around the world as of the publication date. A large number of academic contributors provided entries in the volume. Oddly, the Who's Who excludes artists who work primarily in musicals. The entries add some interpretation and context to artists' careers to accompany the artists' educational profile and major works or credits. Its comprehensiveness, within its scope, make it a useful, if rapidly dating, theater resource.

Asian Theater Resources

8-84. **Encyclopedia of Asian Theatre**. Samuel L. Leiter, ed. Westport, CT: Greenwood Press, 2007. 2 vols.

This attractively bound and moderately illustrated two-volume encyclopedia fills in a gap in many collections for information on theater in Asia, particularly performance outside China and Japan. The scope of the encyclopedia, however, comprises East, Southeast and South Asia while excluding the Middle East. The contributors list includes authorities in Southeast Asian theater, ritual and healing; Sanskrit theater; and Balinese dance drama. An unusual aspect of this resource lies in the taxonomy the editors use to organize the entries. Although alphabetically arranged, the editors use such general topics as acting, directing, and experimental theater as subject headings, and then break each down into national or cultural entries. Because the editors also include entries on individual nations, artists and theatrical styles scattered alphabetically through the general-topic entries, users will have to look in many places throughout the volume to get a full picture of theater in a particular country. Entries on individuals and theatrical styles will be of most interest to a leisurely browser, while the topical entries will aid theater students studying a particular craft or subject. The volume features a bibliography and an index.

8-85. Historical Dictionary of Japanese Traditional Theatre. Samuel L. Leiter. Lanham, MD: Scarecrow Press, 2006 (Historical Dictionaries of Literature and the Arts, no. 4*)*.

The dictionary deals mainly with the traditional Japanese theater forms of Bunraku, Kabuki, Kyogen, and No, or Noh. The volume begins with a chronology that traces key developments in these four pre-modern genres from 1301 through the war periods to the present and includes measures the American occupation took to ban plays with content deemed too feudal. The introduction reproduces some of the material in narrative form and gives readers a broad overview of Japanese theater history, including brief histories of no and bunraku (puppet theater). Alphabetically arranged entries on practitioners, plays, stage props, and theaters associated with each of the four genres follow. An extensive bibliography is organized by subject; and translations of Japanese play titles, plus a glossary of terms not given their own entries is also included.

8-86. Modern Indian Theatre: A Reader. Nandi Hbatia, ed. New York: Oxford University Press, 2009.

This volume offers a series of essays, excerpts, and theoretical statements in English that describes both historical and contemporary style of performance in India with a scope that reaches back to the late nineteenth century. Particular emphasis is placed on performance after the censorial Dramatic Performances Act of 1876 and subsequent breakouts on the "fringe" of Indian theater starting in the 1960s. The book, printed on thin paper, begins with a table of contents organizing the work into broad categories: History and modernity; Colonial and Nationalist influences; "Interrogating the Nation From the Margins;" "Rethinking the Rural/Urban and the Folk/Classical Binaries in Post-Independence India;" "Language, Myth, and Media;" and a broader end chapter of primary sources called "Statements." This volume goes deeper into Indian theater theory and culture than an encyclopedia, and the essays are academic; references to "orientalism" dot the text. The work features a list of sources from which the essays and documents were taken (as well as bibliographies for individual essays) and a contributors list, but no index. This is not an introductory work.

British Theater Resources

8-87. The Cambridge Companion to Medieval English Theatre. 2nd ed. Richard Beadle and Alan J. Fletcher, eds. New York: Cambridge University Press, 2008.

According to the authors, the second edition adds recent scholarship to the first, including the re-translation or re-editing of medieval play manuscripts and observations taken from attempts to reproduce these plays in performance, complete with music and dance. The book includes a chronological table of roughly when these plays were first performed. The volume consists of a series of essays on different aspects of medieval theater, beginning with an overview and continuing through such subjects as the Chester cycle, morality plays, and saints and miracles, as well as an overview of contemporary productions of these dramas and cycles. The final chapter is on medieval drama criticism. A selected bibliography in the back (including videos of stage productions) will lead scholars to more information. An index is also included.

     Cambridge University Press offers similarly organized theater companions, including *The Cambridge Companion to British Theatre 1730–1830, The Cambridge Companion to Greek and Roman Theatre, The Cambridge Companion to English Restoration Theatre* and *The Cambridge Companion to English Renaissance Drama.* Cambridge also offers companions to several individual or grouped playwrights, including Aphra Behn, Sam Shepard, August Wilson, Tennessee Williams, Caryl Churchill, British female playwrights, Anton Chekov, Samuel Beckett, Greek drama, Tom Stoppard, and Harold Pinter.

8-88. The Cambridge History of British Theatre. Peter Thomson, Vol. 1 (origins to 1660), Jane Milling and Peter Thomson, eds. Vol. 2 (1660–1895), Joseph Donohue, ed. Vol. 3 (since 1895), Baz

Kershaw, ed. Cambridge, U.K.: Cambridge University Press, 2004. 3 vols. Print and e-book in Cambridge Histories Online.

Thomson has supervised a massive three-volume history of British theater from its origins to the present. Each volume has its own editor or editors, and Thomson notes in the General Preface that the work does not shoot for seamlessness; in fact, the volumes are broken down into topic chapters. Chapters vary considerably in scope. Each volume opens with a table of contents, a list of contributors, and a timeline that compares developments in theater to milestones in British history. The chapters offer a solid introduction to the topics covered. At the end, each volume contains an index that refers specifically to its own volume and an extensive bibliography. Photos from across the timeline are included. The fact that the history pauses frequently for looks at years and productions will help users get a fuller picture of theater history during these periods, and with the aid of a reference librarian, students who want more information on these specific productions will find it here.

8-89. The London Theatre Guide. Richard Andrews. London: Metro Publications, 2003.

This pocket-size travel book is ideal for theater tourists headed to London. The book presents a list of London theaters, their history, and seating charts. It has a table of contents and brief biographies of noted theater architects; subsequent entries include descriptions of how to buy (or book) tickets, a map of "theaterland," theater superstitions, tours, and theater shops.

8-90. Modern British Drama: The Twentieth Century. Christopher Innes. New York: Cambridge University Press, 2002.

This volume updates *Modern British Drama, 1890–1990* to include the last decade of the twentieth century. Innes covers a wide range of twentieth-century British dramatists in this volume whose organization is part chronological, part thematic. The opening pages place British drama in historical context and trace its influencers. Playwrights are covered in chapters that are thematic; each chapter begins with a list of the playwright's major works and ends with notes referring to related resources. Included are passages about broader theater movements during the century, including the Workers' Theatre Movement in the 1930s. A table of contents, chronology, a brief bibliography for the playwrights, and an index for more focused access by play title, name or movement complete the work.

8-91. Shakespeare's Theatre: A Dictionary of His Stage Context. Hugh Macrae Richmond. London: Continuum, 2002.

This extensive, encyclopedia-like volume serves as a companion to Shakespeare's plays. If students are reading an annotated or lightly annotated edition of the Bard's works, then this book will be of great use to them. Arranged in alphabetical order, the dictionary defines words and figures from Shakespeare's era in the context of his plays. Richmond provides more material at a website (including production photos) devoted to bibliographies of Shakespeare in performance: Shakespeare's Staging at http://shakespearestaging.berkeley.edu/.

8-92. Victoria and Albert Museum Theatre and Performance Resources. London: Victoria and Albert Museum. http://www.vam.ac.uk/collections/theatre_performance/resources/index.html

The theater collection at the Victoria and Albert (V&A) started with a donation by Gabrielle Enthoven in the 1920s and she continued to add to it after the gift. Some of the material was on display at the Theatre Museum in Covent Garden, which closed in 2007. The collection now is housed back at the Victoria and Albert Museum, which maintains this gateway site to U.K. theater research. The website has a guide to theater and performance research (the site's creators consider the playbill the basic primary resource for theater scholarship), links to more resources as well as descriptions of the V&A collection, and an extensive Theatre & Performance Reading List. Navigation through the site is easy; pages are clearly identified, and several articles are brief to accommodate short Web attention spans. The site's interactive features include a program to browse through the prompt book for the play *Diplomacy;* a History of Musicals; an interactive tour through selections from the Costume Collection; and a history of the circus. The site provides "edutainment" for both the novice and the theater buff. Also of great help is the British Library site *Theatre: Reference Sources* under the Help for Researchers category (http://www.bl.uk/reshelp/findhelprestype/refworks/theatre/theatreref.html). The website offers lists of bibliographies of plays and theater books, dictionaries, encyclopedias, theaters, historical surveys, and Shakespeare. It also has links to performing arts websites in the U.K.

German Theater Resources

8-93. Historical Dictionary of German Theater. William Grange. Lanham, MD: Scarecrow Press, 2006. (Historical Dictionaries of Literature and the Arts series).

This resource is another title in this series of alphabetical listings of plays, theaters, and practitioners in a topic of theater history. This volume's scope reaches back to about 970 with the production of six Latin comedies at a cloister Braunschweig and continues through the emergence of modern German theater in the 1700s and the turbulent twentieth century. The work includes Swiss and Austrian artists who worked in the German language. The dictionary follows the pattern set by others in the series: a timeline, a historical introduction that places the entries in context, the entries, and a lengthy bibliography broken down into subjects. In addition to biographies of stage personalities, the dictionary includes descriptions of theatrical styles and movements. Black and white photos are included.

Latin American Theater Resources

8-94. Encyclopedia of Latin American Theater. Eladio Cortes and Mirta Barrea-Marlys, eds. Westport, CT: Greenwood Press, 2003.

This encyclopedia introduces whole nations and scores of theater artists to the history of world theater. Contributors are mainly from the study of Spanish literature and Latin American theater areas. The volume features an overview of Latin American theater history, which includes Chicano and Nuyorican (Puerto Ricans in New York) theater in the United States, followed by several hundred entries categorized by the country of origin of the playwright. The articles on each country cover the general theater cultures, but the reference itself is weighted toward playwrights and playwright-directors with glances at performers and other theater professionals. The organization of the volume makes for easy access by country and the index is by playwright or play title.

8-95. Latin American Dramatists Since 1945: A Bio-Bibliographical Guide. Tony A. Harvell. Westport, CT: Praeger Publishers, 2003.

Harvell has assembled an annotated list of more than 700 playwrights. The playwrights are numbered in a system with a three-letter abbreviation by nationality followed by the place number within each country. Mario Lage, for example, is assigned MEX 057. Nations are presented in alphabetical order, with the playwrights arranged in alphabetical order by nation. Each entry begins with the name, dates of birth and death, and a brief biography. The entries then list plays and dates, as well as where the play is published, if that information is available. The indexes provide access by playwright and by play title. Spanish is necessary because most of the plays listed in the volume are in Spanish.

Russian Theater Resources

8-96. Historical Dictionary of Russian Theater. Laurence Senelick. Lanham, MD: Scarecrow Press, 2007. (Historical Dictionaries of Literature and the Arts Series, no. 14).

This is a reference volume on Russian drama and theater for users with no Russian; the book first presents a transliteration key from Cyrillic to Roman characters with a pronunciation guide. The structure of the volume echoes that of other dictionaries in the series. Users get a chronology of Russian theater history, starting with the first mention of professional performers in 1068. Several illustrations grace the book's midsection. The entries are divided into four categories: people, theaters, subjects (censorship, for example), and plays. The brief entries give students an introduction to many key figures and movements including the contemporary. Reference materials in the back of the book feature the original names in Cyrillic of the plays cited in the text, and an extensive, categorized bibliography with its own table of contents.

Organizations

8-97. The American Society for Theatre Research. http://www.astr.org

The Society issues a newsletter and the semiannual publication *Theatre Survey*.

8-98. The American Theatre Critics Association (http://www.americantheatrecritics.org/about-atca/) is a national association of professional theatre critics. Membership in the association is open to all those who review theatre and performance for publication.

8-99. The International Federation for Theatre Research.
https://www.firt-iftr.org/en/theatre-research-international

The International Federation for Theatre Research exists to facilitate communication and exchange between scholars of theatre and performance research through its conference events, publishing activities, and website. The organization sponsors *Theatre Research International*, published by the Cambridge University Press.

8-100. The Institute of Outdoor Drama. http://outdoordrama.unc.edu/

The Institute of Outdoor Drama is a public service agency that provides national leadership and coordination of the outdoor drama movement. It provides training, research and advisory programs. It performs as a clearinghouse for activities such as auditioning for summer programs.

8-101. The Theatre Library Association (TLA). http://www.tla-online.org/

TLA includes not only librarians but also actors, booksellers, writers, and researchers in its membership. Located in New York, the Association publishes *Broadside*, a newsletter focusing on performing arts collections, and an annual, *Performing Arts Resources*. TLA also has undertaken other publishing projects, especially notable ones in the preservation and historical areas. Its website also has a number of valuable links to resources on theater and related topics in the performing arts.

CHAPTER 9

MUSIC

Cynthia Miller

INTRODUCTION

Library resources for music are of several kinds. They include musical scores and sheet music both in print and online; books, including reference resources, in print and online; sound recordings in several formats, including compact discs and computer audio files, and sometimes LPs and even older formats; and videos in various formats. People interested in music come to the library to get information about music and musicians, to find music they can listen to, and to borrow music that they can perform.

Musical scores include everything from large orchestral works to solo music, and from popular performing editions to multi-volume scholarly collections. Writings about music encompass the fields of music history, music theory, music education, ethnomusicology, musical performance, acoustics, aesthetics, and many other specialized topics. All of these materials exist in print as well as in digital form.

Computer software and online resources for music are plentiful. Today, most musical scores are produced with computer notation software. *Finale* and *Sibelius* are among the most widely-used notation programs. Most professional composers, arrangers, and music copyists use one of these programs to produce their scores. Computer notation programs are also helpful for music historians and music theorists who include musical examples in their papers and publications. It is a simple matter to merge musical examples in computer notation with a text document.

The prevalence and ease of use of computer notation has resulted in a great deal of self-publishing by numerous composers, from little-known artists to Pulitzer Prize winners. Many composers have their own websites where their music is available for sale. This situation has created a new group of online resources for researchers interested in contemporary music and for librarians wishing to acquire that music. Sometimes the only way to obtain music by a particular composer is to visit that composer's website. Researchers may find that the composer's website is also the best place to find an up-to-date list of the composer's works and an informative biography.

Music research has benefited greatly from the development of online searchable databases. These databases give users access to a wealth of resources. Some of the most important music encyclopedias, bibliographies and catalogs of music, and periodical indexes, as well as the full text of many journals, are now online. This has transformed music research in many ways. To give only one example, in print publications cross references must be looked up in another section or volume of a book; in the online world, cross references can easily be consulted through a system of hyperlinks.

A number of great libraries have digitized portions of their vast music collections and made them available online, often to anyone with an Internet connection. The online resources of the Library of Congress and the British Library are discussed below. Many other online resources are also available.

Among them are the online database of the J. Pierpont Morgan Library (http://www.themorgan .org/music/default.asp) and the Gallica collection online at the Bibliothèque Nationale de France (http://gallica.bnf.fr/?lang=EN). A great deal of printed music can be freely accessed online; for example, the complete new edition of the works of Wolfgang Amadeus Mozart is online at http://dme. mozarteum.at/DME/main/index.php?l&l=2. Additional websites offering free access to music scores in the public domain will be profiled in the entries below.

The availability of streaming and downloadable audio has created new resources for library users. Although libraries still acquire CDs, many also subscribe to one or more streaming audio databases, thereby greatly increasing the number of sound recordings accessible to listeners. A number of these audio databases, both open access and those requiring a subscription, will be discussed in this chapter.

The richness and complexity of music resources make music librarianship a specialized profession. For a good discussion of music libraries, readers may wish to consult the chapter entitled "Music Librarianship," by Holly Gardinier, Sarah R. Canino, and Carl Rahkonen, in the *Encyclopedia of Library and Information Sciences* (3rd ed. 2009). The chapter includes a description of the many different types of music libraries, as well as information on the particular needs and requirements of music libraries in carrying out typical library functions, such as collection management and development, acquisition, cataloging, preservation, and access. Librarians interested in the field should be aware of the Music Library Association (http://www.musiclibraryassoc.org/) and the International Association of Music Libraries at http://www.iaml.info/. See entries 9-165 and 9-166 for descriptions of both of these organizations.

This chapter is organized into six main sections: Online Resources, Print Resources, Special Topics, Libraries, Directories and Career Information, and Organizations. Within each of these sections there are several sub-sections organized either by type of resource, e.g., encyclopedias or by topic, e.g., music history. Often, the search for information will involve making use of several types of resources. Librarians and library users should be aware that music is a subject that can be approached from many angles and through many mediums. Although the entries in this chapter are limited to music resources, it is sometimes advisable to consult more general sources, such as newspapers and newspaper databases to retrieve music-related information.

It is a truism that the moment a book of this type is published, it is out of date. Nevertheless, the author hopes that the materials listed here will provide a good introduction to the field and give some clues about where to look for the new materials that are constantly appearing.

INFORMATION SOURCES IN MUSIC

Online Resources

Users frequently go first to the Internet in their search for information. This section lists many of the major online resources for music. In addition to these sources, faculty, students and researchers may wish to consult the website *Online Resources for Music Scholars*, hosted by Harvard College, at http://hcl.harvard.edu/research/guides/onmusic/. This website provides links to many diverse types of electronic resources, including archival collections, online scores and sound recordings, article indexes, discographies and bibliographies, scholarly societies, and musical reference works. Resources are listed in alphabetical order by title, and the database may be searched via several criteria, including keyword, subject, and resource type. This is an excellent site to search when beginning research on almost any musical topic.

Encyclopedias and Dictionaries

9-1. Grove Music Online (GMO). New York: Oxford University Press, 2001-. Online subscription database at: http://www.oxfordmusiconline.com/public/book/omo_gmo

GMO is currently the most up-to-date, scholarly encyclopedia of music in English, and it is the main resource provided by a subscription to Oxford Music Online (entry 9-2). It includes the full text of the second edition of *The New Grove Dictionary of Music and Musicians* (entry 9-27), as well as *The New Grove Dictionary of Jazz*, 2nd edition (entry 9-96), *The New Grove Dictionary of Opera* (entry 9-116), The *Norton/Grove Dictionary of Women Composers* (entry 9-150) and some entries from the forthcoming second editions of *The New Grove Dictionary of American Music* (entry 9-26) and The *New Grove Dictionary of Musical Instruments* (entry 9-99), as well as most entries from the first editions of these works. GMO is updated on a regular basis and currently includes more than 50,000 signed articles and 30,000 biographies. The contributors are internationally recognized scholars. GMO provides a "What's New" link that gives users access to a list of recently-created entries. The interface offers numerous features, including links to outside sources such as RILM (entry 9-3) and Classical Music Library (entry 9-14). Among the many helpful features is the ability to search the full text of a lengthy article for information about a particular aspect of a topic. The composer works lists are also of primary assistance to students and researchers. This feature will be discussed in greater detail in entry 9-64. Overall, GMO is an outstanding contribution to music research.

9-2. Oxford Music Online (OMO). Oxford: Oxford University Press, 2008– . Online subscription database. http://www.oxfordmusiconline.com

This subscription database provides access to a number of resources. A basic subscription includes GMO (entry 9-1), *The Oxford Companion to Music* (entry 9-29), and *The Oxford Dictionary of Music* (2006). *The Encyclopedia of Popular Music* by Colin Larkin (entry 9-125) may also be added to the subscription. By default, a simple search will search the full text of all resources. It is also possible to limit a search to a particular source. Advanced keyword searches using Boolean operators are also possible. See the entry above for GMO (9-1) for discussion of additional features.

Indexes to Periodical Literature

The databases cited below are the most widely-used periodical indexes for music. All are available through online subscriptions. There are a number of additional databases that also provide access to music materials. Among them are JSTOR (entry 2-43), which provides retrospective coverage with full text to journals in music and related subject areas, and the Arts and Humanities Citation Index (entry 2-1). It is also frequently possible to find citations and full text for music-related articles in large, general databases such as Academic Search Premier.

9-3. Répertoire International de Littérature Musicale (RILM). New York: RILM, 1967-. Online subscription database. http://www.rilm.org
Available from EBSCO at http://www.ebscohost.com/pages/contact-ebsco-publishing.
Also available from ProQuest at http://www.csa.com/contactus/index.php.

RILM Abstracts indexes approximately 700 journals comprehensively, as well as music-related articles in 10,000 non-music journals. The journals indexed originate in 151 countries and are in 214 different languages. RILM's Abstracts are supplied by national committees in approximately 60 countries. RILM provides abstracts in the language of the publication and in English translation. In addition to journals, RILM indexes books, dissertations, films, sound recordings, and electronic resources. The indexing is retrospective to 1967. Of the three databases indexing current literature, RILM is the most scholarly in its orientation and has especially good coverage of musicology and music theory, and offers good user support, including online tutorials and a list of RILM subject headings to facilitate searching.

9-4. International Index to Music Periodicals (IIMP). Ann Arbor, MI: Chadwyck-Healey/Pro-Quest, 1998-. Online subscription database. http://iimp.chadwyck.com/marketing.do

Unlike the other periodical indexes discussed here, IIMP did not begin as a print publication. It was established as an online subscription database in 1998. IIMP offers indexing and abstracts of more than 470 music journals and the full text for approximately 160 of those journals. The database also provides selective indexing, and in many cases, the full text of, articles in 33 non-music publications (such as the *New York Times*, the *Washington Post*, the *Village Voice*, and *Current Biography*). IIMP's coverage of pop music of various kinds is strong, as is its coverage of performers, reviews of performances and recordings, and ethnomusicology. Some indexing is retrospective to 1874. For subscribers to Naxos Music Library (see entry 9-18), it is now possible to link from abstracts in IIMP to relevant audio in Naxos.

A related resource is the International Index to the Performing Arts (entry 7-1). This database provides indexing and abstracts for approximately 270 periodicals covering the performing arts, including dance, film, television, drama, theatre, opera, and musical theatre. Subscribers to this database and IIMP have the ability to search both simultaneously.

9-5. Music Index. EBSCO, 1999– . Online subscription database.
http://www.ebscohost.com/public/music-index

9-6. The Music Index: A Subject Author Guide to Music Periodical Literature. Warren, MI: Harmonie Park Press, 1949–2009.

Music Index began as a print publication in 1949 and became an online service in 1999. At the present time, indexing for the years 1949 through 1970 can be found only in the print edition. Music Index currently provides citations from approximately 800 journals from 40 countries. The Index is now updated weekly and, as of mid-2011, includes abstracts. A broad range of subjects is covered, with good coverage of performance and performers, including reviews of concerts and recordings, and popular music.

9-7. Répertoire International de la Presse Musicale (RIPM). H. Robert Cohen. Baltimore, MD: RIPM, 1988– . Print and also online subscription database at http://www.ripm.org.

RIPM was established in 1988 as a print publication to provide indexing for music periodicals from the nineteenth and early twentieth century and became an online service in 2000, but continued release of print volumes is planned through 2012. Currently, 175 journals are indexed. RIPM is sponsored by several international scholarly organizations, including the International Association of Music Libraries, and UNESCO's International Council for Philosophy and Humanistic Studies. In 2009, full-text coverage was begun for some journals; currently, 100 journals are available in full text, and new titles are added every six months. RIPM is an invaluable resource for scholars conducting research in musical activity in the years 1800 to 1950.

Indexes of Music and Thematic Catalogs

The following entries are online resources for locating and identifying particular pieces of music. ThemeFinder (entry 9-12) and Series AII of RISM (entry 9-11) are thematic catalogs. (See heading for Thematic Catalogs under Print Resources for a description of thematic catalogs.)

9-8. Emusicquest. Donald Reese. Lansdale, PA: Emusicquest, 2000– . Online subscription database. http://www.emusicquest.com

This is a subscription database available either online or on CD-ROM. It includes listings from earlier editions of *Music in Print*, published since 1965, and according to the website, is updated regularly. The database can be searched by categories such as sacred choral, secular choral, organ, classical vocal, string, percussion, orchestral, popular music, etc. The entire database can be searched through the Master Index. Each listing includes instrumentation and publisher contact information as well as the date the information was listed in the database and verified. This is a valuable resource but by no means exhaustive. Works may not be currently available from the publishers listed and small publishers are not indexed. More recent works by living composers may not be listed even though they have been published and are available for sale.

9-9. **The Hymn Tune Index: All Hymns Printed Anywhere in the World with English-Language Texts up to 1820, and Their Publication History up to That Date.** Nicholas Temperley. Urbana; Champaign, IL: University of Illinois at Urbana-Champaign, 2001– . http://hymntune.library.uiuc.edu/default.asp

This free online database is a project of the library at the University of Illinois Urbana-Champaign. The database indexes all hymns with English-language texts found in printed sources published anywhere in the world in or before 1820. Users can search the database in several ways: by the name of the tune, by composer, title, text, and *incipit*. The database began as a print publication, published in 1998 by Oxford University Press. It was converted to an online resource in 2001 and was revised and updated in 2006. Additional updates are planned, with a possible extension of the printed sources date.

9-10. **Index to Printed Music** (IPM). George R. Hill. Ipswich, MA: EBSCO, 2004– . Online subscription database. http://www.ipmusic.org/index.php

This online subscription database makes it possible to search for particular works published in scholarly editions, anthologies, and collections. The database continues and expands on Hill's book described in entry 9-62. It is regularly updated, and currently contains approximately 412,000 index records. It is possible to search the Index by title, composer, librettist, poet, and edition or anthology title. The Names Index allows searches by alternate spellings of a name, and thus makes it possible to retrieve all titles associated with all known spellings of the name. A user can also search by a frequently used title, such as *Missa l'hommearmé*, and find the names of all the composers who wrote a Mass with this title, where each Mass is published, and in what library the manuscript of the work is held. At this point, the index includes very few twentieth-century composers, and for these composers, it is better to consult the works lists in Grove Music Online (entry 9-64).

9-11. **Répertoire International des Sources Musicales/International Inventory of Musical Sources** (RISM). Series AII: Manuscripts by Individual Composers after 1600. Freely available online at http://opac.rism.info, or by subscription through EBSCO at: http://www.ebscohost.com/public/rism-series-a-ii-music-manuscripts-after-1600.

RISM is a large catalog of music, music manuscripts, and writings about music, in both print and manuscript, from ancient times to approximately 1850. (See entry 9-38 for a fuller discussion of the contents of RISM.) RISM is organized in three large series, Series A, B, and C, almost all of which are available only in print. Series AII, however, is online and contains approximately 700,000 entries referencing works by almost 25,000 composers. Most of these works are in manuscript form and are held by libraries and archives worldwide. It is possible to search the database by composer and title, and also by *incipit*. Each record provides information about a work, including an identifying *incipit* and the library which holds the manuscript.

9-12. **ThemeFinder.** David Huron. Stanford, CA: Center for Computer Assisted Research in the Humanities, 1996. http://www.themefinder.org

This online thematic catalog is freely available through collaboration between the Center for Computer Assisted Research in the Humanities at Stanford University and the Cognitive and Systematic Musicology Laboratory at the Ohio State University. At present, there are three searchable databases:

Classical and Instrumental Music, European Folksongs, and Latin Motets from the sixteenth century. Together, these total more than 35,000 themes. Searching the database requires some basic knowledge of musical notation. It is possible to search for the title of a work by entering the intervals or notes of a melody, either by note name or scale degree. It is also possible to search by the contour of a melody. Browsable composer work lists display the *incipits* of the themes of each work included in the database.

Recorded Music, Scores, and Sheet Music

In the United States, music published before 1923 is in the public domain and may be reproduced legally. A number of websites offer digitized musical scores, which may be freely viewed, downloaded and printed. One of these is IMSLP–*Petrucci Music Library* at http://imslp.org/wiki/Main_Page. This website offers free downloads of printed music that is in the public domain. The database includes more than 37,000 works by more than 5,000 composers. *Variations,* a project of Indiana University, offers a website where users can view digitized versions of scores in the collection of the William and Gayle Cook Music Library at http://www.dlib.indiana.edu/variations/scores/bae7451/index.html. Also useful is the Choral Public Domain Library at http://www.cpdl.org, which is a repository of public domain editions of choral and vocal music.

Numerous libraries have digitized sheet music in their collections. A large selection can be found at the Sheet Music Consortium, a cooperative project of several libraries, at http://www.digital.library.ucla.edu/sheetmusic. Also of interest is the Charles H. Templeton Sr. collection at Mississippi State University at http://library.msstate.edu/ragtime/.

9-13. American Song. Online streaming service by subscription.

9-14. Classical Music Library. Online subscription streaming service.

9-15. Classical Scores Library. Online subscription database.

9-16. Smithsonian Global Sound for Libraries. Online streaming service by subscription.
All of the above are available from Alexander Street Press, individually by subscription or through Alexander Street's Music Online Reference package. http://alexanderstreet.com/products/music.htm

American Song is a streaming audio service that includes almost 7,000 albums and approximately 116,000 tracks. The database provides access to a very diverse collection of folk, popular, and religious music, including music of many ethnic groups and geographic regions in a wide variety of styles. Labels providing content include Rounder Records, Appleseed Records, Smithsonian Folkways, and many others.

For Classical Music Library, the publisher has licensed recordings of a number of excellent labels, including EMI, Hänssler Classic, Hyperion, and Virgin Classics. As of this writing, the database includes almost 6,000 albums with approximately 90,000 tracks. It is possible to browse the database by performers, labels, time periods, genres, and so on. Like Naxos (entry 9-18), Classical Music Library offers users the ability to create playlists.

A related service is the Classical Scores Library, which currently offers about 25,000 musical scores for online viewing and study. Coverage is best for scores that are out of copyright, and some copyrighted scores have been licensed as well. Some scores may be downloaded and printed, others may not. Many of the scores are coordinated with tracks in the Classical Music Library.

Smithsonian Global Sound for Libraries is offered in partnership with Smithsonian Folkways and includes recordings from that record label. The database also contains the archival collections of Folkways Records, on-site recordings of African music from the International Library of African Music at Rhodes University, and recordings from the South Asian subcontinent from the

Archive Research Centre for Ethnomusicology. The site offers more than 2,800 albums and almost 41,000 tracks.

The publisher also offers Opera in Video, which will eventually contain 250 operas featuring well-known performers. A streaming video service of classical music performances is forthcoming. Also available are several packages of performances and reference sources designed for use in courses on various topics, including classical music, African-American music, jazz, and world music.

9-17. DRAM (Database of Recorded American Music). New York: Anthology of Recorded Music, 2000– . Online streaming service at: http://www.dramonline.org/.

DRAM is a streaming audio service offered to libraries and other institutions. As a nonprofit organization, the purpose of DRAM is to preserve and disseminate important recordings of American music that may not be commercially viable. As of January 2011, the service offers approximately 3,000 albums from 25 different record labels, including all of the recordings of New World Records and Composers Recordings, Inc. The database includes a great variety of music, from opera and contemporary and historic American classical music, to jazz, Native American, and folk music.

9-18. Naxos Music Library. Online subscription streaming service at: http://www.naxosmusiclibrary.com/home.asp.

This online subscription database provides streaming audio for almost 55,000 CDs, with more than 780,000 tracks. Approximately 800 CDs are added to the database each month. All of the recordings on the Naxos and Marco Polo labels are included, as well as selected recordings from numerous other labels. Music includes standard classical repertoire, but Naxos is especially strong in contemporary music, and includes jazz and some world music. The service offers the ability to create playlists, and a glossary, pronunciation guide, and other supplementary resources are included. Libraries can also subscribe to Naxos Sheet Music, which currently offers approximately 45,000 musical scores that can be downloaded and printed.

PRINT RESOURCES
General Guides to Research

The resources listed here serve two purposes. They provide an overview of the field of music research, of the important areas for music research, as well as descriptions of the diverse types of sources necessary to the study of music. They can also serve as a starting point for research projects of all kinds. Everyone from undergraduate music students to seasoned music professionals will find these resources useful.

9-19. Sourcebook for Research in Music. 2nd ed. Phillip D. Crabtree and Donald H. Foster. 2nd ed. rev. and expanded by Allen Scott. Bloomington: Indiana University Press, 2005.

This resource has become a standard reference work since its first publication in 1993, and the second edition has been updated and expanded. It is a compact but thorough compilation of bibliographic materials of central importance for research in music. The book is divided into eight chapters, each of which treats materials relevant to a particular area of music research. An introductory chapter defines common music bibliographic terms in English, French and German, and presents the Library of Congress and the Dewey Decimal systems of music classification. Chapters 2–7 cover basic bibliographical tools for research in music, area studies, dictionaries and encyclopedias of music, sources treating the history of music, current research journals in music, and editions of music. The authors also do a good job of covering those areas of study that have become especially important in recent years, such as performance practice, and gender and sexuality studies. Chapter 8 treats several topics, including guides to writing about music, the music industry, careers in music, digital technology, and grant support for the arts.

9-20. Music Reference and Research Materials: An Annotated Bibliography. 5th ed. Vincent H. Duckles and Ida Reed. New York: Schirmer, 1997.

Vincent Duckles was one of the most important music bibliographers of the twentieth century, and "Duckles," as it is known to all music researchers and students, has been a standard work of music reference and a fixture of music bibliography courses since the publication of its first edition in 1964. The author describes this resource as "a list from which the essential materials for a music reference collection can be selected." In recent years, there has been a great increase in the number of reference titles published, so this selective list comprises a volume of approximately 800 pages. The book is divided into 13 sections covering all types of music reference works. The entries are concise and informative, and include citations to reviews for readers wishing further evaluative comments. An extensive index provides access by title, author, subject, library, institution, state, and country. This is an essential music reference tool for all libraries.

9-21. Music Research: A Handbook. Laurie J. Sampsel. New York: Oxford University Press, 2009.

This book, by a highly experienced and knowledgeable music librarian, introduces music students to the major print and electronic research tools in the field. Ideal for graduate-level music bibliography and research courses, it can also be used in any undergraduate or graduate music course that requires students to engage in library research or to write a research paper. Concise and practical, this unique handbook does not aim to provide an exhaustive introduction to the subject. Rather, it is highly selective and guides students to the most significant English-language research tools and resources, reference titles in major areas, and the principal sources in French, German, Italian, and Spanish. The book's first section, Chapters 1–14, is organized by type of research tool, e.g., encyclopedias, periodical indexes, and discographies. Each chapter in this section includes an overview of the tool it covers; an annotated bibliography that describes the tool's purpose, scope, strengths, and weaknesses; and an evaluation checklist that encourages students to think critically about the tools and materials they discover as they do research. The second section, Chapters 15–16, discusses style manuals and various resources for writing about music and citing sources. Methods for evaluating reference and research tools are emphasized throughout the book. *Music Research: A Handbook* is supplemented by a companion website, http://www.oup.com/us/musresearch, which includes supplemental links, updates to available bibliographies and readings by chapter, research tools listed by composer, and lists of core music journals and major professional music associations.

9-22. Information Sources in Music. Lewis Foreman, ed. München: Saur, 2003.

This book is organized in the form of bibliographic essays on a large number of topics. In addition to chapters on the standard reference sources and periodicals, there are informative chapters on the music publishing business, the music publisher as a research source, libraries of performing organizations, the publication and dissemination of new music, the iconography of music, music in American and British government documents, etc. Although oriented toward British readers, this resource contains a wealth of information, making it of great interest to American audiences as well.

General Encyclopedias and Dictionaries

9-23. The Harvard Concise Dictionary of Music and Musicians. Don Michael Randel. Cambridge, MA: Belknap Press, 1999.

The Encyclopedia of Music in Canada. James H. Marsh, ed. Toronto: The Historica-Dominion Institute, 1999–. Online at: http://www.thecanadianencyclopedia.com/index.cfm?PgNm=EMCSubjects&Params=U1.

A freely available resource, this encyclopedia is part of the larger *Canadian Encyclopedia*. It provides a great deal of information about all aspects of music in Canada, including composition; operas; musicals; ballets; pop, rock and jazz groups; festivals; musical venues; publishers; foundations; and music of various ethnic groups. It is regularly updated. The articles are signed and include selected bibliographies and work lists as well as numerous linked cross references. A related site is the Canadian Music Centre (http://www.musiccentre.ca/), comparable to the American Music Center (see entry 9-176). The Centre collects scores by Canadian composers, and it is possible for ensembles to borrow scores and parts for performance. The site also offers free online streaming of music from the Centre's large archive of recordings by Canadian composers, as well as news about music events, interviews, and other features.

This resource contains entries from the *New Harvard Dictionary of Music* and the *Harvard Biographical Dictionary of Music* (entry 9-36). The majority of entries deal with music and musicians in the classical Western tradition, but the biographical entries include jazz and popular composers and performers. The entries include definitions of musical terms, musical genres and works, descriptions of musical instruments, and short biographies of composers and performers. The articles are brief but informative. This is a useful one-volume reference for students, music lovers, and professional musicians.

9-24. The Harvard Dictionary of Music. 4th ed. Don Michael Randel. Cambridge, MA: Belknap Press of Harvard University Press, 2003.

This dictionary has been an essential reference source since its first edition in 1944. The current edition is based to a large extent on the third edition, with both additions and deletions to reflect recent developments in music scholarship. A large number of topics is covered and ranges from relatively brief definitions of musical terms and identifications of musical works to more lengthy articles on music during various historical periods and in various parts of the world, musical genres and forms, important issues and areas of study, and musical instruments. The longer articles are signed by well-known scholars and include bibliographies. The first and second editions of this work remain useful, since they contain some material that is not included in this or the third edition.

9-25. Die Musik in Geschichte und Gegenwart: AllgemeineEnzyklopädie der Musik. 2nd ed. Ludwig Finscher, ed. Kassel; New York: Bärenreiter, 1994–2007. 27 vols.

This encyclopedia, usually referred to as MGG, remains, in its second edition, an important reference resource that, like the *New Grove Dictionary of Music and Musicians*, attempts to cover all aspects of music. Some 20,000 entries have been contributed by 3,500 internationally known scholars. The 27 volumes of MGG are divided into 10 subject volumes, Sachteil, and 17 biographical volumes, Personenteil. A Supplement volume contains entries on contemporary musicians and on additional topics of more recent interest. Some of the scholars who contributed to New Grove have contributed articles on the same subjects to MGG. Nevertheless, the two encyclopedias do not contain identical information, so for a complete overall survey of a topic or musician, it is useful to consult both resources. MGG is well-organized, with many musical examples and illustrations, some of them in color. Each article concludes with a bibliography. Two index volumes provide page references to all mentions of a topic or person. MGG remains an outstanding resource that can be useful, even to those with a minimum knowledge of German who have a German dictionary at hand.

9-26. The New Grove Dictionary of American Music. H. Wiley Hitchcock and Stanley Sadie. London: Macmillan, 1986. 4 vols.

This is currently the most comprehensive dictionary of American music available. Known as *AmeriGrove*, its coverage is broad, including classical, jazz, and popular music, as well as the music of Native Americans and other ethnic groups. *AmeriGrove* features numerous biographical articles on composers and musicians, as well as articles on important topics, cities, and musical organizations. The signed entries are written by approximately 900 well-known scholars. Each entry includes a bibliography, and there are numerous illustrations. A great deal of the material in *AmeriGrove* has now been included in Grove Music Online, but not all, so it is a good idea to check both sources for the most complete information. A new, six-volume edition of *AmeriGrove* is in progress, and some entries from this new edition have already been incorporated into Grove Music Online (entry 9-1).

9-27. The New Grove Dictionary of Music and Musicians. 2nd ed. Stanley Sadie and John Tyrrell. New York: Grove, 2001. 29 vols.

This is the most recent print edition of the major music encyclopedia in English, and its range is enormous. It contains some 29,000 articles written by approximately 6,000 internationally known scholars. In addition to biographical entries on musicians of every period, country, and background, *New Grove* contains numerous, often lengthy, essays on musical topics of all kinds, as well as extended articles on music and the history of music in various countries and areas of the world. Also included are articles on important cities, musical instruments, organizations, and performing groups, as well as definitions of many musical terms. Most of the articles include bibliographies, and entries for major composers include works lists. In 2008, *New Grove* migrated to Grove Music Online (see entry 9-1). Nevertheless, *New Grove* remains a very useful reference source for people who find that reading long articles is easier with a paper copy and for libraries that may not be able to subscribe to the online version.

9-28. The Norton/Grove Concise Encyclopedia of Music. Rev. ed. Stanley Sadie and Alison Latham. New York: W. W. Norton, 1994.

This encyclopedia is written for a wide audience, including music lovers, students, and music professionals who need a succinct, one-volume reference work. For the most part, the entries are brief but informative and cover many of the same topics found in the multi-volume *New Grove*. These include composers, performers, instruments, terminology, and genres, as well as articles on such subjects as acoustics, music criticism, and music of various countries and regions. Composer work lists are included. Although there are many cross-references, not all of them are clearly indicated in the text.

9-29. The Oxford Companion to Music. Alison Latham, ed. Oxford: Oxford University Press, 2002. Print and also available online from Oxford Music Online at: http://www.oxfordmusiconline.com/public/book/omo_t114.

This is a new edition of a reference work that was first issued in 1938. Like its predecessors, it is written for a broad audience, including music lovers, students, and professionals. The entries are wide-ranging and include composers, performers, titles of works, musical terms, and instruments as well as musical periods, genres and forms. Unlike earlier editions, this new edition provides very few entries on popular or world music, and the focus is almost completely on music of the Western concert music tradition. Although this reference offers very few bibliographic citations, and no works lists for composers, it is, nevertheless, a very useful "quick look-up" reference book for almost any library.

9-30. **The Oxford Dictionary of Musical Terms.** Alison Latham. Oxford: Oxford University Press, 2004.

This pocket-sized dictionary can serve as a handy reference source for musicians, students, and concert-goers. Based on the *Oxford Companion to Music* (entry 9-29), the dictionary includes more than 2,500 entries defining a large number of musical terms in English, French, German, Spanish, and Latin. The entries are generally clear and well-written, and handled in such a way that both professional musicians and music lovers will find them useful. This is a valuable ready-reference tool for any library.

Biographical Encyclopedias and Dictionaries

9-31. **American Song Lyricists, 1920–1960.** Philip Furia. Detroit: Gale Group, 2002. (Dictionary of Literary Biography, v. 265)

This resource includes the major lyricists who wrote for Broadway, motion pictures, and Tin Pan Alley. Lyricists whose most important work came before 1920 or after 1960 are not included. The entries, arranged in alphabetical order, are lengthy and informative. Each includes a bibliography and selected discography. The numerous historical illustrations include pictures of show productions, sheet music covers, actors, singers, composers, and the lyricists themselves. This is a well-written and fascinating book.

9-32. **Art Song Composers of Spain: An Encyclopedia.** Suzanne Rhodes Draayer. Lanham, MD: Scarecrow, 2009.

This outstanding reference work will be of great interest to singers, accompanists, voice teachers, and concert-goers wishing to learn more about Spanish art song. The encyclopedia is organized chronologically, covering composers born between 1775 and the early twentieth century. The entries include not only biographical information, but also extended discussions of composers' works with musical examples. Each entry concludes with a work list, bibliography, and discography. Throughout, the author provides a political, social, and cultural context for the music she discusses. The appendix provides a guide to selected anthologies of Spanish songs. Also included are indexes to song titles and composers, as well as a general index.

9-33. **Baker's Biographical Dictionary of Musicians.** 9th centennial ed. Nicolas Slonimsky and Laura Diane Kuhn. New York: Schirmer Books, 2001. 6 vols.

Nicolas Slonimsky was one of the most important music writers and researchers of the twentieth century. This dictionary, now in its ninth edition, has been an outstanding bio-bibliographical reference source under his editorship. The work is known both for its accuracy and witty writing style. Prior editions were one volume only; this edition has six volumes, with over 1,000 new entries on classical musicians and almost 2,000 new entries on jazz and pop musicians. Entries include work lists, bibliographies, and, for pop and jazz musicians, discographies.

9-34. **Baker's Biographical Dictionary of Popular Musicians Since 1990.** Stephen Wasserstein, ed. New York: Schirmer, 2004. 2 vols.

This resource functions as a supplement to *Baker's Biographical Dictionary of Musicians*, discussed in entry 9-33. It covers musicians who have achieved wide popularity and commercial success since the 1990s. Approximately 575 signed articles are written by 24 contributors, most of whom are newspaper and magazine writers. The focus is on pop, rock, rhythm and blues, and hip hop, with additional entries on rap, country, jazz, and even some classical artists. Entries include selective discographies, bibliographies, and website listings. The appendix provides short essays on various pop music topics and a glossary.

9-35. A Biographical Guide to the Great Jazz and Pop Singers. Will Friedwald. New York: Pantheon, 2010.

The author of this guide is a music critic who has written several well-regarded books on jazz and pop songs and singers. The guide presents biographies of approximately 200 singers of jazz and pop standards from Louis Armstrong to Diana Krall. The entries are arranged alphabetically; and most of them are quite lengthy, offering detailed histories and assessments of the singers' recordings and careers. Friedwald also includes essays on five outstanding singers who are not jazz or pop performers but who have been both popular and influential: Bob Dylan, Mahalia Jackson, Elvis Presley, Bessie Smith, and Hank Williams.

9-36. The Harvard Biographical Dictionary of Music. Don Michael Randel, ed. Cambridge, MA: Belknap Press of Harvard University Press. Print and also available online from Credo Reference at http://www.credoreference.com/book/harvbiodictmusic.

This companion volume to the *Harvard Dictionary of Music* (entry 9-24) contains entries on approximately 5,500 musicians from all historical periods and countries, with an emphasis on American musicians of the twentieth century. The dictionary mainly covers classical musicians although some prominent jazz and pop musicians are also profiled. The articles are unsigned; most are fairly brief and provide selected bibliographies and work lists. The online version of the encyclopedia has not been updated, so more recent composers and musicians will not be found there.

9-37. International Dictionary of Black Composers. Samuel A. Floyd Jr., ed. Chicago: Fitzroy Dearborn, 1999. 2 vols. Also available online from Alexander Street Press at http://alexanderstreet.com.

This outstanding reference work offers information about 185 black composers from around the world. Of the 185 entries, 87 are devoted to composers of classical or art music. The editors decided to put more emphasis on these composers because they tend, for the most part, to receive less public recognition than composers of vernacular music. Composers of vernacular music who have had a substantial influence on the development of various popular genres, such as blues, jazz, gospel, and ragtime are also included. The entries have a unique organization. Each entry begins with a thumbnail biography, followed by a list of works, with publisher and discographic information, and a bibliography. Then there is a longer essay describing the composer's work and importance and providing analytical commentary on between one and four of the composer's pieces. The front matter provides a list of contributors, an alphabetical list of entries with the works discussed for each composer; and a list of composer names, pseudonyms, and variants.

RESOURCES FOR FINDING AND IDENTIFYING MUSIC

The entries in this section give information about where the user can find music, both in published and manuscript form.

Vocal and Instrumental Music

9-38. RISM. Répertoire International des Sources Musicales/International Inventory of Musical Sources. Frankfurt: Répertoire International des Sources Musicale.

Series A. 2 parts. **AI.** 9 vols.; 4 Supp. vols. **AII.** Online, accessible at
http://opac.rism.info.
Also as a subscription database through EBSCO at
http://www.ebscohost.com/public/rism-series-a-ii-music-manuscripts-after-1600.

Series B. 29 vols.; 1 supp. vol.

Series C. 6 vols.

RISM is an international project cataloging music in print, music manuscripts, theoretical writings about music, and libretti in libraries, archives, and other repositories worldwide from ancient times to approximately 1850. The project was begun in 1952 by the International Musicological Society and the International Association of Music Libraries, and is ongoing. RISM consists of Series A, B and C. Series A is devoted to sources by individual composers and is in two parts, AI and AII. Series AI is a catalog of printed music before 1800. It is in nine volumes with four supplement volumes. Series AII is a catalog of music manuscripts between 1600 and 1800. This series is freely available at an open access website and through EBSCOhost. Series B is devoted to bibliographies of collections of various types of music in print and manuscript, as well as theoretical writings. Series C consists of international directories of music research libraries published in six volumes. The online database of Series AII and a number of the printed volumes in Series B provide melodic *incipits*. See entry 9-11 for a description of the online portion of RISM.

Vocal Music

The resources described here provide singers, voice teachers, and coaches with organized lists of songs of all types and in many different languages, with publication and other information necessary to find the songs.

9-39. American Song: The Complete Musical Theatre Companion. 2nd ed. Ken Bloom. New York: Schirmer, 1996. 2 vols.

This resource provides information about more than 4,800 American musicals from 1877 to the fall of 1995. Included are Broadway, off-Broadway, and off-off Broadway productions, and original television musicals, as well as selected nightclub shows, vaudeville and burlesque shows, plays with original songs, shows that closed out of town, and English and French productions of shows by established American writers. Shows are listed alphabetically by title. Information for each show includes the date and place of opening, and the names of composer, lyricist, librettist, producer, director, choreographer, musical director, designers, and cast. There is also a list of songs and notes providing additional information. A song title index and a personnel index provide access to the more than 70,000 songs and 27,000 personnel. An index of shows by opening date is also provided.

9-40. Art Song in the United States, 1759–1999: An Annotated Bibliography. 3rd ed. Judith E. Carman, William K. Gaeddert, Rita M. Resch; with Gordon Myers. Lanham, MD: Scarecrow, 2001.

This is an annotated bibliography of American art songs for voice and piano. The main body of the work treats songs by American composers published in the nineteenth and twentieth century. A separate section by Gordon Myers treats songs published from 1759 to 1810. The book is organized alphabetically by composer, and then alphabetically by the titles of the songs and song cycles. The annotation for each entry supplies the title, poet, publication information, key, range and tessitura, and voice type. In addition there are comments about each work's mood or subject, difficulty for both singer and pianist, and suggestions for use in teaching and programming. The end matter provides a chronological list of the composers whose songs are included in the book; composer, poet, and title indexes; and an index of "special characteristics," such as suitable encore songs, program-ending songs, etc. This is an important resource for singers and teachers of singing and will be of great assistance in introducing them to new repertoire and in helping them put together interesting recital programs.

9-41. From Studio to Stage: Repertoire for the Voice. Barbara Doscher and John Nix. Lanham, MD: Scarecrow, 2002.

This resource lists approximately 3,000 songs organized by category, including art songs in English, Italian, French, German, Russian, and Spanish, as well as folk songs, musical theatre songs, and selections from operas, oratorios, cantatas, and Masses. For each entry information is provided on the range, tessitura, tempo, voice type, and difficulty, together with helpful comments on the music, the quality of voice needed to perform the song well, and performance issues. Publication information, including collections and commonly available editions, is listed for each song. Five indexes provide access by composer, title, poet, vocal range, and level of difficulty. This is a valuable reference source for singers, voice teachers, and coaches.

9-42. A Guide to the Latin American Art Song Repertoire: An Annotated Catalog of Twentieth-Century Art Songs for Voice and Piano. Maya Hoover. Bloomington, IN: Indiana University Press, 2010.

Singers and voice teachers wishing to become better acquainted with the Latin American art song repertoire will welcome this publication. The book is divided into 22 chapters, one for each of the countries covered. Each chapter begins with a short essay discussing the history and the main composers of art songs in that country. This is followed by alphabetical listings of composers, with their dates, and their songs and song cycles. For each song, information is provided about the text, poet, date of publication or copyright, range, and tessitura. Abbreviations for publishers and libraries are also included. The appendices contain keys to the publisher and library abbreviations, lists of suggested repertoire for various levels, and a substantial bibliography. Indexes of subjects and composers, text sources and poets, and song and song cycle titles are provided.

9-43. Index to Poetry in Music: A Guide to the Poetry Set as Solo Songs by 125 Major Song Composers. Carol June Bradley. New York: Routledge, 2003.

This valuable reference source offers comprehensive lists of songs for voice and piano by 125 major composers of the Western classical tradition and identifies the poets who wrote the lyrics. It also identifies which composers set a particular poem and offers publication information for each song when available. Complete lists of the songs of even major composers are usually not given in bibliographies of composers' works. This book goes a long way toward addressing this need by bringing together information that was previously scattered and difficult to find.

9-44. Recent American Art Song: A Guide. Keith E. Clifton. Lanham, MD: Scarecrow, 2008.

This compilation brings additional listings to the Carman bibliography (see entry 9-40), focusing as it does on American art songs for voice and piano composed or published since 1980. The entries are organized alphabetically by composer last name, and then alphabetically by title of song or song cycle. Each entry provides a short biographical note for the composer, and a description of the mood and subject of the song, as well as information about range, tessitura and difficulty. For some songs, the author has added the composers' own comments. Indexes to composers, poets, song cycles and song titles are helpfully supplemented by indexes to songs by voice type and songs by difficulty for each voice type.

9-45. Singer's Repertoire. 2nd ed. Berton Coffin. Lanham, MD: Scarecrow, 2002. 5 vols.

This resource is a reprint of the 1960 second edition. Although it is now somewhat out-of-date, it remains an important reference tool for singers developing their repertoire. It includes 8,200 songs for nine voice classifications. The book is organized in five volumes: Volume 1 lists songs for coloratura, lyric and dramatic sopranos; Volume 2 includes songs for mezzo-soprano and contralto; Volume 3 lists songs for lyric and dramatic tenors; and Volume 4 includes songs for baritone and bass. Volume 5 consists of program notes about each of the songs listed in the previous volumes. Songs are grouped together according to their type, e.g., opera, aria or wedding song, and by language, mood, and singing technique. Information given for each song includes composer, publisher, and range.

9-46. Vocal Chamber Music: A Performer's Guide. 2nd ed. Barbara Winchester and Kay Dunlap. New York: Routledge, 2008.

This book covers a large repertoire: vocal chamber music published from 1650 to 2005. Included in this resource is a list of works scored for at least one voice and one instrument other than keyboard, with up to 12 solo singers and 12 solo instruments. The authors have selected works with English, French, German, Italian, Spanish, and Latin texts, although a few works in other languages are also included. The works are by major composers, and most are currently in print. The entries are listed alphabetically by composer last name, and then alphabetically by work title. Instrumentation and publication information are given for each work.

Song Indexes

Song indexes are resources that enable users to locate individual songs in collections and anthologies. The indexes here reference classical art songs as well as popular songs. There are a number of online song indexes, in addition to those in print discussed below. These include the Song Index at the New York Public Library: (http://legacy.www.nypl.org/research/lpa/songindex/), the UT Song Index:
(http://www.lib.utk.edu/music/songdb/), the California Library System Cooperative Song Index: (http://www.sjvls.org/songs/), and the Seventh String Fake Book Index:
(http://www.seventhstring.co.uk/fbindex.html), which searches the contents of the best-known fake books.

9-47. Literature for Voice: An index of Songs in Collections and Source Book for Teachers of Singing. Tom Goleeke. Metuchen, NJ: Scarecrow, 1984–2002. 2 vols.

This is a valuable index to songs in collections. Volume 1 indexes over 60 collections and Volume 2 indexes an additional 72 collections published, for the most part, between 1984 and 2002. Each volume contains an index of song titles and an index of composers. Volume 1 includes a bibliography of books on topics such as voice production, pronunciation, translations, and interpretation. As the title indicates, this resource will be especially useful for voice teachers needing material for their students.

9-48. The New Broadway Song Companion: An Annotated Guide to Musical Theatre Literature by Voice Type and Song Style. Rev. ed. David P. DeVenney. Lanham, MD: Scarecrow, 2009.

This resource is a guide to songs in musicals for singing actors, teachers, coaches, directors, and producers. The main section of the book is a catalog of more than 300 shows arranged in alphabetical order. Songs in each show are listed with the names of the characters who sing them and annotations indicating the vocal range and style, such as uptempo and ballad. Six indexes provide access to the songs by voice type, vocal arrangement (solos, duets, trios, etc.), and composer and lyricist. This is a highly useful resource for musical theatre performers and those who work with them.

9-49. Popular Song Index. Fourth Supplement: 1988–2002. Patricia Havlice. Lanham, MD: Scarecrow, 2005. 2 vols.

This useful reference tool makes it possible to find in published song collections the music and words of various types of popular songs, including folk songs, pop tunes, spirituals, hymns, children's songs, sea chanteys, and blues. The current edition, the fourth supplement, indexes song collections published between 1988 and 2002. The first edition (1975) covered collections published between 1940 and 1972, the first supplement (1978) indexed collections published between 1974 and 1981. The second supplement (1993) indexes collections published from 1974 to 1981, with the addition of a few previously un-indexed titles from the 1950s and 60s. The third supplement indexes songs published between 1979 and 1987. The book is organized in three sections. The first is an alphabetical list of the song collections indexed with reference codes. The second section is an alphabetical listing of tunes by title and first line, together with the names of the composer and lyricist, when known, and the reference numbers of collections in which the song may be found. The third section is an alphabetical listing of composers and lyricists, together with the titles of the songs they wrote.

9-50. SongCite: An Index to Popular Songs. William D. Goodfellow. New York: Garland, 1995. Supp., 1999.

Together, the main volume and the supplement of this resource index 449 song collections and more than 13,500 individual songs. The collections were published for the most part during the 1990s. The author indexed recently published popular songs, as well as songs that have remained popular over a long period of time. He also attempted to index only those collections that were not indexed in any other resource in print. The titles of the collections are listed in alphabetical order at the beginning of each volume. Three indexes are provided: an index of songs by title and first line; an index of composers; and an index of songs from musicals, films, and television shows. The composer of each song is listed next to its title; there is no information on lyricists.

9-51. Song Finder: A Title Index to 32,000 Popular Songs in Collections, 1854–1992. Gary L. Ferguson. Westport, CT & London: Greenwood, 1995. (Music Reference Collection, no. 46)

This volume indexes 621 song collections dating from 1854 to 1992 and held by the State Library of Louisiana. It is not, however, merely a local resource, as most of these song books are also found in other libraries across the country. Access is by song title only. Many types of songs are indexed, including art songs, hymns, musical theatre songs, popular, rock, and folk music of many kinds. The book is in two parts. The first part is an alphabetical list of the titles of the song collections indexed, together with the letter symbols that represent each title, publication information, and OCLC numbers for use in interlibrary loan requests. The second part of the book is an alphabetical listing of the songs. Below each song title, the letter symbols of the collection(s) in which it appears are provided. In addition, letters (w or m or w, m) indicate whether the book provides both words and music, words only, or music only. If applicable, a foreign language designation is also given.

Instrumental Music

9-52. Chamber Orchestra and Ensemble Repertoire: A Catalog of Modern Music. Dirk Meyer. Lanham, MD: Scarecrow, 2010.

This will be a welcome reference for all chamber ensembles, especially those that feature music of the twentieth and twenty-first centuries. The book, organized like Daniels's *Orchestral Music: A Handbook* (entry 9-56), contains information on almost 4,000 compositions. Composers are listed in alphabetical order, and for each composer, works are listed alphabetically by title. Publisher, date of publication, duration, and instrumental breakdown are given for each work. The appendix organizes the listed compositions into various categories. For example, it is possible to search the appendix for works with a particular instrumentation or duration. Also included is an alphabetical listing by title of all works cited in the catalog.

9-53. **A Conductor's Guide to Choral-Orchestral Works**. Jonathan D. Green. Lanham, MD: Scarecrow, 1994– . 5 vols. Contents:

> A Conductor's Guide to Choral-Orchestral Works: Part I, 1994.
>
> A Conductor's Guide to Choral-Orchestral Works, Twentieth Century: Part II: The Music of Rachmaninov through Penderecki, 1998.
>
> A Conductor's Guide to the Choral-Orchestral Works of J.S. Bach, 2000.
>
> A Conductor's Guide to Choral-Orchestral Works, Classical Period: Haydn and Mozart, 2001.
>
> A Conductor's Guide to Nineteenth-Century Choral-Orchestral Works, 2008.

This is a valuable resource not only for conductors, but for students wishing to acquire an overview of the choral-orchestral literature. For each work, information is provided about the duration, text, required performing forces, and editions of the score and where they may be obtained. Also included are brief biographies of the composers, selected bibliographies and discographies, and notes on various issues of performance. The discussions of the types of difficulties that occur in the works of J.S. Bach are especially helpful and show a great knowledge of these scores.

9-54. **Guide to the Pianist's Repertoire**. 3rd ed. Maurice Hinson. Bloomington and Indianapolis: Indiana University Press, 2000.

Now in its third edition, this volume lists compositions for solo piano by approximately 2,000 composers. A wealth of information is packed into relatively brief entries. In Part I, entries are listed alphabetically by composer. For each composition, the author provides the complete title and work number, date of composition, publisher, length, duration, and level of difficulty with helpful remarks describing the stylistic characteristics of each work. If the composition is found in a collection, the title of the collection is given, and the user may then look it up in Part II, which lists anthologies and collections by type and country. At the end of the book is an extensive bibliography, and bibliographies are also provided within the body of the text for composers and sometimes for particular works. The front matter includes a list of publishers' addresses, and there is an appendix with historical recital programs.

9-55. **The Literature of Chamber Music.** Arthur Cohn. Chapel Hill, NC: Hinshaw Music, 1997. 4 vols.

For this comprehensive survey, the author's working definition of chamber music is music performed by two to nine players, with one player to a part. Music for voice is not included. Music of all periods and styles, from the 17th century to the last years of the 20th century, is covered. Entries are in alphabetical order by composer last name, and then in alphabetical order by title. The author examined music of publishers from all over the world and writes informative descriptions of almost all the works listed. The inclusion of short essays on a variety of topics adds interest to the compilation. No publication information is supplied, but in many cases, other sources, such as the *New Grove Dictionary of Music and Musicians*, or library catalogs, may supply the information.

9-56. Orchestral Music: A Handbook. 4th ed. David Daniels. Lanham, MD: Scarecrow, 2005.

This resource is of great importance to anyone involved with orchestras and orchestral music, including librarians, conductors, programmers, orchestra managers, music critics, discographers, and others. Organized alphabetically by composer and work title, the book gives information about approximately 6,400 orchestral works by almost 900 composers. Entries include information on instrumentation, duration, and publisher. The current edition incorporates listings from the Orchestra Library Information Service database. Eleven appendices provide lists of works requiring various soloists or instrumental groupings, lists of works by duration, works for youth orchestras, a title index, and publisher contact information. The online version of this resource is updated monthly. Available at http://www.orchestralmusic.com.

9-57. Orchestral "Pops" Music: A Handbook. Lucy Manning. Lanham, MD: Scarecrow, 2009.

Conductors, program planners, and music lovers will find this work of particular interest. In addition to reviewing publishers' catalogs, the author surveyed a large number of recent "pops" programs by American orchestras to compile this volume. Included in the listing for each work is information about instrumentation, duration, and publication. Especially helpful are the appendices, which list works by instrumentation, duration, theme (Americana, Black History Month, etc.), title, and publisher contact information.

9-58. Piano Music by Black Women Composers: A Catalog of Solo and Ensemble Works. Helen Walker-Hill. New York: Greenwood, 1992.

This reference source is a catalog of works for solo piano and piano with ensemble by black women composers. The catalog includes only instrumental music that is available in written notation. It is organized alphabetically by composer last name. For each entry, there is a short biography and an address where the composer's works can be obtained, if available. Walker-Hill examined many of the works listed here, and provides information on key, meter, stylistic characteristics, and level of difficulty.

9-59. The Piano in Chamber Ensemble: An Annotated Guide. 2nd ed. Maurice Hinson and Wesley Roberts. Bloomington and Indianapolis: Indiana University Press, 2006.

This resource is an important guide to works of chamber music for piano together with other instruments. The bibliography includes pieces requiring no more than eight instruments, including piano, and composed for the most part from 1700 to the present. The entries are grouped in categories by number of instruments required, and then alphabetically by composer. Each entry is identified by title and publication information, and there is a full listing of publishers' contact information in the front matter. The authors also comment on stylistic characteristics and difficulty of each work. A listing of collections and anthologies for various instrumental combinations and an annotated bibliography are included.

9-60. String Music of Black Composers: A Bibliography. Aaron Horne. New York: Greenwood Press, 1991.

This bibliography is organized first by geographical region and then alphabetically by composer last name. For almost every composer, there is a thumbnail biography; a list of pieces, with publication information; and a bibliography of sources. For some composers, however, very little information is available. When a work has not been published, the author sometimes provides library holdings information, but in some cases, even that information is not available. In spite of these problems, this is a useful resource that brings together in one book information that will give performers and researchers greater access to music of which they might otherwise be unaware. Also of interest are two additional volumes by the same author: *Woodwind Music of Black Composers* (Greenwood, 1990); and *Keyboard Music of Black Composers: A Bibliography* (Greenwood, 1992).

Indexes to Scholarly Editions and Anthologies

9-61. **Anthologies of Music: An Annotated Index**. 2nd ed. Sterling Murray. Warren, MI: Harmonie Park Press, 1992. (Detroit Studies in Music Bibliography, no. 68)

This resource indexes musical works published in 44 anthologies. The anthologies are, for the most part, designed to provide musical examples for college and university music courses. It can often be difficult to locate a particular work in one of these anthologies, and this book addresses that problem. The index is organized alphabetically by composer and title, with a separate listing for each anthology in which a work is published. A genre index makes it possible to locate pieces by type. Approximately 4,670 works are included.

9-62. **Collected Editions, Historical Series & Sets & Monuments of Music: A Bibliography**. George R. Hill and Norris L. Stephens. Berkeley, CA: Fallen Leaf Press, 1997.

9-63. **Historical Sets, Collected Editions, and Monuments of Music: A Guide to Their Contents**. 3rd ed. Anna Harriet Heyer. Chicago: American Library Association, 1980. 2 vols.

The bibliography by Hill and Stephens is currently the most up-to-date print source in which to find music published in monuments of music and historical series. These are multi-volume editions containing works by numerous composers. For each such edition, all of the published volumes are listed, and there is a short description of what each volume contains. A system of cross-referencing makes it possible to find a more complete record of the contents under the composer's name. The collected works of individual composers are cited, but the contents of each volume are not listed. For this information, it is necessary to consult the composer work lists of Grove Music Online (see entry 9-64).

Although now superseded by the online Index to Printed Music (entry 9-10), and by Hill and Stephens, the Heyer volumes are still useful, especially to those librarians who may not have access to the online resource. It indexes more than 1,300 musical works found in editions published before 1979. Volume I lists the editions alphabetically by composer or by title if the edition contains pieces by many different composers. The volumes and the pieces contained in them are then listed in order. Volume II is an index which lists all of the editions in which a composer's works appears in addition to the collected works editions. Volume II also lists citations for publications of works by composers for whom, at the time this book was published, no collected works edition was available.

9-64. **Grove Music Online** (GMO). New York, Oxford University Press, 2001– . Online subscription database at: http://www.oxfordmusiconline.com/public/book/omo_gmo. For a more general discussion of GMO, see entry 9-1.

Composer works lists are among the most valuable features of Grove Music Online. They are especially useful for finding individual works by prolific composers in the collected editions of their works. A works list begins with a list of all scholarly editions of that composer's works. The works are then listed by genre, e.g. dramatic works, orchestral works, chamber works, etc. The citation for a particular work provides a great deal of information, including the opus number or other cataloging number, the work title, and the volume and page citation for one or more collected editions in which the piece is published. Together, GMO and the Index to Printed Music (entry 9-10) provide good online access to music published in scholarly editions.

Thematic Catalogs

Thematic catalogs provide information needed to identify musical works. The main feature of thematic catalogs is that they include "themes" from the works cited, usually in the form of musical notation, referred to as *incipits*. *Incipits* usually include the first few measures of a work or movement, but they may be drawn from other important sections of a work as well. Thematic catalogs are useful, and often indispensable, tools for people who need to identify a musical work by its theme or themes. For online thematic catalogs, see RISM (entry 9-11) and ThemeFinder (entry 9-12). Readers should be aware that there are also numerous thematic catalogs for the works of individual composers.

9-65. The Book of World-Famous Music: Classical, Popular and Folk. 5th ed. rev. and enlg. James J. Fuld. New York: Dover Publications, 2000.

Since the publication of its first edition in 1966, this has been an invaluable source of information about the origins of many well-known pieces of music, including classical works, and popular and folk melodies. For each entry, the author discusses the first known printing, or in some cases, recording, of a work, including the date and place of publication, the composer, if known, and, when applicable, lyricist. In addition, there is other information about the history of the music, and in most cases a short *incipit* is provided.

9-66. Thematic Catalogues in Music: An Annotated Bibliography. 2nd ed. Barry Brook and Richard Viano. Stuyvesant, NY: Pendragon, 1997.

Barry Brook (1918-1997) was an important scholar who made great contributions to the field of musicology. One of these contributions was his work on thematic catalogs, including this one and RISM (entry 9-11). The current work is a bibliography of thematic catalogs and writings about them. Most of the catalogs listed are those of individual composers, but there are also catalogs of library and publisher holdings, as well as entries for compilers of catalogs and for authors who have written about them. Most of the entries are annotated. The introductory material explains the purpose and importance of thematic catalogs, and outlines the history of their development.

RESOURCES FOR FINDING LITERATURE ABOUT MUSIC

Vocal Music

9-67. Choral Music: A Research and Information Guide. 2nd ed. Avery T. Sharp and James Michael Floyd. New York: Routledge, 2011.

This comprehensive resource is an annotated bibliography of literature on choral music published from 1960 through the first decade of the twenty-first century. It is divided into eight main sections and includes monographs and bibliographies, dissertations, work lists, choral and church music journals, journal articles, electronic databases, and websites about choruses and choral music in the Western tradition. This resource will be of interest to a wide audience, including school and church choir directors, educators, as well as scholars and conductors of professional choruses and choirs.

9-68. Researching the Song: A Lexicon. Shirlee Emmons and Wilbur Watkins Lewis. New York: Oxford University Press, 2006.

Singers and others wishing to learn more about the texts of Western art songs will find this book a useful resource. Entries provide information about many literary, historical, and mythological references that occur in songs by German, French, Italian, Russian, Spanish, South American, Greek, Finnish, Scandinavian, British, and American composers. Large song cycles and their origins are discussed, and synopses of relevant large literary works are provided. Thumbnail biographies of poets and lists of composers who have set their songs are provided, often with specific song titles. A bibliography and suggested readings are included.

9-69. **Song: A Guide to Art Song Style and Literature**. Carol Kimball. Rev. ed. Milwaukee, WI: Hal Leonard, 2005.

For the most part, this resource focuses on important song composers from the eighteenth century to the present. It is organized by country, and then chronologically by composer birth dates. For each composer, there is a concise biography outlining his or her contribution to the song repertoire, followed by discussions of individual songs and song cycles. These discussions contain useful information about the poetry and music of the song, and often advice about performance. This resource will be especially useful to singers, accompanists and teachers, and will also serve as a handy reference tool for librarians and music lovers.

Instrumental Music

9-70. **Chamber Music: A Research and Information Guide.** 2nd ed. rev. John H. Baron. New York and London: Routledge, 2002. (Routledge Music Bibliographies).

The second, revised edition of this resource contains approximately 600 additional citations of publications that appeared between 1986 and 2001. The book is organized in six chapters. The first, Basic Reference, contains citations of encyclopedias, dictionaries and periodicals, as well as a listing of bibliographies of music for various chamber ensembles. This section should be of particular interest to performers. Chapter 2, the longest chapter, contains citations to studies of the history of chamber music, both by type of ensemble and by regions of the world. Chapters 3-6 are devoted to analytic studies, performance practice of chamber music, performers of chamber music, and miscellaneous topics, respectively. This edition has four indexes: an author index, a person index, an index of performing groups, and a subject index.

9-71. **The Concerto: A Research and Information Guide.** Stephan D. Lindeman. New York & London: Routledge, 2006. (Routledge Music Bibliographies).

This resource brings together references to writings about the concerto from its beginnings in the sixteenth century to the early twenty-first century. The author includes citations to general studies about the concerto and to more specialized studies organized by time periods, instruments, and by individual composers. Approximately 400 composers are listed. Writings cited include reference works and other books, periodical articles, and dissertations.

The Flute on Record: The 78 rpm Era: A Discography. Susan Nelson. Lanham, MD: Scarecrow, 2006.

This discography is a guide to recordings with flute made during the years 1889–1954. The discography catalogs commercial, private, and unpublished recordings, on cylinders and 78 rpm discs, for over 200 national and international flutists. Flutists are listed in alphabetical order with biographical sketches, followed by recordings listed in chronological order with dates, record label and number, and matrix and take number if known. Also listed are broadcast transcriptions, with dates and media. Where applicable, a list of LP and CD reissues is provided at the end of an entry. This is a thoroughly researched discography and will increase accessibility to these historic recordings.

9-72. String Quartets: A Research and Information Guide. Mara E. Parker. New York & London: Routledge, 2005. (Routledge Music Bibliographies).

This annotated bibliography focuses on one important genre of chamber music, the string quartet. Six chapters cover basic reference works dealing with chamber music in general, as well as the string quartet. The author cites Baron's bibliography (see entry 9-70) and notes that she has attempted not to duplicate his work. The chapter on the history of the string quartet cites general as well as period histories. The longest chapter deals with works about individual composers. There are also chapters on performance, facsimiles, and critical editions. Subject and author indexes are provided.

MUSIC HISTORY, THEORY, AND MUSIC EDUCATION

9-73. Analyses of Nineteenth and TwentiethCentury Music, 1940–2000. David J. Hoek. Lanham, MD: Scarecrow, 2007. (Music Library Association Index and Bibliography Series, no. 34).

For the most part, the audience for this bibliography includes music students and professional musicians searching for analyses of works they are studying. Nevertheless, because not all of the analyses cited are highly technical, music lovers who want to learn more about a work they have heard may also wish to consult this resource. The author has combined the content of Arthur Wenk's book *Analyses of Nineteenth- and Twentieth Century Music, 1940–1985*, with citations to analyses from 1986 to 2000. Analyses cited appear in periodical literature, books, and theses and dissertations in English, French, German, Italian and other European languages. Entries are listed alphabetically by the composer's name whose work is analyzed. Referring to this book provides efficient access to analytical writings about a particular piece of music, in some cases making it possible to circumvent time-consuming searches in several other indexes.

9-74. Music Theory from Boethius to Zarlino: A Bibliography and Guide. David Russell Williams and C. Matthew Balensuela. Hillsdale, NY: Pendragon Press, 2007.

9-75. Music Theory from Zarlino to Schenker: A Bibliography and Guide. David Damschroder and David Russell Williams. Stuyvesant, NY: Pendragon, 1990.

These two volumes are bibliographic dictionaries of important music theorists from early medieval times to the early twentieth century. The entries are arranged alphabetically by the name of the theorist, when that is known. Those treatises that are anonymous are listed by the name of the first modern editor of the work. Each entry begins with a short essay summarizing the ideas and contributions of the theorist or the anonymous treatise. This is followed by a list of original sources, their translations, and a bibliography of secondary literature. The back matter of each volume includes an extensive supplementary bibliography, a topical index, a chronological index, an index to the titles of treatises, and a name index.

9-76. The New Handbook of Research on Music Teaching and Learning: A Project of the Music Educators National Conference. Richard Colwell and Carlo Richardson. New York: Oxford University Press, 2002.

This resource is comprised of 61 bibliographic essays by more than 90 authors organized in 10 parts corresponding to important topics of research in music education. Each essay summarizes the research in a particular area with in-line references. Full citations of references are given at the conclusion of each essay. This resource supplements but does not supplant the similar *Handbook of Research on Music Teaching and Learning: A Project of the Music Educators National Conference,* by Richard Colwell (Schirmer, 1992).

9-77. **Reader's Guide to Music History, Theory, Criticism.** Murray Steib. Chicago: Fitzroy Dearborn, 1999.

An alphabetically arranged series of approximately 500 bibliographic essays by various authors, overseen by an editor and 16 advisors, makes up this useful one-volume reference source. It represents an attempt to organize and summarize important monographs in English on various aspects of Western art music, with some entries on popular and non-Western music. The front matter includes an alphabetical list of entries as well as a thematic list. The thematic list is especially helpful, since it makes it possible for a user to find a list of all articles dealing with a particular topic. This resource is especially designed for students, teachers, and general readers.

9-78. **A Topical Guide to Schenkerian Literature: An Annotated Bibliography with Indices**. David Carson Berry. Hillsdale, NY: Pendragon, 2004.

This is a large-scale bibliographic study of writing by and about the important theorist Heinrich Schenker containing approximately 2,200 entries. The entries are grouped by the 15 major topics, each of which is divided into a number of sub-topics. The author provides a survey of the topical headings in which he explains the types of sources presented under each. An index of topics and sub-topics follows. The bibliographic annotations are well written and informative. Schenker's theories have had an enormous influence on music pedagogy and on a great deal of thinking and writing about music. This is an important resource for all music libraries.

Music History

9-79. **The Norton Introduction to Music History.** New York: W. W. Norton.

The Norton series is used in many college and university courses. It is comprised of six volumes, published separately, which include *Medieval Music* by Richard Hoppin; *Renaissance Music: Music in Western Europe, 1400–1600* by Allan W. Atlas; *Baroque Music: Music in Western Europe, 1580–1750* by John Walter Hill; *Classical Music: The Era of Haydn, Mozart, and Beethoven* by Philip G. Downs; *Romantic Music: A History of Musical Style in Nineteenth-Century Europe* by Leon Plantinga; and *Twentieth-Century Music: A History of Musical Style in Modern Europe and America* by Robert P. Morgan.

9-80. **The Prentice Hall History of Music Series**. Upper Saddle River, NJ: Prentice Hall.

Like the Norton series, the Prentice Hall series covers the history of western music in several separately published volumes, including *Music in Medieval Europe* by Jeremy Yudkin; *Music in the Renaissance* by Howard Mayer Brown and Louise K. Stein; *Baroque Music* by Claude Palisca; *Music in the Classic Period* by Reinhard G. Pauly; *Nineteenth-Century Romanticism in Music* by Rey M. Longyear; *Twentieth-Century Music: An Introduction*, 4th ed. by Eric Salzman; *Music in the United States: A Historical Introduction*, 4th ed. by H. Wiley Hitchcock (entry 9-89); *Music Cultures of the Pacific, the Near East, and Asia*, 3rd ed., by William P. Malm; and *Folk and Traditional Music of the Western Continents* by Bruno Nettl.

9-81. **A History of Western Music**. 8th ed. J. Peter Burkholder, Donald Jay Grout, Claude V. Palisca. New York: W. W. Norton, 2010.

Now in its eighth edition, this remains the most widely-used survey of Western music history. Chapter introductions discuss the history, culture, and technological developments of the time. Sidebars offer timelines, primary source readings, composer biographies, and discussions of various musical concepts and terms. Numerous musical examples and illustrations are provided. The textbook is accompanied by a three-volume anthology of musical examples, a 14-CD set, and a study and listening guide. There is also an associated website where, for a small additional fee, users can access streaming audio, download MP3s, and subscribe to the Naxos Music Library for a semester. The website also offers study and listening guides, composer biographies, glossaries, and listening quizzes.

9-82. Music Since 1900. 6th ed. Nicolas Slonimsky and Laura Kuhn. New York: Schirmer, 2001. Print and also available online from Alexander Street Press at http://alexanderstreet.com.

The sixth edition of Nicolas Slonimsky's well-known chronology is now under the editorship of Laura Kuhn. The longest section of the book is the descriptive chronology, beginning in the year 1900 and continuing through December 2000. The entries, which cite notable musical events, including many world premieres of significant works, are pithy and informative. The second section of the book includes a selection of readings drawn from composers' letters and other writings, as well as declarations and statements about music from governments and other institutions. A glossary of terms and an index are included. This is a highly informative and entertaining book.

9-83. The Oxford History of Western Music. Richard Taruskin. New York: Oxford University Press, 2005. 6 vols.

This well-written resource will make for interesting reading for sophisticated users. Richard Taruskin is a highly-regarded musicologist who has written on Russian music, including the music of Stravinsky, as well as early music. The text is interspersed with numerous musical examples, whichTaruskin discusses both from a technical and aesthetic point of view. Taruskin's guiding idea is that Western classical music is a written tradition, and he shapes his history with this idea in mind. As he points out, this book is not a survey, as his intention is not to cover everything but to show a kind of through line with more substantive discussions of important pieces and musical styles than sometimes appear in books that cover the entire history of Western music. Volume 6 offers an interesting chronology showing important musical dates with parallel events in the other arts, science, and philosophy, and world history. Volume 6 also contains a master index; it would have been useful to have an index for each individual volume.

9-84. Performance Practice: A Dictionary-Guide for Musicians. Roland Jackson. New York: Routledge, 2005.

Performance practice, that is, the playing of musical works in a manner as close to a composer's original idea as possible and consistent with what is known about musical practices of a particular period, is a rich area of study. This dictionary serves as a basic resource and overview of the field, supplying articles on various aspects of performance, such as tempo, accompaniment, ornamentation, and ensemble size and make-up, in addition to entries on musical instruments and individual composers. The explanations are clear and succinct, and there is a sizable number of pictures. Bibliographies are included with every entry. Long entries are divided into sections separated by bibliographical references. An index of theorists and writers listed with the titles of their important writings is included.

Source Readings

Music source readings are selections from primary source documents compiled for use in music history classes. The collections described in the entries below range widely over the entire history of Western music. In addition to these general source readings, there are several books of source readings in particular subject areas. Among these are *Opera: A History in Documents*, by Piero Weiss (Oxford University Press, 2002); *Music Education: Source Readings from Ancient Greece to Today*, 2nd ed., by Michael L. Mark (Routledge, 2002); *Keeping Time: Readings in Jazz History*, by Robert Walser (Oxford University Press, 1999); *To Stretch Our Ears: A Documentary History of America's Music*, by J. Heywood Alexander (W. W. Norton, 2002); *The Pop, Rock, and Soul Reader: Histories and Debates*, by

David Brackett (Oxford University Press, 2005); and *Audio Culture: Readings in Modern Music*, by Christoph Cox and Daniel Warner (Continuum, 2004).

9-85. Music in the Western World: A History in Documents. 2nd ed. Piero Weiss and Richard Taruskin. New York: Schirmer, 2008.

This volume presents a collection of readings similar to those in *Source Readings in Music History* (entry 9-86) but offering somewhat less technical selections intended for a broader readership. Approximately 200 readings are included, organized in eight parts from antiquity to the twentieth century. A sizable number of illustrations is included, as is a glossary of terms.

9-86. Source Readings in Music History. Rev. ed. Oliver Strunk and Leo Treitler. New York: W. W. Norton, 1998. Also published in 7 volumes: Vol. 1: *Greek Views of Music*, Thomas J. Mathiesen, ed.; Vol. 2: *The Early Christian Period and the Latin Middle Ages*, James McKinnon, ed.; Vol. 3: *The Renaissance*, Gary Tomlinson, ed.; Vol. 4: *The Baroque Era*, Wye J. Allanbrook, ed.; Vol. 6: *The Nineteenth Century*, Ruth A. Solie, ed.; Vol. 7: *The Twentieth Century*, Robert P. Morgan, ed.

Selections from this resource are standard reading assignments for courses surveying the history of the classical Western music tradition. The book is made up of writings by composers, theorists, performers, poets, critics, and music lovers from the major periods of music history. The editors have provided an introduction to each musical period, and each source reading includes a biographical profile of the writer. The revised edition is greatly expanded to include readings from twentieth-century sources. Readings dealing with performance and reception history are also given greater prominence, as are writings by women and people of color.

SPECIAL TOPICS IN MUSIC

The entries in this section include reference titles organized by topic. Resources covered include encyclopedias and dictionaries, as well as bibliographies of writings about music. Bibliographies of books, articles, and online resources are good starting points for research on a particular topic.

American Music

9-87. America's Musical Life: A History. Richard Crawford. New York: W. W. Norton, 2001.

This history of American music is written, for the most part, for the general reader. The book begins with Native American music and continues through recent developments in minimalism and hip-hop culture. Very few musical examples are included, and discussions of the music are usually non-technical. Instead, music is considered in the context of history, economics, and economic opportunity, with particular emphasis on performers and the conditions and venues in which they performed. The author shapes the discourse around three categories—the classical, popular and folk—and attempts to give equal weight to each. This is a well-researched history filled with interesting details and numerous illustrations. An extensive bibliography is included.

9-88. Bibliographic Handbook of American Music. Donald William Krummel. Urbana: University of Illinois Press, 1987

This is a scholarly work by one of the music profession's outstanding librarians and bibliographers. It is a bibliography of bibliographies, including highly informative essays and annotations covering approximately 750 publications of music, writings about music, and discographies from the earliest American publications through the mid-1980s. Although it is in need of updating, it has not been superseded, and remains a highly interesting and useful resource for the serious student and researcher.

The reader may also wish to consult *Resources of American Music History: A Directory of Source Materials from Colonial Times to World War II*, by Donald William Krummel, et al. (University of Illinois Press, 1981). This is a state-by-state directory of libraries, archives, and other institutions that hold American music and materials related to musical activity in America. The organization is alphabetical by state and then by the name of the repository. For this project, the editors relied on librarians and archivists at the institutions surveyed to report on their holdings. An index provides access to the names of repositories and personal names. This is a highly useful reference source for students and scholars conducting research in early American music. Also notable is *Early American Music: A Research and Information Guide*, by James R. Heintze (Garland, 1990). This is an annotated bibliography of music and music literature having to do with early American music up to 1820.

9-89. Music in the United States: A Historical Introduction. 4th ed. H. Wiley Hitchcock and Kyle Gann. Upper Saddle River, NJ: Prentice-Hall, 2000.

This is an introduction to the history of music in the United States by an eminent scholar and insightful commentator. The book is organized chronologically, and covers developments in music from the colonial period through the mid-1990s. The music critic Kyle Gann is the author of the final chapter on music since the 1980s. The emphasis is on "serious" music, but nevertheless, the author treats what he refers to as the cultivated and vernacular traditions on a par, reflecting recent trends in music criticism and scholarship. Each chapter concludes with a brief annotated bibliography of basic sources. The book is well-written and authoritative, because, as the author notes, he consulted scores and/or recordings of all of the works he discusses.

9-90. The Music of Black Americans: A History. 3rd ed. Eileen Southern. New York: W. W. Norton, 1997.

This was a ground-breaking history when it was first published in 1971, and it remains an important resource today. The book traces the history of all areas and genres of music to which African-Americans contributed, from colonial times to the late twentieth-century. The coverage is broad and includes folk music, spirituals, black minstrel performers, concert artists and classical composers and performers, ragtime, blues, jazz, rhythm and blues, and rap. The extensive bibliography is divided into sections by century. In addition to books and periodical articles, each section includes a list of selected scores. This is an excellent general introduction to the music of African-Americans.

Jazz

9-91. The Biographical Encyclopedia of Jazz. Leonard Feather and Ira Gitler, with the assistance of Swing Journal, Tokyo. New York: Oxford University Press, 2007.

Leonard Feather was one of the most important jazz critics of the twentieth century. This book is based in part on his three earlier encyclopedias: *Encyclopedia of Jazz*, *The New Encyclopedia of Jazz*, and *The Encyclopedia of Jazz in the Sixties*, and on *The Encyclopedia of Jazz in the Seventies*, which he co-authored with Ira Gitler. Although it is only a single volume, this source provides a great deal of biographical information on approximately 3,300 jazz artists, active from the 1920s to the early twenty-first century. The book does this in part through the skillful use of abbreviations. In addition to names that are often abbreviated, such as musical instruments and record labels, other ordinary words are also abbreviated, and a great deal of information is included in each entry in a kind of short-hand fashion. A complete list of abbreviations is included in the front matter, so that the presentation is always clear. Each entry includes a list of record labels for which the artist recorded, and information about films and videos, festivals, and awards and honors.

9-92. Free Jazz and Free Improvisation: An Encyclopedia. Todd S. Jenkins. Westport, CT: Greenwood, 2004. 2 vols.

This is the only currently available encyclopedia focusing exclusively on free jazz. The author is a jazz critic who has written for *Down Beat* and other publications, and is one of the founders of Jazz .com. Individual artists, groups, record labels, and jazz critics are covered. Entries are often quite lengthy, and include critical commentary on musical styles and albums. The first volume contains an alphabetical list of entries, a guide to related topics, two essays outlining the history of free jazz, and a chronology of important events in that history. The second volume completes the alphabetical listings and offers a list of suggested readings and an index.

9-93. The History of Jazz. 2nd ed. Ted Gioia. New York: Oxford University Press, 2011.

This is a well-researched history of jazz for the general reader. The author begins with the "prehistory" of jazz in the early nineteenth century and continues through developments in jazz during the 1980s and early 1990s. Descriptions of the music are interesting and vivid. They sometimes contain technical terminology, but there are no musical examples. A list of recommended listening is provided in the appendix. The author recommends listening carefully to a few selected works rather than listening casually to entire albums. This is a good introduction to jazz history.

9-94. The Jazz Discography. Tom Lord. Online subscription database. http://www.lordisco.com

This online subscription database, also available in CD-ROM format, was first published as a 26-volume reference book from 1992–2001. It covers more than 400,000 jazz recordings released from 1896 to the present. The Jazz Discography lists not only albums and sessions that were released, but also those that were broadcast on radio and television, and albums that were recorded but not released. The database can be searched by musician name, band leader, session date or number, record label, and tune title. Each listing includes personnel; recording date and place; album title, record label and number, when applicable; and complete track listings. The multi-search function makes it possible to search for two or three musicians simultaneously and discover what recordings they made together. The ability to search by tune title is also interesting since it makes it possible to see the recordings of all musicians who recorded a particular tune.

9-95. Jazz Scholarship and Pedagogy: A Research and Information Guide. 3rd ed. Eddie S. Meadows. New York & London: Routledge, 2006.

This is an annotated bibliography of books and other materials devoted to jazz research, performance, and pedagogy published from the 1920s to late 2004. No articles are included, so the book does not constitute a complete listing of everything published on jazz. This work incorporates material from the author's earlier *Jazz Research and Performance Materials: A Selected Annotated Bibliography*, published in 1995. The current volume is divided into 15 sections, including Reference Works; Jazz in World Cultures; Biographies and Autobiographies; History; Discography; Theses and Dissertations; Pedagogy Materials; Transcriptions; and Jazz Videos and DVDs. The annotations are concise but informative. The section on transcriptions includes knowledgeable annotations on the entries, and the section on pedagogical materials will be useful for both students and teachers of jazz and jazz techniques.

9-96. The New Grove Dictionary of Jazz. 2nd ed. Barry Kernfeld, ed. New York: Grove, 2002. 3 vols. Print and online at Oxford Music Online: http://www.oxfordmusiconline.com.

The second edition of this authoritative encyclopedia is a complete revision and expansion of the first edition, published in 1988. It contains approximately 7,750 entries written by more than 300 contributors. Articles are signed, include bibliographies, and, when applicable, selected discographies. Many of the entries make fascinating reading. The articles on instruments, for instance, contain not only definitions, but also discussions of their use in jazz and the techniques and sounds of various players. The long article on nightclubs in major cities of the world is especially interesting and includes information about their histories, and the musicians who performed there. The full text of this resource has now been incorporated into Grove Music Online (entry 9-1) and some entries have been further updated.

9-97. The Oxford Companion to Jazz. Bill Kirchner, ed. New York: Oxford University Press, 2000.

This book is made up of essays by 59 outstanding authorities in the field of jazz. The essays cover a wide variety of topics, including jazz styles and their history, the role of various instruments, and profiles of important musicians. Also included are articles on the blues, improvisation, composing and arranging, the relationship of jazz and classical music, and many other topics. Although this is not a sequential history of jazz, the historical orientation of many of the essays, together with their careful attention to dates, makes this volume a valuable contribution to jazz history.

9-98. The Penguin Guide to Jazz Recordings. 9th ed. Richard Cook & Brian Morton. New York: Penguin, 2006.

This is an excellent discography of currently available recordings of jazz on CD. It is international in scope, and the editors have reviewed more than 14,000 recordings. Richard Cook was a well-known jazz critic and record producer, and Brian Morton is himself a jazz musician. The artist biographies and the CD reviews are short but informative, and the editors are clearly experts in the field. This book uses the star rating system similar to that of the other Penguin guides. Approximately 200 titles that the authors recommend as a "core collection" are highlighted in the text. An artist index is included.

Musical Instruments

In addition to the books listed here, there are several excellent online resources for musical instruments. These include the musical instrument collection at the Metropolitan Museum of Art at http://www.metmuseum.org. The musical instrument collection at the Boston Museum of Fine Arts at http://www.mfa.org/collections/musical-instruments is also excellent and includes audio clips of some of the instruments being played. Both of these collections may be freely browsed and searched.

9-99. The New Grove Dictionary of Musical Instruments. Stanley Sadie, ed. London: Macmillan, 1984. 3 vols.

The editor outlines the scope of this resource in the preface. The three volumes include entries on classical Western instruments and their makers; modern Western musical instruments, including electronic instruments, and their makers; performance practice in the Western tradition; and approximately 10,000 entries on non-Western and folk instruments. Most of the entries on classical Western instruments are derived from the 1980 edition of *The New Grove Dictionary of Music and Musicians*. The articles on non-Western instruments, on the other hand, were written especially for this dictionary. Numerous illustrations and a sizable number of musical examples are provided. Articles are signed and most include bibliographies. The second edition of this outstanding reference source is forthcoming.

9-100. Origins and Development of Musical Instruments. Jeremy Montagu. Lanham, MD: Scarecrow, 2007.

This is a thorough and comprehensive survey of musical instruments from all over the world, from prehistoric times to the late twentieth century. The author was the curator of the Bates Collection of Musical Instruments at Oxford University and has published a number of books about musical instruments. His discussion and explanations are clear and well-written, and the text is filled with fascinating information. Approximately 120 black and white photographs of instruments from various collections provide additional interest. Electronic instruments, however, are not discussed in great detail. A substantial bibliography is included.

9-101. **Musical Instruments of the World: An Illustrated Encyclopedia**. Diagram Group. New York: Paddington Press, 1976. Rep., New York: Sterling, 1997.

This is a comprehensive survey of musical instruments of the world. Virtually every type of instrument is described and illustrated. The encyclopedia is divided into sections corresponding to the classification system developed by Hornbostel and Sachs, which groups instruments into families according to the way the sound is produced. There are frequently several illustrations for an instrument, some showing change and development in the instrument over time, and some showing how the instrument is played. There are also sections describing and illustrating musical groups of various types and sizes. This is a useful resource, particularly for its numerous illustrations.

9-102. **Musical Instruments: Craftsmanship and Traditions from Prehistory to the Present**. Lucie Rault. Trans. by Jane Brenton. New York: H. Abrams, 2000.

This is a beautiful book, offering a pictorial overview of musical instruments of the world, with emphasis on instruments of Asia and Africa. The photographs are large and of high quality, and the captions are informative. The book is not a comprehensive survey of musical instruments, and the instruments are not categorized according to traditional classification systems. Instead, the author takes a more ethnographic point of view and discusses the meaning and function of musical instruments in relation to human life, the power of nature, and religious rites and rituals. The appendices include a glossary, a list of important collections of musical instruments, and a selected bibliography.

9-103. **Encyclopedia of Keyboard Instruments.** New York: Routledge, 2003–2006. 3 vols.
     Vol. 1: The Piano: An Encyclopedia. 2nd ed. Robert and Margaret Palmieri, eds. 2003.
     Vol. 2: The Harpsichord and Clavichord: An Encyclopedia. Igor Kipnis, ed. 2007.
     Vol. 3: The Organ: An Encyclopedia. Douglas Bush and Richard Kassel, eds. 2006.

These three volumes are excellent reference sources. They offer articles on numerous topics, including instruments, instrument construction, keyboard-related terminology, instrument makers, composers, and performers. The signed articles have been contributed by an international group of well-known scholars. Many articles include bibliographies, and there are many illustrations.

Musical Theatre

Musicals 101: The Cyber Encyclopedia of Musical Theatre, TV and Film. John Kenrick.
http://www.musicals101.com/

This is an entertaining website offering a great deal of information about musicals, with pages on musical theatre history, on staging musicals, and on the elements that go into creating musicals. There are numerous reviews of shows, recordings, books, and DVDs, as well as features on famous composers, lyricists, and performers. This is a great site for musical theatre buffs.

9-104. American Musical Theatre: A Chronicle. 4th ed. Gerald Bordman and Richard Norton. New York: Oxford University Press, 2010.

This resource is a chronicle of American musical theatre history from 1866 through the first decade of the twenty-first century. The presentation, however, is quite different from that of the chronology by Richard C. Norton (entry 9-106). That work is a show-by-show listing, whereas this is a narrative chronology. For most shows, information about producers, composers, lyricists, and book writers is provided, and in many cases, the author discusses the plot, scenes, and musical numbers in some detail and gives a critical evaluation. Four indexes provide access by show title, source (play, novel, etc.) on which a show is based, song title, and personnel. This is a well-researched and well-written reference book that provides extensive information and is enjoyable to read.

9-105. Broadway Musicals Show by Show. 6th ed. Stanley Green and Kay Green. New York: Applause Theatre and Cinema Books, 2008.

This resource profiles more than 300 Broadway musicals from *The Black Crook*, which premiered in 1866, to *Young Frankenstein*, which opened on Broadway in 2007. The entries are organized chronologically by opening date, and include information about writers, principal actors, directors, and choreographers. Titles of important songs, number of performances, date of closing, and recordings are also noted. For each show there is a brief essay describing its plot; history, including revivals; and other interesting information. Indexes provide access by show title, composers and lyricists, directors, choreographers, and major cast members.

9-106. A Chronology of American Musical Theater. Richard C. Norton. New York: Oxford University Press, 2002. 3 vols.

This is a thoroughly researched reference source with a vast amount of detailed information about more than 5,000 musicals produced on major New York stages from 1750 to 2001. The author defines the term "musical" very broadly to include comic operas and operettas, including those in languages other than English, as well as revues, pantomimes, rock operas, and so on. The chronology is organized by year, but a title index provides access to shows by title. There is also an index of songs, in which more than 50,000 songs are listed, and an index of approximately 100,000 persons. This chronology has much more information about early musicals than the Internet Broadway Database (entry 8-51).

9-107. The Encyclopedia of the Musical Theatre. 2nd ed. Kurt Gänzl. New York: Schirmer, 2001. 3 vols.

The second edition of this widely-used reference work has been expanded from two to three volumes, with more than 4,000 entries. The 500 new entries include information about more recent productions, as well as about musical theatre outside New York and provincial British theatre in the nineteenth and early twentieth century. The scope of the work is international, covering, as the author notes, "the plays and people involved in the mainstream of Western musical theatre" over the past 150 years. The encyclopedia includes entries for most successful writers and composers, important performers, directors, choreographers, and designers. The various performances and revivals of works in all countries are documented, and selected recordings and bibliographies are included.

9-108. Historical Dictionary of the Broadway Musical. William A. Everett and Paul R. Laird. Lanham, MD: Scarecrow, 2008.

This one-volume work is a compact reference source covering the Broadway musical from the opening of *The Black Crook* in 1866 to the premiere of *Spring Awakening* in 2006. The dictionary includes approximately 1,000 relatively brief entries, arranged alphabetically, including show titles and genres, composers, lyricists, actors, directors, critics, and awards. The introduction includes a chronology, and the appendix includes a selected bibliography.

9-109. The Musical: A Research and Information Guide. 2nd ed. William A. Everett. New York: Routledge, 2011.

The second edition of this reference book has been expanded and contains more than 1,400 annotated entries describing the numerous resources currently available for research about the musical on stage and screen. The book is divided into 15 chapters, including reference works, general histories, sources dealing with stage, film and television musicals in general, with particular shows, and with the creators and performers of musical theatre. Chapters on periodicals, sets and series of musical theatre works, discographies, and recorded and video anthologies make up the second half of the book. The index provides access by names, titles of shows, and titles of songs.

9-110. Off-Broadway Musicals Since 1919: From Greenwich Village Follies to The Toxic Avenger. Thomas S. Hischak. Lanham, MD: Scarecrow, 2011.

Resources such as the Internet Broadway Database (entry 8-51) have made it easy to find information on Broadway musicals. But there are no comparable sources of information on Off-Broadway shows. So this volume fills an important need. As the author points out, this is not a detailed history of all Off-Broadway musicals; but it does offer profiles and critical evaluations of 381 major Off-Broadway musicals from 1919 through the early twenty-first century. The organization is chronological, with shows grouped by decade and then chronologically within each decade. The chronological list of shows in the front matter makes it easy to see which shows are covered in each decade; there is also an alphabetical list of shows. It would be helpful if these lists were handled as real indexes with a page reference for each show.

9-111. The Oxford Companion to the American Musical: Theatre, Film, and Television. Thomas S. Hischak. New York: Oxford University Press, 2008.

This is an A-to-Z encyclopedia of musicals produced on stage, and for films and television from the mid-nineteenth through the early years of the twenty-first century. There are approximately 2,000 brief but informative entries on shows, performers, composers, lyricists, directors, and choreographers, as well as on genres, such as revues and concept musicals. The listing of shows is selective, and, as befits the title of the book, the emphasis is on those shows that were adapted for more than one medium. The appendix includes a chronology of musicals, a year-by-year listing of Academy and Tony Awards, a guide to recordings, and a selected bibliography. The index provides access to names, titles, organizations, and genres.

9-112. The Rodgers and Hammerstein Encyclopedia. Thomas S. Hischak. Westport, CT: Greenwood, 2007.

This reference work offers approximately 600 entries covering the life and works of Richard Rodgers and Oscar Hammerstein. It includes brief biographies of both men and descriptions of all the musicals they wrote together, as well as those each of them wrote with other collaborators. There are entries for librettists, performers, singers, and other artists with whom Rodgers and Hammerstein worked, as well as information about recordings, films, and revivals. A bibliography and discography are included.

9-113. Showtime: A History of the Broadway Musical Theater. Larry Stempel. New York: W. W. Norton, 2010.

This is a substantial history of the American musical theatre, well-written and thoroughly researched. As the author notes, the book is not simply a chronology; he has instead given the history a shape, discussing shows not from the point of view of a fan, but of a knowledgeable professional. Not every show is discussed, but the author has selected shows both for their individual importance and for their significance as "examples of each of the many styles, genres, subjects, personalities, institutions, movements, and trends" that have a place in musical theater. Many illustrations, musical examples and excerpts from books and lyrics are provided, along with a substantial bibliography, a selected historical discography, and an index. This is an outstanding history of musical theater.

Opera

MetOperaDatabase. http://archives.metoperafamily.org/archives/frame.htm

This database provides complete information about every opera staged at the Metropolitan Opera from its opening night on October 22, 1883 to the present day. The database is updated five days a week during the opera season. Searching the database by singer produces a list of all performances at the Met by that singer. It is then possible to click on one performance and see a complete listing of cast and production members, as well as a review of the production. Links to other Metropolitan Opera features include free audio streaming of selected performances, and paid subscription audio and video services.

9-114. Blacks in Opera: An Encyclopedia of People and Companies, 1873–1993. Eric Ledell Smith. Jefferson, NC: McFarland, 1995.

This reference work covers more than 500 black composers, conductors, singers, choral directors, stage directors, choreographers, lighting designers, producers, and critics. Each entry provides biographical information and a summary of the individual's work in opera, including repertoire and performance history. Bibliographies, including reviews, and a list of recordings, including broadcasts, are also provided.

9-115. Encyclopedia of American Opera. Ken Wlaschin. Jefferson, NC & London: McFarland, 2006.

This encyclopedia covers American opera and operetta from the eighteenth century to the early years of the twenty-first century, with entries on individual works, composers, librettists, singers, arias, and source authors. There are articles on various "firsts:" the earliest American operas published and staged, the first recordings of American operas and operettas, and the broadcasts of American opera for both radio and television. An entry for each of the 50 states describes their opera theatres, companies, premieres, singers, composers, etc. For each work entry, the author documents major performances, recordings, films, and broadcasts. This is a very useful resource and also makes for interesting reading.

9-116. The New Grove Dictionary of Opera. Stanley Sadie, ed. New York: Macmillan, 1992. 4 vols.

This is the leading and most comprehensive English-language dictionary of opera. Entries include articles on composers, librettists, operas, singers, conductors and opera directors. There are also entries on voice types, singing technique, opera-related terminology, cities, opera houses, and opera companies. Articles on individual operas include plot summaries, as well as discussions of production history, relationship to a composer's other works, reception history, and so on. The back matter includes an index of role names and an index of first lines of arias, ensembles, and choruses. This important reference work has been integrated into Grove Music Online (entry 9-1).

9-117. The New Penguin Opera Guide. Amanda Holden, ed. London: Penguin, 2001.

This excellent guide contains articles on approximately 850 opera, operetta, and musical theatre composers, and 2,000 articles on individual operas. This is one of the most comprehensive encyclopedias of its kind. For each composer, there is a concise but informative biography, with emphasis on the composer's operatic output. Following the biography is a list of the composer's operatic works. For each of these, the librettist, and dates of composition are given, together with the dates and places of premieres, a cast list, and orchestration, followed by a plot summary. Each opera entry concludes with publication information, a list of major and currently available recordings, and a bibliography.

9-118. Opera: An Encyclopedia of World Premiers and Significant Performances, Singers, Composers, Librettists, Arias and Conductors, 1597–2000. Franklin Mesa. Jefferson, NC & London: McFarland, 2007.

This unusual encyclopedia provides information not usually found in a single reference source. The entries include both operas and operettas, from the earliest known opera, Jacopo Peri's *La Dafne* of 1597, to Jake Heggie's *Dead Man Walking*, premiered in 2000. Altogether, there are 7,400 entries. Works are listed alphabetically by title in their original languages. Each entry provides the composer's and librettist's names and dates, as well as brief listings of their other works in the genre. Information about world premieres and other important performances follows, including dates, principal singers, and conductors. The book also includes more than 1,300 short biographies of singers, as well as an index to composers, conductors, and premiere theatres and locations.

9-119. Opera: A Research and Information Guide. 2nd ed. Guy A. Marco. New York: Garland, 2001.

The second edition of this annotated bibliography has 2,833 entries, more than three times the number in the first edition, published in 1984. This is an indication of the large increase in literature about opera in the approximately 15 years between the two editions. The author focuses on books in English published through 1999. The largest section of the book deals with composers and their operas. For major composers, there are subsections on editions, thematic catalogs, bibliographies, conference proceedings, and so on. General biographies and books on the composer's entire output are next, followed by monographs, articles and dissertations on individual works. The indexes provide access by opera titles, subjects, authors and main entries, and secondary authors.

9-120. A Short History of Opera. 4th ed. Donald Jay Grout and Hermine Weigel Williams. New York: Columbia University Press, 2003.

The fourth edition of this widely-used history of opera has been revised and expanded, including much greater coverage of twentieth-century opera. The emphasis on national operatic traditions of the previous editions is retained in the section on the twentieth century, so that there is a consistency of organization. Seminal works such as Gershwin's *Porgy and Bess* and Virgil Thomson's *Four Saints in Three Acts* are discussed more fully, as are operas by African-American composers such as Scott Joplin and William Grant Still, and musical theatre works are also given a place. The chapter on opera in the United States covers recent works by Philip Glass, John Adams, John Corigliano, John Harbison, and others. The appendix includes a discussion of Chinese opera and a bibliography of sources cited.

9-121. Who's Who in Opera: A Guide to Opera Characters. Joyce Bourne. New York: Oxford University Press, 1998. Print and also available as part of Oxford Reference Online at: http://www.oxfordreference.com/pub/views/home.html.

In this very readable reference work, the author has profiled more than 2,500 characters in almost 280 operas, operettas and musicals. The entries are arranged alphabetically by characters' names.

Well-known singers have contributed essays on important roles they have played. For example, Bryn Terfel discusses his performance as Leporello, and Placido Domingo writes about one of his most famous roles, Otello. Biographies of these special contributors are given in Appendix 1. Appendix 2 includes a list of all operas discussed, organized alphabetically by composer last name.

Popular Music

9-122. American Popular Music: From Minstrelsy to MP3. 3rd ed. Larry Starr & Christopher Waterman. New York: Oxford University Press, 2009.

This is a good, general overview of the history of popular music in the United States, beginning in the mid-19th century. The book is designed for students taking a college music appreciation course. The text is well-written, and relates developments in popular music to contemporary historical events. Highlighted sections offer discussions of particular songs, some of which are included on the accompanying 2-CD anthology. A glossary of important musical terms, a bibliography, and a timeline are included.

9-123. A Century of American Popular Music: 2000 Best-loved and Remembered Songs (1899–1999). David A. Jasen. New York: Routledge, 2002.

This book offers an overview of some of the most well-known songs of the twentieth century. In deciding what songs to include, the author considered a number of factors, including a song's ranking on the pop charts or in sheet music or record sales, how well-remembered a song is today, and its historical importance. Some songs that are still remembered today but that were not top hits are included, and some songs that were top hits but are not well-known today are not included. Songs are listed alphabetically by title. Information for each song includes composer, publisher, and year and place of publication. In addition, there is a brief paragraph with information about performers and recordings, including record label and number; popularity; and titles of shows and films in which the song appeared. Three indexes offer access by composer, publisher, and year of publication. This is a useful reference book for anyone interested in the history of American popular music.

9-124. Continuum Encyclopedia of Popular Music of the World. John Shepherd, ed. London; New York: Continuum, 2003. 7 vols.

This encyclopedia offers extended articles by well-known scholars. The first volume is divided into two parts. The first part covers the social and culture dimensions of popular music, and the second focuses on the popular music industry. Articles summarize important developments and research in these areas. Each section ends with a bibliography and, where applicable, a discography. Volume 2 is entitled Performance and Production and includes articles on various types of musical groups, notation, technology, recording techniques, musical instruments, as well as topics such as harmony, rhythm, and form. Volumes 3–7 contain articles about popular music in various parts of the world. Additional volumes are planned, including a biography volume that will contain entries for musicians and other important personalities in the world of popular music.

9-125. Encyclopedia of Popular Music. 4th ed. Colin Larkin, ed. New York: MUZE: Oxford University Press, 2006. 10 vols. Print and also available online through Oxford Music Online at: http://www.oxfordmusiconline.com/public/book/omo_epm.

This is a comprehensive and scholarly reference source dealing with all types of popular music from 1900 on. It includes approximately 18,500 entries and is international in its coverage, with emphasis on American and British music. It is organized alphabetically, and no attempt has been made to categorize entries by type or style of music, which makes for, as the editor notes, a very democratic organization. The entries are well-written, with a good balance of factual information and critical evaluation, and filled with cross-references to related articles. Discographies are provided for bands and individual artists, including album titles, labels, and release dates, as well as ratings based on the opinions of respected critics and on the editor's and contributors' evaluations. Volume 9 offers more extensive reviews of selected albums and bibliographies. In addition to the general index, there is a useful song and album title index.

9-126. A Guide to Popular Music Reference Books: An Annotated Bibliography. Gary Haggerty. Westport, CT: Greenwood, 1995.

This resource includes 427 annotated entries organized according to type of resource. Categories include bibliographies, periodical indexes, indexes to printed and recorded music, encyclopedias and dictionaries, discographies, guidebooks, yearbooks, and almanacs. The author examined every source included, and the entries are well-researched and well-written. Appendices include discographies and biographies of individual musicians.

9-127. The Praeger Singer-Songwriter Collection. James Perrone, ed. Santa Barbara: ABC-CLIO, 2006– .

The 20 books issued so far in this series are by various authors. Each book examines the words and music of a major singer-songwriter, active any time from the 1960s to the present, and focusing on the creative history and development of the artist through his or her songs and albums. Among the artists discussed are Stevie Wonder, Dolly Parton, Patti Smith, Frank Zappa, Paul McCartney, John Lennon, and Ice Cube. The analyses are detailed, and substantial; bibliographies and indexes are provided.

Folk, Blues, Ragtime, Country, and Gospel

9-128. A Blues Bibliography. 2nd ed. Robert Ford. New York and London: Routledge, 2007.

The second edition of this bibliography is a revision and expansion of the first edition published in 1999. Materials published between 1999 and early 2006 are included, as are some citations from prior years that were not included in the first edition. The author lists citations to books; journal and newspaper articles, including those in specialist and obscure journals; and some record liner notes. Citations of writings on individual artists, producers, etc., take up the majority of the book. There are also sections on the history and background of the blues, instruments, record labels, regional variations, and lyric transcriptions and musical analysis. A section citing important reference works is especially helpful.

9-129. Country Music Records: A Discography, 1921–1942. Tony Russell. New York: Oxford University Press, 2004.

This discography documents all country music recordings from their beginnings in 1921 to the end of 1942. The author brings together primary research from the files of record companies, interviews with musicians, and information gathered from the 200,000 recordings in the sound archives of the Frist Library of the Country Music Hall of Fame. Entries are organized alphabetically by artist, and each entry includes information about personnel, recording location and date, recording title, and issue label and number. This is an exhaustive reference work that will be of great interest to anyone wishing to learn about the early history of recorded country music.

9-130. Encyclopedia of American Gospel Music. W. K. McNeil. New York: Routledge, 2005.

This book is designed to be a reference source for students, scholars and general readers. The book treats both black and white gospel music traditions as parallel and related strands, and is thus a somewhat unusual resource. The entries were selected by an editorial board of five scholars, editors, music critics, and gospel performers, and written by more than 60 contributors from academic, gospel, and folk music organizations. Entries include artist biographies and articles on performing groups and organizations, musical styles, important record labels, and radio shows. Entries are signed, and most include selected bibliographies and discographies. The index allows access to particular songs and people that may not have separate entries.

9-131. Encyclopedia of the Blues. Edward M. Komara. New York: Routledge, 2006. 2 vols.

The approximately 2,100 entries in this two-volume work range from short definitions and biographical notes to extended articles outlining important blues topics, such as the history of blues bands, musical styles, musical instruments, and geographic areas where development of the blues took place. Indexes include an alphabetical list of entries and a thematic list of entries. The list of contributors is long, including mainly U.S. scholars but also Canadian, British, and international experts.

9-132. Encyclopedia of Country Music: The Ultimate Guide to the Music. Paul Kingsbury, ed. New York: Oxford University Press, 1998.

This resource has been considered the authoritative encyclopedia of country music since its publication in 1998. Almost 1,300 entries by 150 well-known contributors are included, and all entries are signed. The encyclopedia covers mainly North American country music, particularly commercially produced country music of the United States. The entries include biographies of singers, songwriters, producers, recording executives, and radio personalities. Other entries cover important radio and television programs, sub-styles of country music, instruments played in country music, record companies, and organizations. In addition to these entries, there are 10 longer essays about various aspects of country music including its history, its folk and popular roots, and its costumes. Thirteen appendices list best-selling albums and songs, country radio stations in the U.S., Country Music Hall of Fame members, and winners of various awards. This is a valuable reference tool for any library.

9-133. Encyclopedia of Rhythm & Blues and Doo-Wop Vocal Groups. Mitch Rosalsky. Lanham, MD: 2000.

This resource provides information about the recordings of more than 800 groups of four or more singers that performed vocal group harmony, rhythm and blues and doo-wop, from the 1930s through the 1960s. The author includes groups whose lead singer and one other group member were well-known. Groups are listed in alphabetical order. Each entry has three parts: personnel, notes and discography. The notes give information about other group names, other groups the performers appeared with, changes in personnel, etc. The discography lists record label, number, title and date of issue for each album. An appendix offers a complete alphabetical list of individual performers and the names of their groups.

9-134. Folk and Blues: The Encyclopedia. Irwin Stambler and Lyndon Stambler. New York: St. Martin's, 2001.

This volume and its companion volume *Country Music: The Encyclopedia* (1997), together constitute the third edition of the *Encyclopedia of Folk, Country & Western Music*, the first edition of which was published in 1969 and the second in 1983. A burgeoning interest in and a concomitant increase in the number of performers of "roots music," made it necessary to expand this reference source to two volumes. The entries are well-written, professional biographies of performers from the turn of the twentieth century to today. The authors gathered information both from interviews and from published sources. Each biography discusses the artist's early development and influences and then outlines his or her career path, focusing on important appearances and albums. A substantial bibliography is included, as well as an index to main entries and song and album titles.

9-135. **Folk Music in America: A Reference Guide**. Terry E. Miller. New York: Garland, 1986. (Garland Reference Library of the Humanities, vol. 496).

This annotated bibliography offers approximately 2,000 entries, mostly describing sources in English published between 1900 and 1986, with emphasis on more recent material. Included are books, doctoral dissertations, articles in scholarly journals and *Festschriften*, and articles from important encyclopedias. The entries are grouped in nine sections covering music of native Americans, African Americans, Anglo-Americans, and various other ethnic traditions, as well as topics such as psalmody and hymnody, shape-note singing, and traditional instruments and instrumental music. Author and subject indexes are provided.

9-136. **Folk Music: An Index to Recorded Resources.** Jane Keefer. Chapel Hill, NC: ibiblio.org, 1996–2011. Free online database. http://www.ibiblio.org/folkindex

This free online database indexes recorded folk music, as well as printed collections of folk music. The author has amassed information for the database over a long career as a teacher and performer of folk music beginning in the 1970s. The database can be searched by song title or performer. It is also possible to browse printed and recorded collections by publisher and label and recorded sources arranged by performers. Linked cross references make it possible to find identical or closely related songs with different names. The database was updated in 2011. This is a unique resource containing very valuable information.

9-137. **The Penguin Guide to Blues Recordings.** Tony Russell and Chris Smith. London: Penguin, 2006.

This discography documents recordings by more than 1,000 musicians who are primarily blues artists. By blues artists the authors mean those artists who record for blues labels. For the most part, blues-rock, soul, and gospel performers are not covered, unless they also record blues. The entries are arranged alphabetically by artist. Each entry begins with a thumbnail biography of the artist. Then the currently available albums by the artist are discussed in the order in which they were made. Complete information on each album is given, including record label and number, personnel and their instruments, and recording dates. The authors also rate each album according to a system they describe in the introduction, and provide informative commentary, some quite extensive. This is a valuable resource for blues lovers.

9-138. **Ragtime: An Encyclopedia, Discography, and Sheetography.** David A. Jasen. New York: Routledge, 2007.

The author of this resource is a well-known authority on ragtime, and this volume offers an enormous amount of information. The main section of the book is an encyclopedia with entries on composers of ragtime, individual rags, important publishers of ragtime, and longer articles on various periods in the development of ragtime. For individual rags, the composer's name, publisher, and publication date are provided, in addition to a short description of the music. Numerous historic pictures appear throughout. This reference has three appendices. Appendix 1 is a discography of all commercially released ragtime recordings, from the earliest in 1897 through the 1920s, including 78s, 45s, and LPs. Appendix 2 is a Ragtime Piano Rollography. The rags are listed alphabetically with roll labels and label numbers. Appendix 3 is an alphabetical listing by title of all rags published in America. The composer's name, date of publication, publisher's name, and city of publication are given for each title.

Rock

9-139. **Encyclopedia of Indie Rock.** Kerry L. Smith. Westport, CT: Greenwood, 2008.

The author of this resource defines indie rock as a do-it-yourself movement in which rock bands attempted to take control of all aspects of their recordings, rather than putting themselves in the hands of record labels. The introduction offers a timeline and overall history of the indie rock movement. Entries are organized alphabetically by individual artist and band names with entries on indie rock styles and terminology, record labels and publications. Many of the entries are lengthy, including histories of bands and discussions of their albums. The appendices include a list of the most significant indie rock albums and a substantial bibliography.

9-140. Encyclopedia of Rap and Hip-Hop Culture. Yvonne Bynoe. Westport, CT: Greenwood, 2006.

This is a useful reference work for those looking for a basic introduction to some of the important aspects of rap and hip-hop. In the introduction, the author presents a brief history of hip hop and rap. This is followed by alphabetically arranged entries on important rap artists and groups, producers, record labels, films, types and subgenres of rap music, and performance locales. Entries on artists and groups include discographies. The author also defines and discusses various elements of hip-hop culture, such as misogyny in rap music, graffiti, sampling, DJing, etc. An appendix offers a list of albums that are considered among the best of the genre, and there is a selected bibliography of books and internet resources.

9-141. The Essential Rock Discography. Martin C. Strong. Edinburgh: Canongate Books, 2006.

This discography serves as the eighth edition of *The Great Rock Discography*, condensed and updated. In all, approximately 600 bands and artists are included, from the 1950s through the first half of 2006. The author excluded pop and lesser-known rock artists. Albums are given ratings between 1 and 10, based on music reviews, evaluations written by listeners, and the author's opinions. Many of the entries include essays that provide both biographical information and discussion and evaluation of important albums, followed by the discographies with track listings, record labels and numbers.

Another valuable guide to rock is *The Rock Song Index: The 7500 Most Important Songs of the Rock and Roll Era: 1944–2000* (2nd ed. Bruce Pollock. Routledge, 2005). This reference source consists of three indexes. The first is organized alphabetically by song title, the second is an artist index, and the third lists song titles according to the year they came out. Songs were chosen based on a number of criteria, including the relative popularity of a given song, as indicated by its rankings in the pop charts both in the United States and England, critical reviews, and opinions of music professionals, including the author, who is an award-winning journalist, producer, and writer. Each entry in the song title index includes the performing artist, the composer, album title, label, year, and often a short description of and commentary on the song. The author notes that the second edition includes the same number of songs as the first edition, which covered songs recorded between 1944 and 1997. The author added approximately 400 songs from 1997 to 2000, and, therefore, deleted that number from the earlier edition. Songs deleted were those that peaked on the pop charts between numbers 6 and 10.

9-142. Rock's Backpages. Hoskins, ed. London, England: Backpages Limited, 2000– . Online subscription database available at http://www.rocksbackpages.com.

Rock's Backpages is a subscription database of rock journalism from the 1950s to the present. The database includes more than 17,000 articles and reviews from rock magazines, including *Creem, Rolling Stone, New Musical Express*, and *Melody Maker*. The database can be searched by artist, genre, writer, or keyword. Also included are more than one hundred audio interviews with rock artists.

9-143. Rock Music Scholarship: An Interdisciplinary Bibliography. Jeffrey N. Gatten. Westport, CT: Greenwood, 1995. (Music Reference Collection, no. 50)

This is an annotated bibliography of scholarly writing about rock. The author has for the most part excluded popular writing on rock and rock criticism in favor of more analytical and interpretive writing. The focus of the organization is the interdisciplinary nature of rock scholarship, and each of the ten chapters contains entries relating to a particular discipline. Within each chapter, entries are organized by type of resource: articles, chapters, books, dissertations, and films and videos. The entries are substantial and give excellent summaries of the sources they describe. There are two indexes, an author index and a subject index. This is a very useful resource for students beginning serious research on a rock topic.

9-144. What's That Sound?: An Introduction to Rock and Its History. 2nd ed. John Covach. New York: W. W. Norton, 2009.

John Covach has written several well-received books on American popular music. This book is an introduction to rock for college students in introductory music courses. It is organized broadly by decade, beginning with the 1920s and popular music before the advent of rock, through the late twentieth century. The book has a large number of listening guides, and this second edition includes a new feature called "Backstage Pass." These are essays by well-known scholars and critics on such topics as Elvis Presley, The Beatles, and Woodstock. The musical selections are available as iTunes downloads on the companion website. Also available on the website are chapter outlines, interactive listening guides, and quizzes.

Technology

9-145. The Audio Dictionary. 3rd ed. rev. and expanded. Glenn D. White and Gary J. Louie. Seattle: University of Washington Press, 2005.

This is an excellent dictionary with clear, well-written definitions. The third edition has more than 400 new entries, which define terms related to recent developments in audio technology. In addition, entries from the second edition have in many instances been rewritten and brought up to date. A total of 11 appendixes provide more extensive essays on particular topics, such as auditorium acoustics, musical scales and the tuning of musical instruments, and the history of high fidelity. The dictionary will be of interest to students studying music, electronic music, film, and audio engineering, and to music listeners and audiophiles wishing to learn more about the field.

9-146. Encyclopedia of Recorded Sound. 2nd ed. Frank Hoffmann and Howard Ferstler, eds. New York: Routledge, 2005.

Offering more than 3,500 entries, the second edition of this encyclopedia covers a great deal of information about sound recording and its history. The signed entries include articles on recording techniques, equipment, record labels, and recording terminology. There are extended articles on the history of recording of various musical genres, among them jazz, opera, rock, and orchestral music. Entries on musicians who have made important recordings include titles, record labels, and label numbers of their notable albums. The back matter provides an extensive bibliography and biographies of contributors. This is a valuable resource offering information that is not easily available elsewhere.

9-147. The Oxford Handbook of Computer Music. Roger T. Dean, ed. Oxford; New York: Oxford University Press, 2009.

This volume presents a series of essays on many aspects of computer music. The editor notes that the book focuses more attention on developments in computer music since the 1980s when the rapid development of desktop and then laptop computers made working with computer music possible for a great number of musicians. The contributors are well-established experts in the field. The essays are grouped into five broad categories, including the history of computer music, compositional approaches to computer music, the cognition and computation of computer music, and cultural and educational issues in computer music. A helpful chronology lists significant musical events together with parallel technological developments.

9-148. The Routledge Guide to Music Technology. Thom Holmes, ed. New York: Routledge, 2006.

This resource gives definitions of terms used in the field of music technology and audio production, as well as thumbnail biographies of important people in that field. Featured items include a "Technology Firsts" chronology, a timeline of the development of various playback devices, and a history of the development of recording industry charts. A substantial bibliography will guide readers seeking additional information. This is a highly useful reference source for almost any library.

Women in Music

9-149. From Spirituals to Symphonies: African-American Women Composers and Their Music. Helen Walker-Hill. Westport, CT: Greenwood, 2002.

For this biographical-historical study, the author presents chapter-length studies of eight African-American women composers of the twentieth century. In the introduction, the author notes that the composers chosen for this study are representative of various generations, backgrounds, and musical styles. The book opens with a chronology of African-American history and an introductory chapter providing an overview of the history of African-American women composers. The author interviewed all of the composers profiled here and provides detailed information on composers' biographies and on their music. Each biography includes a list of works, a bibliography and discography.

9-150. The Norton/Grove Dictionary of Women Composers. Julie Anne Sadie and Rhian Samuel, eds. New York: W. W. Norton, 1995.

This resource greatly adds to and expands on entries in the second edition of *The New Grove Dictionary of Music and Musicians*. It includes signed entries by well-known scholars covering almost 900 women composers from the Middle Ages to the late twentieth century. The entries include work lists organized by genre, including publication and performance information, and bibliographies. The front matter includes essays on the history of attitudes toward women composers and a detailed chronology.

9-151. "Say Can You Deny Me": A Guide to Surviving Music by Women from the 16th through the 18th Centuries. Barbara Garvey Jackson. Fayetteville: University of Arkansas Press, 1994.

The author conducted a great deal of primary research to compile the information in this book. Approximately 600 composers are listed in alphabetical order; dates of birth and death, and places of origin are given when known. For each composer, titles of works, either published or in manuscript, are listed in alphabetical order, with information about performing forces, publication, and library holdings. Five appendixes are provided, including a key to abbreviations and a bibliography of modern editions, arrangements and facsimile reprints. The general bibliography lists sources and an index provides access to works by medium of performance.

9-152. Women and Music in America Since 1900: An Encyclopedia. Kristine H. Burns, ed. Westport, CT: Greenwood, 2002. 2 vols.

Women working in all areas of music who were born, lived most of their lives, or made major contributions in the United States are included in this encyclopedia. The entries are organized alphabetically, but relatively brief entries for individual musicians are interspersed with longer essays on large topics. Members of an advisory board who worked with the editor developed this list of topics, which include blues, classical music, education, folk music, experimental music, gender issues, gospel, honors and awards, jazz, multicultural music, music technology, and rock and popular music. These essays provide a great deal of interesting information and establish a context for the individual entries. The entries are signed and include cross references and bibliographies. Citations of recordings, including album title, label, and number, are included in the body of each entry. Not all American women musicians active since 1900 are included. The editor notes that the choice of which musicians to include was made on the basis of the significance of their contributions, and not on their popularity. This is a highly useful and very readable reference work.

9-153. **Women & Music: A History**. 2nd ed. Karin Pendle, ed. Bloomington: University of Indiana Press, 2001.

This one-volume history is made up of a series of essays on women composers, performers, teachers, and music librarians from the time of the ancient Greeks to the present. Most of the essays focus on the role of women in Western art music, but there are also chapters on women in popular music and jazz, and in world music. The book is organized by time periods and would be easy to incorporate into a typical survey of Western music history. The essays are by established scholars. Each essay concludes with a list of suggested readings, and the end matter includes a general bibliography and selected discography.

9-154. **Women in Music: A Research and Information Guide**. 2nd ed. Karin Pendle and Melinda Boyd. New York: Routledge, 2010.

This guide is an annotated bibliography covering a wide spectrum of resources on the subject of women in music. Scholarly resources are emphasized, but popular books and journal articles are included as warranted. All types of music are considered, from pop and rock, to classical, to world music. Seventeen chapters group the resources by topic and by type of resource. Topics include feminist analytical methods and viewpoints, historical periods, and women in rock and pop. There are also chapters of bibliographies of individuals and of two or more individuals. Three helpful indexes include an index of names; index of subjects; and an index of authors, editors and translators.

World Music

Global Music Archive at Vanderbilt University.
http://www.globalmusicarchive.org/

The Global Music Archive came about through the initiative of Vanderbilt ethnomusicologist Gregory Barz. The Archive is freely available and currently provides access to approximately 1,600 recorded musical performances from various regions of East Africa. Metadata are provided for each recording, including performers, musical instruments, languages, etc. The site also provides slide presentations on various aspects of the project and a description of future plans for the Archive.

9-155. **Ethnomusicology: A Guide to Research.** 2nd ed. Jennifer C. Post. New York: Routledge, 2011. (Routledge Music Bibliographies)

This guide supplements but does not supersede the bibliography by Schuursma (entry 9-156). It includes resources published for the most part between 1990 and 2010. It provides information on reference and research materials, with chapters on encyclopedias and dictionaries; bibliographies, discographies and filmographies; journals; audio recordings; and film and video recordings. Subheadings within chapters are organized by geographic location as well as other useful categories, such as musical genre, dance, cultural studies, and gender studies.

9-156. Ethnomusicology Research: A Select Annotated Bibliography. Ann Briegleb Schuursma. New York: Garland, 1992.

This is the first general bibliography in English of important ethnomusicology resources. It contains approximately 470 annotated entries for sources published from 1960 to 1990. The entries are grouped into five categories: the history of ethnomusicology as a field of study; theory and methodology; fieldwork theory and method, including technical aspects, such as equipment used; musical analysis; and sources from related fields. Within each of these sections, entries are organized alphabetically by the author's last name. The author entries are clear and well-written, and the name and subject indexes.

9-157. The Garland Encyclopedia of World Music. Bruno Nettl, Ruth M. Stone, James Porter, and Timothy Rice. New York: Garland, 1998–2002. 10 vols. Also available from Alexander Street Press, online at: http://glnd.alexanderstreet.com/.

> Vol. 1: *Africa*. Ruth Stone, ed.
>
> Vol. 2: *South America, Mexico, Central America, and the Caribbean*. Dale Olsen and Daniel Sheehy, eds.
>
> Vol. 3: *The United States and Canada*. Ellen Koskoff, ed.
>
> Vol. 4: *Southeast Asia*. Terry E. Miller and Sean Williams, eds.
>
> Vol. 5: *South Asia: The Indian Subcontinent*. Alison Arnold, ed.
>
> Vol. 6: *The Middle East*. Virginia Danielson, Scott Marcus, and Dwight Reynolds, eds.
>
> Vol. 7: *East Asia: China, Japan, and Korea*. Robert C. Provine, Yosihiko Tokumaru, and J. Lawrence Witzleben, eds.
>
> Vol. 8: *Europe*. Timothy Rice, James Porter, and Chris Goertzen, eds.
>
> Vol. 9: *Australia and the Pacific Islands*. Adrienne L. Kaeppler and J.W. Love, eds.
>
> Vol. 10: *The World's Music: General Perspectives and Reference Tools*. Ruth M. Stone, ed.

Filled with fascinating detail as well as broad cultural overviews, this encyclopedia is a wonderful guide to the music of the world's peoples. Its organization is somewhat different from most encyclopedias. Each of the first nine volumes focuses on a different region of the world. Each volume contains an overall introduction, a section dealing with important issues and processes, and a section containing essays on aspects of music in smaller areas within the larger region. All of the volumes have indexes, and readers looking for specific information will need to make use of these. Volume 10 contains a series of essays by several important ethnomusicologists, in which they describe their personal involvement in ethnomusicology, their influences, and their methodologies. This volume also contains a glossary, bibliographies, discographies, video and filmographies, and a general index.

9-158. Jamaican Popular Music from Mento to Dancehall Reggae: A Bibliographic Guide. John Gray. Nyack, NY: African Diaspora Press, 2011. (Black Music Reference Series, v. 2)

This is an important bibliography covering all aspects of Jamaican popular music. It is comprehensive, listing almost 3,700 publications from all over the world, including books, articles, dissertations and theses, and media materials. The book is divided into four sections. The first lists general works on Jamaican music and culture. The second covers the many genres of Jamaican popular music. The third deals with the export of and developments in Jamaican music in other parts of the world. The fourth and largest section focuses on individual artists, performing ensembles, and music industry personalities. The back matter includes a list of sources consulted, a directory of libraries and archives, and two appendices. Appendix I includes a list of individuals and groups by musical style and/or occupation. Appendix II is a list of individuals and groups by country. Indexes by author and subject are provided. Also notable is *From Vodou to Zouk: A Bibliographic Guide to Music of the French-Speaking Caribbean and Its Diaspora*, volume 1 in the same series and by the same author. Both of these works provide access to a wealth of material not readily available in the past.

9-159. **Selected Musical Terms of Non-Western Cultures: A Notebook-Glossary.** Walter Kaufmann. Warren, MI: Harmonie Park Press, 1990.

Walter Kaufmann was a multi-faceted musician, a composer, conductor, and scholar of the music of India and the Far East. He compiled this useful dictionary over many years. The terms include those used by musicians of Asia, Africa, and Oceania. The terms are listed in alphabetical order, and alternate spellings and cross-references are provided. Definitions are brief but informative and many of them conclude with references to the bibliography at the end of the book. This is a handy ready-reference tool for academic libraries supporting courses in ethnomusicology.

9-160. **Soundscapes: Exploring Music in a Changing World**. 2nd ed. Kay Kaufman Shelemay. New York: W. W. Norton, 2006.

This book is a standard text used in many introductory survey courses in non-Western music. The book is organized in three parts. Listening to Music covers the elements of sound and music with an emphasis on focused listening, Transmitting Music discusses mobility and the global reach of all types of music, and Understanding Music discusses the relationship of music to various aspects of human life. The book provides 84 listening guides to the musical selections contained on three accompanying CDs. The appendix includes a glossary and suggestions for further reading.

LIBRARIES

The libraries described here, the Library of Congress, the New York Public Library, and the British Library, are important resources for music scholars. Their music holdings are unparalleled.

Archival Sound Recordings. London: British Library, 2009– . http://sounds.bl.uk/

This online resource provides access to more than 45,000 recordings of music, speech, and human and natural environments. The database resulted from a project to increase access to the British Library's enormous archive of sound recordings, totaling some 3.5 million items originating in countries all over the world. The online archive includes examples of accents and dialects; poetry, theatre, and other spoken word recordings; classical music; jazz and popular music; sounds of nature and the environment; oral history; and world and traditional music. Anyone with an Internet connection can search the database and listen to approximately 24,000 recordings. U.K. library members may listen to all the recordings and also add information to the metadata via user tags.

9-161. **Catalogue of Printed Music in the British Library.** London: British Library Bibliographic Services Division, 1957–2010. Available in the British Library Integrated Catalogue online at: http://catalogue.bl.uk/F/?func=file&file_name=login-bl-list.

For many years, the *Catalogue of Printed Music in the British Library* was available as a print publication. Print publication ceased as of 2010, and all of the records in the printed catalogue have been incorporated into the online catalogue. The printed music collection is vast and contains music published in every European country from the late 15th century to the present day. Fascinating examples of the earliest printed music have been digitized and can be viewed online. The collection is strongest in music published in the United Kingdom. Like the Library of Congress, the British Library is a national copyright depository, and receives one copy of every piece of music published in the United Kingdom and the Republic of Ireland.

9-162. **Library of Congress: Music Division.** http://www.loc.gov/rr/perform/guide/toc.html

The collection of sheet music and sound recordings at the Library of Congress is the largest in the world. The Music Division's holdings include books, printed music, music manuscripts, sound and video recordings, concert programs, correspondence, and musical instruments. The American music collection is comprehensive because a copy of every piece of copyrighted music must be deposited in the Library of Congress. Some of the Library's collections have been digitized and are freely accessible online at American Memory: http://memory.loc.gov/ammem/browse/ListSome.php?category=Performing%20Arts,%20Music. American Memory is a rich resource (see also entry 2-55). Among its many collections are digitized recordings of African-American music, recordings made by the early inventor Emile Berliner, Civil War era band music, the John Lomax folk music recordings, and recordings of Native American music.

9-163. **New York Public Library for the Performing Arts: Music Division.**
http://www.nypl.org/locations/lpa/music-division

The Music Division of the New York Public Library has a vast music collection. The library contains everything from archival collections to comprehensive holdings of recent published music from virtually every country in the world. The holdings in American music are especially strong and contain scores of many important American composers. The library recently acquired the collection of the American Music Center (entry 9-176), which has further augmented its holdings of scores by American composers. The Rodgers and Hammerstein Archives of Recorded Sound is an important component of the library's research collections. The archives contain approximately 700,000 recordings in all formats. Recordings include music of all types, recorded literature and speech, and videos and videodiscs. Library users are given access to all of these resources on site.

Music Librarianship

9-164. **American Music Librarianship: A Research and Information Guide**. Carol June Bradley. New York: Routledge, 2005.

The author has brought together a well-researched bibliography of writings about music libraries and music librarianship in the United States from the late nineteenth century through the year 2000. The entries are organized in eight chapters covering collection development and management, cataloguing and classification, administration, and general studies. Additional chapters cover the literature on particular libraries and librarians, education for music librarianship, and professional organizations. Brief annotations are supplied for most of the entries, and an author index and subject/name index are included.

9-165. **The International Association of Music Libraries (IAML)** has branches in most developed countries. It currently co-sponsors several ongoing projects, including the *International Inventory of Music Sources/Répertoire international des sources musicales* (RISM) (entry 9-11); *International Inventory of Music Literature/Répertoire International de Littérature Musicale* (RILM), (entry 9-3); *International Inventory of Music Iconography/Répertoire International d'iconographie Musicale* (RIDIM); and *Retrospective Index to Music Periodicals/Répertoire International de la Presse Musicale* (RIPM), (entry 9-7). Since 1954, IAML has published the journal *Fontes Artis Musicae*. The association supports projects and working groups developing standards and principles in areas such as access to music archives, music education, and core bibliographic records in music. The association's website is at http://www.iaml.info/.

9-166. **Music Library Association (MLA)** consists of a national organization and regional chapters, and is a source of information for everyone in the profession. The organization holds annual meetings for members; supports important bibliographical projects such as RILM Abstracts of Music Literature; and issues a number of publications, including the quarterly journal *Notes* and a series of Basic Manuals dealing with various aspects of music librarianship.

DIRECTORIES AND CAREER INFORMATION

9-167. **All You Need to Know About the Music Business.** 6th ed. Donald S. Passman. New York: Free Press, 2006.

This book explains many of the legal and financial complexities of the music business. It is directed to artists but also to independent producers. Sections include advice on how to choose a team of advisors (business managers, personal managers, lawyers, etc.), information on all aspects of record deals, including the calculation of royalties, the songwriting and music publishing business, including copyright basics, touring, and motion picture music. An extensive index makes it fairly easy to find topics.

9-168. **Bridge–New England Conservatory.** http://necmusic.edu/bridge

Bridge, a service of the New England Conservatory of Music, offers online access to job listings by subscription and other opportunities in music and arts administration, including auditions, teaching positions, administrative positions, competitions, grants, scholarships, and festivals. The listings are updated daily. Individual and institutional subscriptions are available; subscriptions are free for students, alumni, faculty and staff of the New England Conservatory.

9-169. **Career Opportunities in the Music Industry.** 6th ed. Shelly Field. New York: Ferguson, 2009.

People who want to work in music in some capacity are the primary audience for this book, earlier editions of which have been favorably reviewed in *Library Journal* and *Booklist*. It is organized by general professional areas, including chapters on recording; radio and TV; touring; music retailing and wholesaling; instrument repair, restoration, and design; publicity; symphonies, orchestras and other areas of classical music; education, church music, etc. Individual jobs within these areas are then described. The author has personal experience in the music industry, and she also conducted interviews with individuals in all areas of the music industry, sent out surveys and questionnaires, and contacted employment agencies, unions, trade associations, orchestras, and other musical groups. The index makes it easy to locate a particular job description quickly.

9-170. **Directory of Music Faculties in Colleges and Universities, U.S. and Canada.** Missoula, MT: College Music Society, 1969– . http://www.music.org/cgi-bin/showpage.pl?tmpl=infoserv/facdir/facdirhome&h=63

The College Music Society publishes this directory annually. The 2010–2011 edition covers almost 1,800 institutions and includes almost 43,000 faculty. The directory contains information about each institution, including the degrees offered, the name, rank, area of specialization, and contact information for faculty and up to five administrators at that institution. Users must be members of the College Music Society to use the online database. This is a very useful reference source providing information about people working in music in higher education. It is a helpful resource for students seeking information on music programs at various schools and for faculty advising them.

9-171. International Who's Who in Classical Music. London: Europa Publications, 2002– .

This resource, published annually, provides biographical and contact information for more than 8,000 prominent figures in the field of classical music, including composers, performers, conductors, directors and managers. The information is provided, for the most part, by the entrants themselves, and includes compositions, recordings, repertoire, honors and awards. The appendices provide addresses for orchestras, opera companies, festivals, competitions, music libraries and music conservatories.

9-172. International Who's Who in Popular Music. London: Europa Publications, 2002– .

Like its companion volume on classical music (entry 9-171), this serial publication provides short biographies of numerous prominent people in the fields of pop, rock, folk, jazz, dance, world and country music. Included is information about recordings, broadcasts, films, and so on. Contact information is also given when available. In many cases, the entrants have provided information for their entries, in others, research is completed by the editorial staff. The appendices supply addresses of recording companies, booking agents, management companies, publishers, festivals, and music organizations.

9-173. Music Vacancy List. College Music Society. Missoula, MT: 1968– .

This is a weekly online publication for members of the College Music Society. The publication announces openings for academic positions in all areas of music, including some announcements for music librarians, at colleges and universities throughout the United States. Also listed are selected non-academic positions for which advanced training in music is needed.

9-174. Musical America. Print and online subscription database. www.musicalamerica.com

This directory requires a subscription for complete access. It provides contact information for performing arts organizations, as well as artist managers, competitions, music schools and departments, and services and products. The database is updated frequently, and the coverage is international in scope. One very useful function is the ability to search for jobs. Listings include performance jobs as well as administrative and teaching jobs. The website also offers travel booking services for helping to manage the logistics of going on tour. Numerous other features are offered including information about grants, a career advice blog, feature articles about up-and-coming artists, and a searchable archive of back issues of the directory. The print version of *Musical America* is published annually.

9-175. Songwriter's Market. 34th ann. ed. Cincinnati, OH: Writer's Digest Books, 2012.

This resource provides aspiring composers and lyricists with information about numerous record producers, record companies, music publishers, managers and booking agents, theaters and publishers of plays, classical performing organizations, and contests and awards. Complete contact information is given for all organizations, together with descriptions of the kind of material they are interested in and a list things they have recently produced, published, etc. Established writers offer insight into various aspects of the creative process and tips for marketing; as well as informative pieces on submission strategies, royalties, copyright, contracts, and using social media to develop career contacts. A section of the book is devoted to lists of publications, venues, grants, and websites of interest. A general index and an index to names are included.

ORGANIZATIONS

ASCAP–American Society of Composers, Authors and Publishers. http://www.ascap.com/

BMI–Broadcast Music, Inc. http://www.bmi.com/

ASCAP and BMI are the two major performing rights licensing organizations in the United States. Both issue licenses to performing organizations and other users of music and then distribute royalties to their members based on the performance history of the members. Both organizations maintain databases of their members' works. These databases are freely available and may be accessed by the name of the writer or composer, the title of the song or work, and publisher.

9-176. **American Music Center**. http://www.amc.net/default.aspx

The American Music Center is an important source of information about American music and American composers. It is also a source of grants in support of composers' creative activities. The Center offers a number of resources, including an online catalog providing access to more than 57,000 works by over 6,000 composers. The Center's online directory offers biographical and contact information for many composers, performers, and ensembles. The AMC also has a 24-hour online radio station, Counterstream Radio, and a web magazine, New Music Box, which features interviews, profiles, discussions, and reviews of recent recordings.

9-177. **The American Composers' Alliance** (ACA) (http://composers.com/) was founded in 1937 by Aaron Copland and several composer colleagues. It has approximately 200 composer members and is dedicated to publishing, promoting, and preserving the music of its members. The ACA maintains an online catalog, which can be searched by composer name and title. The organization holds a yearly summer festival of American music presenting six to eight concerts of new works by composers from across the United States.

9-178. **The American Musicological Society**, founded in 1934, publishes the *Journal of the American Musicological Society* (JAMS) and periodic lists of theses and dissertations in the field. An index to the dissertations is available on the web at the American Musicological sponsored site at www.ams-net.org/ddm/index.php.

9-179. **The Association for Recorded Sound Collections**, a non-profit organization, was founded in 1966 and includes in its membership people in the recording and broadcasting industries as well as librarians in the performing arts. The organization is dedicated to the study and preservation of sound recordings in all formats and from all periods. It publishes the peer-reviewed *ARSC Journal* and *ARSC Bulletin*. See http://www.arsc-audio.org.

9-180. **The International Musicological Society** was founded in 1927 to promote research in musicology. Since 1928 the Society has published the journal *Acta Musicologica*. Information on the Society can be accessed at http://www.ims-online.ch/news.aspx.

9-181. The League of American Orchestras (formerly American Symphony Orchestra League) was founded in 1942 and has a library pertaining to all aspects of the symphony orchestra. The organization promotes symphony orchestras and provides information for musicians, managers, boards and volunteers. It is, according to its website, "the only national organization dedicated solely to the orchestral experience." See http://www.americanorchestras.org/utilities/about_the_league.html.

9-182. The Music Publishers' Association of the United States (http://mpa.org) founded in 1895, is a non-profit organization of music publishers in the United States. Its members are mainly publishers of concert and educational music, and the association works closely with organizations such as the American Choral Directors Association, the American Music Center, the American Music Conference, the American Symphony Orchestra League, the Church Music Publishers Association, the International Confederation of Music Publishers, the International Federation of Serious Music Publishers, the Music Library Association, the Major Orchestra Librarians' Association, the National Association for Music Education, the National Orchestra Association, the Music Teachers National Association, and the Retail Print Music Dealers Association. Also note the National Music Publishers' Association (http://nmpa.org/home/index.asp).

9-183. The National Association for Music Education (formerly Music Educators National Conference) was founded in 1902 and has over 75,000 members. It publishes *Music Educators' Journal*, *Teaching Music Magazine*, and the quarterly *Journal of Research in Music Education* (http://www.menc.org/about/).

CHAPTER 10

FILM, RADIO, TELEVISION, AND VIDEO

Elizabeth S. Aversa

In perhaps no other area of the performing arts has there been a greater convergence of types of materials as in film, radio, television and video. Resources that were once straightforward annual listings of films are now mega-websites where users not only find information about films, but they can find reviews, read synopses, watch trailers, and sometimes see whole films. Where there used to be TV episode synopses, there are now libraries of episodes online for the user's viewing. These resources have changed greatly over the years, and while some annual media have continued to double digit edition numbers, others have disappeared with other publishers taking up the slack by providing new web-based resources. This is a rapidly changing area that needs continuous update, so users of this section of the guide should be especially mindful to check on changes at publisher or web-provider sites.

FILM

Databases and Digital Collections

10-1. Cinema Image Gallery. New York: H.W. Wilson.

The Cinema Image Gallery is one of the most comprehensive collections of still images from movies, television, and the entertainment industry, over 150,000 superior-quality images, along with 4,000 post-art and lobby cards used to promote movies. It presents the history of movie-making; still images of films in production; directors working on-set; set, costume and production design; as well as hair and make-up shots; and rare behind-the-scenes material. The Gallery also offers an extensive TV stills archive, covering comedies, dramas, series, TV movies, game shows, and thousands of pictures of stars.

10-2. Film Indexes Online Proquest Information and Learning. Online subscription database. (Chadwyck-Healey film resources).

This resource is comprised of three valuable resources that have been brought together online under a single portal. The databases are Film Index International, the American Film Institute Catalog, and FIAF International Index to Film Periodicals. Subscribers to Chadwyck-Healey Film Indexes Online can search across these three resources or search the individual databases separately. The databases included are described briefly below:

Film Index International offers records on international films that were released over the past 90 years and indexed by the British Film Institute. The database is updated twice each year and now consists of over 128,000 film records and more than 880,000 records on persons working in the film industry. This is a rapidly growing tool; for example, in 2009, 700 film and 21,000 person records were added. The record on each film includes information on director, cast, crews, year of release, production information, and awards (if any). A synopsis of each film is included. Person records give biographical information, awards (if any), and films in which the individual appeared. There are references from film journals within the records, and also links among the records so that the user can navigate between the records in the database.

American Film Institute Catalog has long been a standard for American film information. Its scope is the history of American film from 1893 to 1974, with records for selected major films from 1975–2008. The print Catalog is updated annually. This database is also updated twice per year.

The International Index to Film Periodicals indexes scholarly film periodicals. This database is provided by the International Federation of Film Archives (FIAF). The index begins in 1972 and extends to present day. It is searchable by topic, not just by film title, and thus adds a type of accessibility unavailable through the Film Index International above.

It is important to note that each of the databases included in Film Indices Online is also available in other formats. See, for example, the American Film Institute Catalog in the listing of open source materials in this section of the performing arts chapter.

10-3. Film and Television Literature Index: With Full Text. EBSCOhost. Online subscription database.

Film and Television Literature Index covers material from some 300 periodicals, which are scanned for pertinent articles. Recently, it has included television periodicals as well. Since it was first issued in 1973, in print as *Film Literature Index*, it has developed an excellent reputation not only for its coverage of some 160 journals from 30 countries but also for its organization and ease of use. Developed originally as a pilot offering at SUNY-Albany with a grant from the New York State Council on the Arts, this work has continued without interruption and occupies a prominent position among such tools. The full text online offering includes *Variety* movie reviews from 1914 to the present.

Open Access Resources

10-4. The American Film Institute Catalog of Feature Films.
http://www.afi.com/members/catalog/

The AFI Catalog has been described as the most authoritative film database on the Web. It is comprised of entries on American feature-length and short films produced from 1893–2011. Nearly 100,000 entries are available. Outstanding Movies of the Year awards from 2000 through 2010 are also included. For each film included, the database yields production information (director, release date, production company, distribution company, names of technical directors), release and premier dates and places, languages, locations, series information (if any), copyright claimant, and MPAA rating. Entries also note genre as well as physical properties (i.e., Dolby, Technicolor, etc.). Bibliographic resources about the films are noted in abbreviated form: title of the source (i.e., variety), date, and page. Full casts of the films are listed by their names and the respective character names. Handily, there are links to related information in the database: click on Twentieth Century Fox Film Corp. in the listing for the distribution company in the "Star Wars" entry, and the number of films in the database distributed by Twentieth Century Fox is revealed. This is an essential place to look.

10-5. Internet Movie Data Base (IMDB). Col Needham, Founder & CEO. http://www.imdb.com

Now 21 years old, this mega-site is the largest film database on the Web, and it now has telephone and iPad apps for both iPhones and Androids. Entries on films include complete cast and crew lists, information on technical and production aspects, and also reviews (many of them for popular movies) from critics and from fans and moviegoers. News articles about films, and photos and videos are included. The website also has user-friendly opportunities to keep track of movies viewed and to communicate the information to friends (the Watchlist and Check-in features). Features include trivia about the films, box office information, such as revenues, and trailers that can be viewed by the user. Users can find a theater "nearby" with the click of the mouse. The database also includes similar, though abbreviated, information on television shows and videos. The user should beware. Between watching trailers and videos, and "just checking" for favorites, this website can keep the user engaged for lengthy periods of time. It is a great resource to grab quick information, such as where a movie is showing or to spend an afternoon updating the list of films, episodes, or videos that were missed. Like its counterpart for Broadway (the Internet Broadway Database, entry 8-51), this is a great addition to free resources in the performing arts. Additional coverage is available in BBC-Film, (British Broadcasting Company http://www.bbc.co.uk/film/), which provides another example of the convergence of media around the performing arts. It offers film information and reviews of both feature and short films; and links to BBC-news, television, blogs, and DVD reviews are all there for the user. Release information is included along with interviews with casts and crew members, and advice for filmmaking. These two sources together will meet audience needs and professional needs for many.

Print Resources

10-6. **The Encyclopedia of Novels Into Film.** John C. Tibbets and James M. Welsh. New York: Facts on File, 2005.

This work will find a welcoming audience in those interested in novels that serve as sources for subsequent motion pictures. Coverage is given to more than 300 novels and their screen adaptations, including a wide range in terms of seriousness of purpose, from *Schindler's List* to *Valley of the Dolls*. Drama, comedy, film noir, science fiction, westerns, suspense, and action all are represented in two-part entries. The first part describes the original novel, while the second provides comparative examination and assessment of the film(s).

10-7. **Filmmaker's Dictionary**. Ralph S. Singleton and James A. Conrad. New York: Crown Publishing Group, 2000.

Like its earlier editions, this volume is concise and compact and filled with the terminology of filmmaking practice. It is written in simple language but provides a useful service of helping the user to become familiar with both technical terms and slang expressions employed by professionals in the field. More than 1500 terms, representing every aspect of the art, are defined. *Filmmakers Dictionary* has abundant cross-references from the entries to other related definitions, making this a convenient and practical dictionary. Most interesting are the almost anecdotal bits of background information attached to many of the definitions.

10-8. **International Motion Picture Almanac.** New York: Quigley, 1929– . Ann.

This has been a leading directory of services and products and an important purchase for film libraries throughout its long history and its issuance under varying titles. It is a treasure-house of miscellaneous information and statistical data. Included is a who's who providing brief biographical sketches of numerous film personalities. There are also sections on pictures, corporations, theater circuits, buying and booking, equipment and suppliers, services, talent and literary agencies, organizations, advertising, world market, press, non-theatrical motion pictures, censorship, and various timely issues.

10-9. **Magill's Cinema Annual**. Detroit: Gale, 1982– . Ann.

Beginning with coverage of the year 1981, this resource has served as a supplement to the extensive multi-volume *Magill's Survey of Cinema* (Salem Press, 1980–1985). The reviews are lengthy and well-constructed, and cover films released in the United States. Entries include production credits, direction, screenplay, cinematography, editing, art direction, music, MPAA rating, running time, and principal characters. Foreign films are included if they were released in this country during the time period. There is also a section of additional films that treats briefly the same number of films that appear in the "Selected Films" category. A number of indices provide excellent access.

10-10. Schirmer Encyclopedia of Film. Barry Grant, ed. Farmington Hills, MI: Thomson Gale, 2006. 4 vols. Print and e-book.

This is a comprehensive resource covering many aspects of film studies: production, national traditions in film, history of film, critical theory, and genres, issues (such as censorship), and technical aspects such as sound and lighting. Main entries are accompanied by sidebars that point to the accomplishments of individuals of different types: actors, directors, etc., in the main articles. There is a full index, a list of recommended readings attached to the entries, and extensive photographs throughout.

10-11. Chris Gore's The Ultimate Film Festival Survival Guide.4th ed. Chris Gore. NY: Random House, 2009.

This work is more of a handbook than a directory in its emphasis on the marketing and selling of films at some 500 festivals held around the world. The author is a knowledgeable film writer and editor who has written and directed films as well as served as judge at different festivals. He offers a manual of steps to follow in submitting a film, marketing the film, and closing the deal, but also lists thousands of festivals to which films might be submitted and contact information, too. The publisher called this resource the "the guerrilla guide to marketing and selling indie films."

10-12. DVD and Video Guide. Mick Martin and Marsha Porter. New York: Ballantine, 2006.

This is a well-known, comprehensive guide to more than 17,000 films, serials, and television programs found on video. Movies and shows are alphabetically arranged in this text. Capsule reviews are furnished, along with a rating system from five stars to "turkey." Included for each film or program are release dates, directors, and principal cast. As in the Maltin guide (entry 10-13), there are indexes by director and cast members.

10-13. Leonard Maltin's 2012 Movie Guide. Leonard Maltin. New York: Signet. Ann.

This is one of the best-known annual guides providing comprehensive and somewhat controversial coverage of motion pictures. Unlike a number of others, it is not limited to films that appear in video. The author is one of the leading film critics, and in this work he treats thousands of titles. Reviews are very brief but informative. Maltin's brief reviews are lively, employing a sense of humor in the capsule commentaries, but they are not without their own critics. Included are release dates, running time, director, major cast, and video availability. Entries are arranged alphabetically and can be accessed through indexes of performers and directors.

10-14. Roger Ebert's Movie Yearbook 2010. Roger Ebert. Kansas City, MO: Andrews McMeel, 2009.

This volume includes the full-length reviews that Ebert published between 2007 and 2009. In addition, it includes interviews, essays, tributes, and a glossary. After 25 years of reviewing and many awards to his credit, Ebert is among the most popular film critics and his reviews are trusted by many readers.

RogerEbert.com (http://rogerebert.com) is a free and addictive website for those who like the film critic. This website shares Ebert's reviews, essays, lists (for example, great movies), and observations of all things having to do with film. Sections on the site are updated with varying regularity, but most lists are up-to-date. Tabs from which users can select to search include: reviews, great movies, people, commentary, one-minute reviews, festivals, Oscars, and even a glossary of terms.

10-15. VideoHound's Golden Movie Retriever. Jim Craddock. Florence, KY: Gale, 2010. Ann.

Since its first issue in 1991, this annual work has joined Maltin's as one of the most popular comprehensive guides to motion pictures on video. It has more titles and, like the other guides, provides capsule reviews along with a rating (ranging from four bones to "woof," the equivalent of a bomb). The reviews are informative and provide interesting facts. Also included in each alphabetically arranged entry are release dates, running time, video availability, and major credits (principal cast members and directors, but also individuals responsible for writing, camera work, and music). About 1000 new movies are added to each edition.

SPECIAL TOPICS IN FILM

Animation

Animation, although its roots go back to much earlier times (around 1800 in the western world, earlier in Asia), is an area of the performing arts that is increasingly important because of the use of it in so many films today. Animation has several common forms, but all of them create an illusion of movement by using sets of photographs, drawings, pictures, or models presented in quick succession.

Traditional animation encompasses full animation such as we see in Disney productions; limited animation in which characters are hand-drawn with sparse backgrounds as in some children's cartoon shows; and live animation that combines live action with hand-drawn animation. There are several types of "stop motion" animation in which real objects such as puppets, models, or cut-outs are moved about and filmed, again creating the illusion of real movement. Computer animation is used in multi-media presentations. Traditional animation takes many images and manipulates them to show movement; computer animation does the opposite.

Animation is not only an art form, but it is a type of craft profession as well. A number of universities offer serious study of animation as well as programs leading to careers in the production of animated materials. Some junior/community colleges and special schools also offer an entrée to this creative area. A few resources are noted here; they will get the searcher started.

10-16. The Animator's Survival Kit, Expanded Edition: A Manual of Methods, Principles and Formulas for Classical, Computer, Games, Stop Motion and Internet Animators. Richard Williams. Faber & Faber, 2009.

This is a comprehensive source in that it offers, from a highly successful animator (*Toy Story* and Roger Rabbit are among his credits) and master class teacher, the basics along with the history of animation. Brief chapters, some just a page or two in length, offer technical how-to advice, as well as historical notes, current perspectives, and just plain interesting information. Hundreds of illustrations show the reader exactly what Williams is referring to; successions of drawings illustrate what he writes about, for example, the handling of "weight" in running and jumping in the animation domain. A very detailed table of contents guides the reader through the content. This is a good resource to start with. The book is marketed with a DVD.

10-17. The Animation World Network. http://www.awn.com/

The AWN is a large animation publishing group with a web presence that gives users a wealth of information on animation. Among its publications are *Animation World Magazine,* an online journal publishing several articles per week and *VFX World Magazine,* also online. The former covers animation issues in general–creative, technical, and business, etc., while the latter is focused on 3-D animation and computer graphics (effects). The Network can also guide users to workshops, tutorials, products and services, as well as publications, competitions and events, jobs (there is a placement function), and much more.

10-18. TheAssociation Internationale du Film d'Animation (ASIFA). http://asifa.net/

The ASIFA was started as an association of animation artists but has grown into a worldwide network with local chapters across the globe. The association is a good source of information on conferences, schools, and animation festivals.

10-19. Best Animations. www.bestanimations.com.

Best Animations claims to offer the best animations on the Web with over 3,000 of the best 3-D animated GIFs.

10-20. Origins of Animation. Washington, D.C.: Library of Congress Motion Picture, Broadcasting and Recorded Sound Division, 1999– . Video and e-book.

A collection of 21 animated films and 2 fragments, spanning the years 1900 to 1921, shows the development of early American animation and reveals the social attitudes of early 20th-century America. The films include clay, puppet, and cut-out animation, as well as pen drawings. They point to a connection between newspaper comic strips and early animated films, as represented by Keeping Up With the Joneses, Krazy Kat, and The Katzenjammer Kids. This work from the Library of Congress Motion Picture, Broadcasting and Recorded Sound Division, is only one of a number of films and publications available from the Division on the subject.

10-21. Society for Animation Studies. http://gertie.animationstudies.org/

Society for Animation Studies is an international organization dedicated to the study of animation history and theory. It was founded by Dr. Harvey Deneroff in 1987. Each year, the SAS holds an annual conference at locations throughout the world, where members present their recent research. One of the foci of the organization is to publish and republish material on animation, including techniques, best practices, and such.

10-22. The World History of Animation. Stephen Cavalier. Berkeley: University of California Press, 2011.

This resource provides history of animation from an international perspective. It is arranged chronologically and provides information on feature films, TV programs, games, web animation, and digital films. Color illustrations are included. The publisher's synopsis claims the work includes "... the more unusual and unheard of artists whose creations have caused wonderment and controversy around the world, as well as offering new insight into old favorites."

History of Film

10-23. America's Film Legacy: the Authoritative Guide to the Landmark Movies in the National Film Registry. Daniel Eagan. London: Continuum International Publishing Group, 2009. Print and e-book.

Each year, 25 films are selected for preservation from the Film Registry. Five hundred are profiled in this tome, selected for historical and artistic significance. Listed in chronological order by date, each entry contains information on cast, director, set, production, and current availability. An essay gives the history and background of the film's story with incisive comments that give details about early filmmaking and culture.

10-24. Encyclopedia of Early Cinema. Richard Abel, ed. New York: Routledge, 2005. Print and e-book.

In this major A-Z work, nearly 1000 entries written by experts from the United States and Europe describe not only the technological advances and their inventors from which cinema would develop, but also the cultural milieu from which cinema was to emerge. The period, "early cinema," refers to the first 20 or 25 years of the cinema's emergence at the end of the nineteenth and beginning of the twentieth century, that is from the early 1890s to the middle 1910s. The entries cover film production, filmmakers, film genres, individual films, technology, developments in film style, and the topic with the largest number of entries, key figures of the various national cinemas. A useful thematic index draws similar topics and concepts together, among them "Cultural Contexts" and "Social Contexts" that show how early cinema was entwined with other forms and practices of mass culture.

10-25. Enser's Filmed Books and Plays: a List of Books and Plays from Which Films Have Been Made, 1928–2001 6th ed. Ellen Baskin, comp. Brookfield, VT: Ashgate Publishing, 2003.

Enser's standard work has been revised and now cumulates the content of the previous issues (first published in 1968) while adding material published through 2001. It is a list of almost 10,000 films (primarily in English) derived from books and plays. Never claiming to be a completely exhaustive listing, the bibliography is accessed through excellent indexes. Entries in the title index give the name of the distributing company and year of registration, as well as author, publisher, and book title. The author index lists works by the authors whose works have been made into films and includes publisher as well as film distributor. There are indications of whether the film was made for TV and whether a film is suitable for juvenile audiences. An effort that complements this coverage is *Books and Plays in Films, 1896–1915: Literary, Theatrical, and Artistic Sources of the First Twenty Years of Motion Pictures*, by Denis Gifford (McFarland, 1991). Gifford lists about 3,000 film presentations derived from artistic or literary works (ballet songs, operas, and comic strips, as well as novels and short stories). Most of these early silent films were relatively short and thus have not received much attention from writers of guides such as this. Arrangement is alphabetical by name of author or creator, after which are listed the films in chronological order. Companies are given and genre is identified.

10-26. From Silents to Sound: A Biographical Encyclopedia of Performers Who Made the Transition to Talking Pictures. Roy Liebman. Jefferson, NC: McFarland, 2009.

This is a most interesting and specialized biographical resource, focusing on actors and actresses who bridged the gap and made the transition from silent film to talking pictures. Coverage is limited to screen personalities who had made at least three silent movies as either a star or major supporting figure and then had appeared in at least one talking picture. A further limitation omits those who had silent film careers in countries other than the United States. The roster of individuals included varies considerably in terms of their current fame and popularity, although they were prominent in their day. Entries vary in length and furnish birthplace, dates, nicknames and pseudonyms along with real names, citations to sources for filmographies, and career description along with excerpts from film reviews. Appendices supply additional listings and the work concludes with a general bibliography followed by an index.

10-27. A History of Narrative Film. 4th ed. David A. Cook. New York: W. W. Norton, 2004.

This continues as the most complete and comprehensive history of cinema on an international basis, focused on the development of narrative film. The first three editions established it as an important information source; it proved to be of use to a variety of patrons from serious students to laypersons. The material in this work is presented in scholarly fashion, well documented throughout, and provides illustrations of major scenes from many of the films described. Fred Davies notes in his review that Cook's aim is to deal with the '"hegemonic control by American distributors of virtually every film market in the world," globalization, and the dominance of CGI . . ."' Inserts on color technologies are provided as well. Detailed information is found on individual filmmakers, and their movies are examined in a critical manner. National cinemas and many films are covered. Film elements are analyzed, and in some cases, public reaction and influence on the field are gauged. The layperson will be especially interested in the quantity of production stills taken from a variety of motion pictures over the years. There are both a good bibliography and a good glossary. (Fred Davies, "Review of David A. Cook, *A History of Narrative Films*," H-USA, H-Net Reviews, October 2004. http://www.h-net.msu.edu/reviews/)

10-28. Historical Dictionary of African American Cinema. Torriano S. Berry and Venise T. Berry. Lanham, MD: Scarecrow Press, 2007. (Historical Dictionaries of Literature and the Arts)

This work adds to the growing number of resources on African American contributions to the performing arts. The dictionary lists films, people, and topics related to African American cinema: events, awards, prizes, and the like, as well as general information about organizations, prizes, and terms. For films, run times, themes, casts and production information is given; for individuals, biographical information includes birth and death dates, brief descriptions of the career, and filmographies with dates. Appendices list NAACP Image Award Winners, African American Academy Award Winners and Golden Globe Winners, and Top Grossing African American Films.

      An earlier work is *African American Films Through 1959: A Comprehensive, Illustrated Filmography* (Larry Richards, McFarland, 1998). This is an important information tool, providing identification, and, in some cases, detailed exposition on 1,324 feature films, short subjects, and musical soundies featuring African-American casts or providing topical treatment of African-Americans. The Negro film industry was flourishing in the 1920s with studios in several of the major cities in this country. Their products were shown in theaters catering to this audience before the time of integration and lasting until the 1950s. Their record of accomplishment represents an important element in the history of American film-making. Each film entry supplies production date, producer, director, company, distributor, cast, type, genre, and so forth along with synopsis of plot and references to reviews. Appendices provide film credits for 1,850 actors and listing of film companies and their films.

10-29. Hollywood's Indian: The Portrayal of the Native American in Film. Peter C. Rollins and John E. O'Connor, eds. Lexington: University of Kentucky, 2003.

This is an expanded collection of essays examining the treatment given to Native Americans in cinema from the silent film era to the present day. Both general history of film development in this regard and specific titles are treated in an effort to provide insight into the nature of changing perspective within American society. A representative set of movies is examined in depth and the essays examine the manner in which the films may represent the attitudes and perceptions held by the movie-going public. Review and exposition of such cultural attributes enables one to understand the issues, conflicts, and forces that shape the final products.

10-30. The Media in the Movies: A Catalog of American Journalism Films, 1900–1996. Larry Langman. McFarland, 2008.

This is a filmography identifying more than 1,000 feature films and serials whose central characters or plots were focused on journalism. Most of the titles treat newspaper reporters and reporting, but radio, television, and photojournalism also are represented, too. Entries are arranged alphabetically and furnish production credits, casts, and brief plot descriptions, and sometimes analysis.

10-31. The New Historical Dictionary of the American Film Industry. Anthony Slide. Lanham, MD: Scarecrow Press, 2001.

Slide's work updates his earlier detailed dictionary of the historical development of the film industry in this country. Coverage is alphabetically arranged. The writing is smooth and the descriptions well-developed. Cross-references are furnished. The work treats many facets of the film industry, with special attention given to business organizations, industrial techniques, and technology. Also covered are producing and releasing companies, film series, genres, organizations, and specific terms peculiar to the field. Some entries include addresses, bibliographies, and archival resources.

10-32. Routledge Encyclopedia of Early Cinema. Richard Abel. Florence, KY: Routledge, 2005.

This alphabetically organized resource of over 800 pages provides information about the first 25 years of film history. This work has worldwide coverage and so is not limited to what happened in the US and UK. It covers the technology of filmmaking during the period covered. Also, style of films, production and distribution in those times, and film companies are all covered in short to medium length entries. More than 150 scholars contributed to this large effort that includes bibliographic sources with the longer articles. A thematic index is helpful to the user.

People in Film

10-33. Art Directors in Cinema: A Worldwide Biographical Dictionary. Michael L. Stephens. Jefferson, NC: McFarland, 2008.

This is a useful biographical dictionary that treats a segment of endeavor that has received little attention. The work describes the lives and achievements of 300 important personalities representing the world of production design. Individuals from all aspects of art direction and design creativity in film are covered on an international basis. Although this activity emanated from the legacy of those who labored for the stage, the demands of motion pictures were monumental in comparison. Entries are well written and readable, and are arranged alphabetically. They vary in length from a single paragraph to several pages; each biographical sketch is followed by a filmography of credits. The work concludes with a general bibliography; a good general index provides access to names, film titles, issues, and studios.

10-34. Halliwell's Who's Who in the Movies. 4th ed. John Walker, ed. New York: HarperPerennial/ HarperCollins, 2006.

The Filmgoer's Companion, which appeared in some 15 editions, is now published as *Halliwell's Who's Who in the Movies.* Since Halliwell's death in 1989, Walker has edited the subsequent editions and continues the tried-and-true format. Arrangement of entries is alphabetical and coverage is given to films, personalities (actors, directors, writers, etc.), and other related elements. It remains a storehouse of information on the cinema even after a long run.

10-35. The New Biographical Dictionary of Film. 5th ed. David Thomson. New York: Alfred A. Knopf, 2010.

The first edition of this work was published in 1976 and was praised by reviewers for its literate and witty, albeit opinionated, coverage of actors and directors. The second edition, published in 1981, updated and expanded the initial effort. Now in the 5th edition, there is alphabetically arranged coverage of actors, directors, and producers on an international scale. This work is still a vital source, entertaining in style but at the same time cogent and effective as a critical tool. Thomson's "obsessive work provides a sharp expression of personal taste, jokes, and digressions, insults, and eulogies." Entries are lengthy and packed with details, and provide references to other entries in the volume. The work retains its charm and continues to be a top-rated biographical dictionary for its clarity, depth, and provocative nature.

Motion Picture Academy of Arts and Sciences. The Oscars. http://www.oscars.org/

The Academy is famous because of the Oscar awards it grants annually, the most prestigious of which are awarded in the live TV presentation of The Oscars. Awards are for acting, producing, directing, writing, costume design, documentaries, and so forth. The awards for technological specialties are given in separate ceremonies prior to the annual TV show.

Dedicated to the advancement of the arts and sciences of motion pictures, the Academy is best known for the Oscars, but it is busy year-round with a wide array of educational, outreach, preservation and research endeavors. Founded in 1927 by 36 of the most influential men and women in the motion picture industry at the time, the Academy is an honorary membership organization whose ranks now include more than 6,000 artists and professionals.

The Margaret Herrick Library is maintained by the Academy. The Library, founded in 1929, contains more than a thousand collections that document the products and activities of companies and organizations as well as the careers of producers, directors, writers, actors, cinematographers, art directors, costume designers, composers, makeup artists, animators, columnists, publicists, executives and others who have made a significant contribution to the industry. Collected material includes production files, scripts, correspondence, clippings, contracts, manuscripts, notes, scrapbooks, costume and production design drawings, storyboards, sheet music, music scores and recorded sound.

Professional Associations and Organizations in Film

10-36. **The American Film Institute** (AFI). http://www.afi.com/about/

The AFI supports a wide range of archival, research, and production activities. AFI preserves the legacy of America's film heritage through the *AFI Catalog of Feature Films*, an authoritative record of American films from 1893 to the present (last ed. 1999) and the AFI Archive, which contains rare footage from across the history of the moving image. AFI honors the artists and their work through a variety of annual programs and special events. For 39 years, the AFI Life Achievement Award has remained the highest honor for a career in film, while *AFI Awards,* the Institute's almanac for the 21st century, honors the most outstanding motion pictures and television programs of the year. Other publications have included *American Film* and *Guide to College Courses in Film and Television.*

10-37. **Los Angeles Film Critics Association** (LAFCA). http://www.lafca.net

Founded in 1975, The Los Angeles Film Critics Association (LAFCA) is an organization of Los Angeles-based, professional film critics working in print and electronic media. The LAFCA sponsors the annual Achievement Awards, honoring screen excellence on both sides of the camera. Over the past three decades, LAFCA has sponsored and hosted numerous film panels and events, and donated funds to various Los Angeles film organizations, especially where film preservation is concerned.

10-38. **The Motion Picture Association of America.** http://mpaa.org/

The Motion Picture Association of America provides both the motion picture rating system and economic reports on the film industry. The organization that was established as a trade organization is also concerned with the protection of intellectual property in the film and video industry.

10-39. Screen Actors Guild (SAG). http://www.sag.org

Established in 1933, with 20 branches nationwide, SAG represents over 125,000 actors who work in film and digital motion pictures and television programs, commercials, video games, corporate/educational, Internet and all new media formats. The Guild sponsors the Screen Actors Guild Awards annually that benefit the Screen Actors Guild Foundation, which provides a meaningful way for SAG members to contribute to the literacy of children in their communities through BookPALS (Performing Artists for Literacy in Schools), its online component, Storyline and the We the Children family-heritage book-writing project.

   Other film industry guilds are the Art Directors Guild (http://www.adg.org) and Director's Guild (http://www.dga.org/); Motion Picture Editors Guild (https://www.editorsguild.com/index.cfm); Writers Guild of America (http://www.wga.org); and The Animation Guild (http://www.mpsc839.org)

10-40. The University Film and Video Association. http://www.ufva.org/

Formerly the University Film Association, the University Film and Video Association publishes the *Journal of Film and Video*.

RADIO

10-41. Music Radio: The Greatest Performers and Programs of the 1920s through the Early 1960s. Jim Cox. Jefferson, NC: McFarland, 2005.

This is a book that will fill the gaps for readers who want to know more about programs and aspects of radio either hard to find or not covered elsewhere. The author provides a number of in-depth chapters on some of the most popular "old time" shows: the Fred Waring Show, the Bing Crosby Show, Your Hit Parade, and the Grand Old Opry are examples. The chapters on the individual shows are separated by chapters on aspects of musical radio: disc jockeys, big bands, house bands, and similar topics are taken up in the individual chapters. There are chapter notes, a bibliography, and an index. This is a rather unique and very helpful work.

10-42. Radio Programs, 1924–1984: A Catalog of over 1800 Shows. Vincent Terrace. Jefferson, NC: McFarland, 1999.

This title expands the author's work treating radio's golden years (1930–1960), published in 1981 and treating 1,500 programs. It retains the solid character and informative approach of the earlier effort in its identification of network and syndicated programs over a period of 60 years. Arrangement is alphabetical by title of the program; entries include story line, cast lists, announcer and music credits, sponsors, program openings, network and syndication information, length, and dates. All types of programming are included, representative of the range of entertainment afforded the public (adventure, comedy, crime, drama, game shows, musicals, mystery, science fiction, and westerns). A name index provides access.

10-43. RadioLovers.com–Free Old Fashioned Radio Shows. http://www.radiolovers.com

This website lists radio programs that can be downloaded without charge. The database provides lists by program or by genre. Soap operas are not included, but one can find variety shows, comedies, dramas, westerns, science fiction, and music programs for which the website developers believe have expired copyrights. Here the user can find Arthur Godfrey, Eddie Arnold, Abbott and Costello, and Hopalong Cassidy, among others. This is both a useful and an enjoyable resource.

TELEVISION AND VIDEO

10-44. Television Cartoon Shows: An Illustrated Encyclopedia, 1949 through 2003. 2nd ed. Hal Erikson. Jefferson, NC: McFarland, 2005. 2 vols.

This resource, one of the many produced by McFarland Publishing, provides information on a sometimes overlooked area of television programming. Entries are arranged alphabetically and there is coverage of individual shows with their histories, themes, synopses, voice credits, and production information. The illustrated work is in two volumes with half the alphabet covered in each. Entries run between one and several (up to 10) pages, and there are essays on the creative, historical, and regulatory aspects of cartoons on television. There is a bibliography and index to both volumes.

10-45. The Complete Directory to Prime Time Network TV Shows, 1946–Present. 9th ed. Tim Brooks and Earle Marsh. New York: Ballantine Books, 2007.

Defining prime time in broad terms as the time period from 6:00 P.M. to sign-off, this now-familiar work furnishes the librarian and patron with a comprehensive listing of all regularly scheduled programs ever aired on network television during the choice hours. First published in 1979, it has been following a pattern of about three years between issues. In addition to network series, it includes the top shows in syndication. Entries are arranged by title of the program and include dates of showing, broadcast history, cast, story line, and memorable episodes. There are several interesting and useful appendices.

10-46. Dictionary of Television and Audiovisual Terminology. Moshe Moshkovitz. Jefferson, NC: McFarland, 2008.

This is a practical dictionary providing coverage of both common technical and slang terminology relevant to the world of television broadcasting and audiovisual production. There is some representation of the vocabulary of electronics and computer science. The author is an academic, who began by compiling a glossary for his students. The dictionary contains over 1,500 words and phrases representing the common speech of professionals in the field and of those writing for publication. Arrangement is alphabetical; acronyms are placed as if words and numbers had been spelled out. Definitions are clear and well-constructed, with many providing examples illustrating the meanings. They vary in length from a few lines to more than a page, depending upon the topic.

10-47. Encyclopedia of Television Shows, 1925 through 2007. Vincent Terrace. Jefferson, NC: Mac-Farland, 2009. 4 vols.

This resource represents decades of research on the part of the author, a well-known expert on radio and television. The scope of the work is the entire history of television, and it provides descriptions of shows from authoritative sources not documented elsewhere. All genres are covered here: children's, talk shows, game shows, opera, plays, women's programming, dance, documentary television, as well as the usual categories. The more than 9,000 entries are arranged alphabetically across the four volumes. A name index to nearly 2,000 names accompanies.

10-48. International Television & Video Almanac. Quigley, 1956– . Ann.

Statistical reporting and information on people and developments make it a useful tool for the study of television. It identifies television stations, shows, networks, personnel, festivals, awards, producers, feature releases, and so forth, and provides information on the television and video industries.

10-49. The Interactive TV Dictionary & Business Index. http://www.itvdictionary.com

This website is a portal to all things related to interactive TV. While there are links to schools, courses, and other commercially available information on this topic, the dictionary feature is free and very useful. The user simply clicks on the letter that begins a term sought, moves to that section of the database, and enters the term. Links abound. This is a good starting point for a search on interactive television.

10-50. Television & Cable Factbook. Washington, DC: Warren Publishing, 1982– . Ann.

This annual publication has proved to be a most useful reference tool for those needing up-to-date information on the television and cable industries. Technical facilities, ownership, personnel, rate, and audience data for all television stations in the United States are among the most useful data and that for which the work is known. Entries are arranged by state, then alphabetically by city, with separate treatment for Canadian and international stations. Cable and TV providers are covered as well. Recently, the publication has been made available online under the title Advanced T.V. Factbook Online; the database offers search capabilities plus cross file searching so that one can search network, cable, and provider information simultaneously.

10-51. The Video Source Book. The Gale Group, Florence, KY: 1998– . Ann.

The Video Source Book, according to the publisher's catalog, continues its comprehensive coverage of more than 130,000 complete program listings, encompassing over 160,000 videos. In this resource, program listings are arranged alphabetically by title. A description of the program and information on how to obtain the title are provided in the entries. Alternate title, subject, credit, awards, and special format indexes are helpful as is the index by distributors.

Emmy Awards

Academy of Television Arts and Sciences. http://emmys.com

The National Academy of Television Arts & Sciences. http:// www.emmyonline.org

The Emmy Award is owned jointly by the Television Academy and the National Academy. The first Emmy Awards, which were devoted solely to local Los Angeles programming, were held on January 25, 1949, at the Hollywood Athletic Club. The Television Academy rejected 47 proposals before accepting the statuette designed by television engineer Louis McManus, whose wife served as its model. Her wings represent the muse of art with the atom and its electrons representing the science and technology of the new medium.

The Academy of Television Arts & Sciences is based in Los Angeles. It honors prime-time programming. Membership is from all fields of television work, from network executives to hair stylists; from performers to cinematographers. In May of 1991, the Television Academy moved into its new headquarters in Los Angeles replete with an enormous fountain dominated by a 27-foot Emmy Award statue. The statue and Hall of Fame Plaza were conceived and overseen by production designer Jan Scott, winner of 11 Primetime Emmy awards, more than any other woman in the history of television. One of its most important components is the ATAS/UCLA Television Archives, which was created in 1965 in conjunction with UCLA's Department of Theater Arts, and contains the largest collection of kinescopes, tapes and films from the earliest days of television.

The National Academy of Television Arts & Sciences is based in New York and administers daytime, news and sports Emmys. The National Academy has members nationwide and has affiliated chapters in major cities that award Emmys for local programming. The National Academy and the Television Academy work closely together on the daytime Emmy honors.

PART FIVE
VISUAL ARTS

CHAPTER 11

VISUAL ARTS

Anna H. Perrault

INTRODUCTION TO THE VISUAL ARTS

With the invention of movable type by Gutenberg in the mid-fifteenth century, the Age of the Printed Work was inaugurated. Shortly after the end of a 500-year hegemony of the printed work, the digital age was begun with the invention of the Internet. Prior to the Renaissance, societal and religious communication was primarily visual representation through art in churches and illuminated manuscripts. Because of the scarcity of hand-written volumes, literacy was only attained by the clergy and the wealthy ruling classes. Printing eventually made literacy possible for all. In the digital age, the visual has returned to the forefront in communication. Just as printing changed the world of the Renaissance, the Internet has had similar revolutionary effects that are being realized today in the twenty-first century.

As with all disciplines in the humanities, the visual arts have been changed by the advent of the World Wide Web. Graphical in nature, the Web is a perfect medium for visual arts information. The Web has opened the door to new and expanded research possibilities for the visual arts scholar and the practicing artist. The digital object is actually a new medium. Not only can it display one-dimensional art forms, but software allows drawing, the capacity to turn or revolve images, zoom in or out, 3-D visualization, and more. The technical capabilities of digitization and the Web have transformed education and libraries, especially in the visual arts. Slide libraries, once an essential component of art education, are now obsolete, with digitized image databases having replaced them, bringing about a paradigm shift for art history. Exhibition catalogs are still printed, but they can also be virtual on the Web, as can the exhibition itself. The *artist's book* is now apt to be a digital production with greater possibilities for creativity than the printed work. While digital images are preferred for instant access on the Web, printed works are still being produced and used in descriptive works for teaching, the history of art, and browsing for ideas.

This introduction to the visual arts and visual arts librarianship begins with a definition of the visual arts, major divisions of the visual arts, and information resources in the visual arts. A literature review of use and users of information resources follows. One section is on arts and museum librarianship. The last section looks to the future with the convergence of libraries, archives, and museums. Throughout the influence of technology on the visual arts is emphasized. We begin by defining what constitutes the visual arts.

Working Definition of the Visual Arts

The term *art* is derived from the Latin word *ars*, which means skill or ability. At the time of the Italian Renaissance, the craft guilds were known as *arti* and the word *arte* denoted craftsmanship, skill, mastery of form, or inventiveness. The phrase *visual arts* serves to differentiate a group of arts that are generally nonverbal in character and that communicate by means of symbols and the juxtaposition of formal elements. The modern definition of visual arts encompasses those formerly known as the *fine arts* (painting, sculpture, drawing, print-making); the decorative arts and crafts; the modern visual arts including photography, video, film-making; and the applied arts: industrial design, graphic design, fashion design, architecture, and interior design.

In the fine arts the material object is formed with the intention of representing an idea, experience, or emotion. The representation is communicated by the creation of emotional moods and through expansion of the range of the aesthetic experience. *Beauty*, as such, is not an integral part of art but more a matter of subjective judgment. The difficulty here is that aesthetics deal with individual taste, a subjective issue from the outset. Nevertheless, certain concepts of balance, harmony, and contrast have become a part of our way of thinking about art as a result of Greek speculation about the nature of beauty.

Style normally refers to the whole body of work produced at a given time in history; however, there may be regional and national styles as well as one basic style for a period. In modern times, attention has even been given to the "styles" of individual artists. Style, like taste, is a subjective phenomenon.

Iconography is the use of symbols by artists to express universal ideas; the Gothic style of architecture, for example, symbolized humanity's reaching out toward God. On a more recent note, designers of graphical software have used "icons" to denote certain functions and messages; an example is the use of a timepiece, clock, or hourglass, to communicate that the user should wait and that processing is taking place.

Major Divisions of Visual Arts

The traditional division of the visual arts is into four main groups: 1) pictorial arts, 2) plastic arts, 3) building arts, and 4) decorative arts and crafts. The *pictorial arts* employ flat, two-dimensional surfaces. The term is most often applied to painting, but it can also include drawing, graphic arts, photography including moving pictures and video, and mosaics. Painting may be done with a variety of materials: oil, tempera, water color, or other media. Drawing is done most often with pencil, pen and ink, wash, crayon, pastel, or charcoal.

The *graphic arts* are produced by the printing process with three basic methods employed. Intaglio, in which the design is hollowed out of a flat surface and ink is gathered in the hollows for transmission to the paper, is exemplified by etching or engraving. Cameo, or relief, in which the design is on a raised surface as in woodcut, mezzotint, aquatint, or drypoint and only the raised surface is inked, is the second method. Last is the planographic method in which a completely flat surface is used and the design is created by using substances that will either attract or repel ink. Lithography is the term often used for this method because the flat surface was frequently made of stone. Graphic arts now include computer and digital art as well.

The *pictorial arts* employ one or more of three basic forms: murals, panels, or pages. Murals involve pictures directly applied to walls of buildings or painted on canvases and permanently attached to the walls. Panels are generally painted on wood or canvas; these are sometimes known as easel paintings. Pages may be illuminated manuscripts or, more often, produced as a result of the printing process. The basic problems of the pictorial artist, regardless of the form used, include surface, design, movement, space, and form. These are commonly solved by the use of line, color, values (light and dark), and perspective.

In the *plastic arts,* of which sculpture is the most obvious example, ideas are expressed by means of three-dimensional objects. This type of art is perhaps the oldest form, predating even cave painting. The materials used include stone, metal, wood, plaster, clay, or synthetics such as plastic. Tools of the artist may include chisels, mallets, natural and chemical abrasives, and punches. The techniques used are determined primarily by the materials and tools available, and include carving, casting, modeling, or welding. The finished product may be free standing or bas-relief, part of a wall or planar surface. In sculpture, the human figure has traditionally provided the most common subject matter, although there was an increased use of abstractions in the twentieth century.

In the *building arts*, architecture, spaces are enclosed in such a way as to meet certain practical needs as in schools, homes, offices, or factories and to make some kind of symbolic statement of basic values. These values may be utilitarian and the symbolic statement very pedestrian or they may be related to the highest aspirations of the human spirit. Factories and gasoline stations are frequently examples of the former, while Gothic cathedrals are often cited as examples of the latter. Architects design buildings of three basic types: *trabeated*, in which a lintel is supported by two posts; *arcuated*, in which arches support rounded vaults and domes; and *cantilevered*, in which only one post is required to support a lintel or beam. The materials used in the construction will determine the type of design used. Wood is useful for trabeated construction, but brick and stone can be better adapted to the requirements of arcuated building. Structural steel and reinforced concrete make possible large-scale cantilevered construction.

The *decorative arts* encompass the professional areas of interior design, industrial design, fashion, and some aspects of architecture. The minor arts are often referred to as "crafts," or "collectibles." They are often classified on the basis of the materials used: ceramics, glass, metals, textiles, ivory, precious gems, wood, reeds, synthetics, and the like. Ordinarily, they follow the same styles as the major art forms. The end products may be useful everyday objects such as coins, clothing, baskets, utensils, and furniture, or they may be ornamental items such as jewelry, stained glass, and many items of interior decoration.

While these definitions still obtain for the tangible arts, forms, formats, and techniques in the arts have altered due to modern technology. Certainly now, drafting and drawing can be accomplished with computer software as well as material tools. Technology has become a tool of the arts and in some cases, the art itself, as in *digital art*. The uses and influence of technology can be seen in the resources treated in the next section.

Art Information Resources

An understanding of the nature of the resources in the visual arts is necessary for the art librarian to develop collections of resources, as is knowledge of the information seeking behavior of those in the visual arts. Beyond the standard books, periodicals, and databases there are different types and formats of materials that define art publications and art library collections.

Catalogs are first-rate sources of art information and necessary acquisitions for the study of art. The *catalogue raisonné* is defined as a systematic, descriptive, and critical listing or catalog of all known or documented, authentic works by a particular artist, or of all his/her known works in one medium. Each entry aims at providing all ascertainable data on the work in question: 1) title, date, and signature, if any, as well as size and medium; 2) present location or owner and provenance, previously recorded owners and history of the work; 3) description, comments, analysis, or literary documentation; 4) bibliographical references to books and periodicals; 5) listings of exhibitions and reproductions. Usually there is also an illustration. The entries are numbered consecutively. These catalog numbers are often referred to in scholarly literature about the artist and permanently identify a particular work. The *oeuvre catalog* is similar but may omit documentation and provenance (Muehsam 1978).

Museum catalogs are defined as catalogs of a museum's permanent collection; exhibition catalogs, on the other hand, include works from many museums or owners' private collections that are brought together for a particular exhibition. Corpus catalogs attempt to do for an entire category of art what the *catalogue raisonné* does for an individual artist. Because of their scope, these often depend on international collaboration. Jack Robertson's "The Exhibition Catalog as Source of Artists' Primary Documents" addresses exhibition catalogs as research resources (1989). The chapter by Susan Wyngaard, "Fine Arts," in the second edition of *Humanities and the Library* (1993), covers exhibition and sales catalogs in considerable depth. Artists' books and ephemera are also discussed in the same chapter. Finally, another approach to the use of exhibition catalogs is presented in Olivia Fitzpatrick, "Art Exhibition Catalogues: A Resource for Art Documentation" (1996). Collection development for exhibition catalogs is addressed in the chapter by Barbara Rominski in *Art Museum*

Libraries and Librarianship (2003). Several articles in the *Encyclopedia of Library and Information Sciences* (3rd ed. 2009) address aspects of exhibition catalogs from collection development and acquisitions to cataloging.

Another special type of document for the art library is the *art book*, by which is usually meant a large format, heavily illustrated work. The term *coffee-table book* came into use in the mid-twentieth century to describe these beautiful, luxurious editions, containing many color plates, although to arts professionals the art book is a serious work of scholarship. The definition of art book has been somewhat broadened to encompass publications in the arts that are illustrated and that include scholarly monographs in art history that are not large format.

Elizabeth Esteve-Coll discusses the art book medium in her provocative keynote paper, presented at the European Conference of the IFLA Art Libraries Section and published as "The Art Book: The Idea and the Reality" (1992). Christopher Lyon in "The Art Book's Last Stand?" provides an in-depth look at the plight of the art book in today's publishing environment (2006). Also in the article are two sidebars, *"A Short History of the Art Book"* and *"Permissions Purgatory"* (49, 51). According to Lyon, commercial publishers have ceased publishing expensive art works that have low sales possibilities. Difficulties with publication of art books are the expense of securing rights permissions for the reproduction of the many illustrations needed with costs in the thousands of dollars, pricing pressures, a shifting from commercial publication to institutional publication, and loss of sales outlets. In most cases the costs for reproduction rights for illustrations can neither be borne by the author nor the publisher. Some museum publications are subsidized by grants. Because of these difficulties the art book is one of the last types of printed monographs to transition to a wholly digital object.

The problems in art publications are explored in *Art History and Its Publications in the Electronic Age*, the report of a study sponsored by the Andrew W. Mellon Foundation (Ballon and Westerman, 2006). The report is optimistic. Among the findings of the study are that there is growing interest in arts publishing by a number of university presses and also a growing interest in electronic distribution upon the part of art historians. A session on "The Aesthetics of Publishing: the Art Book as Object from Print to Digital" was held at the College Art Association of America (CAA) in New York City in February 2007. Among other questions asked of the panel participants was, "Is it possible to transpose the printed art book into the digital realm?" The papers from the session were published in *Visual Resources* (2008).

The prominence of the art monograph and the slowness in embracing digital formats became a subject for research in user studies.

Use and Users of Art Information Resources

Users of visual arts information can be categorized as art professionals including art historians, artists, art educators, critics, curators, and architects; students of the visual arts who are enrolled in art schools, colleges and universities, and secondary schools; and the interested public who are museum goers, collectors, and others for whom art is a hobby or avocation.

Interest in the use and users of art materials is not a new phenomenon. An early article on use of art materials was "The Use of Art Books," by Katherine Patten (1907). Later in the twentieth century, use and user studies became a stream of research in information science. The literature of use and user studies in the visual arts can be divided by user categories. Early studies focused on students and art historians. More recently, attention has turned to studying the information seeking habits of practicing artists, first those in academe, and then most recently those outside of formal education. A sufficient number of studies of information-seeking behavior in the visual arts exist to divide them into distinct categories: studies of art historians and faculty; studies of students in art and design education programs; and studies on practicing artists.

A thorough review by Zach, "Arts Literatures and Their Users," appears in *Encyclopedia of Library and Information Sciences* (3rd ed. 2009). Zach includes music as well as the fine arts and covers the studies in sections on art historians, music scholars, fine artists, musicians, and other artists. In addition to the review of information seeking studies, she includes sections on subject retrieval, image retrieval, and melodic retrieval. The scope of the review included here is selective and concentrates upon studies published since the 1980s. We begin with studies of information seeking behaviors of art historians.

Information Seeking by Art Historians

Although art libraries have a variety of users, students, faculty, staff in the museum, and the general public, art historians are the most frequent and constant users of art libraries. Joan Beaudoin gives an overview of findings from studies in information seeking by art historians in her 2005 article, "Image and Text: A Review of the Literature Concerning the Information Needs and Research Behaviors of Art Historians" (Beaudoin 2005).

Deirdre Stam began the first of several studies on the information seeking behaviors of art historians with her 1984 dissertation "How Art Historians Look for Information" (1984). Stam's contributions continued with an empirical study, "Tracking Art Historians: Information Needs and Information Seeking Behavior" (1989). Stam studied both academic and museum art historians with hopes to improve library services for them. Her findings indicated that both types of scholars interpret an art object in light of existing information and original observation. They depend heavily upon their own personal libraries, but they also make frequent use of libraries although not necessarily librarians, and they often travel for research purposes. Their search for bibliographic material including accidental discovery associated with the search process is crucial to their final product (29). Beaudoin summarized the findings from the studies of Stam, as art historians possess well-honed library skills due to the dependence of their scholarship on library systems. Their heavy reliance on objects, or images of these objects, is a critical difference between their research methods and that of their colleagues in other humanities-based disciplines. Therefore, a broad and deep collection of visual materials with adequate indexing is needed to support their research. While art historians were found to perform much of their work in an online environment, technology seemed to have a limited impact on their research processes beyond the initial phases of information seeking and basic writing tasks. The development of additional technological tools to aid in art historical research and scholarship was still needed. Understanding the particular information needs and research processes of art historians provides an avenue for improving library services to this user group (36). Beaudoin defines the art historian user group's adoption of technology as "relatively slow and hesitant" and explains current art historians "have a vastly different set of tools with which to access information than they did even over a decade ago, so the digital divide among established and emerging scholars must be acknowledged" (2005, 34).

The Getty Online Searching Project, also conducted in the late 1980s and early 1990s, investigated information-seeking practices of art historians and humanists to survey their attitudes toward and use of technology. The Getty vocabulary and thesauri projects grew out of these studies (entries 11-8 through 11-15). Bates described the art historian's methods of information seeking as "berry-picking," the opposite of systematic; that information-seeking is an ever evolving rather than a static process (1989). Footnote chasing, citation searches, browsing journal runs or shelves of materials, author searches, and searches conducted using bibliographies, abstracts, and indices are all examples of the process. These activities fit the information seeking profile of humanists in general. The studies revealed that databases were not tailored to the needs of art historians and they did not make much use of electronic databases and resources (Bates 1989, 409).

Trish Rose conducted an investigation of the research patterns of fifteen art historians with an average of twenty-two in the profession, finding that connoisseurship and iconography are the primary methodological and theoretical approaches to art historical research (Rose 2002). By this time art historians were using computers to search online catalogs, online periodical indices, and searching the Internet for images or current information, but Rose found that 87 percent of art historians' research was still being conducted through print, rather than electronic, resources (39). The study participants judged electronic sources to have images of poor quality and back issues of journals in black and white were no better than photocopies. Many believed that slides and photographic reproductions were superior. Rose explained, "Just as with the introduction of photographic surrogates to the study of art history, the introduction of digital surrogates has not replaced the need to see the original object" (37). Rose found that art historians continue to perceive the Internet as lacking in scholarly merit with the searches they perform having little value (36). Rose recommends that art historians' information seeking be studied at least every five years to keep up with changing technology and changes within the field.

Nemeth reports on the findings of a survey of art historians conducted by the Department of Research Databases at the Getty Research Institute in 2008. The survey had a sample size of 2,077 with 1,976 respondents. The survey sought "to identify the most frequently accessed resources for searching of scholarly literature in art history and to ascertain the most valued features of search tools and content databases" (Nemeth 2010, 223). Among the findings were that the art historians use both field-specific databases and Web search engines and "value a combination of search tools with a range of features . . . A growing demand for open access to full-text and comprehensive searching through a single interface illustrate the increasing expectations of academics" (235). The findings of the study are useful to librarians and producers of field-specific databases and thesauri.

In addition to the empirical studies of the information seeking and research methods of art historians, there have been a number of bibliometric studies of the literature of art history. Cullars has investigated citation practices in the humanities and the arts. His study "Citation Characteristics of Monographs in the Fine Arts" relates to art historians as the authors of those works (1992). A later citation study focused on French and German fine arts monographs (1996). Cullars is referenced elsewhere in this volume for other citation studies in the humanities.

A longitudinal citation analysis for eight disciplines in the humanities was conducted by Knievel and Kellsey (2004, 2005). The eight disciplines were art, classics, history, linguistics, literature, music, philosophy, and religion. The researchers constructed a humanities average for all of the disciplines and give comparative findings among the disciplines. Although all of the disciplines were humanities fields, art showed high use of non-English sources. Art was also the least English-dominated field of all eight humanities fields studied, with only 65.3 percent of citations referring to English materials. An unusually high 6.7 percent of citations were to German materials, and an even higher 11.1 percent of citations were to Italian materials. Art history is a field that is known for using materials in other languages, but the percentages of citation as compared with other humanities fields was surprising. The authors conclude, "The relatively high proportion of foreign language to English citations, however, seems to be a reliable characteristic of the field of art history" (153).

After a spate of studies in the last decades of the twentieth century on art historians, interest in the information seeking behavior in the arts shifted to the study of practicing artists.

Information Seeking Studies of Artists

After her studies of information seeking by art historians, Deirdre Stam turned her attention to artists. In "Artists and Art Libraries" she reports on a study in which she interviewed art librarians about the information seeking habits of artists (1995). Her findings were in line with earlier studies in confirming the importance of browsing, the need for a wide range of resources on many subjects for inspiration, specific visual information, and career and funding information. In keeping with the respondents being librarians, such things as color photocopy machines and better indices to resources are recommended.

Cobbledick tackled what she perceived as persistent preconceptions concerning artists and the reasons that little research has been done with working artists (1996). She proposed to design questions specifically for artists. She divided the sources or types of information into five categories: inspirational, specific visual information, technical information, current developments in the visual arts, and business information. Cobbledick interviewed four artists who were also art faculty of a strong art program at a large Midwestern university. One of Cobbledick's interesting findings is in relation to browsing. All of the artists said they go to the library with a specific need in mind and they may find it by browsing, but it is targeted browsing in a certain subject area. As Cobbledick says, "None of the artists describes happy accidents of serendipitous discovery in the library . . . ," but rather, ". . . happy accidents occur in the studio while working with their various media" (362).

All the artists did consider interpersonal relationships important "extralibrary" sources of information. High quality photocopying machines are mentioned as library needs as well as liberal circulation policies to allow the artists to take items back to the studio. Cobbledick concludes that, "Art reflects the human experience. The information needs of artists are too diverse to be addressed solely within the confines of art librarianship. . . Artists need to have access to the universe of knowledge, not merely to some of its parts, and libraries that would meet their information needs must become access points to that universe" (365). This statement is reinforcement that general library collections can serve the needs of practicing artists.

Dane (1987) and Oddos (1997) both write from their experiences as librarians to characterize the needs of working artists and their findings and recommendations are similar. One characteristic is that working artists are no longer in an educational environment and thus do not have access to in-depth collections of art books and periodicals. Thus, they become users of public libraries or art museum libraries.

A broader study was conducted by Littrell in which she considers visually oriented artists to be those in the music, dance and theater, fashion, fine and decorative arts, and architecture fields (2001). In her qualitative study conducted at Kansas State University, Littrell set out to answer the question "What do artists need from libraries?" She interviewed 27 students and faculty across the visual arts fields. Her findings were that artists from all of the fields have the same use patterns as those in the primary visual arts fields. From the study, she drew up a simple model of the creative process and showed how the library can play a role in that process. The first step in the process is "Finding inspiration"; the second step is "Finding the individual voice," with the third step being "Producing the result" (293). As with others who have studied the information seeking behavior of artists, Littrell found that browsing plays a large role in the creative process: "Browsing is necessary because traditional search techniques are text oriented and artists are notorious for using discovery as a primary tool" (293). In sum, the traditional service in libraries focuses upon texts and objectivism; the creative artist needs to be nurtured with an emphasis on images and quiet for inspiration.

In 2004, Cowan found that there had been six studies of artists' use of information resources, of which only three had actually sought information directly from artists (Cobbledick 1996; Frank 1999; VanZijl 2001). Cowan considers that the research using academic populations has a bias when it comes to the information needs and behavior of practicing artists. Furthermore, the respondents in the studies were all library users and the studies focused on the use of library resources. Cowan says, "There is an assumption that art librarians know what artists need and want, and how they go about looking for it" (16). She wanted to "understand whether and how the nature of artists' work might influence the way they seek information, and the kinds of information they seek" (14). Cowan interviewed one artist about what informs her work. From the interviews the main themes that emerged were the Natural Environment; the Work itself; Relationships; Self-inquiry; and Attentiveness. "The artist receives sensory information in all these ways. She thinks of her work as "visual poems" that reflect the experience of being in a certain physical location" (18). Cowan discovered that to artists information seeking is not problem oriented or the search for some "thing." What informs an artist's creative process is "highly personal, self-reflexive, and characterized by process and sensory feedback. She perceives the process of finding out what she needs in order to do her work as moving, relational, organic, dialogic, and iterative"(20). Cowan concludes that "Information seeking is a creative process that begins and ends outside of the walls of any library" (20). These findings differ somewhat from the findings of other studies, but the research was conducted with only one subject.

A thorough literature review of "The Information-seeking Behavior of Visual Artists," was conducted by Hemmig (2008). He found that the majority of the studies focus on those with academic affiliations: teachers, art historians, or students, that population readily available to art librarians. Very few studies focus on the information needs of working artists or a community of artists. In his review, Hemmig found that the results of studies conducted from the 1970s up into the first decade of the twenty-first century are consistent for the most part in depicting the information seeking behavior of visual artists. These findings can be summarized as—

- The information needs of artists are different from those of art historians and students
- Artists require information for several different purposes: inspiration, specific visual image needs, technical knowledge, marketing and career guidance, and knowledge of current trends in the art world
- Artists also require information on subjects not related to art
- Browsing is a frequent method of finding information, images, or ideas leading to inspiration
- Public libraries appear to best satisfy the needs of practicing artists
- Students use art periodicals more than practicing artists (Hemmig 355–356)

Hemmig also published the findings of a study he conducted on "The Empirical Information Seeking Behavior of Practicing Visual Artists (2009). From his findings, Hemmig concluded that the model of the information seeking behavior of practicing artists that had emerged from his review of the literature did indeed fit in all respects. The findings of his study suggest that "use of electronic sources is increasing generationally" (696) and that there "may be gender specific tendencies in creative information use" (697).

A variation on the studies of practicing artists is a study conducted by Mason and Robinson on "The Information-related Behaviour of Emerging Artists and Designers" (2011). The findings were that emerging artists are by necessity very cost conscious and use the Internet and social networking tools; that "Browsing is very important, but not a predominant means of accessing information; and, Inspiration is found from a very diverse and idiosyncratic set of sources, often by serendipitous means" (1). The artists need career and marketing advice which they did not get during their formal education. They rely a great deal on personal interactions, with the Internet now very prominent. They are enthusiastic users of libraries and traditional resources also. The findings of the study are consonant with those of earlier studies, but also picture a younger generation of artists who are more integrated into the digital age. A preference for social networks as a source of information can be added to the list of information seeking characteristics found in earlier studies.

What Art Students Need and Expect from Libraries

The primary student user group in the fine arts is composed of art history graduates, undergraduates, and studio art majors. Toyne (1975, 1977), Pacey (1982), Day and McDowell (1985), and Frank (1999) all published articles focused on the needs of students. Philip Pacey provides an accurate and entertaining look at the library needs of the art and design school student in his classic article, "How Art Students Use Libraries–If They Do" (1982). Toyne and Pacey were art librarians and offer advice from their own observations. Both stress the students' need for resources on a broad range of subjects for browsing and inspiration, not just art information. Day and McDowell conducted interviews of art students representing a variety of art and design fields at one school. Their findings agree with Pacey in that art students and art historians do not use libraries in the same way. Students' information needs are wide ranging; they are looking chiefly for visual resources and browsing is their main mode of information seeking.

Polly Frank conducted a qualitative study aimed at generalist librarians in academic libraries who might not often encounter student artists (1999). She sought an answer to the question, "What can the generalist learn from students regarding how they actually use academic libraries for artwork-related problems?" (445). Frank discusses her findings in detail with many examples from the students she interviewed. As in other studies, she found that student artists used browsing as their chief approach to library collections and that the collections are used broadly, not just the art collection or looking for images, but all media formats. The article fulfills the author's intention in providing insight into what student artists expect and need from academic library collections, not just art libraries.

Bennett also endeavored to find ways that the librarian can reach students in studio art and architecture (2006). Students in these fields "remain on the fringes of library outreach and have always been difficult groups to target" (38). While many see the library's role as supporting browsing and the creative process, these students more often need assistance in traditional academic courses they take outside of their field. Through interviews with students and teachers, Bennett became aware that supporting them in areas such as grant and fellowship research, basic image research, gallery research, copyright issues, and finding free resources beyond the library's collection, were all ways the librarian can serve students in the visual arts. The article by Bennett has a good bibliography on library instruction for art and architecture.

The last group of studies reviewed here is those of faculty in schools of art.

Studies of Arts Faculty

A few information seeking studies focus on arts faculty who may or may not be either artists or art historians. Jacquelyn Challener interviewed eleven artists and sixteen art historians teaching in five liberal arts colleges and three universities to discover their information needs and the resources they use for their own work and for teaching (1999). Challener found a large number of them used computers and about fifty percent of them used computers in teaching. Also about half had their own personal libraries. All used slides in the classroom, also journal articles and reserve materials. They used libraries frequently and consulted with librarians (3).

By 2007, Tori Gregory found that studio art faculty were using journals more than books (Gregory 2007). Their use of print versus electronic sources was about 50/50 (63). Google images were the most frequently used source for images, while magazines were the most popular print source (63). Gregory summarized the findings of previous studies: "Studio art faculty are likely to buy books that interest them, and may not use the university library at all; many studio art faculty prefer browsing over using the library catalog; studio art faculty are somewhat hesitant to approach librarians for assistance and consult peers or colleagues first; studio art faculty are not likely to request bibliographic instruction for their students" (61).

The findings of information seeking studies of arts faculty are similar to those of practicing artists, which indeed many of them are. The most useful findings to art librarians are those that relate to art faculty as teachers. Quite a few of the researchers recommend that librarians be more proactive in liaising with art faculty, especially with regard to students in art education programs.

Arts and Museum Librarianship

Unlike literature, philosophy, and religion, where conventional techniques of librarianship and library research will cover most situations, the visual arts pose several distinct problems. As a result, art, or visual arts, librarianship has emerged as a specialized branch of the field. The growth in the field of visual arts is rapid even when compared to the explosive growth of the Internet as a whole. Not only do we have text and resource-finding tools available, but a variety of image collections are now accessible through the Internet.

A good introduction to art libraries and art librarianship is an article by Kathryn M. Wayne in the *Encyclopedia of Library and Information Sciences* (3rd ed. 2009). The article begins with a history of art librarianship followed by a section on current trends. The article is a succinct treatment of the field for those who are new or not yet in the profession.

The chapter "Fine Arts" in Lester Asheim's now-classic text, *The Humanities and the Library* suggests some basic tenets that still hold (1959). First, different types of art libraries serve differing purposes, although the subject matter contained in them may be similar. Museum, art school, and departmental public and university libraries serve diverse, though sometimes overlapping, clienteles, and hence the institutions will have varying policies and practices in terms of management, collection development, user education, public services, and organization (100–150).

Kim Collins, who has worked in both types of art libraries, compares the two on various points in "Patrons, Processes, and the Profession: Comparing the Academic Art Library and the Art Museum Library" (Collins 2003). The museum library is different from the academic art library in that museums are most often independent institutions, whereas the art library is situated within a larger library system. The museum library must also support staff from museum departments other than curatorial, such as education, public relations, development, and administration. Also, like the academic art library, the art museum library often serves the general public and teachers at all grade levels (80). In comparing the two types of art libraries, Collins covers many basic facts and issues in art librarianship that librarians in both types of libraries should be cognizant of.

Both art and museum librarianship are also covered in *The Handbook of Art and Design Librarianship* (2010). The *Handbook* is divided into four sections: Roles and Responsibilities, Materials and Collection Management, Teaching and Learning, and Learning Spaces, Promotion and Sustainability. This book is written for the professional. It can also be helpful to library users needing art or media resources.

Another work written for the professional is *Art Museum Libraries and Librarianship,* edited by Joan M. Benedetti (2007). The Benedetti book is thorough in the treatment of all facets of art museum librarianship. Experts in various aspects of museum librarianship have written informative essays on such topics as management, security, automation, cataloging, space planning, building collections, promotion and fund raising, marketing, and professional development. The last section contains profiles of fifteen of a variety of museum libraries. This work is an excellent handbook for art librarians.

More specific topics are addressed by Elizabeth Lorenzen in "Selecting and Acquiring Art Materials in the Academic Library: Meeting the Needs of the Studio Artist" (2004). Changes transpiring in the worlds of the artist and library acquisitions are reviewed for how these changes may affect the way that librarians acquire monographic art collections. Sarah Falls of ARTstor addresses access to various types of art information in "Art Libraries: Creating Access to Unique Collections" (2009). Falls reports on changes to long-running indexing products, art auction catalogs, and art libraries. Chen covers art history by periods in "Great websites for art history," providing practical advice for finding visual arts information and also reviewing museum collections and other resources on the Web (2009). A list of the websites mentioned in the article is at the end.

Librarians are often consulted on matters of copyright relating to text or image reproduction and use. Cultural institutions are deeply involved in copyright compliance with digital materials and all professional staff needs to be knowledgeable about the subject. Copyright and permissions are probably considered the thorniest issues in dealing with collections and clientele in cultural institutions. One of the most useful guides is *Copyright & Cultural Institutions: Guidelines for Digitization for U.S. Libraries, Archives, & Museums* (2009). The usual topics of the duration of copyright ownership, fair use, rights and permissions, licenses and the Digital Millennium copyright Act are covered. The guide has FAQ like questions in each chapter that answer common queries. The last two chapters contain case studies which help to understand various types of rights management.

Another guide to compliance management is *Permissions, a Survival Guide: Blunt Talk about Art as Intellectual Property* by Susan Bielstein, an executive editor at the University of Chicago Press (2006). Bielstein has a thorough knowledge of the subject and uses examples and anecdotes from her experiences, many of them humorous. The guide is written for a general audience covering the history of copyright, the basics of copyright law, and most used provisions, such as fair use. Financial, procedural, and legal details throughout the book are also summarized in a final chapter. In addition, there are sample copyright and use permission letters, a permissions log and summary, and a directory of image banks and artists' rights organizations. Unlike the first guide above that is focused on digitization, the Beilstein guide is devoted to all aspects of securing permissions to reproduce both textual and digital materials. It may be well to have both guides on the topic.

Exhibits are a central focus in museums for showcasing collections and for educational purposes. Exhibits are also a source of funding and a draw for visitors to the permanent collections. In the majority of museums, exhibitions are crafted by curators and staff. The curator is usually the creator of the exhibit, but art librarians play several roles in the staging of exhibits and even may be the primary person responsible for the exhibit. Several works concern museum exhibitions. In *What Makes a Great Exhibition?*, every aspect of staging exhibitions is covered (2007). Subjects include the definition of an exhibition, appropriate/successful exhibition settings, exhibition design, effective presentation of video, appropriate wall-mounted captioning, white cubes, and more. Art students, those in museum studies programs, and art librarians should all have access to this work.

Art libraries also have exhibits and displays. An introductory, basic work is *Displays and Exhibitions in Art Libraries* from ARLIS/UK & Ireland (2009). Based on responses to a 2008 ARLIS survey, this handy spiral-bound publication provides a brief but informative overview of display and exhibition design and development. The book provides ideas through case studies from a variety of European institutions, e.g., the British National Art Library and the Van Gogh Museum. Topics such as establishing goals, project planning, design, promotion, and evaluation are covered. Additional resources in the handbook include an exhibition proposal example and a glossary of terms. The book is useful for all art librarians and can be used as a professional development tool.

In "What Might It Mean for Museums to Become Interactive?" Bremen has written about the possibilities of museums using new technologies to become more interactive with visitors, both onsite and through the Web by use of phone apps and "viral loops" (2011). Nancy Proctor has pointed out that museum goers are now actively participating in social media, Flickr, YouTube, Facebook, and Twitter, with more new possibilities arising every day (2010). According to Proctor, some museums are integrating social media into exhibits through crowd sourcing with "citizen curators" who post their own photographs to add to exhibits or evaluate works through online forums (2010, 36). The role of curator is becoming more one of storytelling for stimulating interest, and with social media the curator is interacting beyond the museum. More ideas can be found in Nina Simon's book, *The Participatory Museum,* which provides detailed advice on structuring exhibits to encourage the most effective kind of participation (2010).

For further reading, The *Encyclopedia of Library and Information Sciences* (3rd ed. 2009) has articles on all aspects of art and design libraries, museums and museum libraries, archival practices, media and visual resources, and digital libraries.

Convergence of Libraries, Archives and Museums

In 2003, the American Library Association, the Society of American Archivists, and the American Association of Museums entered into a formal relationship to meet three times a year at their respective professional conferences to discuss issues of mutual concern and share information. Although the three organizations had engaged in informal contact for years, this agreement is an acknowledgement of the growing overlap of missions and services of the three types of cultural institutions.

Even before the merger of the Department of Library Programs in the U.S. Department of Education and the Institute of Museum Services into the Institute for Museum and Library Services (IMLS) in 1996, the term *cultural heritage institutions* had come to be descriptive of libraries, archives, and museums. Having the umbrella of one agency has facilitated increased cooperation between the three types of institutions. The rapid pace of digitization of printed and cultural artifacts into digital texts and images has pointed up the commonalities among the three. In June 2006, a conference sponsored by the Rare Books and Manuscripts section of the ALA Association of College and Research Libraries and funded by IMLS was held in Austin, Texas. The theme of the conference was "Libraries, Archives, and Museums in the Twenty-First Century: Intersecting Mission, Converging Futures?" The papers from the conference were published as an issue of *RBM: A Journal of Rare Books, Manuscripts, and Cultural Heritage* (Spring 2007*)*. In that issue, Robert Martin, former director of the IMLS, looks at the differences among the three types of institutions and suggests "common themes" for collaboration: focusing on users; finding out who they are and why they are accessing digital collections; making practices and policies more uniform; and adjusting to meet users' expectations. Martin points out that "The boundaries between types of cultural heritage institutions that we now accept as common are simply lines that we ourselves have drawn. And we can *re*-draw them . . .

nowadays the general public sees little significant difference between libraries, archives, and museums. This perception is driven in part by the experience of people who use our resources in the digital environment" (82). All three types of institutions collect everything in terms of formats, but have different standards and methods of classifying materials. Digital collections offer the most possibility for cooperation and it is digital collections that are bringing the different institutions closer.

One sign of increasing convergence with archives, libraries, and museums is that many schools of library and information science have begun to develop courses, tracks, concentrations, or joint degrees for archival and museum work. Meta-data and archival cataloging are now included in cataloging courses. Museum informatics is a stream of research and courses in museum informatics are now offered in information schools. The extent of the development of curricula in all of these areas is demonstrated in two issues of the *Journal of Education for Library and Information Science* devoted to "Digital Library and Digital Curation Curricula" (January 2011 and April 2011). In the introduction to Part One, Jeffrey Pomerantz observes that the disciplines of library and information science, archival studies, and museum studies "have come to realize that they increasingly share overlapping educational goals" (January 2011, 1). Students increasingly are interested in courses in all of the areas.

With digitization, librarians have taken on added responsibilities and become more involved in preservation and conservation. As many major museums have aged, recognition has come that institutional history needs to be preserved. These activities have broadened the mission of visual arts libraries into that of image libraries and archives. Sarah Falls makes the point that digital images are being used by teachers and students in many disciplines now and that the art librarian has become a point of contact for the "digital image, visual culture research, and visual literacy, regardless of the disciplinary origin of the image" (226). The clientele of art libraries is broadening and "Art libraries are ripe ground for innovation and evolution to serve the users of the future that include an ever expanding range of disciplines, interests, and research needs" (229).

Works Cited

Ballon, Hilary and Mariet Westermann. 2006. *Art History and its Publications in the Electronic Age.* Houston: Rice University Press and CLIR. Connexions website: http://cnx.org/content/col10376/latest/

Bates, Marcia J. 1989. "The Design of Browsing and Berrypicking Techniques for the Online Search Interface," *Online Review* 13 (October): 409.

Beaudoin, Joan. 2005. "Image and Text: A Review of the Literature Concerning the Information Needs and Research Behaviors of Art Historians." *Art Documentation* 22, 2 (Fall): 34–37.

Benedetti, Joan, ed. 2007. *Arts Museum Libraries and Librarianship.* ARLIS/NA, co-published with the Scarecrow Press. (Occasional Paper no. 16)

Bennett, Hannah. 2006. "Bringing the Studio into the Library: Addressing the Research Needs of Studio Art and Architecture Students." *Art Documentation* 25 (Spring): 38-42.

Bielstein, Susan M. 2006. *Permissions, a Survival Guide: Blunt Talk about Art as Intellectual Property.* Chicago: The University of Chicago Press.

Bremen, Sara. 2011. "Wikipedia Links and Viral Loops." *Curator* 54 (April): 117–122.

Challener, Jacquelyn. 1999. "Information-Seeking Behavior of Professors of Art History and Studio Art." Master's Research paper, Kent State University. ED 435405.

Chen, Ching-Jung. 2009. "Great Websites for Art History." *Collection Building* 28 (4): 155–158.

Cobbledick, Susan. 1996. "The Information-Seeking Behavior of Artists: Exploratory Interviews," *Library Quarterly* 66, 4 (October): 343–372.

Collins, Kim. 2003. "Patrons, Processes, and the Profession: Comparing the Academic Art Library and the Art Museum Library." Co-published simultaneously in *Journal of Library Administration* 39 (1): 77–89; and *The Twenty-First Century Art Librarian* (ed., Terrie L. Wilson). The Haworth Information Press, Inc., 2003: 77–89.

Couch, Nena and Nancy Allen, eds. 1993. *The Humanities and the Library*. 2nd ed. Chicago: American Library Association.

Cowan, Sandra. 2004. "Informing Visual Poetry: Information Needs and Sources of Artists." *Art Documentation* 23 (Fall): 14-20.

Cullars, John. 1992. "Citation Characteristics of Monographs in the Fine Arts," *Library Quarterly* 62, 3 (July): 325–342.

Cullars, John. 1996. "Citation Characteristics of French and German Fine Arts Monographs. *Library Quarterly* 66, 2 (April): 138–160.

Esteve-Coll, Elizabeth. 1992. "The Art Book: The Idea and the Reality," *Art Libraries Journal* 17(3): 4–6.

Falls, Sarah E. 2009. "Art Libraries: Creating Access to Unique Collections." *Public Services Quarterly,* 5 (3): 223–229.

Fitzpatrick, Olivia. 1996. "Art Exhibition Catalogues: A Resource for Art Documentation," *An Leabharlaan* 12: 117–120.

Frank, Polly. 1999. "Student artists in the library." *Journal of Academic Librarianship* 25(6): 445-55.

Gluibizzi, Amanda and Paul Glassman. 2010. *The Handbook of Art and Design Librarianship*. London, UK: Facet Publishing.

Gregory, Tori F. 2007. "Under-served or Under-Surveyed: The Information Needs of Studio Art Faculty in the Southwestern United States." *Art Documentation* 26 (Fall): 57–66.

Hemmig, William S. 2008. "Literature of Information Seeking Behavior of Visual Artists: A Literature Review." *Journal of Documentation* 64 (3): 343–362.

Hemmig, William S. 2009. "The Empirical Information Seeking Behavior of Practicing Visual Artists." *Journal of Documentation* 66 (4): 682–703.

Hirtle, Peter B., et al. 2009. *Copyright & Cultural Institutions: Guidelines for Digitization for U.S Libraries, Archives, & Museums.* Ithaca, NY: Cornell University Library.

Knievel, Jennifer E. and Charlene Kellsey. 2004. "Global English in the Humanities? A Longitudinal Citation Study of Foreign Language Use by Humanities Scholars." *College & Research Libraries* 65, 3 (2004): 194–204.

Littrell, Laura. 2001. "Artists: the neglected patrons?" in *Proceedings of the Tenth National Conference of the Association of College and Research Libraries*, March 15-18, Denver, CO. ACRL, Chicago: 13-21.

Lorenzen, Elizabeth A. 2004. "Selecting and Acquiring Art Materials in the Academic Library: Meeting the Needs of the Studio Artist." Co-published simultaneously in *The Acquisitions Librarian*, No. 31/32: 27–39; and *Selecting Materials for Library Collections* (Audrey Fenner, ed.). The Haworth Information Press: 27–39.

Lyon, Christopher. 2006. "The Art Book's Last Stand?" *Art in America* 94, 9 (September): 47–55.

Marincola, Paula. 2007. *What Makes a Great Exhibition?* Philadelphia, PA: Philadelphia Exhibitions Initiative, dist. by Reaktion Books and The University of Chicago Press.

Martin, Robert. 2007. "Intersecting Missions, Converging Practice." *RBM: A Journal of Rare Books, Manuscripts, and Cultural Heritage* 8, 1(Spring): 80–88.

Milne, Christine and Annamarie McKie, eds. 2009. *Displays and Exhibitions in Art Libraries*. ARLIS/UK & Ireland.

Muehsam, Gerd. 1978. *Guide to Information Sources in the Visual Arts*. Santa Barbara, CA: ABC-CLIO.

Nemeth, Erik. "Complementary Value of Databases for Discovery of Scholarly Literature." *College & Research Libraries* 71, 3(May 2010): 223–235.

Pacey, Philip. 1982. "How Art Students Use Libraries–If They Do." *Art Libraries Journal* 7(Spring): 33–38.

Patten, Katherine. 1907. "The Use of Art Books," *Bulletin of the American Library Association* 1 (July): 183.

Pomerantz, Jeffrey, guest ed. "Digital Library and Digital Curation Education, Part One." *Journal of Education for Library and Information Science* 52, 1(January 2011): 9–31. Part Two. JELIS 52, 2(April): 79–121.

Proctor, Nancy. 2010. "Digital: Museum as Platform, Curator as Champion, in the Age of Social Media." *Curator* 53 (January): 35–43.

Robertson, Jack. 1989. "The Exhibition Catalog as Source of Artists' Primary Documents." *Art Libraries Journal* 14 (Spring): 32–36.

Rominski, Barbara. 2007. "Exhibition Catalog Exchanges as Part of the Collection Development Program at the San Francisco Museum of Modern Art Research Library." In *Arts Museum Libraries and Librarianship*. Joan Benedetti, ed. ARLIS/NA, co-Published with the Scarecrow Press. (Occasional Paper no. 16)

Rose, Trish. 2002. "Technology's Impact on the Information-Seeking Behavior of Art Historians. *Art Documentation* 21, 2(Fall): 39–42.

Simon, Nina. 2010. *The Participatory Museum*. Santa Cruz, CA: Museum 2.0.

Soussloff, Catherine M., et al. 2008 a. "The Aesthetics of Publishing: The Art Book as Object from Print to Digital." *Visual Resources*, 24 (1): 39–58.

Stam, Deidre Corcoran. 1984. "How Art Historians Look for Information." *Art Documentation* 3(Winter): 117–119.

Stam, Deidre Corcoran. 1989. "Tracking Art Historians: Information Needs and Information Seeking Behavior." *Art Libraries Journal* 14(Fall): 13–16.

Stam, Deidre Corcoran. 1995. "Artists and Art Libraries." *Art Libraries Journal* 20: 21–24.

Tomlin, Patrick. 2011. "Every Man His Book? An Introduction to Open Access in the Arts." *Art Documentation, 30*(1): 4–11.

Van Zijl, Carol and Elizabeth Gericke. 2001. "Methods Used by South African Visual Artists to Find Information." *Mousaion* 19 (1): 3–24.

Wayne, Kathryn M. 2010. "Art Librarianship." *Encyclopedia of Library and Information Sciences*, 3rd ed. New York: Taylor & Francis. 1: 1, 260–269.

Weijsenfeld, C. and M. Wolffe. 2009. "Changing Times and Art Librarians." *Art Libraries Journal,* 34(4): 36–41.

Wyngaard, Susan. 1993. "Fine Arts," in the second edition of *Humanities and the Library*, edited by Nena Couch and Nancy Allen. Chicago: American Library Association: 11–38.

Zach, Lisl. 2010. "Arts Literatures and Their Users." *Encyclopedia of Library and Information Sciences*, 3rd ed. New York: Taylor & Francis. 1: 1, 313–320.

Further Reading

Lanzi, Elisa. 2010. "Work of Art." Chicago: American Library Association. *Encyclopedia of Library and Information Sciences,* 3rd ed. New York: Taylor & Francis. 1: 1, 5665–5678.

Marty, Paul F. 2006. "Meeting User Needs in the Modern Museum: Profiles of the New Museum Information Professional." *Library & Information Science Research,* 28(1): 128–144.

Marty, Paul F., W. B. Rayward, and M. Twidale. 2003. "Museum Informatics." *Annual Review of Information Science and Technology,* 37: 259–294.

Whiteside, Ann Baird, Pamela Born, and Adeane Alpert Bregman, comps. 2000. *Collection Development Policies for Libraries & Visual Collections in the Arts.* Laguna Beach, CA: Art Libraries Society of North America, 2000. (Occasional paper, no. 12).

INFORMATION RESOURCES IN THE VISUAL ARTS

ARTS IN GENERAL

Because of the international nature of the arts, databases and digital collections for the arts have a global focus. Many of the databases and digital collections treated in this chapter may be provided in large research institutions. Listings in this chapter for open access resources provide wide coverage for art history and contemporary information. Like other areas in the humanities, publication of monographs, especially in art history, has continued to a greater extent than in the sciences, technology, and the social sciences, and this trend is reflected in the number of printed books and sets included in this chapter.

Databases

11-1. Allgemeines Kunstlerlexikon—World Biographical Dictionary of Artists. Munich: De Gruyter Saur. Online subscription database.

 Allgemeines Kunstlerlexikon (AKL). [Artists of the World]. Munich: De Gruyter Saur, 1991–. Print edition to be completed in 2020.

 The Artists of the World: Bio-Bibliographical Index A-Z. Leipzig, Germany: K.G. Saur, 2000. 10 vols.

The online edition of the Allgemeines Kunstlerlexikon is a comprehensive, authoritative art history database. The background of the database needs to be explained as one element in a series of related publications published by K.G. Saur. All art librarians are familiar with and frequently use the multi-volume *Allgemeines Lexikon der Bildenden Kunstler von der Antike bis zur Gegenwart* (1907–1950, 30 vols.), referred to as "Thieme-Becker," and its successor *Allgemeines Lexikon der Bildenden Kunste des XX. Jahrhunderts* (1953–1962, 6 vols.), known as "Vollmer."

 Thieme-Becker is considered the most complete and scholarly biographical reference work in the entire art field in print. It includes nearly 50,000 artists from all countries and all time periods. The emphasis is on painters and engravers, but architects and sculptors are also covered. Articles vary in length but generally provide good depth of coverage, with the longer ones signed by the contributors. Locations are provided for works of art and this title is known for the bibliographies accompanying the majority of entries. These include references to books, catalogs, and periodical articles. Entries are arranged alphabetically by names of personalities. Thieme-Becker was extended by a supplementary effort by Hans Vollmer, entitled *Allegemeines Lexikon der bildenden Kunstler des XX Jahrhunderts* (Seeman, 1953–1962, 6 vols.). Although there is some overlap with Thieme (which included a few living persons at time of publication), the concentration on twentieth century artists by Vollmer includes about 6,000 brief biographies with bibliographical references. After the six volumes published by Seeman, K.G. Saur Verlag took over the publication and issued new editions of volumes 1–3 and volumes 5 and 6 in 1992. The title was then recast as *Allgemeines Kustlerlexikon* (AKL), forecast to consist of approximately eighty volumes, with three volumes being published each year. K.G Saur subsequently published the ten volume set, *The Artists of the World: Bio-Bibliographical Index A-Z*, an index to AKL and over 200 other relevant works, published in Germany and abroad, in all totaling some 500 volumes. The entries include the briefest biographical data: artist's name, life dates, artistic profession, country code, name variant, and 1-3 bibliographic citations.

 Allgemeines Kunstlerlexikon (AKL) [Artists of the World] is now the standard art history reference work for scholars, students, librarians, gallery owners, auctioneers, collectors, and all those interested in the art of the world. It is the successor of the traditional standard works on art history, the *Thieme-Becker* and the *Vollmer*. The print edition of AKL continues. The content of the AKL database contains biographical profiles from all volumes of Thieme-Becker, all volumes of Vollmer, and all volumes of AKL published to date; additionally it includes full-text articles from all volumes of AKL published to date, 135,000 previously unpublished brief biographies from the AKL editorial database, and 13,000 artist profiles from the AKL archive that are unpublished in the book edition of AKL. The database includes over one million biographical profiles of artists. Ranging in scope from antiquity to the present, information on the arts from all over the world is covered in more than 180,000 full-text articles. The database is searchable, with a multitude of search criteria options, and is updated two to three times annually.

11-2. Art Source. EBSCO Publishing/ Wilson, 2011-. Online subscription database.

Art Source was formed in the merger of EBSCO Publishing and H.W. Wilson in 2011. The Wilson databases *Art Abstracts*, *Art Full Text*, and *Art Index Retrospective* were merged with the EBSCO *Art & Architecture Complete* database to form Art Source. All of the databases are also available separately as well as within the Art Source database. The separate databases from each company are treated in the two entries below.

11-3. Art & Architecture Complete. EBSCO Publishing. Online subscription database. http://www.ebsco.com

The "Complete" in the title obtains for the wide number of disciplines and fields indexed as well as the range of resources covered. More than 800 periodicals and over 230 books are fully indexed in *Art & Architecture Complete* with selective coverage for another 70 publications. Major subject areas covered include art, antiques, archaeology, architecture and architectural history, art history, decorative arts, painting, sculpture, photography, printmaking, costume design, interior and landscape design, and graphic arts. The database is appropriate for both academic and public library users.

11-4. Art Full Text. New York: H.W. Wilson. Online subscription database.
Art Index Retrospective. H.W. Wilson. Online subscription database.

The long-running Wilson-printed *Art Index* was replaced by Art Full Text. This bibliographic database indexes and abstracts articles published world-wide from periodicals in Dutch, English, French, German, Italian, Japanese, Spanish, and Swedish. Coverage includes art reproductions that appear in indexed periodicals, museum bulletins, yearbooks, and more. This is the database most likely to be found in public libraries. The Art Index Retrospective database includes the contents of the *Art Index* from 1984 back to the beginning.

11-5. Arts and Humanities Search. Detroit: Thomson/Reuters. Online subscription database.

Also known as the *Arts and Humanities Citation Index* (entry 2-1), this multidisciplinary database is a module within the *Web of Knowledge* subscription database. International in scope, Arts and Humanities Search covers 1,300 of the leading arts and humanities journals. Implicit citations are added for material such as painting, musical compositions, literary works, films and records, along with dance, music, and theatrical performances. Dates covered are from 1980 to the present and the database is updated weekly. The database is most suitable for academic research.

11-6. ARTbibliographies Modern. Detroit, MI: CSA/Proquest. Online subscription database.

As the title implies, the database does not furnish full text, but indexes journal articles, books, essays, exhibition catalogs, dissertations, and exhibit reviews of English and foreign-language materials beginning with the late 1960s. The bibliography is comprehensive for modern art, with more than 13,000 new entries being added each year. Coverage includes famous and lesser-known artists, movements, and trends from the late nineteenth century onwards. The bibliography thoroughly covers all arts fields including illustration, painting, printmaking, photography, sculpture, and drawing. In the design fields, crafts, ceramic and glass art, calligraphy, computer and electronic art, graphic and museum design, fashion, video art, and theatre arts are included. In addition to the traditional art forms, ethnic arts and modern forms such as performance art and installation works, body art, graffiti, artists' books, and more are included.

11-7. FRANCIS. France: Institut de l'Information Scientifique et Technique of the Centre National de la Recherche Scientifique (INIST-CNR), Nancy, France: 1991-. Online subscription database.

Art, art history, and archaeology are covered in the FRANCIS database for the Humanities and Social Sciences which contains 2,600,000 records from 4,300 journals dating from 1972 to the present. FRANCIS continues the content indexed by the earlier *RAA (Repertoire d'Art et d'Archeologie)*, published from 1973 to 1989 and *RILA (International Repertory of the Literature of Art)*, published from 1975 to 1989, both of which were merged to form *The Bibliography of the History of Art* (entry 11-87), which was subsequently subsumed by the *International Bibliography of Art* (entry 11-15). A fuller entry for FRANCIS is included in chapter 2 of this guide (entry 2-13).

The J. Paul Getty Trust. http://getty.edu

The J. Paul Getty Trust is an "international cultural and philanthropic institution that focuses on the visual arts in all their dimensions, recognizing their capacity to inspire and strengthen humanistic values." The Getty Trust is a major influence and benefactor in the area of art information. There are four Getty programs: the Museum, Research Institute, Conservation Institute, and Foundation. The Museum consists of The Getty Center Los Angeles and the Getty Villa, Malibu. The Getty aims "to further knowledge and nurture critical seeing through the growth and presentation of its collections and by advancing the understanding and preservation of the world's artistic heritage. The Getty pursues this mission with the conviction that cultural awareness, creativity, and aesthetic enjoyment are essential to a vital and civil society." The Getty Research Institute is responsible for the database projects in entries 11-8 through 11-11. The Getty Search Gateway is a search interface, an easy way to find the numerous databases and publications of the Getty (http://search.getty.edu/gateway/).

"With involvement in virtually all aspects of art and the history of art, the J. Paul Getty Trust is a dominant force in the field." (Constance Gould. *Information Needs in the Humanities: An Assessment* (RLG 1988, 15))

Four Vocabularies or Thesauri are maintained by the Getty Research Institute (entries 11-8 through 11-11). The Getty vocabularies contain structured terminology for fine art, architecture, decorative arts, archival materials, and other material culture. The vocabularies are available on the Getty Web site, free of charge, for searching individual terms and names. The data are updated every two weeks. The Getty vocabularies are made available via the Web to support limited research and cataloging efforts only. Licensing is required for more extensive use of these tools. Contributors of significant numbers of records to AAT, ULAN, TGN and CONA are currently given a fee-free license for the data.

11-8. Art and Architecture Thesaurus Online (AAT). Los Angeles, CA: The Getty Research Institute. Online database. http://www.getty.edu/research/conducting_research/vocabularies/aat/index.html

AAT contains terms, synonyms, definitions, and relationships for objects, styles, materials, and other topics related to art, architecture, and other material culture. The three main areas of use are for cataloging, search tips for databases, and information for researchers. The AAT contains around 34,000 concepts and 131,000 terms.

11-9. Thesaurus of Geographic Names Online (TGN). Los Angeles, CA: The Getty Research Institute. Online database. http://www.getty.edu/research/tools/vocabularies/tgn/index.html

One of the four Getty vocabularies, the TGN is a controlled vocabulary list for geographic names derived from lists of thousands of geographic names used by the various Getty cataloging and indexing projects. TGN contains names, variant names, and hierarchical context for current and historical cities, towns, nations, empires, physical features, and archaeological sites. The thesaurus is constantly growing due to contributions from the user community and the Getty Vocabulary Program editors. Its purpose is to standardize terminology needed for cataloging and retrieval of information about the visual arts and architecture.

11-10. The Union List of Artist Names (ULAN). Los Angeles, CA: The Getty Research Institute. http://www.getty.edu/research/tools/vocabularies/ulan/index.html

Also one of the four Getty vocabularies, the ULAN is a controlled vocabulary list for artist names derived from lists of thousands of artist names used by the various Getty cataloging and indexing projects. ULAN contains names, variant names, and biographical information for artists, architects, studios, firms, and repositories of art needed for cataloging and retrieval of information about the visual arts and architecture.

11-11. Cultural Objects Authority File (CONA). Los Angeles, CA: The Getty Research Institute. Online database under development. http://www.getty.edu/research/tools/vocabularies/cona/

CONA, a new vocabulary being developed, is a thesaurus in structure and includes titles, attributions, and other information for works of art and architecture. CONA comprises authority records for cultural works, including architecture and *movable works* such as paintings and sculpture. The minimum fields in a CONA record are the types of information typically captured in a visual resources catalog, repository catalog records, or included on a museum wall label.

The Getty Research Institute has published a number of guides on cataloging, metadata, controlled vocabularies, records, standards, and tools that promote best practices for managing information in libraries, archives, and museums. Many are issued in both print and e-book formats. The next two entries are e-books on these topics that are useful to catalogers, curators, staff in archives and museums, systems designers, and students in information science and museum studies. Other similar titles from the Getty Research Institute not treated here are *Introduction to Metadata* (2008); *Introduction to Imaging* (2003); and *A Guide to the Description of Architectural Drawings* (2000). All are available online.

11-12. Introduction to Controlled Vocabularies: Terminology for Art, Architecture, and Other Cultural Works. Patricia Harpring. Los Angeles, CA: The Getty Research Institute, 2010. Print and e-book.

This work is not a database, but is an accompaniment to the use of the Getty vocabularies, *Art & Architecture Thesaurus* (11-8), *Getty Thesaurus of Geographic Names* (11-9), and the *Union List of Artist Names* (11-10). The Library of Congress's Authority File, the *Conservation Thesaurus*, *Nomenclature for Museum Cataloging*, and *Thesaurus for Graphic Materials* also are discussed. The print and online publication defines the characteristics, scope, and uses of controlled vocabularies for art and cultural materials and explains how vocabularies should be integrated in cataloging systems and utilized for indexing and retrieval. Topics covered are the standards governing the construction and use of controlled vocabularies; the function, structure, and types of thesauri and taxonomies; and the links and relationships between terms in a thesaurus and between thesauri. The author is the managing editor of the Getty Vocabulary Program. Examples and illustrations are drawn from the Getty's collections. The book includes a bibliography, a glossary, and an appendix listing source terms to use when constructing controlled vocabularies. Although written primarily for catalogers, it makes a good supplement to cataloging texts and is useful to students in information science and museum studies and systems.

11-13. Categories for the Description of Works of Art. (CDWA) Rev. ed. Murtha Baca and Patricia Harpring, eds. Los Angeles, CA: The Getty Research Institute, 2009. E-book.

CDWA "describes the content of art databases by articulating a conceptual framework for describing and accessing information about works of art, architecture, other material culture, groups and collections of works, and related images. CDWA provides a framework to which existing art information systems can be mapped and upon which new systems can be developed. The work includes discussions, basic guidelines for cataloging, and examples. It is intended for use by curators, researchers, information managers, systems vendors, and others using CDWA as a basis for making decisions about the content of both new and existing databases. Also edited by Murtha Baca is *Introduction to Art Image Access: Issues, Tools, Standards, and Strategies* (Getty 2002).

11-14. Grove Art Online. New York: Oxford University Press. Online subscription database.

In 2003, the Oxford University Press began publishing Grove Art Online which contains the complete printed *Grove Dictionary of Art* (1996). The printed *Grove Dictionary of Art* is a 34 volume monumental work containing 41,000 articles written by 6,700 art historians and specialists worldwide. The work is considered to be the largest international collaboration in the history of art publishing. Although the *Dictionary* was published in 1996, the database is constantly updated with new material and image links. The database has 45,000 articles on every aspect of the visual arts, including 21,000 biographies of artists, architects, patrons, collectors, dealers, theorists, writers, and scholars. More than 5,500 art images and line drawings are displayed within the text of the articles. The interface is user friendly with thematic guides to key topics. Even if libraries own the printed *Grove Dictionary*, the updated database is a necessary acquisition. The database is a *Choice* Outstanding Academic Title and a *Forbes* Best of the Web selection. Grove Art Online is also included in Oxford Art Online (entry 11-16).

11-15. International Bibliography of Art (IBA). Detroit, MI: CSA/Proquest. Online subscription database. www.csa.com

IBA is the successor to the *Bibliography of the History of Art* that was maintained by the Getty Research Institute until 2009 (entry 11-87). The database covers "visual arts in all media, plus decorative and applied arts, museum studies and conservation, archaeology and classical studies, antiques and architectural history, and related fields. American art from the colonial era to the present, European art from late antiquity to the present, and global art since 1945 are covered." Indexed are at least 500 core journals, plus detailed coverage of monographs, essay collections, conference proceedings and exhibition catalogues. As befitting the name, at least 60 percent of records are from non-English-language publications (principally German, French, Italian and Spanish).

11-16. Oxford Art Online. Oxford: Oxford University Press. Online subscription database. Updated quarterly. http://www.oxfordartonline.com/public/

Oxford Art Online is published in partnership with the Bridgeman Art Library. This resource provides a comprehensive searchable database of approximately 45,000 articles, over 100,000 images, 500,000 bibliographic citations, and hyperlinks. It covers all aspects of the visual arts worldwide from prehistory to the 1990s, including painting, sculpture, graphic arts, photography, and more. Subscriptions to Oxford Art Online include *Benezit Dictionary of Artists* (entry 11-23), *Grove Art Online* (entry 11-14), *The Oxford Companion to Western Art*, *Encyclopedia of Aesthetics*, and the *Concise Oxford Dictionary of Art Terms*. Subscriptions to the Oxford Art Online provide a complete library of basic coverage for the arts. The database will most likely be found in research libraries and special libraries in the arts.

11-17. Oxford Reference Online Premium. Oxford: Oxford University Press. Online subscription database. http://www.oxfordreference.com (See also entries 2-23, 5-11.)

Oxford Reference Online Premium is a different database from Oxford Art Online above (entry 11-16). Reference Premium is a broader online collection of over one hundred reference titles for all subjects with an interface that allows searching all titles included in the subscription. Art titles in the database include *The Grove Encyclopedia of Art*, *The Oxford Dictionary of Art and Artists*, *The Concise Oxford Dictionary of Art Terms*, *The Oxford Dictionary of Art*, *A Dictionary of Modern Design*, *A Dictionary of Modern and Contemporary Art*, *The Oxford Companion to the Garden*, *The Oxford Companion to the Photograph*, and *The Oxford Companion to Western Art*. The individual titles in both Oxford Art Online and Reference Premium have not all been treated in the individual entries in this Guide. It is likely that research libraries will maintain subscriptions to Reference Premium, the broader database which includes the arts titles as well as many other subjects, providing access to indexing and full text across all of the titles.

Digital Libraries and Collections

11-18. ARTstor. www.artstor.org. Digital library. Access by membership fees.

The Andrew W. Mellon Foundation, founders of the JSTOR database, started ARTstor as a non-profit entity in 2000 to enhance scholarship and teaching in the arts. Part of its mission is "to create an organized, central, and reliable digital resource that supports noncommercial use of images for research, teaching and learning." The project was begun to address technical problems with digitization, issues with standardization and copyright, and the challenge of bringing together a collection from artifacts and objects scattered around the world. ARTstor is a repository of one million images in the arts, architecture, humanities, and social sciences. Collections comprise contributions from outstanding museums, photographers, libraries, scholars, photo archives, and artists and artists' estates. ARTstor contains dozens of collections from a wide variety of cultures across all major time periods including a collection of 190,000 old master drawings originally photographed at over 100 different repositories, twenty years of contemporary New York City gallery shows, archives of Islamic textiles, the restored Ghiberti "Gates of Paradise," African masks, medieval manuscripts, images of all exhibitions shown at MOMA, and many others. For a fee, non-profit organizations can become members of ARTstor, securing access to over one million images with more constantly being added. Additionally, ARTstor provides the technology for users to create presentations, zoom in on the artwork, and save personal collections. This excellent resource is vital for all study and research in the arts fields.

11-19. Catalog of Art Museum Images Online. (CAMIO) OCLC. Online subscription database. www.oclc.org

According to the website, this online collection features 95,000 art images in the various art genres such as photographs, prints, sculpture, paintings, decorative arts and utilitarian objects, drawings and watercolors, costume jewelry, textiles, architecture, and more. The images are posted in JPEG format. The image collections, ranging from 3000 B.C. to the present, come from the contributions of twenty-five prominent museums, such as the Smithsonian and the Metropolitan Museum of Art.

11-20. Art Museum Image Gallery. New York: H.W. Wilson, Co. Online subscription database.

Over 165,000 superior quality images can be accessed through this database. All images are rights cleared for use in educational settings, providing essential images for programs in art history, studio art, and design. The images are accompanied by detailed descriptions that may include curatorial text, provenance data, and related multimedia content where available. The publisher claims that the Gallery is the largest image database available in comparison with some of its leading competitors and that the image count is nearly all unique, rather than images being counted multiple times. Users can search by keyword, artist, title of work, year of creation, subject, ownership, type of object, and/or culture or nationality. Coverage is global of both fine and decorative arts from 3000 B.C. to the present day, and art from the cultures of Africa, Asia, Europe, and the Americas, including Native American and Meso-American peoples. The database serves the interests of research in a wide variety of fields including cultural studies, area studies, women's studies, archaeology, history, religion, social studies, literature, and theater departments and community theater research on set design, period costumes, and period furniture.

Printed Monographs and Sets

11-21. The Art Lover's Almanac: Serious Trivia for the Novice and the Connoisseur. Helen Hume. San Francisco: Jossey-Bass, 2003.

The Almanac is an easy-to-browse, yet comprehensive guide to art history, art terminology, art collecting, museums and more. The work contains lists of information under various topics, divided into eleven chapters, each with lists of information, suggestions, little-known facts, definitions, illustrations, and quotations. Some of the chapters in the book are: About Art, Art from Many Cultures, and Naïve, Folk, and Outsider Art. The author is a well-known artist, scholar, and art educator.

11-22. ART WORKS. New York, NY: Thames & Hudson, dist. W. W. Norton. Pap. Monographic series.

Each book in the ART WORKS series explores a theme. Titles published are *Autobiography* (2004), *Money* (2004), *Place* (2005), and *Perform* (2005), with more planned. The design and organization of the volumes is that of an exhibition divided into several chapters or "rooms," reflecting the title's theme. Each volume contains high quality reproductions of the work of fifty or more artists, along with short explanatory notes and quotations. Each volume has an introductory chapter authored by professors, art historians, curators, and artists. The last chapter is a discussion about the theme of the volume. Each work includes a useful bibliography, artists' biographies, an illustration list, and an index of artists. The audience for the volumes may vary according to interests, but they are suitable for students, artists, art collectors, and the general public.

11-23. Benezit Dictionary of Artists. New York: Oxford University Press, 2006. 14 vols. Print and online. French language, 4th ed. OUP, 1999. 14 vols.

The *Benezit* has been the standard and most authoritative biographical work in the visual arts for over a century now. Originally published in French in 1911, the *Dictionnaire Critique et Documentaire des Peintres, Sculpteurs, Dessinateurs, et Graveurs de Tous les Pays*, is known by the name of its compiler, Emmanuel Benezit. A new edition of *Benezit* was issued in 1976 (Paris: Grund) in ten volumes. A fourth edition in French was published in 1999 by the Oxford University Press. The 2006 English language edition is an update of the 1999 French fourth edition with more than 5,000 new and updated entries. In addition to the print volumes, the Oxford University Press has made the English edition available electronically within Oxford Art Online (entry 11-16) with content updated three times a year. The online Benezit contains over 175,000 entries including wide coverage of lesser-known artists worldwide. Valuable features of the work include 11,100 images of artists' signatures, monograms, and stamps. Entries often contain auction records, museum holdings, exhibition information, and bibliographies. An easy to use, attractive interface with quick search from any page and image tabs provides quick access to artists' signatures. The dictionary can be found in academic libraries and special libraries in the arts.

11-24. EYE on Art. Detroit MI: Gale. http://www.gale.cengage.com/

The title is a series of short volumes exploring several aspects of the art world targeted towards middle and high school students. Series titles include: Anime; Architecture; Art Conservation; Art Deco; Art in Glass; The Artist's Tools; Claude Monet; Computer Animation; Cubism; Folk Art; Graffiti; Graphic Art; Impressionism; The Jeweler's Art; Manga; Pablo Picasso; Photography; Post Modern Art; Pottery; Renaissance Art; Romanticism; Sculpture; and Surrealism. Each chapter features illustrations and sidebars containing key concepts and other pertinent information. A bibliography of books, periodical articles and websites, along with a comprehensive index conclude each volume. The series is suitable as an introduction to the subject for students and the general public.

11-25. The Handbook of Art and Design Terms. D. Edwards. Upper Saddle River, NJ: Pearson/ Prentice Hall, 2004.

This is a basic introductory art and design text containing around 640 entries to meet the information needs of students in art, design, architecture, and other disciplines. Some entries contain cross-references. There is also a selected bibliography of art, design, and architecture publications.

11-26. International Directory of Arts, 2011. 35th ed. München: De Gruyter Saur, 2010. 3 vols. Print and e-book.

The International Directory of Arts (IDA) is a reference directory that has the contact information for over 145,000 museums and public galleries, universities, academies and schools, associations, the art and antiques trade, numismatics, galleries, auctioneers, restorers, art publishers, art journals, antiquarian and art booksellers, and art and antiquity fairs. The directory also lists details of museum specializations, as well as their curators and senior staff.

11-27. The Thames & Hudson Dictionary of Art Terms. 2nd ed. Edward Lucie-Smith. London: Thames & Hudson, 2004.

The dictionary contains 2,000 entries that span all periods of time to the present and 400 illustrations defining the vocabulary of art and art history. Some entries have cross-references. International in coverage, topics include painting, sculpture, architecture, photography, the decorative, applied and graphic arts from around the world.

11-28. Who's Who in Art: Biographies of Leading Men and Women in the World of Art Today. 34th ed. Charles Baile de Laperriere and Lynda Murray, eds. Caine, Wiltshire: Hilmarton Manor Press, 2010.

This source contains biographies of the leading British men and women in the current art world, including artists, sculptors, designers, architects, critics, writers, lecturers, curators, and photographers. The biographies are written by the artists themselves and only those that wish to be included are published. Special features include contact information, histories of leading British arts organizations, and appendices of the artists' monograms and signatures.

11-29. Women Artists in the 20th and 21st Century. Uta Grosenick, Ilka Becker, et al. Koln; New York: Taschen, 2001.

This resource covers nearly one hundred female artists working in France, Germany, Japan, Poland, Scandinavia, South Africa, and Spain, the United States, and other countries. Each entry is six pages long and includes biographical information and examples of the artist's work, often with color.

Open Access Resources

11-30. Absolutearts.com. World Wide Arts Resources Corporation. http://www.absolutearts.com/

This website gives access to 50,000 pages of searchable art sites such as galleries, museums, art services, government and non-profit organizations. Research resources include the ability to search for art from "Portfolio Artists and Galleries," which includes over 100,000 works of art. Users also have the ability to browse or search the "Art History Resources—Artists, Art Movements, Biographies, and Artwork," an index of more than 22,000 artists, including detailed biographical information. The website also includes links to "Art Resources across the World Wide Web."

11-31. Artcylopedia. http://www.artcyclopedia.com/

The focus of this website is on "museum quality art" in the Western tradition. The site is an online index of artists, art movements and art news, from an international perspective. Included are original articles, reproductions of art works and sculpture, definitions of important art terms, and a searchable index, which includes links to more than 2,000 other art websites. One of the features of the site is the Art Museums Worldwide tool, an interactive map to search for worldwide museum listings.

11-32. ArtLex Art Dictionary. Michael Delahunt. http://www.artlex.com/

This free online dictionary includes entries for over 3,600 terms relating to art and visual culture, thousands of supporting images, and pronunciation notes. Entries also include quotations and cross-references. The website provides usage suggestions, resource links, and a bibliography.

11-33. ArtSource. Interactive Learning Paradigms. http://www.ilpi.com/artsource/

According to the website, ArtSource is "an index of networked resources on art and architecture." Contents include architecture resources, art and architecture programs, art and architecture libraries, art journals online, artist's projects, electronic exhibitions, events, general resources, image collections, museum information, new media, organizations, vendor information, and virtual ceramics exhibits.

11-34. AskArt and Artist's Blue-book. http://www.askart.com/AskART/index.aspx

Focusing on American artists from the early sixteenth century through the present, AskART is an online database covering more than 200,000 artists. The database began including international artists' auction results in 2007. The site is divided into directories: Artist Directory, an alphabetized searchable directory of over 185,000 artists, living and deceased, also groups, "top artists" in each alphabetical category; Museum Directory, a searchable directory of museums in the United States, alphabetized by museum title; and an Association Directory, an alphabetized listing of professional associations, museums, and dealers operating in the United States.

11-35. Smithsonian Institution Research Information System (SIRIS). http://www.siris.si.edu/

The Smithsonian Institution Research Information System site allows access to the catalogs of the vast Smithsonian collections. Searching for information is by six catalogs: the Library catalog, Archives and Manuscripts catalog, Peter A. Juley & Son collection catalog, Art Inventories catalog, Research/

bibliographies catalog, and the Smithsonian Chronology catalog. SIRIS provides online access to the following databases and catalogs: Smithsonian Libraries; Archives, Manuscripts, & Photographic Collections; Smithsonian American Art Museum Research Databases; Specialized Research Bibliographies; History of the Smithsonian; Directory of Airplanes; Museum Collections; and Image Gallery.

11-36. Web Gallery of Art. http://www.wga.hu/

This resource is a virtual museum and searchable database of European painting and sculpture of the Romanesque, Gothic, Renaissance, Baroque, Neoclassic, and Romantic periods (1000 AD–1850 AD). It contains over 26,000 reproductions. Picture commentaries and artist biographies are available. Online services include guided tours, period music, a catalog, and free postcards.

SPECIALIZED TOPICS IN THE ARTS
Art Sales and Pricing

Special libraries and special collections of all types need sales and provenance information for books and art objects. These resources are generally expensive and only large libraries or well supported art and museum libraries can afford subscriptions. More information is now available on the Internet with auction sites such as eBay.

11-37. Price It! Antiques and Collectibles. Gale Cengage. Online subscription database. http://www.gale.cengage.com/PriceIt/

This database is an identification, research, and pricing tool for collectors, dealers, appraisers and anyone interested in the trade. Price and sales data are provided from eBay, TIAS.com, land-based auction houses, and antique businesses. The database has 127 searchable categories with 41 million records and more than 60 million images. It is marketed to public libraries.

11-38. Art and Rare Book Sales/Auction Catalogs. (SCIPIO) OCLC. Online subscription database.

Produced by the OCLC Online Computer Center, SCIPIO is a searchable bibliographic database that covers art objects, collection sets, estates, furniture, jewelry, painting, rare books, rugs, sketches, sculpture, and textiles. Researchers can search by keyword, auction house, date of sale, sale code, title of catalog, and/or year. This database is updated daily and contains over 300,000 records dating from the late sixteenth century to the present.

11-39. Antique Collectors' Club. http://www.antiquecollectorsclub.com/us

The Antique Collector's Club has been in the publishing industry for over forty years and is the publisher of *Antique Collecting* magazine, as well as scholarly books and price guides. Publications cover antiques, architecture, art, decorative arts, fashion, gardening, and nature, with a focus on British antiques, architecture, and art. The publisher's website includes a list of useful links related to publication topics.

11-40. Art Dealers Association of America. (ADDA) http://www.artdealers.org/

The ADAA produces a *Collectors Guide* that serves as an introduction to the art world for would-be collectors available for download at http://www.artdealers.org/collectorsguide.html

11-41. Art Market Research: a Guide to Methods and Sources. Tom McNulty. Jefferson, NC: McFarland, 2006.

The basics of art collecting are covered in this book, including terminology, artwork analysis, documentation, database researching methods, and online resources. The book is recent enough for most of the information to still be useful and not be outdated.

11-42. artnet. http://www.artnet.com/

Boasting a network of over 2,200 galleries worldwide and more than 166,000 artworks by over 39,000 artists, artnet is a valuable resource for buyers, sellers, and researchers of fine art. The site offers a comprehensive archive of fine art auction results from around the world, of everything from the Old Masters to contemporary art. Price databases and market reports and alerts are available by a modest subscription fee.

11-43. Bridgeman Art Library. http://www.bridgemanart.com

Founded in 1972, according to the website, the Bridgeman Art Library "works with museums, art galleries and artists to make the best art available for reproduction by providing a central source of fine art images." The images are from large museums and galleries, historical societies, and universities throughout the world. With images from over 8,000 collections, more than 29,000 artists, and over 500 contemporary artists with over 17,000 works, the result is an outstanding archive of images, all of which are available for licensing. Bridgeman passes along five percent of the reproduction fee back to the museum or collection, thus assisting in financing conservation and future exhibitions. The arts are broadly included, not just fine arts, but design, antiques, maps, architecture, furniture, glass, ceramics, anthropological artifacts and many other categories. "Each image has been catalogued with full picture data and key-worded to make searching the website easy, even for those with little art knowledge. " In addition to the reproductions, the Bridgeman Artists' Copyright Service assists artists and their estates to administer their copyright and sell reproduction licenses for their work.

11-44. The International Art Markets: The Essential Guide for Collectors and Investors. James Goodwin. Philadelphia: Kogan Page, 2008.

The contributors examine the countries represented in the secondary art markets of three major auction houses: Christie's, Sotheby's, and Bonham's. While coverage of the markets of the United States and Great Britain dominate, this work is truly international with fifty-eight experts' comments that focus on the art markets in more than forty countries. An emphasis in the work is a rationale for investing in art when other financial assets are losing value. The contributions vary but can include art history; art market history including taste, fashion, value, artists, art types, subjects, sales, prices, and records; market structure and performance including auctioneers, dealers, trade associations, museums, exhibitions, fairs, training and education; and taxes and regulations. Diagrams, graphs, and charts support the contributors' key points, but no reference apparatus such as a bibliography and references.

11-45. Kovels.com. http://www.kovels.com/

Kovels publishes price guides on a wide variety of antiques and art media. Free resources available on the website include: a calendar of nationwide antiques and collectibles events; an antiques and collectibles price guide with over 750,000 price listings; reviews of reference books on antiques; a searchable directory of appraisal services, auctions, clubs and publications, matching services, museums and archives, and repairs, conservators, and parts.

11-46. Printworld Directory of Contemporary Prints and Prices. 13th ed. Bala Cynwyd, PA: Printworld Inc., 2010.

The most up-to-date resource available for fine art print and price information, this 1,300 page directory includes 5,000 detailed biographies of the artists, along with contact information and full documentation accompanying each print. International artists are organized alphabetically with newer artists listed separately in their own index.

11-47. Christie's. http://www.christies.com/
  Sotheby's. http://www.sothebys.com/

The two most famous auction houses in the world are Christie's in London and Sotheby's in New York. Both houses have sales offices internationally. The websites provide monthly auction results, catalogs, online magazine and publications, press releases, a sold lot archive, and sale and topical videos, real estate listings, storage and other services, and more. With the websites collectors, dealers, and connoisseurs can learn a great deal free of charge.

Organizations in Visual Arts

Within the United States, the variety of national, regional, and state organizations concerned with art information is too large for an exhaustive listing, but the major organizations are listed here. More specialized organizations are treated in the appropriate sections in this chapter. A listing of art libraries societies worldwide can be found on the ARLIS/UK & Ireland site at http://www.arlis.org.uk/resources.php?link=4

11-48. The American Federation of Arts. (AFA) http://www.afaweb.org/

The AFA was founded in 1909 to broaden public art appreciation, especially in areas of the country not served by large museums. The program of the organization includes circulating museum collections and preparing curricula on visual arts education. The Federation advises on the publication of the *American Art Directory*, *Sources of Films on Art*, and *Who's Who in American Art*. The AFA publishes catalogues for the many exhibitions in the exhibitions program. In 2009, the *AFA: a Century in the Arts* was published.

11-49. Art Libraries Society. Bromsgrove, United Kingdom. http://www.arlis.org.uk

Founded in 1969, ARLIS/UK & Ireland: the Art Libraries Society is a professional organization for people involved in providing library and information services and documenting resources in the visual arts, including librarians, archivists, libraries, publishers and specialist library suppliers. The Society maintains close links with art libraries societies worldwide, including ARLIS/North America, ARLIS/ANZ (Australia and New Zealand) and with individual art libraries societies in Europe as well as in Canada and Japan. ARLIS/UK & Ireland is an institutional member of IFLA and participates in the Section of Art Libraries, which it helped to establish. The Society publishes *Art Libraries Journal*.

11-50. Art Libraries Society of North America (ARLIS/NA). http://www.arlisna.org/

The ARLIS began as the counterpart to the British Art Libraries Society. Founded in 1972, ARLIS/NA serves as a forum for communication, cooperation, new ideas, projects, and programs for art librarians. The website provides information about the society's mission, organization, conferences and events, and publications. It also provides access to resources and subject guides in the arts including links to art libraries, image banks, electronic journals, and to other arts organizations. ARLIS/NA celebrated its twenty-fifth anniversary in 1997. Its history was chronicled by notable author Wolfgang M. Freitag in "ARLIS/NA at Twenty-five-a Reminiscence," an entertaining recount of how ARLIS/NA was founded (Art Documentation 1997).

ARLIS/NA is the publisher of the journal *Art Documentation*. ARLIS-L is an electronic forum for the dissemination of information and the discussion of issues of interest to art information professionals. Postings routinely include job vacancy announcements; conference, workshop, and meeting information; announcements of awards, honors, and prizes; news items from groups and individuals in the Society; new publications and web sites; copyright and information policy issues, and more. Anyone may subscribe. listserv@lsv.uky.edu.

11-51. Artists Rights Society (ARS). http://www.arsny.com/

ARS is the preeminent copyright, licensing, and monitoring organization for visual artists in the United States. Founded in 1987, ARS represents the intellectual property rights interests of over 50,000 visual artists and estates of visual artists from around the world (painters, sculptors, photographers, architects, and others).

11-52. Association of Art Museum Directors. http://www.aamd.org/

This website provides information about the Association of Art Museum Directors and its advocacy efforts, conferences, and publications. The site is also home to the AAMD Object Registry Database, which is comprised of two subsections: New Acquisitions of Archeological Materials and Works of Ancient Art and Resolutions of Claims to Nazi-Era Cultural Assets.

11-53. College Art Association. (CCA) http://www.collegeart.org/

The CAA website includes links to museums worldwide. It has a directory of affiliated societies and information about subscriptions to industry publications, annual conferences, grants, internships, fellowships, and advocacy activities and news.

11-54. International Association of Art Critics. (AICA) http://www.aica-int.org/

Following two international congresses at UNESCO in the late 1940s, the AICA was founded in 1950 under the patronage of UNESCO. AICA comprises various experts anxious to develop international co-operation in the fields of artistic creation, dissemination, and cultural development. The goals of the AICA include contributing to mutual understanding of visual arts and aesthetics in all cultures; promoting art criticism as a discipline and contributing to its methodology; and defending impartial freedom of expression and thought. The AICA Press publishes online and print editions on its congresses and a wide range of topics internationally.

11-55. The National Art Education Association. (NAEA) http://www.arteducators.org/

The NAEA was founded in 1947 to promote the study of the problems of teaching art as well as to encourage research and experimentation in the visual arts. Affiliated with the National Education Association, the NAEA has 8,000 art teachers, supervisors, and students as members. It publishes *NAEA* and many publications/resources for K–12 art teachers.

11-56. Visual Artists and Galleries Inc. (NAGA) http://www.VAGA.org

VAGA is an artists' rights organization and copyright collective representing reproduction rights (copyright) for approximately 500 American artists and, through agreements with affiliated organizations in other countries, thousands of foreign artists worldwide.

11-57. Visual Arts Resource Association (VRA). The International Association of Image Media Professionals. http://www.vraweb.org/

According to the website, the VRA grew out of groups in both the College Art Association and ARLIS/NA. The association is a "multi-disciplinary organization that provides leadership and advocates for standards in the field of image management within the educational, cultural heritage, and commercial environments." VRA offers educational tools and opportunities through publication programs and educational activities. The VRA publishes a scholarly journal, *VRA Bulletin,* an online newsletter (*Image Stuff*), the annual *Sourcebook and Directory of Members*, and occasional Special Bulletins.

11-58. **The Special Libraries Association: Museums, Arts, and Humanities division of Special Libraries Association** (http://units.sla.org/division/dmah/)

Two organizations for the library and information professions have special interest groups for arts and humanities: The Special Libraries Association: Museums, Arts, and Humanities division and The American Society for Information Science & Technology (ASIS&T)-SIG on Arts and Humanities (http://www.asis.org/SIG/ah.html).

ARTS BY FORM AND MEDIUM
Digital Arts and Media

11-59. **Art of the Digital Age.** Bruce Wands, ed. New York: Thames & Hudson, Inc., dist. by W. W. Norton, 2006.

A large format book, this printed work is the first major illustrated survey of digital art. The history of digital art is traced through a Timeline of Digital Art and Technology which begins with the ENIAC in 1946 and goes to 2006. Chapters cover specific types of digital art: digital imaging; digital sculpture; digital installation and virtual reality; performance, music, and sound art; software, database, and game art; net art; and the future of digital art. There are 250 stunning original illustrations of the art of over 100 artists. As befitting the subject and the editor, a digital artist himself, the emphasis is technical, describing the processes and techniques used to create the works. The book contains a brief glossary, a short bibliography, suggestions for further reading, a detailed index, and Web sites for digital art resources and artists' websites. It is appropriate for academic, public, and special libraries.

Form and Technique Reference Guides

11-60. **The Anatomy & Figure Drawing Artist's Handbook.** Viv Foster. Hauppauge, NY: Barron's, 2009.

This resource is a guide to anatomy and figure drawing that covers a variety of techniques and materials. It includes step-by-step projects and a section on developing technique, with many color illustrations.

11-61. **An Artist's Handbook: Materials and Techniques.** Margaret Manning Krug. New York: Abrams Studio, 2007.

This guide covers drawing and painting materials and their use. Photographs show materials and demonstrate techniques. A variety of historical and contemporary techniques are discussed and exercises are included.

11-62. **The Arts of Asia: Materials, Techniques, Styles.** Meher McArthur. New York: Thames & Hudson, 2005.

Although primarily concerned with medium, this work also discusses the history and culture of Asia through examining its visual art. Countries covered include Afghanistan, Burma, Cambodia, China,

India, Indonesia, Japan, Korea, Laos, Malaysia, Pakistan, Philippines, Sri Lanka, Thailand, Tibet, and Vietnam. Illustrations, an index, and bibliographies are included.

11-63. **The Grove Encyclopedia of Materials and Techniques in Art.** Gerald W. R. Ward. New York: Oxford University Press, 2008. Print and e-book.

Arranged alphabetically, this comprehensive resource contains approximately 1,440 articles and entries and covers traditional as well as new media art forms and techniques. Cross references, indices, illustrations, and a bibliography are provided.

Painting, Drawing, and Print

11-64. **Understanding Art: A Reference Guide to Painting, Sculpture, and Architecture in the Romanesque, Gothic, Renaissance, and Baroque Periods**. Armonk, NY: ME Sharpe Reference, 2000. 2 vols.

Designed to make each style easily accessible, this two-volume work provides clear analysis of techniques used to create typical art forms. In addition to the magnificent photographs of major artistic achievements on every page, there are also analytical drawings and photographic details of the works to illustrate the artistic principle under discussion. Illustrations, a bibliography, and an index are included.

11-65. **The Practical Encyclopedia of Acrylics, Oils, and Gouache**. Ian Sidaway. London: Lorenz Books, 2004.

This is a guide to basic as well as advanced techniques in painting media. Projects and exercises are included.

11-66. **The Practical Encyclopedia of Drawing.** Ian Sidaway and Sarah Hoggett. London: Lorenz Books, 2005.

This work is a comprehensive guide to a variety of drawing media and techniques, including composition, line drawing, measuring, observing, pastels, pencils, pens, perspective, shading, sketching, texture, and using negative spaces. The work includes illustrations and an index.

11-67. **Understanding Paintings: Themes in Art Explored and Explained.** Alexander Sturgis and Hollis Clayson, ed. New York: Watson-Guptill, 2000.

This resource discusses the history of painting according to genre. Subjects discussed include genre and abstraction, history painting, landscape, myth and allegories, the nude, portraiture, religious art, and still life. The work has illustrations and an index.

11-68. **National Watercolor Society** (NWS). http://www.nationalwatercolorsociety.org/

The NWS was founded in 1920 as the California Watercolor Society. After two name changes it became the National Watercolor Society in 1975. The NWS is foremost an exhibiting society with annual exhibitions, lectures and orientation programs. The slides of its annual exhibitions are available through a rental program. There are also traveling shows that visit collegiate and public galleries and museums throughout the United States and Canada. In October 2010, NWS held the grand opening for a building in Los Angeles that is its center for offices, gallery, workshops, and a place to house a growing permanent collection.

11-69. Water Color Art. http://www.watercolorart.net/apr.html

This website provides information and resources related to art appraisal, auctions, authentication, conservation, and research.

Photography

11-70. A Consumer Guide to Materials for Preservation Framing and the Display of Photographic Images. Image Permanence Institute (IPI). https://www.imagepermanenceinstitute.org/resources/publications

The Image Permanence Institute is a department of the Rochester Institute of Technology's College of Imaging Arts and Sciences. This brochure, written for the average consumer, discusses the frame package, photo decay, best practices, and display recommendations. Four other guides in the series deal with preserving and framing of family photos: A Consumer Guide to Traditional and Digital Print Stability; A Consumer Guide for the Recovery of Water-Damaged Traditional and Digital Prints; A Consumer Guide to Modern Photo Papers; A Consumer Guide to Understanding Permanence Testing. The guides are all free to download in PDF format and include a bibliography and illustrations.

11-71. Encyclopedia of Nineteenth-Century Photography. John Hannavy, ed. New York: Routledge/Taylor & Francis, 2008. 2 vols.

For use in photo-historical research, this encyclopedia set is international in scope. It contains alphabetically listed entries of biographies, themes, terminology, techniques, and other topics. The resource contains image reproductions, extensive bibliographies, and a sixty-four page index.

11-72. Encyclopedia of Twentieth-Century Photography. Lynne Warren, ed. New York: Routledge/Taylor & Francis Group, 2006. 3 vols. Print and e-book.

Mostly dedicated to art photography, this three-volume set contains more than 525 entries on a range of topics in photography and the history of photography. Included are lists of exhibitions and major works, family and fashion photography, and the development of photography. Aesthetic, critical, technological, and business concepts are covered. Biographies, photographic examples, appendices, glossary, indices, and bibliographies are included.

11-73. Fundamentals of Photography: The Essential Handbook for Both Digital and Film Cameras. Tom Ang. New York: Alfred A. Knopf, 2008.

This handbook provides a comprehensive guide to the fundamentals of photography in both analog and digital technique. It contains over 1,000 images (most in color) that explain concepts in context, a glossary, copyright FAQ, and references. The work is designed for beginning as well as advanced users.

11-74. Issues in the Conservation of Photographs. Debra Hess and Jennifer Jae Gutierrez, ed. Los Angeles: Getty Publications, 2010.

This anthology includes key writings that address the philosophical and practical aspects of conserving photographs. The book includes 72 texts, many of which have never been published before, chronicling the key issues of photo conservation from the nineteenth century through the present.

11-75. Photography Collections Online. George Eastman House. http://geh.org/

This website provides access to a digital storehouse of the George Eastman photography holdings. Photography collections are organized as follows: Indexed by Photographer, Stereo Views, Lantern Slides, Subject, and Books and Albums. Other resources on the site include: A Collection Guide: Photography from 1839 to Today; a sampler of The Gabriel Chrome Collection; the Pre-Cinema Project; and the Technology Collection, which contains images of photography and related equipment. The project is supported by grants from Irv Schankman, National Endowment for the Humanities, Pew Charitable Trusts, and the Getty Grant Program.

11-76. Photographs of the Past: Process and Preservation. Bernard Lavedrine, et al. Trans. John McElhone. Los Angeles, CA: Getty Conservation Institute, 2009.

The history of photographic processes is covered in this work first published in France in 2007. Each process is described in detail with its history, materials, and methods of use such as glass, papers, negatives, and more. Then up-to-date information on preservation and conservation of the materials produced by the process are given including causes of deterioration, lifelines of materials by format, and storage options. The work is a reference and manual that should be owned by most professionals and can be used by anyone involved in the care of photographs.

11-77. Photographs: Archival Care and Management. Mary Lynn Ritzenthaler, Diane Vogt-O'Connor, et al. Rev. ed. Chicago: Society of American Archivists, 2006.

The first edition of this important guide was published in 1984. This updated edition encompasses the preservation of digital images and an expanded and updated section on preservation and archival procedures. Intended to serve as a manual and "compendium of practice," there are chapters on reading and researching photographs; on description and cataloging; on accessioning and arrangement; and a new chapter on digitization. Also, users will find new features such as boxes of "tips" and "terminology." Sample forms and memos are included such as the "Sample Intellectual Property Permission" and "Sample Digital Publication Project Checklist. " The revision has been accomplished by a team of Mary Lynn Ritzenthaler and Diane Vogt-O'Connor, with additional contributions by Helena Zinkham, Brett Carnell, and Kit Peterson of the Library of Congress. The work is suitable for anyone working with photographs, regardless of the type of collection, for beginners as well as experienced practitioners.

Sculpture

11-78. A Century of American Sculpture. Lucy Rosenfeld. Atglen, PA: Schiffer Publishers, 2002.

For over a century the majority of America's major sculptors chose the company Roman Bronze Works to cast their sculptures. This premier American foundry has cast the work of sculptors from Saint-Gaudens to the cowboys of Remington and Russell. The work covers biographical information on over 120 sculptors. Examples in over 700 photographs from the firm's archives are included.

11-79. Collecting Sculpture in Early Modern Europe. Nicholas Penny and Eike D. Schmidt. Washington, DC: National Gallery of Art, 2008.

This resource surveys the practice of collecting sculpture from the late medieval era to the nineteenth century. Case studies examine acquisition methods, value as determined by individual collectors, and the use of artwork as interior and exterior decorations and studio models. The work contains illustrations and an index.

11-80. Display and Displacement: Sculpture and the Pedestal from Renaissance to Post-Modern. Alexandra Gerstein. London: Courtauld Institute of Art Research Forum, in association with Paul Holberton Pub., 2007.

This illustrated resource collects eight essays on the role of the pedestal in sculpture. Topics include varieties of pedestals, pedestal inscriptions, politics, gender, and contemporary trends in the use of pedestals.

11-81. Encyclopedia of Sculpture. Antonia Bostrom, ed. New York: Fitzroy Dearborn, 2004. 3 vols.

The rationale for purchasing this reference work is that it is aimed at the non-specialist and provides a survey that is international in scope. At the time of its publication, it was the most complete reference on the subject of sculpture. It covers the entire history of three-dimensional art in 760 detailed entries on artists, major works, movements, media, techniques, regions, and nations. Entries on individual sculptors include lists of selected works and their years of completion. There is a general index and thematic and author indices. The work was named one of The Top 20 Reference Titles of the Year by American Libraries in 2004.

11-82. Human and Divine: 2000 Years of Indian Sculpture. Balraj Khanna and George Michell. London: Hayward Gallery, 2000.

This resource was produced to accompany the traveling museum exhibit by the same name. Items in the exhibition date from ancient times to the early twentieth century and are made of bronze, ivory, marble, stone, terracotta, and wood. The early history of Indian sculpture is outlined in the context of culture and religion. Forms, styles, and meanings of Indian sculpture are discussed. A chronology, glossary, list of works discussed, and a map are included.

11-83. The International Sculpture Center. http://www.sculpture.org

The International Sculpture Center is a nonprofit organization created to promote the creation, understanding, and appreciation of sculpture. The ISC's website includes information on gallery and museum exhibitions, competitions, job listings, commissions, scholarships, grants, schools and programs, sculpture-related services and supplies, and sculpture parks.

11-84. National Sculpture Society. http://www.nationalsculpture.org/nssN/index.cfm

According to the website, in 1893, Daniel Chester French, Augustus St. Gaudens, Stanford White, and J.Q.A. Ward, among others, established the National Sculpture Society to "spread the knowledge of good sculpture." The NSS serves as a link between the public, sculptors and collectors. Its members promote "the knowledge of excellence in sculpture inspired by the natural world and create, interpret, exhibit, collect and support the evolving tradition in American sculpture." NSS programs include *Sculpture Review* magazine, *the NSS News Bulletin*, scholarships, the Alex J. Ettl Grant, and rotating exhibitions.

11-85. Sculpture: From Antiquity to the Present Day. Jean Luc Daval and Georges Duby, eds. London: Taschen, 2002.

This resource explores the creation, discovery, historical, and political background of sculptural works. Comparisons are drawn between eras and genres.

11-86. Thais—1200 Years of Sculpture. http://www.thais.it/scultura/default.htm

Thais is an image archive in English and Italian of 1200 years of sculpture from the Romanesque through the modern era. The archive can be searched by art period, artist, and location of the sculpture.

HISTORY OF ART

Databases

11-87. **Bibliography of the History of Art** (BHA). Getty Art History Information Program and Institut de l'information scientifique et technique (France). Santa Monica, CA: J. Paul Getty Trust, Getty Art History Information Program: Centre national de la recherché scientifique, 2001–2007.

Although the Getty Research Institute ceased maintaining the BHA in 2009, it still provides access to the *Bibliography* and to the *Répertoire de la litterature de l'art* (RILA) for no charge on its Web site at http://library.getty.edu/bha. The databases, searchable together, cover material published between 1975 and 2007. *RILA* covers the years 1975–1989. It was produced at the Sterling and Francine Clark Art Institute, and Michael Rinehart was the editor-in-chief. In 1982, Getty began to support *RILA* and in 1990 the Getty began to collaborate with INIST-CNRS to produce the BHA, which was a merger of *RILA* and the *Répertoire d'art et d'archéologie.* For material published after 2007, see the International Bibliography of Art (IBA), entry 11-15. The Getty Web site offers both basic and advanced search modules for BHA and *RILA*, and they can be searched easily by subject, artist, author, article or journal title, and other elements. The Getty Search Gateway allows users to search across several of the Getty repositories, including collections databases, library catalogs, collection inventories, and archival finding aids (http://search.getty.edu/gateway/).

11-88. **Index to 19th Century American Art Periodicals**. Mary M. Schmidt. OCLC FirstSearch. Online subscription database.

Originally an online resource through the Research Libraries Group, the index is now available through OCLC. This resource contains information on artists, illustrators, painting, sculpture, drawing, photography, architecture, and design exhibitions and sales, decoration, and collecting. All articles, poems, illustrations, and advertisements are indexed. There are over 26,000 records from 1800–1899.

Printed Resources

11-89. **African American Art and Artists**. Samella S. Lewis. Berkeley, CA: University of California Press, 2003.

This book provides a comprehensive overview of the lives and work of African American artists from 1610–2002. Along with traditional media, this resource also includes installation art, mixed media and digital/computer art. A bibliography and an index follow the conclusion.

11-90. **African Americans in the Visual Arts**. 2nd Rev. ed. Steven Otfinoski. New York: Facts on File, 2011.

Part of the A to Z of African Americans book series, this work has alphabetically arranged biographical entries on more than 190 African American artists. It includes an introduction, bibliography, indices, photographs, and a list of further readings.

11-91. **American Art to 1900: A Documentary History.** Sarah Burns and John Davis. Berkeley, CA: University of California Press, 2009.

The history of American art is told in this book through images of primary documents arranged chronologically and then thematically. The documents are from published and unpublished sources including newspapers, magazines, advertisements, pamphlets, broadsides, poems, speeches, and sermons. The authors of the documents are a wide variety of personages including artists, collectors, critics, educators, poets, politicians, and editorial writers. The documents include diaries and letters from artists about exhibitions, their struggles, and work-related business. Sarah Burns and John Davis have written comments to provide historical and social context to the documentary sources. All aspects of art are discussed including the art market, collecting, and art education. A detailed index is provided and cross references are given in the comments. Each document has bibliographic information. There are a small number of images in the book as the documents are the primary focus. The work is an essential addition to collections on the history of art in America.

11-92. Animal & Sporting Artists in America. F. Turner Reuter, Jr. Middleburg, VA: The National Sporting Library, in association with Red Fox Fine Art, 2008.

The author claims this is the "first comprehensive, scholarly work" devoted solely to American sporting artists. In keeping with this statement, the work includes biographical entries for 2,384 painters and sculptors and over 400 images, many of which have not been previously published. Perhaps the most outstanding feature of the work is its coverage of lesser-known and obscure artists as the criteria for inclusion demand that an artist need only have produced one drawing, painting, or model of an animal or sporting subject, although they must have been included in a least one verifiable reference source. Entries include name, life dates, education, training, work experience, exhibitions, and works in public collections. The writing has a personal tone and much of the commentary is drawn from the author's experiences with sporting art. The work is well researched with an extensive bibliography. The author is an expert in the subject matter as curator of fine arts at The National Sporting Library and also an innkeeper, art dealer, gun enthusiast, and gentleman farmer. The work is unique in its thorough treatment of the subjects and is appropriate for all libraries with clientele having similar interests.

11-93. Art Beyond the West: The Arts of Africa, India, and Southeast Asia, China, Japan, and Korea, The Pacific, and the Americas. Upper Saddle River, NJ: Prentice Hall, 2006.

This work provides an introductory survey of non-western art, including its historical, cultural, and socio-economic contexts. The author provides detailed analysis of each major style through its respective cultural context. The artists are arranged within a geographic and chronological framework, from early civilization to modern day. The book contains maps, time charts, a wide selection of images, a glossary, index, and detailed bibliography.

11-94. Atlas of Egyptian Art. Prisse d'Avennes. New York: American University in Cairo Press, 2007. Print and e-book.

An examination of the work of Emil Prisse d'Avennes, a nineteenth-century Frenchman well-known for documenting monuments of ancient Egypt, Nubia, and the Islamic world, this collection is dedicated to ancient Egyptian art, architectural features, and sculpture. The work contains photographs, illustrations, cross references, and bibliographies.

11-95. Atlas of World Art. John Onians, ed. New York: Oxford University Press, 2004.

This work provides a detailed chronology of art history by geographic region from the Paleolithic era to the present. The book is divided into seven chronological sections. Each section is then categorized by broad land masses and finally divided by region or country. The work is notable for its more than 300 maps depicting trade routes, migrations, borders, natural resources, and human settlements. An index is included.

11-96. Bibliography on American Prints of the Seventeenth through the Nineteenth Centuries. Georgia Brady Barnhill. New Castle, DE: Oak Knoll Press, 2006.

Most useful for research libraries, print collectors and dealers, this is an annotated bibliography of almost 2,000 citations to books, book chapters, and articles on a variety of topics in early American printmaking. The bibliography is arranged topically, with sections ranging from Artists and Publishers, Collecting and Collectors, and ending with Wood Engraving. Each citation includes a short summary of the work, along with references for further study. An index of authors is included.

11-97. Encyclopedia of African American Artists. Dele Jegede. Westport, CT: Greenwood Press, 2009.

Part of the Artists of the American Mosaic series, this encyclopedia discusses the works of sixty-six African American artists. The entries are arranged alphabetically and focus on artists of the twentieth and twenty-first centuries. Essays range from three to six pages and include discussion of the author's purpose and message, along with biographical information including artistic influences. A list is provided of galleries and museums which house the artist's work as well as a print bibliography. The entire volume contains a composite bibliography and index.

11-98. Gardner's Art Through the Ages: A Global History. 13th ed. Helen Gardner, Fred S. Kleiner, and Christin J. Mamiya. Belmont, CA: Wadsworth, 2010.

A classic, standard reference work, this resource covers the art and architecture of Africa, China and Korea, Japan, Oceania, South and Southeast Asia, Western Europe, the Islamic world, and Native American art. Maps and a fold-out timeline are included.

> Grove's Dictionaries is the well-known publisher of the *Grove Dictionary of Art* (1996) and the *New Grove Dictionary of Music and Musicians* (entry 9-27), *the New Grove Dictionary of Opera* (entry 9-116), and the *New Grove Dictionary of Jazz* (entry 9-96). The Grove art dictionaries are now distributed by the Oxford University Press in print and are incorporated into Oxford Art Online (entry 11-16). All of these publications and databases have been given wide acclaim for their thoroughness, authoritativeness, and ease of use.

11-99. The Grove Art Series. Jane Turner, ed. New York: Oxford University Press, 2000. Print and e-book.

The Grove Art Series is a separate set of titles of five biographical encyclopedias updated from the 34-volume *Grove Dictionary of Art* (1996). Series titles include: *From Renaissance to Impressionism, From Monet to Cezanne, From David to Ingres, From Expressionism to Post-Modernism,* and *From Rembrandt to Vermeer.* Each title includes an index, cross-references, bibliographies, appendices, and illustrations.

11-100. The Grove Encyclopedia of American Art. Joan Marter, ed. New York: Oxford University Press, 2011, 5 vols. Print and e-book.

For this new encyclopedia Marter has updated the content of Grove Art Online (entry 11-16) by commissioning articles on new topics, such as digital and performing arts. Existing content was also updated, all to reflect current trends in the twenty-first century with a more international perspective. The new content in turn is being incorporated into Grove Art Online. Artists, major movements, institutions, critics, and the architecture found in major cities of the United States are covered, as are new media and methodologies, including digital art, performance art, and installation art. The decorative arts are not included in this new edition because they were covered in the separate *Grove Encyclopedia of the Decorative Arts* (entry 11-147). The set is a definitive work which should be included in academic and public libraries for students, researchers, and the general public. Subscribers to Grove Art Online may want to own the printed set as well.

11-101. The Grove Encyclopedia of Classical Art and Architecture. Gordon Campbell, ed. New York: Oxford University Press, 2007. 2 vols. Print and e-book.

The two-volume set includes over 800 entries on every art form dating back to the fall of the Roman Empire. This is a comprehensive resource including entries on all subject areas in the classical arts, namely philosophers, rulers, writers, artists, architecture, ceramics, sculpture, etc. Entries are arranged alphabetically, and there are illustrations, maps, line drawings, and 32 color plates. The work is a *Library Journal* Best Reference selection.

11-102. The Grove Encyclopedia of Islamic Art and Architecture. Jonathan M. Bloom and Sheila S. Blair. New York: Oxford University Press, 2009.

A comprehensive encyclopedia of Islamic art and architecture beginning with the seventh century, this resource contains over 1,600 entries, indices, bibliographies, and illustrations. The work covers Islamic art and architecture from the Middle East to Central and South Asia, Africa, and Europe. The work is a *Library Journal* Best Reference selection, a *Booklist* Editors' Choice selection, and a *Choice* Outstanding Academic title.

11-103. [Grove] **Encyclopedia of Latin American and Caribbean Art**. Jane Turner, ed. New York: Grove's Dictionaries, 2000.

This volume is another Grove comprehensive encyclopedia containing biographical entries, art movements, from pre-history to the present in a variety of genres edited by Jane Turner. The artistic development of each country is examined in survey articles. The work contains bibliographies, illustrations, and indices for Latin American art and artists outside of the United States. There is also an entry for Latin American artists of the USA.

11-104. The Grove Encyclopedia of Northern Renaissance Art. Gordon Campbell, ed. New York: Oxford University Press, 2009. 3 vols. Print and e-book.

Another set drawn from the *Grove Dictionary of Art* and updated, this work deals with all aspects of art historical and cultural information about Northern Renaissance artists, artisans, architects, craftsmen, philosophers, rulers, countries, cities, centers of production, painting, sculpture, jewelry, theory, criticism, historiography, collecting, and patronage vital to the flourishing of art in this period. It offers fully updated articles and bibliography in 1700 A-Z entries, as well as more than 500 illustrations, maps, drawings, diagrams, and color plates.

11-105. Guide to the Literature of Art History, 2. Max Marmor and Alex Ross, ed. Chicago, IL: American Library Association, 2004.

The work is a supplementary volume to the *Guide to the Literature of Art History* (1980). It is an annotated bibliography of the leading art and architecture books and journals from around the world, published from 1980–2000. This edition consists of new titles, volumes, editions, and reprints, along with cross-referencing to the GLAH 1. Two additional chapters concern art preservation and law.

11-106. Historical Dictionaries in Literature and the Arts; A to Z Guide series. Lanham, MD: Scarecrow Press. Monographic series.

These two series by Scarecrow Press cover all major subject areas. The Historical Dictionaries are hardbacks, while the A to Z are paperback editions of the same titles. The books have brief A-Z entries that describe the main people, events, politics, social issues, institutions, and policies surrounding the subjects of each work. Extensive bibliographies in each are divided into broad subject areas and entries are cross-referenced to make locating information easy. The titles in the arts series are:

>*Animation and Cartoons*, 2009
>
>*Architecture*, 2009
>
>*Baroque Art and Architecture*, 2010
>
>*Neoclassical Art and Architecture*, 2011
>
>*Renaissance Art*, 2007
>
>*Rococo Art*, 2011
>
>*Romantic Art and Architecture*, 2011
>
>*Surrealism*, 2010

11-107. A History of Art in Africa. 2nd ed. Monica Blackmun Visona, Robin Poynor, Herbert M. Cole. New York: Prentice Hall, 2007.

This resource is a comprehensive regionally based chronological survey of the arts and cultures of Africa written by four respected scholars in the field of African art. It covers art from pre-history to contemporary art and contains a glossary, index, annotated bibliography, and illustrations.

11-108. History of Italian Renaissance Art. 6th ed. Frederick Hartt and David G. Wilkins. Upper Saddle River: NJ: Prentice Hall and Harry Abrams, 2007.

A chronology of painting, architecture, and sculpture in Renaissance Italy, this book covers works and their creators by city and region. A glossary, bibliography, and index are included.

11-109. History of Modern Art: Painting, Sculpture, Architecture, Photography. H. Harvard Aranson and Peter Kalb. Upper Saddle River, NJ: Pearson Prentice Hall, 2003.

A survey of modern art, this resource discusses trends and influences in architecture, painting, photography, and sculpture from the mid-nineteenth century to the present day. A bibliography, glossary, illustrations, and index are included.

11-110. Impressionism: Origins, Practice, Reception. Belinda Thompson. New York: Thames & Hudson, 2000.

A very concise, but informative source, Part I covers the origin of impressionism and part II covers the practice and reception finalizing the end of impressionism and its legacy. The source includes a chronology, bibliography, a list of illustrations, and an index.

11-111. Janson's History of Art: The Western Tradition. 8th ed. Penelope J.E. Davies, Walter B. Denny, Frima Fox Hofrichter, Ann M. Roberts, and David Simon. Upper Saddle River, NJ: Pearson Prentice Hall, 2010. 2 vols.

This resource is organized by period, including the Northern European Renaissance, the Italian Renaissance, the High Renaissance, Baroque art, and stylistic divisions for the modern era. A chapter on Islamic art and its relationship to Western art is also included. Discussion focuses on objects, their manufacture, and visual character.

11-112. Lives of the Great Modern Artists. Rev. and expanded ed. Edward Lucie-Smith. London: Thames & Hudson, 2009.

First published in 1999 as *Lives of the Great 20th Century Artists*, this work contains biographies of 105 well-known twentieth and twenty-first century artists by style, including lists of important works, self-portraits, and photographs. The book consists of short biographies of artists, grouped by era and style, and illustrated with major works, self-portraits, and photographs.

11-113. Masterpieces in Detail. Rainer Hagan and Rose-Marie Hagan. New York: Taschen, 2010. 2 vols.

The authors provide answers to numerous questions about 100 world-renowned works of art in a two volume set. Entries reveal hidden details in the works of art, and provide insight on the fashions and lifestyles of the artists and their subjects. Includes color reproductions of each work of art discussed. Volume 1 covers works *From Antiquity to the Renaissance* and Volume 2 covers artwork *From Rembrandt to Rivera*.

11-114. MediaArtHistories. Oliver Grau, ed. Cambridge, MA: The MIT Press, 2007.

The guiding premise of this volume of essays is that media art is not new, but it has its roots in a number of influences in art history and is trans-disciplinary or cross disciplinary. According to the author, new media art has relationships to cultural and media studies, film studies, computer science, and philosophy and deserves recognition in traditional art history as a contemporary discipline. The title, which joins together two terms symbolically, makes the point that media are part of art history and should be included within that field. Art history needs to broaden to become more inclusive of works produced through technology that are "immaterial." One of the essays by Christiane Paul is on the concerns of preserving dynamic works and the work of video and performance artists. The book is divided into sections: Origins: Evolution versus Revolution, Machine-Media-Exhibition, Pop Meets Science, and Image Science. The chapters on the history of media art are interesting in the devices that are described as forerunners of media art such as ingenious Islamic automated devices of the thirteenth century, magic lanterns, and phantasmagorias. The work makes an important scholarly contribution to the field. It is suitable for undergraduates and researchers in media and art history and according to the author's viewpoint should be read by both.

11-115. Modern Chinese Artists: A Biographical Dictionary. Michael Sullivan. Berkeley, CA: University of California Press, 2006.

Many of the entries on 1,800 artists in this dictionary are brief due to the difficulties in securing information in China. The work is an expansion of *Art and Artists of Twentieth-Century China* (Univ. California Press, 1996). The scope of inclusion according to the author is those "who grew up, or were trained, in China . . . even if they subsequently went abroad to work" and ". . . who attained some reputation in China in the twentieth century and opening years of the twenty-first" and whose artworks "are likely to appear in collections, exhibitions, and auctions abroad" (xi). Included are practitioners of traditional painting (guohua), but not artists whose work is limited to calligraphy. The organization is alphabetic by Romanized transliterations, but names are also given in Chinese; characters. Information may include birth and death dates; education; preferred medium and style; address or academic affiliation; honors and awards; exhibitions or publications of work; professional, social, and political activities. Each entry includes a bibliography. Some entries have photographs of the artist or portraits. The work is the only reference on Chinese artists in a western language. With increasing interest in China and Chinese art, this book is an essential acquisition for art libraries and general academic and public libraries as well.

11-116. Oxford Dictionary of American Art and Artists. Ann Morgan. Oxford: Oxford University Press, 2007. Pap.

Oxford has produced a number of paperback reference guides, of which this title serves as an example. It is best suited as a personal guide for the home or for museum visits as its inexpensive paperback format and small type would make carrying around easy. There are 1,000 well-written entries that combine biographical details, descriptions of representative works, and critical views. However, an index and a bibliography of works consulted are missing. The author is an independent scholar, although the work does not seem designed for research, but rather as a quick reference.

11-117. Silhouette: The Art of the Shadow. Emma Rutherford. New York: Rizzoli, 2009.

Although some forms of the silhouette date back to antiquity, the technique was at its height of popularity in the eighteenth century before the advent of photography. Not many works are focused on the silhouette and this one does justice to the art form. The author traces the history of the silhouette in five chapters. The book is heavily illustrated and the various techniques and media discussed. The focus is on the silhouette within British and American arts, crafts, and design. The author discusses the difficulty in categorizing the art form as the matter has been argued over time, as art or craft. The silhouette was a common type of portraiture in all walks of society before photography and never much respected as it is such an easy technique. The book is a well-designed, attractive publication. The hardcover book appears to have been made with durability in mind. While it has a bibliography, there is no index. *The Art of the Shadow* is recommended as suitable for a general audience and for library collections supporting both undergraduate and graduate research in art history, design, and the decorative arts.

11-118. The Queer Encyclopedia of the Visual Arts. Claude J. Summers, ed. San Francisco, CA: Cleis Press, 2004.

This resource contains approximately 200 scholarly essays arranged alphabetically on the contributions of gay, bisexual, and transgender artists to the visual arts. Comprised mainly of biographies, topics also include art styles, ethnic art, and historical periods. It also contains illustrations, bibliographies, and indices.

11-119. St. James Guide to Hispanic Artists: Profiles of Latino and Latin American Artists. Thomas Riggs, ed. Detroit, MI: St. James Press, 2004.

This volume includes biographical and career information, on 375 of the most well-known Hispanic, Latino, and Latin American artists of the twentieth and twenty-first centuries. Arranged alphabetically by artist, each entry begins with a biographical summary, and continues with a list of individual and group exhibitions, public and private collections containing the artist's work, a bibliography of publications, both by and about the artist, and ending with a critical essay. The guide includes indices to artists by nationality and medium, as well as 256 black and white reproductions of the art. This is a useful resource for researchers and as a collection-development aid for librarians.

11-120. Signatures and Monograms [series]. John Castagno. Lanham, MD: Scarecrow Press.

John Castagno is a multimedia artist and sculptor and also a researcher who has been producing works on the signatures, marks, and monograms of artists for over twenty years. The books are organized either by period or geographic area. All entries direct researchers to biographical and bibliographical sources and offer additional references. The works in this series have become the standard reference source for galleries, museums, libraries, and collectors around the world to identify, authenticate, or verify signatures and works of both well-known and little-known artists. Many of the titles have been updated several times. Below is a partial list of works in the Signatures and Monograms series:

> *Abstract Artists: Signatures and Monograms, an International Directory* (2007)
>
> *American Artists II: Signatures and Monograms, From 1800* (2007); III, (2009)
>
> *European Artists II: Signatures and Monograms, From 1800* (2007); III, (2009)
>
> *African, Asian, and Middle Eastern Artists: Signatures and Monograms from 1800: A Directory* (2009)
>
> *Artists' Monograms and Indiscernible Signatures III* (2009)
>
> *Latin American Artists' Signatures and Monograms: Colonial Era to 1996* (1998)
>
> *Old Masters, Signatures and Monograms: A Directory, II* (2009)

11-121. **The Visual Arts: A History**. 7th ed. Hugh Honour and John Gleming. Upper Saddle River, NJ: Pearson Prentice Hall, 2005. 2 vols.

This resource presents the art of Asia, Africa, the Pacific Islands, Europe, and North and South America dating from pre-history to the present. Illustrations include photographs, architectural plans, and maps.

11-122. **Who Was Who in American Art, 1564–1975, 400 Years of Artists in America.** Peter Hastings Falk, ed. Madison, CT: Sound View Press, 1999. 3 vols.

The first edition of *Who Was Who in American Art* was published in 1985. This work cumulated biographical information from the original thirty volumes of *American Art Annual* (1898–1933) and the four subsequent volumes of *Who's Who in American Art* (1936–1947). The 1985 edition included information on 25,000 deceased personalities associated in some way with American art. Included among the entries are painters, sculptors, printmakers, illustrators, photographers, cartoonists, critics, curators, educators, and craftspeople whose creative activity spanned a fifty-year period from the 1890s to the 1940s. Entries include name, profession, last known address, dates of birth and death, education, location of works, exhibitions, awards, memberships, and references to the volume of either of the two source works in which the artist was last covered. The revised edition of the work brings the number of entries to 65,000 and the scope is considerably broader, encompassing artists active from the sixteenth century well into the twentieth. "How to read an entry" describes how the entries were compiled. Not only does the new edition add entries from *Who's Who in American Art* from 1950–1973, but the compilers searched through other biographical dictionaries, exhibition catalogs, city directories and lists from various libraries and museums. The guide to bibliographical sources includes complete citations for the hundreds of references used to find data on the artists. In addition to the two editions of the *Who Was Who*, editor Falk and his team have produced a number of other reference works on art including the *Exhibition Record* Series and the *Dictionary of Signatures and Monograms* (1988).

Open Access Resources

11-123. Arthistory.net

A one-stop resource for Art History, Archaeology and Architecture resources on the web, the site has three divisions: Famous Artists, Art Styles and Periods, and Art Mediums. A click on each of these brings up lists of links to the information.

11-124. Art History Resources on the Web. Dr. Christopher L.C.E. Witcombe. http://arthistoryresources.net/ARTHLinks.html

Dr. Christopher L.C.E. Witcombe is a professor of Art History at Sweet Briar College. This is his personally maintained website that contains a vast number of links to art history resources from Prehistoric Art through contemporary art. The site is categorized by period and by nationality.

11-125. Art Resources. New York: Art Resource, Inc. http://www.artres.com/c/htm/Home.aspx

This fine art image database contains high quality images of architectural works, painting, sculpture, and minor arts from worldwide museums, monuments, and commercial archives.

11-126. Arthistoricum.net-Virtual Library for Art History. Germany: German Research Foundation (DFG). http://www.arthistoricum.net/en/home

This art history resource provides access to electronic journals, dissertations and theses, images, and historic texts. Thematic portals group information about art history, architecture, photography, works on paper, and garden history. Tutorials regarding art history research on the web are designed for beginner and advanced researchers. A database of primary art resources is also provided.

11-127. Heilbrunn Time-line of Art History. New York: The Metropolitan Museum of Art. http://www.metmuseum.org/toah/

This site provides a timeline of art history, as well as world maps, thematic essays, art works, subject indices, and bibliographies by thematic category.

11-128. Mother of All Art History Links Pages. http://www.umich.edu/~motherha/

The Michigan School of Art and Design maintains this site. As the title implies, the site provides links to other websites in a number of categories including art museums, image collections and online art, fine arts schools and departments, art history departments, textual resources and linguistic resources, and research resources. Most anyone can find websites they did not already know about from this resource.

11-129. Perseus Digital Library. Tufts University Library. http://www.perseus.tufts.edu/hopper/

This vast digital library collection mostly covers history, literature, and culture of the Greco-Roman world, including Greek and Latin texts and translations. Perseus features a large database of images, such as coins, vases, and sculpture. The collection also contains additional resources for textual studies and English word searches of the texts. See also entry 6-81.

11-130. Old Stones, the Monuments of Art History. M.D. Gunther. http:// www.art-and-archaeology.com

Images of stone monuments from around the world are mounted on this site, organized geographically. The materials include original photographs, images, essays, timelines, and links to related art history pages.

Iconography

11-131. Index of Christian Art. Online subscription database. http://ica.princeton.edu

According to the website, Charles Rufus Morey founded the *Index of Christian Art* in 1917. Since that time it has developed into the most important archive of medieval art for the iconographer, being a "thematic and iconographic index of early Christian and medieval art objects." The Index records "works of art produced without geographical limitations from early apostolic times up to A.D. 1550 (extended in the case of the Morgan and Princeton Library projects to include their manuscript holdings up to the middle of the sixteenth century)". As is to be expected, there is a particular emphasis and focus on art of the western world. More recently this focus has been expanded to include Coptic Egypt, Lebanon, Ethiopia, Syria, Armenia, and the Near East.

The index is divided into three components: the Subject file, the Photographic file, and the Database. The combined resources contain materials primarily related to Christian art and over 26,000 terms related to Christian iconography, and Jewish, Islamic, and non-ecclesiastical subjects. Besides iconographic descriptions of works of art, the database includes bibliographic records and information such as style, school, location, and more.

11-132. Lexikon Iconographicum Mythologiae Classicae (LIMC). Zürich: Artemis,1981–2009. 8 vols. Supp. 2 vols.

After almost thirty years, the LIMC is complete. The set has two volumes of indices. Descriptive entries are arranged alphabetically in four volumes of text, with the remaining four volumes containing black-and-white illustrations indexed to their respective entries. LIMC provides access to the entire iconographical tradition of classical art, cataloging representations of mythology in the plastic arts of antiquity. The work was produced through an international collaboration and gathering of information and photographs with a total of 46,250 documents by the 38 countries that participated. International scholars contributed in one of four languages in English, German, French, or Italian. A history of LIMC is in volume 8 (1, xiv–xvii), which contains even more illustrations than the previous volumes. The U.S. LIMC Center is at the Alexander Library of Rutgers University which has developed a database of the indexed material held in the United States.

11-133. The Continuum Encyclopedia of Animal Symbolism in Art. Hope B. Werness. New York: Continuum, 2004.

This encyclopedia examines animal symbolism and its significance throughout world cultures and history. Animal entries begin with zoological information. The work includes cross references, an index, appendix, and bibliography.

11-134. The Continuum Encyclopedia of Native Art. Hope B. Werness. New York: Continuum, 2003.

This resource covers aesthetics, anthropology and mythology within tribal or indigenous non-Western art. Symbols, meanings, and significance of art are identified and discussed in context. The work contains illustrations, indices, maps, and references.

11-135. Dictionary of Subject and Symbols in Art. 2nd ed. James Hall. Boulder, CO: Westview Press, 2007.

An update of the 1974 version, this work provides entries on religious and secular symbols and subjects from antiquity to the Renaissance. Religious, classical, and historical themes are discussed. There are an index, bibliography, and illustrations.

11-136. 1000 Symbols: What Shapes Mean in Art and Myth. Rowena Shepherd and Rupert Shepherd, ed. New York: Thames & Hudson, 2002.

Each entry in this source gives a blue outline drawing of the symbol. Each symbol in a table/index is easily searched by general themes. These thematic chapters include: Heaven and Earth, Characters and People, and Objects and Artifacts. Each symbol explanation covers worldwide pertinent cultural meanings.

11-137. Symbols and Allegories in Art. Matilde Battistini. Los Angeles: J. Paul Getty Museum, 2005.

This work examines symbols found in great works of western art, especially fifteenth through seventeenth century European art. Entries are divided thematically into four sections: "time," "man," "space," and "allegories." Bibliographic references, appendices, and indices are included.

11-138. Symbols and Rebuses in Chinese Art: Figures, Bugs, Beasts, and Flowers. Jing Pei Fang. Berkeley, CA: Ten Speed Press, 2004.

This work is an alphabetical catalog of hundreds of symbols in Chinese art and their meanings. Folklore, history, myths, and religion are used to explore the significance of each symbol. It includes more than 200 illustrations of symbols and artwork in various media.

DESIGN AND DECORATIVE ARTS

Databases

11-139. Design and Applied Arts Index (DAAI). CSA/Proquest. Online subscription database.

DAAI is an index of well over 200,000 records of news articles, reviews, and articles from periodicals covering the areas of architecture, design, crafts and other applied arts. The content is limited to publications from 1973 onward and each record includes an abstract, as well as bibliographic information.

11-140. Designinform (composed of **Design Abstracts Retrospective, Design ProFILES, and ReVIEW** (DASR, DP, ReVIEW). Design Research Publications. Online subscription database(s). http://Designinform.co.uk

These three connected databases offered as Designinform, formerly distributed by CAS/Proquest through 2009, provide access to biographical information about notable persons in the fields of design and architecture, abstracting and indexing of journals about architecture and the applied arts, and fully indexed, digitized copies of nineteenth- and early twentieth-century art journals. In addition, the paid content of the three databases that compose the Designinform product, the Designinform Research Guides offer lengthy lists of links to free internet sources of biographical information about architects, artists and designers, and freely accessible digitized art and design journals.

Printed Resources

11-141. Abitare: 50 years of Design: the Best of Architecture, Interiors, Fashion, Travel, Trends. Piazza, ed. New York: Rizzoli International Publications, 2010.

A compilation of the classic articles from *Abitare*, the influential Italian design magazine, this volume brings together the very best of the *Abitare* universe, focusing on the most noteworthy design developments of the last 50 years, with emphasis on the 1960s and 1970s. *Abitare* is the source of all things hip, important, and avant-garde, as well as must-know information and must-have objects, many of which have become design classics fifty years later. The rationale of this important compilation was to cover the growing influence of Italian design but also to gather the most interesting trends worldwide, from the mod fashion in London, and the rise of alternative lifestyles in New York and San Francisco, to the development of industrial design in Milan.

11-142. Design Dictionary: Perspectives on Design Terminology (Board of International Research Design). Michael Erlhoff and Timothy Marshall, eds. Basel: Birkhäuser Verlag, 2008.

This work collects contributions from 110 authors across the globe to provide an internationalist perspective on design, emphasizing the essential terminology and categories.

11-143. Design Encyclopedia. New ed. Mel Byars, ed. New York: The Museum of Modern Art, 2004.

This reference work, a comprehensive, heavily illustrated treatment of design across the past 130 years, explores its subject in terms of key figures, movements, and materials. Global in scope, this new edition contains not only detailed biographical information about key designers, but also focuses on interior design and many of the decorative arts (furniture production, ceramics, metal, and glass).

11-144. Dictionary of Modern Design. Jonathan Woodham, ed. New York: Oxford University Press, 2004.

This dictionary includes more than 2000 entries for significant names, products, and places in design from the last 150 years. In addition to the attempt at a global focus, in terms of geography as well as subjects within design, the book also serves as a useful reference tool because of its included time-lines and large bibliography.

11-145. Early American Decorative Arts, 1620–1860: A Handbook for Interpreters. Rev. ed. Rosemary Troy Krill. Lanham, MD: AltaMira Press, 2010.

This handbook is of particular use to those working directly with decorative art objects in a curatorial capacity. The contents of the book reference the Winterthur Museum collections, some of which have been digitized and are accessible online, as a sort of case study to guide those responsible for interpreting decorative arts to the public, although the notes and bibliographies about each sort of object may also be of use to a more general academic audience.

11-146. Elements of Design: A Practical Encyclopedia of the Decorative Arts from the Renaissance to the Present. Noel Riley, ed. New York: Free Press, 2003.

A vast survey of decorative design from the years 1400–2000, this work is especially important to researchers who wish to compare the development and repetition of design throughout history. Each section represents a different era of design and is subdivided into types of decorative art: ceramics, furniture, glass, metalwork, textiles, and wallpapers. Modern eras also include fashion and industrial design. Each page contains several full-color photographs depicting the designs of the time period, a helpful resource for artists and crafters. A thorough glossary is included.

11-147. Grove Encyclopedia of Decorative Arts. Gordon Campbell, ed. New York: Oxford University Press, 2006. 2 vols.

This reference work on the decorative arts contains 3,000 entries and focuses primarily on acknowledged art objects as collected by museums rather than including folk art materials. Its geographic coverage, while not only of Western Europe, is heavily weighted in that direction. Its included detailed bibliographies include a variety of publications, including foreign-language and local press materials that may not be included within less thorough works.

11-148. Materials & Techniques in the Decorative Arts: an Illustrated Dictionary. Lucy Trench, ed. Chicago: The University of Chicago Press, 2000.

The materials and techniques, the behind-the-scenes aspects of producing decorative objects, are explained in the entries of this work. Trench makes the point that many of the materials and techniques have not changed since antiquity or at least in the last several hundred years. A number of illustrations from Diderot's *Encyclopedie* emphasize this point. The entries are written by conservators, scientists, and art historians. For materials, the entries typically begin with a description of the properties of the material in scientific detail, followed by examples of the techniques for use and how it is used in decoration or manufacture, and finished objects fashioned from the material. Each entry contains cross references to related topics. There is a general bibliography and others by topic. The users of the work will be craftsmen and decorators, collectors, historians, curators, conservators, scientists, students, and anyone interested in the manufacture and use of decorative objects.

11-149. Theory of Decorative Art: An Anthology of European & American Writings, 1750–1940. Isabelle Frank, ed. New Haven: Yale University Press, 2000.

Theory of Decorative Art provides an historical contextualization for theoretical debate about separation of "decorative arts" and "fine arts," expressed through writings of noted designers, architects, critics and historians from the mid-eighteenth century through the middle of the twentieth century.

11-150. World Design: The Best in Classic and Contemporary Furniture, Fashion, Graphics, and More. Bernd Polster, ed. San Francisco: Chronicle Books, 2000.

A good compendium of international design, this work includes profiles on designers of various fields, including fashion and graphic arts. A twentieth-century timeline with important dates pertaining to the design field is at the back of the book, along with a list of design museums and institutes.

Open Access Resources

11-151. Design Addict. Design Addict. http://designaddict.com

Describing itself as the portal for design lovers, Design Addict is an ideal place to start exploring twentieth and twenty-first century design. The site assembles brief information on designers and their works in the form of three indices, Designers, Producers, and Objects. Topics are wide-ranging, covering furniture, lighting, dinnerware, glass, ceramics, plastic, wood, and metalware. The site also provides a links directory, a calendar of exhibitions, and a blog that reviews new design.

11-152. Digital Library for the Decorative Arts and Materials Culture. http://decorativearts. library.wisc.edu/

This website for decorative and applied arts has four sections: Documents, Images, Resources, and Materials Culture. Most impressive are the links to primary source materials, which acknowledge the arts historian's need for contextual research.

11-153. Museum of Early Southern Decorative Arts (MESDA). http://www.mesda.org/

This museum site offers access to images and descriptions of fine art and folk art, concentrating on the regional decorative arts of the preindustrial South. The collections of furniture and decorative arts at MESDA are of both rural and urban origin and are of both free and enslaved creators, presenting a diverse perspective as regards Southern decorative arts. The website for the museum also includes access to the MESDA Craftsmen Database, a database of Southern artists and artisans searchable by name, trade, location, and dates active.

11-154. Online Collections at Winterthur. Winterthur Library. http://www.winterthur.org/?p=605

Although the online portal to the Winterthur Museum, Garden and Library collections by no means allows comprehensive access to the museum's peerless collection of American decorative arts, the site does provide guides to the collections as well as some digital content. As more of the museum's collections are available digitally, the Winterthur Digital Collections will become richer. Already, the Winterthur Quilt Collection is accessible within the Digital Collections (including descriptions as well as high-quality images).

11-155. Victoria and Albert Museum. http://www.vam.ac.uk/index.html

The Victoria and Albert Museum, the self-proclaimed 'greatest museum of art and design,' has digitized much of the collections which are accessible through the museum's website. The digitized content not only includes high quality images of art and design objects, but also full bibliographic data including subjects, which can be used to find related objects, as well as detailed physical descriptions and historical summaries.

DESIGN SPECIALIZED BY TOPIC
Graphic Design

11-156. Artist's & Graphic Designer's Market: Where and How to Sell Your Illustration, Fine Art, Graphic Design & Cartoons. 36th ed. Cincinnati, OH: F & W Publications for Writer's Market, 1994-. Ann. Print and online.

This guide provides contact information for artists and designers seeking to sell their services and work, as well as information to aid in networking, marketing, and grant-seeking.

11-157. Creative Type: A Sourcebook of Classic and Contemporary Letterforms. Cees W. de Jong, Alston Purvis, and Friedrich Friedl. New York, NY: Thames & Hudson, dist. by W. W. Norton, 2005.

Although the work includes a section on classic typefaces, the worth of the book is in the contemporary typefaces produced between 1985 and 2004 and the examples and commentary on them. The authors are de Jong, a Dutch former publisher and now design consultant; Purvis, an American graphic design scholar; and Friedl, a German former typesetter and now professor of typography. Contemporary designers are covered by Purvis while Friedl's essay is an analysis of the themes and printing innovations introduced in each decade of the twentieth century. The digital era of typography of the last few decades is compared to the classic period. The three essays address the central point of the work in that contemporary designers draw inspiration from the typefaces of the past "to satisfy the needs of the present." The information on the thirty-four contemporary typefaces has brief biographical and historical information, followed by samples and photographs, with brief statements by the designer. The work is translated from the Dutch, but coverage includes Europe and the United States. This is an informative work for students and professionals in graphic arts and historians of art and the book. It is a beautifully designed book, with full-color images of font families, posters, advertisements, magazine covers, and other illustrations. An index to the typefaces is included with a full list of available forms and a list of Web sites to consult for purchasing individual fonts. The work is recommended for art and design collections, especially for libraries supporting programs in graphic or communication design.

Many works are available on the history of typographic design. Two others that can be recommended are *Twentieth-Century Type* by Lewis Blackwell (Yale University Press, 2004); and *Modern Typography* by Robin Kinross (London: Hyphen Press, 2004).

11-158. Graphic Artists Guild Handbook: Pricing & Ethical Guidelines. 13th ed. Newton Abbot: Graphic Artists Guild, distr. David & Charles, 2010.

The Handbook is considered the main source of reference for design professionals. Chapters cover salaries, legal issues, contracts, professional relationships, and references and resources. The Guild "intends to promote and protect the social, economic, and professional interests of its members."

11-159. Graphic Design: A New History. Stephen J. Eskilson. New Haven: Yale University Press, 2007.

It is the author's belief that histories of graphic design have not paid enough attention to the social context in which the designs were created. As he states, "This book is predicated on the idea that graphic design and typography are the most communal of art forms, and I strive to show how deeply they are embedded in the fabric of society of every era" (p. 10). Thus, this historical treatment of graphic design focuses more upon social and technological currents and their interplay with graphic design. The work may be considered an alternative to the more comprehensive and authoritative *Meggs' History of Graphic Design* (entry 11-160). The worth of the book may lie in the analysis which is concentrated in the period from Art Nouveau to the early twenty-first century and heavily illustrated with examples that provide a visual record of creative achievement in the field. The history of the relationship between design and manufacturing are covered. Chapters cover the movements of Modernism, Constructivism, the Bauhaus, International Style, and post-modernism through examining the work of prominent designers. For the up-to-date ending, Eskilson examines the impact of web design on typography and motion graphics such as the film title sequence and music video. The work contains 480 illustrations, mostly in color and also includes a brief glossary, a bibliography and an index. It is suitable for teachers and students in the design fields and the general public. A website designed to help instructors and students achieve a broader understanding of the field of graphic design contains discussion questions, essay topics, and online quizzes at http://yalepress.yale.edu/yupbooks/eskilson/index.asp.

11-160. Meggs' History of Graphic Design. 4th ed. Philip B. Meggs and Alston W. Purvis. Hoboken, NJ: Wiley, 2006.

Meggs' has been the standard text in the history of graphic design as attested to by the number of editions. The work is comprehensive in its approach, following the development of a wide range of what may be considered design, including typography, graphic arts, industrial design, the interplay of "art" and "design," and the impact of technologies across time on design. The newest edition includes more than 1,000 images as well as a section on modern type design.

11-161. Indie Fonts. Richard Kegler, James Grieshaber, and Tamye Riggs, eds. Buffalo, NY: P-Type Publications, 2002, 2003, 2007. 3 vols. with accompanying CD.

The title of this set gives a hint that these are digital fonts designed to suit innovative digital publications. Over 2000 fonts are displayed from eighteen "foundaries" with names such as Chank, fontBoy, Typodermic, GarageFonts, P22, and Atomic Media. Specimen pages for each foundary and a CD display thirty-three fonts. The type specimens are more than interesting, but the set has other features such as a character keyboard reference chart we all need when word processing. There are a glossary and further readings. For serious business there is an essay on the ethics of font use and intellectual property. The work is useful for anyone in graphic design or typophiles interested in digital font design.

11-162. Science Fiction and Fantasy Artists of the Twentieth Century: A Biographical Dictionary. Jane Frank. Jefferson, NC: McFarland, 2009.

While there is a plethora of works on comics and manga artists (in chapter 5), there are not many resources devoted to the often overlooked genre of science fiction and fantasy art. Only one previously published reference book focuses specifically on artists and illustrators. This text, *Biographical Dictionary of Science Fiction and Fantasy Artists* (1988) by Robert Weinberg is still useful but in need of updating. Weinberg is a guest author for one of the historical overviews in the current work. Artists included in the work by Frank are primarily twentieth-century commercial illustrators in the science fiction and fantasy publishing industry. The mass market paperback is the primary vehicle for science fiction and fantasy artists as well as other mass market genres such as romances, Westerns, horror, and so forth. There are 350 artists profiled in the work in thorough, detailed biographical entries. Information was provided directly by the artist, indirectly (via the artist's Web site), or the artist's family or estate. Also extensive bibliographic citations of works published for each artist's listing are provided. An appendix contains a chronological listing of the most prominent awards won by the artists, such as the Hugo and the World Fantasy Award. A general index follows the appendices, listing artists, authors, publishers, titles, and subjects. The work is suitable for both academic and public libraries. Collectors, dealers, and enthusiasts may want to purchase their own copies.

11-163. Thames & Hudson Dictionary of Graphic Design and Designers. 2nd ed. Alan Livingston and Isabella Livingston. London: Thames & Hudson, 2003.

This dictionary of design serves best as an introduction to key figures and terminology in the field of graphic design, with accompanying bibliography and timeline that may be of use to students. The newest edition includes forty additional entries as well as a total of 485 illustrations.

11-164. The Typographic Desk Reference. Theodore Rosendorf. New Castle, DE: Oak Knoll Press, 2009.

Manuals and reference works on typography abound. The subject has always held a fascination for those in literature and design. The key word in the title of this work is "reference." It is divided into four sections: terms; glyphs; anatomy and form; and classifications and specimens of type. A section for further reading includes citations to books, journal articles, information on type founders and distributors, websites, and an index. A proofreader's chart is included in the section on glyphs. Throughout each section there are simple drawings that accompany the text for clarification and example. A neat feature is the placement of small images in the margins that illustrate the terms in the text so that readers can visualize as well as read about the meaning of a term. The book seems to be designed as a personal reference guide; it is attractively designed and set in Adobe Caslon in a small, handbook size. The work is a good acquisition for students in the graphic arts as well as typophiles, authors, historians, and others interested in this aspect of journalism and the book arts. Other similar but larger, more in-depth works are Robert Bringhurst's *The Elements of Typographic Style* (Hartley & Marks, 2004) or James Felici's *The Complete Manual of Typography* (Peachpit Press, 2003).

Ceramics, Pottery, Glass

11-165. An Illustrated Dictionary of Ceramics. George Savage and Harold Newman. New York: Thames & Hudson, 2000.

Pottery is among the oldest of man-made vessels. The range of ceramic types and terminology from antiquity to the present are covered in this dictionary. The physical nature of pottery and porcelain, the materials, processes, types, and decorative patterns are all covered. Many specialized terms are explained as well as foreign terms. A list of the principal English and continental factories, with their dates, marks and other information associated with them, provides a master list of the notable names in the history of pottery and porcelain. Collectors will want to own this work as well as libraries serving the design fields.

11-166. Dictionary of Glass: Materials and Techniques. 2nd ed. Charles Bray. Philadelphia: University of Pennsylvania Press, 2001.

This dictionary covers all essential terminology related to materials and techniques of glass art, and includes both illustrations and diagrams, as well as a bibliography and lists of relevant glass-related resources, material suppliers, schools, and museums.

11-167. Potter's Dictionary of Materials and Techniques. 5th ed. Frank Hamer. Philadelphia: University of Pennsylvania Press, 2004.

This newest edition of the *Potter's Dictionary of Materials and Techniques* provides the expected comprehensive reference of great use for any level of practicing potter, including updates from previous editions that deal with new types of glazes and colorings, as well as new techniques. As with previous editions, this volume is thoroughly illustrated with photographs as well as hundreds of diagrams.

11-168. Corning Museum of Glass, Rakow Research Library. http://www.cmog.org

The mission of the Rakow Library at the Corning Museum of Glass is to acquire everything published on the subject of glass in every format, in every language. So it follows that the Rakow Library has an incredibly comprehensive collection of materials on glass from antiquity to the present day. The catalog of the Library and information about the museum holdings are available online, including images and physical descriptions of the items. The website also includes an extensive and unique index, Article Index, to articles on virtually every conceivable aspect of glass, as well as glass glossaries, and bibliographies.

11-169. Glass Art Society (GAS). http://www.glassart.org/

The GAS is an "international nonprofit organization founded in 1971 whose purpose is to encourage excellence, to advance education, to promote the appreciation and development of the glass arts, and to support the worldwide community of artists who work with glass. GAS members are artists, students, educators, collectors, gallery and museum personnel, writers, and critics, among others." The Society publishes the *GAS Directory and Resource Guide*, member names and contact information, educational programs; *GASnews*; and *The Glass Art Society Journal* with lectures, presentations and proceedings from the annual conference.

Fashion and Costume

11-170. Berg Fashion Library. Online subscription database. Dist. by Oxford University Press. http://www.bergfashionlibrary.com

According to the website, the Berg Fashion Library provides access to over sixty Berg fashion titles including e-journals, *Fashion Theory, Fashion Practice*, and *Textile*. The ten-volume *Encyclopedia of World Dress and Fashion* (entry 11-180) is included as well as a dictionary of key terms and an A to Z of fashion. Users will find an extensive image bank, including 1,600 images from the Victoria & Albert Museum's fashion collection and 2,000 images from the print Encyclopedia. The Berg Fashion Library is the "first online resource to provide access to interdisciplinary and integrated text, image, and journal content on world dress and fashion, updated three times a year." It will be of use to anyone working in, researching, or studying fashion, anthropology, art history, history, museum studies, and cultural studies. The Berg Fashion Library website won the 2011 Dartmouth medal, the 2011 Frankfurt Book Fair Digital Award, and the 2011 Bookseller FutureBook Award for Best Website.

11-171. A to Z of the Fashion Industry. Francesca Sterlacci and Joanne Arbuckle. Lanham, MD: Scarecrow Press, 2009.

Both a substantial introduction to the history of fashion and a thorough reference work with entries on many essential elements in the world of fashion: designers, brands, trends, and even labor, this volume also includes a bibliography of relevant sources. The work may be appropriate as a general reference work for students and enthusiasts.

11-172. The Complete Costume Dictionary. Elizabeth J. Lewandowski. Lanham, MD: Scarecrow Press, 2011. Print and e-book.

Lewandowski combed a wide variety of sources to compile this comprehensive dictionary that includes more than 20,000 fashion and costume terms that span the globe from the earliest record of fashion to the twenty-first century. The work includes 300 illustrations and a number of appendices that list the terms by country of origin, period, and type of clothing. The work can be an essential resource for costume and fashion historians, theater professionals, textile preservationists, period re-enactors, and students in all of these fields.

11-173. **Contemporary Fashion.** 2nd ed. Taryn Benbow-Pfalzgraf, ed. Detroit: St. James Press, 2002.

Following on an earlier edition considered to be a key reference work dealing with the industry of fashion through the latter half of the twentieth century, this new edition treats fashion through biographical entries for notable designers and information about significant companies, including statements of philosophy behind design.

11-174. **Costume and Fashion Source Books.** Chelsea House, 2009. 8 vols. Print and e-book.

11-175. **Fashions of a Decade: 1920–1990.** Chelsea House, 8 vols. Print and e-book.

11-176. **A History of Fashion and Costume.** Chelsea House, 2005. 8 vols. Print and e-book.

11-177. **Famous Fashion Designers.** Chelsea House, 2011. Print and e-book. Monographic Series.

As can be seen from the list of titles in this entry, Chelsea House has made fashion and costume a specialty. These sets are all similar in that they are very well illustrated with color and black and white photographs and images. In addition to being visually eye-catching, the sets provide well-written commentary on the social and historical role of fashion by eras. Included are illustrations from publications, plays, and movies of the time period, giving authentic indications of the dress and culture as well as essays on the role of particular pieces of clothing and designers.

Famous Fashion Designers is a series with separate volumes, each devoted to the career and influence of one designer. Sidebars feature quotes from the designers who are twentieth century and contemporary. These sets are useful to those in theater and cinema, students of fashion, teachers in the arts, and a general audience.

11-178. **Dictionary of Fashion History.** Valerie Cumming, C.W. Cunnington, P.E. Cunnington. New York: Berg, 2010.

This new reference work, based on the canonical *A Dictionary of English Costume* (1960), serves as both reissue and supplement in its thorough (and now, up-to-date) collection of fashion terms and fashion history.

11-179. **Encyclopedia of Clothing and Fashion**. Valerie Steele, ed. Farmington Hills, MI: Charles Scribner's Sons, 2005. 3 vols.

This comprehensive three-volume reference work includes hundreds of articles about materials and trends in clothing, as well as an index, outline, and timeline. It was a RUSA Outstanding Reference Sources selection in 2006.

11-180. Encyclopedia of World Dress and Fashion. Joanne B. Eicher, ed. New York: Oxford University Press, 2010. 10 vols. Print and online subscription database.

This work provides a truly comprehensive treatment of fashion and clothing in terms of chronology and geography. It is arranged geographically and written by 600 experts from around the world. All aspects of dress and fashion are covered from pre-history to the present. The work is an essential resource for students and researchers in fashion and textiles as well as art history, museum studies, anthropology, history and cultural studies. It was a *Booklist* Editor's choice, a RUSA Outstanding Reference Sources selection in 2011, and winner of the Dartmouth Medal.

11-181. Free Stylin': How Hip Hop Changed the Fashion Industry. Elena Romero. New York: Oxford University Press, 2011. Print and e-book.

An interdisciplinary work researched through interviews with scholars, urban designers, business persons, music experts, and music celebrities, the work traces twentieth-century fashion styles and urban fashion from the late 1970s to the present.

11-182. Greenwood Encyclopedia of Clothing through American History, 1900 to the Present. Amy Peterson and Ann T. Kellogg, gen. eds. Westport, CT: Greenwood Press, 2008. 2 vols.

11-183. Greenwood Encyclopedia of Clothing through American History, 1620–1899. Amy T. Peterson, ed. Westport, CT: Greenwood Press, 2009.

11-184. Greenwood Encyclopedia of Clothing through World History. Jill Condra. Westport, CT: Greenwood Press, 2007. 3 vols.

These sets are all amply illustrated with fascinating examples. Each begins with a chronology of events that have influenced fashion and clothing design during the time periods covered. The emphasis is upon women's clothing as might be expected, but all types of clothing are represented, from the glamorous to the mundane, for servants as well as the ruling classes. The age range covers clothing for infants through teen's clothing. The studies of clothing include the context of social, political, economic and religious history as they pertain to each time period and place.

11-185. Twentieth Century American Fashion. Linda Welters and Patricia Anne Cunningham, ed. Oxford: Berg Publishers, 2005.

This work provides a detailed description of the history of twentieth-century fashion in the United States, focusing on elements in American culture. The book examines how different influences such as gender, public policy, and family values have impacted twentieth-century fashion. It has separate chapters focusing on the Gilded Age, American Jazz, the Space Age, Television in the 1980s, and the influence of Hip-Hop on contemporary fashion. Index included.

11-186. Costume Page. Julie Zetterberg Sardo. http://www.costumepage.org/

Although the content of the page is delivered by an enthusiast rather than a scholar of fashion and costuming, the Costume Page website provides a comprehensive list of links that divide neatly into two categories: those regarding the "study of costume" including links to reference materials and museums, and those focused on the actual practice of "making costume."

11-187. Fashion Era. Pauline Weston Thomas and Guy Thomas. http://www.fashion-era.com/

This fashion enthusiast site provides a detailed, popular, illustrated review of fashion and trends through the nineteenth and twentieth centuries.

11-188. Fashion.net. http://www.fashion.net/

Clearly intended for the contemporary fashion enthusiast, and visibly commercial in intent, Fashion .net provides comprehensive lists of links to fashion designers and labels, as well as links to publications about and by the industry including magazines and blogs. Arrangement of designers by region allows for geographic focus by design.

Folk Art and Crafts

11-189. Hobbies and Crafts Reference Center. EBSCO. Online subscription database through EBSCOhost.

It would be difficult to find any hobby or craft that is not included in this comprehensive database. The full text of more than 760 magazines and books, 720 instructional videos and more than 140 full-text hobby reports are included on more than 140 specific topics. The video "How to Knit a Basket Weave Stitch" calls to mind the famous college course "underwater basket weaving." The topics range from the broad, as in antiques and genealogy, to the daring, as in bungee-jumping or hang-gliding, to the sedentary, such as embroidery and quilting. Every public library could use this fun database that was introduced with a clever brochure/poster.

11-190. American Craft Council Online. http://www.craftcouncil.org

The mission of the American Craft Council is to "promote understanding and appreciation of contemporary American craft." The site includes its library catalog which lists thousands of books, exhibition catalogs, and periodicals. The site also includes links to organizations, magazines, museums, and craft schools. A nice feature is the calendar of the American Craft Council that lists shows for both the public and wholesalers.

11-191. American Folk Art: A Regional Reference. Kristin Congdon and Kara Hallmark. Santa Barbara, CA: ABC-CLIO, 2011. 2 vols. Print and e-book.

A collection of essays of the life and work of 300 artists, both well-known and other practicing artists who have not yet received wide attention, this work is organized by region, with an essay on the region and profiles of the artists. At least one photograph is provided for each of the artists' work. The book places the artists in their local contexts and highlights the importance of place for creative work. It makes an important contribution to an understanding of who folk artists are.

11-192. Encyclopedia of American Folk Art. Gerard Wertkin and L. Kogan, eds. New York: Routledge, 2004.

This resource provides a detailed look at 300 years of what is considered non-academic art in America. It contains cross-references, bibliographies, indices, and illustrations.

11-193. Native Village Arts and Crafts Library. http://www.nativevillage.org/

Although the links focus on North American native peoples, there are links to Japanese, Caribbean, and Aboriginal artisans. Many of the links feature videos of artists at work, as well as instructions for making pieces, such as dream catchers and cornhusk dolls. The links are not categorized in any discernible fashion, which makes it more difficult for users to find appropriate information. However, a patient researcher will find links that would be valuable for teaching and scholarly pursuits alike.

11-194. Outsider Art Source-book: International Guide to Outsider Art and Folk Art. 2nd ed. John Maizels, ed. Herts, England: Raw Vision, 2009.

Intended as a guide to the subject of outsider art through biographical data on 130 artists and information on their work, as well as inclusion of entries for different "environments" and "movements," the *Outsider Art Source-book* is one of few extant reference volumes on the subject. Also included are lists of galleries, collections, journals, organizations, and web resources devoted to outsider art.

11-195. Outsider, Self-Taught, and Folk Art Annotated Bibliography: Publications and Films of the 20th Century. Betty-Carol Sellen. Jefferson, NC: McFarland, 2002.

This is a specialized reference work encompassing art and artists from outside academic traditions. The annotated bibliography covering works from 1900 to 1999 includes indices.

Industrial Design

11-196. Design Meets Disability. Graham Pullin. Cambridge, MA: The MIT Press, 2009.

The author's thesis in *Design Meets Disability* is that there should be more collaboration in developing products for the disabled between the medical, engineering, and technological sectors with trained designers. In chapters such as Feeling Meets Testing and Identity Meets Ability, the implication is that better design may influence societal attitudes toward the disabled. Also, more needs to be focused upon fitting assistive devices to individuals, rather than a reliance upon universal design for all. Not just in design of assistive devices but also in general, it is suggested that the design and fashion fields should become more sensitive to the needs of the disabled as design can impact identity. Pullin gives examples of design to be emulated and also suggests designers capable of the kind of design he envisions. The work is especially suitable for special libraries serving art and industrial design students and also health sciences libraries.

11-197. Ultra Materials: How Materials Innovation is Changing the World. George M. Beylerian and Andrew Dent. New York: Thames & Hudson, Inc. Dist. by W. W. Norton, 2007.

The authors of this work are the founders and officers of *Material Connexion* which is a subscription library database for design-related businesses, particularly architecture, industrial design, and fashion. Material Connexion maintains a library with the materials in New York City. The work provides a broad overview of current materials, excluding natural materials, suited to those fields and highlights the most innovative designers and the most unique materials. The work is divided into two sections. The first half is comprised of essays on the current state of materials development, innovative products, and interviews and profiles of "Material Maestros," artists that use ultra materials. The second half of the work is a catalog of hundreds of materials with descriptions and illustrations of use. There is much to learn about innovative uses of these ultra materials with names such as Ninitol (a shape memory alloy), Tenara (a fiber made from a chemical used in Teflon), and Fabrican (spray on fabric in a can). The work looks to the future in which materials research expands into nanotechnology and sustainable green design principles. In addition, the second section includes a glossary and directories of designers, design publications, material organizations, competitions, and fellowships. The work is replete with captivating illustrations of unique products, innovative materials, and extraordinary buildings. Although the names may sound industrial, the book can be understood by the audience it is written for: students, teachers, and professionals in the art and design fields.

Jewelry and Metalcrafts

11-198. Answers to Questions about Old Jewelry: 1840–1950. 7th ed. Jeanenne Bell. Iola, WI: Krause, 2009.

The 7th edition from Jeanenne Bell, who was an appraiser on the popular PBS series *Antiques Roadshow*, has a section on Modernist jewelry and an expanded section on Mexican jewelry along with prices and photos of collectible American and English jewelry.

11-199. Encyclopedia of American Silver Manufacturers. 5th ed. Dorothy T. Rainwater. Atglen, PA: Schiffer Pub., 2004.

This title is a basic reference work related to silver manufacture. It includes more than 2,300 illustrations of maker's marks and lists more than 1,600 manufacturers.

11-200. Jewelrymaking Through History: An Encyclopedia. Rayner W. Hesse, Jr. Westport, CT: Greenwood Press, 2007.

Hesse's Encyclopedia provides an alphabetical listing for different pieces and types of jewelry, providing descriptions, historical information, and images for each. The work also includes abbreviations and a timeline.

11-201. Masters: Gemstones: Major Works by Leading Jewelers. Marthe Le Van, ed. New York: Lark Books, 2008.

Each chapter in this book is devoted to one master designer of original jewelry set with gemstones. It focuses on their work, career, style, advancements and contributions in the field. The book also contains a glossary of terms and index of featured jewelers.

11-202. Treasures in Gold: Masterpieces of Jewelry from Antiquity to Modern Times. Gianni Guadalupi, ed. Vercelli, Italy: White Star Publishers, 2008.

This book covers the art of goldsmithing throughout history (starting with the ancient Egyptian pharaohs) and includes compelling stories behind each work of art. It is organized chronologically, with full-color photographs and a chapter devoted to master jeweler, Cartier.

Textiles and Weaving

11-203. Textile Technology Complete (TTI). EBSCO. Online subscription database. http://EBSCOhost.com

Formerly the Institute of Textile Technology's *Textile Technology Digest*, this database traces the body of knowledge in textile science and technology as far back as the early years of the twentieth century. The database contains indexing and abstracting for more than 470 periodical titles and for thousands of titles drawn from sources such as books, conferences, theses, technical reports and trade literature. Subject coverage includes manufacturing techniques, textile end products, chemicals and dyes, the properties of natural and synthetic fibers and yarns, environmental issues, and the related areas of chemistry, biology, and physics. Coverage spans the domestic and international arenas and includes publications covering the major resources from the scientific community, as well as the apparel, home furnishings, flooring, and polymer industries. The database also includes full text for nearly 50 journals, as well as over 50 books and monographs.

11-204. **Handweavers Guild of America, Inc.** (HGA) http://www.weavespindye.org/

Founded in 1969 to inspire creativity and encourage excellence in the fiber arts, the HGA in Suwanee, Georgia brings together weavers, spinners, dyers, basketmakers, fiber artists, and educators. HGA provides educational programs, conferences, and an award-winning quarterly publication, *Shuttle Spindle & Dyepot* with an online companion to the printed version available to members only, on topics dealing with design, history, techniques, artists, shows, and more.

11-205. **TextileMuse**. Arthur D. Jenkins Library at the Textile Museum. Washington, DC. http://www.textilemuseum.org/

The Textile Museum in Washington, DC announced in 2011 that it is moving to the George Washington University for expanded exhibition space and support through affiliation with the University. TextileMuse is the publicly-accessible online catalog of holdings at the Textile Museum's Jenkins Library which supports perhaps the most significant museum of textiles in America. The Arthur D. Jenkins Library is a "rich storehouse of literature and visual resources that reflect and interpret the Textile Museum's collections and support research in the broader field of textile studies. While international in scope, the Library's holdings emphasize the traditional cultures of the Americas, Africa, and Asia."

ARCHITECTURE

This section contains resources in architecture, landscape architecture, interior design, and community and urban design.

Several discernible trends are at work in architecture and allied fields in the twenty-first century. By slightly different names, the *eco movement, sustainable architecture,* and *green building* design are all under the "green" umbrella. These involve building design and construction, landscape and environmental planning, and urban planning and design.

The "Aging in place" or "lifelong communities" movement in urban planning and design fits under sustainable architecture. In this case the sustainable is for both the built environment and the sustenance of the people within that environment. Although demographers have warned for decades that the world population is aging, the trend toward accessible housing in planning and zoning policies is just now beginning to accelerate. "Aging in place" and "lifelong communities" are becoming more common in revitalizing areas of large cities where senior populations are concentrated. Building construction is becoming "age friendly," which means design that benefits all ages and not just the aged. More places to sit down; using school buses during the day to transport seniors; vehicles designed to make it easier for older people and people with disabilities to get in and out are just a few of the accommodations that are becoming more common.

Although not as cutting-edge as the eco movement, historic preservation also fits under that umbrella. Urban planning and community design need to incorporate structures from the past into community scapes for the future, in order that visual appeal and emotional appeal are planned into revitalized communities.

These trends have changed the focus of the architecture and design fields at the beginning of the twenty-first century and occasioned new approaches and publications.

Databases

11-206. **Avery Index to Architectural Periodicals**. Columbia University; J. Paul Getty Trust. CSA/ Proquest. Online subscription database. Updated weekly.

The Avery Index to Architectural Periodicals is a comprehensive listing of journal articles published internationally germane to architecture and design. The online index contains over 638,000 records dating back to 1934 and is one of the largest listings of journal articles including over 440,000 entries surveying over seven hundred American and international journals. Some major areas of coverage included are architectural design, history of architecture, interior design, and city and urban planning.

Open Access Resources

11-207. archINFORM: International Architecture Database.
http://eng.archinform.net/index.htm

According to the website, "This database has become the largest online-database about worldwide architects and buildings from past to present." The contents are concentrated on architecture of the twentieth century and include records of interesting building projects from architecture students, and on "more than 29,000 built and unrealized projects from various architects and planners." With the indices or by using a query form, it is possible to look for a special project using an architect's name, town, or keyword. Most entries give name, address, keywords and information about further literature. Some entries include images, comments, links to other websites or internal links. The site has several mobile phone apps to become connected to the same information, automatically reading the user's location (without asking!) and giving a list of architecturally significant buildings nearby.

11-208. Architects USA. SearchUSA. http://www.architectsusa.com/

Architects USA is an internet directory of over 20,000 architectural firms in the USA. Architects can register with the website and potential clients can search for firms. By helping clients find an architect that fits their needs "the end results should be better architecture."

11-209. InformeDesign. University of Minnesota Harrington College of Design/American Society of Interior Designers. http://www.informedesign.org/Default.aspx

InformeDesign content is concerned primarily with "the connection between human behavior and design and the use of this evidence to inform practice in future design endeavors." The substantial content freely accessible through InformeDesign includes research summaries of articles in more than 200 scholarly journals. Also available is access to webcasts and online courses, a glossary of relevant terminology, and a calendar marked with upcoming design seminars and conferences.

11-210. Inhabitat. http://inhabitat.com/

Inhabitat was started by NYC designer Jill Fehrenbacher as a forum for investigating emerging trends in product, interior, and architectural design. The site is a weblog devoted to the future of design, tracking the innovations in technology, practices and materials that are pushing architecture and home design towards a smarter and more sustainable future. The site is extremely well designed with a slogan, "green design will save the world." This has sections for architecture, interiors, energy, products, technology, transportation, fashion, and art. The editors are young professionals and there is a shop with ecofriendly products to buy and a photo gallery.

11-211. Pritzker Architecture Prize. Hyatt Foundation. http://www.pritzkerprize.com/

The Pritzker Architecture Prize, considered the highest honor to be earned within the field, is awarded to a living architect for "significant achievement." The Pritzker website includes biographical information about, and images of selected works by, each prize winner since the honor's inception, as well as videos of each full award ceremony.

Printed Resources

11-212. Almanac of Architecture and Design. 11th ed. James P. Cramer, ed. Atlanta, GA: Greenway Communications, 2010.

This almanac covers the entire field of architecture and design: awards and honors, leadership in design, records and achievements, building types, sustainable/green design, historic preservation, design education, organizations, design resources, and obituaries.

11-213. Archispeak: An Illustrated Guide to Architectural Terms. Tom Porter. London, New York: Spon Press, 2004.

Archispeak is a term coined to describe the language of design jargon that is commonly found in architectural literature and journalism. This unique illustrated guide helps students understand the nuances of this specialized language and help them in communicating their own design ideas.

11-214. Architect's Handbook of Professional Practice. 14th ed. Joseph A. Demkin, ed. Hoboken, NJ: Wiley, 2008.

Developed by the American Institute of Architects, this manual contains updated practice reports and case studies, expanded practice topics, and practice profiles of architectural firms. It is an essential resource for professionals and students of architecture.

11-215. Dictionary of Architecture and Landscape Architecture. 2nd ed. James Stevens Curl. New York: Oxford University Press, 2006.

The *Dictionary of Architecture and Landscape Architecture* is primarily a comprehensive treatment of the history of Western architecture, with more than 6,000 entries covering as many years. Included within the new edition are definitions of landscape terms and biographical information about modern architects.

11-216. Phaidon Atlas of Contemporary World Architecture. New York: Phaidon Press, 2004.

Because of, or perhaps despite, its awe-inspiring size, this work is a unique global pictorial review of the variety of architectural products finished between 1998 and 2004. The scope of architectural projects contained in this volume is impressive, too, as it ranges from private dwellings to large commercial and public building projects, each of which is described through photos, drawings, and explanatory text. The back of the book has comprehensive indices such as a "world data section illustrating the global economic and demographic context of the practice of architecture." The work is unusual, but is suitable for a general audience as well as for special libraries and research libraries serving architecture programs.

11-217. Oxford Companion to Architecture. New York: Oxford University Press, 2009. 2 vols. Print and e-book.

All aspects of architecture, from architects, building types, and movements and styles, to materials, aspects of design, and definitions are covered in 1,500 A-Z entries in this work. The *Companion* has over 150 illustrations, including architectural plans and line drawings. The set is a good reference source for professionals.

ARCHITECTURAL SPECIALTIES

Architectural History

11-218. SAH Architecture Resources Archive (SAHARA). Society of Architectural Historians. Online subscription database. http://www.sah.org/index.php?src=gendocs&ref=HOME&category=Sahara%20HOME

The SAHARA is an archive of architectural and landscape images from throughout the world. Funded by a grant from The Andrew W. Mellon Foundation, and built in partnership with ARTstor, SAHARA "includes not only high quality images but also rich, searchable metadata for each of those images." The SAHARA collection has been developed "for all who study, interpret, photograph, design and preserve the built environment worldwide." SAH members can use the archive to store their own digital photographs or download images from the archive for teaching and research. See also entry 11-235.

11-219. American Art Museum Architecture: Documents and Design, by Eric M. Wolf. New York: W. W. Norton, July 2010.

Wolf presents case studies of six major museums: the Frick Collection, the Museum of Modern Art, and the Whitney Museum of American Art in New York; the Menil Collection in Houston; the Georgia O'Keeffe Museum in Santa Fe; and the Art Institute of Chicago. The case studies trace the development of the museums and analyze areas of the museum such as exhibition, storage, administration, dining areas, and research, as well as spaces for events and large-scale exhibitions. An introduction traces the history of museums as cultural agencies up to the nineteenth century in Europe. The history of art museums in the United States is covered from after the Civil War to the present. Challenges in the design and functions of museum buildings today are discussed. The book is large format with many photographs and architectural drawings, a bibliography, and an index.

11-220. Encyclopedia of 20th Century Architecture. R. Stephen Sennott, ed. New York: Fitzroy Dearborn, 2004. 3 vols.

The emphasis is on the United States, modernism, and urbanism in this encyclopedia covering architecture from 1900–2000. The work includes over 1,200 entries about persons, places and architectural topics arranged in alphabetical order with entries ranging from 1,000 to 4,000 words. Entries include bibliographies and illustrations. The set is a good reference work for academic and public libraries and general readers.

11-221. Encyclopedia of Architectural and Engineering Feats. Donald Langmead. Santa Barbara, CA: ABC-CLIO, 2001.

This book provides an overview of major architectural and engineering works, awesome accomplishments, and significant innovations in architecture. Over 200 achievements are listed from pre-history to the present. Included are a glossary of terms, index and black and white illustrations.

11-222. Essential Humanities: Western Architecture Timeline. Essential Humanities. http://www.essentialhumanities.net/s_art_arch_time.php

This remarkably straight-forward web resource provides a timeline of the large movements or styles of architecture throughout the course of the history of Western civilization. The deceptively simple timeline is very easy to read, color-coded, and provides examples of each sort of architecture, neatly mapping architectural styles to different epochs. There is a History of the World site as well. The timelines are useful for students and the general public.

11-223. **European Architectural History Network** (EAHN). Delft, the Netherlands. http://www.eahn.org/site/en/home.php

The *EAHN* networks' mission is to support research and education by providing "a public forum for dissemination of knowledge about histories of architecture." The site has sections with links to libraries, museums, databases, societies and associations, as well as news, editorials, and articles.

11-224. **A Global History of Architecture**. Francis D.K. Ching et al. New York: Wiley, 2006.

The outstanding feature of this work is its unusual organization. Instead of proceeding along a linear timeline from antiquity to present that includes all areas of the globe or proceeding through time by separate regions, the work progresses through time by switching the focus to different regions in "timecuts." Sometimes the progression is east to west and other times west to east. The period between 1500 to 1700 starts in Japan and works its way to England and then back to the Far East so that the reader gets a real sense of the economic, political, religious, and technological forces at work around the world that shaped architecture. Ching is the author of several works on architecture among them, *Architecture: Form, Space, and Order* (Wiley, 2007) and *Design Drawing* (Wiley, 2010).

11-225. **Greenwood Encyclopedia of Homes Through American History.** Thomas W. Paradis, ed. Westport, CT: Greenwood Press, 2008. 4 vols.

This set covers ten historical periods of housing in the United States, beginning with the homes of Colonial America in 1492 and ending with homes of the suburban era in the 1970s. Entries cover the homes from a historical, social, and political perspective.

11-226. **Grove Encyclopedia of Classical Art and Architecture.** Gordon Campbell, ed. New York: Oxford University Press, 2007. 2 vols.

This work offers more than 1,000 articles concentrating upon all aspects of the arts during the Greco-Roman periods. The publication combines information from *Grove Art Online* (entry 11-14) with updated entries (45,000 entries by over 6,700 contributors). Included are abbreviations, a thematic index in Vol. 1, a cumulative index in Vol. 2, and illustrations.

11-227. **Historical Dictionary of Architecture.** Allison Lee Palmer. Metuchen, NJ: Scarecrow Press, 2008.

This historical overview of architecture includes cross-referenced entries for significant people, buildings, styles and movements, and materials. Also included is a chronology of architectural developments and bibliography to guide the reader to additional sources. As it is one volume, the coverage is not in-depth, but is well suited to be a personal handbook or a quick reference tool.

11-228. **Icons of American Architecture: From the Alamo to the World Trade Center.** Donald Langmead. Santa Barbara, CA: Greenwood Press/ABC-CLIO, 2009. 2 vols. Print and e-book.

Twenty-four buildings and structures are analyzed in this work to ascertain what makes a structure an architectural icon. The essays on each structure include descriptions of their roles in fiction, film, music, and popular culture worldwide. At least one image is shown for each structure. Such well-known structures included are the Brooklyn Bridge, the White House, the Hotel del Coronado, the Washington Monument, and more. Sidebars also feature additional structures. Because of the prominence of the structures, the work is suitable for public and academic libraries.

11-229. **International Confederation of Architectural Museums** (icam)
http://www.icam-web.org

ICAM is an affiliate of the International Council of Museums (ICOM, entry 2-85) and has special links with the International Council on Archives (ICA). icam and its members aim to: "Preserve the architectural record; Raise the quality and protection of the built environment; Foster the study of architectural history in the interest of future practice; Stimulate the public appreciation of architecture; and Promote the exchange of information and professional expertise." icam publishes *icam print,* a journal that covers topics presented at conferences along with other major topics within the field.

11-230. Islamic Art and Architecture: 650–1250. 2nd ed. Richard Ettinghausen, Oleg Grabar, and Marilyn Jenkins-Madina. New Haven, CT: Yale University Press, 2001.

Early Islamic Art and Medieval Islamic Art are covered in this work that addresses architecture in text as well as in drawings and photographs. The architecture of North Africa and the Middle East has not been the sole subject of many works, making this book an important contribution to the subject.

11-231. Understanding Architecture (Original Title: Capire l'Architettura). Marco Bussagli. Armonk, NY: M.E. Sharpe, 2005. 2 vols.

This book covers the history of architecture from all periods throughout the world and also the great architects from the medieval period to present. Volume 1 focuses on people and space, building and typologies, techniques, materials, structures and style. Volume 2 focuses on civilizations, architectural achievements and outstanding figures. Also included are an index of names, color photographs, drawings and maps.

11-232. World History of Architecture. 2nd ed. Michael Fazio, Marian Moffett and Lawrence Wodehouse. Boston: McGraw-Hill, 2008.

The second edition of this notable reference work seeks to provide a global perspective of the development of architecture from prehistory to the present. In addition to the expected entries for significant works of the Western world, *World History of Architecture* also focuses on areas and times that have received less coverage, including the pre-Columbian Americas, and the Middle and Near East. The volume also includes a substantial glossary of key architectural terms including those relevant only to certain areas or time periods, maps indicating significant architectural sites, and a bibliography.

11-233. Great Buildings Collection. *Architecture Week.* http://www.greatbuildings.com/

This website is maintained by *Architecture Week* and documents thousands of current and historical buildings by leading architects from around the world. The site allows for searching by name of building or architect, and also allows for browsing more than 1,000 great buildings. The site also contains an alphabetical list of master architects.

11-234. Society of Architectural Historians. Chicago, IL. http://www.sah.org

The Society of Architectural Historians was founded in 1940 to "advance knowledge and understanding of the history of architecture, design, landscape, and urbanism worldwide." The Society serves scholars, professionals in allied fields (including architecture, historic preservation and planning), and the interested general public by sponsoring the pursuit and presentation of scholarly research, publications, and professional information about the built environment and supporting the preservation of historic places and cultural heritage. The Society publishes the *SAH Newsletter* and the quarterly *Journal of the Society of Architectural Historians.*

11-235. Society of Architectural Historians, Great Britain. http://www.sahgb.org.uk/

The Great Britain Society extends membership to "individuals from all walks of life who are interested in the history of architecture from all places and all time periods." The Society "exists to encourage an interest in the history of architecture, to provide opportunities for the exchange and discussion of ideas related to this subject." It publishes the journal *Architectural History*, original research, and significant source material for the study of architectural history. The Society awards the Hawksmoor Essay Medal and the Alice Hitchcock Davis Medallion for outstanding writings in architectural history.

Building and Construction

In the latter twentieth century, architecture and building construction began to embrace the eco movement with green design and construction. Several national green building rating systems and guidelines are in place, among them Leadership in Energy and Environment Design (LEED), The Natural Step, Green Globes, and the National Association of Home Builders (NAHB) National Green Building Program A wealth of rapidly changing information about site planning, building materials, water, energy, and more is available. The entries in this section reflect the green building trend.

11-236. BuildingGreen Suite. BuildingGreen, Inc. Online subscription database. http://www .buildinggreen.com/

The BuildingGreen web resources include access to green product listings, articles related to green building, and hundreds of green building case studies, searchable by name, owner, or location of the project, or by energy type and building details. This is a substantial resource for those working in the field as well as students of green building.

11-237. Advanced Architectural Modelmaking. Eva Pascual i Miro. New York: W. W. Norton, 2010. (Rep. of Spanish 2009 Parramón Ediciones imprint).

This "definitive" practical manual for architectural modelmaking covers necessary materials and techniques for construction of scale models.

11-238. Dictionary of Architectural and Building Technology. 4th ed. Henry J. Cowan. London: Spon Press, 2004.

This dictionary includes over 6,000 technical architectural and building terms for the professional. The fourth edition has added 1,750 new entries and over 330 entries have been updated. Also included are additional illustrations.

11-239. Dictionary of Architecture and Construction. 4th ed. Cyril M. Harris, ed. New York: McGraw-Hill, 2006.

This dictionary is considered the authority on architectural terminology. The 4th edition features over 25,000 definitions and terms in architecture and construction and contains over 2,500 illustrations.

11-240. Dictionary of Ecodesign: An Illustrated Reference. Ken Yeang. New York: Routledge, 2010.

This dictionary of the terminology of green building is a basic reference source for all professionals working in the many fields and disciplines that involve ecodesign. It is useful for students, professionals, and the general public.

11-241. Extreme Architecture: Building for Challenging Environments, by Ruth Slavid. London: Laurence King, August 2009.

At the rate of population growth in the world, it may be necessary in the future to live in areas of the world not now inhabited because of intimidating environmental challenges. Ruth Slavid, editor for British magazine, *The Architect's Journal*, has put together 45 examples of architecture designed for extreme environments to show that living in such places is possible. Examples include case studies of designs in Antarctica, the Netherlands, Fiji, southern Chile, and Sweden. The book is organized by environmental concern with five sections: hot, cold, high, wet, and space. Each example begins with a large photograph of the structure in situ. For each example the height above sea level, average annual rainfall, and average temperatures are given. Each project is illustrated including exterior and interior photographs and site plans. The index lists projects by name, architect or firm, and by country. While aimed at students and professionals, the work is fascinating enough for a general audience and will certainly be of interest to those concerned about the environment.

11-242. Green Builder. Sustainable Sources. http://www.greenbuilder.com/general/env.dir.html

Sustainable Sources links to websites and publications focused on sustainable design and construction. Major topics include: intentional communities, general environmental sites, energy and solar related sites, sustainable forestry, permaculture, water, parks and wilderness, sustainable future, environmental law, and more. Sustainable Sources maintains the *Green Building Professionals Directory*, an online database.

11-243. Green Building A to Z: Understanding the Language of Green Building. Jerry Yudelson. Philadelphia, PA: New Society, 2007.

Green Building A to Z includes both an historical review of the recent emergence of the green building movement and an overview of important issues underpinning the potential success of sustainable building practices. As such, this work provides an approachable introduction to the subject without overwhelming the reader with technical specifications as some other such publications. It is most useful for the background and historical information as some terms may need updated definitions.

11-244. Green Building Fundamentals: A Practical Guide to Understanding and Applying Fundamental Sustainable Construction Practices and the LEED Green Building Rating System. 2nd ed. Michael Montoya. Upper Saddle River, NJ: Prentice Hall, 2011.

While also functioning as a practical guide to sustainable building practices, this work is, first and foremost, a preparation manual and includes a study guide for the Leadership in Energy and Environment Design (LEED) Green Associate examination. As such, it will likely find its market in aspiring green building professionals and students of sustainable building. It may also be useful to lay persons planning buildings.

11-245. Green Building Materials: A Guide to Product Selection and Specification. 3rd ed. Ross Spiegel. Hoboken, NJ: Wiley, 2010.

This practical checklist of acceptable materials for green buildings and achieving LEED building certification has been updated in the newest edition to include lists of green product standards, labeling and certification. The third edition also includes sample specifications for aspects and functions of green buildings, as well as an appendix of additional sources for more information about green product selection, certification, and use.

11-246. Green Building Through Integrated Design. Jerry Yudelson. New York: McGraw-Hill, 2009.

This manual for professional practice approaches green building as a holistic process; as such, the inclusion of case studies and guiding questions for each stage of design and building are intended to direct the user, in a step-by-step process, to successful project completion and, ultimately, LEED certification.

11-247. **Illustrated Dictionary of Building Design + Construction**. Ernest Burden. New York: McGraw-Hill, 2005.

Burden's Illustrated Dictionary of Building Design + Construction contains almost 5,000 definitions and greater than 1,500 illustrations related to the process of building design and construction. As with nearly all current building construction reference works, this volume includes coverage of green building and focuses more on illustrating terms or concepts than on in-depth written explanations.

11-248. **Rematerial: From Waste to Architecture,** by Alejandro Bahamón and Maria Camila Sanjinés. New York: W. W. Norton, June 2010.

Recycling of waste products finally seems to be gaining traction in the twenty-first century, but there is still a long way to go. Not many works have addressed the problem of pollution from building and construction waste. The authors of this work focus on the reuse of trash to offset the environmental impacts of construction and garbage and express their hope that the architecture profession will come to embrace the reuse of such materials. They give examples from all over the world of how waste materials have been recycled by architects and young designers to create projects that are not only purposeful but that work within the local environmental and social context. *Rematerial* features projects that rescue diverse, discarded materials, including both natural and manufactured materials from paper cups to cargo containers, and are then transformed into imaginative, attractive, efficient buildings and projects that are sustainable, innovative, and even novel. The projects range from a simple shelter made of tires in Cape Town, to railroad ties used for the façade of the Azkoitia Municipal Library in Spain, to a classroom space with a recycled cardboard structure in Essex. A plan, site plan, elevation, or preliminary sketch and color photographs are included for each project along with a two-page diagram that details how the waste materials were recycled and used. The book is made from recycled materials and contains a bibliography and a list of the architects whose work has been featured. Another work on the topic, *Building with Reclaimed Components and Materials* by Bill Addis, is more technical and practical (Earthscan, 2006). These works are appropriate for design libraries as well as large public libraries.

11-249. **Sustainable Construction: Green Building Design and Delivery.** 2nd ed. Charles J. Kibert. Hoboken, NJ: Wiley, 2008.

Written by one of the experts responsible for the LEED standards, *Sustainable Construction* tracks not only the historical development of green building and a number of different green building metrics, but also presents best practices in sustainable building including LEED 2009 standards. This work is likely to be a valuable reference tool for students of green building and professionals working in the field.

Standards and Codes

11-250. **2010 ADA Standards for Accessible Design**. United States Department of Justice, 2010.

The Department of Justice published revised regulations for Titles II and III of the Americans with Disabilities Act of 1990 (ADA) in the Federal Register on September 15, 2010. These regulations adopted revised, enforceable accessibility standards called the 2010 ADA Standards for Accessible Design went into effect on March 15, 2012.

11-251. Architectural Graphic Standards. 11th ed. American Institute of Architects. Hoboken, NJ: John Wiley & Sons, 2007.

According to the publishers description, "Since 1932, the ten editions of the AIA standards have been referred to as the 'architect's bible.'" The work is designed to answer any question about building and construction and contains over 8,000 illustrations. The 11th edition, to commemorate the 75th anniversary of the work, has been "thoroughly reviewed and edited by hundreds of building science experts and experienced architects." Additions include: ". . . new structural technologies, building systems, and materials; emphasis on sustainable construction, green materials, LEED standards, and recyclability; expanded and updated coverage on inclusive, universal, and accessible design strategies; computing technologies including Building Information Modeling (BIM) and CAD/CAM; and new standards for conducting, disseminating, and applying architectural research." The work is an essential reference for both professionals and architecture libraries.

11-252. Guide to Green Building Rating Systems: Understanding LEED, Green Globes, Energy Star, the National Green Building Standard, and More. Linda Reeder. Hoboken, NJ: Wiley, 2010.

The title of this work is self-explanatory. A number of different standards and certifications for building design and home products are in place. The author provides comparisons between the various rating systems to assist the reader in finding the rating system best suited to their needs. Students, professionals, and libraries serving education programs all need this resource.

11-253. LEED. U.S. Green Building Council. Washington, DC. http://www.usgbc.org

LEED is an internationally recognized green building certification system. The U.S. Green Building Council, a Washington DC-based, nonprofit coalition of building industry leaders developed and administers the LEED green building rating system. LEED is designed to "promote design and construction practices that increase profitability while reducing the negative environmental impacts of buildings and at the same time improving occupant health and well-being." In the United States and in a number of other countries around the world, LEED certification is the recognized standard for measuring building sustainability. Achieving LEED certification is the best way to demonstrate that a building project is truly "green." The LEED rating system offers four certification levels for new construction, Certified, Silver, Gold, and Platinum, that correspond to the number of credits accrued in five green design categories: sustainable sites, water efficiency, energy and atmosphere, materials and resources, and indoor environmental quality. LEED standards cover new commercial construction and major renovation projects, interiors projects, and existing building operations. Getting certified allows architects, builders, and owners to take advantage of a growing number of state and local government incentives and can help boost interest in a project. A number of websites offer information about LEED certification including the National Resources Defense Council at http://www.nrdc.org/buildinggreen/.

11-254. Multitasking Architectural Database for Computer Aided Design (MADCAD). Compu. Tecture. Online subscription database. http://www.madcad.com/index.php

MADCAD is a state-of-the-art subscription based reference online database, containing building codes, knowledge-based design solutions, and guidelines to meet the codes. MADCAD contains building, electrical, mechanical, plumbing, fire, and maintenance codes and published standards, including but not limited to ASCE, ASME, ASTM, BHMA, BOCA, ICBO, ICC, IEEE, NFPA, SBCCI, and others. Electronic subscriptions for each of the standards are required for access through MADCAD, but the advantage to MADCAD is that all of the standards and codes can be searched through one site in a combined search result. MADCAD also gives access to comprehensive state and local codes, a very valuable asset to the database.

Historic Preservation

11-255. **Blue Shield Network**. http://www.ancbs.org/

Blue Shield is the cultural equivalent of the Red Cross. The Blue Shield is an emblem specified in the 1954 Hague Convention, Convention for the Protection of Cultural Property in the Event of Armed Conflict, for marking cultural sites to give them protection from attack in the event of armed conflict. The Association of National Committees of the Blue Shield (ANCBS), founded in December 2008, is coordinating and strengthening international efforts to "protect cultural property at risk of destruction in armed conflicts or natural disasters." The Blue Shield network consists of organizations dealing with museums, archives, audiovisual supports, libraries, as well as monuments and sites. The International Committee of the Blue Shield, founded in 1996, comprises representatives of the five non-governmental organizations (NGOs) working in this field: the International Council on Archives (www.ica.org); the International Council of Museums (www.icom.museum, entry 2-85); the International Council on Monuments and Sites (entry 11-258)(www.icomos.org); the International Federation of Library Associations and Institutions (www.ifla.org); and the Co-ordinating Council of Audiovisual Archives Associations (www.ccaaa.org). Blue Shield issues statements, news releases, and reports on the effects of armed conflicts and natural disasters upon cultural sites throughout the world.

11-256. **Historic American Buildings Survey** (HABS) /**Historic American Engineering Record** (HAER) /**Historic American Landscapes Survey** (HALS), 1933-. Library of Congress. http://memory.loc.gov/ammem/collections/habs_haer/index.html

The Library of Congress' *Historic American Building Survey*, *Historic American Engineering Record*, and *Historic American Landscapes Survey,* all material collections now digitized, have been bundled into an online, freely accessible, searchable, or browsable database of the photographic and textual record of American achievements in architecture and engineering.

11-257. **International Council on Monuments and Sites** (ICOMOS). http://international.icomos.org

The ICOMOS is an international non-governmental organization of professionals, an interdisciplinary network of experts among which are architects, historians, archaeologists, art historians, geographers, anthropologists, engineers, and town planners dedicated to the conservation of the world's historic monuments and sites. ICOMOS issues World Reports annually and Heritage at Risk special reports on endangered sites. The aim of these reports is to identify threatened heritage places, monuments and sites, present typical case studies and trends, and share suggestions for solving individual or global threats to cultural heritage sites.

11-258. **National Register of Historic Places** (NRHP) **Database.** National Register of Historic Places. U.S. National Park Service, Department of the Interior. http://nrhp.focus.nps.gov

The National Register is well known to local preservationists and tourists alike. The NRHP Database allows access to documentation associated with properties listed in the National Register that have been digitized, including registration forms, photographs, and maps. The database is also searchable by location (by city, county, or state), resource name, and/or National Park Service park name if searching for an NPS park.

11-259. **National Trust for Historic Preservation** (NTHP). National Trust for Historic Preservation, Washington, DC. http://www.preservationnation.org/resources/

The NTHP is a U.S. government agency. The website offers useful resources significant in historic preservation, including funding sources for projects, case studies, links to conferences and training, and resources to aid in advocating for historical preservation. The NTHP publishes the *Forum Journal* which covers topics about the conservation and restoration of buildings and historic sites in the U.S. It also publishes *Preservation*, a magazine that covers the same topics.

11-260. **Illustrated Dictionary of Architectural Preservation: Restoration, Renovation, Rehabilitation and Reuse**. Ernest Burden. New York: McGraw-Hill, 2004.

This dictionary lists the major works and names of world famous architects who practiced during the eighteenth century to the present. Indices of two dozen architectural histories and four encyclopedias were searched to compile the architects who are included in this book. It also lists many historic preservation architectural firms still practicing today. Listing is alphabetical with cross-references and over 2,000 photos.

11-261. **National Center for Preservation Technology & Training** (NCPTT). Natchitoches, Louisiana. https://www.ncptt.gov

The U.S. Congress passed the Historic Preservation Act Amendments of 1992, creating the National Center for Preservation Technology and Training, its advisory board and grants program. The NCPTT "advances the application of science and technology to historic preservation." Working in the fields of archeology, architecture, landscape architecture, and materials conservation, the Center engages in training, education, research, technology transfer, and partnerships. NCPTT's research has benefitted many historic sites and monuments including the Statue of Liberty, Congressional Cemetery, and a number of National Parks. Topics with links on the site include cemetery conservation; archaeology and collections; architecture and engineering; disaster recovery; heritage education and more. The site also has podcasts, videos, PTT reports, and a product catalog. All can be accessed from the site free of charge.

Interior Design

11-262. **American Furniture: Understanding Styles, Construction, and Quality**. John T. Kirk. New York: Harry N. Abrams, 2000.

Styles of American furniture design from the seventeenth to the early twentieth century are covered in this work. In addition to a multitude of examples illustrated throughout, the author dedicates a section of the book to wood and "how it affects design . . ." Color and black and white plates are well produced. Notes are at the end of the work.

11-263. **Dictionary of Furniture.** 2nd ed. Charles Boyce. New York: Facts on File, 2001.

This is an updated version from the original edition published in 1988 and includes more than 2,000 entries about furniture design, styles, construction, materials, designers, and manufacturers throughout the world.

11-264. **Encyclopedia of Furnishing Textiles, Floorcoverings and Home Furnishing Practices 1200–1950**. Clive Edwards. Burlington, VT: Lund Humphries, 2007.

The focus in this work is on British and American materials, although some continental and Indian materials used in these two countries are included. Informative entries include such facts as patents, technology used to produce the materials, examples of how the materials were used, and quotations from contemporary sources. Many entries include useful cross-references and suggestions for further reading. An extensive bibliography includes theses and dissertations. The work has been criticized for the poor quality of the illustrations and there are only twelve pages in color; but it is still useful for the prodigious amount of information on the subject. Anyone with an historical interest in the textile trades, the history of interior decoration and living quarters, the investigation and preservation of historic textiles and upholstery, and details of everyday life will find useful tidbits in this work.

11-265. Encyclopedia of Furniture Materials, Trades and Techniques. Clive Edwards. Brookfield, VT: Ashgate Publishing Company, 2000.

Although the author regards this work as a history rather than a technical guide, it is organized in 1,700 A-Z entries covering the years 1500–2000. Many of the entries are for synthetic materials, such as latex, nylon, olefins, and so forth, and do contain technical details about production, marketing and adoption, and patents. Cross references and brief citations are provided in the entries to the book's extensive bibliography. The work is like a dictionary in that it does not have many illustrations and no index. Edwards subsequently authored the encyclopedia in entry 11-264.

11-266. Encyclopedia of Wood. U.S. Department of Agriculture. New York: Skyhorse Pub., 2007.

This technical volume deals with the properties of wood and is more a manual than encyclopedia with its inclusion of information about stress grading of varieties and other mechanical and chemical attributes. It is an essential reference to the professional woodworker or furniture maker.

11-267. Encyclopedia of Wood: a Tree-by-Tree Guide to the World's Most Versatile Resource. 2nd ed. Aidan Walker. New York: Facts on File, 2005.

Included in this work is a "Directory of the Wood" in which each type is briefly described in six categories: impact, resistance, stiffness, density, workability, bending strength, and crushing strength. The descriptions are accompanied by large color photographs of the wood color. Other topics discussed are tree growth, structure, forest growth, timber processing and more. There are glossaries and indices. This work is useful not just to architects and interior decorators but to anyone interested in furniture and trees.

11-268. Furniture: Great Designs from Fine Woodworking. Matthew Teague, ed. Newtown, CT: Taunton Press, 2006.

This book features over 65 favorite project articles from the last fifteen years of *Fine Woodworking* magazine with full drawings and diagrams for woodworkers, designers, and decorators.

11-269. Great Lady Decorators: The Women Who Defined Interior Design, 1870–1955. Adam Lewis and Jeremiah Goodman. New York: Rizzoli. Dist. in the U.S. by Random House, 2010.

Women invented the business of interior design in the nineteenth and early twentieth century. The entries contain brief biographies and a review of the accomplishments of twelve women who are considered to be pioneers in the founding of interior design as a professional field. The book is heavily illustrated and contains much social history as projects of the women are profiled.

11-270. History of Interior Design. 3rd ed. John Pile. New York: Wiley, 2009.

This expanded 3rd edition of *History of Interior Design* provides an historical overview of interior design from ancient times to the present and includes a CD-ROM with additional material in the form of a timeline with over 100 illustrations. The new edition also focuses on non-Western and "domestic vernacular" interiors.

11-271. Source-book of Modern Furniture. 3rd ed. Jerryll Habegger and Joseph H. Osman. New York: W. W. Norton & Co., 2005.

This sourcebook is intended for interior-design and architecture professionals and provides a concise reference of high quality works of modern furniture and lighting. It contains twenty-two chapters of different products, e.g., wall lamps, chaise lounges, modular seating with detailed information regarding each work: model name, year of design, manufacturer, materials and dimensions. It also contains three separate indices of designers, model names, and manufacturers.

Landscape Architecture

11-272. Gardening, Landscape and Horticulture Collection (InfoTrac). Gale/Cengage. Online subscription database. http://www.gale.cengage.com/pdf/facts/GardeningCollection.pdf

One of the Gale InfoTrac collections, the *Gardening, Landscape and Horticulture Collection,* much like EBSCO's *Garden, Landscape & Horticulture Index* (entry 11-273), is heavily concentrated in horticulture, but there are also resources dealing with landscape planning, design, and conservation.

11-273. Garden, Landscape & Horticulture Index. EBSCO. Online subscription database. http://www.ebscohost.com/academic/garden-landscape-horticulture-index

Although this EBSCO database focuses on horticulture, the indexing and abstracting of content does cover areas of architectural overlap and intersection, such as landscape design. The majority of the more than 500 titles that are covered by this database are in English and are from publications dating back only to the early 2000s.

11-274. The American Society of Landscape Architects (ASLA) http://www.asla.org

The ASLA is the official organization for American landscape architects. The website, while serving as a community for practicing architects, also acts as a resource for students and people interested in the field. The site provides lists of firms, suggested resources, information on state and federal licensure, as well as general professional information.

11-275. Dictionary of Landscape Architecture and Construction. Alan Jay Christensen. New York: McGraw Hill, 2005.

This area-specific reference includes more than 7,500 terms and definitions related to landscape architecture, planning, landscape ecology, and construction.

11-276. Encyclopedia of Gardens: History and Design. Candice A. Shoemaker, ed. Chicago: Fitzroy Dearborn, 2001. 3 vols.

The purpose of this work is to provide description and analysis of a range of subjects and individuals related to the history of gardens and garden design. Entries are arranged in alphabetical order in three broad categories: individuals, architects, designers, plant collectors, writers, patrons, and horticulturists; places, countries, regions and gardens; and topics, garden elements, periods, and styles. Each entry includes a critical essay, a summary biography, a list of principal works, a chronological synopsis of major development in the site's history, and a list of further reading. This also has black-and-white illustrations, plans, photos, designs and a color plate section.

11-277. Encyclopedic Dictionary of Landscape and Urban Planning: Multilingual Reference in English, Spanish, French and German. Klaus-Jurgen Every, ed. Berlin: Springer, 2010.

This multilingual work is perhaps the most ambitious and comprehensive dictionary for landscape architecture terminology currently in print. The two volumes contain a total of more than 10,000 terms, defined and appropriately cross-referenced in American and British English, Spanish, French, and German. Three indices at the end of the second volume in Spanish, French, and German in order of the English entries allow for any user to find a term in any of the four languages.

11-278. Illustrated History of Landscape Design. Elizabeth Boults and Chip Sullivan. Wiley-Blackwell, 2010.

The contents of this work are drawings and illustrations with a minimal amount of accompanying text. The organization is by century, with a selection of examples from a few countries and landscape forms. Each chapter has a chronology with entries on political, scientific, and artistic achievements that influenced landscape design. The book is very attractive and was a *Choice* outstanding reference book selection in 2010. It can be enjoyed by students, professionals, and the general public.

11-279. Landscape Design: A Cultural and Architectural History. Elizabeth Barlow Rogers. New York: Harry N. Abrams, 2001.

Information about landscapes from prehistoric times to recent design history, along with the off-and-on relationship of landscape design with architectural design, is included in this work. As a comprehensive survey of the history of landscape design, the work reveals human interaction with the land. It is an invaluable resource for scholars, architects, and garden enthusiasts. Hundreds of pages of plans, color and black and white photos, drawings, illustrations, are included, all with useful captions, dated and with credits.

11-280. Residential Landscape Architecture: Design Process for the Private Residence. Norman K. Booth and James E. Hiss. Englewood Cliffs, NJ: Prentice Hall, 2005.

Focusing on the design process, this work includes many high color, in-depth illustrations, plans, diagrams, and differing points of perspective to instruct people both new to landscape architecture as well as those more experienced within the field. This is achieved through a solid focus on the fundamentals of the field, as well as knowledge of the standards and history of residential landscape construction.

11-281. Shaping the American Landscape: New Profiles from the Pioneers of American Landscape Design Project. Charles A. Birnbaum and Stephanie S. Foell, eds. Charlottesville, VA: University of Virginia Press, 2009.

The Pioneers of American Landscape Design is a project of the National Park Service Historic Landscape Initiative, Library of American Landscape History catalog of landscape records in the United States at Wave Hill published in 2000. *Shaping the American Landscape* is a replacement for the title published in 2000. This biographical collection focuses on more than 150 significant professionals in twentieth-century American landscape architecture and related fields. Each entry includes biographical information, a discussion of the architects' approach and methodology, and representative plans and photographs of major projects. Vital issues in landscape preservation and ecologically sound design are emphasized. The significant, still extant works of the profiled individuals are included as a reference tool within the volume.

Urban and Community Design

The literature of urban planning and design is voluminous. The resources in this section relate most directly to the design fields of architecture, buildings, environmental design, and landscape architecture. Many broad treatments are not included.

11-282. GreenFILE. EBSCO. www.greeninfoonline.com

GreenFILE is a free multidisciplinary database that covers all aspects of human impact to the environment. It is designed to be used by professionals, students, and the general public and includes government documents and reports. The connections between the environment and a variety of disciplines such as agriculture, education, law, health, and technology can be seen in search results from over 470,000 records and full text for more than 5,500 records. Topics covered include global climate change, green building, pollution, sustainable agriculture, renewable energy, recycling, and more.

11-283. Environmental Systems Research Institute, Inc. (Esri) http://www.esri.com

The Esri site is all about GIS technology. According to the website, GIS allows users to "view, understand, question, interpret and visualize data in many ways that reveal relationships, patterns and trends in the form of maps, globes, reports and charts." In 1982, Esri introduced ARC/INFO, the first commercial GIS product. Today it's the Web and Web GIS. With the advent of GIS, architects and planners have moved from two-dimensional drawings to three-dimensional models that have completely changed the processes of modeling for urban development. The technology has become pervasive in research and every-day living from Google maps, to advances in medical treatment, to letting our friends know our location by the minute. Esri licenses its GIS software. The site has product support and "galleries" in which there are map templates and tools. Esri offers a GIS dictionary, white papers, technical reports, a GIS wiki, blogs, and email discussion lists on the Esri site.

11-284. Index to Current Urban Documents. ILM Corporation. Online subscription database. http://www.urbdocs.com/

The Index to Current Urban Documents provides full-text access to more than 27,000 reports and published research products from government, civic, research and planning organizations across the United States and Canada, with specific subject emphasis on financial, architectural and planning content.

11-285. Cities and Buildings Database. UW (University of Washington) Libraries Digital Collections. http://content.lib.washington.edu/buildingsweb/index.html

This collection of freely accessible images of buildings and cities is of global scope and is connected to sufficient metadata within the database to allow for searching by building name, location, style, date of construction, and responsible architect. This is an excellent site for browsing and is geared towards students as well as general interest.

11-286. Environmental Design Library. UC (University of California) Berkeley Library. http://www.lib.berkeley.edu/ENVI/

The UC Berkeley Environmental Design Library site is an entryway to the materials within the actual UC Berkeley Library, but also provides substantial free bibliographies and links to free web resources in areas of architecture, city planning, environmental planning, landscape architecture, and urban design.

11-287. Urban Land Institute. (ULI) . http://www.uli.org/

In addition to being the web face of the nonprofit ULI, the ULI site also allows access to ULI research publications in areas of urban planning/development and sustainable building, as well as a substantial freely accessible database of innovative, financially successful case studies in development. http://casestudies.uli.org/

11-288. Contemporary Urban Planning. 9th ed. John M. Levy. Boston: Longman, 2010.

As with earlier editions, this latest update of *Contemporary Urban Planning* addresses influential factors to urban planning, including economic and environmental issues. The ninth edition specifically addresses timely issues, including the housing crisis in 2008 and the federal response. This work is likely most useful as a general overview or an introductory text to urban planning.

11-289. Designing for the Homeless: Architecture that Works. Sam Davis. Berkeley, CA: University of California Press, 2004.

Davis gives a brief explanation of the rise of homelessness in the United States and how the population of homeless people has changed, necessitating new approaches to the problem. Housing needs to be designed to include on-site support services to assist the homeless to begin to take care of themselves. Many of the ideas he advances are from his own projects. A few, recent works concentrate on architectural design for housing the homeless. This work is appropriate for libraries serving schools of architecture and degree programs in sociology and urban studies, as well as public libraries.

11-290. Encyclopedia of Urban Studies. Ray Hutchinson, ed. Thousand Oaks, CA: Sage, 2009. 2 vols.

This comprehensive reference work about urban studies contains entries for different subjects, individuals, locations, as well as related areas of study and practice such as urban planning and urban ecology. In addition to the thorough indexing and cross-referencing of entries, the first volume also contains an alphabetical reader's guide to the content.

11-291. Inclusive Housing: A Pattern Book: Design for Diversity and Equality. Center for Inclusive Design and Environmental Access. Edward Steinfeld, et al. W. W. Norton, 2010.

Inclusive housing design extends the design to do more than just accommodate special needs but rather provides convenience for everyone. The projects in the work include the neighborhood as well as the dwelling design for both detached and attached housing. One of its main ideas for aging in place is that urban housing must take into account the neighborhood and the property the building(s) is on to create socially supportive neighborhoods for aging in place The authors observe that their book focuses on the urban environment whereas much of accessible design is for suburban environments. The book covers the concept of the "neighborly house," and livable neighborhoods, presenting the rationale in terms of changing household needs, affordability, social interaction, and security. The book is based on the new urbanist concept of the "urban transect," with models for block layouts at different levels of density, and for lot and house components. The overall philosophy is that an accessible house in auto-dependent surroundings is not really accessible at all. Despite its forward-looking focus, the examples presented are all traditional design. The work is appropriate for schools of architecture and academic programs in gerontology and disability studies, as well as for public libraries.

11-292. Public Art by the Book. Barbara Goldstein, ed. Seattle: Americans for the Arts in association with University of Washington Press, 2005.

This book is intended to be a handbook for those involved in the production or support of public art. The book has 32 essays from twenty-two authors that review recent public art projects, organized into sections on planning, funding, categories of projects, best practices, legal issues, and resources for further study. As a practical manual the book has many useful examples of forms, contracts, fact sheets, policies, and ordinances, that illustrate the permissions and bureaucracy, not to mention political persuasion, involved in the planning process and staging of public art. This reference has a substantial bibliography of resources published from 1970–2004. The majority of the illustrations are black and white with eight pages of color plates. It is useful for students, practitioners, artists, governmental administrators, and those supporting public art.

11-293. Routledge Handbook of Urban Ecology. Ian Douglas, ed. Abingdon, Oxon, England: Routledge, 2011.

The *Routledge Handbook of Urban Ecology* is fairly unique in its collective approach to addressing urbanism and urbanization, specifically as regards the relationships between humans and urban planning and development, as well as the relationship with the wider ecosystem. This interdisciplinary approach is reflected in the handbook's collection of articles contributed by 50 researchers and professionals in the field.

11-294. Skinny Streets and Green Neighborhoods: Design for Environment and Community. Cynthia Girling. Washington, DC: Island Press, 2005.

Skinny Streets and Green Neighborhoods relies on an exploration of eighteen case studies as a means to address the need for integrating sustainable building practices and landscape design with the larger, surrounding environment. This volume shows the interrelated areas of practice of urban planning and ecology, landscape design, and green building and construction, and delivers its readers practical advice premised upon the overlap.

Organizations

11-295. American Institute of Architects (AIA). http://www.aia.org/

The AIA supports research in architecture, aligned with the AIA initiatives of Integrated Practice, Sustainability, and Diversity. Specific research agenda areas include: Social, Technological, Environmental, Cultural, Organizational, Design, and Educational to integrate research and "evidence-based design" in education and practice. The professional association for architects in the USA, the AIA publishes *The Architect's Handbook of Professional Practice* (entry 11-215).

11-296. Association of Collegiate Schools of Architecture (ACAS). https://www.acsa-arch.org/

The Association of Collegiate Schools of Architecture is a nonprofit, membership association founded in 1912 to "advance the quality of architectural education through support of member schools, their faculty, and students by encouraging dialogue among the diverse areas of discipline; facilitating teaching, research, scholarly and creative works, through intra/interdisciplinary activity; by articulating the critical issues forming the context of architectural education; and by fostering public awareness of architectural education and issues of importance." The association maintains a variety of activities such as scholarly meetings, workshops, publications, awards and competition programs, support for architectural research, policy development, and liaison with allied organizations.

11-297. Association for Women in Architecture (AWA). http://www.awa-la.org/

The AWA, founded in 1922, is dedicated to advancing and supporting the positions of women in architecture and allied fields. The AWA provides support to its members, especially those starting out in their professions and running their own firms, by developing educational programs, lectures and tours, and by providing opportunities for mentoring and mutual support. The AWA also raises money for annual scholarship awards to women students in architecture and allied fields.

11-298. **International Union of Architects (IUA).** http://www.uia-architectes.org/

The IUA is a global network dedicated to the profession of architecture. It is a federated network of national professional organizations from around the world that sponsors congresses and publications.

Author/Title Index

Authors, titles, and names of organizations, agencies, libraries, and other entities are included in this index. All authors and titles are indexed by chapter entry number unless they occur within the narrative portions of the chapter, in which case page numbers are given. An "n" after the entry number indicates that the author or title is found within the annotation to that entry. Only titles for printed works and journals are italicized.

PAL, 5-46
Palgrave Connect, 2-44, 5-12
Palgrave Studies, 5-12n
Palisca, Claude V., 9-82
Palmer, Allison Lee, 11-227
Palmer, Carole L., (p. 10, 20)
Palmer, Donald, (p. 68, 70)
Palmer, Gene V., 6-100n
Palmer's Index to the Times (1790–1905), 2-38n
Paradis, Thomas W., 11-225
Paravisini-Gebert, Lizabeth, 6-46n
Parini, Jay, 5-32n
Paris Metro Tales, 6-149n
Paris Tales, 6-149n
Parker, Jeff, 6-203n
Parker, Linda L., (p. 9, 21)
Parker, Mara E., 9-72
Parker, Mary, 6-140
Parkinson, Stephen, 6-130
Parshalls, Adris E., 4-77
Participatory Museum, (p. 353, 355)
Partridge, Christopher, 4-105
Passman, Donald S., 9-167
Paton, Stewart, 6-248
Patte, Daniel, 4-72
Patten, Katherine, (p. 346, 355)
Patterson, David, 6-172
Patterson, Michael, 8-69
Pauly, Reinhard G., 9-80n
Payne, Roberta L., 6-126n
Peake, Arthur, 4-47n
Peake's Commentary on the Bible, 4-47n
Pearl, Nancy, 5-73n
Peek, Robin P., (p. 23)
Pendergast, Sara, 5-109n, 6-17
Pendergast, Tom, 5-109n, 6-17
Pendle, Karin, 9-153, 9-154
Penguin Guide to Blues Recordings, 9-137
Penguin Guide to Jazz Recordings, 9-98
Penner, Katherina, (p. 86, 87)
PENNsound, 5-193
Penny, Nicholas, 11-79
Penzler, Otto, 6-104n
Percy, G. D., 6-16
Performance Practice, 9-84
Performing Arts, 7-13, 7-15
Performing Arts Business Encyclopedia, 7-14
Performing Arts Encyclopedia, 7-7
Performing Arts Fergusin Career Launcher, 7-15n
Performing Arts Yearbook, 7-2
Periodicals Archive Online, 2-29, 2-38n
Periodicals Index Online, 2-28, 2-38n
Permissions, a Survival Guide, (p. 352, 354)
Perper, Timothy, 5-107n
Perriam, Christopher, 6-134
Perrone, James, 9-127
Perseus Digital Library, 6-81, 11-129
Persoon, James, 5-175n

Petersen, Robert S., 5-102n
Peterson, Amy, 11-182, 11-183
Peterson Jr., Bernard L., 8-71
Peterson, Nadya L., 6-103n
Petrucci Music Library, 9-12n
Phaidon Atlas of Contemporary World Architecture, 11-216
Phi Sigma Tau, 3-45
Philosopher's Index, 3-6
Philosophical Perspectives, 3-43
Philosophy (Bynagle), 3-34
Philosophy Around the Web, 3-22
Philosophy Documentation Center, 3-54b
Philosophy News Service, 3-23
Philosophy of Religion—A Guide to the Subject, (p. 85, 86)
Philosophy on the EServer, 3-12
Philosophy Research Index, 3-7
PhilPapers, 3-13
Photographs, 11-77
Photographs of the Past, 11-76
Photography Collections Online, 11-75
Piano in Chamber Ensemble, 9-59
Piano Music by Black Women Composers, 9-58
Pile, John, 11-270
Pinch, Geraldine, 4-116n
P. J. Kennedy and Sons, 4-79
Plantinga, Leon, 9-79n
Play Finder, 8-64n
Play Index, 8-29, (p. 30 box)
Playography na Gaelig, 8-34n
Poetry Archive, 5-195
Poetry Criticism, 5-9n, 5-181
Poetry Daily, 5-197
Poetry for Students, 5-182
Poetry Foundation, 5-198
Poetry in a Provisional State, 6-167n
Poetry of Our World, 6-26
Poetry 180, 5-194
Poetry Society of America, 5-199
Poetryclass, 5-196
Poet's Market, 5-183
Poets.org, 5-200
Poiesis, 3-8
Pointe, 8-1n
Poitrass, Gilles, 5-122n
Polish Literature from 1864–1918, 6-99
Polish Literature from 1918–2000, 6-99
Polish Romantic Literature, 6-99
Pollock, Bruce, 9-143
Polster, Bernd, 11-150
Pomerantz, Jeffrey, (p. 354, 356)
Poole's Index to Periodical Literature, 2-38n
Pop, Rock, and Soul Reader, 9-84n
Poplawski, Paul, 6-12n
Popular Song Index, 9-49
Porter, James, 9-157
Porter, Marsha, 10-12
Porter, Stanley E., 4-76n

SUBJECT/KEYWORD INDEX

The purpose of this index is to provide access to both broad topics and keywords from titles. The organization places page references in parentheses first followed by entry numbers. Entry numbers indicate the subject is found somewhere within the entry, not necessarily in the title.

ABOUT THE AUTHORS

ANNA H. PERRAULT is Professor Emerita in the School of Information at the University of South Florida in Tampa and Librarian Emerita from Louisiana State University. She holds MA and MS degrees in English literature and Library Science from LSU Baton Rouge and a PhD in Library and Information Studies from The Florida State University. Among awards received are the ALISE Doctoral Dissertation Award, the Library Acquisitions Practice and Theory Research Award, and the ALCTS "Best of LRTS" Award. She is co-author with Ron Blazek of two editions of *United States History: a Selective Guide to Information Sources* for Libraries Unlimited. Perrault has authored numerous publications on collection analysis and assessment projects in academic libraries.

ELIZABETH S. AVERSA is Professor in the School of Library and Information Studies at The University of Alabama where she served as director for eight years (2003–2011). She previously served as director of the School of Information Sciences at The University of Tennessee Knoxville and as dean at The Catholic University of America. In addition to her academic work, Aversa has experience in public and state librarianship and in the corporate research department of the Institute for Scientific Information (ISI), now Thompson Reuters. Aversa earned the PhD at Drexel University and the MLn and BA at Emory University. She has published three books, including co-authoring the 3rd, 4th, and 5th editions of *The Humanities*; she has also published articles in *JASIS&T, Scientometrics, Advances in Librarianship, Proceedings of the International Conferences on Webometrics, Informetrics and Scientometric Meetings,* and in many additional titles.

CYNTHIA MILLER is Music and Performing Arts Librarian at the University of Alabama. She holds an MLIS degree in library science from the University of Alabama and a PhD in music from the City University of New York. She has held teaching positions at Minnesota State University Moorhead, Ball State University, and Brooklyn College. Her audio-visual presentations on music, published by Clearvue/EAV, are used by schools and colleges throughout the United States. Dr. Miller is also a composer whose works are performed both in the United States and abroad.

SONIA RAMÍREZ WOHLMUTH is an instructor in the Department of World Languages at the University of South Florida where she has taught courses in Spanish language and linguistics since 1996. She has also taught for the School of Information at the University of South Florida. Wohlmuth has an MA in Spanish from the University of Illinois, an MA in Library and Information Science from the University of South Florida, and in 2008 she received a PhD in Romance Linguistics from the University of Florida. She has published articles on library services for the Spanish-speaking and on Spanish as a global language.